DISCARD

Twentieth Century Sociology

TWENTIETH CENTURY SOCIOLOGY

Edited by

GEORGES GURVITCH

and

WILBERT E. MOORE

Essay Index Reprint Series

BOOKS FOR LIBRARIES PRESS
FREEPORT, NEW YORK

Copyright 1945 by Philosophical Library, Inc.

Reprinted 1971 by arrangement

INTERNATIONAL STANDARD BOOK NUMBER:
0-8369-2110-0

LIBRARY OF CONGRESS CATALOG CARD NUMBER:
78-134090

PRINTED IN THE UNITED STATES OF AMERICA

PREFACE

Nineteenth Century Sociology was characterized by a limited number of problems more or less dogmatically accepted and differently resolved in conflicting "schools." The initial tendency to link if not to identify sociology with "philosophy of history" or "theory of evolution" (as exemplified by Auguste Comte, Herbert Spencer, and even Karl Marx) was overcome only slowly and step by step. The field was marked by eternal discussions between the partisans of "order" or the admirers of "progress"; between the defenders of the "individual" or of "Society," contrasted with each other as isolated entities; between the promoters of psychology as against sociology, and vice versa; and among the proponents of a "predominating factor" in social life, such as the geographical, biological, anthropo-racial, demographic, technological, and so on (not one of which as a matter of fact when taken separately belongs to the social reality). These conflicts threatened to compromise the scientific character of early sociological research. The practice of seeking and formulating "sociological laws" on which different sociologists could never agree completed the rather dismal picture of sociology in the first century of its birth.

Twentieth Century Sociology, as the reader will see, is characterized first of all by a gradual elimination of all the uncritically accepted problems that worried the sociologists of the past century. Finally none of the old "main topics" in sociology remained, because every one of them was revealed to be improperly posed and badly formulated. It is symptomatic of a new trend toward maturity in sociology that real progress reports can be primarily devoted either to the central body of verified positive-empirical research on strictly descriptive or typological bases, or to the formulation of sounder and more fundamental problems, accepted only after careful anaylsis but with a studied neglect of the haphazard array of conflicting opinions and schools.

The present Symposium, which was undertaken as a venture in stocktaking, spontaneously and encouragingly reconfirmed the predominant trend of contemporary sociology toward critical but constructive assessment. The emphasis in the papers here presented is on the new problems and positive results. It is not primarily a current history crowded with battles and skirmishes. Differences in points of view and even in fundamental positions may be found reflected in the analysis of the various fields of sociological inquiry (Part I), or in the portrayal of the status of sociological scholarship in different countries (Part II). But without any pressure or direct suggestion by the editors all contributors elected to concentrate their efforts on the essential issues and verified positive achievements of sociology, rather than on their more or less traditional formulations and contrasting solutions. In typically Twentieth Century manner the contributors find no real conflict between empirical investigation and theoretical analysis, which in all mature sciences always support and presuppose each other. Thus in this Symposium, as in the Twentieth Century Sociology itself. the "logic of sociological problems" seems definitely to have superseded the "logic of sociological systems and schools," which was always very superficial.

Each contributor was asked (1) to set forth the major trends in the special field discussed, (2) to discuss these trends critically, and (3) to summarize the present position of the field with particular emphasis on problems requiring further research. The papers are divided roughly along these lines by centered Roman numerals. The subject matter and the authors' methods of exposition have not of course lent themselves equally well to such a uniform division. We have not attempted to impose an arbitrary and essentially artificial uniformity on papers dealing with diverse topics from divergent points of view. Nor have we sought to maintain any particular position with respect to the proper subject matter and methods of sociology.

The result of the long-distance collaboration among the authors are of course less uniform and consistent than they would have been had all the chapters been written by the editors or by any other single author or close collaborators. As for ourselves, we not only admit but insist that the results are better and more nearly representative of the contemporary state of the science precisely because the book is a collective work.

The papers in Part I are intended to cover the greater part of the special fields in sociology, while those in Part II review the principal tendencies in those countries or regions where the science has been actively developed. It would be naive to suppose that either section is "complete." Our aim has not been encyclopedic. We believe however that the coverage is representative, although specialists may perhaps quarrel with the amount of attention accorded to the various recognized fields and areas of sociological research.

Although the book will probably be most frequently used as a reference work for sociologists, sociologists-in-training, and interested professionals in related fields, it may well serve as a text in those advanced and unduly rare courses that emphasize topics, difficulties, and achievements rather than a randomly detailed chronology.

The editors are grateful for the willing response of prominent and competent scholars asked to collaborate with us in writing this book, and for their punctual fulfillment of their promises despite heavy burdens of wartime teaching and research. If the book is found to have merit, the credit naturally belongs primarily to the individual authors and not to us as collectors.

There remains the assignment of the editors' individual responsibilities. The organization of the Symposium was originally undertaken by the senior editor, Georges Gurvitch, who drew up the list of chapters, suggested their general scope, and invited contributors. The junior editor, Wilbert E. Moore, was primarily responsible for matters of form and for preparing the manuscripts for the printer, including the translation of Professor Roger Bastide's paper from the French. Moore also assumed the bulk of the proof-reading. All the chapters have been reviewed by both editors, and we jointly subscribe to all editorial decisions. Each author of course has complete responsibility for his own paper.

GEORGES CURVITCH
WILBERT E. MOORE

Table of Contents

PREFACE .... V - VII

PART ONE

CHAPTER	PAGES
I. SOCIOLOGY AND THE SOCIAL SCIENCES *By Huntington Cairns*	3-19
II. RESEARCH METHODS IN SOCIOLOGY *By Ernest W. Burgess*	20-41
III. THE PRESENT POSITION AND PROSPECTS OF SYSTEMATIC THEORY IN SOCIOLOGY *By Talcott Parsons*	42-69
IV. INTERPRETIVE SOCIOLOGY AND CONSTRUCTIVE TYPOLOGY *By Howard Becker*	70-95
V. SOCIOCULTURAL DYNAMICS AND EVOLUTION *By Pitirim A. Sorokin*	96-120
VI. SOCIAL CAUSATION AND CHANGE *By Robert Morrison MacIver*	121-138
VII. SOCIOLOGY OF GROUPS *By Logan Wilson*	139-171
VIII. SOCIAL ORGANIZATION AND INSTITUTIONS *By Flofrian Znaniecki*	172-217
IX. SOCIAL PSYCHOLOGY *By James W. Woodard*	218-266
X. SOCIAL CONTROL *By Georges Gurvitch*	267-296
XI. SOCIOLOGY OF LAW *By Roscoe Pound*	297-341
XII. CRIMINOLOGY *By Jerome Hall*	342-365
XIII. SOCIOLOGY OF KNOWLEDGE *By Robert K. Merton*	366-405
XIV. SOCIOLOGY OF RELIGION *By Joachim Wach*	406-437
XV. SOCIOLOGY OF ECONOMIC ORGANIZATION *By Wilbert E. Moore*	438-465
XVI. HUMAN ECOLOGY *By Emma Llewellyn and Audrey Hawthorn*	466-499

Table of Contents

PART TWO

CHAPTER		PAGES
XVII.	FRENCH SOCIOLOGY By Claude Lévi-Strauss	503-537
XVIII.	AMERICAN SOCIOLOGY By Robert E. L. Faris	538-561
XIX.	BRITISH SOCIOLOGY By J. Rumney	562-685
XX.	GERMAN SOCIOLOGY By Albert Salomon	586-614
XXI.	SOCIOLOGY IN LATIN AMERICA By Roger Bastide	615-637
XXII.	ITALIAN SOCIOLOGY By Costantino Panunzio	638-652
XXIII.	SPANISH SOCIOLOGY By Alfredo Mendizábal	653-670
XXIV.	RUSSIAN SOCIOLOGY By Max M. Laserson	671-702
XXV.	EASTERN EUROPEAN SOCIOLOGY	703-754
	A. Polish Sociology By Eileen Markley Znaniecki	703-717
	B. Czechoslovak Sociology By Joseph S. Roucek	717-731
	C. Rumanian Sociology By A. Manoil	732-740
	D. Sociology in Yugoslávia By Joseph S. Roucek	740-754

PART ONE

CHAPTER I

SOCIOLOGY AND THE SOCIAL SCIENCES

by

HUNTINGTON CAIRNS

I

Sociology's constant concern with its relations to the other social sciences, which began at the very moment of its establishment as a separate branch of inquiry, has been prompted, in part at least, by a desire to achieve for itself greater order and system in a field of extraordinary elusiveness. But the realization of that desire has been impeded by two obstacles. First, the subject matter of the social sciences is unusually intricate, in the sense that it so far has defied organization at anything like the level achieved in the organization of the subject matter of the physical sciences. Explanation in the realm of the physical sciences is on a much firmer foundation than explanation in the social sciences. One consequence of this higher degree of conceptualization in the physical sciences is that their advances can be made on purely theoretical lines, and the advances often outstrip for long periods of time the possibility of application to concrete data. Second, sociologists have never agreed on the domain of their subject matter nor on their attitude toward it. In many sciences the subject matters which are studied are frequently altered. The transformation of geometry in the Nineteenth Century from an apodeictic science of space of one occupied exclusively with formal structure is an illustration. But in such cases the continuity of investigation is usually uninterrupted. This means that the later investigation, which may be directed towards a subject matter which has been fundamentally revised, builds for the most part upon data already accumulated. Sociology does not exhibit a comparable continuity. In both its theory and its subject matter it displays a mutative quality that forcibly indicates a relatively rudimentary stage of development. As a consequence of this excessive individualism, the larger claims that sociology advances are consistently disappointing in their results. It is not clear whether the time has arrived when this unsatisfactory condition can be brought to an end. But it appears possible, in view of the data accumulated, to indicate some of the main lines that must be followed if the sociologist is to achieve the order and system which the physical scientists have already attained.

The Field of Sociology. At the outset it will be assumed that, although the data of the physical sciences and the data of human society are different, their susceptibility to treatment by the ordinary means of scientific method is the same. This means that the search for facts, the formulation of hypotheses, measurement, and the regard for system are methods applicable alike to both the natural and the social spheres. It will be assumed also that the subject matter of the social sciences is human activity and its products. If we look at the particular social sciences we see that each studies some aspect of human activity, and that none studies human activity as a whole. The same state of affairs does not exist in the natural sciences. There are many natural sciences, each studying a facet of physical reality. But over and above them all is something that in the Nineteenth Century was called "science" and today the "philosophy of science," which purports or hopes to explain the world in its totality, and which is a synthesis of the researches of the separate sciences. In this attitude science competes with art, philosophy, history and religion, each of which also asserts an explanation of the world in its fullness. But the social sciences possess no general science charged with the exclusive function of examining and synthesizing the conclusions of its separate fields.

Until sociologists themselves define the object of their study it will have to be assumed that sociology is what the men who call

SOCIOLOGY AND SOCIAL SCIENCES

themselves sociologists write about. This does not mean that sociology does not have a distinguishing trait. It means only that no word has yet been specified to denote that trait. An examination of the standard texts in the field reveals such a uniformity in the selection of topics for treatment that the implication is inescapable that human activity is being viewed in an aspect which admits of a systematic approach. But the topics covered are clearly not limited to the psychological, economic, historical, legal, anthropological, political, religious, or ethical aspects. What is left is a multitude of topics — among them the structure of society, social causation, institutions, societary change, group contacts, progress, interests, social forces, social control, assimilation, human nature, isolation, competition, social interaction, conflict, social ethics, the crowd and crime. Some of those topics are studied by other social sciences, but no social science except sociology studies all of them, and no other science approaches any of them solely from the point of view of the sociologist. Inasmuch as the various social sciences are studying the not-too-clearly differentiated parts of a whole, separations and classifications must be provisional and temporary. Even so, there remains something distinctive which is properly termed sociological. No satisfactory word exists to name it, and no concept has been devised to embrace it. Insofar as it may be caught in a single phrase, the sociological attitude seems to represent an emphasis upon the facts of human activity in general, in which the role of specific factors, such as geography or economics, is given full recognition, but the activity is not seen exclusively from the point of view of any one of them.

Notwithstanding its preoccupation with the methods of science, sociology still possesses a national quality which is not characteristic of any of the advanced sciences. Its practice and point of view shift from country to country; thus we have English, French, German, Russian, Italian and Japanese sociologies, to name but a few. This is a limitation sociology shares with philosophy. However, it is possible that in the case of philosophy this characteristic is inescapable, on the ground, as stated by Bosanquet, that philosophy "being, like language, art, and poetry, a product of the whole man, is a thing that would forfeit some of its essence if it were to lose its national quality." (1) Such a defense is not open to sociology if its ideal, like that of the other sciences, is an impersonal one.

---

1. Bernard Bosanquet, "Science and Philosophy" in *Proceedings of the Aristotelian Society* N.S. Vol. XV, (London: Williams and Norgate, 1915), p. 2.

TWENTIETH CENTURY SOCIOLOGY

Nationalism in sociology is a symptom of its fumbling immaturity, and a warning of the extensive labors still demanded before it can meet the numerous requirements of scientific method.

Comte and His Successors. The issues raised in the consideration of the relations of sociology to the separate social sciences have been subjected to extensive analysis by sociologists, but they have not been brought to a satisfactory termination. Comte conceived of five fundamental sciences—astronomy, physics, chemistry, physiology and social physics—arranged in a serial order, which was both logical and historical. Each successive science was regarded as dependent on those that preceded it in the series for methods and conclusions. The first, astronomy, was held to consider the most general, simple, abstract, and remote phenomena, that which influences all others without being influenced by them. The last, social physics, or sociology, examines the most particular, complicated and concrete phenomena, and that which is of the greatest inmediate interest to man. The phenomena in this field depend, more or less, upon the phenomena of the anterior domains, but exercise no influence on them. Between astronomy and sociology the degrees of specialty, complexity and individuality of the phenomena are in proportion to the place of the science in the series. (2) This, in brief, is his idea of the "filiation" of the sciences, from which developed the conception of the "hierachy of the sciences." It was subjected to attack by Fiske and Spencer, and defended in part by Mill, Littré and Ward. There is an element of truth in the idea, but it would not be supported in its entirety today by anyone. It is now seen that some sciences are filiated (crystallography and mineralogy) and many in part at least are interdependent (crystallography and geometry). It would be rash, in view of the surprising connections between the different domains of investigation exhibited by the history of science since Comte's time, to assert that any is independent.

Sociology in Comte's hands thus became the final science, (3) the only one, inasmuch as it dealt with the human and social, that supplied a truly universal point of view. It employed the results of all the previous sciences, and occupied fully the domains of all the other social sciences. In Comte's view social phenomena are indivisible and must therefore be studied as a whole by a single science. The conclusions of such a subject as economics, for example,

---

2. *Cours de philosophie positive,* (Paris: Bachelier, 1852), Vol. 1, p. 76.
3. *Ibid.,* Vol. 6, Chap. 58-59.

SOCIOLOGY AND THE SOCIAL SCIENCES

represent nothing but "profound misconstructions of the valuable tokens of common sense." (4) Not only workers in the other social sciences, but sociologists as well have repudiated Comte's insistence upon the all-inclusive character of sociology. Yet here again Comte's position has an element of truth. In practice social phenomena have been departmentalized for the purposes of study. But are they in truth divisible? It is possible that all the labors of all the social scientists will never add up to an understanding of the social process. Until social phenomena are seen as a whole the social scientist can not know whether the directions taken in the separate departments are pointed towards the possibility of ultimate explanation. The sociology studied in the three volumes of Herbert Spencer's *Principles of Sociology* is no longer for the most part the sociology set forth in current treatises. Spencer's sociology has largely passed over into anthropology, and some parts of it are not studied at all. That may well be the fate of sociology once again in another two generations. Modern science has taught us the advantages to be derived from the study of the specific; but unless that study is guided by system the likelihood in sociology of reaching a general theory appears remote.

Spencer, instead of repudiating the separate social sciences in favor of sociology, as Comte had done, accepted them as legitimate subsciences whose results would be synthesized by the parent science into a general theory of society. The highest achievement in sociology was "to grasp the vast heterogeneous aggregate" (5) so that it could be seen in its entirety. This idea has been widely accepted, both in the United States and abroad, and is still a vital one. It was justified by Small, who accepted it on the ground that it was an accurate description of what sociologists did in fact, notwithstanding their formal definitions and protestations to the contrary. He insisted that all sociologists endeavored to reach judgments of a higher degree of generality than the subject matter of any single branch of social science was competent to authorize. It therefore followed that sociology was "an attempt to organize and generalize all available knowledge about the influences that pervade human associations." (6) Closely allied to this conception

---

4. *Ibid*, Vol. 4, p. 271.
5. *Principles of Sociology*, (New York: D. Appleton and Co., 1882) Vol. I, p. 462.
6. *General Sociology*, (Chicago: Chicago University Press, 1905), 27.

was Ward's (7) doctrine that sociology is not a synthesis of the special social sciences but a compound which their synthesis created. It is not any of the social sciences nor all of them. The special social sciences are the units of aggregation that are combined to create sociology, but they lose their individuality as completely as do chemical units, and the resultant product it wholly unlike any of them, and is of a higher order.

The alternative conception that sociology is a distinct science, with no thought of a suzerainty over the special social sciences, was advocated by Giddings. (8) Its province is co-extensive with the entire field of all the social sciences, but it is content to study exhaustively the elementary and generic phenomena of the field, leaving the endless forms of combination to other investigators. It is therefore not the sum of the social sciences, but their common basis. Its principles are the postulates of special sciences, and as such they act to coordinate the whole field. The special social sciences thus become differentiations of sociology. This view has now shifted to the later one that sociology is both basic to all the other social sciences and at the same time is merely a specialism coordinate with other specialisms. Sociology is "regarded neither as the mistress nor as the handmaid of the social sciences, but as their sister." (9)

Historically, sociology may thus be regarded from the point of view of its major practitioners as the sole social science, as a synthesis of the separate social sciences, and as the basic social science. Other views are sometimes taken of the question, notably that it is none of the things just outlined but is merely a method utilized by all the social sciences for studying social phenomena. Sociologists have attempted to show that the various views are not in conflict but are supplementary to each other. (10) Before examining the question closely it will be well to ascertain briefly the nature of the relationship between sociology and the separate social sciences, as it reveals itself in practice.

---

7. *Pure Sociology*, (New York: The Macmillan Co., 1903) p. 91.

8. *Principles of Sociology*, (New York: The Macmillan Co., 1896), p. 26 *et seq.*

9. Harry Elmer Barnes and Howard Becker, *Social Thought from Lore to Science*, (New York: D. C. Heath and Co., 1938), Vol. I, p. x.

10. Harry Elmer Barnes, *Sociology and Political Theory*, (New York: Alfred A. Knopf, 1924), pp. 22-23; Charles A. Ellwood, *Sociology in its Psychological Aspects*, (New York: D. Appleton and Co., 1912), pp. 30-31.

SOCIOLOGY AND THE SOCIAL SCIENCES

II

Interdependence of Sociology. When sociology is considered by sociologists or other social scientists in relation to a particular social science, as distinguished from the social sciences generally, the tendency today is to regard them as interdependent. Formerly, it used to be held, at least by sociologists, that a social science was dependent upon sociology when its subject matter was historically posterior or when the elements which it studied were differentiations of general sociological concepts. Thus political science was regarded as a dependent sociological science, because political organization was a late development in social evolution, and could be understood only after social organization and the nature of society in general had been grasped. Similarly, economics was held to rest upon sociology because the concepts it handled, *e. g.* value, were treated with greater generality by sociology. There was a natural disinclination on the part of political scientists and economists, particularly since their fields had been established long before the advent of sociology, to accept such a proposal, and they contented themselves with either ignoring or denouncing it. However, in practice the proposal offered great difficulties. There was at hand for neither the political scientist nor the economist a body of established sociological knowledge to which they could turn for positive guidance. It was true that sociologists had occupied themselves with a subject matter which also fell to some extent in the political science and economic domains. But their conclusions were hopelessly diverse and conflicting. It seemed to the political scientist and economist that they should not be forced to choose among the competing claims of sociologists, and that before they were asked to accept a conclusion the minimum condition should be met that it be an established one in the sociological field.

For the most part sociologists have now abandoned their ideas of a world State in favor of a good neighbor policy which recognizes the interdependence of the various social sciences. The movement in general has been a reciprocal one, with benefits flowing to each of the sciences. Sociologists recognize the advantages to be gained through the study of anthropological investigations of primitive types of social organization; jurisprudence, in its insistence upon the practical working of law, its conception of law as a social institution, its emphasis upon social purposes, and its functional outlook, reveals the vast obligation it is under to sociology; economists have recognized the assistance sociology can render in the clarification of the problems of social control, social adaptation, social forces, competition, and collective behavior, and sociologists have always leaned heavily upon economics for an understanding of economic phases of society; sociology looks to political science for the data of political organization, and political science derives from sociology its knowledge of the social structure of which political organization is but a part; history turns to sociology for its general view of the principles of social organization as the basis for the proper distribution of its facts, and sociology looks to history for some of its most significant data; finally, ethics derives much of its factual subject matter from the researches of sociologists.

Thus in practice the relationship of sociology to the other social sciences is one of general but discriminate borrowing. There is no question of sociology as the sole social science, as a synthesis, or as other social science studies, although there is an extensive overlap among all the social sciences. This, in itself, is sufficient to negative the idea that it is merely a synthesis; not since Comte has it been seriously urged that it is the sole social science, and nowhere in practice is there any substantial evidence that it is treated as the basic social science. In the natural sciences the practice of discriminate borrowing is widespread, and is one of the basic factors in their continued success. The relatively new and successful science of molecular physics was devised by Waterston, the great Scottish physicist, through an extension of the general principles of Newton to the molecular world. There are no absolute boundaries for the various sciences, and those which have been sketched may be crossed at any point for revitalization and additional sustenance.

III

Integration of the Social Sciences. This observation does not, however, exhaust the inquiry. Sociologists in their insistence upon characterizing their science as a synthetic or basic social science had their eyes upon a vital point. If the aim of the social sciences is the full explanation of social phenomena it is not likely that this will be achieved by the piecemeal methods now prevailing. Human behavior and its products, or to use a shorthand expression, culture, must be considered for the purposes of knowledge a single domain, and it is the object of the social sciences ultimately to isolate all

SOCIOLOGY AND THE SOCIAL SCIENCES

the significant factors and relationships which, when seen synoptically, will yield the explanation of that domain. As it stands now each social science gives a partial account of part of that area. Their accounts are not complete in detail, nor is it possible to assemble them into a coherent whole. The extent of their partiality is even unknown. Because science has reached a general physics it can bring its energies to bear on diminishing the importance of the individual element, by accounting for it as an instance of the general. When the individual element proves refractory, a modification in the general theory becomes imperative. Thus the wave theory of light accounted for many phenomena, but it left out color as perceived. If sociology had been in truth the basic social science, as some of its advocates claimed, the chaotic condition of the social sciences would not now prevail.

As a method, specialization has much to recommend it. Without it, knowledge is apt to be superficial. Cosmic explorations of the universe are never more than high school botanical outing parties which result in an indiscriminate assemblage of four-leaf clovers, dried snake skins and congealed sap. Science, as Santayana has pointed out, confined itself at its second rebirth to concrete discoveries—the earth's roundness and motion about the sun, the laws of mechanics, the development and application of algebra, the invention of the calculus, and a hundred other steps forward in the various disciplines. "It was a patient siege laid to the truth," he writes, "which was approached blindly and without a general, as by an army of ants; it was not stormed imaginatively as by the ancient Ionians, who had reached at once the notion of nature's dynamic unity, but had neglected to take possession in detail of the intervening tracts, whence resources might be drawn in order to maintain the main position." (11) It so happened, as discoveries accumulated, they fell insensibly into a system, and philosophers like Descartes and Newton arrived at a general physics. That happened because the entities and relations which were chosen for study turned out to be the entities and relations which would explain nature. We have no evidence that the entities and relations which the social sciences study are those which will yield a comparable result in that department of inquiry. But specialization can also lead to an undue stress upon the significance of trifling points. Above all, specialization may cost the perception of the unity of knowledge,

---
11. *Life of Reason*, (New York: Charles Scribner's Sons, 1905), Vol. 5. p. 6.

upon which adequate explanation in the end turns. The task confronting the social scientist is the reconciliation of the advantages of departmentalization and universality. The former will give to the discrete social sciences an autonomy justified by the distinctive character of their subject matter, with the attendant benefits flowing from an exhaustive study of a limited order of facts, and the latter will weld the specialities into that synthesis and system which alone yield unity.

Sociology and the social sciences have parcelled out for study among themselves parts of a whole which, if an exploration of the entire process is to be reached, must when gathered together explain the whole. But there is no claim on the part of social scientists that that is the case. The continual emergence of new areas of study, the constant shifting of points of view, both indicate the existence of numerous lacunae. There is no concerted effort to discover them systematically, and little lamentation of that fact. There is a blind faith that the haphazardness which had such a triumphant resolution in physics will have a similar issue in the social sciences. But in physics the specific discoveries that occurred before the end was even envisaged were signposts that the physicists, if not on the main road, were on highways leading to it. Notwithstanding the vast amount of research which has been accumulated, there are few, if any, comparable discoveries in the social sciences that warrant any such encouragement in that field.

Obstacles to Integration. Two difficulties stand in the way of a possible solution. First is the idea prevalent among some workers in the field that sociology ought consciously to endeavor to become the basic social science. Its task then would be to supply the framework of a social science upon which the particular social sciences could build. It would be under the further obligation of testing and systematizing the conclusions of those sciences, of suggesting explorations in new directions for them, and of synthesizing the final results into a unified whole. However, against this proposal there are a number of weighty objections. While the subject matter of sociology, because of its generality, might suggest that it alone among the social sciences is peculiarly fitted for the undertaking, that may not be true in actuality. A general science is not necessarily a basic science, and we are without knowledge whether the entities and relations which sociology studies are sufficiently fundamental for them to be accepted as the structure of a general theory. If

SOCIOLOGY AND THE SOCIAL SCIENCES

they are not, there is no reason why the task should be assigned to sociology, in preference to some other science. Further, sociology has a distinctive subject matter which, until the contrary is established, must be taken as warranting the energies devoted to it by sociologists. The analysis of that subject matter would suffer were the interests of sociologists to be diverted into the new undertaking. That it suffers even now by the endeavors of sociologists to occupy themselves with problems which are studied in the other disciplines is only too apparent. To enlarge further the burden that sociologists are now carrying would be an ill turn, both to them and to the social sciences generally.

Second is the idea, advanced by some sociologists that sociology and the other social sciences ought to attempt a radical revision of their approach to their subject matters, with the object of discovering a focal point common to all the disciplines which would allow the advantages of specialization but at the same time indicate the path towards integration. The history of thought contains many illustrations of similar efforts. From Aristotle's constant search for the universal type in the individual phenomenon to the Tenth-Century encyclopaedia of the Brethren of Purity, with its assumption of a world soul, to Humboldt's *Kosmos*, with its insistence upon the unity of nature, we have witnessed the power of integration generated by concepts which permeate numerous fields of research. We have seen the same occurrence in the social sciences. Comte's law of the three stages and Spencer's application of the principle of evolution provided concepts on which all the then-known facts of social existence could be hung and united, like pearls upon a string. No such concepts are available, or at least appeal, to the social scientist today, nor does it appear likely, in view of the prevailing skeptical mood, that any will appear. Progress, institutions, relations, human nature, these and many others have been tried and found wanting. Concepts of the type which would meet the requirements of such a proposal undoubtedly could be devised, at least as tentative working hypotheses. In fact, the movement of social science thought, in its insistence upon culture as the subject matter common to all the disciplines, is a step in that direction. However, as matters now stand, the choice of such concepts would be fortuitous and not based upon knowledge. We possess no such synoptic view of the social sciences which encourages us to believe that we are now at a stage of analysis where we can with any certainty select the basic concepts upon which an integrated structure of knowledge can be erected. Moreover, assuming adequate knowledge for the formulation of such concepts, the requirement that the disciplines abandon their present orientation and substitute a radically new point of view is one that is scarcely likely to be met. To surrender a conceptual approach which has already yielded material successes in favor of largely adventitious assumptions would be too hazardous an undertaking to enlist many adherents.

The Philosophy of the Social Sciences. One possible solution for these difficulties presents itself. A new discipline might be created, a philosophy of the social sciences, whose subject matter would be the special sciences themselves, and whose task would be the critical analysis of their practices and assumptions and the construction ultimately of a theory that would answer the problems of society in their totality. This solution of the difficulties that now embarrass the social sciences appears to be a fruitful one. In the domain of the exact sciences a similar solution has already led to a ferment of activity and considerable progress in the analysis of the obstacles that confront the workers in those disciplines. Four journals, one in the United States, one in England and two in Germany, have been founded to explore the problems of the philosophy of science, and the First International Congress of the Philosophy of Science was held in Paris in 1935. The subject itself is taught in most of the important universities and colleges of the world. That the social sciences stand in need of a comparable discipline seems self-evident. It would possess much the same aims as the philosophy of science, but inasmuch as its subject matter would be different its propositions also would be different. To the extent that there was an overlap of subject matter, as in the analysis of such basic concepts as order, law, and causation, which are common to the thought of both the exact and the social sciences, the propositions might be identical. Also, since a philosophy of the social sciences would aim at what is abstract and universal, while the special social sciences in view of their partiality can only intimate it, the propositions of the philosophy of the social sciences would in large measure be such as would not occur in the special social sciences. A philosophy of the social sciences should therefore lead to knowledge of a kind which has heretofore remained unexplored in the social sciences.

A philosophy of the social sciences would be concerned with three sets of problems, which may be classified as methodological, critical and synoptical. (12) On the methodological side, the business of a philosophy of the social sciences would be to analyze the methods employed by each of the separate social sciences, to isolate the characteristics, if any, peculiar to the domain, to propose corrections, to harmonize the practices with the tested procedures of other disciplines, and in general to make certain that the methodology of the social sciences is as rigorous, so far as its subject matter permits, as that which obtains in the physical sciences. In its critical aspect, a philosophy of the social sciences would analyze the basic concepts and the primary postulates, both express and implied, of the separate sciences, and would endeavor, insofar as they are ascertained to be necessary, to develop a rational justification for them. This is a task which is performed to a limited extent by the separate sciences for the concepts and postulates that each employs; but here again the analysis is incomplete because of its partiality. In its synoptic or synthetic phase, a philosophy of the social sciences would attempt to make some kind of a whole from the results of the various sciences. At this point gaps in the structure of the social sciences may appear and new problems, even new disciplines to explore them, may be suggested.

Sociology and the Philosophy of the Social Sciences. Historically, sociology has been, and is today, a descriptive science. That is to say, it is non-explanatory and its propositions are of equal rank logically and do not serve as bases for one another. It is a science based directly on detached facts not united by a universal hypothesis, (13) and inasmuch as the other social sciences are also descriptive sciences, its propositions are not corroborated by the propositions established in those fields. Its facts are therefore unrelated, and, as Aristotle observed long ago, might just as well have been otherwise. As hypotheses are introduced into sociology it will pass over into an explanatory science, and its facts and propositions will become integrated. Until such hypotheses are developed, therefore, the special task of sociology is classification. It is a

---

12. C. D. Broad, *Scientific Thought*, (New York: Hartcourt, Brace and Co., 1923), p. 11. *et seq.;* Morris R. Cohen, *Reason and Nature*, (New York: Harcourt, Brace and Co., 1931), p. 147 *et seq.;* A. Cornelius Benjamin, *Logical Structure of Science*, (London: Kegan Paul and Co., 1936), p. 36 *et seq.; idem, An Introduction to the Philosophy of Science*, (New York: The Macmillan Co., 1937), p. 33 *et seq.*

13. W. Stanley Jevons, *The Principles of Science*, (London: The Macmillan Co., 1892). p. 526.

science with a distinct subject matter which, it is assumed, is susceptible of manipulation in accordance with the logical conditions which have to be satisfied in other branches of inquiry.

Sociology thus differs materially from the proposed philosophy of the social sciences. The subject matter of the philosophy of the social sciences is primarily the social sciences themselves, their methods, assumptions and propositions. Ultimately, its subject matter is also culture, but its concern with the data from that field is critical, and directed towards what the individual social sciences do with culture. It leaves to the separate social sciences the formulation of propositions related to their fields, and inquires only into the validity of the methods through which they are reached, and the soundness of the assumptions on which they are based. Its final end, like that of the separate social sciences, is knowledge, but its propositions will not be limited to segments of the subject matter, which is necessarily the case with the separate sciences, but will purport to possess complete generality. If a proposition put forward by social science today has that generality, it is unknown and accidental, since no social science professes to occupy the entire field. The philosophy of the social sciences is thus distinct from sociology in its current activity as a descriptive science, but it has some similarity with attitudes from which sociology has been viewed in the past. It does not wish to suppress the other social sciences as Comte desired, but, on the contrary, depends upon them for its very existence. In its ultimate product it may be a synthesis of the social sciences, as Spencer insisted, or a compound as Ward maintained, or it may be something else. The answer to that question will have to await the analysis of the character of the propositions developed by the philosophy of the social sciences.

In its direct concern with sociology, the philosophy of the social sciences will raise many questions to which sociologists have never been oblivious. Sociologists are as aware as their critics of the shortcomings of sociology, and their efforts to correct the aberrations and deficiencies of their science have been of a notable order. Their contributions to methodology do not suffer by comparison with those made by students of any other science, including the exact. The justification of the philosophy of the social sciences in raising many of the same questions already considered by sociologists might rest on the ground that they have never been satisfactorily answered, and therefore an inquiry into them by the philosophy of the social sciences is legitimate. But the ultimate justification lies in the fact

SOCIOLOGY AND THE SOCIAL SCIENCES

that the philosophy of the social sciences raises appropriate questions from a point of view which differs from that of the sociologist. Many factors contribute to that difference; but essentially it is perhaps again the difference between the general and the particular. The sociologist has but one section of a vast field before him, while the philosopher of the social sciences must endeavor to encompass the whole domain. The sociologist, to borrow an Aristotelian analogy, is the physician. It is the particular case that is treated, not the universal; Socrates or Callias, not man in general. It is not directly man the physician cures, but directly Callias and indirectly man because Callias is a man. (14) The sociologist wants to know what is, in fact, the situation in his field; in determining that he contributes to the general problem. Again, there is the question of bias. Is there any excuse for the existence of the subject of inquiry called sociology? John Stuart Mill, after an extensive *a priori* examination of the problem, answered it in the negative. (15) It may be taken for granted that all authors of sociological works would answer the question affirmatively.

It is no doubt true, as Cohen (16) has observed, that it is difficult for anyone but a specialist to know what *are* the results of any one special science. But the implied criticism has a reciprocal force. Sociologists who write on methodology are not specialists in that field, and their knowledge of its results ought not to be assumed to be more profound than the philosopher's knowledge of the conclusions of sociology. In any event, the philosopher will insist upon satisfactory answers to questions which the sociologist customarily ignores or minimizes. Is the current emphasis of sociology upon the concrete a mistake? Should the society studied be, in Hobbes's phrase, this or that society, the presently existing United States or Europe or other area. Perhaps the insight of the *Leviathan* was due to the circumstance that it analysed an ideal State, constructed logically from certain assumptions which Hobbes admitted were completely unhistorical. Again, should the sociologist assume, as he does, a uniformity of social phenomena comparable to the physicist's assumption of the uniformity of nature? Is history the foundation of sociology in the same sense that it is held by some to be the foundation of the natural sciences? In the exact sciences there is no overlap of classes: a line is either straight or curved.

---

14. *Meta.* 981 a 20.
15. *A System of Logic*, (New York: Harper and Bros., 1864) pp. 547 *et seq.*
16. *Ibid*, p. 147.

TWENTIETH CENTURY SOCIOLOGY

In the natural and social sciences classes frequently overlap. What is the exact boundary between animal and vegetable, State and Association? Does it follow, as Croce (17) argues, that the universals of all these sciences are quite arbitrary, that therefore the sciences cannot be unified (hence their ineradicable plurality) and must remain unsystematic, a mass of sciences without close relations among themselves, and even worse, that no logical distinctions are possible in any of them? Since Aristotle pointed out that goodness was predicable under all the categories, which was incompatible with the theory of classification, the problem has been a persistent one in philosophy. In modern logic an attempt is being made to treat the overlap as normal, in defiance of the traditional rules of classification, and the results may have repercussions in sociological methodology, which follows, consciously or unconsciously, the customary practices. Problems of this kind will constitute the focal point between sociology and the philosophy of the social sciences, and their full or even partial solution ought to further materially the expansion of sociological analysis.

That this proposed solution will be attempted appears inevitable. One of the factors that has been held responsible for the emergence of the philosophy of science is the various crises which science experienced in the last century. The formulation of alternative systems of geometry by Lobachevski and Riemann and the shock of the relativity theory were two among several major turning points in scientific thought which provoked a sense of instability among scientific workers. Science became self-critical, and, as Benjamin has pointed out, a philosophy of science is inevitable whenever a science becomes self-critical. The social sciences are self-critical today, but for different reasons. They have suffered no obvious breakdowns at all comparable to those which occurred in Nineteenth-Century science. But they display the doubts and hesitations that are usually the mark of incipient sciences; they are torn by distracting alternatives. If, as Russell has suggested, the internal development of science may be summed up as the passage from contemplation to manipulation, the social sciences, except in relatively unimportant matters, have not yet made that passage, and that in itself has bred distrust. Moreover, the concern of the social sciences over their

---

17. *Logic as the Science of the Pure Concept,* (London: The Macmillan Co., 1917), p. 334. For an attempt to develop the idea of the overlap of classes systematically see R. G. Collingwood, *An Essay in Philosophical Method,* (Oxford: Clarendon Press, 1933) *passim.*

SOCIOLOGY AND THE SOCIAL SCIENCES

relations with each other may be viewed merely as a phase of the self-critical mood which today has gripped all the sciences. It has been found that the problems raised by that same concern in the exact sciences appear most likely to be answered by a new discipline, whose sole task is to respond to that and similar problems. No reason suggests itself why the same solution is not available to the social sciences.

SELECTED BIBLIOGRAPHY

Barnes, Harry Elmer, *Sociology and Political Theory*, (New York: Alfred A. Knopf, 1924).

Barnes, Harry Elmer, *The New History and the Social Studies*, (New York: Century Co., 1925).

Benjamin, A. Cornelius, *An Introduction to the Philosophy of Science*, (New York: The Macmillan Co., 1937).

Broad, C. D., *Scientific Thought*, (New York: Harcourt, Brace and Co., 1923).

Cohen, Morris R., *Reason and Nature*, (New York: Harcourt, Brace and Co., 1931).

Dewey, John, *Logic: The Theory of Inquiry*, (New York: Henry Holt and Co., 1938).

Ellwood, Charles A., *Sociology in Its Psychological Aspects*, (New York: D. Appleton and Co., 1912).

Flint, Robert, *Philosophy as Scientia Scientiarum*, (London: Blackwood, 1904).

Friend, Julius W. and James Feibleman, *The Unlimited Community, a Study of the Possibility of Social Science*, (London: George Allen and Unwin, 1936).

Giddings, Franklin H., *The Principles of Sociology*, (New York: The Macmillan Co., 1896).

Lynd, Robert S., *Knowledge For What?* (Princeton: Princeton University Press, 1939).

Malinowsky, Bronislaw, *A Scientific Theory of Culture*, (Chapel Hill: University of North Carolina Press, 1944).

Ogburn, William Fielding and Alexander Goldenweiser, *The Social Sciences and Their Interrelations*, (Boston: Houghton Mifflin Co., 1927).

Peirce, Charles Sanders, *Collected Papers* Vol. I, (Cambridge: Harvard University Press, 1931).

Huntington Cairns is the author of *Law and the Social Sciences*, (New York: Harcourt, Brace and Co., 1935) and *The Theory of Legal Sciences*, (Chapel Hill: University of North Carolina Press, 1941), both of which are directly concerned with the integration of the social sciences. Born in 1904, he practiced law in Baltimore from 1926 to 1937, and during the last two years of his practice he also taught at University of Maryland Law School. In 1937 he was appointed Assistant General Counsel of the United States Treasury Department. He resigned in 1943 to become Secretary, Treasurer and General Counsel of the National Gallery of Art in Washington, positions which he now holds. He is the author of numerous articles and books and is a frequent contributor to the law reviews and scientific journals.

CHAPTER II

RESEARCH METHODS IN SOCIOLOGY

by

ERNEST W. BURGESS

A crucial issue in sociology centers around the relative values for research of its two basic methods, statistics and case study. The questions raised by this issue ramify out and are involved in almost every consideration of sociological method. They are implicit or explicit in (1) conceptions of the nature of the subject matter of sociology, (2) the problem of the applicability of scientific method to the study of human behavior, (3) the sifnificance of concepts for sociological research, (4) the conditions underlying the independent development of cases studies and statistics, (5) the emergence of sociometry as a combination of conceptualization and measurement susceptible both to case study and statistical procedures, and (6) the ways in which statistical and case study methods may be interrelated.

I

The Nature of Sociology. An early and recurrent problem in sociology is the wide difference of opinion upon the nature of society and of its relation to the individuals which compose it. Is society to be treated as a reality and to be studied then through social processes such as communication, collective representations and social control or is it to be considered as an aggregate of individuals and therefore to be analyzed in terms of their behavior and mental processes? If society is organic and exists in the interaction and the intercommunication of its members, then quite different methods of study are indicated than if society is atomistic, i.e., a mere collection of individuals.

The so-called realists devised conceptions and viewpoints on methodology in keeping with their assumption of the reality of society. Examples of their concepts or methods are: Comte, the social consensus; Durkheim, collective representation; Simmel, social forms of interaction; Weber, ideal type analysis; Sumner, folkways and mores; Small, the group; Cooley, sympathetic introspection; and Park, collective behavior. With the exception of Durkheim in his work on *Suicide* the others made little or no use of statistical data.

The nominalists, so-called because of their refusal to consider society in itself as the object of study, found the explanation of why men behave together, in the physiological and mental process of its individual units. Aristotle and others posited man as possessing a social instinct. Tarde specifically identified the instinct of imitation as explaining man's social behavior. Giddings coined the alliterative phrase "the consciousness of kind" and was logically consistent in substituting the term "pluralistic" for "collective" behavior. Floyd H. Allport, rejecting interpretation by "instincts," substituted "prepotent reflexes" — a distinction with little if any difference — and maintained the nominalist position by characterizing the terms "the group" and "institution" as fallacies.

Both Giddings and Allport made considerable use of statistics. Giddings, in fact, was the first general sociologist to emphasize the importance of statistics for sociological research. Allport, professionally trained as a psychologist, has made several statistical studies of "group" behavior, and has proposed the J curve for the study of rule and custom as individual variations of behavior distributed upon a continuum of conformity.

The conflict between the realist and nominalist school of sociological thought was valuable in defining issues important for methodology. The victory of the controversy went to the realists, at least in the sense that the distinctly social aspects of human behavior cannot be studied adequately merely by the analysis of mental processes within individauls but require examination of the social processes involved in their interaction. From the more detached position of the present, the battle might be said to have ended with a consolation prize for the loser.

By this figure of speech is meant that there actually are aspects of human behavior which may best be studied under the conception of society as an aggregate of independent individuals, and other aspects which can only be adequately defined and examined by the opposing conception of society as a reality of which its members are products.

The distinction between the individual and the group aspects of society has been dramatically posed by the implications of the contrast between the concepts of the "community" and of "society." In something like ideal type analysis the community may be considered according to the nominalist conceptions of individuals taken in the aggregate with their resulting behavior determined not at all or in a minimal degree by communication and culture. Entire fields of sociology have been developed according to this conception and by the use of the method appropriate to it, such as population problems, social economics, human ecology and mass behavior. In all of these areas statistical procedures have been predominantly employed.

On the other hand, the conception of society as an organic unity in which it members are incorporated by communication and culture is one that is basic in the fields of personality study, social organization, personal and social disorganization and collective behavior. In these areas the chief and characteristic method of study by sociologists has been the case study.

Before examining the ways in which statistical and case study methods have developed it is desirable to consider the problem of the applicability of scientific method to human behavior.

Scientific Method and Human Behavior. A problem of persistent interest for sociology as well as for psychology and the other social sciences has been the applicability to human behavior of the scientific methods as developed in physics and biology. It is to the point that Comte, the founder of sociology, and Quetelet, the founder of statistics, each called the new science he was instituting "social physics." Comte later substituted the term "sociology" for his original designation.

Some sociologists implicitly or explicitly have conceived of sociology as having different objectives and as employing other methods than those of natural science. A decreasing group consider

RESEARCH METHODS

sociology as social ethics with the responsibility for shaping the social values of our time. H. G. Wells expressed this viewpoint in extreme form in stating that the proper and distinctive method of sociology, "its very backbone," in short, "is the creation of Utopias and their exhaustive criticism." Another group, best represented by George E. Howard, author of *Matrimonial Institutions*, thinks of sociology as limited to the use of the historical method. Howard in fact suggested that "history is past sociology and sociology present history." (1)

Sociologists in general, however, interested in creating a natural science distinct from social ethics or history, realized the presence of three conditions in the study of human subjects which were absent in the examination of organic and inorganic objects. First, man was both observer and observed which intensified the problem of objectivity in research upon human behvior. Second, the observer could communicate with his subjects and receive their communications which both opened a new lead to discoveries and at the same time introduced many and difficult problems of research method. Third, human behavior is often apparently more complex and certainly more difficult to be brought under controlled conditions for observations, comparison, and experimentation.

One way of meeting these problems was to admit tacitly or avowedly the insuperable nature of these objections and to seek out areas where they did not apply. One such field was that of population. Studies of vital statistics, of fecundity, of growth and movement of population, could be carried on with the same objectivity and somewhat the same precision as those of physics and biology. For example, Raymond Pearl devised a mathematical formula for the growth of countries and cities which he applied to different times and places. Samuel A. Stouffer constructed a mathematical formula for population movements in relation to distance by testing the hypothesis that "the number of persons going a given distance is directly proportional to the number of opportunities at that distance, and inversely proportional to the number of intervening opportunities." (2)

Studies in human ecology dealing with the types of organization which arise from temporal and spacial relations of the inhabitants

---

1. *History of Matrimonial Institutions*, VII.
2. "Intervening Opportunities, a Theory Relating Mobility and Distance," *American Sociological Review*, 5: 845-867, 1940.

of a given area gave little or no attention to problems of communication and culture.

A second reaction was to recognize as insuperable the obstacles to the application of scientific method in areas of human behavior involving communication and to employ other methods without claiming scientific validity for them. The point stressed was that acquaintance with and understanding of human behavior was significant whether or not the methods employed could be considered as scientific. A wide range of studies of a descriptive type present concrete materials which are revealing and convincing but where there is no assurance that a second observer would make the same report or arrive at the same conclusions. Illustrative studies are *Middletown* and *Middletown in Transition* by the Lynds, *The Hobo* by Nels Anderson and *Street Corner Society* by William F. Whyte.

A third reaction to the obstacles in the way of the application of scientific method to human behavior was the attempt to define and to systematize methods of observation and interpretation appropriate to descriptive studies. Charles H. Cooley recognizing the need for such technique thought that he had discovered it in sympathetic introspection and urged its extensive use. Cooley himself does not seem to have realized the difficulties involved in trying to put one's self in the place of another person and the fallacies in interpretations which almost inevitably result. He would have been on sounder methodological ground if he had emphasized that sympathetic introspection is a universal human phenomenon and urged its study, not only from the standpoint of its function as a fundamental fact of human behavior but also on its relation to misunderstanding, bias and prejudice.

Other investigators, becoming more sophisticated, sought to explain a research worker's points of view and even his conclusion by the injection of his own temperament, attitudes and values into his studies. They pointed out that if the personal equation of the research worker was difficult to control in the physical and biological sciences, it was almost impossible to do so in the social sciences. The social scientist is not only observing his society but he is a product of it. Thus the problem of the personal equation becomes the problem of the social equation, i.e., the cultural background, the class membership and the experiences of the sociologist.

Not all sociologists were content to abandon the attempt to apply scientific methods to the most human aspects of behavior, namely those which are the result of communication. They saw no reason

RESEARCH METHODS

why the central procedures of every natural science — observation, comparison, and even communication — might not be applicable ultimately to the entire gamut of human conduct. The problem was how to be guided by the two essential criteria of scientific method, first the formulation of a working hypothesis and second the use of an objective method of verification or disproof of the hypothesis that can be repeated by other workers in the field.

Important, however, for each science is the discovery and invention of a chief instrument that is appropriate for the study of its particular phenomena. For astronomy this is the telescope, for chemistry the test tube, and for biology the microscope.

There are those who feel that significant advance in sociology and the other social sciences awaits a discovery of a similar instrument designed to bring under observation and examination what is most significant in human behavior.

Some investigators are convinced that the social microscope has been discovered and requires only further perfection and the development of auxiliary instruments. This instrument they assert is the personal document, or in its most complete and perfected form, the life history.

The place of the life history in sociology may be better understood by an analysis of the nature of the microscope as an instrument of research in biology. The principle of the microscope is simple, that of enlargement, so that what was previously invisible to the naked eye may be clearly perceived. The great discoveries which the microscope has made possible—the activities of bacteria and other microorganisms — result from observation through lenses that magnify. Persons must, of course, be trained to make accurate and discriminating observation. Auxiliary instruments must be devised like the slide, the smear, and the culture. But the essential need which the microscope met in the biological sciences was to get beneath the surface of the externally observable to what could not be perceived without its use.

In the psychological and social sciences there is also the necessity of penetrating underneath the surface of the readily observable in human behavior. The basic nature of mind and society is communication, both the intercommunication which goes on between man and his fellows and internal communication which is called thinking. Therefore an instrument is needed for psychological and sociological research which provides the investigator access to the inner life of the person and to the web of intercommunications between persons. This is the virtue of the personal document that it is the record of a personal communication, which like the finding of the microscope recorded upon a slide provides an objective record of behavior. In the case of the microscope it is physiological behavior. In the case of the personal document it is mental and social behavior.

The functional nature of the microscope and the personal document is the same. There are differences which of course should not be ignored or minimized. The microscope is a physical instrument, the personal document is recorded communication. In that sense it is similar to the slide which records the findings of the microscope; and the interview by which the document was secured may be said to correspond to the microscope.

Accordingly the perfection of the interview and of its recording is of signal importance for sociological research. In the development of the interview method the chief source of divergence is between the advocates of the guided and the unguided interview. In the guided interview a set of questions is prepared in advance on which data are to be obtained. The purpose is to obtain from a number of subjects statements which can be compared. The assumption is that the interviewer knows best what data should be sought. In the unguided interview the interviewer stimulates the person to talk with a minimun of questioning so that the latter introduces and stresses what he believes to be important.

The personal document and the interview provide the social scientist with his appropriate instruments. How important is a frame of reference or a conceptual system to their effective use?

The Role of Concepts. The question of the role of concepts in social research has divided students into two camps. The historical tradition of general sociology from Comte to the present has been to develop conceptual systems for the analysis of social change, social structure and social function. These have been regarded as more or less adequate to interpret past events and to forecast in general terms the future.

The group of sociologists, more numerous in Germany than in the United States, who follow the sociology of knowledge stress the importance of studying society through an understanding of past, current and emerging ideologies. They stress the relativity of conceptual systems in time and in space, perceiving their role both as products of past and present historical periods and as precursors of future epochs.

RESEARCH METHODS

The exponents of the sociology of knowledge are, in a sense, the sociological philosophers of history. They are, however, more sophisticated and critical. They not only perceive their own works as the articulation of the movement of thought of a period but they evaluate a given contribution in relation to the cultural environment, class position and life experiences of the author. In this way they attempt to correct for the influence of the personal and social equations upon the conclusions reached by the writer. Max Scheler, taking a larger social setting, attempted to establish a definite relationship between different forms of thought and certain types of groups necessary for their origin and elaboration.

Karl Mannheim in *Ideology and Utopia* developed the thesis that "there are modes of thought which can not be adequately understood as long as their social origins are obscured." (3) He continues, "Only as we succeed in bringing into the area of conscious and explicit observation the various points of departure and of approach to the facts that are current in scientific as well as popular discussion can we hope, in the course of time, to control the unconscious motivations and presuppositions which, in the last analysis, have brought these modes of thought into existence." (4)

The outstanding value of the sociology of knowledge for social research inheres in its function of manifesting the intimate interaction and interdependence of social life and social science. The understanding of this relation is essential to the investigator in grasping the nature and limitations of research and in appreciating the conditions which permit and handicap objectivity.

Sociologists are divided upon the question of the importance of concepts for individual research projects. There are those who would concentrate upon conceptual analysis in the belief that advance in the understanding of personality and society is achieved by the discrimination, the adequacy and the richness of the concepts employed. There are others as represented by W. F. Ogburn who hold that emphasis should be directed not to concepts but to hypotheses and their verification or disproof.

A third position vigorously and persuasively urged by George Lundberg is that of the operational definition of the concept. The value of a concept for research is the definition which it receives in the operation of the research. An example in the field of psychol-

---
3. *Ideology and Utopia,* p. 2.
4. *Ibid.,* p. 5.

ogy was the definition of intelligence as that which intelligence tests measure. Mental tests, unquestionably, have made one of the great contributions to psychological research in our generation but they did undoubtedly narrow and destroy the meaning of intelligence. Only now are psychologists regaining perspective upon the nature and scope of intelligence. They are realizing that the mental tests were a measure of abstract thinking and omitted consideration of mechanical ability and the capacity for dealing with people.

If the operational movement is to develop widely in sociology as seems probable, it would be well if the mistake made with mental tests be avoided. This might be done if the operational definition be clearly and unmistakably disassociated from the commonly accepted meaning of the concept.

There has been, especially since World War I, a notable attempt among sociologists to bridge the too evident gap between conceptual analysis and data gathering. The first great impetus to inductive studies in the light of a conceptual system was given by W. I. Thomas and Florian Znaniecki in the *Polish Peasant in Europe and America.* This trend received further momentum and upon an even larger sociological front by the work of Robert E. Park and his students. The problems arising from this union of conceptualization and inductive research will be considered in their different phases under the discussion of the case study, statistics, and sociometry.

II

The Development of the Case Study Method. The methodological use of the life history and other personal documents was introduced into sociology by W. I. Thomas and Florian Znaniecki in their work *The Polish Peasant in Europe and America.* The significance of the life history for research was appraised by them as "the *perfect* type of sociological material." (5) Thomas and Znaniecki conceived of their task as a scientific study of social life which would take into account both the objective and the subjective factors in behavior. They sought to test their theories and hypotheses by the use of personal documents and thus derive laws and generalizations applicable to other situations of social change.

As Blumer points out they did not actually achieve this goal.

---

5. See Vol. II, pp. 1833-34.

RESEARCH METHODS

Their conceptual scheme was not entirely or chiefly derived from their data and their data did not in any precise and conclusive sense verify their concepts and hypotheses. Yet he adds that the concepts are not unrelated to the personal documents and that the interpretations make the materials more significant. (6)

There has been general recognition by sociologists of the value of personal documents as data, but much controversy as to their significance for scientific method. All agree as to their worth for descriptive studies and for exploratory investigations in giving insight and leads for further studies.

The argument in favor of a significant role for the case study as an instrument of psychological and social science is ably presented by Gordon W. Allport in his monograph, *The Use of Personal Documents in Psychological Science*. On the basis of a survey of the literature and of a series of studies carried on under his direction he asserts that personal documents must be admitted as valid scientific method since they "can be shown to enhance understanding, power of prediction, and power of control, above the level which man can achieve through his own unaided common sense." (7)

Applicable to personal documents are two methods of interpretation (1) nomothetic or the comparative study of documents in order to arrive at generalizations and (2) idiographic, or the appreciation of the individual case in all its individuality and completeness. Allport asserts that prediction can be made upon the basis of the ideographic study of a single case, a claim that has been challenged by others. Further research is necessary to decide this issue.

A persuasive argument for the use of the life history for personality study is presented by John Dollard in his treatise on *Criteria for the Life History*. His goal is the description and analysis of the total individual in his total culture. He contends for a genetic study of personality not independently by separate disciplines but jointly by the points of views and techniques of cultural anthropology, psychology, psychiatry, and sociology.

The questions arising from the study of the life history and other personal documents have proved to be perplexing. There is no doubt that an autobiography is revealing but it may raise many questions which it cannot answer. The different methods of interpre-

---

6. Herbert Blumer, An Appraisal of Thomas and Znaniecki, *The Polish Peasant in Europe and America*, (New York: Social Science Research Council 1939).
7. *The Use of Personal Documents in Psychological Science*, p. 185.

tation proposed in practice — sympathy, empathy, recipathy, insight, and intuition — appear to involve a common difficulty in the control of the personal equation of the analyst. The same problem also appears although to a lesser degree in the method of conceptual analysis where personal documents and skill in their use depend upon the investigator's formal training in a discipline, his previous clinical experience and his personal history. (8)

A significant method of analyzing cases including personal document has been projected and developed by Simmel, Toennies, Emile Durkheim, Marcel Mauss, Max Weber, and several younger French and American sociologists, namely by means of ideal types. The ideal type is a construct of the investigator which he obtains by abstracting from concrete cases a characteristic in which he is interested, accentualizing it and defining it clearly, unambiguously, and uncomplicatedly by other characteristics. Thus Weber defines the ideal type of the charismatic leader who is imputed to be endowed with superhuman qualities. Ideal type analysis is often polar in the sense of making antithetical abstractions as the contrast between the charismatic leader and the leader who exerts influence due only to official position or between the economic man and the philanthropic man.

The concepts of *Gemeinschaft* and *Gesellschaft* as defined by Simmel and by Toennies also illustrate the method of analysis by ideal types. Here the polar distinction is between the intimate and traditional form of association of the village and the formal association which involves contractual relations. Somewhat the same antithesis is seen in the contrasting conceptions of primary contacts as in the rural community and secondary contacts as in the city.

Ideal type analysis may be thought of as a method *sui generis*, and as such it has a list of imposing achievements in the psychological and social sciences. These include the conceptions of the economic man from which the deductive science of classical political economy was derived, of the community as a distribution of individuals over an area of human ecology, of the transition from the sacred to the secular society, of charismatic *versus* official leadership, of the introverted and extroverted types of personality and of the six types of men (Spranger).

Ideal type analysis may be brilliant and provocative as in

---

8. See discussion by Paul Wallin in Paul Horst, *The Prediction of Personal Adjustment,* pp. 220 ff.

RESEARCH METHODS

Simmel's sociology of the stranger, Max Weber's analysis of the religious basis of capitalism, or Sorokin's classification of the pure types of culture as sensate and ideational, but there ever remains the question of the degree to which the extremes of the ideal construction are actually represented by concrete phenomena. This objection does not trouble the ideal type analyst since he maintains that only approximations can be found in society. The question of measurement then becomes what degree of approximation.

This demand for measurement has led to a development of scales by which different degrees of the characteristics may be given values. The process of this development is interesting to trace. C. G. Jung, as a result of his clinical studies proposed the ideal types of extrovert and introvert. Concrete-minded critics pointed out that some persons were neither extrovert nor introvert but combined these traits. Consequently, a third category, that of ambivert was introduced. But obviously the ambivert is a hybrid term and not an ideal construction. This concession, however, to common sense and to the statistical conception of the normal curve of distribution was a realization that extremes are few in number and that the great majority of cases normally fall around the middle. The next step was to recognize the relativity of introversion-extroversion in the sense that this characteristic constitutes a continuum. Consequently, it was feasible to devise a series of questions presumably indicative of extroversion and introversion under the assumption that the sum total of "introvert" replies would indicate the degree of introversion of the subject.

A particularly interesting case of the transition from ideal type analysis to scale construction is provided by Spranger's ideal-type classification of men grouped according to their predominant value system as theoretical, economic, esthetic, social, political, and religious. No doubt something is gained by pigeonholing persons under these rubrics. Yet there are at least two serious limitations. First, the classification is subjective and the influence of the personal equation is not ruled out. Second, while it may be revealing for those persons where one of these values is clearly predominant, it may appear to be arbitrary and unrewarding where two or more values are about equal in strength.

To meet these deficiencies Gordon W. Allport and P. E. Vernon made a Personal Values Scale. (9) By answers to a series of ques-

---

9. G. W. Allport and P. E. Vernon, "A Test for Personal Values," *Journal of Abnormal and Social Psychology*, 26: 231-248, 1931.

tions and situations a person could be given a total score upon each of the six values. This means, however, that ideal types as such disappear. The scale implies that what is being measured are six characteristics, each of which is a continuum. Since each characteristic is theoretically independent of the others a person may conceivably receive a score on any one trait ranging from the lowest to the highest value in the continuum. If the scores on each characteristic for a large number of persons correspond to a normal curve of distribution, many persons will receive middle scores and only a few very high and very low scores. This result is taken by the statistically-minded student to expose the inherent fallacy in the ideal type method, namely its application without qualification in the classification of phenomena.

If, however, the scale derived from the ideal-type analysis proves valuable then the worth of this prior conceptualization must be conceded.

Spranger's ideal type classification assumed that his six values were mutually exclusive and this was implied also in the Allport-Vernon Scale. This assumption was tested by W. L. Lurie (10) who subjected the answers to questions based on Spranger's types to factor analysis and found four instead of six main attitudes, namely, the social, the Philistine, the theoretical and the religious.

The examples of ideal type analysis of extroversion-introversion and of personal values indicate that this type of conceptualization, valuable as it is for descriptive and analytic studies, readily prepares the way for tests and scales which become instruments for statistical treatment. This is an illustration of the way in which by natural stages case-study may pass over into highly refined statistical procedure.

The Growth of Statistical Method. The statistical method in great part received its original impetus from the necessity of controlling and manipulating population data. The phenomena of birth and death and of migration all dealt with the behavior of the individual as a biological organism and were not concerned with his attitudes and values.

As studies developed in the field of population and social economy statistical methods became increasingly important. Interest developed in the adequacy and representativeness of the sample of

---

10. "A Study of Spranger's Value Types by the Method of Factor Analysis," *Journal of Social Psychology*, 8: 17-37, 1937.

the population selected, in correlating variables hypothetically in a cause and effect relation, and in determining the reliability of significances ascertained. The great contributions to statistical methods were made by men who were biologists but interested in population studies and vital statistics, as Karl Pearson and his disciples. More recently psychologists working with mental and educational measurements, personality tests and attitude scales have made significant contributions, as those of C. Spearman, T. L. Kelly, and L. L. Thurstone. Sociologists have increasingly used statistical methods in their studies but their contribution to research methods have been minor with certain exceptions to be pointed out later. Statistical methods peculiarly adapted to the requirements of sociological data remain to be worked out.

A comprehensive and systematic quantitative structure for all sociological situations and concepts has been formulated by S. C. Dodd in his book, *Dimensions of Sociology*. In this volume he applies the S-theory and its algebraic formulae to 1500 records of the results of quantitative research by sociologists. Critics assert that this conversion of sociological terminology and social situations into S-symbols actually provides descriptive rather than calculating equations.

This restatement of sociological terminology and social situations into S-equations has been vigorously approved by George Lundberg and others as a marked advance. It has been criticized by many as a nominal rather than a real change, e.g., that it is only classification and marks no real gain in method. Dodd, however, challenges this objection. (11) Whatever be the merits of Dodd's work it is symptomatic of a growing interest of sociologists in the discovery and invention of mathematical formulae appropriate to social research.

The main research method relied upon by students of personality, social organization and disorganization, and collective behavior has been the personal document. Through letters, interviews, and life histories data have been obtained by which the processes of personal and social interaction might be analyzed. Once a process or situation is identified and defined then it is possible but often difficult to develop statistical methods for more precise and accurate measurement as in the case of ideal type concepts already discussed.

Present statistical methods appear to be relatively adequate

---

11. "Of What Use is Dimensional Sociology," *Social Forces*, 22: 169-182, 1943.

TWENTIETH CENTURY SOCIOLOGY

for dealing with the data of population studies and human ecology. This does not mean, of course, that new formulae and new techniques have not been devised. An illustration of the invention of a mathematical formula in population studies is the one earlier mentioned by S. A. Stouffer of intervening opportunities as determining the relation of distance to internal migration. Work in human ecology also has stimulated the development of many devices in the plotting of data upon maps. In fact, Erle F. Young, a sociologist and author of the first social data base map, has devised a model for a spot mapping machine which makes it possible to plot mechanically by different symbols the street location of addresses within a large city.

One interesting line of research development largely statistical in nature is the study of social trends. This method of study was highlighted by the work of the President's Commission on Social Trends, published under the title *Recent Social Trends* which presented the main economic, social and political trends in American society from 1900-1929. The data in this volume provide a base from which further projection of the trends may be made.

Sociometry. A recent development of quantitative devices in the wake of conceptual analysis is called sociometry. It is most characteristically exemplified in the work of J. L. Moreno, M.D., a psychiatrist rather than a sociologist. His conceptualization of inter-personal relations, though expressed in original terminology, is sociological rather than psychiatric which perhaps explains why his procedures have been followed by sociologists more than by psychiatrists. Sociometric methods in use by sociologists actually antedate Moreno as indicated by the social distance scale of Bogardus used in studies of Americanization and race prejudice, but Moreno took the lead in the systematic development of sociometric procedures according to a guiding ideology. He is, for example, the founder of the Sociometric Institute and of *Sociometry*, a journal for the promotion of these methods.

Sociometry should be distinguished from social statistics in the same way that biometry, psychometry, and econometry are similarly to be differentiated from biological, psychological, and economic statistics. Statistical methods in general are common to all four fields, but within each field the significant biological, psychological, economic, and social forms and processes need to be defined, analyzed, and charted in a way that is susceptible to measurement. This measurement may or may not be statistical in the sense that the conventional formulae and procedures are followed. If non-statistical

RESEARCH METHODS

it may be graphic as in the plotting of friendship choices or status relationships.

Sociometry is contributing to bridging the gap between social analysis and statistics. In the past, analyses of social processes have not been for the most part oriented toward measurement, and statistical studies too often have dealt with aggregates of atomistic items about individuals and not with relationships and processes within groups of interacting persons.

While sociometry is in some respects narrower than statistics, in others it is far broader. Conceived of as the union of conceptual analysis and of measurement it includes a wide range of recent developments in sociology of significance for research. Among these are: (a) field theory, (b) class structure analysis, and (c) scale construction.

The field theoretical approach according to Levin is "instrumental in integrating divergent physiological, psychological and sociological facts on the basis of their interdependence." He states "to explain social behavior it is necessary to represent the structure of the total situation and the distribution of forces in it." (12) It is exemplified in a systematic way in the work of psychologists, as Kurt Levin and B. J. Brown, rather than that of sociologists. But the effects of its influence in sociology are appearing.

The notion of social classes and of class conflict is long standing in sociology, but the use of class structure systematically as a research method significant for understanding society and personality is recent. Foremost in pushing community study by means of an analysis of class position have been W. Lloyd Warner and his associates in a series of studies in Ireland, New England, Chicago, and the South. Particularly interesting methodologically is the study by Warner, Adams, and Jonker reported in *Color and Human Nature* in which the personality development of Negroes in a Northern city was analyzed in terms of shades of complexion and levels of class position.

Scale construction in sociology and in psychology have had so great a vogue that absorption with its mechanics has often eclipsed attention desirable and essential for prior conceptualization. Sociologists have been responsible for several of these scales including those for social adjustment, home background, family

---

12. Kurt Levin, "Field Theory and Experiments in Social Psychology," *American Journal of Sociology*, 44: 868-896, 1938-1939.

relations, marital adjustment, morale, social distance, social status, social insight, and for many on attitudes and opinions.

The date is now overdue for a critical evaluation of the present status of scale construction especially in the field of attitude and opinion. Actually so-called tests of attitudes are examinations of opinion. The loose use in these tests of the term attitude beyond its conceptual significance has been a barrier to searching studies of attitude that would be valuable for the understanding of the processes in the formation of opinion and in the motivation of behavior. While opinions are formulations of attitudes, the knowledge of the opinion that is static and readily discernible does not necessarily give much understanding of the attitude which is dynamic and predictive of action under changing conditions.

In general, however, developments in the field of social measurement are more and more in terms of a conceptualization of interpersonal relations and social processes.

III

Interrelation of Case-Study and Statistics. Our discussion has indicated the increasing use in research of the methods of the case-study and of statistics. Statistical methods have reached a high degree of technical perfection but they still seem inapplicable to many social problems. Case-studies are revealing but difficult to focus upon the crucial verification of hypotheses. We have noted the signal importance of the case-study and of personal documents for the social sciences in giving the research worker access to the peculiar subject-matter of human behavior. But what are the limits to the use of case study as a scientific method? These may be briefly stated as follows:

1. *A useful adjunct to statistics.* Almost all sociologists agree upon the usefulness of the case-study for the exploration of the problem, for disclosing leads, for deriving hunches, and for raising questions and hypotheses. All these are valuable for further research, quantitative as well as qualitative. Certain investigators conclude that this service to statistical study is the upper limit of the value of the case study for sociological research.

2. *Valuable for the interpretation of statistical findings.* Sometimes the findings of a statistical study are interesting but unintelligible. Case-studies focused upon these findings may reveal their meaning and even suggest further research.

RESEARCH METHODS

3. *A continuing complementary relation.* Some investigators think of statistics and cases-studies as mutually complementary. They perceive in any problem the possibility of case-studies suggesting problems for quantitative study which require interpretation by more intensive case-study indicating more problems for statistical analysis, with this process of interaction continuing until all the questions on a given subject are answered.

4. *Case-study as a scientific method.* The claims for the case-study as a scientific method in its own right have been ably set forth by Gordon W. Allport. An excellent case has been made but it is doubtful that these claims have been conclusively demonstrated as valid. It has been noted that the ideal type method — one peculiarly appropiate to case-studies — readily can be converted to scale construction with gain in precision and accuracy.

One of the tasks for further investigation is the possibilities of its use as a scientific method. Its value as a scientific instrument has been indicated as essential to all sociological inquiries concerned with the subjective aspects of human behavior. Is it also a scientific method to be used in putting hypotheses to the test of data?

R. C. Angell has, perhaps, made the most thorough-going attempt to subject analysis of case-study records to the test of empirical findings. He secured from his students fifty personal documents upon interpersonal relations within families adversely affected by the depression before and after this experience. He then intuitively graded these families by three levels of integration and adaptability before the depression and by three types of vulnerability to the depression. He was then able to show an association between the levels of integration and adaptability of the family before the depression and the way in which it reacted to the depression.

At the present time a Committee on Appraisal of the Social Science Research Council is making a restudy of the Angell cases to determine first if a second trained investigator using intuitive methods will arrive at the same or similar conclusions, and second whether a rating scale or a rank order method would give different results.

It is by such experiments that the method of the case-study may be perfected and its most promising use in connection with statistical procedures determined.

Certain of the most ardent supporters of the case-study method like Gordon W. Allport believe that the highest value of the personal document lies not in its further nomothetic development but rather in its ideographic or clinical behavior in each individual case.

Another way in which the interrelations and the distinctive values of case-study and statistical methods are being tested is in the area of predictive studies of personal adjustment. These have been carried on by psychologists and sociologists in predicting success in school, in a vocation, in marriage, and in the reformation of criminals. The procedure consists of five steps: (1) setting up a criterion of success, such as grades received for college success; (2) selecting the factors assumed to make for success; (3) establishing a sharp line dividing the time between the factors present *before* and the success achieved *after*; (4) correlating the individual factors with the criterion of success, (5) combining the factors with predictive value into a prediction score by which predictions of success or failure may be made upon the careers of individuals not in the original study.

Studies have shown the feasibility of predicting the risk group to which a person belongs. This statistical prediction is upon the assumption, however, that factors operate in the individual case as in the average of all cases in the sample of the population upon which predictions are based. This assumption does violence to the clinically-minded person who perceives in each case a unique configuration of dynamic factors.

It is however, possible to compare the findings on clinical or case study prediction with the results of statistical prediction. Do interview data permit superior prediction of success in school, in vocation, in marriage, and in criminal rehabilitation?

So far the data available in comparison of statistical and case study predictions appear to indicate the superiority of quantitative methods. This seems in large part due to the difficulty of controlling the personal equation of the clinical investigator who tends to judge cases on the basis of his training or personal experience.

This paper has attempted to show that research methods have developed in sociology to meet the dual opportunity which its subject matter presents to study its phenomena both in its external and in its internal aspects. In accepting these two challenges the respective methods of statistics and case study had their origin and development.

But this separation of outer and inner aspects of behavior is, of course, arbitrary as the two are separable only in abstraction. This is the reason why in much research both methods must be used to

RESEARCH METHODS

secure valid and significant answers to questions raised for research. (13)

In conclusion it is in point to indicate present trends in methods of sociological research:

1. There has been an increasing tendency to inductive research which has been gaining in momentum during the past twenty-five years. This gain in research studies has, however, not as yet been accompanied by a synthesis of methods as a basis for further research. This is doubtless, in part, due to the recent invention of new methods which have not been incorporated in the training of the student.

2. Conceptual analysis is increasingly evident as a preliminary to the planning of research and to the determination of hypotheses and methods. Nevertheless, much so-called research is fact finding and makes little or no contribution to the sum total of sociological knowledge.

3. There has been interestingly enough little or no attempt to create a behavioristic movement in sociological research. Yet the stage seems set for this development. The motion picture and the sound track would seem to provide the essential equipment, especially for studies of group behavior. The pictures and motion pictures of Balinese behavior by Gregory Bateson and Margaret Mead furnish evidence of the value for research of these records of human behavior.

4. There is growing recognition that problems to be studied are interdisciplinary even if methods of research are best developed within the discipline. This fact means that the adequate study of a problem like that of crime or race prejudice demands the employment of concepts and methods of two or more disciplines. This drive to the integration of points of view and of research techniques of the different psychological and social sciences was one of the reasons for the founding of the Social Science Research Council in 1923 and one of its continuing objectives.

In a provocative volume *Knowledge for What?* Robert S. Lynd makes a convincing argument for breaking down departmental overspecialization with concentration of men from different disciplines upon the study of important problems.

Many difficulties have impeded attempts to develop integrative

---

13. See R. E. Park, "The Spacial Pattern and the Moral Order," Chapter I in the *Urban Community*.

TWENTIETH CENTURY SOCIOLOGY

research including departmental isolation, barriers of terminology to communication and the tradition of individual research. Examples of successful integration to date appear to be of two types. In one case the research worker combines in his training two disciplines as Dollard who united sociology and psychiatry in his study of *Caste and Class in Southern Town*. The second is where two investigators of different disciplines who have familiarity with the concepts and techniques in each other's field collaborate in a project.

5. There seems every indication of the continued growth both of the statistical and the case study methods. Particularly promising are the prospects that both methods will be used in the same research project to the enhancement of the understanding of the problem.

SELECTED BIBLIOGRAPHY

Allport, Gordon W., *The Use of Personal Documents in Psychological Science,* (New York: Social Science Research Council, 1942).

Bernard, L. L., *The Fields and Methods of Sociology,* (New York: Farrar and Rinehart, 1939).

Angell, Robert C., *The Family Encounters the Depression,* (New York: C. Scribner's Sons, 1936).

Blumer, Herbert, *An Appraisal of Thomas and Znaniecki, The Polish Peasant in Europe and America,* (New York: Social Science Research Council, 1939).

Cooley, Charles H., "Roots of Social Knowledge," Chapter 9 in *Sociological Theory and Social Research,* (New York: Henry Holt and Co., 1930).

Dodd, S. C., *Dimensions of Society,* (New York: The Macmillan Co., 1939).

Dollard, John, *Criteria for the Life History,* (New Haven: Yale University Press, 1935).

Durkheim, E., *The Rules of Sociological Method,* (Chicago: University of Chicago Press, 1938).

Giddings, F. H., "Pluralistic Behavior," *American Journal of Sociology,* 25: 9-20, 385-404, 539-61.

Horst, Paul, *The Prediction of Human Adjustment,* (New York: Social Science Research Council, 1941).

Lundberg, George, "Quantitative Methods in Social Psychology," *American Sociological Review,* 1: 38-60, 1936.

Lundberg, George, *Foundations of Sociology,* New York: The Macmillan Co., 1939).

Lynd, R. S., *Knowledge for What?* (Princeton: Princeton University Press, 1939).

MacIver, R. M., *Social Causation,* (Boston: Ginn and Co., 1942).

Mannheim, Karl, *Ideology and Utopia,* (New York: Harcourt Brace and Co., 1936).

Mead, George H., *Mind, Self and Society,* (Chicago: University of Chicago Press, 1934).

RESEARCH METHODS

Moreno, J. L., *Who Shall Survive?* (Washintgon: Nervous and Mental Disease Publishing Co., 1934).

Park, R. E., "Symbiosis and Socialization," *American Journal of Sociology*, 45: 1-25, 1939.

Park, R. E., "Sociology," Chapter I in Wilson Gee, *Research in the Social Sciences*, (New York: The Macmillan Co., 1929).

Parsons, Talcott, *The Structure of Social Action*, (New York: McGraw-Hill Book Co., 1937).

Reckless, W. C., *The Etiology of Delinquent and Criminal Behavior*, (New York: Social Science Research Council, 1943).

Rice, Stuart A., ed., *Methods in Social Science, A Case Book*, (Chicago: University of Chicago Press, 1931).

Shaw, Clifford R., and H. D. McKay, *Juvenile Delinquency and Urban Areas*, (Chicago University of Chicago Press, 1942).

Shaw, Clifford, "Case Study Method," *Publications of the American Sociological Society*, 21: 149-157, 1927.

Stouffer, Samuel A., *An Experimental Comparison of Statistical and Case History Methods of Attitude Research*, Ph. D. Thesis, University of Chicago, 1930.

Thomas, W. I., and F. Znaniecki, *The Polish Peasant in Europe and America*, New York: A. A. Knopf, 1918-1920).

Thomas, William I., and Dorothy S. Thomas, *The Child in America*, (New York: A. A. Knopf, 1928).

Warner, W. Lloyd, and Paul Lunt, *The Status System of a Modern Community*, (New Haven: Yale University Press, 1942).

Webb, Sidney and Beatrice, *Methods of Social Study*, (London: Longmans Green and Co., 1932).

Weber, Max, *The Protestant Ethic and the Spirit of Capitalism*, (London: G. Allen and Unwin, 1930).

Znaniecki, F., *The Method of Sociology*, (New York: Farrar and Rinehart, 1932).

Ernest Watson Burgess: Professor of Sociology, University of Chicago; former president (1934) American Sociological Society; member: Social Science Research Council since 1938, American Association for the Advancement of Science, American Statistical Association, American Association of Social Workers; Associate Editor: "American Journal of Sociology"; Advisory Editor: "Journal of Legal Sociology," "Social Forces," "Sociology and Social Research"; Editor: *Urban Community*, 1926; *Personality and the Social Group*, 1929; *Human Side of Social Planning*, 1935; Compiler: (with C. Newcomb) *Chicago Census Data by Local Communities*, vol. I, 1920, vol. II 1930, 1931-33.

Author: *The Belleville Survey* (with J. J. Sippy), 1915; *The Lawrence Social Survey* (with F. W. Blackmar), 1916; *The Function of Socialization in Social Evolution*, 1916; *Introduction to the Science of Sociology* (with R. E. Park, 1921); *The Workings of the Indeterminate Sentence Law and the Parole System in Illinois*, (with A. A. Bruce, A. J. Harno and John Landesco), 1928; *Predicting Success or Failure in Marriage* (with L. S. Cottrell), 1939.

CHAPTER III

THE PRESENT POSITION AND PROSPECTS OF SYSTEMATIC THEORY IN SOCIOLOGY

by

TALCOTT PARSONS

I

The General Nature and Functions of Systematic Theory. It is scarcely too much to say that the most important single index of the state of maturity of a science is the state of its systematic theory. This includes the character of the generalized conceptual scheme in use in the field, the kinds and degrees of logical integration of the different elements which makes it up, and the ways in which it is actually being used in empiricial research. On this basis the thesis may be advanced that sociology is just in the process of emerging into the status of a mature science. Heretofore it has not enjoyed the kind of integration and directed activity which only the availability and common acceptance and employment of a well-articulated generalized theoretical system can give to a science. The main framework of such a system is, however, now available, though this fact is not as yet very generally appreciated and much in the way of development and refinement remains to be done on the purely theoretical level, as well as its systematic use and revision in actual research. It may therefore be held that we stand on the threshold of a definitely new era in sociology and the neighboring social science fields.

"Theory" is a term which covers a wide variety of different things which have in common only the element of generalized conceptualization. The theory of concern to the present paper in the first place constitutes a "system" and thereby differs from discrete "theories," that is, particular generalizations about particular phenomena or classes of them. A theoretical system in the present sense is a body of logically interdependent generalized concepts of empirical reference. Such a system tends, ideally, to become "logically closed," to reach such a state of logical integration that every logical implication of any combination of propositions in the system is explicitly stated in some other proposition in the same system.(1)

In a highly developed system of theory there may be a wide variety of different types of generalized concepts and functions which they may serve. A thorough discussion of the possibilities cannot be undertaken here, so attention will be confined to those most vital to the general status of the scientific field. The two most general functions of theory are the facilitation of description and analysis. The two are most intimately connected since it is only when the essential facts about a phenomenon have been described in a carefully systematic and orderly manner that accurate analysis becomes possible at all.

The basic category of all scientific description seems to be that of empirical system. The empirical references of statements of fact cannot be isolated from each other, but each describes one aspect or feature of an interconnected whole which, taken as a whole, has some measures of independent significance as an entity. Apart from theoretical conceptualization there would appear to be no method of selecting among the indefinite number and varying kinds of factual observation which can be made about a concrete phenomenon or field so that the various descriptive statements about it articulate into a coherent whole, which constitutes an "adequate," a "determinate" description. Adequacy in description is secured in so far as determinate and verifiable answers can be given to all the scientifically *important* questions involved. What questions are important is

---

1. For a fuller development of this view of theory, see the author's *The Structure of Social Action*, (New York: McGraw-Hill Co., 1937), especially Chaps. I and XIX.

largely determined by the logical structure of the generalized conceptual scheme which, implicitly or explicitly, is employed.

Specific descriptive propositions often refer to particular aspects or properties of an empirically existent set of phenomena. Such propositions are, however, empirically meaningless unless the "what" which they qualify is clearly and determinately conceived and defined. This "what," the interconnected empirically existent phenomena which constitute the field of description and analysis for a scientific investigation, is what is meant by an empirical "system." It is that which can, for scientific purposes, be treated at the same time as a body of phenomena sufficiently extensive, complex and diversified so that the results of their study are significant and not merely truistic, and sufficiently limited and simplified so that the problems involved are manageable and the investigator does not get lost in the maze.

The functions of a generalized conceptual scheme on the descriptive level seem to be performed mainly in terms of two types of conceptual elements. The first consists in what is called the "frame of reference." This is the most general framework of categories in terms of which empirical scientific work "makes sense." Thus, in classical mechanics, three-dimensional rectilinear space, time, mass, location, motion are the essential elements of the frame of reference. Every descriptive statement, to be applicable to a mechanical system must be referable to one or more "particles" each with a given mass, capable of location in space, changing its location in time through motion, etc. Besides providing the specific categories in terms of which a system is described, the function of the frame of reference is above all to provide a test of the determinacy of the description of a system. It is a logical implication of the structure of the conceptual system that there is a limited number of essential categories, specific values for which must be obtained before the description can be determinate. Its use is the only way of locating the important gaps in available knowledge.

The second level is that of the structure of systems as such. Phenomena which are significantly interrelated, which constitute a system, are intrinsically interrelated on the structural level. This fact seems to be inherent in the most general frame of reference of empirical knowledge itself, which implies the fundamental significance of the concept of system as that is taken for granted here. Structure is the "static" aspect of the descriptive mode of treat-

SYSTEMATIC THEORY

ment of a system. From the structural point of view a system is composed of "units," of sub-systems which potentially exist independently, and their structural interrelations. Thus a system in mechanics is "made up" of particles as its units. The structure of the system consists in the number of particles, their properties, such as mass, and their interrelations such as relative locations, velocities and directions of motion.

The functions of the frame of reference and of structural categories in their descriptive use are to state the necessary facts, and the setting for solving problems of dynamic analysis, the ultimate goal of scientific investigation. Besides the immense possibilities of variation in the scope of analysis, there are two aspects of the goal itself; first, the "casual explanation" of past specific phenomena or processes and the prediction of future events; second, the attainment of generalized analytical knowledge, of "laws" which can be applied to an indefinite number of specific cases with the use of the appropriate factual data. The attainment of the two goals, or aspects of the same goal, go hand in hand. On the one hand, specific causal explanation is attainable only through the application of some generalized analytical knowledge; on the other, the extension of analytical generalization is only possible by generalization from empirical cases and verification in terms of them.

In both respects scientific advance consists especially in the gradual widening of the scope of dynamic analysis. Even the simplest rational practical activity would be impossible without the ability to establish a dynamic relation between a single, simple "necessary condition" and a consequent effect under the assumption that in a relevant degree "other things are equal." This, applied in a particular case, implies some degree of generalization that this *kind* of factor is a necessary condition of the kind of effect, thus, that "boiling" for a certain length of time — i. e. a generalized *type* of antecedent process — is necessary if potatoes are to "cooked" — i. e., reach a certain kind of observable state. This *kind* of common sense analysis merges gradually into science in proportion to the complexity of the system of dynamically interdependent variables which can be treated together, and to the breadth of applicability to particular situations of the analytical generalizations commanded.

Sometimes one aspect is predominant in the development of a body of scientific knowledge, sometimes the other. Where, however, breadth of applicability can be attained only through extreme simplicity in the relations of variables, only a secondary order of scientific significance can be attributed to the results. For where only very simple relationships, or only those of two or three variables, can be involved in a dynamic generalization it must inevitably remain undesirably abstract in the sense that in very few cases of concrete empirical systems, will these relationships and these variables be the only or the predominant ones involved in the solution of the pressing empirical problems. Hence, the ideal of scientific theory must be to extend the dynamic scope of analysis of complex systems as a whole as far as possible. It is the attainment of this ideal which presents the greatest theoretical difficulties to science.

Put a little differently, the essential feature of dynamic analysis in the fullest sense is the treatment of a body of *interdependent* phenomena simultaneously, in the mathematical sense. The simplest case is the analysis of the effect of variation in one antecedent factor, but this ignores the reciprocal effect of these changes on this factor. The ideal solution is the possession of a logically complete system of dynamic generalizations which can state all the elements of reciprocal interdependence between all the variables of the system. This ideal has, in the formal sense, been attained only in the systems of differential equations of analytical mechanics. All other sciences are limited to a more "primitive" level of systematic theoretical analysis.

For this level of dynamic analysis to be feasible, there seem to be two essential necessary conditions. On the one hand, the variables need to be of an empirical character such that the particulars within the generalized categories are in actuality the relevant statements of fact about a given state of the empirical system as indicated by the structure of problems of the science. On the other hand, the formal logical character of these concepts must be such as to be susceptible to special types of technical manipulation The only kind of technical manipulation so far available which makes simultaneous dynamic analysis of interdependence of several variables in a complex system possible in a completely rigorous sense, is the mathematics of the differential calculus and some of its more refined derivatives.

To be susceptible of this type of analytical manipulation a variable must be of a very particular sort — it must vary only in numerically quantitative value on a continuum. This requirement greatly narrows the range of observational possibility. In many cases even where numerical continua can be observed they are not necessarily the variables of greatest empirical significance.

The most essential condition of successful dynamic analysis is continual and systematic reference of every problem to the state of the system as a whole. If it is not possible to provide for that by explicit inclusion of every relevant fact as the value of a variable which is included in the dynamic analysis at that point, there must be some method of simplification. Logically, this is possible only through the removal of some generalized categories from the role of variables and their treatment as constants. An analytical system of the type of mechanics does just this for certain elements *outside* the system which are conditional to it. But it is also logically feasible *within* the system. This is essentially what happens when structural categories are used in the treatment of dynamic problems.

Their function is to simplify the dynamic problems to the point where they are manageable without the possibility of refined mathematical analysis. At the same time the loss, which is very great, is partly compensated by relating all problems explicitly and systematically to the total system. For the structure of a system as described in the context of a generalized conceptual scheme is a genuinely technical analytical tool. It ensures that nothing of vital importance is inadvertently overlooked, and ties in loose ends, giving determinacy to problems and solutions. It minimizes the danger, so serious to common-sense thinking, of filling gaps by resort to uncriticized residual categories.

It should be noted that in mechanics the structure of the system does not enter in as a distinct theoretical element. For descriptive purposes, it is of course relevant for any given state of the system. But on the dynamic plane it dissolves into process and interdependence. This calls attention to the important fact that structure and process are highly relative categories. Structure does not refer to any ontological stability in phenomena but only to a relative stability — to sufficiently stable uniformities in the results of underlying processes so that their constancy within certain limits is a workable pragmatic assumption.

Once resort is made to the structure of a system as a positive constituent of dynamic analysis there must be a way of linking these "static" structural categories and their relevant particular statements of fact to the dynamically variable elements in the system, This link is supplied by the all-important concept of *function*. Its crucial role is to provide criteria of the *importance* of dynamic factors and processes within the system. They are important in so far as they have functional significance to the system, and their specific importance is understood in terms of the analysis of specific functional relations between the parts of the system and between it and its environment.

The significance of the concept of function implies the conception of the empirical system as a "going concern." Its structure is that system of determinate patterns which empirical observation shows within certain limits, "tend to be maintained" or on a somewhat more dynamic version "tend to develop" according to an empirically constant pattern (e. g. the pattern of growth of a young organism).

Functional significance in this context is inherently teleological. A process or set of conditions either "contributes" to the maintenance (or development) of the system or it is "disfunctional" in that it detracts from the integration, effectiveness, etc., of the system. It is thus the functional reference of all particular conditions and processes *to the state of the total system as a going concern* which provides the logical equivalent of simultaneous equations in a fully developed system of analytical theory. This appears to be the only way in which dynamic *inter*dependence of variable factors in a system can be explicitly analyzed without the technical tools of mathematics and the operational and empirical prerequisites of their employment.

The logical type of generalized theoretical system under discussion may thus be called a "structural-functional system" as distinguished from an analytical system. It consists of the generalized categories necessary for an adequate description of states of an empirical system. On the one hand, it includes a system of structural categories which must be logically adequate to give a determinate description of an empirically possible, complete empirical system of the relevant class. One of the prime functions of *system* on this level is to insure completeness, to make it methodically impossible to overlook anything important, and thus explicitly to describe *all* essential structural elements and relations of the system. For if this is not done implicit, uncriticized allegations about the missing elements will always play a part in determining conclusions and interpretations.

On other hand, such a system must also include a set of dynamic functional categories. These must articulate directly with the structural categories — they must describe processes by which these particular structures are maintained or upset, the relations of the system to its environment are mediated. This aspect of the system must also be complete in the same sense.

On a relatively complete and explicit level this type of generalized system has been most fully developed in physiology (2) and more recently if less completely in psychology. The anatomical structure of the organism is an essential fixed point of reference for all physiological analyses of its functioning. Function in relation to the maintenance of this structure in a given environment is the source of criteria for the attribution of significance to processes such as respiration, nutrition, etc., and of their dynamic interdependence. In recent psychology, it is "character structure" or personality which plays the role analogous to that of anatomical structure in biology while "motives" in relation to situations are the dynamic elements.

II

Unsatisfactory Types of Theory in Recent Sociology. It is the primary thesis of this paper that the structural-functional type of system is the one which is most likely and suitable to play a dominant role in sociological theory. In varying degrees it has, through largely implicitly and in a fragmentary fashion, been in actual use in the field. But until quite recently the predominant trends of thought in this field have been such as to prevent its emergence into the central explicit position which would allow it to develop freely all its potentialities for fruitful integration of the science. On the one hand, there has been a school of empiricism which was blind to the functions of theory in science — often mistakenly thinking it was following the model of the physical sciences. On the other hand, what has gone by the name of "theory" has consisted mainly in conceptual structures on quite a different level from what is here meant by a generalized theoretical system.

---

2. For the place of structural-functional analysis in physiology, see especially W. B. Cannon, *The Wisdom of the Body,* (New York: W. W. Norton and Co., 1932).

TWENTIETH CENTURY SOCIOLOGY

One major strand of thought in the history of sociological theory has been that closely associated with, indeed merging into, the philosophy of history. The central interest here has been in the establishment of a highly generalized pattern in the processes of change of human societies as a whole, whether it be linear evolutionism, cyclical or dialectic process, etc. Perhaps the evolutionary anthropologists like Tylor and Morgan have been most prominent here. But it also, in certain respects, includes Marx and his followers, Veblen and many others.

The element of generality which justifies calling these writers particularly theorists lies in the comprehensiveness of the empirical generalizations they have formulated and attempted to establish. The theory of analytical mechanics, or of general physiology, on the other hand, does not *as such* contain any empirical generalizations at all. It is a set of *tools* by which, working on adequate data, both specific empirical solutions and empirical generalizations can be arrived at. To make empirical generalization the central focus of theory in a science is to put the cart before the horse. In proportion as a generalized theoretical system is really perfected, and, what necessarily goes with it, empirical research and knowledge of fact builds up, it becomes possible to attain more and more comprehensive empirical generalizations. Indeed it can be said that any system of sound empirical generalizations implies a generalized theoretical systems.

But concentrating theoretical attention on this level of empirical generalization to the exclusion of the other is very risky. Such systems have had a notorious tendency to overreach the facts and their own analytical underpinning and by and large have not, in the meanings originally meant by their authors, stood the test of competent criticism. On this level no competent modern sociologist can be a Comtean, a Spencerian, or even a Marxian.

The prominence of this tendency has had two very serious unfavorable consequences. First it has, by focussing attention at the wrong place, impeded the progress of the subject. It has attempted to attain, at one stroke, a goal which can only be approached gradually by building the necessary factual foundations and analytical tools. It is not surprising that such ill-advised attempts should lead to difficulties. As these have become increasingly formidable and evident, the second consequence has appeared. Since "theory" has been so largely identified with such attempts at com-

SYSTEMATIC THEORY

prehensive empirical generalization, their failure has discredited not only themselves, which is only right and proper, but also everything else which has gone by the name of theory. This reaction has contributed greatly to a kind of "empiricism" which has blindly rejected the help of theoretical tools in general. While one tendency, it may be said, has sought to create a great building by a sheer act of will without going through the requisite of technical procedures, the other has tried to make a virtue of working with bare hands alone, rejecting all tools and mechanical equipment.

A second major strand of "theoretical" thinking in sociology has been that which has attempted to assess the importance of various "factors" in the determination of social phenomena. Usually it has taken the form of attempting to prove the exclusive or predominant importance of one such factor — geographic, biological, economic or what not.

This type of theorizing, though in a different way, also puts the cart before the horse. It also involves a kind of generalization which can only be soundly established as a *result* of the kind of investigation in which generalized theory, in the present sense, is an indispensable tool. If it is sound it, like the other, will *imply* a system of theory, and will depend upon it. But it is unlikely that such an uncriticized implicit system will be as adequate as one which has been carefully and explicitly worked out in direct relation to the facts.

Indeed a very large part of this "factor" theorizing has had the effect, if not the function, of evading the problem of a generalized theory of *social* systems. It has tended to do this in two ways. The major trend, particularly in Anglo-Saxon countries, has been to attribute the principal role to factors which are not specific to social systems, notably the environmental (e. g. geographical), and the biological and the economic.

In the first two of these cases the most important elements of theoretical generality have already been thoroughly worked out by investigations in other fields which have high prestige in the scientific world. Though on principle new discoveries in any field of application should lead to revision of the theoretical structure of a science, in fact in the case of biology for instance there was little chance of the human social tail being able to wag the dog of all known lower organic species. If, on the one hand, it was assumed that men, being organisms, were subject to biological laws, and on the other that the theory of natural selection was fully established as explaining the process of development of organic species in general, the predominant tendency would naturally be simply to seek in human social development examples of the working of the principles of natural selection without too much attention to the distinctive features of human society in other respects. Thus both economic competition and international rivalries have been widely interpreted in these terms. This has led to widespread neglect of the fundamental canon of science, the need to study in the very first instance the facts of the *particular* phenomena.

This unfortunate effect has been reinforced by another circumstance. Until recently it has been rare to find very much insight into the senses in which scientific theory on practically all levels is abstract. Thus natural selection has been interpreted as a generalized description of *the* process by which change in organic species came about—not as the formulation of *certain elements* in the process which might have a more or less dominant role relative to others in different cases. The effect of this tendency to "empirical closure" of a system is to make its application to any given field, especially a new one, a rigidly simple question of whether it "applies" or not. Application is interpreted in "all or none" terms—it is either a case or not. If it is in any sense a case then there is no incentive to look further and study the interdependence of the factors thus formulated with others which might be involved, since the latter are assumed not to exist or to be important. (3)

A slightly different though closely analogous situation occurs when the factors singled out are of certain types predominantly observed in human social behavior, but are treated in such a way as to ignore major elements of the context in which they operate in social systems.

A leading example of this type is the kind of theory which lays primary emphasis on rational adaptation of means to given ends in technological or economic contexts. This tendency has been predominant in the whole "utilitarian" tradition of social thought since Locke and in a modified form is decisive for Marx and Veblen. As I have shown in other connections this mode of treatment of social action as a whole has implied a very specific form of generalized theoretical system which has very seriously broken down in the course

---

3. The above is what Whitehead has called the "fallacy of misplaced concreteness."

of the last generation of theoretical work. (4) The key to this process of breakdown is the emergence into a position of central prominence, of certain modes and factors in the integration of social systems which could not be taken account of in utilitarian terms.

The utilitarian type of factor analysis is analogous to the environmental and biological in that it singles out elements which also can be treated in complete abstraction from social systems as such. Actual rational behavior is not, of course, observed apart from social situations. But the implicit conceptual scheme is such that other elements of a "social" rather than a biological or enviromental character, enter only in the role of conditions of the situation in which people act. They become, that is, theoretically equivalent to the physical environment and are thus deprived of any distinctive theoretical role in the social system of action itself.

All of the above factor theories have impeded the development of a theory of social systems by imposing an implicit generalized conceptual scheme which denied the empirical relevance of a distinctively social system—as a generalized theoretical system or a class of empirical systems. There would be no objection to this if the resulting theoretical structures had proved to be adequate for the solution of the pressing ranges of empirical problems which have dominated social science. At point after point, however, this empirical inadequacy has come to be exposed and has necessitated theoretical reconstruction. (5) A common strategy has been the retreat from one lost factor theory to another—thus from a rational utilitarian type to a bio-psychological instinct theory or one of natural selection. None of these has, however, provided more than temporary relief from the relentless pressure of empirical criticism and developing empirical knowledge.

It is not surprising that in this atmosphere attempts should have been made to elevate the neglected distinctively "social" elements into a dominant factor in the same sense—to oppose a "sociologistic" (6) theory to an economic or biological one. The most notable

---

4. See Talcott Parsons, *The Structure of Social Action,* Chaps. III, XII.

5. Two conspicuous fields are the breakdown of the theories of social evolution of the Spencerian type, and the growing dissatisfaction with an individualistic utilitarian interpretation of the modern industrial economy.

6. A term used by P. A. Sorokin in *Contemporary Sociological Theories,* (New York: Harper and Bros., 1928).

example of this possibility is what is in part the actual significance, but still more the predominant interpretation placed upon Durkheim's famous formula that "society is a reality *sui generis*" which "constrains" the thought, feelings and actions of individuals. If however this alternative is taken as simply another "factor" theory it involves the same theoretical and empirical difficulties which all other similar constructions do. It throws light on some empirical problems but only at the cost of increasing difficulties in other directions. (7)

Not the least deleterious effect of the "factor" type of theorizing, to which it is even more subject than the empirical generalization type, is the division of the field into warring "schools" of thought. On this basis every school has some solid empirical justification but equally each, as a result of the need for closure of the system, involves insuperable difficulties and conflicts with other interpretations of the same phenomena. Professional pride and vested interests get bound up with the defense or promotion of one theory against all others and the result is an impasse. In such a situation it is not surprising that theory as such should be discredited and many of the sanest, least obsessive minds become disillusioned with the whole thing and become dogmatic empiricists, denying as a matter of principle that theory can do anything for science. They feel it is, rather, only a matter of speculative construction which leads away from respect for facts and that thus the progress of science can consist *only* in the accumulation of discrete, unrelated, unguided discoveries of fact.

Such empiricists often invoke the supposed authority of the natural sciences. But the whole history of science shows that this is a gross misinterpretation. Perhaps the most extraordinary view is the relatively common contention that the glory of physics is mathematical method, while at the same time "theory" is an unnecessary impediment. But mathematics in physics *is* theory. The greatness of Newton and Laplace, of Einstein and Heisenberg is as theorists in the strictest sense. A science of physics without higher mathematics would be the real equivalent of the empiricists' ideal for social science. This shows quite clearly that what we need is not a science purified of theoretical infection—but one with the nearest possible

---

7. It is the author's contention that progress toward the formulation of a genuine structural-functional system is a far more important aspect of Durkheim's work. See *Structure of Social Action*, Chaps. VIII-XI and Section III below.

SYSTEMATIC THEORY

aproach to an *equivalent* of the role of mathematical analysis in physics. The trouble with sociology has not been that it has had too much theory but it has been plagued with the wrong kinds and what it has had of the right has been insufficiently developed and used to meet the need.

III

Approaches to a Generalized Social System. In various partial aspects of the field of human social behavior highly developed theoretical schemes of what are here considered the right kind have existed. This is notably true of economic theory especially since the discovery of the principle of marginal utility, and of psychological theory especially since Freud.

Economics has directly followed the methodological model of analytical mechanics and has been able to do so because, uniquely among social disciplines, it can deal primarily with numerically quantitative continua as variables. It has proved possible in principle to describe the state of a price economy in terms of the values of the variables of a system of simultaneous differential equations, though it is not possible operationally to ascertain the exact values of the variables nor would it be mathematically possible to solve the equations because of their excessive complexity. Hence most actual working economic analysis has had to fall back on more "primitive" analytical methods, and use the system of differential equations only as a methodological model.

But even more serious than this limitation has been the difficulty of fitting economic theory into the broader context of the social system as a whole. This was not a serious problem to the classical economists since they implicitly assumed a "utilitarian" system which gave economic "factors" the dominant dynamic role. (8) The general direction of solution seems to be that technical economic analysis makes sense only in the context of an "institutional" structure of social relationship patterns which is not as such part of the system dynamically treated by economic theory, but must constitute a set of constant data for it. Exactly what this means when the institutional data are treated on structural-functional terms while the economic data are not, remains on the whole an unsolved problem.

---

8. See *Structure of Social Action,* Chaps. III and IV.

It is significant that concern with economic theory as well as training in mathematics and physics constituted the background of by far the most important attempt so far made to build up a generalized analysis of social systems as a whole in a dynamic analytical system on the model of mechanics—that of Pareto. (9) Pareto's attempt undoubtedly put systematic theoretical thinking about social systems on a new level; it is unique in the literature for its comprehensiveness and the sophistication of its understanding of the physical science model. And yet it must be regarded as a relative failure.

Pareto started with the view that economic theory had become a genuine dynamic system, but it was, relative to concrete social problems (including those which are usually classed as "economic"), empirically inadequate because unduly abstract. Hence he sought to analyze the most important missing variables in a total social system in terms of their dynamic interdependence with those of economics. He took the "logical action," which is involved in the economic as well as certain other phases of the orientation of action, as a starting point and attempted to analyze the remaining residual category of nonlogical action inductively in order to reveal the principal variables.

The result is highly complex and not very satisfactory. He isolated three variables which are very heterogeneous relative to one another. The most satisfactorily analyzed, the "derivations," proves to be empirically the least significant. Even this, however, cannot be reduced to variation on a continuum but its values must be treated in terms of a four-fold qualitative classification. The same is true of the most important, the "residues," except that here the classification is far more complex and its basis of principle in the structure of social systems of action far less clear. Indeed it gives the impression of a great deal of arbitrariness. Finally, with the fourth variable, social heterogeneity, Pareto shifts to an althogether different level. The first three referred immediately to elements of the motivation or orientation of the action of individuals. The fourth refers to an aspect of the structure of a system of social relationships. Its appearance may be taken as an indication of the extreme difficulty of operating in this field without

---

9. *Cf.* L. J. Henderson, *Pareto's General Sociology: A Physiologist's Interpretation,* (Cambridge: Harvard University Press, 1937); Parsons, *Structure of Social Action,* Chaps. V-VII.

SYSTEMATIC THEORY

structural categories. Its relevance to Pareto's principal empirical generalizations is very clear and it serves the function of giving empirical relevance to his analytical scheme. But strictly speaking it has no place in the latter as a variable but should, with the aid of the relevant data, be derivable from the system of variables.

It was said above that Pareto's attempt was a *relative* failure. He certainly succeeded in avoiding all the principal theoretical difficulties discussed above. His system is an extraordinarily useful instrument of criticism. It also, when skillfully used as by Pareto himself, yields important though rather general empirical insights. But it has signally failed to work as a direct source of detailed analytical tools in detailed research. What is successfully established is too vague and general. The gaps have to be filled by arbitrary *ad hoc* constructions and classifications or by the introduction of structural categories which are merely tolerated, not systematically developed.

The conclusion is that Pareto took what is, in the present state of sociological knowledge, the less fruitful alternative. A structural-functional system must sacrifice much of the dynamic flexibility Pareto aimed at. But it can hope to counterbalance this by a great gain in explicit systematic determinacy and precision in detailed analytical use.

The other alternative, the structural functional type, also has important antecedents. The most important of these are the following four:

1. The developments of modern dynamic and clinical psychology which conceive the human individual as a dynamic structural-functional system. Psychoanalytic theory has been the most important single influence in this field but stands by no means alone. This psychological theory is highly important both as a methodological model for that of a social system and as itself providing some of the most essential components of it.

2. Modern social and cultural anthropology, especially that with something of a "functional" slant though by no means confined to those writers, usually designated as belonging to the functional school. Probably Malinowski's is so far the most important single name. Perhaps the basic point is that the scale of non-literate societies has been small and there has been no established division

into different specialisms in dealing with it. Hence the anthropologist, when dealing with a society, was more likely than other social scientists to see it as a single functioning system.

3. Durkheim and his followers. As has been noted above Durkheim in many respects tended to set a "sociologistic" factor theory over against the individualistic factor theories current in his day. But along with this heading there is a more important strand in his thought which gained increasingly in strength in the course of his carrer. This was a genuinely structural-functional treatment of the social system—with a gradual clarification of the more important elements of it. This is above all evident from the way in which he treated empirical problems, in his analysis of the stability of a system of functionally differentiated roles in his *Division of Labor*, in his study, *Le suicide*, and in his interpretation of religious ritual in the *Elementary Forms of the Religious Life*.

4. Max Weber. In part Weber can serve as a type case of the more generalized thinking of the historical disciplines in the institutional field. But also, in reaction against the individualistic factor theories of his time, he went much farther than any other writer toward the underpinning of empirical study of comparative institutions with a generalized theoretical scheme. Incomplete though this was, it converged with Durkheim's scheme and supplemented it in the directions where comparative structural perspective is most important. (10)

IV

Outline of a Structural-Functional Theory of Social Systems. Limitations of space forbid following out the substantive problems in the devolpment of the present state of the structural-functional theory of social systems. It is, however, contended that, developing with particular clarity though by no means exclusively in the above four sources, we now have the main outline of an articulated system of structural-functional theory available and in actual use. The

---

10. In addition to the *Structure of Social Action*, Chaps. XIV-XVII, see the author's introduction to Weber's *Theory of Social and Economic Organization* (translated from *Wirtschaft und Gesellschaft*, Part I) to be published by William Hodge and Co., Edinburgh.

SYSTEMATIC THEORY

final section of this paper will be devoted to an exceedingly bare and general sketch of this main outline. Of necessity most of the details will have to be omitted. As in every developing theoretical structure, there are innumerable difficulties and unsolved problems which also cannot be entered into.

The first essential of a generalized theoretical system is the "frame of reference." For the social system in question it is quite clear that it is that of "action" or perhaps better "actor-situation" in a sense analogous to the organism-environment frame of reference of the biological sciences.

The actor-situation frame of reference is shared with psychology, but for a social system it takes on the added complication introduced by the treatment of a plurality of *inter*-acting actors in situations which are in part discrete, in part shared in common.

The unit of all social systems is the human individual *as actor*, as an entity which has the basic characteristics of striving toward the attainment of "goals" of "reacting" emotionally or affectively toward objects and events and of, to a greater or less degree, cognitively knowing or understanding his situation, his goals and himself. Action is, in this frame of reference, inherently structured on a "normative," "teleological" or possibly better, a "voluntaristic" system of "coordinates" or axes. A goal is by definition a "desirable" state of affairs, failure to attain it a "frustration." Affective reaction includes components of pleasurable or painful significance to the actor, and of approval or disapproval of the object or state which occasions the reaction. Finally, cognitive orientation is subject to standards of "correctness" and "adequacy" of knowledge and understanding.

This essential "normative orientation" of action directs attention to the crucial role of the "patterns" which define the desirable direction of action in the form of goals and standards of behavior. This system of normative patterns seems to be best treated as *one* very important element of the "culture" of the group, which also includes cognitive patterns of "ideas," symbols and other elements. From the present point of view, however, a social system is a system of action; i. e., of motivated human behavior, not a system of culture patterns. It articulates with culture patterns in one connection just as it does with physical and biological conditions in another. But a "system of culture" is a different order of abstraction from a "social system" though it is to a large degree abstraction from the same concrete phenomena (11)

In all this, the point of view of interpretation of action has a peculiar duality. One essential component is its "meaning" to the actor, whether on a consciously explicit level or not. The other is its relevance to an "objective" concatenation of objects and events as analyzed and interpreted by an observer.

In a sense this basic frame of reference consists in the outline of the structural categories of human personality in a psychological sense, in terms of the particular values of which each particular character structure and sequences of action must be described and analyzed. But the structure of social systems cannot be derived directly from the actor-situation frame of reference. It requires functional analysis of the complications introduced by the interaction of a plurality of actors.

Even in abstraction from social relationships, features of the situation of action, and the biologically determined needs and capacities of an individual provide certain fixed points of determination in the system of action. The functional needs of social integration, the conditions necessary for the functioning of a plurality of actors as a "unit" as a system sufficiently well integrated to exist as such, impose others .

But functional needs, whether their ultimate sources be biological, socio-cultural or individual are, so far as they are dynamically relevant to this conceptual scheme, satisfied through *processes of action*. The need to eat is biologically determined, but the human processes of food production and the variations in the social customs of food taste and consumption are no more biologically determined than any other social phenomena such for instance as the production and enjoyment of symphonic music. Hence, the ultimate "source" of needs is not relevant except in so far as it affects the structure and orientation of social systems of action, especially by providing "foci" around which attitudes, symbols and action patterns cluster.

A structure is a set of relatively stable patterned relationships of

---

11. For the distinction between action and culture, see *Structure of Social Action*, Chap. XIX, pp. 762 ff. This view differs from that of culture and social system set forth in Kluckhohn and Kelly, "The Concept of Culture," to be published in Ralph Linton, ed., *The Science of Man in the World Crisis*, Columbia University Press.

SYSTEMATIC THEORY

units. Since the unit of social system is the actor, social structure is a patterned system of the social relationships of actors. It is a distinctive feature of the structure of systems of social action, however, that in most relationships the actor does not participate as a total entity, (12) but only by virtue of a given differentiated "sector" of his total action. Such a sector which is the unit of a system of social relationships has come predominantly to be called a "role." (13) Hence, the previous statement must be revised to say that social structure is a system of patterned relationships of actors in their capacity as playing roles relative to one another. Role is the concept which links the subsystem of the actor as a "psychological" behaving entity to the distictively *social* structure.

Two primary questions arise in following on beyond this point. First, what is the nature of this link, what is social structure from the point of view of the actor playing his roles within it? Second, what is the nature of the "system" of the patterned relationships of social structure?

The clue to the first question is found in the normative-voluntaristic aspect of the structure of action. From the point of view of the social system, a role is an element of generalized patterning of the action of its component individuals. But this is not merely a matter of statistical "trend." It is a matter of goals and standards. From the point of view of the actor, his role is defined by the normative expectations of the members of the group as formulated in its social traditions. The existence of these expectations among his fellows constitutes an essential feature of the situation in which any given actor is placed. His conformity with them or lack of it brings consequences to him, the sanctions of approval and reward, or of condemnation and punishment. But more than this, they constitute part of his own personality. In the course of the process of socialization he absorbs—to a greater or less degree—the standards and ideals of his group so that they become effective motivating forces in his own conduct, independently of external sanctions.

From this point of view the essential aspect of social structure lies in a system of patterned expectations defining the *proper* be-

---

12. In the sense in which a given brick as a whole is or is not "part" of a given wall.
13. This concept has been used above all by Ralph Linton in *The Study of Man*, (New York: D. Appleton-Century Co., 1936). See especially Chap. VIII.

havior of persons playing certain roles, enforced both by the incumbents' own positive motives for conformity and by the sanctions of others. Such systems of patterned expectations, seen in the perspective of their place in a total social system and sufficiently thoroughly established in action to be taken for granted as legitimate, are conveniently called "institutions." The fundamental, structurally stable, element of social systems then, which, according to the present argument, must play a crucial role in their theoretical analysis, is their structure of institutional patterns defining the roles of their constituent actors.

Seen from the functional point of view, institutionalized roles constitute the mechanism by which the extremely varied potentialities of "human nature" become integrated in such a way as to dovetail into a single integrated system capable of meeting the situational exigencies with which the society and its members are faced. Relative to these potentialities they have two primary functions: first, the *selective* one of bringing out those possibilities of behavior which "fit" the needs and the tolerances of the particular patterned structure and by-passing or repressing the others; secondly, through interactive mechanisms the maximum of motivational backing for action in conformity with the expectations of roles must be secured. Above all, *both* the disinterested motives associated with "conscience" and "ideals" and the self-interested ones must be mobilized in the interest of the *same* directions of behavior.

The second main problem is that of the structure of institutions themselves as a system. They are resultants of and controlling factors in the action of human beings in society. Hence, as a system they must at the same time be related to the functional needs of their actors as individuals and of the social systems they compose. Thus, the basic structural principles, as in the case of anatomy, is that of functional differentiation. The functional reference, however, is in the social case more complex since *both* the functional needs of the actor and those of the social system are intertwined.

Any scheme for analyzing such a functionally differentiated structure is necessarily complex and there is presumably no single "right" one. A basic three-fold scheme has, however, proved very useful and seems of highly generalized significance. (14) In the first place, there are "situational" institutions or patterns. These are

---

14. See "Toward a Common Language for the Area of Social Science," Part II, mimeographed for use by students in Harvard College.

SYSTEMATIC THEORY

cases of the organization of roles about aspects of the situation in which actors and social systems are placed. Leading examples are kinship roles, organized about the biological relatedness of individuals through descent, and in part at least, political institutions organized about solidarity with respect to the use and sufferance of force within a territorial area.

The second class are "instrumental" institutions, patterned about the attainment of certain classes of goals as such. For example, a given technology like that of modern medicine is pursued within the framework of an institutionalized role, that of physician. Finally, third, there are "integrative" institutions, those primarily oriented to regulating the relations of individuals so as to avoid conflict or promote positive cooperation. Social stratification and authority are primary examples.

Since relative valuation of personal qualities and achievements is inevitable in a system, it is, thus, essential that these valuations be integrated in an ordered system of ranking, the system of stratification of a society. Similarly the potentialities of deviant behavior and the need for detailed coordination of the action of many people are, in any at all complex society, such that spontaneous response to unorganized controls cannot be relied upon. Some persons and organized agencies must be in a position within limits to repress deviance or its consequences or to insure effective cooperation. Again, it is essential to the integration of a society that such control over others be institutionally ordered and regulated, should constitute a system of roles of legitimate authority. This is both an important factor in the effectiveness of the control since it makes possible appeal to a sense of moral obligation, and makes it possible to regulate authority which, if misused, has serious, disruptive potentialities.

The importance of conceiving institutions as a functionally differentiated system lies in making it possible to place changes in any one part of it in the perspective of their interdependence in the system as a whole. In so far as the system is adequately formulated in generalized terms and is structurally complete, it ensures explicit attention will be given to every major possibility of the repercussions of a change in different directions.

Dynamic analysis is not, however, possible in terms of the systematic treatment of institutional structure alone. This involves the possibility of generalized treatment of the behavioral tendencies of the human actors, in the situations in which they are placed and subject to the expectations of their institutionalized roles. In the most general terms such generalization depends on a theory of the "motivation" of human behavior.

The ultimate foundations of such a theory must certainly be derived from the science of psychology. But both because the "idiosyncratic" element in the behavior and motivation of individuals is so great and because the levels of abstraction current in psychology have been what they have in general, it has not been possible to derive an adequate theory of the motivation of socially structural mass phenomena through the simple "application" of psychological generalizations. The relationship between the psychological level and behavior in social systems is complex, but light is thrown on it in terms of the psychological implications of the conception of role.

This is above all true in two directions. The early tendency of psychology was to consider "personality" as largely an expression of genetic constitution or of unique idiosyncracy. Study of socialization in a comparative perspective is, however, demonstrating that there are important elements of uniformity in the "character structure" of those who have been socialized in the same cultural and institutional system, subject to variations according different roles within the system. (15) Though the limits of applicability of this conception of a character structure appropriate to a given role structure are as yet by no means clear, its general theoretical significance is established. In so far as it applies, the pattern of motivation to be used in explaining behavior in an institutionalized role is not derived directly from the "propensities of human nature," in general. It is a matter of such components *organized* into a particular structure. Such a structured personality type will have its own appropriate patterns of motivation and tendencies of behavior.

The other principal direction of development is different. It concerns the area within which there is, in any given social system, a range of flexibility in behavior on a psychological level. Evidence, particularly from complex societies, points to the view that this range is relatively wide for large proportions of the popu-

---

15. See, for instance, Abram Kardiner, *The Individual and His Society*, (New York: Columbia University Press, 1939), and various recent writings of Margaret Mead.

lation and that the distribution of character types more or less successfully fulfilling the requirements of a given role also covers a wide range.

The fundamental mechanism here is what may be called the "structural generalization of goals" and of other aspects of orientation. As W. I. Thomas puts it, one of the fundamental functions of institutions is to "define the situation" (16) for action. Once a situation is institutionally defined and the definition upheld by an adequately integrated system of sanctions, action in conformity with the relevant expectations tends, as pointed out, to mobilize a wide variety of motivational elements in its service. Thus, to take one of the most famous examples, the "profit motive" which has played such a prominent part in economic discussion is not a category of psychology at all. The correct view is rather that a system of "free enterprice" in a money and market economy so defines the situation for those conducting or aspiring to the conduct of business enterprise, that they must seek profit as a condition of survival and as a measure of the success of their activities. Hence, whatever interests the individual may have in achievement, self-respect, the admiration of others, etc., to say nothing of what money will buy, are channeled into profit-making activity. (17) In a differently defined situation, the same fundamental motives would lead to a totally different kind of activity. (18)

Thus, in analyzing the dynamic problems of a social system, it is not enough to apply "psychology" to the behavior of individuals in the relevant "objective" situations. It is necessary to qualify the interpretation of their "reactions" in terms of the evidence on at least two other problems—what can be known about a character structure "typical" of that particular social system and particular roles within it, and what will be the effect of the structurally generalized goals and orientations resulting from the "definitions of the situation" current in the society.

---

16. See especially his *The Unadjusted Girl*, (Boston: Little, Brown, and Co., 1927), Introduction.

17. See Talcott Parsons, "The Motivation of Economic Activity," *Canadian Journal of Economics and Political Science*, 6: 187-202, May, 1940. For a further analysis of the relation of role-structure to the dynamics of motivation see Talcott Parsons, "Propaganda and Social Control," *Psychiatry*, 5: 551-572, November, 1942.

18. See B. Malinowski, *Coral Gardens and their Magic*, (London: G. Allen and Unwin, 1935), vol. I, Chap. I, Sec. 9.

But with due regard of this type of qualification, it remains true that the basic dynamic categories of social systems are "psychological." The relation of psychology to the theory of social systems appears to be closely analogous to that of biochemistry to general physiology. Just as the organism is not a category of general chemistry, so a social system is not one of psychology. But within the framework of the physiological conception of what a functioning organism is, the *processes* are chemical in nature. Similarly, the *processes* of social behavior as of any other are psychological. But without the meaning given them by their institutional-structural context they lose their relevance to the understanding of social phenomena.

However sketchy and inadequate the above outline may be, it may be hoped that it does give an idea of the main character of the emerging structural-functional theory of social systems. It remains to raise the question of what aspect of that theory may be considered specifically sociological.

It is of course possible to consider sociological theory as concerned with the total theory of social systems in general. It seems, however, undesirable to do this since it would make of sociology such an extremely comprehensive discipline, including as it would have to, for instance, both the major part of psychology and all of economic theory. The most important alternative is to treat sociology as the science of institutions in the above sense or more specifically of institutional structure. This would, as here conceived, by no means limit it to purely static structural analysis but could retain a definite focus on problems of structure, including structural change. Dynamic, particularly psychological, problems would enter into sociology in terms of their specific relevance to this context. (19)

This view leaves room for a clear distinction from psychology as the general science of human personality structure and motivation. It is quite clear that many of the concrete problems of psychology in this sense are not sociological at all. For example, sociological considerations would be secondary and peripheral in the whole field of clinical psychology. The two sciences are, however, necessarily

---

19. This is in slightly modified form essentially the view put forth in *Structure of Social Action*, Chap. XIX. Institutions are those elements of the structure of social systems which most distinctively embody the patterns of "common value integration" of a system of action.

SYSTEMATIC THEORY

closely interdependent and data concerning the role structure of the social system are at least implicity involved in practically all concrete psychological problems. This, however, is not an unusual situation in the relationship of different sciences.

This view also makes it possible to distinguish sociology from economic theory. Economic theory is concerned with certain distinctive dynamic processes which go on within social systems. A situation where it is relevant in more than the broadest respects is confined to certain distinctive types of social systems, notably those where there is an important degree of primary orientation to considerations of optimum utilization of resources and of cost. Such a situation presupposes in the first place a distinctive institutional structure. In the second place, as a consequence of this, it presupposes the organization of motives about certain types of structurally generalized goals. But, given these conditions, the distinctive dynamic consequences of economically oriented action must be analyzed in terms of a specific technical conceptual scheme. As Pareto and many other have been well aware, this scheme is highly abstract and the larger aspects of the dynamics of total economic systems will inevitably involve interdependence with non-economic variables.

In some respects analogous to the distinctive features of a market or price economy is the emergence in complex social systems of certain prominent functionally differentiated structures. Perhaps the most important of these is that of government. It is always possible to make a study of such structures and the relevant social processes the subject of a relatively independent science. So far, however, in none of these cases has a distinctive analytical scheme appeared which would give that science a theoretical status analogous to that, for instance, of economics. Thus, it is highly questionable whether "political theory" in a scientific rather than an ethical and normative sense should be regarded as a fundamental element of the theory of social systems. It seems more logical to regard it as a field of application of the general theory of social institutions but one which is sufficiently differentiated to be treated as an independent discipline for many purposes. The same general considerations apply to other aspects of structural differentiation, such, for example, as that of religion.

Finally, there is a question as to whether anthropology should be considered in a theoretical sense an independent science. As the study of non-literate societies, it is of course a pragmatic field of specialization of considerable significance, in some ways analogous to the field of government. In so far, however, as its theoretical concern is with the study of social systems as such, there seems to be no reason to regard social anthropology as a distinctive theoretical discipline. In the relevant respects, it must be regarded as a branch of sociology, and its other aspects of economics, government and so on. There is, however, one problem, analysis of which might modify this view. To many of its proponents, the distinctive feature of anthropology is that it is the science of *culture*, not of social systems. It is implicit in the above analysis that culture, though empirically fundamental to social systems and in one sense a component of them, is not in the theoretical sense exclusively a social phenomenon. It has been pointed out above that the study of the structure of cultural patterns *as such* and of their structural interdependence is a legitimate abstraction from the concrete phenomena of human behavior and its material consequences which is quite different from their study in the context of interpendence in a social system. It is perfectly clear that this study is not equivalent to the study of institutions as aspects of a social system. If the focus of theoretical interest of anthropology is to develop in this direction, two important consequences would seem to follow. First, it is quite clear that its traditional primary concern with non-literate peoples cannot be upheld. The culture of non-literate peoples is neither more nor less a subject for the differentiation of a science than is their institutional structure. Secondly, it is particularly important to clarify the generalized relationship between culture and social structure. A great deal of confusion appears to be prevalent on this point among both sociologists and cultural anthropoligists.

SELECTED BIBLIOGRAPHY

Cannon, W. B., *The Wisdom of the Body*, (New York: W. W. Norton and Co., 1932).

Durkheim, Emile, *The Elementary Forms of the Religious Life*, trans. by Joseph Ward Swain, (London: G. Allen and Unwin; New York: The Mcmillan Co., 1915).

Durkheim, Emile, *The Rules of Sociological Method*, trans. by S. A. Solovay and J. H. Mueller, and ed. by E. G. Catlin, (Chicago: University of Chicago Press, 1938).

SYSTEMATIC THEORY

Freud, Sigmund, *Beyond the Pleasure Principle*, authorized trans. from 2nd German edition by C. J. M. Hubback, (London: International Psychoanalytical Press, 1922).

Freud, Sigmund, *The Ego and the Id*, trans. by Joan Rivers, L. and Virginia Woolf, (London: Hogarth Press, 1935).

Kardiner, Abram, *The Individual and His Society*, (New York: Columbia University Press, 1939).

Malinowski, Bronislaw, *Coral Gardens and Their Magic*, (New York: American Book Co., 1935), Vol. I.

Malinowski, Bronislaw, *Crime and Custom in Savage Society*, (New York: Harcourt, Brace and Co., 1926).

Malinowski, Bronislaw, *The Foundations of Faith and Morals*, (London: H. Milford, Oxford University Press, 1936).

Mead, Margaret, *And Keep Your Powder Dry*, (New York: W. Morrow and Co., 1942).

Pareto, Vilfredo, *The Mind and Society*, trans. by A. Bongiorno and A. Livingston, (New York: Harcourt, Brace and Co., 1935, 4 vols.).

Parsons, Talcott, *The Structure of Social Action*, (New York: McGraw-Hill Book Co., 1937).

Weber, Max, *Gesammelte Aufsaetze zur Religionssoziologie*, (Tuebingen: J. C. B. Mohr, 1920-1921, 3 vols.).

Weber, Max, *Wirtschaft und Gesellschaft*, (Tuebingen: J. C. B. Mohr, 1925). English translation of Part I under title, *The Theory of Social and Political Organization*, to be published by Wm. Hodge & Co., Edinburgh.

Whitehead, A. N., *Science and the Modern World*, (New York: The Macmillan Co., 1925).

Talcott Parsons, A. B. Amherst, 1924; graduate study at the London School of economics, particulary with Malinowski, Hobhouse and Ginsberg; graduate study at the University of Heidelberg (Germany) 1925-27; Ph. D. University of Heidelberg 1927. Instructor in Economics, Amherst College, 1926-27; Instructor in Economics, Harvard University, 1927-31; Instructor in Sociology, 1931-36; Assistant Professor, 1936-39; Associate Professor, 1939-44; Professor 1944—; Chairman, Department of Sociology, 1944—. Staff, School for Overseas Administration, Harvard University, 1943—. President, Eastern Sociological Society, 1941-42. Translator of Max Weber's *The Protestant Ethic and the Spirit of Capitalism;* author of *The Structure of Social Action*, and of numerous papers in scientific journals and symposia.

CHAPTER IV

INTERPRETIVE SOCIOLOGY AND CONSTRUCTIVE TYPOLOGY*

by

HOWARD BECKER

I

Once upon a time, a waggish occupant of an Orthodox Presbyterian pew drew a startling conclusion from the two-hour sermon through which he had just suffered: "Gin we are all puir sinners, we maun juist sin. What else can we do?" Tradition has delivered no account of the dominie's reply to this heretical query, but it can be taken for granted that the good man, after the first shock of dazed astonishment, succeeded in convincing both himself and his audacious hearer that the Divine Author of the Scheme of Salvation had made suitable provision for exceptions to the general rule.

---

*With the permission of the author, this paper has been abridged by about three-fifths. Illustrative materials have been mainly eliminated from the two sections here published, and the entire concluding section (about one-half of the total), consisting of the application of the principles here set forth, has been omitted. A complete mimeographed version may be secured gratis on application at the University of Wisconsin, Department of Sociology and Anthropology.—*The Editors.*

INTERPRETIVE SOCIOLOGY

Where the Sociological Dispensation is concerned, however, it is gravely to be doubted whether any exceptions to Interpretive (1) Sinning are possible. In fact, if I could find someone carrying out the role of minister among a gathering of the sociologically elect (and there are persons who sometimes come uncomfortably close to playing such a part), I should ask him, not jocularly, but seriously: "Inasmuch as we all interpret the conduct of our fellows, whatever our confession of faith, why should we not interpret with full awareness of what we are doing?" A professor of the strictly positivistic sect (2) thus interrogated would roll up his eyes in holy horror, denying that he had ever committed the sin of interpreting, of imputing motives, of "understanding" the meaning of conduct, or of inferring what lies behind overt action. Almost certainly he would mumble something about mysticism (3), electron-proton combinations (4), fallacies of folk belief, animism, and behaviorism. After listening awhile to this assortment of words conveying blame or dispensing praise, I might attempt to convince him that the kind of interpretation of which I spoke has nothing

---

1. "Interpretive" is used in preference to the longer "interpretative," and is assigned a meaning closely akin to but not wholly identical with "understanding" as it occurs in the writings of Max Weber and others. See especially Max Weber, *Gesammelte Aufsaetze zur Wissenschaftslehre,* (Tuebingen: Mohr—Paul Siebeck—1922), pp. 405-450, 503-523, *et passim;* Florian Znaniecki, *Social Actions,* (New York: Farrar and Rinehart, 1936), esp. pp. 1-34; Howard Becker, *Systematic Sociology on the Basis of the* Beziehungslehre and Gebildelehre *of Leopold von Wiese,* (New York: John Wiley and Sons, 1932), pp. 57-59, particulary footnote 10 (hereafter cited as Wiese-Becker); Talcott Parsons, *The Structure of Social Action,* (New York: McGraw-Hill Book Co., 1937) pp. 84-86, 583-585, 588-589, 634, 635-639, 681, 765; Alexander von Schelting, *Max Webers Wissenschaftslehre.* (Tuebingen: Mohr—Paul Siebeck,—1934) pp. 325-329, 353-404; R. M. MacIver, *Social Causation,* (Boston: Ginn and Co., 1942), pp. 263-265; *et al.*

2. Robert Bierstedt is one of the most shrilly orthodox. See his article, "The Means-End Schema in Sociological Theory," *American Sociological Review,* 3: 665-671, October, 1938. Bierstedt follows Lundberg, as do also Ozanne, Bain, and a number of others. The older sages are of course Watson, Weiss, Bernard, and "ithers o' that ilk."

3. "Mysticism," to many of these gentry, simply means "not orthodox Watson behaviorism." The term is only a name-calling device. Perhaps it is time for the rest of us to take counter-measures.

4. Here I have in mind effusions such as those of George A. Lundberg, *Foundations of Sociology,* (New York: The Macmillan Co., 1939). See my critical review, "The Limits of Sociological Positivism," *Journal of Social Philosophy,* 6: 362-370, July, 1941, esp. p. 366.

"mystic" about it, but on the contrary is utterly matter-of-fact and everyday.

Here, reduced to its barest, most obvious terms, is what is meant by interpretation, no more and no less: the interpreter puts himself in the place of the actor as best he can, and the degree to which he views the situation as the actor views it determines his success in predicting the further stages of the conduct. In order to achieve this end, we make use of certain interpretative devices, and among these is what we may technically call the contruction of models (5) of motivation in accordance with which his tactics are shaped. Models of motivation are constructs in two senses: (a) the observer selects and combines, for the purposes in hand, certain criteria regarded as significant for the solution of his special problems; and (b) those selected and combined criteria go beyond the immediately perceivable sense data, inasmuch as certain other criteria, either not observed at the time, very infrequently observed within the limits of ordinary experience, or directly accessible only "within" qualified observers, are built into the combination in such a way that a coherent structure usable for predictive purposes result (6). Granting that constructs of this kind include meanings not encountered at the level on which the physicist operates, it is nevertheless true that they are in many respects equivalent to the constructs characterized as follows by Bridgman, high priest of the operationists:

> There are many sorts of constructs: those in which we are interested are made by us to enable us to deal with physical situations which we cannot

---

5. By "model" I do *not* mean *"desirable* structure" or anything remotely similar, but something of which a chemist's model of a carbon ring is a good illustration. It should be unnecesary to make these simple-minded comments, but persistent misunderstanding of "ideal," "paradigm," and the like have put me on my guard. A little good will on the part of critics, plus careful study of various possible uses of English words, would make such pendantic defensiveness unnecessary.

6. In his unpublished doctoral dissertation, one of my graduate students, W. L. Kolb, has put this very shrewdly:

"To the reader of mystery stories, the fundamental similarity of this... to the deductions of the fictional master sleuths—and of the reader who inevitably tries to beat them at their own game—should be apparent... The specific overt act of murder (let us say) may be interpreted within many contexts of motive, but as the clues continue to pile up which point to other overt actions, it gradually becomes apparent that these series of actions are understandable only through one context (which is a construct) of motive." (*The Peasant in Revolution: A Study in Constructive Typology,* University of Wisconsin Library, 1943, p. 34.)

INTERPRETIVE SOCIOLOGY

directly experience through our senses, but with which we have contact indirectly and by inference. Such constructs usually involve the element of invention to a greater or lesser degree. A construct containing very little of invention is that of the inside of an opaque solid body. We can never experience directly through our senses the inside of such a solid body, because the instant we directly experience it, it ceases by definition to be the inside. We have here a construct, but so natural a one as to be practically unavoidable. An example of a construct involving a greater amount of invention is the stress in an elastic body. A stress is by definition a property of the interior points of a body which is connected mathematically in a simple way with the forces acting across the free surface of the body. A stress is then, by its very nature, forever beyond the reach of direct experience, and it is therefore a construct. (7).

Without pushing the analogy off its feet — for biped analogies cannot be made to go on all fours without absurdities — it can nevertheless be said that the physicist's concept of stress bears some similarity to our concept of attitude or motive, more especially when we regard the latter as a sort of stress imposed on a given actor prior to the immediate situation in which his conduct is observed. If, however, practicing the asceticism proper only to an orthodox member of that conventicle of the positivist sect once presided over by Parson John Broadus Watson, we restrict ourselves to the sense data directly given in the immediate situation, we are unable to make predictions of any kind. Exhibit: A man is chopping wood at the rate of forty-five stroke a minute, using a four-pound axe with a three-foot handle. Having recorded these and many similar data, and comparing the results with records of woodchoping gathered elsewhere, we discover that the actor concerned is exceeding the ordinary rate by about fifteen strokes. What are the reasons, if any, for this discrepancy between the "stimulus," whatever it may be, and the ensuing "response"? (8)

If we are not orthodox behaviorists, we may of course try to discover by inferential means the stress entering as an effective factor into the performance of the given task. In other words, we may try to find what the effective attitude of the man in question toward woodchopping is, and we may learn that he has certain ends in view

---

7. P. W. Bridgman, *The Logic of Modern Physics*, (New York: The Macmillan Co., 1932), pp. 53-54.

8. Howard Becker, "The Limits of Sociological Positivism," *Journal of Social Philosophy*, 6: 367-369, July, 1941.

with relation to which woodchopping is merely a means. (9) Perhaps he has quarrelled with his wife because the coffee was cold and is working off a fit of temper, or a visit to his physician has convinced him that his waistline is much too large, or that the threatened coal famine he has read about in the newspaper has made him think of a cozy wood fire next December, or that he is to get $25.00 a cord for red oak in stove lengths rather than the accustomed rate of forty cents an hour, or that he is obsessed by the delusion that he is battering in the heads of Japanese soldiers on Saipan.

Having provisionally determined the end to which the action is directed, we may then, perhaps predict the length of time the action will be pursued, this prediction serving as a check on the inference. If the woodchopper is merely getting the taste of cold coffee out of his oral equipment and an excess of adrenalin out of his bloodstream, we may hazard the guess that fifteen minutes will see the end of the furious axe-swinging, and if our doughty axeman does quit his job within a time not too far away from our quarter-of an-hour estimate, our construct is rendered more plausible than it was at the beginning. We have therefore interpreted, as we might say, with some degree of success, and the *plausibility* of the interpretation may be brought to a fair degree of *probability* by the analysis of other evidence made avaliable to us after the burst of woodchopping is far enough in the past for the aggrieved husband to talk without gasping for breath. (10)

To be sure, we most certainly would not accept the actor's interpretation of his own conduct at face value, for along with the "gift of tongues," with the capacity for speech, the human being has also been endowed with the ability to lie, both to himself and to others. In short, deceit and self-delusion are always possibilities; other corroborative evidence would have to be sought and found before our fair degree of probability could become reasonable certainty. (11) Nevertheless, the basic necessity in this little piece of interpretation is the ascertaining, by whatever resources of observation

---

9. Be it noted, however, that if woodchopping is a means of affectively irrational character (as it is in this case), means and ends are fused in such a way that even analytic separation by the observer has little practical value. A repetition of the clammy coffeepot may lead to an affective display of radically different type; e.g., the actor may use the axe on his wife.

10. See Wiese-Becker, *op. cit.*, pp. 57-59, footnote 10.

11. Viz., a very high degree of probability.

INTERPRETIVE SOCIOLOGY

and inference at our disposal, of the actor's "definition of the situation." (12)

Note, by the way, that definition of this kind does not *necessarily* involve the element of choice (13) — at least, not of choice with full awareness of the alternatives. Situations may be defined by the actors concerned with varying degrees of clarity, and a considerable amount of additional data may have to be obtained and analyzed before the investigator can determine the end toward which the conduct was actually directed. Regardless, however, of whether or not the actor can put into words the purpose that governed his woodchopping or similar activity, it still remains true that the purpose is his own, that the end pursued is the end he envisages, no matter how dimly. If the investigator's constructs are to possess any degree of analytic utility, they must be constructs imputing a certain "state of mind" (14) to the actor which is meaningful in the light of the actor's own traits, the elements of the situation, and the overall value-system (or systems) within which those traits and elements function and from which they derive their ulterior significance.

Returning to our woodchopping illustration: What was the fulcrum on which the interpretative lever rested? What would strike the casual observer as problematic in the conduct of our irate husband? What might bring even the extreme behaviorist to indulge

---

12. MacIver, *op. cit.*, prefers "dynamic assessment," but Znaniecki uses "definition of the situation" in his most recent writings, and it seems unwise to deviate from his well-established terminology now.

13. Not that we are trying to dodge the fact that choice frequently does occur! As choice, purpose, and related terms are used here, they have nothing to do with the high-school debate "dilemma" of "free will *versus* determinism." See R. M. MacIver, *op. cit.*, pp. 240-241.

14. W. L. Kolb, in the dissertation previously quoted (footnote 6), says this:

"If we are to credit the positivists with any theoretical sophistication whatever, we must assume that when they state that man is a biological organism 'endowed' with a nervous system (here the reference is to Bierstedt, *op. cit.*, pp. 666-667) they are not implying that the origin of the nervous system is supernatural. It is not unfair to expect, then, that the positivists will be willing to allow that their opponents conceive of "mind' as something produced in naturalistic fashion. If this is recognized, the utilization of the concept of 'mind' becomes a matter of recognizing the nature and limitations of scientific systems. For the purpose of a systematic analysis of social action it is unnecessary to go beyond the concept of mind . . ." (pp. 48-49).

in the collecting of sense-data in the hope that somehow an intelligible pattern might emerge from the jumble if only a sufficient number of similar cases could be tabulated and the right formula aplied? Well, even the positivist doing his best to restrict himself to the immediate situation would probably contrast the rate of forty-five strokes a minute with a "normal" rate of about twenty-five, and would feel that an increase of eighty percent was in some way "intresting." In thus regarding the conduct as worth further observation, our behaviorist has been indulging in a little covert interpretation—that is to say, he vaguely feels that here is something "abnormal" that should be looked into further. He may say to himself, as it were, "I never saw a man chop so fast. I wonder what he's up to?"

If he does thus lapse from the ascetic creed of his positivistic sect, he may be making use of an implicit construct; namely, the construct of "the rational man." (15) Indeed, he may mutter to himself, "That fellow surely isn't working for wages. No man in his senses would make the chips fly like that even if the boss were looking on." Aha! "No man in his senses!" The problem-setting although hitherto covert interpretation has here become more or less explicit. Our behaviorist has ingenuously admitted that he is using a construct of rational motivation as a measuring rod by means of which he imputes irrational motivation to the woodchopper whose mighty swings he is watching. Should he beat his breast in an agony of remorse when his sinful deviation from the pure doctrine is called to his attention, he can perhaps be consoled by the remark with which this essay began, "We're all poor sinners."

Inasmuch as we all interpret, usually by drawing upon constructs of rational conduct, even though these are only of problem-setting and negative character, the way out of the impasse is simply to make such constructs definite, to devise them in accordance with sound rules of method, and to carry them beyond the realm of the merely plausible by searching for further corroboration and applying crucial checks.

Although this is not a suitable context for the exhaustive discus-

---

15. *Cf.*, on this point my essay "Irrational Factors in International Relations," in Brown, Hodges, and Roucek, *Contemporary World Politics*, (New York: John Wiley and Sons, 1939), esp. pp. 572-573. See also my "Historical Sociology" in Barnes, Becker, and Becker, *op. cit.*, pp. 519-524. Manifestly, much of what I say in these passages directly or indirectly refers to Max Weber's formulations.

INTERPRETIVE SOCIOLOGY

sion of sound rules of interpretive method, (16) it may be said that among these rules should be included those governing: (a) selective attention to social actions rather than to human actions in general; (b) preliminary focus on what seem to be the major features of the end or purpose held in view by the actor or actors concerned; (c) tentative characterization of the social situation plus analytic distinction between the chief factors in that situation; and (d) working specification of the salient aspects of the value-system or systems entering into the situation, the ends pursued, and the meanings assigned to the situational conduct by those involved in it. *Seriatim*, now:

(a) Trite but true it is that man is not born human; conduct defined as characteristic of man in any society of which we have knowledge is the outcome of the planned or unplanned inculcation of social meanings by other human beings. In this broad sense, therefore, all conduct is social, but we can nevertheless distinguish between those actions which are more or less specifically directed toward the actions of other persons and those which have to do primarily with technology, aesthetics, and similar systems, objects, or actions which are social only in a derived and secondary sense (17). Following the general principle of scientific division of labor, it seems expedient to restrict our interpretive and predictive efforts to man in his social capacities rather than to man as a biological entity, physical object, or what not. Accordingly, our field of interest should be limited by defining it about as follows:

---

16. In my estimation, Znaniecki's *Social Actions*, 1936 (cited in footnote 1) is the best single presentation of interpretive procedure in English. Talcott Parson's *Structure of Social Action*, 1937 (likewise cited in footnote 1) is also excellent, but falls short of maximum usefulness because it makes little reference to Znaniecki's work, published over a year earlier. To be sure, Parsons focuses on Marshall, Pareto, Durkheim, and Weber primarily. It should be noted that Znaniecki's 1936 work is largely an elaboration of his 1925 *The Laws of Social Psychology*, (Chicago: University of Chicago Press, printed in Poland).

If I have any strong objection to Znaniecki's presentation in *Social Actions*, it has to do with his lack of explicit attention to *general* value-systems, although his inductive evidence abounds in relevant implications. In *The Social Role of the Man of Knowledge*, (New York: Columbia University Press, 1940), he does deal with value-systems and at length.

17. I owe this distinction to Znaniecki, in whose *The Laws of Social Psychology* (1925) I first encountered it, but Weber's essay on interpretation, dating from 1913, contains the same distinction in so many words, and his earlier writings abound in differentiations that involve it.

TWENTIETH CENTURY SOCIOLOGY

The term "action" is to be used to designate that kind of conduct to which those involved in it assign meanings communicable to others by means of symbols, even though these symbols may be non-verbal or implicit or both, and even though the actions focussed on may not be outwardly observable or may consist only in refraining from a given course of conduct. The kind of action which we choose to call "social" conforms to these requirements, but in addition is determinably and intentionally directed toward the conduct of others by the actor or actors concerned (18). In the foregoing sentence "determinably" is to be taken as "ascertainable through direct and inferential evidence," and "intentionally" has the meaning of "in accordance with a motivational model or construct of the actor's other-regarding purpose or end, regardless of whether or not the actor himself is fully aware of the goal pursued." Finally, we add the obvious proviso that the action under analysis must continue for a length of time sufficient to permit accurate indentification of it.

(b) The ends or purposes of the action may be differentiated in several ways; the analytic utility of any or all of these ways depends on the aspect of the action which the investigator has singled out as problematic. For some varieties of problem it may be sufficient to set up a fourfold classification.

First, we may distinguish the pursuit of ends by any means regarded as conforming to the principles of economy of effort, efficiency, and absence of undesirable effects. For example, if the action is combat and the purpose is annihilation of the opponent, the situation may be defined in such a way that, as it were, "no holds are barred"; anything from poisoning to terroristic inducement of insanity may be held suitable. Following a well-established sociologi-

---

18. It will be recognized that this definition is much the same as that occurring on the very first page of Max Weber's famous *Wirtschaft und Gesellschaft*, (Tuebingen: Mohr—Paul Siebeck—,1922). I incorporated it, without, however, making full use of it, in Wiese-Becker, *op. cit.*, pp. 57-58.

Note that social actions in their "dynamic" aspects are social processes; in their "static" aspects, social structures. Almost the entire Wiese-Becker treatise is devoted to the analysis of actions from the process and structure standpoints. Nothing that is said here is intended to supplant analysis of the process-structure type; indeed, interpretive sociology and constructive typology run parallel to and continually interweave with process-structure analysis. Great as is my admiration for Max Weber's work, for example, I am not a man of one gospel, or two, or . . . *n as* gospel.

INTERPRETIVE SOCIOLOGY

cal tradition this might be called "purposive rationality," (19) but the term seems ambiguous. The rationality consistis only in the fact that any expedient whatever may be planfully and systematically used for the achievement of the end; "expedient rationality" would appear to be better fitted to designate such conduct.

Second, we may single out another kind of rationality in which the principles of economy of effort and so on are followed up to a given point, or as far as a certain limit; this limit is set by the character of the end itself. Instance: although the action may be combat and the purpose the annihilation of the opponent, action and purpose may be integrally bound up with a code of sportsmanship. It is said that many American soldiers when first encountering Japanese in the present war were themselves killed because of their readiness to "give the guy a break"—their conception of a fair fight kept them from plunging the bayonet into a Japanese grovelling on his face, with the consequence that the groveller disposed of both his sportsmanlike conqueror and himself with one grenade. The creed of the Marquis of Queensbury suffered speedy eclipse when the risks of observing it were fully realized. But while it lasted the restraint it imposed provided an excellent example of what has been called "value-rationality," but which perhaps might be better termed "sanctioned rationality" in indication of the fact that ends of certain kinds do not provide sanction for any means whatsoever of their attainment (20). Love, or *caritas*, the topmost value in the Christian scale, offers another illustration: "If you do not love the Lord your God with all your heart, with all your soul, and with all your mind, and your neighbor as yourself, I'll cut your throat" has long been a classic example of a basic contradiction of means and ends.

As counterweights, so to speak, of expedient rationality and sanctioned rationality, we may also distinguish two varieties of irrationality, the traditional and the affective. Traditional irrationality is marked by the dominance of means over ends or, otherwise put, by

---

19. From Rudolph von Ihering or Ihering's *Das Zweck im Recht*, (2 vols., Leipzig: 1877-83, translated as *Law as a Means to an End*) and Weber's adaptation.

20. Expedient rationality plus allegiance to the national state is made the basis of the "ethics of responsibility" by Weber, whereas he bases the "ethics of sentiment" primarily on sanctioned rationality of New Testament character. See "Politik als Beruf," *Gesammelte Politische Schriften*; (Munich: Oldenbourg, 1920), pp. 396-450, esp. pp. 441-442.

a state of affairs in which actions formerly regarded as mere means became ends in themselves. Pratices once of strictly utilitarian character are elevated to the level of ceremonials or rituals. Witness: the carrying of an axe with a number of rods lashed about the handle was once a vital aspect of Roman military discipline; the *lictor*, a sort of combined scourger and executioner, did not carry this bulky bundle about with him for mere ceremonial display; he expected to put its parts to use and often did so. With the passage of time, however, the *fasces* became an emblem of unchanging justice lavishly displayed, for example, as a decorative motif in American law courts and (with an olive branch intended to evoke the notion of mercy in the background) as the central symbols of the "tails" side of the American ten-cent piece. In the latter role, to be sure, the *fasces* also serves as an embodiment of the conception of "many in one"; alongside the axe and rods our dime carries the motto *E pluribus unum.* To the ordinary American this imagery is of course not much more than a dimly understood artistic convention, but to the Italian Fascist the erstwhile tools of the lictor's trade have become the revered sign of the corporative state, under the aegis of which violence for its own sake is widely practiced and is invested with the aura of a tradition which, although in part spurious from the standpoint of the detached observer, is nevertheless defined as genuine by the blackshirted adherents of the Fascist faith. "If men define situations as real, they are real in their consequences." (21) Traditional irrationality, then, is not a matter of the remote, the faraway, the medieval, or the so-called primitive; the modern world affords many instances.

Affective irrationality is a variety somewhat more "private" than the sort identified with the publicly accessible symbols of the traditional. The irate husband blowing off steam on the woodpile is indulging in an emotional outburst, to speak popularly — more precisely, in an affective release or discharge. Obviously it is virtually impossible to find examples of the *purely* affective (22); empirically

---

21. W. I. Thomas and Florian Znaniecki, *The Polish Peasant in Europe and America,* (1-vol. ed., New York: Alfred A. Knopf, 1927—1st printing, 1918— p. 79). This phrase, in content at least, is probably Znaniecki's; his *Cultural Reality* (1919), based on his earlier Polish writings (1910, 1912, *et seq.*) elaborates its significance in a very profound way.

22. Because very little if any human conduct, in the proper sense of human, is devoid of symbolic reference; the purely affective would be the purely biological, i.e., the nonsymbolic.

it may manifest itself merely as an accessory of the expedient or the sanctioned modes of rational conduct or as a component of irrationality of primarily traditional character. It may be said, however, that when it is encountered as the *chief* phase of an action viewed from the angle we are now utilizing, it represents a fairly complete fusion of means and ends; even analytic separation is impracticable.

Epitomizing: expedient rationality is unrestrained in the means adopted; sanctioned rationality has ends of a sort which inevitably bar certain means; traditional irrationality elevates means to the rank of ends; and affective irrationality manifests a coalescence of means and ends (23). In each of these four, be it remembered interpretation always follows the definition of the actor or actors involved in the given situation.

Turning now to the attitude, wish, or tendency, in the narrower sense, which becomes manifest in the action: what convenient pigeonholes can be devised for its preliminary analysis? Here few words need be wasted; the well-established distinction between tendencies to achieve the ends of response, recognition, security, and new experience (24) can be used as long as it is clearly recognized that these must stand at the beginning and not the end of the interpretive task. That is to say, they do not necessarily represent common-human or universal personal-social impulses, drives, or wishes that need no closer specification in terms of socially meaningful trend, means-ends patterning, situational orientation, and location and direction within general value-systems. When they are used as interpretive guides rather than interpretive finalities they are eminently warranted, but validation by any or all the empirical cheks applicable to them is absolutely indispensable if scientific method is to replace arbitrary speculation and dogmatic assertion (25).

(c) The need for these classifications will perhaps become clearer as we turn to the situational and value-system aspects of these social actions. The situation, broadly considered, has at least four distinguishable analytic elements: the social object, the social method, the

---

23. This formulation, good or bad, is my own. The fourfold classification, however, is Max Weber's.

24. Again, Thomas and Znaniecki, *op. cit. passim*. After about 1925, Thomas disavowed the "four wishes" because of their all-too-frequent finalistic use by the smaller fry of the sociological swim. Znaniecki retained them, but rechristened them "tendencies" ("wish" and "attitude" had previously been used synonymously by both Thomas and Znaniecki).

25. *Cf.* Wiese-Becker, *op. cit.*, pp. 171-174.

social instrument, and the social response (26). In some situations, the actor may include the reflected self among the vital elements of his definition, e.g., he may try to secure a response from the object which testifies to the high regard in which he, the actor, is held, and thus experience a heightening of his self-esteem. But the reflected self therefore does not always enter in an essential way into the actor's definition of the situation. Inasmuch as the sociologist's interpretive endeavor deal with the situation defined by the actor as the inevitable starting point, it is sometimes possible to work with only four analytic elements rather than five.

(d) Let us now take note of the fact that any situation is a whole within the context of at least one larger whole. This statement holds good regardless of whether we are dealing with the situation as defined by the actor or as defined by the detached observer, although it must be granted that ordinarily the participant, and in many cases the observer, does not—yea, sometimes cannot—put the whole-within-a-whole state of affairs into words. Non-verbal symbols (27) may be the only clue to the situational context; facial expression, hand gestures, habitual modes of dress, postures, and the like provide the evidence. More inclusive social frameworks impinge on social situations in the narrower sense, and even though these frameworks are sometimes ignored or, more properly speaking, remain vaguely marginal to the situation as defined by the actor and in all too many instances by the observer, the interpretive sociologist must take them into his reckoning.

Our discussion has already reckoned with them implicitly, for the rationalities and irrationalities we have considered can be regarded as aspects of value-systems as the latter are viewed from the standpoint of the actor rather than as conduct congruent with interpersonal patterns within which a large number of actors play their social roles (this congruent conduct may or may not enter directly into their immediate definitions). Sanctioned rationality

---

26. Znaniecki, *Social Actions*, chapter III.

27. To which Mead, among others, pays insufficient attention. For suggestions that the concept of symbolism needs revision, see Suzanne Langer, *Philosophy in a New Key*, (New York: The Macmillan Co., 1942). Charles Morris, "Foundations of the Theory of Signs," *International Encyclopedia of Unified Science*, I, 2 (1938) is also of the highest importance, although it relates chiefly to language. See "Bibliographical Appendix," in Barnes, Becker, and Becker, *op. cit.*, pp. 890-892, 895-898.

and traditional irrationality, for example, can be regarded by us as modes of conduct manifesting the existence of a sacred society —that is, of an interpersonal network of relations having its chief characteristic the eliciting from participants of a certain emotionally tinged unwillingness or inability to respond to the new. Expedient rationality, on the other hand, may be thought of as the intrapersonal phase of a secular society, i.e., of a web of meaningful connections between persons unwilling or unable to refrain from responding to the new so long as their actions pattern and are patterned by such a structure (28).

Overall social frameworks of these contrasting types are of course never existent in unmixed form; only for analytic purposes can the sharp distinction between absolute conservatism and absolute innovation be maintained. Granting all this, it is still of the utmost utility, in many instances, to be able to specify the extent to which the given society approximates one or the other of these polar extremes, for no one who remains within the confines of what we call sanity can entirely dissociate an immediate situation from its ulterior bearings; the definition of the situation will inevitably although indirectly take in some of the societal fringes. Indeed, the fringes, paradoxically enough, may determine the way in which the strands of action interweave to form the central pattern.

In nuce, interpretive sociology cannot dispense with the analysis of social situations as parts of larger wholes, and for many purposes a simple two-fold classification of these encompassing structures can be utilized; appropriate labels are "sacred society" and "secular society." (29).

With this outfit of analytic tools at our disposal, we ought to be able to do a fairly workmanlike job.

—if indeed it ever began. Last-ditch defenders of Revelation might

II

Most of our scientific brethren, if tackled by the inquiring reporter, would assert confidently that the Age of Miracles is over

---

28. For fuller discussion of the bearing of "sacred society" and "secular society" see my chapter (I) "Changing Societies as Family Contexts" in Becker and Hill, eds., *Marriage and the Family*, (Boston: D. C. Heath and Co., 1942), particulary the references in the footnotes and the chapter bibliography.

29. These have been drawn from and utilized in numerous concrete researches by my graduate students and myself, and of course have many antecedents and contemporary parallels. See *ibid*.

try to refute such assertions by twisting scientific Scripture to their purposes; for example, they might try to quote Heisenberg in support of loaves and fishes or turning water into wine. Nevertheless, the informed scientist would smile indulgently, and properly point out that the principle of indeterminancy has nothing to do with the miraculous. (30).

So far so good. Still, there is ample evidence to show that although scientists scoff at the Age of Miracles, they apparently do not think that the Age of Prophecy is forever in the past. Men who have spent their lives peering through microscopes and manipulating microtomes, or shooting beams of light through tourmaline crystals, sometimes fancy themselves to be Ezekiels or Hoseas. When one of these scientists is dealing with his own special field, his conditional predictions are marked by the utmost caution, but when called upon to prophesy about affairs concerning which he knows no more than any reasonably intelligent person, he casts scientific scruples to the wind. Without the flickering of an eyelash he will oblige the inquiring reporter with lengthy replies to "What will Hitler do next?" or "Will Churchill retire from public life when the war is won?"

This incidental disparagement of physicists and biologists has been by way of illustration only, for many practitioners of the social sciences also drape the mantle of the prophet about themselves at the slightest provocation. Only a few members of the social-scientific fraternity feel upset when called upon to provide or witness prophetic displays; unfortunately, the greater number of social scientists can stomach almost anything. The minority members feel queasy because they have come to think that no single science, nor indeed any combination of sciences at the disposal of mere mortals, can successfully prophesy the beginning, course, and consequences of any *particular* action at any *particular* time (31). The reasons for this conviction are many and various; I mention two only: (a) the literally innumerable array of factors involved in any unique phenomenon if uniqueness is taken seriously; and (b) the vast range of the weights or inten-

---

30. For many of the moot points in this whole section, I should like earnestly to ask the reader to refer to my chapters II and XV in Barnes, Becker, and Becker, *op. cit.*, as well as to my article, "Supreme Values and the Sociologist," *American Sociological Review*, 6: 155-172, April, 1941.

31. F. Znaniecki, *The Laws of Social Psychology*, p. 69.

sities assignable to these factors on any empirical basis, even if the factors themselves were limited in number.

If the goal of the scientist's activity is "the systematic statement of the probability of the hypothetical or actual recurrence of phenomena which, for the purposes in hand, are regarded as identical," (32) then *ipso facto* the scientist is forever barred from the effort to deal with the unique as the unique.

Among students of social affairs, only a few ever attempt to deal with the unique as such. Among these are ethnographers who, because they are doing field work in situations where scientific division of labor is difficult or impossible, and where the population to be studied rarely numbers more than one or two hundred persons having a relatively simple past (because in the absence of written records bygone days lose their complexity), therefore attempt the gathering of "all the facts." Ethnographers who try to do this are not necessarily naive; in many cases they know full well that they cannot possibly achieve their objective and are content to do the best they can, in the realization that unless they collect whatever data their focus of attention makes perceivable at the time, such data may be forever lost in the hurly-burly of change thrust upon the simpler peoples by the impact of a ruthless Western civilization.

Also among those who try to amass all the information they can lay hands on are the historians, some of whom it is not easy to absolve from the charge of naïveté. Granting the presence of numerous honorable exceptions, it still remains true that many of those who traffic with what is called history (33) actually think that they can pile up, single handed, everything that can possibly be relevant about a given time, place, and people. They do not recognize that selection is inevitable, nor that facts are facts only for those who are prepared by equipment and training to perceive them. Moreover, when they do establish a division of labor they base it on content or chronology rather than on problem-choosing.

---

32. H. P. Fairchild, ed., *Dictionary of Sociology*, (New York: Philosophical Library, 1944), "Science." This is a condensation of the formulation in my "Supreme Values and the Sociologist," *loc. cit.*

33. Some historians apparently think that anything falling in the "past" should be enclosed in a field which is theirs exclusively. This may be, if any historian is a Diogenes Teufelsdroeckh, a Professor-of-Things-in-General. May I point out, however, that the "past" begins . . . now? The writing of that very "now" is irrevocably a "historical" fact. The "past" is a large order, my friends.

Stated differently: historians split up the past along the lines of political history, social history, or intellectual history, regarding the lines as somehow given in the data instead of being arbitrarily imposed, or else they chop time-sequences into convenient chunks, ordinarily selecting these by country and century, e.g., eighteenth-century England or eleventh-century France.

Very seldom indeed, and then only among historians tainted by contact with social scientists, is a specific problem singled out as a center about which relevant facts are systematically arrayed. Only the honorable exceptions mentioned above seem to be aware of the indefensible position in which most historical endeavor now finds itself; viz., that if history is to be something other than a grandiose hodgepodge of information now more efficiently collected by geographers, economists, and other social scientists, it must have some governing principle of selection; "all the facts" leads only to absurdity.

In all essentials, the task of history is do depict the past in such a way that every one of its phases is sharply distinguishable from every other, and that as opposed to generalization without primary regard to time and place, history is charged with the duty of particularization with special reference to dates, localities, personalities, and actions in unique configurations and time-series (34). With all of this we can heartily agree, for basically nothing is absolutely identical with anything else; only confusion can develop if social scientists fail to recognize that "identical" means simply "identical for the purposes in hand." To communicate or engender what is sometimes called "historical sensitivity" is no mean feat (35); unless we are made thoroughly aware that no

---

34. *Cf.* Alexander Goldenweiser, "The Relation of the Natural Sciences to the Social Sciences," in Barnes, Becker, and Becker, *op. cit.*, for a discussion of historical method as set forth in the writings of Wilhelm Dilthey and Heinrich Rickert.

35. "The vitally necessary function of the idiographic historian should be plain to every unprejudiced social scientist; the 'thisness' of events *must* be made clear.

"If you wish to appreciate to the full the characteristic essence of the culture of the Scottish Border, let us say, you steep yourself in . . . that culture. In so doing you acquire kinds of sensitivity that may enable you to communicate, to others less sensitive or less erudite, some notion of what it meant . . . to grow up an heir to The Debateable Land north of the Cheviots . . There is no need to justify such immersion in and absorption of the particular . . . (Howard Becker, in Barnes, Becker, and Becker, *ibid.*, pp. 20, 24-25).

section of the past or present is or can be the same as any other section, we shall continue to perpetrate the fallacy of prophesying on the empirical level instead of abandoning this false lead and bending our efforts toward predicting on the typical level—but again, more of this later.

Some historians apparently hold that the goal of particularization can be reached by assembling variegated facts, much as a child picks up shells on the seashore, and then "letting the facts speak for themselves." In the terminology of the present essay, "full particularity," rather than selective attention to crucial differentials, is held to be the way in which that sense of the unique which is the distinguishing mark of historical awareness can best be evoked. Can full particularity ever be achieved? To me at least the answer is "Manifestly not." Not only would the search for "all the facts" about even a simple physical object carry us to the outermost confines of the cosmos, (36) spatially speaking, but from the temporal standpoint we are likewise confronted with an infinite *regressus*. The historian properly insists on dating the events with which he deals, but there is no good reason why he should confine himself to a given year, month, and day. Why not hours, minutes, and seconds? And why stop at the second? Modern stroboscopic photography enables us to freeze events in divisions of one hundred-thousandth of a second and even less; where is the logical terminus if full temporal particularization is the task in hand?

All this is obviously nonsensical, but the reasons why it is nonsensical may not be so obvious. Clearly, the historian particularizes only up to a certain point; anything beyond that is superfluous. This superfluity resides in the fact that the *absolutely* unique is ineffable, incommunicable. Unless the historian wishes to be a sort of James Joyce raised to the *n*th degree, in which case he alone could understand himself, and then only in a kind of mystic union achieved in a single flash of awareness, he must make use of the ordinary devices of communication. His language may be poetically evocative at times, but nevertheless he attempts to communicate within a universe of discourse. In such a universe only the *relatively* unique is effectively present, and its presence is vouchsafed only by the simultaneous presence of the *relatively* general. All forms of significant symbolism—and all communication is necessarily symbolic—are of general character (although

---

36. *Ibid.*, p. 23.

the generality may be limited to a very few instances). This is true even of proper names, as Korzybski insists. Mary (1944) is not the same as Mary (1941), although for ordinary purposes the two can safely be regarded as identical. Using the generalities of symbolic communication, the historian manipulates them in such a way that relatively unique description results. If the person, occurrence, or whatnot described is set against the background of other persons and occurrences so that characterization regarded as adequate is brought about, that phase of the historical endeavor which distinguishes it from the social sciences *per se* is made manifest.

Assuming, with perhaps undue confidence, that the foregoing analysis is accurate, we can now ask this question: "What do historians do when they prophesy?" Answer: "They are indulging in illicit generalization." (37). All too often unaware of the problem that has governed their selection of facts, or unable or unwilling to specify it, and so innocent, methodologically speaking, that they think it possible to particularize without open or covert reference to general contexts, they make guesses, lucky or unlucky as the case may be. Given the gullibility of the public, and the elastic language in which the guesses are cast, most of them are lucky. When an eminent historian intones: "I said that something terrible would happen and now look at the mess we're in," most of us forget that grandmother said that much.

Lacking prophetic inspiration, the scientist had better confine himself to the job of prediction; this, in spite of current misconceptions, has nothing to do with prophecy, forecasting, or foretelling. Strictly, it refers only to the "before-saying" (pre-diction) of certain kinds of recurrence.

Take note, now, that to predict the recurrence of phenomena is, in a certain sense, to control that recurrence if it should be possible to reinstate or reconstruct the circumstances under which previous recurrences have taken place. Of course, the scientist may not have any interest whatever in bringing about actual recurrence; he may be quite content to say that "if and when" certain factors are combined in certain ways, the results are predictable.

---

37. Sometimes historians make direct mention of "historical generalizations," or "what we learn from history." These same historians, however, are often the first to insist that "history does not repeat itself." These statements add up to what? Differently worded: Can historians eat their cake and have it too?

INTERPRETIVE SOCIOLOGY

This is conditional prediction; it is the prototype of all scientific research, however complex and esoteric. Experiment is the supreme test of prediction, but when a number of experiments sufficient to diminish chance to insignificance have been performed — and a very small number, under certain circumstances, may suffice—the scientist has achieved all the control he seeks: "When this is done, these—within a small range of variation—*must* be the consequences."

Bear in mind, moreover, that the scientist may get the prediction he is after even when he is not able to reinstate the conditions of previous recurrences, i.e., when actual manipulative experiment is impracticable or impossible. He may, in other words, attain hypothetical prediction through mental reconstruction and extension or projection of such reconstruction. Evidence: because of the study of the heavens over a long period, astronomers are able to say that time, space, and motion are in certain definite relations with each other. Hence they are able to say that if the mass of the moon were altered by so and so much, its orbit and its cycle would be changed in proportionate amounts. Without much doubt this "if the mass of the moon were altered" is hypothetical—at least, until such time as a rocket ship can be successfully landed on one of the greener spots of the lunar surface. Hypothetical prediction is therefore prediction, on the basis of previously observed recurrences, of related phenomena never yet specifically observed but defined as identical for the purpose in hand.

Orientation toward the future has characterized all the varieties of prediction, whether hypothetical or actual, thus far discussed, and this orientation has prevailed both with regard to the predictive act itself and with regard to the phenomena predicted. Worded differently: there has been an effort to make clear the implications of actual prospective prediction and of hypnothetical prospective prediction. Only in the predictive act itself, however, need there be a prospective reference; the phenomena under examination need not recur in the future.

A number of sciences make extensive use of retrospective prediction: astronomy paleontology, geology, archaeology, zoology, botany, philology, ethnology, sociology, and several other sciences frequently following the same pattern. In sociology the frequency would be much greater if it were not for the fear of treading on ground made holy by the footsteps of historians who, incidentally, rarely suffer from such an excess of humility that they refrain from supplying the voice from the burning bush themselves.

Still another reason for the failure to make full use of hypothetical retrospective prediction is the prevailing confusion between the logic and psychology of the matter. From the strict logical point of view, there is not a particle of difference between prospective and retrospective prediction. Psychologically, retrospective prediction may of course swing wide the door to juggling the evidence, playing deceitful tricks on oneself, rationalization, and the rest of the seven devils. Diabolical machinations are certainly much easier when the events to which predictive techniques are applied have already occurred; may of us readily succumb to the besetting temptation to reconstruct the earlier recurrences and functional interrelations in such a way that the solution appears inevitable. In all essentials, the problems thereby raised are the same as those which appear when a small boy gets hold of the book containing the answers to his arithmetic homework; fearful and wonderful may be the gyrations through which he goes, and his solution usually has a certain flavor of the miraculous about it, as his teacher soon discovers. Many scientists, however, have grown up, and in any case their results are closely scrutinized by a jury of their peers who thereby play the restraining role of the schoolma'am.

Detaining us for the moment at this stage of the exposition looms one all-obstructing barrier which we must either demolish or avoid; namely, the objection that hypothetical retrospective prediction is useless because the recurrences to which it applies are past and done. "Call it prediction if you want to," say the critics, "but admit that such turning of intellectual handsprings is solely for your own gratification. We are neither amused nor instructed thereby." Promptly I reply that what can be learned about the interdependence of social actions, situations, and value-systems by the application of interpretive sociology and constructive typology to the task of retrospective prediction may eventually be of much use when prospective prediction of the actual variety is undertaken. The determination of what are sometimes called "causal sequences" in a collection of apparently discrete events and structures turned up by digging into the past may turn out to be of the highest utility in stating what is likely to take place "if and when" other events and structures, which for the purposes in hand can be regarded as identical with the earlier set, make themselves evident in the future. Sociologists are not prophets, for they regard unique configurations and happenings as forever beyond scientific grasp. Nevertheless, by the use of techniques adapted to legitimate prediction they hope to be able to state the limiting conditions under which any phenomenon, however unique, will inevitably be placed. Moreover, explicit attention to the logic of prediction, which is essentially the logic of probability, lifts their analyses out of the vague, epistemologically ambiguous situations in which reference to "causal sequences" would otherwise place them. By pouring their results in the predictive mold, they make it possible for others to check the validity of their conclusions in ways which would otherwise be barred. With Whittier, the sociologist must say, "I know not what the future hath of marvel or surprise," but with all due humility, the sociologist can also assert that some advance statement of the probable range of the marvelous and surprising can be provided. (38).

In the discussion of the ways in which the historian can approach his only feasible goal, the depiction of the *relatively* unique, I said that selective attention to the data of the "past" was the only way to escape from the futility of trying to seize the absolutely unique by gathering "all the facts." Such selective attention is necessarily directed toward the materials bearing on a problem of the kind just posed. Delineation of the relatively unique on a selective basis I have elsewhere termed "culture case study," for every case study, whether of a single personality or of a nation, must take account of the cultural margin which surrounds or even interweaves with social actions.

A general value-system is for our purposes the most important part of this cultural context, but the value-system must often be analytically extracted from language, music, the dance, the graphic and plastic arts, and other aspects of culture representing its less thoroughly formalized phases, as well as from law, religion, moral codes, and similar cultural products which have been more completely crystallized. It is frequently necessary, therefore, to make selective historical studies of relatively unique configurations and time-sequences out of which it may then become possible to distill a general value-system and other distinguishable parts of the cul-

---

38. This topic has been discussed at greater length in my "Supreme Values and the Sociologist," previously cited. A briefer version occurs under "Prediction, sociological" in H. P. Fairchild, ed., *op. cit.*

tural context which qualify or essentially modify the means used for the attainment of given ends, the ends themselves, and the various elements of social situations.

The harsh remarks about the shortcomings of historians in which I have already indulged do not apply to those students of the past—and many of them are historians by profession—who carry out what I have called culture case studies; one of the greatest drawbacks of contemporary American sociology, to name no other social science, is its almost complete lack of this kind of historical sophistication. The necessity for culture case study in sociology arises from the fact that generalization based on hand-picked illustrative fragments torn from their contexts is thoroughly unscientific and has long since been discredited. If the sociologist is really a scientist his ultimate goal will be prediction, as already noted, and prediction, retrospective or prospective, must always be couched in "if and when" terms. Now, "if and when" always refer to situations that either have already occurred or can be envisaged in terms of what has already occurred. The "geologic strata" of time-sequence cannot be arbitrarily juggled; if the constructed types of sociology are to have predictive power, they must be developed without primary regard to their generalizability. If they prove to be generalizable *in spite of* the fact that they are first of all designed to yield a shorthand description and analysis of the social actions, *etcetera*, permeating a particular historical configuration, in close relation with a broadly stated problem and its derivative hypothesis, so much the better, but such generalizability must not be the all-controlling aim of the endeavor.

In short, the initial conclusions of a culture case study are limited to the interpretation of social actions within the area and period studied, but the basic method used—namely, constructive typology—may enable these configurations to be transferred, after appropriate modification, to other areas and periods. Dated and localized types must be accumulated before there is any thoroughgoing attempt to build types of relatively undated and nonlocalized form.

This result achieved, it may then be posible to restate the constructed types in "if and when" terms, and to search the record for other cases that will provide a checkup on the validity of the retrospective or prospective predictions made. This constitutes a

INTERPRETIVE SOCIOLOGY

genuinely comparative method, (39) even though the initial comparison is only between earlier and later cultural configurations which the unwary might be tempted to think of as necessarily the "same" society. (40) Only when small-scale validation of this pragmatic variety has been secured can there be any talk of far-reaching generalizations, and it is altogether too much to assume that these generalizations will hold for all cases whatsoever. The sociologist predicts, but he does not prophesy.

On the foundation provided by culture case studies of this kind, interpretation in and through the use of constructed types proceeds. That is to say, after the delineation of the relatively unique aspects of the datable and localizable configurations set up as the poles of an empirical continuum has gone as far as is necessary for particularization, the next step is the construction of types adequate to the interpretation and conditional prediction of "if and when" recurrences. (41)

---

39. A generation or two ago, social scientists made a great to-do over the "comparative method," for to this method alone they attributed the apparent success of the theory of organic evolution. Following the vulgarized biology of that day, social scientists meant by the comparative method the collection of "facts" supporting a given "theory." In virtually every instance, these "facts" were items torn from the web of relations which gave them whatever legitimate scientific meaning they might have had. Such items were then jammed into the framework of the so-called "theory," and the result was Spencer's euhemerism or Frazer's totemism and exogamy or Morgan's unilinear social evolution.

Strictly speaking, however, this was merely the illustrative method. A genuinely comparative method has since been developed, chiefly by the functional anthropologists and historical sociologists, but it needs clearer statement.

40. Wholes, it should be remembered, are wholes by definition only. To the man who sits on it a chair is a whole, but to various natural scientists it may be regarded as a conglomerate of other wholes—cells, molecules, atoms, and whatnot. To students building a rally-day bonfire, it is just a minor part of a splendid heap of fuel.

41. At the risk of wearying the reader, let us say again that the conception of science underlying constructed types is that scientific activity is essentially predictive; even though predictions must often be cast in retrospective rather than prospective terms, and even though they are frequently hypothetical rather than actual, the logic of scientific prediction, which is at bottom probability logic, is consistently followed. This point needs stressing, for some interpretations of "ideal types" (of which constructed types represent a closely related offshoot) do not hold the basically probable character of the "ideal type" clearly enough in view. (It is for this reason, among many others, that "constructed type" may eventually become the preferred term. At present it is restricted largely to my own writings and to those of the graduate students who have worked with me.)

It is now high time to offer a clear statement of what is meant by a constructed type. Such types are made up of criteria (so-called elements, traits, aspects, and so on) which have discoverable referents in the empirical world or can legitimately be inferred from empirical evidence, or both. The construction of these types should always take place in relation to an explicit problem and should be oriented toward a clear-cut hypothesis; the type of highest usefulness is not merely classificatory. Although not always constructed with sufficient care, and sometimes lacking possible empirical approximations (referents) and precise validation, (42) constructed types abound in sociological research. Clans, castes, closes, nations, sects, cults, and like social structures are constructed types; individuation, superordination, accommodation, exploitation, and similar social processes are often in the same category. It should be pointed out, however, that the construct and the empirical approximation are not the same thing; no constructed caste will be exactly matched by a given empirical caste as it exists on a given day and hour. In this sense, therefore, nothing but "exceptions" to constructed types exist. It was with this background in mind that I earlier made the statement that the sociologist will not attempt to predict the emergence, course, or consequences of any particular social action at any particular time; this would throw him into the morass of the absolutely unique. If he is to predict rather than prophesy, he must work on the basis of constructed types derived from culture case studies. (43)

---

42. The problem of validation is thoroughly dealt with, in my opinion, in only one study, W. L. Kolb's unpublished dissertation (previously cited, footnote 6).

43. It must be borne in mind that constructed types are not necessarily averages, although every average, in the special technical sense of the mean (not the mode or the median), has some of the attributes of a constructed type. Exhibit: the "average graduate of a woman's college" who reputedly bears only six-tenths of a child during her entire reproductive period does not exist in the flesh; she is not an empirical instance but is computed from empirical instances. (The problem of the "empirical possibility" of the constructed type arises here, but space for its consideration is lacking.) The same non-existence holds for the extremes of a frequency distribution as long as more than one item is found in the given cell; a frequency distribution can be thought of as made up of many means arranged along a continuum, each being computed from a cell including two or more items. This being the case, it is possible to maintain that the constructed type may deviate widely from empirical phenomena ordinarily encountered, and yet that it represents a mean of some empirical phenomena falling on the same continuum as do the ordinary kind.

INTERPRETIVE SOCIOLOGY

Much has been written by others and by myself on the problems of constructed types as such. Here I have endeavored only to point out that such types are tools to be used in conjunction with other tools. For fuller discussion of types themselves, the reader is referred to the writings listed in the footnotes and to the bibliography.

In conclusion, let me say only that there is no infallible, patented method of sociological analysis. Interpretive sociology and constructive typology are *useful*. Why say more?

SELECTED BIBLIOGRAPHY

Becker, Howard, "Constructive Typology in the Social Sciences," and "Historical Sociology," in Harry Elmer Barnes, Howard Becker, and Frances Bennett Becker, eds., *Contemporary Social Theory*, (New York: D. Appleton-Century Co., 1940), Chaps. 2 and 15.

Parsons, Talcott, *The Structure of Social Action*, (New York: McGraw-Hill Book Co., 1937).

Schelting, Alexander von, *Max Webers Wissenschaftslehre*, (Tuebingen: J. C. B. Mohr, 1934).

Weber, Max, *Gesammelte Aufsaetze zur Wissenschaftslehre*, (Tuebingen: J. C. B. Mohr, 1922).

Weber, Max,*Wirtschaft und Gesellschaft*, (Tuebingen: J. C. B. Mohr, 1922).

Znaniecki, Florian, *Social Actions*, (New York: Farrar and Rinehart, 1936).

Howard Becker, Ph. D., is Professor of Sociology at the University of Wisconsin. He has served on the staff at the University of Pennsylvania and Smith College, and has lectured at Columbia, Harvard, and Stanford. He is the author of *Systematic Sociology on the Basis of the* Beziehungslehre *and* Gebildelehre *of Leopold von Wiese* (1932), and, with Harry Elmer Barnes, of *Social Thought from Lore to Science* (1938, 2 vols.); editor, with Harry Elmer Barnes and Frances Bennett Becker, of *Contemporary Social Theory* (1940), and, with Reuben Hill, of *Marriage and the Family* (1942)*; Perverted by the Fuehrer's Grace* (1945; in press); contributor to scientific journals and symposia.

CHAPTER V

SOCIOCULTURAL DYNAMICS AND EVOLUTIONISM

by

PITIRIM A. SOROKIN

I

Shift in the Study of the "What" of Sociocultural Changes:
1. *The Nineteenth Century.* Today's conception of sociocultural dynamics differs markedly from that of the eighteenth and the nineteenth centuries. We still use Comte's term "social dynamics," but we mean by it something different from what Comte and the social and humanistic thinkers of the nineteenth century meant. Sociology, social and humanistic sciences of the twentieth century, compared with those of the preceding two centuries, have experienced a notable shift in their study of the *"what," "how", and "why" of sociocultural change, and of its uniformities.*
Sociocultural change is a complex manifold. It has several different aspects each of which can be the subject matter for a study of social dynamics and the attention of investigators can be concentrated now on one, now on another of these aspects. The aspects of sociocultural change which received intensive study in the eighteenth and nineteenth centuries are quite different from those now

at the center of attention. The dominant stream of social thought of the eighteenth and the nineteenth centuries concentrated largely on a study of various *linear trends* believed to be unfoldig in the course of time, and in mankind as a whole. It operated mainly with the humanity at large, and sought to discover "the dynamic laws of evolution and progress" governing the main course of human history. It paid little attention to the *repeated* sociocultural processes — those which are repeated either in space (in various societies), in time, or in both. In contrast to the dominant interest of the eighteenth and nineteenth centuries, the main interest of the philosophic, social and humanistic disciplines of the twentieth century has been increasingly concentrated on a study of sociocultural processes and relationships which are either *constant,* appearing wherever and whenever sociocultural phenomena are given, or are *repeated* in space, time, or both, in the form of rhythms, fluctuations, oscillations, "cycles" and their periodicities. Such is the main difference in the study of the "what" of sociocultural change in the centuries compared. Let us now concisely comment on this shift.

The dominant current of the scientific, philosophical, social and humanistic thought of the eighteenth and the nineteenth centuries was a firm belief in the existence of perpetual linear trends in the change of sociocultural phenomena. The central content of the historical process of mankind was conceived as an unfolding and ever fuller realization of this "trend of progress and evolution," of steady "historical tendencies" and of "the law of sociocultural development." Some delineated these trends as unilinear, others as "spiral," still others as "oscilating and branching", with minor deviations and temporary regressions; nevertheless in all these varieties the conception of a linear direction of the central sociocultural process remained intact. (1) Consequently the main ambition and central preoccupation of scientific, philosophical, social and humanistic thinkers in these centuries consisted in the discovery and formulation of these "eternal laws of progress and evolution," and in an elaboration of the main stages or phases through which the trend passes as it comes to fuller realization in the course of time. Discovery, formulation and corroboration of the existence of such trends and their stages was the focal point of biology and

---

1. On the four varieties of linear conceptions of sociocultural change *cf.* my *Social and Cultural Dynamics,* (New York: American Book Co., 1937), Vol. I, Chap. 4.

sociology, of philosophy of history and social philosophy, and of the other social and humanistic sciences of the nineteenth century. If in some disciplines like history they did not occupy a very large space in the actual narration of historical events, they served as the guiding stars and referential principles for ordering and interpreting the concrete factual material. In this sense, the social thought of the eighteenth and nineteenth centuries was indeed stamped by a faith in linear laws of evolution and progress.

In the *physico-chemical sciences* this faith expressed itself in an emergence and rapid acceptance of the principle of enthropy of Carnot-Clausius as a perpetual and irreversible direction of change in any thermodynamic system (2) as well as in the whole universe.

In *biology* the belief discussed expressed itself in an emergence and general acceptance of the "law of evolution," almost unanimously interpreted in the sense of a linear trend (in its unilinear, spiral, branching, oscillating variations) of a progressively growing differentiation and integration; of a passage from the simple to the complex; from "the lower to the higher"; from "the less perfect to the more perfect", "from amoeba to man", from reflexes and instincts to intelligence and reason; from the solitary individual to the family, the tribe, the modern state; and, in spite of narrow-minded and reactionary politicians, we or our descendants will yet see the whole human race brought together into a "Society of Nations," a "Federation of the World." "Throughout the course of evolution there has been a continual elimination of the least fit and a survival of the fit . . . the elimination of the antisocial and the increase of specialization and co-operation." (3) The linear

---

2. On the enthropy *Cf.* R. Clausius, "Le second principe fondamental de la théorie mécanique de chaleur," *Revue des cours scientifique,* 1868, p. 158; P. Duhem, *L'évolution de la mécanique,* (Paris: 1902); H. Poincaré, *Thermodynamique,* (Paris: 1892).

3. E. G. Conklin, *The Direction of Human Evolution,* (New York: Charles Scribner's Sons, 1925), pp. 15, 17, 75, 78. Conklin's conception of bio-social evolution is quite typical of the prevalent conception of biological evolution in the nineteenth and partly in the twentieth century. In a similar linear manner though not so anthropomorphically biological evolution was interpreted by the rank and file of biologists of the nineteenth century. The formulae of evolution of Milne-Edwards, K. von Baer, Herbert Spencer, and E. Heckel run along the same lines. The concepts of biological evolution of J. Arthur Thompson, J. S. Huxley, C. L. Morgan, Sir Arthur Smith Woodward and many biologists of

SOCIOCULTURAL DYNAMICS

interpretation of biological (and social) evolution was and still is (though less pronounced now) the main dogma of biology.

The same is true of the dominant conception of sociocultural change in the *philosophy, social philosophy, and philosophy of history* of the eighteenth and nineteenth centuries. The conceptions of Herder, Fichte, Kant and Hegel are typical in this respect. Herder and Kant both saw the central trend of historical process as a progressive decrease of violence and war, as a steady increase of peace area and as a growth of justice, reason and morality in the course of time. (4)

For Fichte the whole of human history is a sequence of five stages: an ever fuller realization of freedom, truth, justice and beauty. For Hegel the central trend of the historical process consists in a progressive growth of freedom, beginning with freedom for none at the dawn of human history, passing through the stages of freedom for one, then freedom for some, and ending with the stage of freedom for all. (5)

In the *sociology and social philosophy* of the nineteenth century the general conceptions of social dynamics held by Turgot, Condorcet, Burdin, Saint Simon, and Comte, and of evolution by Herbert Spencer, are fully representative. For Comte the whole process of history is but a steady passage from the theological, through the metaphysical, to the positive stage of human mentality, culture, and society. Consequently, Comte's "social dynamics" hardly deals at all with repeated sociocultural processes; it is devoted almost entirely to a formulation and corroboration of his "law of the three stages." Spencer's "social dynamics" is simply an application of his formula of evolution — progress, according to which the whole sociocultural universe passes in the course of time from an indefinite, incoherent homogeneity to a definite, coher-

---

even the twentieth century are also similar. They are all not only linear but identify evolution with progress. *Cf.* E. Haeckel, *Prinzipen der generellen Morphologie,* (Tuebingen, 1906); J. C. Smuts, *Holism and Evolution,* (New York: The Macmillan Co., 1925); and two symposia on evolution: *Creation by Evolution,* (New York: The Macmillan Co., 1928), and *Evolution in the Light of Modern Knowledge,* (New York: D. Van Nostrand Co., 1925).

4. *Cf.* Herder's *Outlines of a Philosophy of the History of Man,* tr. by T. Churchill, (London: 1803); Kant's *The Idea of a Universal History on a Cosmo-Political Plan,* tr. by T. DeQuincey, (Hanover: Sociological Press, 1927).

5.*Cf.* Fichte's *Characteristics of the Present Age* (1804) and Hegel's *Philosophy of History,* tr. by J. Sibree, (New York and London: 1900).

[99]

ent, heterogeneity, with a progressively growing differentiation and integration of human personality, culture and society. (6)

Dominated by this linear conception of sociocultural change, most sociologists and social scientists of the nineteenth century reduced their study of a dynamics of sociocultural phenomena, even in purely factual investigations, mainly to a discovery and formulation of various linear trends, successive stages of development, historical tendencies, and laws of evolution of the phenomena investigated. As a result most of the "uniformities of change," they discovered, assumed a linear character. Here are a few examples out of many. (7) Ferdinand Toennies's theory of the passage of human society in the course of time from the *Gemeinschaft* to the *Gesellschaft* type is a linear theory. Emile Durkheim's theory of a gradual change from a state of society based upon the "mechanical" solidarity, to one based upon "organic" solidarity, with a subsidiary trend of replacement of "repressive" by "restitutive" law is also a linear theory. Similar in its linearity is the social dynamics of Lester F. Ward which posits a progressively increasing teleological, circuitous, artificial, self-directed and self-controlled character of human adaptation in the course of time; or H. T. Buckle's dynamics of a "diminishing influence of physical laws and of an increasing influence of mental laws" as time passes by; or Herbert Spencer's and Durkheim's laws of the passage of societies from the "simple" to the "compound" ("doubly compound," "triply compound," an so on), in the course of their history. No less linear is J. Novicow's law of the evolution of the struggle for existence from the earliest form of a bloody "physiological extermination," through a less bloody "economic," then "political" struggle, to a final bloodless form of purely "intellectual" competition; or

---

6.*Cf.* Auguste Comte, *Cours de philosophie positive*, (Paris: 1877), Vol. I, pp. 8 ff. and through all volumes. About the theories of his predecessors, *cf.* R. Mathis, *La loi des trois états*, (Nancy: 1924). See also Herbert Spencer, *First Principles*, (London: 1870), Chap. 22 *et passim; Principles of Sociology*, (London: 1885), 3 Vols. Though the Spencerian formula of evolution-progress includes the opposite process of dissolution, Spencer fails to deal with the dissolution aspect in his study of sociocultural evolution-progress. Such a neglect of this opposite process is also symptomatic of the preoccupation we have noted.

7.*Cf.* the bibliography of the works of all the authors mentioned in my *Contemporary Sociological Theories*, (New York: Harper and Bros., 1928) and *Social and Cultural Dynamics* (all four volumes). Reproduction of such a bibliography in this short article would occupy an unduly long portion.

the alleged historical trend of a progressive widening of the area of peace and of shrinking of the area of war in the course of history, claimed by dozens of social scientists; or Novicow's, William F. Ogburn's, and Hornell Hart's law of acceleration of the tempo of change; or A. Coste's law of the five stages of evolution of social structures from the "Burg" to the "City", "Metropolis", "Capitol,". and finally to a "World Center of Federation"; or P. Mougeolle's "law of altitude" according to which the most densely inhabited areas and the cities descend, in the course of time, from the zones of high altitudes to those of low altitudes; or similar historical trends of the westward, eastward or northward movement of civilization with the passage of time (according to different authors); or A. Gobineau's historical trend from the pure and unequal races to the progressively blended, and equal ones with the degenerated "human herds, benumbed in their nullity," and the end of human civilization as a terminal point of the trend; or L. Winiarsky's law of social enthropy leading progressively to greater sociocultural equalization of castes, orders, classes, races, and individuals, with the final state of a dead sociocultural equilibrium and the end of mankind's history; or the perennial trend towards a bigger and better equalitarianism interpreted as the positive trend of history (in contradistinction to its interpretation as a death of society and culture) by a crowd of sociologists, anthropologists, political scientists, ethicists, philosophers and historians. Even such social dynamics as those of E. De Roberty and of Karl Marx were not quite free from this linear "obsession" of the nineteenth century: if Marx himself did not give a clear-cut theory of successive stages of social evolution, he nevertheless postulated one eschatological linear trend of history: the trend towards socialism as the final stage of social development of humanity. His followers, from Engels, Bebel and Kautsky to H. Cunow and a legion of lesser Marxists, manufactured a series of historical laws in the evolution of economic, political, mental, religious, familial and other sociocultural phenomena, with appropriate stages of development.

Like Marx, E. De Roberty and certain others were little concerned with the manufacturing of various eternal trends and stages of devevlopment, but even they assumed the growth of conceptual thought in one or more of the four forms as formulated by De Roberty (scientific, philosophical or religious, aesthetic and rationally applied thought) as a central tendency of the historical process. G. de Greef, together with many political scientists, posited a trend of political evolution from the earliest regimes based upon force to social organization based on free contractual relationships. G. Ratzenhofer's and Albion Small's trend from the "conquest state" to the "culture state"; or the somewhat opposite trend, claimed by P. Lilienfeld, from the earliest type of decentralized and unregimented political groups to regimes of centralized, autocratic, and regimented political control; or L. T. Hobhouse's trend of social development from a stage of society based upon kinship, through one based on authority, toward a final stage built upon citizenship; or F. H. Giddings' "zoogenic, anthropogenic, ethnogenic and demogenic" stages of sociocultural development (the latter stage divided into linear substages: military-religious, liberal-legal and economic-ethical); all of these are further varieties of the linear type of trends so extensively manufactured by social scientists of the nineteenth and beginning of the twentieth centuries. To these may be added the dozens of historical trends manufactured by sociology and athropology, law and history, concerning the evolution of the family, marriage and kinship — all of them with uniform stages of development: from promiscuous "primitive" sex relationships to the monogamic family (passing through three or four or five stages, according to the fancies of the authors like J. Bachofen, J. F. McLennan, Sir John Lubbock, F. Engels, A. Bebel, L. H. Morgan, and many others); from the patriarchal to the cognatic family based upon equality of the sexes; from the patrilineal to the matrilineal system of descent and kinship, or *vice versa;* from equality to inequality of the sexes, or *vice versa*: —all sorts of trends were claimed. These and all the other social and humanistic sciences vociferously "discovered" a host of eternal historical trends with their stages of development: from fetishism or totemism to monotheism and irreligiosity; from religious and magical superstitions to a rational scientific mentality; from ethical savagery to the rational ethical man; from primitive ugliness to a bigger and better beauty; and so on and so forth. Writers in *political science* unhesitatingly formulated a series of various "laws of political progress-evolution" from " autocratic monarchy to democratic republic" or *vice versa* (depending upon the political sympathies of the scholar); from "direct democracy to representative democracy" or *vice versa;* from primeval anarchy to centralized government or *vice versa;* from "government of force" to that of "social service"; all with various intermediary stages definitely following one another in a more or less uniform sequence. In *economics* likewise a large number of eminent thinkers were busy with economic trends and stages of development through which all peoples were supposed to be passing. F. List's five stages of economic development: barbarian, pastoral, agricultural, agricultural-manufacturing-commercial; B. Hildebrand's theory of the three stages: *Naturalwirtschaft, Geldwirtschaft* and *Creditwirtschaft*; Karl Buecher's law of the three stages: closed self-sufficing, city, and national economy; and Gustav Schmoller's theory of five stages may serve as typical examples of this linear "economic dynamics." The economics of the last century treated in the same linear fashion economic evolution from collective to individual agriculture or vice versa; from primitive collectivism to capitalst individualism, or *vice versa;* and so on, up to the still narrower trends allegedly given in the process of economic change.

Archeology and *history* likewise were dominated by the same linear conceptions of historical change. If in the actual narrative of historical events a discussion of such trends, tendencies and laws of evolution-progress did not occupy a very large space in factual historical works, such trends and laws (assumed by the archeologists and historians) served as the guiding stars and referential principles for the ordering of chaotic historical material and especially for interpreting it. The archeological and historical "law of technological evolution" with its standardized stages: Paleolithic, Neolithic, Copper, Bronze, Iron and Machine Age is one of their linear laws serving as a fundamental referential and ordering principle. The idea of progress itself, interpreted linearly, is actually another such principle — an idea which served as the veritable foundation for the bulk of historical works in the nineteenth cenury. Even the explicitly factual histories openly inimical to any "philosophizing" in history did not escape it. The *Modern Cambridge History* provides a typical example of this: in spite of the aversion of its editors and authors to any philosophy of history we read in its opening pages: "We wish to discover the tendencies which are permanent . . . . We are bound to assume as a scientific hypothesis on which history is to be written, a progress in human affairs. This progress must inevitably be towards some end." (8)

8. The *Cambridge Modern History*, (Pop. ed., New York: The Macmillan Co.; Cambridge: Cambridge Univ. Press, 1934), Vol. I, p.4. Note that the work was executed in the 19th century. A contemporary example is that of H. Fischer's *History of Europe*, (London: Longmans, Green and Co., 1905) where an aversion to historical generalizations, is contradicted with "the fact of progress is written plain and large in the pages of history." Vol. I, p. vii.

TWENTIETH CENTURY SOCIOLOGY

It is hardly necesarry to add that in other supposedly purely factual narratives, the historians of the nineteenth century, from Mommsen, L. von Ranke, Fustel de Coulanges, F. Guizot up to the authors of *Cambridge Modern History* actually formulated a large number of linear laws of evolution, in all fields of social and cultural life. (9)

To sum up: sociology, the other social, philosophical, and even natural sciences of the nineteenth century viewed the central problem of physical, biological and sociocultural dynamics in a fairly simple way — the probem was one of discovering and formulating the linear trends believed to be unfolding in the course of time. In the field of sociocultural change the task assumed an almost unbelievably easy character; it simply amounted to drawing a unilinear or oscillating or branching or spiral main line from the "primitive" man, society or culture to the present time. The whole historical process was thought of as a kind of well-ordered college curriculum, with primitive man or society as a freshman, subsequently passing through the stage of sophomore, junior, senior (or others when the classification contained more than four stages), and then graduating either in the class of "positivism" or "freedom for all" or any other final stage suggested by the fancy and taste of the scholar.

2. *The Twentieth Century.* In the eighteenth and the nineteenth centuries there were already voices sharply criticising this dogma and offering different theories of sociocultural dynamics. In the twentieth century these voice multiplied and finally became dominant. The first result of this change has been an increasing criticism of the assumptions underlying the linear theory of sociocultural change and of the linear laws formulated by the bio-social sciences of the preceding century. These criticisms have been based on logical as well as factual grounds. On the logical side critics of the linear theories of change have indicated, first, that the linear type of change is only one of many possible types; second, that in order for a linear motion or change to be possible, the changing unit must either be in an absolute vacuum, free from interference of external forces, or these forces throughout the whole

---

9. Thus in the quoted *Cambridge Modern History* we read: "The practical applications of scientific knowledge will go on extending and . . . future ages will see no limit to the growth of man's power over the resources of nature, and of his intelligent use of them for the welfare of his race." Vol. XII, p. 791.

process of change must remain in such a "miraculous balance" that they mutually and absolutely neutralize one another at any moment and thus permit the changing unit to move for ever in the same main direction, whether the movement is rectilinear, spiral or oscillating. Evidently, both of these suppositions are factually impossible; even the "material point" of mechanics moves neither in absolute vacuum nor amidst forces that incessantly mutually anull one another; even material bodies are under the influence of at least two main forces: inertia and gravitation, which change their rectilinear and uniform motion (due to the intertia) into a circular or curvilinear motion. This is true of material particles as well as of the heavenly bodies. When we consider that man, society and culture are much more complex "bodies," that they are subjected to the incessant influence of inorganic, organic and sociocultural forces, their linear change throughout the whole of historical time becomes still less probable. Add to this the undeniable fact that each of these "units of change" itself incessantly changes in the process of its existence and thus tends to upset the direction of the change, and the assumption of eternal linearity becomes impossible. For these and similar reasons the theories of eternal linear trends have been increasingly rejected and replaced by what can be called the *principle of limit* in the linear direction of change. According to this principle, only some sociocultural phenomena, and these only for a limited period of time (which is different for different sociocultural units) change in a linear direction. Due to the immanent change of the units themselves and to an incessant interference of countless forces external to them, their temporary linear trends are found to be broken and replaced by "turns and deviations," a total process which results in numerous non-linear forms of sociocultural change. (10) Third, many of the other underlying assumptions of the linear theories such as the Spencerian principle of the "instability of the homogeneous," have been found to be invalid — logically and factually. Fourth, the logical structure of the linear theories themselves has been proved to be self-contradictory. For instance, Spencerian theory states that the supreme uniformity in any change, beginning with the motion of material bodies and ending with sociocultural processes, is a rhythm in which the phase of evolution is always followed by that of dis-

---

10. See a systematic analysis of this in my *Social and Cultural Dynamics*, Vols. I, ch. 4 and IV, ch. 12-16, *et passim* throughout all volumes.

solution; integration by disintegration; differentiation by de-differentiation. When logically applied to the change of the sociocultural phenomena this theory contradicts any unlimited linear theory of evolution. It presupposes that the "evolution" and its trend must be supplanted by "dissolution," and its trend, opposite or different from the trend of evolution. Dominated by the linear conception Spencer neglects this demand of his own theory and, by stressing only the evolutionary trend, not only contradicts his own principles but gets into a series of other difficulties. (11) With some variation the same can be said of practically all the linear theories of change. Fifth, the operation of linear theories with "mankind" as a unit of change is unsatisfactory. Most of these theories trace their linear trend in the history of mankind as a whole. Putting aside the important consideration as to whether "mankind" — in no way united in the past in any real system — can be taken as a unit of change, the linear trends "from the beginning of human history to the present time" can hardly have any real meaning. It is obvious that such a trend could not be realized in the life-history of every human being because billions of human beings in the past lived and died without reaching the later steps of the trend and without passing through its alleged stages. Likewise an overwhelming majority of human groups have lived and disappeared without reaching any of the advanced stages of the trend, and thousands of contemporary groups still live at their earliest stages. On the other hand many groups have never passed through the early stages of the trend but have emerged at once with the characteristics of the latest stages.

Furthermore, an enormous number of societies and groups have been passing through the stages different from those formulated by the respective "laws of evolution-progress" and in temporal order different from that assumed by these "laws." Other groups have shown a regression from a supposedly later stage to the earlier one. Finally, in any individual, group or in mankind as a whole at any given moment we can find a co-existence of several stages of the trend beginning with the earliest and ending with the latest. When all such individuals and groups deviating in all these ways from the "law of evolution" and its stages are excluded from the "mankind" to which the law supposedly refers, there remains only a very small faction of humanity (if any) whose "historical change"

---

11. On this *cf.* my *Dynamics,* Vol. IV, pp. 670-693 *et passim.*

SOCIOCULTURAL DYNAMICS

conforms to the alleged universal trends and laws of linear development. For this reason alone these trends and laws are, at best, merely partial uniformities applicable to a very small fraction of mankind and in no way universal laws of sociocultural evolution.

To these and similar logical criticisms of the assumptions and principles of the various linear theories of sociocultural change a heavy weight of factual criticism has been added. The essence of this factual criticism consists in a large collection of relevant data which clearly contradict the alleged trends and laws. Sociologists, psychologists, philosophers, historians, ethnologists and others have factually shown that the empirical life-histories of individuals, of various societies and groups do not follow the alleged trends and the alleged stages of development. The factual evidence openly contradicts the assumption that any universal and perpetual linear trend or any universal stages of evolution applicable to the whole mankind, to all groups and individuals, exists.

As a result of the logical and factual criticism of the linear dynamics of the last two centuries the enthusiasm for a discovery and formulation of such trends and laws has notably subsided in the twentieth century. Attempts to continue such a dynamics have not entirely disappeared, of course, but they have become fewer and fewer and more and more restricted to specific societies, to limited periods of time, and to many other limits and qualifications.

Having found the linear sort of social dynamics little productive, the attention of investigators has shifted to different aspects of sociocultural change, and first and foremost, to its *constant and repeated features: forces, processes, relationships and uniformities.*

The concentration on the *constant features* of sociocultural dynamics in the twentieth century sociology and social science has manifested itself in many ways. First, study has been increasingly concentrated on the *constant forces or factors* of sociocultural change and the *constant effects* in sociocultural life and organization. The partisans of the Mechanistic and Geographic schools, for example, have investigated various forms of energy from this standpoint (W. Ostwald, E. Solvay, L. Winiarsky, W. Bekhtereff and others) or specific cosmic forces like climate, the sun-spots and other geographic factors (Ellsworth Hunington, W.S. Jevons, H.L. Moore and others) and have formulated their constant effects on social and cultural phenomena, beginning with economic changes and ending with the rise and fall of nations. The adherents of biological and psychological schools in sociology and social science have taken heredity, race, instincts, reflexes, various physiological drives, vital processes, emotions, sentiments, wishes, "residues", ideas, as such constant forces and have attempted to show the constant sociocultural effects of each such constant bio-psychological variable (Sigmund Freud, psychoanalysts, hereditarists like F. Galton, Karl Pearson and others, racialists like H. S. Chamberlain, O. Ammon, V. de Lapouge, C. Lombroso, E.A. Hooton; behaviorists like John B. Watson; psychologists like William McDougall, C.A. Ellwood, E.A. Ross, E.L. Thorndike, W.I. Thomas, Vilfredo Pareto, L. Petrajitsky, H. Blueher, William Trotter, Graham Wallas, Lester F. Ward, William Graham Summer, Gabriel Tarde, Thorstein Veblen and others). Other sociologists have taken for such constant variables a series of sociocultural conditions like density and size of the population, "invention," "economic," or "religious" or other factors, up to "mobility," "moral density," "social anomie," and tried to unravel their constant effects upon other sociocultural phenomena. All such studies try to elucidate the constant role of each of these "factor-variables" in the behavior of men, in social structure and cultural life; the constant functions of each of these factors; and finally how and why these constant factors themselves fluctuate and change.

In the second place, this concentration on the *constant and repeated* features of sociocultural change has manifested itself in an intensive study of the *constant and ever repeated processes in the sociocultural universe*. A large part of sociology of the twentieth century is preoccupied with the study of such ever-repeated processes as isolation, contact, interaction, amalgamation, acculturation, invention, imitation, adaptation, conflict, estrangement, differentiation, integration, desintegration, organization, disorganization, diffusion, conversion, migration, mobility, metabolism, etc., on the one hand; and on the other, by an investigation of such repeated processes as they bear on the problems of how social groups emerge, how they become organized; how they recruit and lose their members; how they distribute them within the group; how they change; how they become disorganized; how they die and so on (Gabriel Tarde, Georg Simmel, Leopold von Wiese, Robert E. Park, Ernest W. Burgess, E.A. Ross, Emory Bogardus, Corrado Gini, P. Carli, Pitirim Sorokin, and almost all the writers of text-books in sociology). In this way sociology of the twentieth century has given care-

SOCIOCULTURAL DYNAMICS

ful study of the main sociocultural processes ever-repeated in the life history of any society at any time.

The third manifestation of this concentration on the repeated processes has been a most intensive study of the *constant and repeated meaningful-causal-functional* relationships between various cosmo-social, bio-social and sociocultural variables as they appear in the everchanging sociocultural world. Though these relationships were investigated in the nineteenth century their study in the present century has been enormously intensified. The main endeavors of the goegraphic, biological, psychological, sociologistic and mechanistic schools in sociology of the twentieth century have consisted exactly in the discovery and formulation of the causal-functional or meaningful-causal uniformities of relationship between two or greater number of the variables: between climate and mentality or civilization; between the sun-spots and business or criminality; between heredity and this or that sociocultural variable; between technology and philosophy, or the fine arts; between density of the population and ideologies; urbanization and criminality; the forms of the family and the forms of culture; social division of labor and forms of solidarity; social *anomie* and suicide; business conditions and criminality, insanity, internal disturbances or wars; between forms of religion and forms of political or economic organization and so on and so forth, beginning with the narrowest and ending with the broadest variables. These studies have yielded a large number of formulas of causal-functional or meaningful-causal uniformities repeated in the dynamics of various societies and in the same society at different periods. They have also tested many generalizations of this kind formulated before and have either found them spurious altogether or in need of serious corrections.

Finally, the fourth manifestation of this concentration on the *constant and repeated* aspects of sociocultural change has been a study of *ever repeated rhythms, oscillations, fluctuations, cycles and periodicities* in the flow of sociocultural processes. Preoccupied with a discovery of the linear trends, nineteenth century sociology and social science paid little attention to these repeated features of sociocultural change. With few exceptions (like Hegel, Tarde, G. Ferrara, Daniliévsky and a few others) social scientists and sociologists of that century neglected to follow the footpath of the Chinese and Hindu social thinkers, of Plato, Aristotle, and Polybius, of Ibn-Khaldun and G. Vico, to mention only a few, who concentrated their study of dynamics mainly on these repeated cycles, rhythms, oscillations, periodicities, instead of investigating eternal linear trends. The twentieth century has resumed the work of these thinkers and has continued it with an ever increasing energy. Among the social and humanitarian disciplines of this present century the earliest and most intensive study of cycles, rhythms, fluctuations and periodicities appeared in the theory and history of the fine arts and then in economics, with its investigation of business cycles. The rank and file of sociologists and other social and natural scientists somewhat lagged in the transfer of their attention and energy to the study of these repeated uniformities. Even at the present time, a large number of sociologists are hardly aware of this decisive shift of attention from a hunt for linear trends to that of repeated rhythms and periodicities. Nevertheless, with some lag, all the social, philosophical and even natural sciences have increasingly undergone and are undergoing this transfer of interest. With a considerable retardation, the natural sciences have opened even now a special Institute for the Study of Cycles in the field of physico-chemical and biological phenomena. As to the totality of the philosophical, social, and humanistic disciplines of the twentieth century, they have already produced a large body of scientific studies of sociocultural rhythms, cycles and periodicities in the field of the fine arts and philosophy, ethics and law, economic, political, religious, and other sociocultural processes. A mere summary of the uniformities of rhythm and tempo, of types and periodicities of fluctuations, and of other important results of these studies would occupy a few hundred pages as it did in my Dynamics. (12) A series of rhythms with two, three, four and more phases, periodic and non-periodic, short-time and long-time, in narrow and broad, simple and complex sociocultural processes has been discovered and analysed: in the fine arts by W.M.F. Petrie, O.G. Crawford, P. Ligeti, H. Woelfflin, F. Mentré, J. Petersen, E. Wechssler, W. Pinder, P. Sorokin and many others; in philosophy

---

12. The fullest concise survey and analysis of the main studies of sociocultural rhythms, cycles, periodicities and uniformities of tempo is probably given in my *Social and Cultural Dynamics*, Vol. IV, ch. 6-11, *et passim*, throughout all four volumes. As mentioned, most sociologists have lagged in the transfer of their attention and energy to the study of these phenomena. In most texts, even the most recent, there is little, if any, space devoted to social rhythms, cycles, fluctuations and periodicities, in spite of an exceedingly large scientific monographic literature devoted to them in sociology, social, humanistic, philosophical and natural sciences of the twentieth century.

by K. Joel, Sorokin and others; in economic processes by a crowd of economists beginning with M. Tugan-Baranovsky and ending with Wesley Mitchell and Joseph Schumpeter; in political processes by O. Lorenz; in fashions by A.L. Kroeber; in the life-history of vast sociocultural systems and supersystems by L. Weber, Alfred Weber, Oswald Spengler, Arnold J. Toynbee, and Sorokin, to mention only a few. The linear time-sequence of the stages or phases of sociocultural processes has also been put on a more sound basis by this study of rhythm and sequence of phases. Instead of hunting for some vague and questionable sequence of stages of a linear process throughout human history, as the social scientists of the nineteenth century did, twentieth century investigators, concentrating on recurrent processes, have been able to demonstrate the existence of many rhythms with a definite temporal sequence of phases repeated again and again. Finally, these studies have contributed greatly to our knowledge of periodicities and durations of various sociocultural processes. To sum up: in the field of rhythms, cycles, tempi, and periodicities, sociology and the social sciences of the twentieth century have found a field of dynamics yielding more fruitful and more certain results than the search for eternal historical trends as it was carried on in the nineteenth century. There is hardly any doubt that rhythms and repeated processes will be studied still more intensively by social scientists of the next decades and in all probability will yield more significant results than those obtained by the social science of the nineteenth century.

Such in brief have been the main changes in the study of the *"What"* of social dynamics as we pass from the dominant current of sociocultural thought of the nineteenth to that of the twentieth century.

II

Development in the Study of the "Why" of Sociocultural Change. Parallel to the outlined shift in the study of the *"What"* of sociocultural change several developments have also occurred in the study of the *"How"* and *"Why"* of this change. Again, these developments do not represent something absolutely new, totally unknown to sociology and social science of the nineteenth century. They are rather the result of a shift in the main interest and dominant pattern of thought, a further clarification of what was less clear in the nineteenth century; and a more conspicuous differentiation of what was less differentiated then.

The first of these developments consists in an *increasing weight given to the sociocultural variables as the factors of sociocultural change*. Although theories emphasizing the important role of geographic, biological and psychological factors in sociocultural change continue to develop, they have hardly added much to what they gave in the preceding century. The main gains and the main contributions have been made by sociologistic theories which have taken various social and cultural factors as the main dynamic forces of sociocultural change. Careful studies of changes in the incidence of suicide or crime, of business fluctuations, war and revolution, of changes in political regimes, of styles in the fine arts, or of the dynamics of vast cultural and social systems have increasingly emphasized the finding that the main factors of such changes lie in these sociocultural phenomena themselves and in the rest of the sociocultural conditions amidst which they occur and function. Geographic and biological forces external to them have been found to play the role of only subsidiary factors which may facilitate or hinder or even crush the respective sociocultural systems but, as a rule, do not determine their normal life career, the main ups and downs, the basic qualitative and quantitative changes in their life-history. This trend of factorial analysis has naturally culminated in *several systematic theories of immanent sociocultural change* according to which each sociocultural system bears within itself the seeds of its own change and disintegration. In this way the old theories of immanent change of Plato and Aristotle, of Polybius and Vico, of Hegel and Marx, of Mommsen and Comte, somewhat neglected in the preceding century, have reappeared and are growing in this century. (13)

This growth has resulted in a second development in the sociological thought of this century, namely in giving an *increasing weight and a more specific role* to the *immanent* or *internal* forces of any given sociocultural system in its life career (change) and in giving a *decreasing weight and less specific function* to the factors *external* to the sociocultural system. (14) The dominant

---

13. On these theories and on the principles of immanent change *cf.* my *Dynamics*, Vol, IV, ch. 12 and 13, which give probably the fullest survey and analysis of this problem in sociological literature.

14. This does not apply to sociocultural congeries. See on the difference between the system and congeries in my *Dynamics*, Vol. IV, ch. 1-4.

SOCIOCULTURAL DYNAMICS

tendency of the factorial analysis of social science in the nineteenth century was to explain a change in a given sociocultural phenomenon, be it the family or business system, literature or music, science or law, philosophy or religion, through the factors external to the phenomenon studied (geographic, biological and other sociocultural conditions external to the given sociocultural system). The growing trend of the twentieth century in such problems is to look for the basic reasons for the main changes in the life-history of a given sociocultural system in the totality of its actual and potential properties and in its connections with the other sociocultural phenomena. All the external forces (geographic, biological and sociocultural) with which the system is not connected directly are to be taken, as a rule, only as subsidiary factors, either hindering or facilitating (sometimes even killing) the unfolding of the potentialities of the system. (15)

A third development in the field of the *"Why"* of sociocultural change has been an *increasing care and precision in the study of the role of specific factors (variables) in specific sociocultural changes and especially of the role of sociocultural factors.* Twentieth century sociology has not discovered any new factor of sociocultural change unknown to sociology of the nineteenth century. But in the study of the causal connections of factors, whether geographic, biological, or especially sociocultural factors, what the nineteenth century vaguely called "economic," "religious," "ideological," "juridical" or other factors, have been more clearly defined by sociology of the twentieth century. In the interest of precision these vast and somewhat vague factors have been broken into several more specific and precise "independent variables" and much more carefully studied in their causal connection with a series of more specified "dependent sociocultural variables." By breaking the vast and vague "economic factor" of Marxism into

---

15. On this *cf.* the volume and chapters of my *Dynamics* cited above. It is to be noted that many sociologists and social scientists are not fully aware of these developments and like Molière's hero talk prose without being aware of it. In their studies these scholars stress and emphasize the decisive role of sociocultural factors in causation of this or that socio-cultural change: but at the same time they oppose the principles of immanent change and immanent factors in it, remaining avowed "externalists" in their standpoint. They seemingly do not realize that, with few exceptions and reservations, the emphasis on the sociocultural factors of sociocultural change as the main factors, is already an avowal of the immanent theory of sociocultural change.

such variables as "export," "import," "price of commodities," "level of wages and incomes," "budget of expenditures," "business index" and so on, and by investigating the connections of each of such variables with a specified form of crime, mental disease, suicide, or change in political ideologies, sociology of the twentieth century has given us more definite knowledge of the relationship between these variables than sociology of the preceding century. Other vast factors have been given a similar treatment by the sociology of our century.

An increase of precision in the factorial analysis has also resulted from the richer, more relevant body of factual material which has been collected by sociology and social science of the twentieth century. Since its main ambition has been to be a "fact-finding" sociology it has amassed a much more numerous, systematic and relevant series of facts of the sort necessary for the establishment and testing of any causal hypothesis. This bigger and better body of factual material has permitted sociology and social science of the twentieth century to test more vigorously the validity of causal hypotheses. As a result, some of the previous theories of causation of sociocultural change have been found to be fallacious, others have had to be narrowed and qualified, and still others have been found to be more valid than they had been thought before. (16) To this increasing trend towards a greater precision and validity of theories of the *"Why"* of sociocultural change we are indebted for the solid acquisitions of contemporary sociology but from it also stems one of contemporary sociology's greatest vices, as we shall see — the vice of sacrificing an approximate validity to a misleading preciseness.

The main development in sociology and social science of the twentieth century, however, has been a *growing split and increasing separation of two contrasting, partly conflicting approaches to the study of the causal-factorial problem of the "Why" of sociocultural change.* In a less conspicuous and explicit form the split already existed in the nineteenth century. In the twentieth it has deepened, widened, and become an open conflict. One approach consists in an uncritical application of what are supposed to be the methods and principles of causal-functional analysis of the natural, particularly the physico-chemical, sciences. The other approach con-

---

16. See the facts and theories in my *Contemporary Sociological Theories*, passim, and in my *Dynamics*, passim.

SOCIOCULTURAL DYNAMICS

sists in a specific sociocultural conception of causality essentially different from that of the natural sciences, designed and fitted for a study of the peculiar nature of sociocultural phenomena, their causal and functional relationships in both static and dynamic aspects. The basic assumption of those who espouse "natural science causation" in the field of sociocultural phenomena is that these phenomena in their componential structure are similar, even identical, with the physico-chemical and biological phenomena; therefore it is assumed that the methods and principles of causal analysis of the natural sciences, so fruitful there, must be adequate also for causal analysis of sociocultural phenomena in both static and dynamic aspects. In accordance with these premises the partisans of this "natural science causality in social phenomena" of the twentieth century have tried to be, first, "objectivistic, behavioristic and operational" in the choice of their factors or "variables" (of change) taking for these something material and tangible. Second, their procedure has been "mechanistic and atomistic" in the sense that they have taken for the variable any "transsubjective" factor regardless of whether it is an inseparable part of some real unity or an isolated phenomenon. Beginning with the causes of crime or "happiness in marriage" and ending with much larger phenomena, factorial analysis of this kind tries to take one by one a long or short series of possible factors (for instance, in marriage-homogamy or happiness, stature, color, economic status, religion, occupation, income, climate, race, nationality, etc., etc.) and to weigh, even quantitatively, their relative causative importance in the phenomenon under investigation assigning to each a very precise "index of influence." The procedure is similar in other causal analyses. Third, quite consistently with these premises, they borrow various principles of the natural sciences for ordering and "processing" their data: the principles of physics and mechanics (from the Einsteinian theory of relativity to the recent theories of microphysics); the principles of chemistry and geometry, of biology and mathematics (currents of contemporary "social physics," "social energetics," "geometrical or topological sociology," "quasi-mathematical theories of social dimensions and causation," "sociometrical," "reflexological," "endocrinological," "psychoanalytical," "biological" and other sociologies of causation and change). Fourth, some of these partisans try especially industriously to use a "precise quantitative method" of causal analysis in the form of various pseudo-mathematical procedures and complex statistical operations firmly believing in the possibility of discovering truth through complex mechanical operations prescribed by their pseudo-mathematics and pseudo-statistics. (17)

As a result of this faith in an alleged (18) "natural science causality" the theoretical and concrete studies of sociocultural causation and the factorial analysis of the twentieth century has produced a plethora of "research" filled with figures, diagrams, indices, complex formulae — looking very precise and "scientific" — of the simple and multiple causation of existence and change of whatever sociocultural phenomenon they happen to be investigating.

In spite of all the noisy claims of the partisans of this current trend, the real results of their laborious efforts have been rather disappointing. Carefully analyzed, their assumptions and premises happen to be a variety of the crudest materialistic metaphysics, inconsistent and selfcontradictory, a distortion of the methods and principles of the natural sciences, logic, and mathematics. The actual results obtained through their "precise looking" manipulations and formulae as a rule turn out to be either a painful elaboration of the obvious; or the formulae, all too often misleadingly precise, happen to be mutually contradictory, with high indices for the same factors in one set of studies and low indices in others, with high positive coefficients of correlation between the same variables in some of the researches and low or negative coefficients in others.

---

17. For the literature on this natural science causality cf. my *Sociocultural Causality, Space, Time*, (Durham: Duke University Press, 1943), chaps 1, 2; *Contemporary Sociological Theories*, Chaps. 1, 11. Typical of the recent works where these tendencies are carried almost to absurdity are: S. C. Dodd, *Dimensions of Society*, (New York: The Macmillan Co., 1942); E. D. Chapple and C. M. Arensberg, *Measuring Human Relations*, (Provincetown: Journal Press, 1940); P. Horst, P. Wallin, L. Guttman and Others, *The Prediction of Personal Adjustment*, (New York: Social Science Research Council, 1941); the most crude and naive statement of the metaphysics of this group can be found in G. A. Lundberg, *Foundations of Sociology*, (New York: The Macmillan Co., 1939).

18. "Alleged" because what they profess to be the methods and principles of the natural science happen to be as a rule their own primitive distortion of these principles. Their "mathematics" are pseudo-mathematics; their geometry and topology have no relationship to real geometry and topology; their "physics," "chemistry," and "biology" are simply amateurish home-made concoctions foreign to any real physics, chemistry and biology. This is repeatedly and explicitly stated by real mathematicians, physicists, chemists, and biologists who have reviewed these works.

SOCIOCULTURAL DYNAMICS

The logico-mathematical untenability of most of these premises together with the virtual sterility of the results achieved have provoked a notable and growing reaction against this amusing game of "natural science causality" in social phenomena on the part of other sociologists and social scientists. Following the footpath of the great social thinkers of the past, like Plato and Aristotle, and some of the eminent nineteenth century social scientists like Comte himself, H. Rickert, W. Dilthey and others, they clearly and convincingly point out a series of reasons for their rejection of this "game." First, they state that each of the mature natural sciences has methods, principles and techniques of analyzing causal relationships peculiar to itself and adapted to the nature of the phenomena they study; the methods, principles and techniques of the purely mathematical sciences are different from those of physics or biology; the methods and techniques of biology differ from those of physics or chemistry; even within the same science the methods, principles and techniques of microphysics are not the same as those of macrophysics. Therefore they argue, it is not permissible to assume the existence of some general "natural science methods, principles and techniques" and to apply them uncritically to the study of sociocultural causation. Second, they indicate that the nature and componential structure of sociocultural phenomena are radically different from those of physical and biological phenomena; therefore, the study of sociocultural causation requires a set of methods, principles and techniques different from those applicable to physical or biological phenomena and fit to grasp the peculiar character of the causal relationships in the sociocultural universe. Third, they hold that, in view of the "immaterial" component of these phenomena, an indiscriminate operation with "objective", "material," "behavioristic," "operational" variables, taken atomistically and mechanically, is impossible here because each and any of the sociocultural variables (including those with which the "natural science sociologists" operate, like religious, economic, juridical, ethical, aesthetic, political) is incorporated "objectively" in a multitude of the most different "material vehicles" — different physically, chemically, biologically, perceptually, materially — and none of these variables is limited, in its objective manifestations, to one definite class of material phenomena; therefore, nobody, not even the "natural science sociologists" can take any "objective" material vehicle as the invariable index of any of these factors, classes or sets of sociocultural phenomena; if and when such an attempt is made the result is the gravest sort of blunder. The fourth objection is that no atomistic study of any sociocultural factor in its relationship with other variables is possible because the same sociocultural factor A has quite a different relationship to the variable B when A and B are part of one sociocultural system (unity) and when they are isolated phenomena (congeries), when A is given in one sociocultural constellation and when it is given in another: for instance the factor of racial similarity (A) exerts a tangible influence upon choice in marriage (B) in a society with a high estimation of racial similarity or dissimilarity; and it exerts little, if any, influence in a society giving little or no value to the racial similarity or dissimilarity; objectively the same act, say A giving B one thousand dollars, may mean socioculturally dozens of different things, from payment of a debt or salary to a charity donation or a bribe. Similarly the causal relationship of such an act to other actions of A and B, and with other sociocultural phenomena may vary enormously from a close causal connection to nil, from connections with C or D, or with M and N, to connections with dozens of other sociocultural variables. Fifth, it must be recognized that causal relationship of sociocultural phenomena are generally quite different when we deal with united sociocultural systems as distinguished from atomistic and singularistic congeries of sociocultural phenomena. For these and many other reasons we hardly ever have a purely causal relationship between sociocultural phenomena in the sense that they exist in physical, chemical, or even biological phenomena; instead we most often find either a meaningful and typological relationship (the *Sinn-Ordnung, Sinn-Zusammenhaenge, Verstehende*, and ideal type relationship of W. Dilthey, H. Rickert, Max Weber, T. Litt, T. Geiger and of others of the Dilthey-Max Weber school); or the relationship of the "dynamic group assessment" (MacIver) or what I call meaninfull-causal relationships. A study of these peculiar relationships through a mechanical application of the dogmatic rules of statistical technique, the methods of induction, or through other mechanically applied rules and techniques of this or that natural science is hardly possible. Such an attempt results mainly in a sort of misleading preciseness. Instead we need a different approach, we need techniques in which "the meaningful component" of sociocultural phenomena (absent in physico-biological universe) is fully taken into account, since this component has to play the leading and decisive role as the main "clue" or "key" to the unravelling of the simplest

SOCIOCULTURAL DYNAMICS

as well as the most complex networks of meaningful-causal, static and dynamic relationships in the sociocultural universe.

In accordance with this trend of thought a number of sociologists and social scientists of the last twenty years have endeavored to construct a systematic theory of sociocultural causation. Some of them have attempted to apply it concretely to the study of several actual sociocultural systems — vast and narrow — not dodging even several predictions as to the further development of these small and vast sociocultural processes. (19)

Though these conceptions of the specific sociocultural causality at the present moment are approximate and tentative, with their further elaboration during the coming decades they promise to put the problem of causal analysis in the social sciences on a much more solid and sound basis than it has hitherto been. With the tool improved, the results of its use are bound also to be more significant and fruitful than they were before.

Such in brief are the main differences in the sociocultural dynamics of the nineteenth and the twentieth centuries.

---

19. The most recent analysis, summary, and a system of sociocultural causation is given in R. M. MacIver, *Social Causation*, (Boston: Ginn and Co., 1942) and in my *Sociocultural Causality, Space, Time* and *Social and Cultural Dynamics*, Vol. IV, et passim.

SELECTED BIBLIOGRAPHY

Possibly the most complete bibliography is given in Pitirim A. Sorokin's *Social and Cultural Dynamics*, (New York: American Book Co., 1937-41, 4 vols.).

Adams, Brooks, *The Law of Civilization and Decay*, (New York: The MacMillan Co., 1897).

Chambers, F. P., *Cycles of Taste*, (Cambridge: Harvard University Press, 1928).

Deonna, W., *L'archeologie*, (Paris: 1912, 3 vols.).

Ellwood, C. A., *Cultural Evolution*, (New York: Century Co., 1927).

Ermatingen, E., *Philosophie der Literaturwissenschaft*, (Berlin: 1930).

Ferrari, G., *Teoria dei periodi politici*, (Milano-Napoli, 1874).

Ibn-Khaldun, *Prolégomènes historiques*. (Paris: 1862, 3 vols.).

Joél, K., *Wandlungen der Weltanschauung*, (Tuebingen: 1928-31, 3 vols.).

Ligeti, Paul, *Der Weg aus dem Chaos*, (Muenchen: 1931).

Mathis, R. *La loi des trois états*, (Nancy: 1924).

Ogburn, William F., *Social Change*, (New York: Viking Press, 1922).

Pigou, A. C., *Industrial Fluctuations*, (London: Macmillan and Co., 1927).

TWENTIETH CENTURY SOCIOLOGY

Schumpeter, Joseph, *Business Cycles*, (New York: McGraw-Hill Book Co., 1939).

Sims, Newell L., *The Problem of Social Change*, (New York: Thomas Y. Crowell Co., 1939).

Spengler, Oswald, *The Decline of the West*, (New York: Alfred A. Knopf, 1929, 2 vols).

Spranger, E., *Die Kulturzyklentheorie und das Problem des Kulturverfalls*, (Berlin: 1926).

Tarde, G., *Social Laws*, (New York: 1899).

Toynbee, Arnold J., *A Study of History*, (London: Oxford University Press, 1934-39, 6 vols).

Vico, G. *Principi di una Scienza Nuova*, (Milano: 1854).

Ward, Lester F., *Dynamic Sociology*, (New York: 1883, 2 vols.).

Weber, Alfred, *Kulturgeschichte als Kultursoziologie*, (Leyden: 1935).

Weber, Louis, *Le rythme du progrés*, (Paris: 1913).

Weber, Max, *Gesammelte Aufsaetze zur Religionssoziologie*, (Tuebingen: 1922, 3 vols.).

Pitirim A. Sorokin was born January 21, 1889 in Russia. Magistrant of Criminal Law (1915), Dr. of Sociology (1922) University of Petrograd. Professor of Sociology, University of Petrograd, Psychoneurological Institute, Agricultural Academy, 1918-1922; University of Minnesota, 1924-1930; Harvard University, since 1930. President of International Institute of Sociology, 1937. Honorary member of several scientific societies and Academies of Science. Author of many works, including: *Sistema soziologii*, 2 vols.; *Sociology of Revolution; Social Mobility; Contemporary Sociological Theories; Principles of Rural-Urban Sociology; Source Book in Rural Sociology; Social and Cultural Dynamics*, 4 vols.; *Crisis of Our Age; Man and Society in Calamity; Time Budgets of Human Behavior; Sociocultural Causality, Space, Time; Russia and the United States*, etc. A number of these works are translated into several foreign languages.

CHAPTER VI

SOCIAL CAUSATION AND CHANGE*

by

ROBERT MORRISON MacIVER

I

Dynamic Assessment and Social Conjuncture. The social sciences are not concerned with the particular behavings of individuals but with the inter-related activities that constitute or reveal group behavior. In the study of social causation we are not confronted with the endless task of explaining how or why different individuals act differently in different situations. It is a question of how *we* behave. And the "we" is not to be construed distributively, as though one were asking about the ways in which like animals react to like stimuli or independently satisfy like needs. It is the "we" of associated beings; whose ways of behaving, whether like, complementary,

---

* Acknowledgment is made by the editors with thanks for permission to republish the following selection of pages from *Social Causation* by Professor R. M. MacIver, 1942. This acknowledgment is addressed to the author as well as to his publishers, Ginn and Company.

The original form of citations has been kept in this paper.

unlike, or opposed, are inter-related and in some measure interdependent. The social sciences are concerned with the modes of behavior characteristic of social beings who belong within the same culture, who possess the same institutions, who together face the same problems, who pursue common causes, who when they act in like ways, are still subject to influences that pass from one to another and envelop them all. Hence in the study of social causation our interest centers in the like or converging dynamic assessments that underlie group activities, institutional arrangement, folkways, in general the phenomena of social behavior. These like or converging assessments we shall speak of as group assessments.

That the group to some extent and for some purposes acts as a unity in the assessment of situations is evidenced in many ways. Anthropological and sociological studies make it very clear that whenever a people or tribe takes over any doctrine, creed, myth, or philosophy from another people or tribe it endows the borrowed cultural form with its own imprint. The creed, for example, is selectively different for every distinctive group, no matter what uniformity of ritual or acceptance of a single authority may prevail. The characteristic difference holds whether the creed in question be the Christianity of modern civilization or the belief in the "guardian spirit" found among American Indian tribes. Wherever it is allowed to express itself, there is a style of the group as well as of the individual, a manner of living, a manner of thinking, a manner of acting. This style the group is always seeking to perpetuate by establishing conventions and standards, by institutionalizing in an at least semi-compulsive form the main lines of its system of assessment, though individual variations and deviations forever play upon them. The thought-forms, the valuational constructs, thus perpetuated among the members of a group serve as the group focus of dynamic assessment.

We may now distinguish three types of social phenomena according to the manner in which these socially conditioned thought-forms are related to them. Our first type includes changes in mores, styles, usages, in the modes of living, in the tides of opinion, and in such statistical facts as the birth-rate, the crime rate, the suicide rate, the frequency of marriage, and so forth. These phenomena do not express the concerted or collective activity of the group to which they refer. The crime rate is not the objective — nor any part or aspect of the objective — of the persons who commit the crimes, as a revolution or a celebration is the objective of those who participate in it. The crime rate is, in effect, a way of saying how many people in a given population have acted alike in violation of a criminal code — or rather have been convicted of acting alike in this respect. Similarly, when the opinions or attitudes of a number of people change at the same time in the same direction the registered volume of change expresses a consensus only, not a collective action but the aggregate of many individual actions. The rate or the volume of change is nevertheless a social phenomenon inasmuch as it is responsive to group or community conditions and is moreover in some measure dependent on suggestion, imitation, intercommunication, leadership, and other social interactions. Through such interactions the varieties of individual assessment become congruent and tend to fall into conformity. Thus also the way is prepared for phenomena of the second type.

Our second type includes statutes, regulations, administrative policies, organized social movements, political revolutions and demonstrations, social agreements of every sort. The distinctive feature of this type is that individuals who are more or less in accord in their assessment of a situation take concerted action, either directly or through agents to bring about a single or common objective, some change in the social structure or in the conditions to which they are together subject. Here congruent individual assessments are the basis of a collective determination. A particular objective is formulated and "blue-printed." It is of the kind that admits actualization through a specific agency in fulfilment of a preconceived design.

Our third type embraces the vast array of phenomena denominated as social resultants, the product of social conjuncture. It includes the greater structures of the social order, the extent of the division of labor, the modes of politico-economic control we call capitalism, socialism etc., the changing equilibrium of economic organization, the business cycle, the volume of unemployment, the various patterns and exhibits of social disorganization. Under this type we should perhaps distinguish two sub-types. There are social phenomena that partly correspond to some preconceived design but in the process of actualization many uncalculated changes have occurred, so that the final result is in important respects different from the "blue-print," and often much more complicated. Again, it frequently happens that around the formally established institution there is woven a subtle network of unplanned usages that in time become an integral part of the operative system. For example, around the law court and the law there develops a scheme of customary practices — what one writer calls the "law-ways." (1) On the other hand there are social resultants that in no measure depend on any preconceived design. Take, for example the fluctuations of business activity commonly referred to as the business cycle. No one plans a business cycle, no group engineers it; the most men hope for is to control or limit it. Under all conditions the multifarious activities of economic life, complicated also by social processes and political regulations, produce unplanned effects. Whether these effects constitute an orderly scheme of things, a precarious moving equilibrium, or a realm of confusion; whether they lead men to bless the "invisible hand" or to demand a social revolution, they belong equally to our third type. So do the various rhythms, patterns, waves that are forever manifesting themselves within a complex society. Certain statistical facts also find place here, instead of under type two. Contrast, for example, the unemployment rate with the crime rate. The former does not presume any kind of like behavior, like objective, like dynamic assessment, on the part of those who fall within the category. The volume of unemployment is a social phenomenon not because it expresses the purposes of social beings but because it is an unpurposed aspect and product of a social system, of complexly interdependent activities falling under our first two types.

In sum, we have distinguished three causal types of social phenomena, as follows:

TYPE ONE. DISTRIBUTIVE PHENOMENA

Directly expressive of the like or converging assessments of a number of people, as they issue in separate activities of a like nature, together constituting an aggregate or ratio of the same order, such as a crime rate or an opinion trend.

TYPE TWO. COLLECTIVE PHENOMENA

Directly expressive of the like or converging assessments of a number of people, as they issue in concerted and unified action, such as a legal enactment or an organizational policy.

TYPE THREE. CONJUNCTURAL PHENOMENA

Arising from the variant assessments and activities of interde-

---

1. K. N. Llewellyn, "The Normative, the Legal, and the Law-jobs." *Yale Law Review* (June 1940), Vol. 49, pp. 1355-1400.

SOCIAL CAUSATION AND CHANGE

pendent individuals and groups, as they issue in unpurposed resultants, such as the business cycle under a capitalistic system.

In all complex social processes phenomena of all three types are combined. Obviously, phenomena of type one are implicated in the phenomena of type two. Obviously, many phenomena of type two are responses to the problems created by the phenomena of type three. Political systems are usually classified according to the manner in which phenomena of type two are organized and controlled, under such names as democracy, dictatorship, oligarchy, and so forth. Another line of distinction takes primary account of the range of phenomena that fall respectively under type one and under type two. On this basis we distinguish socialist from capitalist systems, co-operative societies from other economic corporations, and so forth. The causal relationships that exist between phenomena of type two and those of type three have been a main issue of politico-economic controversy. Some economic doctrines, including laissez-faire, marginal utility, and equilibrium economics of all sorts, announce a socially advantageous harmony; others deny it or assert its inadequacy.

Our immediate concern is with the fact that back of all these phenomena lie the socially interdependent assessments made by individuals as members of a group, whether they act collectively or distributively. The dynamic assessment is for us the preparatory stage of the particular nexus we call social causation. It is that which differentiates it from every other form of causation. It is also that which enables us to attack the peculiar problem of the relation of factors in social causation. These statements we shall endeavor progressively to justify.

The causal role of dynamic assessment is to bring into a single order of coherent relationships the objectively diverse factors involved in social behavior. We begin with the dynamic assessment, while recognizing that back of it lie causal factors of another order. Our problem is not how the evaluating and synthesizing function of conscious being, in its manifold embodiments, is derived and constituted as a psycho-physical system in the realm of universal nature. Our problem is how it operates in the realm of social behavior. We are not asking what determines the focus but what the focus determines. We can see that it is forever being modified and conditioned by the organic processes, by the state of the nerves, the bloodstream, the digestion, by the biological effects of emotional experience, by the rise and fall of the atmospheric pressure, and so forth. Nevertheless for the study of social causation we can take it as a datum, since, however determined, it inaugurates another kind of causal nexus, that on which our interest happens to be centered.

The assessing process, whether it take effect as an individual or as a collective activity, is a function of the personality of the social being, as it apprehends alternatives of behaving, as it discerns their relation to the value-system it incorporates. This personality is constantly changing, is perhaps never fully engaged in any conscious action, is evoked in different degrees and in different aspects by the particular challenges and demands of the occasion. It has nevertheless some coherence and unity through time. A split personality, in the strict sense, is a relatively rare phenomenon. The character type and the character idiosyncrasy are on the whole quite persistent. Otherwise we could not have the complex ordered relations of men. Sometimes there is bewilderment, lack of orientation, cleavage, whether associated with nervous disturbances and other organic impairments or more directly with tense conflict situations. But sometimes the contradictions attributed to personality are such only because different behavings are compared too abstractly. For example, the envisaged alternatives may be of a momentary nature or of superficial content. Shall I go to this party or stay at home? Shall I read this novel or that one? Such assessments involve only a narrow range of the personality. The action taken with respect to them may be no criterion of the principle of action when larger alternatives are under review. Shall I choose this career or that? Shall I marry this girl? Shall I offend my conscience to please my friends or offend my friends to satisfy my conscience? The presented alternatives vary with every situation. But the mode in which the alternatives are selected and presented, delimited and assessed, is revelatory of the personality structure. The value-system is incorporated in personality, finding partial, variant, and aspectual expression in the flux of behavior.

When we turn to consider the group convergence, under our first two types, we are no longer concerned with the elusiveness and complexity of the individual personality. We now enter an area in which the signs are somewhat easier to discern, in which we can neglect the more subtle variations of the value schemes of different individuals, in which the data are equally open to many observers. What is there in this area that corresponds to the individual personality as a focus of behavior? We might speak of a group personality except that the concept is so liable to misconstruction. But as back of the individual assessment there is a relatively coherent personality, so back of the like and converging assessment of many individuals there is a relatively coherent culture complex. It is a commonplace of observation that every group tends to have and to hold its distinctive culture even though it may be only a variation of a circumambient culture. Anthropologists have dwelt on the "patterns" of this complex, historians have described its manifestations over groups of every scale and through greater or shorter spans of time, sociologists have found a "trend of consistency" in its various aspects or have sought to portray its coherence through the conception of an "ideal type." (2)

Social conjunctures are so numerous, variant and complex that we must here be content merely to indicate a few familiar types. Wherever men get together for any purpose, unintended and unforeseen processes are set in motion. The most universal of all social phenomena — the effect on one social being of the presence of another, the effect of the congregation on each member of it — is a social resultant in this sense. Here we can include a vast range of phenomena stretching from the heightened animation of lovers to the accelerated tempo of urban life. Another type of social resultant that has been the object of frequent comment arises from the manner in which the means men have designed become converted into ends, while the ends they have struggled for undergo a process of degeneration into means. (3) Men build organizations and they find that the frame of organization somehow holds them in its grasp. They develop institutions to serve their particular purposes, and they sometimes end by worshipping them. Seeking to preserve institutions from change men turn them into the sanctuaries of bureau-

---

2. As examples, R. Benedict, *Patterns of Culture,* (Boston, 1935); V. L. Parrington, *Main Currents of American Thought* (3 vols., New York, 1930); W. G. Sumner, *Folkways* (Boston, 1940), Chap. I; Max Weber *Wirtschaft und Gesellschaft* (Tuebingen, 1925), Chap. I.

3 See, for example, R. K. Merton, "The Unanticipated Consequences of Purposive Social Action," *American Sociological Review* (December, 1936), Vol. 1, pp. 894-904, and the same writer's "Bureaucratic Structure and Personality," *Social Forces* (May 1940), Vol. 18, pp. 1-9; E. C. Hughes, "Institutional Office and the Person," *American Journal of Sociology* (1937), Vol. 43, pp. 404-413; E. T. Hiller, "Social Structure in Relation to the Person," *Social Forces* (Octorber, 1937), Vol. 16, pp. 34-44.

crats. Or they overthrow the established order, and something else comes into being than the shining goals they sought. Again, we may cite as a well-recognized type of social resultant the unpurposed consequences of technological advance. Men invent aeroplanes, and thereby revolutionize the art of war. They devise the assembly line for automobiles, and the consequences reach into home and school and church. They develop the electron tube, and the remotest hamlet responds to the newest voices of the city.

Since the causal sequence is continuous without end we could logically extend the range of the social conjuncture to include all social phenomena whatever. For they are all the unpurposed consequences, near or remote, of prior behavior in prior situations. A war of a thousand years ago is a determinant, co-operative with countless other things, of the composition of the population today. An advance in sanitation changes incalculably the relation of city and country — and everything else besides. Every birth has consequences of which the parents could not dream. In this sense every being and every event is the product of an inconceivably complex conjuncture. We must merely recognize this truth and pass it by. Such conjunctures, bred in the "dark backward and abysm of time," are beyond investigation. We can at best deal only with dynamic moments of the endless process. For practical reasons we limit ourselves to the conjunctures that are the near unpurposed sequels of purposive actions. Man schemes and contrives under conditions that change and divert his actions into new conditions for new scheming and contriving. But through it all he contributes the causal factor that distinguishes the area of social causation from all others, the factor of dynamic assessment.

These considerations show once more how unavailing is the simply quantitative approach that seeks to attach particular weights to the several "factors," attributing to each so much push or pull in a total push or pull. We have just seen that the factors are dynamic only within the conjuncture, and therein they are dynamic, not as such, not as separate items of reality, not in their intrinsic properties, but only as they are subjectively apprehended and assessed. Only in the dynamic assessment is there anything that can be called the weighting of factors. And this weighting employs no objectives scales. It varies with every mood as well as with every situation. In so far as there is weighting it is relative to a value scheme. And we do not weight ends and means and conditions as coordinate items. Means are also costs in the value reckoning.

SOCIAL CAUSATION AND CHANGE

They limit as well as facilitate desires, and even in facilitating they usually involve a reduction of the immediate net satisfaction we should gain had our desires a magic potency. Utilities from this point of view are also relative disutilities. Since in varying degrees they constitute the minuses of net attainable satisfactions they are forever changing the equilibrium of our effective desires. How much they do so is endlessly contingent and can be learned only, and then within limits, by the most careful analysis of the particular behavior of men and groups, in which we judge how far their objectives and motives are evoked by the various facilities and opportunities at their command. The total apprehended situation, including conditions as well as specific means, controls the value assessment and the direction of the value quest.

Since none of the primary components of the dynamic conjuncture have as such any independent efficacy we must assign that efficacy to the conjunction itself, to the consummation of the dynamic assessment. There are unfathomed psycho-organic processes involved in the formulation of the dynamic alternatives, in the choice between them, and in the passage of decision into action. These are not here our concern. Our concern is with the process wherein changing assessments, changing means and changing conditions are interrelated so as to bring out social action, as revealed in an institutional reform, a group movement, a statistical fact, and so forth. If a like change of attitude or of overt behavior is at the same time manifested by many individuals we can for our present purpose ignore the psychological complexities of their variant assessments. We can look for some significant difference between the conditions to which they alike respond, the means they alike possess, the cultural complex they alike reveal, and the comparable conditions, means, and cultural complexes of those who do not manifest the change of attitude or of overt behavior. We can thus bring the social phenomena within the universal formula of causal investigation. Since the difference is so often one of degree — increase or decrease of crime, competition, division of labor, radicalism, and so forth — we can endeavor to trace the spread or development of the phenomenon, as one traces a rising or receding tide. We may discover why it rises here and recedes there — and our explanation will be no longer the listing of a congeries of factors but the exposition of a coherent pervading cause that is not any of the factors nor all of them together nor even any combination of them.

TWENTIETH CENTURY SOCIOLOGY

II

The Goal of Causal Knowledge in Sociology. One conclusion that has emerged in the course of our enquiry is that the discovery of the causes of social phenomena is progressive and always approximate, always incomplete. We seek to trace the routes of specific transitions within the larger flux. What we designate causes are the various conjunctures of things in the process of creating some difference that arrests our attention; effects are then particular properties — or differences — manifested by things in their various conjunctures. We want to relate the difference as closely as possible to the pertinent conjuncture. But our knowledge of the conjuncture, however far we probe, remains imperfect — its unique configuration is not wholly discerned. A simple illustration will serve. We hear some story, say of a quarrel between two of our friends. We are curious, we are also somewhat disturbed, anyhow we want to know the truth of it. We enquire concerning the occasion and the ground of the quarrel. We receive different versions of the story. We approach the parties to the quarrel, and they too give us different accounts. We get all the "facts" we can. We form our own conception of what really happened. We revise it as we learn more about the previous relations of our two friends. We know something of their personalities, of how they respectively react to various situations. So we get nearer to the truth, but some of it eludes us. There remains an element of conjuncture, an area of uncertainty, a process of reconstruction, a question of emphasis. Who will dare to claim that he has the whole truth? And if this is so in an affair so close to us, what of causes of larger conflicts, of labor disputes, of wars, and so forth? Everywhere, behind the changes of human affairs, there is the problem of knowing the unique conjuncture from which the event proceeds.

Some who are hotfoot for absolute and final certainty, for the whole truth wholly demonstrated, reject this conclusion. They refuse to accept partial knowledge. They refuse to employ methods that do not yield verifiable exactitude. Perhaps the very assumption of potential exactitude is mistaken, or at least irrelevant, for some important aspects of knowledge. The causal problem is not one of how much, but of how, and we should seek to answer accordingly. In any case we should remember that the rejection of partial truth, because it is only partial, is still the rejection of truth — just as much as the rejection of an imperfect light, in preference to none at all, is the choice of darkness instead. This in effect is what the demand for complete objective verification — not merely for objective evidences of subjective data — amounts to. Extreme positivists of this type regard all subjective phenomena as tainted, unfit for scientific consumption. The consequence is that they are quite unable to deal with the issues that mainly concern the social scientist, and least of all do they help us in the quest of causation. We may quote on this head the judicious words with which two of the ablest and best equipped investigators of our day conclude their study of the family in the depression:

"It will be observed that in the foregoing discussions the writers have taken an eclectic point of view with reference to research . . . It should be obvious . . . that a scrupulous limitation of research to that which will yield immediately an order of verification comparable to what is required in the more developed natural sciences would result in almost no knowledge about the effects of depression on the family. Some of us are extremely interested in helping push sociological research more in the direction of verification. But that cause will not be served by an insistence on an exclusive technique which too often may yield trivial results where valid, and pretentious nonsense where invalid." (4)

In the search for causes we advance to fuller and more precise knowledge, employing whatever methods are available and helpful to this end. We have shown throughout this work that the basic method is a form of the method of comparison, the successive analysis of comparable situations in order to demarcate our phenomenon and to segregate the particular complex of things to which it immediately belongs. This method calls for all the precision and all the ingenuity we can muster. We cannot, for example, be satisfied with an explanation that equally covers other phenomena besides the one we are endeavoring to explain. The causal conjuncture must be seen in its specific relation to the specific phenomenon. Thus if we were to assign the characteristic gang of modern American cities to the complex of poverty, deteriorated urban neighborhood, and so forth, we could no less adduce these factors to account for the prevalence of crime in general, drug addiction, desertion, sidewalk peddling, and various other phe-

---

4 Stouffer and Lazarsfeld, *The Family in the Depression*, p. 201.

nomena of slum areas. Our explanation would lack specific relevance. The modern urban gang is a distinctive development, and is the outcome of a distinctive complex of attitudes, opportunities, conditions, and means. To expose this complex, to reveal it in its particular operation, and also in its gestation, this is the kind of problem that in its endless varieties continually challenges the student of social causation.

Causal attribution is therefore the progressive revision of an hypothesis. The process of revision, as already set forth, is also a process of verification. What, we may finally ask, are the tests by means of which, at each stage of the investigation, we can check the adequacy and the validity of the causal hypothesis? In setting up this hypothesis we are claiming that certain things, as coexistent or successive, do not merely coexist, do not merely succeed one another, but are bound together by virtue of their interdependent dynamic properties. Now there are, to begin with, some obvious tests of this claim. Supposing, for example, we put forward the thesis that modern industrial capitalism is a product of democratic conditions, it would be immediately refuted by the fact that this form of capitalism has strongly developed under non-democratic conditions in Germany and in Japan. If, again, we claimed that modern industrial capitalism is the result of technological advance, a reference to the association of technological advance with state-socialism, fascism and communism would show the lack of precision in the claim. These are gross instances, but in many more refined ways the method of comparison can be employed to show that an alleged nexuxs does not hold or at least is improperly stated. On the other hand where certain phenomena are found constantly associated over a wide range of situations the claim of a causal nexus between them is strengthened. Thus we find a rather constant association between economic depression and a decrease in the number of marriages. We cannot conclude that under all social conditions economic depression and a decrease in the marriage rate go together. We can, however, claim that, given a certain type of socio-economic organization, the onset of a depression acts as a check on the marriage rate. As we have shown, this claim becomes the starting point of further investigation in which we seek to define the causal nexus more precisely.

We see here the role of the statistical test in the verification of the causal hypothesis. It does not furnish any positive proof, but by giving us exact formulations of the correlations of variables it provides important clues as to where and how we should look for causal connections. There are simple instances in which it leads us immediately to a causal nexus. Thus there is a very high positive correlation between the temperature and the frequency with which the cricket chirps. (5) Below 45 degrees Fahrenheit the cricket does not chirp. Over a considerable upward range of temperature there is a steady increase in the number of chirps for each additional degree of warmth. The conclusion is inescapable — and can, of course, be experimentally confirmed — that the relation is not coincidental but causal. The rise in temperature causes, under the given conditions, the increase in chirping. The correlation of variables belonging to social situations is generally much less conclusive, but it is still very servicable in a number of ways. In the first place, it enables us to dispose of many false trails to the causal nexus. We conjecture, for example, that the increase of suicides under modern civilization is due to the sharp changes from prosperity to adversity reflected in the movements of the economic barometer. We discover a correlation of, say, +.4 between suicides and business failures. So far, we are not discouraged from pursuing the trail. But when we apply the principle of multiple correlation and make the proper adjustment for age differences, the positive correlation betwen business failures and suicides falls to a quite insignificant figure. "What appeared to be a relationship between business failures and suicides was in fact largely a relationship between average age and suicide rates." (6) So it becomes apparent that there was no such definite nexus as we had supposed. In the second place, the appeal to statistics often helps us to delimit the group or the situation to which a particular phenomenon should be referred. The group has various constituents, and the situation has many aspects. The causal connection may not be predicable of the whole group as such or of the whole situation as a conjuncture. There is, for example, a decline of the marriage rate during a depression. The impact of the depression does not bear equally on all classes of the population, nor does it follow that the decline of the marriage rate for different groups is proportionate to the economic hardship or loss they respectively suffer. Possibly the decline shown for the community as whole may

---

5 F. E. Croxton and D. J. Cowden, *Applied General Statistics* (New York, 1939), pp. 651-653.

6 Ibid., p. 769

mask the fact that the marriage rate of certain subgroups has been unaffected; it is even possible that the rate for some subgroups may have moved upwards. Further statistical analysis, by relevant categories, will resolve these questions, will enable us to construct a group typology according to the mode in which the contracting of marriage is affected by adverse economic changes — and thus bring us nearer to the central issue, our final why: Why do people in the face of certain new situations act thus and thus?

It is at this point we must resort to other methods of investigation than that of statistical analysis. We have insisted on the primary experimental fact that back of every social change there is a reassessment of a situation by individuals or groups and a readjustment, in terms of that reassessment, of activities relating means to valuations. This is the unifying process that brings into one dynamic synthesis the inner or subjective order of urges, values, and effective goals and the outer orders of environmental reality. But the unity is achieved on the condition that the outer loses for this synthesis its sheer externality and becomes the outer of the inner, operates in this relation no longer as its full biophysical reality but instead as a selectively conceived system of opportunities and obstacles, areas of advance and retreat, things celebrated and things deplored, the soil of memories and expectations and hopes and fears. So conceived, so presented to the dynamic assessment, the social environment bears the multitudinous evidences of social action and social change. These are objective evidences for the social scientist. He can detach them from the meanings they have to the social agent. He can count and measure them, can subject them to statistical analysis. But when he is through with that, he must reinvest himself, constructively, with his own role as social agent. Otherwise, though he may learn how much a war has cost in men and treasure, he will never learn why men fought the war; what passions and persuasions moved them, what they sought. Otherwise, though he may trace the fluctuations of the marriage rate and of the birth-rate, he will not discover the forces that control and liberate and direct the behavior of human beings.

These forces, as reflected in social or socially conditioned behavior, pertain to the cultural complex. Is this complex, in specific instances, beyond the reach of scientific method, for the discovery of the causal nexus and for the verification of the causal hypothesis? If it were so, the social sciences could never advance towards the goal of causal knowledge. The methods of science as applied to

SOCIAL CAUSATION AND CHANGE

the phenomena of the external world, and particularly as employed in statistical analysis, assure us of the probability that there is a connection between, say, a depression and a decline in the number of marriages. Shall we stop there? Shall we disregard every hypothesis, however obvious and understandable, as to the kind of connection? A change of fortune interposes no physical or biological barrier to mariage. Statistical evidence may show us that under certain social systems a change of fortune interposes no cultural barrier. If it is otherwise in our present Western society we can very properly enquire where, and how, and under what conditions. Thus every method of scientific investigation brings us to the verge of our final problem. It is not the external aspect of a social system, it is the socially accepted scheme of valuation, that deters from marriage during a depression. The inference is here simple and indubitable. That there is a prevailing scheme of valuation is established by the like preferences men exhibit, by the like changes of behavior to which they resort when the conditions of choice are altered by new circumstances.

The dynamic assessment that lies back of overt behavior is thus a fact as validly attested as any other. The scientific difficulty is not the establishment of the mere fact but the determination of the specific scheme of effective valuation dominant in any process of decision. It is never directly revealed to us and though sometimes the discovery of it is a simple enough inference it is often highly precarious. Often we have some inkling of it but the evidence is insufficient to enable us to compass its subtlety and its full scope. Often the objective is clearly indicated while the motivation remains obscure. But there is abundant evidence that every group has its characteristic mores, or standards of valuation, and that the like and common activities of the group express various aspects of a relatively coherent cultural complex. Such a phenomenon as the decline of marriage during a depression is not an isolated manifestation; it is in accord with various other changes of behavior to which at such time people resort, according to their circumstances, in order to maintain as nearly as possible their prior status or standard of living. We pointed out in another context that the decline of the birth-rate was a particular expression of a general readjustment of values and means that has many other manifestations.

The verification of a hypothesis of social causation is consequently conducted on two levels. We employ statistical analysis and other methods common to all the sciences in order to learn whether and to what extent and in what areas and over what length of time the phenomenon under consideration is associated with certain other phenomena. These methods furnish a test that any hypothesis must first pass before it can be accepted as a legitimate claimant for further investigation. If it meets this requirement, we continue the search on another level. We seek to discover whether it depends on the dynamic response of social beings to changing situations. Again we appeal to evidences, but the interpretation of them follows different lines and requires the application of different methods. These evidences are of various kinds — the other overt activities of those whose behavior in some particular respect is being investigated, the oral, written, and gestural communications of the participants the expressed opinions of those who are in direct or indirect contact with them, the past behavior of the individuals or groups concerned, the behavior of other individuals or groups in comparable situations, and so forth.

We may distinguish two main types of evidence that lead us beyond the data of correlation to the socio-psychological nexus. One consists of the depositions, avowals, confessions, justifications, and other testimonies offered by agents, participants, or witnesses, professedly or ostensibly giving their own answers, on the ground of their inside or close-up knowledge, to the question of causation. The reliability of such declarations can be examined in various ways familiar to historians, anthropologists, psycho-analysts, judges, detective agents, and in fact to all men in so far as they are students of human nature. The other main type of evidence consists of those indications, other than direct testimony, that help us to place the particular behaving in its meaningful context. If a hungry man steals bread it is not necessary to search for the configuration of values that explains his action. If somewhere in our Western civilization a man who has had sudden financial reverses postpones the date of his marriage, the search for an explanation, unless the circumstances are unusual, is not likely to occupy us long. But often the quest is not so easy. We seek for the explanation that is most consistent with the personality and life history of the individual or with the cultural complex of the group, as it bears on the specific situation within which the behavior takes place. But we cannot know the situation fully, as it is presented to or selectively conceived by individual or group, and we cannot fully follow the cultural complex through the subtle

SOCIAL CAUSATION AND CHANGE

processes of readjustment to ever changing conditions. We must here essay the task of projecting ourselves by sympathetic reconstruction into the situation as it is assessed by others, with such aid as we can obtain from the two types of evidence. There must always be, as we have already shown, this process of reconstruction.

What we reconstruct is the relatively coherent scheme of things to which the phenomenon under investigation belongs. Every act is the act of a personality, and every personality is bred within a social system, and every social system exhibits its cultural complex. Everywhere there is some unity embracing the individual life, and beyond that the life of the group, and beyond that the life of the nation, and beyond that there extends the widening area within which men communicate with and influence one another, so that to the synthetic historian continents and epochs have their characteristic being. Every social phenomenon is an expression of some meaningful system. We piece the system together from myriad evidences — not as outsiders but as in some degree ourselves participants. Experience and history provide us, in the measure in which we can learn their lessons, with the background of knowledge into which we seek to fit the specific social phenomenon. The particular methods we have already cited enable us to narrow the margin of error. But complete certitude eludes us. The unity, however coherent, exhibits deviations and conflicts. The systems we construct do not integrate all the manifestations we discover within them. The particular phenomenon may be the offspring of the system, but every birth is difference as well as likeness.

That is why the verifications of any significant hypothesis of social causation is never complete, but only approximate. The goal of causal knowledge is never attained, though our endeavors can bring us always nearer. What we cannot fully apprehend is that which is intrinsically dynamic. We measure its manifestations, but it is always revealing new aspects, turning in new directions, entering into new conjunctures, which we did not foresee, perhaps could not have foreseen. In the study of social causation, as no doubt elsewhere, we are in the presence of an intrinsic dynamic in this sense. In this context we may call it simply human nature. We pursue its endlessly changing responses to endlessly changing situations; we discover continuity in change and change in continuity; we measure concomitances of factors and regularities of sequence; we infer the pattern of the scheme of values that every group sustains and

TWENTIETH CENTURY SOCIOLOGY

forever reconstructs, adjusting means to ends and ends to means through all the vicissitudes of its experience. As we follow these trails and indications, not in one instance but in multitudes, we gain a widening and deepening knowledge. From many angles we attack the problem of understanding human nature and its works. And if this human nature possesses any basis of identity through all its changeful manifestations these angles must converge towards a point they never reach, the goal of causal knowledge.

SELECTED BIBLIOGRAPHY

Broglie, Louis de, *La physique nouvelle et les quanta*, (Paris: 1938).

Eddington, A., *Philosophy of the Physical Sciences*, (New York: The Macmillan Co., 1939).

Durkheim, Emile, *The Rules of Sociological Method*, (Chicago: University of Chicago Press, 1938).

Dodd, Stuart C., *Dimensions of Society*, (New York: The Macmillan Co., 1942).

Halbwachs, Maurice, *Les causes du suicide*, (Paris: 1930).

Hawkins, D. J. B., *Causality and Its Implications*, (London: Sheed and Ward, 1937).

MacIver, Robert M., *Social Causation*, (Boston, etc.: Ginn and Co., 1942).

Ogburn, William F., *Social Change*, (New York: Viking Press, 1922).

Sims, Newell L., *The Problem of Social Change*, (New York: Thomas Y. Crowell Co., 1939).

Sorokin, Pitirim A., *Social and Cultural Dynamics*, (New York: American Book Co., 1937-1941, 4 vols.).

Sorokin, Pitirim A., *Sociocultural Causality, Space, Time*, (Durham: Duke University Press, 1943).

Whitehead, A. N., *Science and the Modern World*, (New York: The Macmillan Co., 1925).

Robert Morrison MacIver, Lieber Professor of Political Philosophy and Sociology of Columbia University, was born in Stornoway, Scotland. He received his education at Edinburgh and Oxford, and taught first at the University of Aberdeen, then at the University of Toronto, where he was head of the Department of Political Science, then at Barnard College, and finally in the Faculty of Political Science of Columbia. He has been awarded honorary degrees by Columbia and Harvard, and has a D. Phil., from Edinburgh. Author of the following books: *Community* 1917, *Elements of Social Science* 1921, *The Modern State* 1926, *Society, a Textbook of Sociology* 1931 and 1937, *Leviathan and the People*, 1939, *Social Causation* 1942, *Towards an Abiding Peace* 1943.

CHAPTER VII

SOCIOGRAPHY OF GROUPS

by

LOGAN WILSON

Introduction. The group concept has been called pivotal in sociology. It would be presumptuous for sociologists to take credit, however, either for having originated the basic concept or for having discovered most of the phenomena to which it now refers. As a matter of fact, the prior existence of an extensive terminology and a considerable body of knowledge on the common-sense level has not only been acknowledged but also incorporated with very little alteration into many sociologists' treatises on human groups. From this perspective, ordinary language is accepted as adequate for descriptive purposes, human groupings are taken as ready-made data reasonably well defined and classified through cultural accretion, and the task of the sociologist is simply perceived as that of further clarification and refinement of analysis. From another perspective, this whole procedure is regarded at best as being of dubious scientific merit and at worst as being an encumbrance to the development of sociological theory. A different process of abstraction has been proposed as an alternative.

These and other points of view with reference to group behavior may be reserved for later comment. It is more pertinent at this early juncture to observe that at various times in the course of its

TWENTIETH CENTURY SOCIOLOGY

theoretical development, sociology has meant many different things to many different men. Originating in the philosophy of history, the discipline was for a long time replete with *ad hoc* generalizations about the nature of society. Grandiose schematizations of society and culture have not been wanting, but the lack of serviceable frames of reference has been conspicuous. Empirical work, particularly in the field of group description and analysis, has tended, like the apocryphal horse, to gallop off in all directions.

Within the past several decades, nonetheless, careful conceptualization has appeared and has been coupled to the task of guiding and systematizing empirical inquiry. There is still no uniform and universal consensus as to the scope of sociology, but since the turn of the century, a number of fairly explicit and widely accepted conceptions have been in use. Giddings was one of the first sociologists to define the whole field as a study of the elements and principles of social actions, social relations, and social groups. More recently and more specifically it has been noted by Znaniecki that there are prevalent in sociological theory four leading schemata. Accordingly, the same basic facts about man in society can be subsumed under a systematic theory of social actions, of social relations, of social persons, and of social groups. Concerning this last category, Znaniecki states:

> The fourth and most developed branch of sociology is the *theory of social groups*. A group, of course, is not a 'society' in the old sense of the term; it is not an entity fully including a number of bio-psychological individuals and unifying them in a community of their total cultural life. It is simply one of the many cultural systems these individuals construct and maintain by their activities. There are, e.g., many thousands of various groups maintained by the inhabitants of a big city, from the municipal groups in whose maintenance all of them participate, down to the small family groups kept up by only a few individuals each; and new groups are being constructed all the time. (1).

Regardless of the analytical framework used, the group factor is an important one. It is no accident, therefore, that a large segment of sociological literature belongs under the heading of group description and analysis. Related concepts and data, together with methods and techniques pertaining to the study of group phenomena may be properly designated as the sociography of groups.

The term *sociography* occurs only rarely in treatises by Amer-

---

1. Florian Znaniecki, *The Method of Sociology*, (New York: Farrar and Rinehart, 1934), pp. 120-121.

SOCIOGRAPHY OF GROUPS

ican sociologists, but it deserves a wider usage. There is no equivalent word which serves equally well to indicate those studies focusing upon groups as basic rather than incidental objects of sociological inquiry.

Sociographic studies occupy, rather curiously, an anomalous and vaguely defined sphere in terms of prevailing topical arrangements. The literature is so enormous and so variously conceived that it almost defies exploration and classification, yet even a cursory examination of accessible published materials reveals certain trends during the last four decades. Within recent years sociography has become one of the most highly developed branches of sociology. A resumé of major sequences in this development will be useful in understanding the present status of the field.

I

by reference to individuals; the other argued for the existence of some mystic bond having an independent "reality" of its own.

Group Theory in France. Group theories and sociographic studies in France developed largely in connection with Durkheimian sociology. Emile Durkheim and his followers reacted strongly against Le Bon's unscientific prejudices about "crowds" and his mysterious "crowd psychology" (much of which had nothing at all to do with crowds). In his first work on *The Division of Labor in Society* (1893; English translations, 1915 and 1933), Durkheim found a theoretical linkage between his concept of mechanical and organic solidarity and the group problem. Organic solidarity flows from the differentiation of society into particular groups connected with the social division of labor. He also recognized, however, that this pluralism of groups can have diverse consequences, depending on the measure of integration in the whole of society. Thus, in his work, *Le Suicide* (1897), Durkheim showed the causal relation between the increase of suicide rates and the disintegration of groups in the nineteenth century. In the Preface to the second edition of

At the beginning of the twentieth century the speculations of Hegel, Comte, and Spencer were still dominant in the efforts of European social scientists to formulate group theory. Social interaction as a key concept had not been evolved, and the problem of the group was being approached largely from two incorrect points of view. One of these tried to account for group phenomena solely

The Division of Labor (1902), Durkeim affirmed the necessity for a stable institutional basis of group integration as the only means for minimizing the *anomie* and psycho-social isolation of the individual in modern society. (2)

Durkheim's pupil, C. Bouglé, in his two books, *Les Idées Egalitaires* (1899) and *Essais sur le régime de Castes* (1907), described the pluralism of free and criss-crossing groups in a given society as an indispensable sociological prerequisite of a democratic order. The theoreticians of French syndicalism, inspired by Proudhon and by Durkheimian sociology, were very much occupied with sociographic descriptions of different worker groups and their roles as centers of autonomous law creation. At the same time, the works of the social anthropologists, Marcel Mauss and Lucien Levy-Bruhl, showed the error made by Durkheim in considering primitive society as homogeneous and groupless. Reaching the same conclusions arrived at elsewhere by Lowie and Malinowski, they found primitive society to be a complex microcosm of groupings, such as age groups, sex groups, magical brotherhoods, clubs, and so on.

More recently, René Maunier in his *Essais sur les Groupements Sociaux* (1929) has utilized former studies in this field, and has insisted that every type of human society can be characterized as a peculiar complex of groups. Social functions are related to forms of group life, and Maunier has tried to classify all groups in three large categories according to the predominant criteria of kinship, locality, and activity. Georges Gurvitch has, in various of his works (see especially his *Idée du Droit Social*, 1932; *Essais de Sociologie*, 1938; *Sociology of Law*, 1942), developed theses concerning group theory. Every type of society is regarded as a macrocosm of groups and every group as a microcosm of the forms of sociability, or social ties and bonds. The particular patterns of a group depend upon the general social conjuncture and the place it occupies in the total society. Gurvitch has classified groups according to the criteria of scope, duration, function, attitudes, dominant organizational principle, form of constraint, and degree of unity. He has recognized, nonetheless, that all classifications (even those founded on pluralistic and interrelated criteria) are only general and abstract

---

2. For the bearing of his sociological realism upon group theory, see *The Rules of Sociological Method*, (8th ed.), Ed. by George E. G. Catlin in Eng. trans., (Chicago: The University of Chicago Press, 1938), pp. 103-104.

SOCIOGRAPHY OF GROUPS

frames of reference to be filled out by concrete sociographic descriptions.

Group Theory in England. In England at the turn of the century, such group theory as existed was being developed largely by the anthropologists. Their approach was primarily evolutionary and highly speculative, as may be witnessed in the schematizations of Frazer, Lang, Tylor, Lubbock, and Hartland. The works of Graham Wallas and Leonard T. Hobhouse dealt primarily with society at large. Westermarck and Briffault focused upon the family group, but from a predominantly institutional aspect. Later English anthrologists, such as Pitt-Rivers, Malinowski, and Radcliffe-Brown have incidentally dealt with specific primitive groups in their broader researches in social organization. In his influential but misleading book, *The Group Mind*, McDougall speculated on the "degrading" as well as "ennobling" effects of human aggregations and set forth a good many generalizations on group self-consciousness, continuity, interaction, and organization. Although many of McDougall's incorrect assumptions persisted until quite recently, they were thoroughly criticized as early as 1921 by another Englishman, Morris Ginsberg. (3)

Group Theory in Germany. In Germany theoretical developments during the present century were initially influenced by folk psychology (as set forth by Wundt and others) and by the instigator of sociology as a special science in that country, Ferdinand Toennies. Toennies' basic contribution is found in the key concepts of his famed book, *Gemeinschaft und Gesellschaft*, published in eight successive editions between 1887 and 1935. As implied in the title, his work is a treatise on "community" and "society." Traditionalized, face-to-face, intimate group organization of the village is typologized under *Gemeinschaft*, whereas "emancipated," contractual, impersonal group organization of the city is represented by *Gesellschaft*. These two concepts, as is generally known, are still widely used by sociologists, particulary in the field of rural-urban sociology. (4)

---

3. *The Psychology of Society*, (London: Methuen and Co., 1921). See especially Chap. IV, "The Theory of a Social or Group Mind."

4. Charles P. Loomis has translated and supplemented his main work under the English title, *Fundamental Concepts of Sociology*, (New York: American Book Co., 1940). An analysis of the later theoretical significance of the concepts, *Gemeinschaft* and *Gesellschaft* is given in Talcott Parsons' *Structure of Social Action*, (New York: McGraw-Hill Book Co., 1937), pp. 686-694.

TWENTIETH CENTURY SOCIOLOGY

One of the first German sociologists to bridge the theoretical gap between the individual on the one hand and society and culture on the other was Georg Simmel. He swept aside both the organic theory and the atomistic theory and found the focus of sociology in the forms of social interaction. From a truly sociological perspective he recognized groups not as substantive entities of individuals but as systems of dynamic relationships. His writings deal with many different types of groups. (*e. g.*, secret societies, etc.) and the characteristics and processes common to them. Processes of superordination and subordination, and subtle aspects and effects of power relationships are analyzed. (5)

Simmel's artificial separation of form and content (6) proved not to be feasible, and his actual procedures departed frequently from his tenets. Although he never erected a synthetic theory of the forms of association, his monographs show considerable insight into group behavior. His analyses of the relations between the number of members and the sociological forms of the group are particularly keen. (7) In much detail he pointed out how changes in group size affect formal organization, interaction processes, and other aspects. Analysis begins with the monad, or single person (not individual *per se*) as the smallest unit, because the person himself exists only in relationship. The next unit in size is the dyad, which form, with but a few highly institutionalized exceptions, also has no super-individual unity. The triad is less dependent upon immediate participants for its structure, absorbs less of the person, and can continue its existence if one element drops out. Simmel shows much discernment in his more or less introspective analysis of small groups, and foreshadows the later work of Leopold von

---

5. For a good summary and analysis of his contributions, see Nicholas A. Spykman, *The Social Theory of Georg Simmel*, (Chicago: The University of Chicago Press, 1925). Theodore Abel's *Systematic Sociology in Germany*, (New York: Columbia University Press, 1929) contains a chapter, "The Formal Sociology of Georg Simmel"; Abel's treatment, however, rather underrates the importance of Simmel's basic ideas.

6. See "The Number of Members as Determining the Sociological Form of the Group," *American Journal of Sociology*, 8: 1-2, July, 1902. See also a second article in the series, *op. cit.*, 8:158-196, September, 1902.

7. His main ideas pertaining to the group are found in his *Soziologie*, (Leipzig: Duncker und Humbolt, 1908). The articles cited above were translated by Small and later incorporated by Simmel into his *Soziologie*.

SOCIOGRAPHY OF GROUPS

Wiese and Howard Becker. Simmel's analyses dealt mostly with either very small or very large groupings.

Interaction between human beings is conceived as occupying social space. Some groups, such as churches, have a life principle which is non-spatial and therefore are not spatially exclusive; territorial groups, such as states, however, are mutually exclusive categories. Problems of sociological boundaries, and spatial influences on group perspectives are considered in a general way. The tendency of groups to persist is noted within the time category. Factors contributing to the persistence of the group are listed as follows: gradual change in membership, permanency of locality, common symbols, protection by means of law, honor and morality, and the formation of special preservative organizational features. Stable and unstable groups are typologized. Simmel's observations about the social personality anticipate many later developments in sociological theory, and his generalizations pertaining to the individual and the group are very cogent. His analysis of the group was from a primarily static and structural point of view, but he also considered the group from the point of view of functionalism. Whereas Simmel's theory is largely speculative and non-empirical in its basis, his process of abstraction is indeed subtle, full of insights and leads for further exploration.

Max Weber was much less concerned with the sociology of the groups than was Simmel, but in his *Wirtschaft und Gesellschaft*, (Tuebingen, 1922), as well as elsewhere, Weber does comment on primary groups, secondary groups, and associations. Strongly influenced by Toennies in these conceptions, Weber viewed the primary group (*Vergemeinschaftung*) as a "social relation based upon the subjective feeling, affective or traditional, of belonging together" (*cf.* Giddings' "consciousness of kind"). The secondary group (*Vergesellschaftung*) is a "social relation based upon a rationally motivated balance or combination of interests." The association (*Verband*) is a "social relation in which the maintenance of order is guaranteed by the activities of a leader and an administrative staff." As the intepretations of Abel, Parsons, and others have demonstrated, Weber ascribed no super-individual "reality" to these structures in any organic or metaphysical sense, but rather viewed them as action patterns. Unlike Simmel, Weber centers his focus not upon social relations *per se*, but upon their concrete manifestation in economic, religious, political and other phases of social behavior. As a consequence, his contingent analysis of group phenomena is cast in another framework of reference.

The most systematic formal treatment of group phenomena in German sociology is that of Leopold von Wiese. (8) From the point of view of the sociologist, Wiese recognized that plurality patterns have no elements other than social relationships; avoiding both the fallacies of reification and those of atomism, he has developed a schema (with later amplifications and revisions by Howard Becker) which purports to form a "working theory of the group" on a logical basis. The objective of schematization is to extract the most frequently recurrent social processes conditioning the patterns. The criterion of structural purpose is avoided as a non-sociological focus in the categorization of the three main types of plurels: crowds, groups, and abstract collectivities. Taxonomically, the degree of sociation is uppermost as a criterion. "The differentiating factor is the distance which in the neuropsychic organizations of members separates the plurality pattern from tangible human beings. In other words, the three chief types of plurality patterns are distinguished by their different degrees of abstractness." (9)

A major concern is not to delimit the total range of all conceivable groupings but to formulate ideal-typical categories which will be of utility in determining group-like traits encountered in empirical exploration. Various modes of sub-classification and cross-classification are discussed. For example, plurality patterns may be regarded as: (1) amorphous or organic, (2) transitory or relatively permanent, (3) bio-social or strictly social, (4) regulated or elected, (5) positive or negative (see Chapter XXXIII in *Systematic Sociology*. Natural areas, villages, cities, regions, and so on are identified as locality patterns. Then there are ideological plurality patterns such as utopias and heavens which may exert a profound influence on social behavior. From another perspective, divisions may be made on the basis of the number of members. Wiese's broader schemata, with its inclusion of such primary abstract collectivities as the State, the Nation, the class, such secondary abstract collectivities as industries and political parties, such marginal plurality patterns as the judiciary and the bureaucracy,

---

8. See his *Systematic Sociology* (On the basis of *Beziehungslehre* and *Gebildelehre*, adapted and amplified by Howard Becker), (New York: John Wiley and Sons, 1932). Note especially chapters 32-41, inclusive.

9. *Ibid.*, pp. 419-420.

SOCIOGRAPHY OF GROUPS

and such mixed plurality patterns as the university, the factory, and the penal system is indeed a comprehensive theory of social organization.

Wiese's definition of the group distinguishes it from certain other aggregations and shows that the members are not as total personalities elements of the group, but rather, that the group is merely a combination and intensification of relations between them. As an ideal type the group has the following characteristics: "(1) relatively long duration and relative continuity; (2) organization based on division of function among members; (3) neuropsychic patterns, symbolic of the group, present in its members; (4) the growth of traditions and customs as the group grows older; (5) interaction with other plurality patterns." (10) General aspects taken into consideration are the genesis, components, membership (including the significance of numbers — optimal limits, etc.), and means of preservation of the group.

Wiese's treatment of group analysis is discursive rather than definitive. Broad suggestions are made for discovering social processes which predominate, for classifying them within a system of social processes, and for the use of questionnaires, participant-observer methods, and other approaches. His principal contribution is taxonomic and formally analytic. Triads, medium and large sized groups are discussed in terms of structural characteristics with reference to means and ends, but the dyadic group comes in for most detailed classification.

A scheme for the formal classification of the chief varieties of the dyadic group (given here in abbreviation) appears as follows:

Our main concern thus far has been to trace leading developments

CLASSIFICATION OF DYADIC GROUPS[11]

A. Superior-subordinate
B. Aider-aided
C. Teacher-pupil
D. Pairs primarily conditioned by the economic order. nomic order.

1. Typical (Genuine) Pairs
   A. Sexual pairs
   B. Generation pairs
   C. Friendship pairs
II. Atypical (Derivative) Pairs

---

10. *Ibid.,* p. 490.
11. *Ibid.,* p. 509. (Reference is made in a later footnote to an extended development of the dyadic concept by Becker and Useem).

in European sociological theory concerning group conceptualization, and these developments have been brought to their highest point in the work of Wiese. In addition to the developments cited in more or less systematic theory, there have been innumerable contributions in the field of empirical research. The vast amount of material, its inacessibility, and the borderline character of much of it, however, prevent reference here to trends exemplified by concrete studies. All that can be said at this point is that European contributions to the development of the sociography of groups have been greater on the side of conceptual clarification than on the side of empirical research.

Group Theory in the United States. In the United States, as elsewhere, there has been a general trend in the development of sociology as a science away from philosophic generalizing about society and culture toward more specialized lines of analysis. Prominent in this change has been an increasing amount of attention paid to sociology as a theory of groups, and a more inductive and penetrating analysis of the group as a factor in social behavior. The role of the group concept in American sociology prior to 1920 has been set forth at some length by Walter B. Bodenhafer, who has shown how it was utilized by leading sociologists in this country during the first two decades of the present century. (12)

Bodenhafer attributes the growing importance of the group concept during the period considered to an increased theoretical recognition of the fundamental importance of the group in a rising collectivism which was displacing individualism in American life, to the development of class consciousness, to the growth of occupational alignments, and to other forces which gave impetus from the outside to sociological inquiry. Lester F. Ward, although a pioneer American sociologist, rather strangely enough was highly individualistic in his approach; however, his perspective serves as an interesting point for contrast with that of other promoters of the new discipline. Neither his first work, *Dynamic Sociology* (2 vols., 1883) nor any of his later writings up to the year 1913 give more than secondary importance to group analysis. The individual rather

---

12. See his series of four articles, "The Comparative Role of the Group Concept in Ward's *Dynamic Sociology* and Contemporary American Sociology," *American Journal of Sociology*, 26:273-314, November, 1920; 26:425-474, January, 1921; 26:588-600, March, 1921; 26:716-743, May, 1921.

SOCIOGRAPHY OF GROUPS

than the group was his starting point, and the importance of interaction patterns was largely ignored. His principal concern with any form of collectivity was the State, and his work attests the fact that he lacked a fundamental understanding of the principles of social organization, as may be seen in his omission altogether of the significance of smaller groupings. Thus, from the point of view of both systematic theory and empirical research, Ward contributed very little to the development of the group concept and its application.

In contrast to Ward, Franklin H. Giddings assumes the group as the starting point of sociological analysis. Both aggregation and association are essential to social life, and in terms of social origins, the family is made the basis from which the larger aggregations evolve. The two main types of aggregation are the ethnical and the demotic, based correspondingly upon the chief bonds of blood kinship and upon habitual intercourse, mutual interests, and cooperation. Giddings subscribed to the idea of unilinear evolution with reference to the development from family to tribe, to confederation of tribes to nation of folk. He made "consciousness of kind" the central subjective factor in social organization. (13) The over-all organization of voluntary groups for specified ends he called the construction of society and he considered political organizations to be the most important voluntary groups (see *The Principles of Sociology*). Little attention was paid by Giddings to the roles of primary groups, but he did deal with miscellaneous types of intermediate groups. One of his last works (14) contains a number of concrete suggestions (unusual for that period) for the study of groups for-

---

13. "Consciousness of kind" belongs with "folkways and mores," "primary group," etc. as one of the popularized terms of sociology. Theodore Abel has given a detailed analysis of the concept, and has shown that the phenomenon itself occurs predominantly in sentiment relations and in closed groups. It is the main factor involved in the determination of feelings of "social distance," and many other qualitative choice situations. The order of importance of factors in the consciousness of kind is as follows: social status, group membership, personality. Of possible combinations, status and group membership are the most important. Consciousness of kind functions in the inception as well as in the development of social relations. (See Abel's article, "The Significance of the Concept of Consciousness of Kind," *Social Forces,* 9: 1-10, October, 1930).

14. *The Scientific Study of Human Society,* (Chapel Hill: University of North Carolina Press, 1924).

tuitously or incidentally assembled, mentioning specific items to be noted and procedural techniques.

Edward A. Ross has recognized that there are many relations between individuals which do not involve groups, and that the group concept is not sufficiently inclusive to constitute the sole theoretical basis around which to organize the framework of sociology as a science. A study of the forms of association would yield a social morphology, but Ross conceived the domain of sociology more broadly as a science of association or processes. In his earlier writings (*Social Control*, 1901; *Fundamentals of Sociology*, 1905; *Social Psychology*, 1908), he ascribed importance to the group and to group relations, but his use of the group concept has never assumed major importance. Originally treating the group simply as a product of the gregarious instinct, Ross eventually came around to the vaguely sociological view that "whatever marks off certain persons from others, or establishes a community of interests is a group maker," and he has classified groups under three heads: local groupings, likeness groupings, and interest groupings. The blood bond and the place bond are stressed as unifying factors, and there is some attention given to likeness groups, common experience groups, fraternal groups, and interest groups. Further, he generalizes:

> Human groups are often the end-products of our social processes. *Domination* begets large aggregates, such as realms and empires. *Socialization* prepares people to cohere when a motive for uniting presents itself. *Adaptation* smoothes away obstacles to the formation of a group, or makes the members more harmonious and cooperative among themselves. *Stratification* causes the we-feeling to spread among those of the same social layer. *Opposition* causes those on the same side of the cleft to stand together, from sympathy and in order to prevail. (15).

Charles H. Cooley's conception of primary groups (16) is so familiar as to require no review here but the theoretical significance of his conceptualization should be emphasized. The implications of the group in personality formation as implied in the "looking-glass self" have had much influence on later writings about socialization as a process and upon theories of the social personality.

---

15. *Principles of Sociology*, 3rd ed., (New York: D. Appleton-Century, 1938) p. 677.

16. See *Social Organization*, (New York: Charles Scribner's Sons, 1923). For a critique of the primary group concept see Ellsworth Faris, "The Primary Group: Essence and Accident," *American Journal of Sociology*, 38:41-50, July, 1932.

SOCIOGRAPHY OF GROUPS

(17) Even in his earliest work, Cooley looked upon society and the individual as collective and particularized aspects of the same thing, and completely eschewed any false separation of the individual and society in looking at the total situation. The importance of the group, particularly the primary group, was generally known before Cooley's time, of course, but had not received sufficient emphasis in sociology and social psychology. His contribution was not only in calling attention to the importance of primary groups, but also in showing their place in the theory of social psychology. In informal style, Cooley points out in *Social Process* (1918) that with increased social differentiation and specialization, human beings remain as dependent as ever upon the group system as a whole, but less and less identified with any one group, while concurrently depending as much as ever for "moral health" upon intimate associations with primary groups such as the family, neighbors, and friends. Furthermore, the voluntary associations of modern life are chiefly impersonal, and specialized interest groups leave the larger segment of the participant's personality outside the group sphere. Cooley's own work was of a highly generalized, non-empirical character, but he recognized the importance of first-hand investigation of actual groups and encouraged the undertaking of such inquiries. (18)

Albion W. Small has been credited with formulating the clearest definition of the group, as reflecting the older and less technical usage:

> The term 'group' serves as a convenient sociological designation for any number of people, larger or smaller, between whom such relations are discovered that they must be thought of together. The 'group' is the most general and colorless term used in Sociology for combinations of persons. A family, a mob, a picnic party, a trade union, a city precinct . . . the civilized or uncivilized population of the world may be treated as a group. Thus a 'group' for Sociology is a number of persons whose relations to each other are sufficiently impressive to demand attention. The term is merely a commonplace tool. It contains no mystery. (19)

---

17. The related contributions of Baldwin, Mead, and others are deliberately omitted from the present discussion because of space limitations.

18. Chapter X, "Case Study of Small Institutions as a Method of Research," in *Sociological Theory and Social Research*, (New York: Henry Holt and Co., 1930) cites studies by Read Bain, R. C. Angell, and other students of Cooley as exemplifying the sort of thing he had in mind.

19. Albion W. Small, *General Sociology*, (Chicago: The University of Chicago Press, 1905), p. 495.

TWENTIETH CENTURY SOCIOLOGY

Small disavowed any claim for sociology as a master science, and increasingly regarded it as a study of group aspects of human phenomena. Social processes were treated by him as interactions within and between groups, and they became simply the dynamic aspects of group relations. Like Cooley, as Bodenhafer has stated, Small assumed no disjunction between society and the individual, and, following Baldwin, made self-consciousness a group product instead of an individual datum.

This summary review of the ideas of leading earlier American sociologists (20) gives some perspective of trends in group theory during the first two decades of the twentieth century. Mention should be made here also of W. I. Thomas and Florian Znaniecki's *The Polish Peasant in Europe and America* (1918-1920). Although this work is noted chiefly for its use of the life-history method and for its theory of disorganization, it is likewise a worthwhile contribution to the empirical study of group behavior, and as an example of the collection of materials through direct and systematic observation stands in marked contrast to the speculative type of enterprise which was so characteristic of Thomas's contemporaries. (21)

These earlier American sociologists were for the most part prone to let their generalization stem from introspective experience rather than from controlled observation, and group theory still had a long way to go after two decades of enterprise. As late as 1921, for example, there appeared in the leading sociology journal an article using the instinct hypothesis as the prime explanatory factor in group theory. (22) In 1924, the psychologist Floyd H. Allport in his *Social Psychology* espoused an individualistic stand and vigorously opposed what he called the "group fallacy." Yet, these earlier American sociologists did succeed very effectively in establishing

---

20. Many of their views are not particulary noteworthy *per se*, but of importance chiefly because of the influence they had upon later sociological inquiry. William Graham Summer made some contribution to a qualitative analysis of intergroup relations (particularly the antagonistic aspects), but is excluded from treatment here because of the fact that group concepts were dealt with only incidentally from his perspective.

21. The works of Charles A. Ellwood, Emory S. Bogardus, and L. L. Bernard are also noteworthy in any comprehensive study of earlier trends in group theory, but space limitations prevent their consideration here.

22. Herbert A. Miller, "The Group as an Instinct," *American Journal of Sociology*, 27:334-343, November, 1921.

within the ranks of their own discipline the basic importance of the group concept in the understanding of social behavior.

Bodenhafer has correctly concluded (23) that the idea of personality as a social product was firmly established in sociology, and that the false dichotomy of extreme realism and extreme nominalism had become obsolescent. It is also true, however, that these theorists were confused in their terminology and inconsistent in their perspectives. Few explicit techniques for group study were formulated or applied; speculative generalizations served in lieu of hypotheses to be tested; and finally, no division of labor was worked out between sociology and the other social sciences for the study or group behavior.

II

Systematic Group Theory. Let us now abandon the historical perspective from which earlier theoretical developments have been considered, and focus attention upon the contemporary status of sociological knowledge with reference to group theory and methodology. As has been noted, earlier theorizing succeeded in pointing up the importance of the group concept, but, with some notable exceptions, failed in developing any explicit conceptualizations and specific formulations for group study. Contemporary sociologists have had to proceed, therefore, without benefit of very much systematic orientation from their predecessors. A major problem confronted has been that of establishing structural points of reference which would provide means for locating the person in social space. Its solution makes the following procedures necessary: "(1) the indication of a man's relations to specific groups, (2) the relation of these groups to each other within a population, and (3) the relation of this population to other populations included in the human universe." (24) These procedures, Sorokin recognizes in his discussion of social space, social distance, and social position, merely pose problems for inquiry.

Definition and Classification. Common awareness of such problems leads into the related problems of group classification. If sociology is to be a science, generalizations must be established, and

---

23. See the last article in Bodenhafer's series in *American Journal of Sociology,* 26:716-743, May, 1921.
24. Pitirim A. Sorokin, *Social Mobility,* (New York: Harper and Bros., 1927), p. 5.

generalizations imply the use of adequately defined classes. Accordingly, a number of sociologists have addressed themselves to the task of establishing more or less comprehensive systems of group classification, and one finds in the literature a variety of taxonomic approaches. The lack of uniformity in them flows in part from the fact that there is no property of phenomena which may not be taken as a reference point.

Earle E. Eubank has given a rather complete summary of classifications which have been used. (25) The seven main types listed from the literature (up to the year 1932) by Eubank are as follows: (1) Ethno-anthropological classifications, such as those used by sociologists as well as anthropologists in dealing with the ethnic or racial divisions of mankind. (2) General social classifications: *e. g.*, Park and Burgess's types of plurels: the family, language groups, local and territorial communities, conflict groups, and accommodation groups. (3) Classifications based on culture levels: societal groupings viewed from an evolutionary perspective as higher and lower, elementary and highly evolved, etc. (4) Classifications based on structure: *e. g.*, Herbert Miller's "vertical groups" and "horizontal groups." (5) Classifications based on function: *e. g.*, institutional as well as "shot-gun" categories, such as Snedden's kinship groups, political groups, company groups, service groups, party groups, religious groups, sociability groups, and "class" groups. (6) Classifications based on the extent of social contact: Sumner's we-group or in-group and they-group or out-group, Cooley's primary group (with secondary group by implication), temporary and relatively permanent groups, Wiese's crowds, groups, and abstract collectivities. (7) Classifications based on the nature of the bond which holds the group together; spontaneous and predetermined groups, independent and dependent groups, *Gemeinschaft* and *Gesellschaft*, ethnic and demotic groups, etc.

In his own treatment of the plurel as a sociological concept, Eubank sets forth three sub-types. Plurel is used as a convenient name "by which to designate any plural number of things referred to as a whole, in contra-distinction from the single units of which the whole is composed . . . From the standpoint of the nature of the connection (whether in mind or in fact) between the several units which constitute a given plurel, three classes are discernible: (1) the

---

25. See *The Concepts of Sociology*, (Boston: D. C. Heath, 1932), Chap. VIII, "Concepts Pertaining to the Human Plurel," pp. 116-171.

SOCIOGRAPHY OF GROUPS

category (class), based on *similarity* (college professors, war veterans); (2) the aggregation, based on *proximity* (crowds, congregations); the *interactivity*, (or group) based upon interaction (the family, the club)" (Page 117). The group is defined as an entity of two or more persons in active or suspended psychic interaction. Eubank's discussion helps to clarify some of the confusion concerning the common language use of the word group in an inexact sense, and to show some less ambiguous uses of the term in a more technical sense.

Yet, a prevailing ambiguity of conceptualization and classification with reference to the group in the whole field of sociology is witnessed in the way the subject is handled in introductory or general textbooks. Those authors who organize the subject matter of sociology primarily in terms of social processes (*e. g.*, Dawson and Gettys) may be expected to give only an incidental topical treatment of groups, but the number of writers who give very little discussion of the subject within other frameworks is indeed surprising. (26) Moreover, the majority of textbooks which do take up the group explicitly and in some detail, manifest an uncertainty and inconsistency about where to place it within their schemes of topical organization. The net result in most instances is a hodgepodge of classifications and generalizations. (27)

---

26. At the other extreme is Emory S. Bogardus's *Sociology*, (New York: The Macmillan Co., 1941), which organizes every chapter around the group concept. The actual use made of the concept in this textbook is so broad, however, that in certain contexts it is rather meaningless. For Bogardus's use of the social distance scale in interpreting intergroup relations, note his article, "Social Distance and Its Practical Implications," *Sociology and Social Research*, 22:462-476, May-June, 1938.

27. Curiously enough, the difficult theoretical task of organizing the whole field of sociology seems to have become the lot primarily of writers of introductory texbooks. In facing this task, some authors apparently have proceeded without any clearly formulated frame of reference or even without awareness of the need for one, whereas others whose treatises are deficient in this respect have implicitly excused themselves by reference to the rather chaotic state of knowledge in the field itself.

It is of interest to compare, for example, the handling of the group concept in the following recent textbooks: R. L. Sutherland and J. L. Woodward, *Introductory Sociology*, (Chicago: J. B. Lippincott Co., 1940); W. F. Ogburn and M. F. Nimkoff, *Sociology*, (Boston: Houghton Mifflin, 1940); Kimball Young, *Sociology*, (New York: American Book Co., 1942); J. L. Gillin and J. P. Gillin, *An Introduction to Sociology*, (New York: The Macmillan Co., 1942); J. L. Bernard, *An Introduction to Sociology*, (New York: Thomas Y. Crowell Co. 1942).

TWENTIETH CENTURY SOCIOLOGY

As a matter of fact, there are only two books by American sociologists which are devoted entirely to an analysis of the group *per se*. These are B. Warren Brown's *Social Groups* and Grace L. Coyle's *Social Process in Organized Groups*. (28) Brown's work discusses the varied nature of groups, the significance of contact, the physical basis of groups and the bases of homogeneity, structure, group dynamics, the interaction of elements within the group, and interrelations between groups. The principal value of this treatise is that it pulls together generalizations about the group which were in sociological use prior to 1926. Coyle's volume is also essentially a work of interpretation and synthesis. Much more specifically than Brown, however, she takes up the following problems: the organized group in the social setting, process of group formation, the determination of members, the evolution of structure, function of leadership, process of communication, morale, the process of collective thinking, and some social functions of organized groups. Both of these treatises are reasonably systematic and comprehensive, but they are based largely upon *ad hoc* generalization derived from common sense observation, and, as a consequence, do not attain a very high level of sociological abstraction.

Systematic Sociography. Empirical research in the sociography of groups still goes on without benefit of much guidance from adequate and comprehensive group theory, but (aside from the earlier work of Wiese) Chapin, Sanderson, Lundberg, and others have made recent contributions toward the development of a more scientific approach. Although Chapin does not always distinguish clearly in an analytical sense between the societal and the cultural aspects of group phenomena, his *Contemporary American Institutions* (29) represents a forward step in the treatment of concrete data (obtained by controlled observation) within an analytical framework. A systematic basis for the classification of groups according to the nature of social contact, and devices for ascertaining and graphically representing group interaction are set forth. His system of classification may be noted in the following table:

---

28. B. Warren Brown, *Social Groups*, (Chicago: The Faithorn Co., 1926), and Grace L. Coyle, *Social Process in Organized Groups*, (New York: Richard R. Smith, 1930). In addition to these works, Richard T. LaPiere's *Collective Behavior*, (New York: McGraw-Hill Book Co., 1938), is in a sense a systematic treatment of the forms of group behavior, but it is written primarily from the point of view of the psychology of social interaction.

29. F. Stuart Chapin, *Contemporary American Institutions*, (New York: Harper and Bros., 1935).

TABLE I. GROUP TYPES AS DIFFERENTIATED BY NATURE OF SOCIAL CONTAC (30) (CHAPIN)

Type of Group	Type of Sensory Contact	Frequency of this Contact	Emotional Intensity of this Contact	Means of Communication	Interdependence and Relationship	Specific Examples of Type
Primary Contact Group (Intimate Contact Group)	Face-to-face, direct sense perceptions of auditory, olfactory	Repeated with same persons at many of same points of contact	Intimate and personal, informal	Oral language, gesture, posture, facial expression	Concrete perceptual elements in the social configuration	Family group, play groups, neighborhood groups
Intermediate Group (Superficial contact group)	Face-to-face, direct sensory perception, auditory, visual	Occasional contacts with different persons at different points	Superficial, formal	As above	Same as above but concrete conceptual elements added	School-room class; audience; local units of Y.M.C.A., Y.W.C.A. Scouts; church, clubs, etc.
Secondary contact Group (Artificial contact Group	Derivative or indirect sense perception, mediated by mechanical means	Contacts at infrequent intervals	Highly impersonal through artificial devices of communication	Telephone, telegraph, radio, printed materials	Abstract conceptual or symbolic elements in the social configuration	Head-quarters of a national society, regional council, board of directors executive committee etc.

30 *Ibid*, p. 162.

[157]

As an outgrowth of his empirical work with rural groupings, (31) Dwight Sanderson has seen the need for more systematic bases for group description and classification, and has attempted to construct inductive categories. Acknowledging that description is only the beginning of analysis, he nonetheless points out the following objectives of group description: (1) for understanding the relation of individuals to the group, and the influences of the group on individuals; (2) for clinical use as ideal types to be used as models in group formation; (3) for determining optimum relations between group structure and functions (with reference to size, power distribution, etc.); (4) for understanding the relation of a given group or group class to other kinds of groups; (5) for policy determination. Sanderson's outline for the description of groups is presented here in abbreviated form:

---

31. *Cf.*, the studies of rural locality groups by Kolb, Brunner, Taylor, Douglass, Zimmerman, and other rural sociologists.

SOCIOGRAPHY OF GROUPS

OUTLINE FOR THE DESCRIPTION OF GROUPS (32)

I. Identity
    A. Group limits (exclusive, restricted, inclusive)
    B. Entrance and exit: voluntary, involuntary, by election
    C. Identification of members: how recognized

II. Composition
    A. Size or number of elements
    B. Homogeneity or diversity of membership
    C. Stratification or uniformation
    D. Permanent or shifting membership; stability or instability

III. Inter-group Relationships
    A. Independent and autonomous
    B. Federated, semi-autonomous
        (etc.)

IV. Intra-group Relationships
    A. Forms of interaction between members
        1. Personal or impersonal, representative, fiduciary
        2. Contacts - frequency and character of
            (etc.)
    B. Spatial relationship (area covered, density or dispersity of group, place of meeting)
    C. Temporal relationships
        1. Temporary, continuous, or seasonal group
        2. History and traditions

V. Structure and Mechanism
    A. Leader, type and origin (how selected and if from group)
    B. Sub-groups, committees
    C. Stated aim and purpose, with or without; unity or diversity; broad or specialized.
    D. Code of behavior for members, definite or lacking (etc.).

---

32. "Group Description," *Social Forces*, 16:313-314, March, 1938.

According to Sanderson's opinion, these "major sets of characters suggest the bases of an adequate description of a group. Elsewhere he has given "A Preliminary Group Classification Based on structure" (33) in which he uses three main categories: involuntary groups, voluntary groups, and delegate groups, with rather elaborate sub-divisions and examples of each. In his comments recognition is given to the fact that classification, description, and analysis are all related aspects of the same problem.

The group concept has been dealt with very systematically by George A Lundberg in his *Foundations of Sociology*. (34) Subsuming groups under the major heading "The Principal Sectors of Society," Lundberg discusses the following topics: a classification of human plurels, types of organic plurels, the classification of groups, types of groups, technic of scientific definition of groups. Like most other theorists, Lundberg is not entirely successful in distinguishing the group from the aggregation or class, but he follows the recent tendency to stress interaction as the distinctly sociological criterion of the group as a variety of human plurel. Non-sociological categories such as age, sex, geographic location, etc., are deemed useful only to the extent that they correlate to a high degree with interactional phenomena. Lundberg correctly points out the futility of the concrete-abstract dichotomy prevailing in some conceptualizations, but erroneously assumes that his epistemological position is the only tenable one. Eschewing most classificatory schemes as being non-scientific, he regards Dodd's S-Theory as affording a satisfactory operational basis for group theory. (35) While stating that criteria of plurel definition and classification may be varied to "suit the needs of empirical research as they arise," Lundberg nonetheless insists upon the desirability of rigorous definition, with

---

33. *Social Forces,* 17: 1-6, December, 1938.

34. See Chapter IX, "Types of Groups, in *Foundations of Sociology,* (New York: The Macmillan Co., 1939), pp. 339-374.

35. See Stuart C. Dodd, *Dimensions of Society,* (New York: The Macmillan Co., 1942). Despite the enthusiasm of Lundberg and a few other sociologists for Dodd's ambitious theorizing in his self-styled "quantitative systematics for the social sciences," the reception of this work has been on the whole very unfavorable. The general consensus is that it merely develops a formal system of notation which is of dubious value in the research process. *Cf.* the reviews of the treatise by Ethel Shanas (*American Journal of Sociloogy,* 48: 214-230, September, 1942), E. T. Bell (*American Sociological Review,* 7:707-709, October, 1942), and Talcott Parsons (*Ibid.,* 709-714).

the description of phenomena in quantitative units as a model procedure.

In his article, "Some Problems of Group Classification and Measurement," (36) Lundberg has essayed a formal schematics of group interaction patterns on a strictly logical basis, and explores certain theoretical possibilities of permutation and combination as over against the numerous empirical modes which have been in actual use. A similar type of procedure has been set forth more exhaustively by Karl Menger as a "survey of all forms of organization conceivable in given situations." (37) Although Menger's theory appears to be mostly an exercise in formal logic, he claims that it "may eventually prove of considerable practical importance."

Current Empirical Approaches. Shifting the focus of examination from the delimited literature of group theory to the highly ramified literature of empirical research, one encounters a critical problem of a different magnitude. In the first place, the number and variety of empirical inquiries is so enormous that comprehensive and systematic presentation within brief compass is impossible. In the second place, the investigation of specific groups is the common meeting ground of research of all the social sciences, and only a detailed exposition could differentiate between the non-sociological and the distinctly sociological. About all that can be done here is to point out some of the principal methodological approaches which are in current use, and to indicate some of the main types of groups which have been given special research attention.

The experimental approach to group study has been pursued more intensively on the whole by social psychologists than by any other investigators. Earlier studies of group behavior under conditions of more or less controlled observation have been summarized by the Murphys in their book, *Experimental Social Psychology.* (38) Reference is made to Moede's experiments in rivalry in the group, and to the work of Mayer, Schmidt, and other German educators with the school as a laboratory for group effects; there

---

36. *American Sociological Review,* 5: 351-360, June, 1940.

37. "An Exact Theory of Social Groups and Relations," *American Journal of Sociology,* 43:790-798, March, 1938.

38. Gardner and Lois B. Murphy, *Experimental Social Psychology,* (New York: Harper and Bros., 1931). See Part III, "General Laws of Interaction in Our Own Society," pp. 445-558. Note also the revised edition of this work brought out by the same authors, together with Theodore M. Newcomb, in 1937.

is also a citation of the studies by F.H. Allport and Donald Laird in social facilitation as approaches to the problem of the individual in the group situation. Studies of social behavior in the cooperating group have been made by H.T. Moore, M.H. Landis, H.E. Burtt, and numerous others. An excellent summary of results which have been obtained from studies of the behavior of children in groups may be found in an article by John E. Anderson. (39) The findings are arranged according to a developmental series showing the normal transition of the infant from solitary activity in the presence of others to the highly complicated process of participation in which the older child engages. Reference is made to studies of social organization, social attachments, motivation within the group, and to differentiation of function within the group. A notable feature of most of these studies is the rigorous use of controlled observation in the study of specified variables, in contrast to the introspective and speculative procedures employed by earlier — as well as later — psychologists and sociologists. The methods and specific techniques used are varied, and hence what may be called the experimental approach is not necessarily identified with any particular modes of manipulating data and is not to be taken as mutually exclusive with reference to other types to be considered.

In general, research in the sociography of groups utilizes the methods and techniques found elsewhere in the social as well as the physical sciences. Some of these methods are more applicable than others, of course, and thus are more extensively used in group study. Nonetheless, certain modes of inquiry have been variously advocated as being peculiarly well adapted to this field. One of these is topological psychology, as set forth most comprehensively by Kurt Lewin and J.F. Brown. (40) Borrowing the basic idea of topology from mathematics, Lewin and his followers have attempted to build a systematic construction of social space within which the "movement" of persons and groups in life situations may be graph-

---

39. "The Development of Social Behavior," *American Journal of Sociology*, 44:839-857, May, 1939.

40. See Kurt Lewin, *Principles of Topological Psychology*, (New York: McGraw-Hill Book Co., 1936), and J. F. Brown, *Psychology and the Social Order*, (New York: McGraw-Hill Book Co., 1936). Consult also the experimental studies by Lewin and his students at the University of Iowa; e. g., Kurt Lewin and Ronald Lippitt, "An Experimental Approach to the Study of Autocracy and Democracy; a Preliminary Note," *Sociometry,* 1: 292-300, January-April, 1938.

SOCIOGRAPHY OF GROUPS

ically represented. The life space is supposedly made a dynamic structure where all problems of position and locomotion may be adequately treated. From the point of view of causation, representation and explanation are not separated. Despite the claims topologists make for unique methodological insights into group locomotion, goals, unity, stratification, and so on, topology is in large part merely a pedagogical or graphic mode of representing findings which are obtained by well-known and fundamentally different procedures. Thus far, topological psychology *as such* has yielded no new problems, insights, or data.

A superficially similar but much more fruitful approach to the study of the group is found in sociometry. Directing attention toward actual situations rather than toward abstractions, sociometry is purported to be first a theory and then a method. (41) The adherents of sociometry maintain that it is not only a novel set of sociographic techniques for using spatial symbols (numbered circles, meshworks of various kinds of connecting lines, special charts, formulas, etc.) to represent such group relationships as attraction and repulsion, but also a method for discovering these relationships and using the derived knowledge for purposes of prediction and control. Most of the methods employed are either implicitly or explicitly quantitative (as the meaning of the term *sociometry* indicates), and hence they have been applied most widely to those aspects of group behavior which lend themselves most easily to quantification. Chapin gives a classification of the leading types of studies as follows:

> The measurement of interaction within the social group may be further broken down into five sub-types of rating scale. There are first those scales or procedures that attempt to measure informal friendship constellations and

---

41. The most comprehensive monograph in the field is Jacob L. Moreno's *Who Shall Survive? (New Approach to the Problem of Human Interrelations,* (Washington, D. C.: Nervous and Mental Disease Publishing Co., 1934). This volume describes some of Moreno's concrete studies and also sets forth his theory; for Moreno's more recent theoretical formulations, note especially the following articles in the journal, *Sociometry*: "Remarks on the Foundation of the Sociometric Institute," 2:v-ix, May, 1942; "Sociometry in Action," 2:298-315, August, 1942; "Sociometry and the Cultural Order," 6:299-344, August, 1943.

seem to get at the latent culture patterns of a group of people. Illustrations of this technique are afforded in the recent work of Moreno, Lundberg, Loomis, and Franz. These are studies within institutions, villages, the school room, and other groups . . . In the second place there have been rating scales and experimental studies that center upon the description and analysis of the informal play groups of children and young persons. Illustrations of this technique are afforded by the work of Parten, Thomas, Arrington, and Newstetter and his co-workers. The third type of measurement of social interaction as embodied in its effects upon social institutions is through the study of formal organizations, and designated by a scale to measure social participation. Here I have in mind my own work in 1924 and more recently described by results in 1939. The fourth type of effort to measure the interaction process or its results is seen in the various scales to measure social distance by Bogardus in 1925, by Dodd in 1935, by Chapin in 1934, and most recently by Zeleny. Finally, the fifth sub-type of measurement of social interaction or its effects is illustrated by Williams' scale for the grading of neighborhoods in 1916, and most recently (1933) by the extremely interesting scale by Jessie Bernard to measure neighborhood folkways. (42).

As the preceding remarks show, sociometric techniques have wide applications. Ogburn, Queen, Thomas, Thorndike, and others have used them in the study of larger cities; Kirkpatrick, Burgess, and Cottrell have used them for studying marital pairs and family groups; however, these applications are primarily to statistical categories or classes of individuals rather than to interacting groups. Most empirical studies in this country have been made since the middle of the past decade. The May 1942 issue of the journal, *Sociometry*, lists eight studies of resettlement communities by Loomis and Davidson. Other types of communities studied have been the primitive community, the rural community, the urban community, and the closed community; these inquiries total about three dozen. About the same number of studies has been made within the last fifteen years of educational institutions, ranging from kindergartens and nursery schools, through boarding schools, summer camps, college and universities. About half a dozen studies have been made of fraternities and sororities. Other groupings so studied

---

42. F. Stuart Chapin, "Trends in Sociometrics and Critique," *Sociometry*, 3:252-253, 1940. This article gives full citations on the references included in the quotation above. See also George A. Lundberg, *Social Research*, (New York: Longmans, Green, 1942), Ch. X, "Sociometric Methods in Ecology and Interpersonal Relations," pp. 325-332.

SOCIOGRAPHY OF GROUPS

are religious congregations, department stores, ethnic groupings, and so on. (43)

Sociometry has been criticized as a faddish cult, but objective appraisal indicates that it is one of the most significant developments in the field of group study. The vogue of sociometry is in part a result of the fact that it enjoys the scientific asset of specific and readily communicable techniques of observation and description. Moreover, in the process of observation and delineation, sociometric methods have resulted in the discovery of hitherto obscured sources of group adjustment and maladjustment. Yet, sociometry also has its limitations, some of which are acknowledged and some of which are not acknowledged by sociometrists. Techniques employed in observation and representation are applicable primarily to highly restricted variables within small groups. Important problems of meaning and motive are largely side-stepped or ignored, and elaborately objective superstructures of methodology are frequently erected upon highly subjective initial data (*e. g.*, when the inexpert verbalizations of lay informants are used). On the whole, however, the sociometric approach appears to be a definite step in the advancement of sociography as a science.

---

43. The following titles may serve to indicate the range of recent work: Charles P. Loomis, "Social Relationships and Institutions in Seven New Rural Communities," Washington, D. C.: Social Research Report, No. XVIII, Bureau of Agricultural Economics, January, 1940; *idem.*, "Culture of a Contemporary Rural Community," (with Olen Leonard), Washington, D. C.: Rural Life Studies No. 1, Bureau of Agricultural Economics, November, 1941; George A. Lundberg, "Social Attraction Patterns in a Rural Village—A Preliminary Report," *Sociometry*, 1:77-80, July-October, 1937; Lundberg and Margaret Lawsing, "The Sociography of Some Community Relations," *American Sociological Review*, 2:318-335, June, 1937; Florence B. Moreno, "Sociometric Status of Children in a Nursery School Group," *Sociometry*, 2: 395-411, August, 1942; Francis M. Vreeland, "Social Relations in the College Fraternity," *Sociometry*, 2:151-162, May, 1942; Irwin T. Sanders, "The Social Contacts of a Bulgarian Village,"*Rural Sociology*, 4:315-327, September, 1939; *idem.*, "Neighborhoods and Neighborly Relations in a Bulgarian Village;" *Social Forces*, 17:532-537, May, 1939; Leslie D. Zeleny, "Sociometry of Morale," *American Sociological Review*, 4: 799-808, December, 1939; *idem.*, "Objective Studies of Group Leaders," *Sociology and Social Research*, March-April, 1940, 326-336; Helen H. Jennings, *Leadership and Isolation: A Study of Personality in Inter-Personal Relations*, (New York: Longmans, Green, 1943); Albert J. Murphy, "A Study of the Leadership Process," *American Sociological Review*, 6:674-687, October, 1941; Wilber I. Newstetter, "An Experiment in the Defining and Measuring of Group Adjustment," *American Sociological Review*, 2:230-236, April, 1937.

TWENTIETH CENTURY SOCIOLOGY

The need for obtaining data on group relations through direct observations has led in recent years to a more systematic formulation of what is known as the participant-observer method or technique. Essentially a mode of approach rather than a definite method or technique, it represents an attempt by social scientists to conceptualize and objectify procedures which have long been employed rather loosely by novelists, journalists, and others. (44) Another frame of reference, the typological approach to group study, although rarely employed by sociologists, appears to afford many possibilities for the comparative study of groups. An example of this type of treatment is found in the present writer's book, *The Academic Man*. (45) In this monograph the social system or group organization of the university is described and analyzed as a typological construct with which the deviations of specified university groupings may be compared and contrasted.

Group research of an empirical type might also be classified from the point of view of the data studied. Whether the community is to be regarded as a social group depends upon the frame of reference used and the identifiable elements found in direct observation. In the vast literature on the community one finds the concept used in the sense of a locally organized society and also as a locality group. As E.T. Hiller has pointed out: "While the phraseology of this literature is suggestive of the idea that a community is a group, the actual treatment does not distinguish a group from the total local societal system, comprising culture complexes and interrelations characteristic of society in the abstract." (46) Although *community* is one of the most vaguely defined concepts in sociology, the methods employed in community analysis are in the main those used for the study of groups. (47) The fact that the

---

44. See Florence R. Kluckholn, "The Participant-Observer Technique in Small Communities," *American Journal of Sociology*, 46:331-343, November, 1940; note also Edward Y. Hartshorne, "Undergraduate Society and the College Culture," *American Sociological Review*, 8:321-332, June, 1943, for suggestions as to applications in the study of informal groups in colleges and universities.

45. Logan Wilson, *The Academic Man*, (New York: Oxford University Press, 1942).

46. "The Community as a Social Group," *American Sociological Review*, 6: 189, April, 1941.

47. For community theory, note the following: R. M. MacIver, *Community, A Sociological Study*; Dwight Sanderson, *The Rural Community;* Carle C. Zimmerman, *The Changing Community; American Journal of Sociology*, 46, May, 1941.

SOCIOGRAPHY OF GROUPS

physical locus of most groups is within the community makes its territorial limits a convenient basis for defining the boundary lines of concrete inquiry, but likewise frequently results in a confused frame of reference between geographic and social space. (48) There are, accordingly, numerous generalized studies of group behavior as delimited by the confines of a particular village, town, or city, and similarly, specialized studies of the prison, hospital, or some other particularized form.

The task of classifying group researches according to the nature of the data explored is, of course, an endless one. Since the data of sociological inquiry are, in the language of Bertrand Russell, "soft" rather than "hard," what is perceived depends upon the perspective. Within a single monograph, there may be present one or many taxonomic points of reference. Some studies concentrate upon the relations between personality and the group as the focus (49), others stress the size of the group in relation to interaction (50), still others emphasize the intensity and quality of group interaction as reflected in morale (51), *esprit de corps*, and so on.

---

48. For example, the neighborhood has been variously taken as an areal concept and as a primary-group concept, and many community studies do not clearly differentiate between ecology and sociography. Monographs on the community *per se* are too numerous to cite here, but the following titles are illustrative of inquiries which concentrate upon group interaction within specified communities: Mirra Komarovsky, "A Comparative Study of Volunteer Organizations of Two Suburban Communities," *Publications of the American Sociological Society,* 27: 83-93, May, 1933; Lloyd A. Cook and others, "Teacher and Community Relations," *American Sociological Review,* 3:167-174, April, 1938; A. I. Tannous, "Group Behavior in the Village Community of Lebanon," *American Journal of Sociology,* 48:231-239, September, 1942. For an attempt to distinguish between "real" and "fictitious" groups, see P. A. Sorokin, C. C. Zimmerman, and C. J. Galpin, *A Systematic Source Book in Rural Sociology,* (Minneapolis: Univ. of Minnesota Press, 1930), Vol. I. p. 307 f.

49. See E. W. Burgess, ed., *Personality and the Group,* (Chicago: University of Chicago Press, 1929); *American Journal of Sociology,* 44, May, 1939.

50. See C. Horace Hamilton, "Some Factors Affecting the Size of Rural Groups in Virgina," *American Journal of Sociology,* 36: 424-434, November, 1930; Howard Becker and Ruth H. Useem, "Sociological Analysis of the Dyad," *American Sociological Review,* 7: 13-26, February 1942.

51. See Robert E. Park, "Industrial Fatigue and Group Morale," *American Journal of Sociology,* 40:349-356, November, 1934; T. North Whitehead, "Social Relationships in the Factory: A Study of an Industrial Group," *The Human Factor* 9: 3:16, November, 1935; F. J. Roethlisberger and W. J. Dickson, *Management and the Worker,* (Cambridge: Harvard University Press, 1940); and also the miscellaneous studies by Delbert C. Miller, Leslie D. Zeleny and others.

The most exhaustively studied of all groups from a sociological point of view is the family, and in the literature on the family may be found almost every conceivable emphasis. The literature of social anthropology also contains manifold treatises on the family and more extended kinship groups.

In short, an examination of the literature does bear out our introductory statement that group classification, description, and analysis is one of the most extended phases of sociological inquiry. The ramified character and uneven quality of the research, however, makes any discriminating appreciation of the results which have emerged extremely difficult.

III

If there were anything in sociology which had such unequivocal utility and universal acceptance as the atomic theory in physics, the Periodic Table of Mendelyev in chemistry, or even the Linnaean system in botany, this discourse possibly would have been shorter, and the array of conceptualizations certainly neater. Whether the conceptual schemes of natural science afford the only appropriate models for social science is a moot point which need not be discussed here. The point of direct relevance is that in sociology many useful approaches exist side by side, and are by no means mutually exclusive. Some of the earlier ideas of this century have been displaced as erroneous, others survive and are still utilized. Even at the present time, the sociography of groups lacks an integrated body of theory and is characterized by some crude empiricism, but inquiry has come a long way since the few decades ago when psychologists and sociologists were arguing abut "the ennobling vs. the degrading" effects of the crowd and were spinning words around the "group mind."

This advance is seen in the more careful definition of terms, the use of controlled observation, the diminution of a tendency toward unfounded generalization, the common realization of a need for systematization, the development of more effective methods and techniques of study, and the conjoining of theory and application. Yet, group description and analysis is in the main today part art and part science. (52) The latter, moreover, is on the level of a

---

52. To say that many studies are non-scientific and that others do not attain a high level of scientific abstraction is not to condemn them. The Gestaltist approach is not a rigorously scientific method, but it has been used very successfully to gain insight into particular configurations; one notable illustration is Willard Waller's study of divorce (the broken dyad).

SOCIOGRAPHY OF GROUPS

descriptive science which stresses the relations of symbols to events rather than on the level of an explanatory science which stresses the relations of symbols to one another. There are few "laws" of group behavior that are known to have a universal application.

Despite the fact that simple, useable definitions of the group are available (*e. g.*, Wiese's), some investigators persist in the use of vague, subjective concepts which fail to make the observed data independent of the observer, and others would perpetrate the fallacy of misplaced abstractness with concepts indiscriminately appropriated from physical science. (53) In current sociological literature one finds no consensus as to the meaning of the *group* —ethnic minorities, propaganda recipients, street car passengers, white-collar workers, and so on, are variously referred to as "groups." There seems to be no general understanding that the group is a plurel with some kind of internal structure.

Furthermore, the lack of an adequate classificatory system precludes the full view of group inter-relations, and postpones any consideration of society as a "coordinated set of differentiated groups." Most of the make-shift empirical schemes of classification and analysis have logical inconsistences, but the logically consistent schemes tend to have the shortcoming of limited applicability. Neither approach has succeeded in reducing to an ordered and verifiable symmetry the multitude of ways in which society has *already* classified its members.

There are many other problems yet to be solved. Since groups are functioning wholes, there is a need for more comprehensive and exhaustive studies of particular groups. Focusing their attention upon one aspect of the group over a short time span, or else shifting their focus from one recurrence to another, few sociologists have taken the time and trouble to study the finer configurations of any given group. Here the Gestalt perspective has much to recommend it. Likewise, the participant-observer approach over a long period of years would yield insights not disclosed by the meth-

---

53. This fallacy is illustrated by the following definition: "From this point of view, *any* social group may be regarded as a system of energy flowing through intersecting channels, eddying around every person and between persons in myriads of forms in different sizes, degrees, directions, and durations. These dynamics stand in the same relation to the more obvious social events that the atomic structure of matter stands to our understanding of the events of the 'physical' world." George A. Lundberg and Margaret Lawsing, "The Sociography of Some Community Relations," p. 334.

ods of summary statistical compilation. Sociometry has yielded techniques for the exact study and representation of limited relationships, but these techniques need to be extended, and others of comparable specificity should be devised for inquiry into complex situations. The structures and functions of informal groups have received some analysis; in view of their social importance they deserve wider investigation, and more means must be evolved to get at areas of hitherto inaccesssible data. Similarly, the same systematic observation which has been applied to surface organization should be given to inner workings and to inter-group relations.

Finally, there are two cleavages requiring correction. One is the tendency to separate qualitative insight and quantitative technique. The other (more serious in scope) is to separate theory and application. A corollary of this separation has been a neglect of applied aspects, stemming in part from the understandable desire of sociologists to gain more scientific status for their field in living down its earlier reputation as a refuge for reformers and "do gooders." The purification process has gone so far in some quarters, however, that it threatens to emasculate utility. Although the banner under which work is carried on is socially unimportant, there is no net gain for sociology when this evasion results in the lay referral of practical problems of group organization to psychiatrists, psychologists, educationists, and welfare workers. Yet, many sociological concepts have been incorporated in the therapeutic work of Moreno, in the industrial studies of Mayo, Roethlisberger, and Dickson, and in the group work approaches of Coyle, Slavson, Newstetter, and others. Sociologists are collaborating with anthropologists (see the journal, *Applied Anthropology*) in solving problems of community organization. Working with economists and other specialists, sociologists in the U.S. Department of Agriculture are doing theoretically sound work of a practical nature. These are encouraging trends. All in all, no other phase of sociological inquiry promises as much practicable significance as the sociography of groups.

SELECTED BIBLIOGRAPHY

The American Journal of Sociology, 44, May, 1939.

Becker, Howard and Ruth H. Useem, "Sociological Analysis of the Dyad," *American Sociological Review*, 7:13-26, February, 1942.

Bodenhafer, Walter B., "The Comparative Role of the Group Concept in Ward's *Dynamic Sociology* and Contemporary American Sociology," *American*

SOCIOGRAPHY OF GROUPS

Journal of Sociology, 26:273-314, November, 1920; 26:425-474, January, 1921; 26:588-600, March, 1921; 26:716-743, May, 1921.

Burgess, E. W., ed., *Personality and the Group,* (Chicago: University of Chicago Press, 1929).

Chapin, F. Stuart, "Trends in Sociometrics and Techniques," *Sociometry,* 3:245-262, 1940.

Coyle, Grace L., *Social Process in Organized Groups,* (New York: Richard R. Smith, 1930).

Eubank, Earle A., *The Concepts of Sociology,* (Boston: D. C. Heath, 1932).

Jennings, Helen H., *Leadership and Isolation: A Study of Personality in Inter-Personal Relations,* (New York: Longmans, Green, 1943).

Lundberg, George A., *Foundations of Sociology,* (New York: The Macmillan Co., 1939).

Lundberg, George A., "Some Problems of Group Classification and Measurement,"*American Sociological Review,* 5:351-360, June, 1940.

Lundberg, George A., and Margaret Lawsing, "The Sociography of Some Community Relations," *American Sociological Review,* 2:318-335, June, 1937.

Moreno, Jacob L., *Who Shall Survive?* (Washington, D. C.: Nervous and Mental Disease Publishing Co., 1934).

Roethlisberger, F. J., and W. J. Dickson, *Management and the Worker,* Cambridge: Harvard University Press, 1940).

Sanderson, Dwight, "Group Description," *Social Forces,* 16:309-319, March, 1938.

Sanderson, Dwight, "A Preliminary Structural Classification of Groups," *Social Forces,* 17:1-6, December, 1938.

Simmel, Georg, *Soziologie,* (Leipzig: Duncker und Humblot, 1908).

Wiese, Leopol i von, and Howard Becker, *Systematic Sociology,* (New York: John Wiley and Sons, 1932).

Logan Wilson, Ph. D. (Harvard), is Professor of Sociology and Dean of Newcomb College (Tulane University), New Orleans, Louisiana. He has formerly had teaching and research affiliations in sociology with University of Kentucky, Tulane University (College of Arts and Sciences), University of Maryland, University of Texas, Massachusetts Community Study Project, and Harvard University. Professor Wilson is a member of the American Sociological Society, Southern Sociological Society, Southwestern Political and Social Science Association, Ohio Valley Sociological Society, and the Louisiana Academy of Sciences; he is a member of the Executive Committee of the Southwestern Sociological Society, the Membership Committee of the American Sociological Society, and the Advisory Board of the *Journal of Legal and Political Sociology.* He has written *The Academic Man,* (New York: Oxford University Press, 1942), and has contributed articles to: *Journal of Criminal Law and Criminology, Social Forces, American Sociological Review, The Southwestern Social Science Quarterly, The American Journal of Psychology, Proceedings of the Louisiana Academy of Sciences, Journal of Social Philosophy, Bulletin of the AAUP, Sociology and Social Research,* etc.

CHAPTER VIII

SOCIAL ORGANIZATION AND INSTITUTIONS

by

FLORIAN ZNANIECKI

I

Lack of Coherent Theory as Symptom of a Period of Transition. A malicious critic of sociology could hardly find a better way of arousing scepticism about its scientific status than by collecting the definitions given by sociologists of "social organization," on the one hand, of "institutions," on the other hand, and comparing the various ways in which relationships between "organization" and "institutions" are conceived. That is how we tried to begin our survey of this part of twentieth century sociology — and it proved to be the worst possible beginning. It is absolutely impossible to introduce any logical order into the present terminological chaos. The efforts made by some theorists have demonstrated this conclusively. For instance, Hertzler, before building his theory, conscientiously tried to construct a kind of "composite sociological conception" of social institution as defined in sociological literature.

SOCIAL ORGANIZATION

(1) Anyone who may be tempted to repeat this performance should first read carefully the relevant paragraph in Hertzler's book.

Undoubtedly, terminological confusion is a defect of sociology as a science, as has often been stated, and certain groups of sociologists are trying to remedy it. But how serious is this defect? Is it symptomatic of a lack of objectively valid knowledge of the phenomena designated by such divergent terms? Or does it merely manifest a lack of professional agreement among sociologists as to the use of particular terms? We believe the latter to be the main source of the prevalent confusion. Sociologists have not yet generally and fully accepted the professional standards of symbolic communication which are recognized as binding in older and more stabilized sciences. Many a sociologist who uses a new type of approach to a certain field of research is inclined to overemphasize those aspects of his data which he investigates, making little or no effort to connect his investigation constructively with that of other sociologists who have used different approaches to the same field; and his terminology expresses his exclusiveness.

· We have decided, therefore, to consider existing definitions as purely heuristic devices which symbolize preliminary attempts to circumscribe a field of research with reference to certain theoretic problems that sociologists have been trying to solve. From this point of view, the lack of terminological agreement among twentieth-century sociologists becomes highly instructive, for it indicates a rapid and many-sided development of scientific problematization. This development has been guided by the assumption that there is a field of investigation commonly designated by the combined terms "social organization and institutions," and that this field, however vaguely circumscribed and diversely conceived, has an objective order. A comprehensive and well-systematized theory of this order was completed before the end of the nineteenth century: Herbert Spencer's *The Principles of Sociology*. (2) Most of the important new problems which emerged during the last decade of the nineteenth and the first decades of the twentieth century can't be either genet-

---

1. Joyce O. Hertzler, *Social Institutions*, (New York: McGraw-Hill Book Co., 1929), p. 7.

2. First edition, 3. vols., (London, 1876-1896). As we have no access to this edition and subsequent editions have different paginations, we quote not volumes and pages, but paragraphs, which are numbered consecutively throughout the work..

ically traced back to his great work or at least logically referred to it.

From the very first, several divergent trends branched off from the original stem, each progressively embracing a wider and still wider range of facts. Following these trends, we find all of them eventually reaching a stage when it becomes obvious that, whatever the objective order in this field of investigation, it is much more complicated than originally thought: neither an improved modification of the Spencerian theory nor any of the synthetic theories which have been substituted for it can give a systematization of the inductive knowledge about this field, still less furnish an adequate heuristic framework for further research.

During the twentieth century, however, another special branch of sociological investigation, at first narrower in scope and relatively neglected, has been rapidly expanding and perfecting its methods. In the last two decades or so, it has successfully approached on a limited scale many of the specific problems within the field we are discussing. By now, we believe, it is ready to take over the task which none of the existing theories of "social organization and institutions" are capable of performing. It cannot yet offer a synthesis of existing factual knowledge, but it does offer at least a way of building gradually by inductive methods a new and coherent theory on firm factual foundations.

The Sociological Synthesis of Herbert Spencer. Two leading methodological principles of universal applicability are used by Spencer in constructing his sociological synthesis. First, sociology — like every science — is an objective, comparative study of natural *systems;* secondly, social systems — like all systems — evolve in the course of time and must be investigated in the very *process* of their evolution.

The systems which sociology investigates are "societies." A society is a system which includes as elementary units biopsychological individuals who inhabit a definite geographical area for a length of time encompassing the life-periods of a number of successive generations. These individuals aggregate in space, forming more or less numerous and lasting groups. However, "the mere gathering of individuals into a group does not constitute them into a society. A society, in the sociological sense, is formed only when, besides juxtaposition, there is cooperation . . . Cooperation . . . is at once

SOCIAL ORGANIZATION

that which cannot exist without a society and that for which society exists." (3) And cooperation implies organization.

A society is like an individual living body and unlike an anorganic system, in that it is a unity of differentiated and mutually dependent parts, each of which cooperates with the others for the benefit of the whole. The organization of a society involves both a differentiation individually, in classes, or in groups, of the human beings who compose it and a specialization of their activities. The total combination of these unlike and mutually dependent parts constitutes the structure of the society; their specialized and mutually dependent activities are functionally combined with reference to a common aim, which is the maintenance of the society as a unity in existence. There is a definite parallelism between social structures and functions and the structures and functions of individual organisms, in that both include sustaining, distributing, and regulating organs. (4)

In the course of social evolution, many numerically small and spacially isolated societies with a simple organization become integrated into numerically larger societies covering extensive territories, and this progressive integration is accompanied by a growing complexity of organization. In such large and complex societies, each part develops a structural differentiation and a functional specialization within itself, thus becoming a system within the more inclusive system. "As it is true of a society that the maintenance of its existence is the aim of its . . . specialized parts, so it is true of its specialized parts that the dominant aim of each is to maintain itself." (5)

The so-called "social organicists," who put biological and social systems in the same category, consistently use the term "organ" to denote such "parts" of a society. Spencer, however, recognizes "society" as a distinct category of organic system and uses the biological parallel merely for heuristic purposes, as helpful in describing similarities between the two categories; he drops the term "organ" as soon as the parallel has fulfilled its purpose and substitutes the term "institution."

But some of Spencer's terms have caused misunderstandings. Words like "cooperation" and "aim" seem to imply purposeful

---

3. *The Principles of Sociology,* No. 440.
4. *Ibid.* No. 238 to No. 255 (Part II, Ch. VI, VII, VIII, IX).
5. *Ibid.,* No. 444.

volition. However, Spencer rejects this implication: although the human beings who are the units of a society are conscious beings, it need not follow that they must be aware in advance of the total result to be achieved by their combined activities and intentionally aim to achieve this result. Purposive, consciously organized cooperation does indeed exist, but the bearing of its results upon the maintenance of society is seldom, if ever, fully anticipated by the agents. The telic character of social organization grows by a natural process which follows the general laws of evolution; the individuals who participated in it not only did not plan it, but are not even fully aware of it after it has evolved. It takes sociology to discover it, just as it takes biology to discover the telic character of the organization of a living body. (6)

If sociology is a science of societies as organized systems and if the specialized parts or institutions which together constitute the organization of a society are mutually dependent, one would expect Spencer to devote his main effort to a comparative study of particular societies as total systems. Whereas we find that the main bulk of his work is given to a comparative study of specific institutions abstracted from the total organization of the societies in which they are found. Spencer has been widely criticized by anthropologists and historians for this tendency to isolate institutional phenomena from their concrete social and cultural background. And there is no doubt that his abstractions have often been hasty and his generalizations superficial. But he did not use this approach without reason. He thought that few generalizations can be drawn from a comparative study of total societies that are not already implied in his general theory of society as a category of organic system. (7) But an analytic and genetic investigation of institutions as common components of all societies seemed to offer a wide and fruitful field for sociological comparison and generalization. And certainly few scientific works in any branch of knowledge contain so many theoretically significant hypotheses as Spencer's systematic comparative studies of the six general classes into which

---

6. Emile Durkheim, as Harry Alpert points out, tried to clarify this situation by explicitly requiring that, in studying social institutions, problems of causation and problems of function be treated separately. See Harry Alpert, *Emile Durkheim and His Sociology*, (New York: Columbia University Press, 1939), pp. 106-7.

7. *The Principles of Sociology*, Nos. 256-263.

SOCIAL ORGANIZATION

he subdivides social institutions. It does not detract from the importance of this work that most of his specific hypotheses have been either rejected or greatly modified: the essential point is that, unlike many speculative doctrines in the history of social thought, they could be tested by facts and were considered to be worth testing.

Present Survivals of Spencer's Theory. Before discussing the new trends which by inductive research have progressively invalidated the Spencerian synthesis, we may note how much of this synthesis is still explicitly or implicitly accepted in current sociological reflection. This can best be ascertained by comparing the content of general textbooks of sociology and of systematic works on social institutions destined for the use of college students. From this point of view we have surveyed most of the textbooks published in America since 1920. Lack of space does not permit us to substantiate our conclusions by specific references. We can merely state that, although these books differ widely in principles and methods of scientific systematization and almost every one of them contains some original and valuable contributions to sociological theory, yet in the majority of them the following Spencerian ideas are accepted as at least approximately valid, even if the part played by these ideas in the total work differs from case to case.

1. "Societies" exist as a definable logical class of separate entities, each of which can be identified and circumscribed in such a way as to be clearly distinguishable from other entities of the same class.

2. The elementary units of a society are biopsychological human beings who are completely incorporated into it (though they can leave it and move into another society).

3. The human beings who are included in a society form a demographic whole, i. e., compose the integral population of a definite geographical area.

4. A society is organized and its organization consists of institutions in which individuals participate by regularly performing differentiated and interdependent activities.

5. Every society has at least three out of the six Spencerian kinds of institutions which are essential for its continued existence as well as for the existence of the individuals who are included in it. These are: domestic institutions (often simply termed "the fam-

ily"), political institutions (sometimes fused together into "the State") and industrial institutions (the term "economic institutions" being usually added or substituted). Most textbooks also accept as essential the institutions which Spencer called "ecclesiastical," though the term and the very concept may be changed to that of "the church" or to that of "religious institutions." The remaining two Spencerian classes of institutions — "ceremonial" and "professional" — have not received such wide recognition, while other kinds of institutions which Spencer did not recognize as distinct categories are added to the list.

Thus, the essential nucleus of Spencer's theory of society is still being transmitted to most college students, notwithstanding the new problems raised and the new discoveries made in the course of the last fifty years which, as we shall see, make it theoretically untenable.

Society vs. the Individual. During most of this period, two seemingly contradictory philosophies were struggling for predominance. One of them, sometimes called "social realism," assumed an objective reality of society, irreducible to any combination of individuals, and often asserted that the human individual as a conscious being had no existence apart from the concrete existence of society. The other philosophy, called by its opponents "social atomism," claimed that the individual was the only objective, empirically ascertainable entity and that society was a subjective conceptual construct, if not a mere name, to which nothing real corresponded but a plurality of interacting individuals.

However, when these philosophies were applied to the methodical study of social phenomena, their opposition proved much less radical than it had seemed in ontological speculation. For the postulate that social phenomena had an objective existence and were irreducible to individual phenomena did not necessarily lead to the conclusion that *society* in the sense of an all-inclusive unity of social phenomena was objectively real; while the contrary postulate that social phenomena were ultimately founded in facts of interaction between individuals did not preclude the possibility that they were a synthesis rather than a mere combination of facts of interaction and that they had to be studied as a specific kind of objective data. It must also be kept in mind that the ontological antithesis between "individual" and "society" was subjected during the period

SOCIAL ORGANIZATION

under discussion to penetrating criticism by such thinkers as Fouillée, Royce, Cooley, and others.

Society as a Psychological Whole. We shall follow first the evolution of social realism, which began with attempts to supplement or to supersede the conception of society as an objective reality, embodied in Spencer's *Principles.* The chief point of contention was the adequacy of the organic analogy in describing the unity of human societies. Another analogy had been initiated long before, but was fully developed only toward the end of the century. It was psychological rather than biological. The unity of society was conceived as parallel or similar to the unity of an individual's conscious life, if not to an individual "mind" or "soul."

However, the attempts to develop a systematic theory of "society" as a "psyche", an integral, conscious entity, were few and not very successful. (8) The conception of a psychological unity of society generally meant that the individuals belonging to a society were bound together by a community of ideas, emotions, and volitions which made each of them think and act not as an isolated, self-contained mental unit, but as component of a larger whole. This conception was used to supplement rather than to supplant the Spencerian theory, since the latter did not seem to fit the facts when applied to simpler societies and folk communities. According to Spencer's general evolutionary hypothesis, "lower," "primitive" or "savage" societies, representing earlier stages of evolution from aggregates to systems, "from incoherent homogeneity" to "coherent heterogeneity," should have been less unified than more developed societies. But this logical deduction was discredited by observation, which showed that lower societies had a high degree of unity, that their individual members were more completely absorbed by the group than members of a higher society, apparently not because of their greater dependence upon others for a living, but because of their psychological inability to live without full participation in collective life.

The result of such considerations was a distinction between two

---

8. Three of these attempts may be mentioned: Zygmunt Balicki, *Social Psychology*, (see below under Polish Sociology).; William McDougall, *The Group Mind.* (New York-London: G. P. Putmans's Sons, 1920); and John Elif Boodin, *The Social Mind,* (New York: Macmillan Co., 1939.) The last is the best from the sociological point of view, and it is the one in which the theory of the psychological unity of collective life is the least influenced by analogy with individual psychological unity.

contrasting socio-psychological types: a later type, corresponding to the Spencerian organized "society," and an earlier type, variously conceived by various thinkers, but possessing one feature which all of them recognized as essential: its unity was not dependent upon the structural or functional differentiation of individuals, classes, or specialized groups, but upon intellectual, emotional, and volitional communion. Thus, Ferdinand Toennies, who follows Wundt's conception of "will" as a dynamic and integrating force of individual as well as of collective life, (9) in his book *Community and Society* (10) distinguishes two fundamental types of social unity corresponding to two types of "will." The "community" type is the expression of original, spontaneous will, leading individuals to share their total conscious lives; the "society" type is a manifestation of reflective, selective will, leading individuals to pursue their separate, though interdependent, ends. His concept of "society" in so far agrees with Spencer's "society" as it emphasizes functional and structural differentiation; but his idea of social unity is in a sense the reverse of Spencer's, for the type of organization which a society represents is accompanied by a decrease of social coherence as contrasted with the "community" type, which has no equivalent in Spencer's theory.

Emile Durkheim in his *Division of Labor in Society* (11) accepts for later stages of social evolution the Spencerian concept of social organization as including a differentiation of functionally interdependent parts within a society, as well as Spencer's correlation between the complexity of his kind of organization and the size and degree of integration of geographically located collectivities. But he introduces the concept of "solidarity" as a unifying socio-psychological force and thus explains why primitive societies, which lack a complex organization, nonetheless manifest a high degree of unity. For solidarity can be founded on uniformity as well as on differentiation, on a consciousness of psychological similarity as

---

9. Wilhelm Wundt's theory that such cultural phenomena as language, myth and religion, mores, social organization, law, are products of collective will as a psychological force is applied in his voluminous work *Voelkerpsychologie*, (latest edition, Leipzig: 1912-1921).

10 *Gemeinschaft und Gesellschaft*, (Leipzig: 1887): English translation by C. P. Loomis, entitled *Fundamental Concepts of Sociology*, (New York, etc.: American Book Co., 1940).

11. *De la division du travail social*, (Paris: Alcan, 1893): English translation by George Simpson, (New York: The Macmillan Co. 1933).

SOCIAL ORGANIZATION

well as on a consciousness of mutual dependence. There are thus two types of solidarity: "mechanical" (an unfortunate term, later dropped by Franch sociologists) and "organic." Under either type, individuals are psychologically parts and products of society, though the conscious bonds which unite them differ.

General typologies of "societies" have always been popular, but we cannot follow their later developments. Georges Gurvitch in his study "Forms of Sociability" (12) gives a conclusive criticism of this kind of typology by showing through intensive analysis that there are multiple and various types of common bonds uniting individuals, any or all of which may coexist in diverse and changing combinations within the total collective life of a society.

Expansion of Institutional Research. In any case, the interest in synthetic conceptions of the unifying principle of human "societies" is philosophic rather than scientific. The majority of sociologists have been much more interested in that large field of empirical social phenomena which Spencer tried to cover in his systematic survey of institutions. And though most of his generalizations were soon found to conflict with the results of historical and anthropological investigation, analytic comparative studies of these phenomena, with considerable emphasis on adequate scientific methods, constituted for more than two decades the central and perhaps the most productive part of sociology.

In these inductive studies, the contrast between social realism and individualism became associated with different philosophies of culture. The French sociological group, of which Durkheim was the original leader and which later became organized into the French Sociological Institute, connected the postulate of the objective reality of society with the objectivity of cultural phenomena in general as empirical data irreducible to natural phenomena, whereas in American thought the individualistic approach to society was associated with a naturalistic conception of culture. (13)

The French Sociological Group soon desisted from attempts at

---

12. *Essais de sociologie,* (Paris: Librarie du Recueil Sirey, 1938): first essay, "Formes de la sociabilité," pp. 11-112.

13. A different type of individualistic approach might have evolved out of Gabriel Tarde's "intermental Psychology". But Tarde had no continuators in France. And although Edward Allsworth Ross and later Charles A. Ellwood started to work on problems initiated by Tarde, each of them eventually developed a different problematization of his own.

sociological synthesis of the kind outlined in Durkheim's *Division of Labor*. Although Durkheim himself continued to philosophize (14) and his philosophy affected somewhat his methodological approach, yet the monographic part of his work remained essentially scientific, as was also the work of other members of the group. The most important methodical innovations of the whole group may be summarized in two heuristic principles: 1. the objective reality, unity, and inherent order of society must be postulated in all sociological investigations, but a vast amount of monographic research must be done before a valid general theory of societies, their organization, and their evolution can be constructed; 2. in order to discover what societies objectively are, we must begin by finding out what they are in the experience of their own members.

Now, what is a society to its members? No individual can experience fully and adequately the society in which he participates. There are, nonetheless, two ways in which individuals become aware of their society:

a. By means of those collective representations which symbolize the society as a whole. These symbolic representations have a character of supreme sacredness; indeed, according to Durkheim's famous theory of religion, all representations of divine entities are symbols of society. Two studies may be referred to as examples of this theory: Durkheim's own analysis of Australian totemism, (15) and Czarnowski's study of the cult of St. Patrick as the national hero of Ireland, embodying the supreme values of Irish national society and symbolizing its unity. (16)

b. More important from the point of view of our problem is the fragmentary but continual and many-sided awareness which every individual has of a collective power underlying most cultural values

---

14. The evolution of Durkheim's own sociological theories has been excellently described by several authors, especially by Talcott Parsons in his *The Structure of Social Action*, (New York: McGraw-Hill Book Co., 1937) and by Harry Alpert in the study quoted above.

15. *Les Formes élémentaires de la vie religieuse*, (Paris: Alcan, 1912): English translation, *Elementary Forms of Religious Life*, by Joseph Ward Swain, (New York: The Macmillan Co., 1915). The significance of this work greatly transcends the particular problem to which we are referring, for it forms the beginning of a sociological theory of knowledge developed in many other contributions of the French group.

16. Stephan Czarnowski, *Le Culte des héros et ses conditions sociales*, (Paris: Alcan, 1919).

SOCIAL ORGANIZATION

and patterns of action within the range of his experience, making him conform with standards and norms independent of his subjective perceptions and impulses. Society is the reality manifested in this collective power, the common source of all internal compulsion and external coercion to cultural conformity. The objectivity which cultural values and patterns have in individual experience is social objectivity; it is founded on the collective sanctions (positive and negative) which society gives to the values and patterns.

In this sense, all cultural phenomena which are collectively recognized are social phenomena: words and rules of language, religious objects and rites, concepts, methods, categories and principles of knowledge, works and styles of art, technical instruments, products and methods of production, economic values and forms of exchange, companionate customs, mores, laws regulating human intercourse, standards and norms of class distinction and occupational differentiation, political systems, principles, and ideals.

This field of research is obviously wider than that covered by Spencer's concept of institution. A Spencerian institution as a part of organized society includes, besides objects of human experience and patterns of human action, also the men who specialize in using these objects and performing these patterned actions. For Spencer, art was not a social institution, but the artist was. When he used the term "ecclesiastical" rather than "religious" institution, he made it clear that religion as such was not an institution but that priesthood was.

The French group, however, did not follow Spencer in assuming that the institutional system of society necessarily involves a differentiation and specialization of the men composing this society. If it does not, then the concept of institution can be extended to all cultural values and patterns which individuals are made to accept and to follow under social pressure, for this pressure is always exercized by men associated together, whether the sanctions used to produce conformity are formal and applied by special functionaries or informal and applied by the collectivity at large. In this light, the phenomena which constitute a living language or a system of knowledge can be scientifically approached in a similar way as, *e. g.*, the phenomena commonly called "economic institutions" or "legal institutions."

While we notice among the French group some hesitation about extending the term "institution" to all cultural values and patterns which are collectively maintained and imposed upon individuals under collective sanctions, the sociological methods applied in their investigation are essentially similar. We can safely say that the sociological work of the French group consisted mainly in monographic research concerning cultural phenomena which, however different in empirical content, could with respect to their social significance all be included under the same concept and called institutions, as many of them actually were called.

The principle that social phenomena should be studied as objective realities irreducible to the psychology of individuals led to many important and original discoveries. Besides the works of authors mentioned before, we need only refer to those of Lucien Lévy-Bruhl, Célestin Bouglé, Marcel Mauss, Georges Davy, Maurice Halbwachs, François Simiand, and Paul Fauconnet among the men who were directly connected with Durkheim; and there were and still are many more who later came under the influence of this group and made first-rate contributions.

Furthermore, this approach to social phenomena has thrown a new light on individual psychology. Such books as *Social Frames of Memory* (17) by Halbwachs, *Morbid Consciousness*, (18) and *Introduction to Collective Psychology* (19) by Charles Blondel tended to confirm the validity of the principle of social realism by showing that whatever lasting order can be found in the psychological life of human individuals is determined by the social order.

Nevertheless, the original goal set before sociological theory in the nineteenth century — a general theory of societies as systems — became more and more unattainable as this monographic research progressed. While developing the new heuristic conception of society as experienced by its members — a synthesis of collectively maintained cultural institutions — the French group would not discard the idea, inherited from Spencer, that society in the institutional sense is coextensive with a definite natural conglomerate of biopsychological human beings, the integral population of a circumscribed geographic area. Durkheim himself clung to this idea for years after in his *Division of Labor* he had treated demographic processes as the chief causes of change from an earlier type of social solidarity and cultural unity to a later type. Of course, the researches of human geographers and demographers had long before established the

---

17. Maurice Halbwachs, *Les Cadres sociaux de la mémoire*, (Paris: Alcan).
18. Charles Blondel, *La Conscience morbide*, (Paris: Alcan).
19. Charles Blondel, *Introduction à la psychologie collective*, (Paris: Colin).

SOCIAL ORGANIZATION

existence of a certain observable order in the special distribution of the peoples who inhabit definite geographic areas and in the materials, instruments, and products of their activities. Marcel Mauss applied to studies of this order the term "social morphology," which clearly implied the assumption that society is a spacial system of material things as well as an institutional system of cultural values and patterns of action, and that the same people who as organisms are included in the former, as conscious agents maintain the latter.

Both the progress of institutional research and the advance of research bearing upon the spacial order of demographic aggregates have invalidated this assumption once and forever.

Society vs. Civilization. On the one hand, intensive investigation of social phenomena within every large territorial collectivity discloses a diverse multiplicity of cultural values and patterns which have behind them strong, often informal but sometimes formal, social sanctions and yet are not only unconnected but often incompatible with each other. They cannot, therefore, be considered as belonging to the institutional order maintained by this society as a whole.

On the other hand, extensive investigations bearing on several large collectivities show that many of the values and patterns which have the collective support of the population of a circumscribed territory are not limited to this population, but are also recognized and supported by populations of other territories.

A joint statement by Emile Durkheim and Marcel Mauss expresses their final realization that the total complex of cultural phenomena which receive collective support among the people of a territorially circumscribed "society" does not constitute a separate system:

"One of the rules which we follow here, while studying social phenomena in themselves and for themselves, is not to leave them in the air, but to refer them always to a human group that occupies a definite portion of space and is capable of being geographically represented. And it seems that the largest of all these groupings, the one which includes within it all the others and consequently frames and embraces all the forms of social activity, is the one which constitutes the political society . . .

"However, there are (social phenomena) which have no such clearly defined frames; they pass above political frontiers and extend over spaces which cannot be easily determined . . .

"Political and juridical institutions, phenomena of social morphology, are parts of the constitution belonging to each people. On the contrary, myths, stories, money, trade, fine arts, techniques, instruments, languages, words, scientific knowledge, literary forms and ideals, all these travel . . .

"There are not only isolated facts, but complex solidary systems which are not limited to a determined political organism . . . To these systems of facts, which have their own unity, their own way of being, it is convenient to have a special name: the name *civilization* seems to us the most appropriate." (20)

Social Morphology vs. Human Ecology. If at the time the above note was published it was still possible to believe that "society" as a whole had a spacial structure coextensive at least with the limits of some political system, such a belief was shattered by the progress of research in human ecology, i. e., of inductive investigation of the spacial order discoverable among the population of an area and representing the combined result of three kinds of variables: geographic conditions, biological forces, and material techniques. The lack of coincidence between the ecological order and the institutional order was realized by leaders of this type of research, who ceased altogether to speak of "society" as a spacial system. The ecological "community" of Park and Burgess, the "metropolitan area" of McKenzie, the "region" of Odum (a concept recently extended to vast ecological complexes, partly overlapping political frontiers as well as ethno-cultural divisions) are certainly not spacial "components" of societies.

Of course, many problems still remain to be solved concerning relationships between the ecological order and the socio-cultural order. Ecologists are inclined to assume that the ecological order is primary, the socio-cultural order secondary; whereas the French group developed certain theories (such as Czarnowski's theory that human representations of space are culturally determined) which could be used as heuristic principles for the opposite line of approach. But since neither order can any longer be considered inherent in a "society" as a closed and inclusive whole, nothing remains of this realistic concept but "the State" as traditionally defined by political philosophers — a territorially and demographically limited and institutionally organized entity. And as the age-old identification of "the society" with "the State" survives only in totalitarian ideologies, the problem of social organization and insti-

---

20. "Note sur la notion de civilization," *L'Année Sociologique,* XII, (Paris: Alcan, 1913), pp. 46-50.

SOCIAL ORGANIZATION

tions as originally defined by social realism must be completely redefined.

Institutions as a basic form of the moral order. Long before the realistic conception of society began to disintegrate in consequence of inductive scientific research, it aroused the opposition of religious and moral philosophers, who objected to the naturalism of Spencer in the first place and later to the cultural relativism of the French sociological group. Much of this opposition was theoretically unproductive, since its dependence upon traditional dogmas and ethical standards interfered with scientific innovation. There were, however, some scientifically significant attempts to develop a sociological theory which, while taking into consideration new scientific work in this field, could be reconciled with the established principles of religion and ethics. Probably the most important of these attempts was Maurice Hauriou's. It is of interest to us not only because Hauriou has been influential even outside of France, but also because he used the term "institution" in the most inclusive sense as a universal sociological category. For him the "institution" — not the "society" — is the repository of all the social order which is justifiable by ethical standards, a key to the solution of conflicts between radical individualism and radical collectivism, an instrument of synthesis of naturalism and idealism. (21)

Every institution represents the enduring realization of an objective idea — not merely of a subjective aim — as a task or an enterprise to be fulfilled in the empirical social world. Hauriou distinguished two general classes of institutions, which he calls *"institution-groupe"* and *"institution-chose."* Any social group, from the family to the church, the State or the nation, is an "institution-groupe" in so far as it serves an objective idea. There are

---

21. Hauriou's criticism of contemporary sociological trends by the standards of religious and ethical philosophy is expressed in his book *La Science sociale traditionnelle* (1896), where the institution is already called the "fundamental social phenomenon" (196). This concept is developed further in his later works, especially *L'Institution et le droit statutaire* (1906) and *La Théorie de l'institution et de la fondation* (1925). For a brief but adequate English summary of his theories, see Georges Gurvitch, *Sociology of Law*, (New York: Philosophical Library, 1942), pp. 139-147. In the following discussion, we quote Hauriou's two main terms—"institution-groupe" and "institution-chose"—in their original French, for it is difficult to translate them without risking misunderstandings; and we particularly want to prevent any confusion between the concept "institution groupe" and the entirely different concepts "group institution," "institutional group" and "institutionalized group" which are defined later in this chapter.

four stages or levels in the process of its realization: the growth of "communion" among the individuals who share an idea and tend to act for it solidarily as a whole; the formation of an organized superstructure which embodies the group's power of collective action and makes it a lasting corporate unit; the development of a moral order of voluntary cooperation between the members and the organized superstructure, which transforms the latter into a "collective moral person"; and, finally, the external recognition of the group already internally incorporated as a "juridical personality," a social unit in relation with other units. "Institution-chose" (*e. g.*, property) is an order of relations between separate social units — individuals or groups — which does not bind them together into a unified whole.

Some of Hauriou's generalizations about social groups are sociologically significant, whether groups be called "institutions" or simply "groups"; and they might have served as heuristic hypotheses for comparative studies of social groups, of their genesis, organization, structure, and mutual relationships. But, as Gurvitch points out (p. 146), Hauriou did not develop this aspect of his theory. His real purpose in extending the concept of institution to groups was not to promote objective sociological research in this field, but to indicate that the internal order of social groups as well as the external order of social relationships is ultimately founded upon a transcendental ideal order, in its objective essence independent of men, though dependent upon them for its empirical realization. Gurvitch finds that Hauriou after 1916 reverts to St. Thomas in his philosophy of law; however, his general social philosophy seems to have been from the very first a modernization of St. Thomas. Everything in human life that manifests an order, however relative and limited, has a pre-appointed place in the total order of the universe, is ideally "instituted" above space and time, though it becomes a real "institution" only in historical duration and extension.

There is a striking parallelism between Hauriou's use of the concept of institution and the more recent use of this concept as a philosophic category by American sociologists (see below). But there are also essential differences, inasmuch as American sociologists emphasize the relative and varied historical content of man's cultural life rather than any universal form of absolute order.

Individualistic Theories of Institutions. The individualistic approach to institutions was originally due to the influence of Dar-

SOCIAL ORGANIZATION

winism. Under Darwin's strictly biological theory of evolution, in contrast with Spencer's cosmic philosophy of evolution, there was no place for "society" as a genetically new category of system, irreducible to its individual components. The ultimate entity in which everything pertaining to mankind originates and to which everything must be scientifically reducible is the individual human organism, a unit and a link in the animal species *Homo*. Human societies, like everything mankind has produced, have to be explained in terms of these entities. The explanation must, of course, take fully into account the psychological development of the human species, the growing capacity of the human organism to react to its environment consciously and purposefully. But inasmuch as man is essentially an animal, his survival as an individual and as a species depends on certain traits of his biological nature. Among the traits which have been most favorable to his survival are those which make him associate with other human beings. He is not the only animal who associates with others of his kind; and the study of associations of lower animals, initiated by Darwin, continued by Espinas, Kropotkin, and many others, throws some light on human associations. But human associations differ from those of lower animals in that they have been evolving in consequence of man's psychological evolution and in that their evolution in turn has been a condition and a factor of psychological evolution. (22)

The sociologists who applied these premises to the study of human societies, while rejecting Spencer's theory of society as a super-individual organic entity, accepted in principle the reality of Spencer's "institutions"; their main effort was directed towards explaining institutions, their origin, persistence, and generality, by biopsychological forces inherent in "human nature." These forces were variously termed: "needs," "wants," "desires," "wishes," "interests." The term "need" originally emphasized the biological aspect of these forces: it denoted what the scientist knew was a necessary condition for the normal life of a human individual, as judged by the scientist's standards of normality, whether the individual himself was aware of what he "really needed" and acted in accordance with his needs or not. "Interest," on the contrary, an essentially psychological term, denoted a combination of the indi-

22. Franklin H. Giddings, in Book III of *The Principles of Sociology*, (New York: The Macmillan Co., 1896) outlines a systematic theory of the "Historical Evolution of Society" as a continous process leading from "Zoogenic Associations" through "Anthropogenic" and "Ethnogenic" to "Demogenic Associations."

vidual's own perceptions, representations, feelings, and volitions which stimulated his activity, whether the results of this activity were necessary, unnecessary, or even harmful to his normal life, as judged by the standards of the scientific observer.

This difference in point of view was minimized by two assumptions based upon the principle of "survival of the fittest," as applied to collectivities. The sociologists who started with the concept of "needs" assumed that individuals living collectively learn in most cases to "want" or "desire" what they "really need" and act accordingly, and consequently that activities which satisfied their needs, as defined by scientists, became collectively patterned and produced institutions. The sociologists who used mainly the concept of "interests" assumed that interests would be general and permanent and consequently would be recognized and institutionalized by a collectivity only when they led to activities compatible with a life which was both organically and psychologically "normal." This was, for instance, the implicit assumption underlying Albion W. Small's famous classification of "interests" under six basic categories: "health, wealth, sociability, knowledge, beauty, rightness." (23)

The most influential theories explaining the institutional order by biopsychological forces were those of Lester Frank Ward and William Graham Sumner. Ward's genetic theory of institutions was expressed in his *Pure Sociology* (24) but takes up only a few sections of this work. Briefly speaking, "desires of associated men" act as "social forces" (p. 103); "social" synergy, a process of equilibration of originally colliding or conflicting forces which ends in collaboration and cooperation (p. 175), is the constructive principle of the social order (184-5); human institutions are structures produced by social synergy and these constitute the social order (pp. 185-193). Ward gives very few empirical data to support these generalizations. The idea that the social processes formative of the social order originate in collision and through successive stages lead to positive cooperation was later accepted (with certain modifications) by Park and Burgess (25) and became widely popularized in later textbooks.

---

23. *General Sociology,* (Chicago: University of Chicago Press, 1905), Ch. XXXII, pp. 443-481.
24. (New York: The Macmillan Co., 1903).
25. Robert E. Park and Ernest W. Burgess, *Introduction to the Science of Sociology,* (Chicago: University of Chicago Press, 1921), Ch. VII,VIII, IX, X, XI.

SOCIAL ORGANIZATION

Sumner's *Folkways* (26) is a work entirely devoted to the problem of the genesis of the social order. It is full of ethnological and historical material; and although as a scientific theory it is poorly systematized and in parts methodically defective, it contains important hypotheses concerning the origin, duration, relationships, and changes of folkways and mores, which have stimulated many later sociologists. Sumner's leading ideas are familiar to all students of sociology and therefore will be only briefly mentioned here.

Since human individuals living in a collectivity have similar basic needs and environmental conditions, the ways of satisfying these needs which after trial and error have proved relatively successful spread by imitation, become individually stabilized as habits, collectively uniformized as customs, and authoritatively transmitted by the old to the young. This is the process of formation of folkways. Folkways become mores when, because of faith in some doctrine of truth and right - some "world philosophy" - they come to be considered essential for societal welfare. Out of mores evolve institutions. Unfortunately, the definition of institutions in *Folkways* is too vague for methodical use; nor does the work contain any general survey of institutions as distinct from folkways and mores. But Albert Galloway Keller developed and organized Sumner's inadequately formulated conceptions in *The Science of Society*, with the later collaboration of Maurice R. Davie. (27)

Throughout both *Folkways* and *The Science of Society*, the principle of causal dependence of the social order on biopsychological forces is maintained. Societal evolution from tentative individual activities to folkways, to mores, to institutions, implies a psychological evolution from animal needs to conscious human interests. "There are four great motives of human action which come into play when some number of human beings are in juxtaposition under the same life conditions. These are hunger, sex passion, vanity and fear (of ghosts and spirits). Under each of these motives there are interests. Life (in a society) consists in satisfying interests." (28) Obviously, only the first two "great motives" go directly back to animal needs; the other two can be only indirectly derived from them and are specifically human. The development of

---

26. (Boston: Ginn and Co., 1907).
27. Vols. I-III, (New Haven: Yale University Press, 1927-8). Vol. IV contains only organized factual material.
28. *Folkways*, p. 18.

institutions is genetically determined by the interests corresponding to these four great motives; their permanence and universality are due to the fact that they continue to serve these interests. Consequently, institutions can be classified into four essential categories: institutions of societal self-maintenance, of societal self-perpetuation, of societal self-gratification, and of religion (though ultimately religion is included under the category of "self-maintenance" with industrial and political institutions).

This theory, as fully developed, is based primarily, if not exclusively, on data derived from lower societies and early periods of historical civilizations. (29) But the progress of inductive sociological research, especially of research bearing on complex modern civilizations, shows that neither the concept of need nor that of interest (want, wish, desire) can provide an adequate theoretic framework for a genetic explanation, analysis, and classification of those phenomena which sociologists include under the term institution, still less for the study of their functional relationships within a vast modern collectivity.

Disintegration of Biopsychological Theories of Institutions. In the first place, no sociologist can fail to recognize that, whatever may have been the "basic needs" or general "interests" of the individuals composing "primitive" societies, new needs or interests have appeared in the course of cultural evolution; and any explanation of modern institutions in biopsychological terms must take account of these new developments. For instance, Ballard (30) finds it necessary to add to the four traditional classes of institutions, assumed to be rooted in universal human needs and fully recognized by the people of every society, newer institutions like the school, the public library, the social settlement, the health center, the recreation center. In Chapter XXX, he discusses such "emergent social institutions" as the research organization, the museum, the motion picture, and the newspaper — all of which must be considered as serving needs or interests relatively recently developed in highly civilized societies.

But what is the reason for not including the alcohol drinking center, the bordel, the gambling "joint," the opium smoking center,

---

29. Indeed, the authors of *The Science of Society* leave out of consideration nearly all the work done by sociologists concerning modern societies and ignore contemporary sociology in general.

30. Lloyd Vernon Ballard, *Social Institutions*, (New York: D. A. Appleton-Century Co., 1936).

whether legally licensed or not, in the list of institutions? They also serve widely spread and persistent human "needs" or at least what the people who try to satisfy them consider as their needs. Is it because other people in the same society disapprove of these phenomena that they are not dignified with the name of "institution"? But what about an international congress on symbolic logic? Although probably only two or three people in a million know about it, presumably none would disapprove, if they did know. Is it an institution? If not, why not?

Secondly, it has often been noticed that particular social phenomena which sociologists classify as institutions of the same category— *e.g.*, particular families or economic enterprises or religious sects — serve widely divergent "needs" or "interests." Nay, even the same institutions may be instrumental in satisfying not only different but conflicting interests; see Chapin's analysis of local political institutions. (31)

Thirdly, the application of psychological interpretation to historical processes leads to the conclusion that the same kind of psychological forces which in certain periods are presumed to form and maintain institutions, in other periods may revolutionize or dissolves these institutions. This is what, according to Barnes, is happening just now to social institutions. (32) Even during the same period, similar needs, wishes, desires, interests can be discovered in processes of social organization as well as in processes of social disorganization.

Already fifteen years ago Hertzler, though using the less inclusive concept of "needs" rather than the more inclusive concept of "interests" as "causes of institutions" and broadly assuming that "the totality of the institutions and their essential parts found among a given people constitute the social organization of that people," was sufficiently aware of the vast empirical variety, complexity, and fluidity of the phenomena denoted by this word to refrain from classifying institutions in terms of needs. He "merely called attention" to what he termed "the major or pivotal institutional fields, in which the multiplicity of institutions operate, each of which includes its numerous special institutions" (p. 47). And

---

31. F. Stuart Chapin, *Contemporary American Institutions*, (New York: Harper and Bros., 1935), pp. 27-65.
32. Harry Elmer Barnes, *Social Institutions in an Era of World Upheaval*, (New York: Prentice-Hall, 1943).

while recognizing the "interdependence of institutions," Hertzler made no attempt to construct a synthetic theory of the organization which the totality of institutions found among a given people is supposed to constitute. (33)

And somewhat later Hamilton, (34) who refers "institutions" to "interests" rather than to "needs," reaches (apparently by strictly empirical methods) the following definition: "Institution is a verbal symbol which . . . connotes a way of thought or action of some prevalence and permanence . . . embedded in the habits of a group or the customs of a people . . . it is the singular of which the mores or the folkways are the plural . . . The world of use and wont, to which imperfectly we accommodate our lives, is a tangled and unbroken web of institutions . . . The range of institutions is as wide as the interests of mankind." But, judging from the fact that many individual interests never become institutionalized, it would seem that the range of interests in their empirical variety and changeability is even wider than the range of institutions. And if so, the concept of interest in its psychological sense obviously cannot serve as an instrument for generalizing about institutions.

On the other hand, a consistent application of radical biological empiricism results in consequences which not only do not help construct, but actually preclude the construction of any theory of institutions whatsoever: this is the conclusion which must be drawn from one of the most original works in this field, Floyd Allport's *Institutional Behavior.* (35) Briefly speaking, the terms used to denote institutions, *e. g.*, "university, industry, church or State," refer to activities or habits which individuals in certain relationships perform. But the activities of these individuals can be scientifically, objectively investigated only as given to the investigator in sensory observation. Such investigation logically leads to theoretic conclusions concerning the behavior of human organisms in response to certain stimuli, primarily the behavior of other human organisms, but to no conclusions whatever about "institutions." For,

---

33. *Social Institutions,* (New York: 1929).

34. Walton H. Hamilton, "Institutions," in *Encyclopedia of the Social Sciences,* New York: The Macmillan Co., 1935), 4: 84-89. It is a different matter if the "interest" is conceived, as in MacIver's theory, as the object of psychological attitudes. *Cf.* Robert Morrison MacIver, *Society: Its Structure and Changes,* (New York: Ray Long and Richard R. Smith, 1931), p. 49.

35. Floyd Henry Allport, *Institutional Behavior,* (Chapel Hill: The University of North Carolina Press, 1933).

SOCIAL ORGANIZATION

according to Allport, "We cannot experience an institution as a reality when we merely examine or study individuals disinterestedly, but only when we try to do something through individuals by organizing them (or conceiving them as organized) in the direction of some ulterior, common end" (p. 21).

Allport believes that this subjectively teleological approach serves as a methodological aid to scientific study in that it helps the scientist understand "the meaning of the institutional field," find the individuals of whose relationships the field consists (p. 24), and observe what these individuals are actually doing. But a scientist who follows the standards of scientific reasoning can never ascribe objective reality to anything that he knows to be his own teleological construction motivated by practical interests, only to what he logically infers from observable facts when guided exclusively by theoretic considerations. A dilemma is ineluctable. Either the scientist conceives the activities of certain individuals as organized "in the direction of some ulterior common end," because of objective evidence that they are so organized, or else he conceives them as organized only because he wishes they were. If he chooses the first alternative, he must admit as objective evidence what he learns from these individuals as conscious agents about *their* idea of an institution, *their* common ends, *their* attempts to achieve these ends by organized cooperation, and the results of these attempts as experienced by them. Even then, of course, he should not look for the fulfilment of any purpose of his own by these individuals, for this would conflict with his objectivity as a disinterested observer.

But Allport refuses on principle to recognize as objective the kind of evidence mentioned above. He must, therefore, take the second alternative. In which case, as a scientist, he has no right to circumscribe an "institutional field," to speak of the "meaning" of this field, to use this "meaning" in choosing certain individuals to be investigated out of the two billion possible choices and then to select specific actions of theirs as relevant to his investigation, to the exclusion of thousands of other actions which each of these individuals performs in the course of a month. Obviously, biological individualism is totally unfit not only for the study of institutions, but even for the study of "institutional behavior." (36)

---

36. We have to omit from this discussion the works of those authors who investigate the psychology of individual participation in institutions (Charles Hubbard Judd) or individual reactions to institutional stimuli (Jacob Robert Kantor), but do not construct a theory of institutions as such.

Institution as a Philosophic Category. However, although attempts to base a systematic theory of institutions on biopsychological foundations have failed, American sociologists have gone on constructing systematic theories of institutions. In surveying their theories, we find that the bulk of their empirical data is derived not from biology or psychology, but from history and cultural anthropology, and that each institution or institutional field is a concept intended to cover a logical class of data taken from these sources. Indeed, it often seems as if sociologists accepted a definite classification of historical and anthropological data before attempting to use a biopsychological approach to their field and then classified human "needs," "wishes," "desires," or "interests" *ex post* to fit into this ready conceptual framework.

In fact, the several categories of institutions listed in systematic studies of this subject correspond approximately to certain subdivisions of culture commonly recognized by anthropologists and historians, in most cases forming distinct fields of specialized sciences. "Political institutions" correspond to the specific field of political science; "economic institutions" to the field covered by economics (and also by a still unformed, but badly needed historico-comparative science of material techniques). The range of "religious institutions" is as wide as that of descriptive history and comparative theory of the religions of the world. The treatment of cultural patterns of marriage and family organization as a separate class of phenomena was initiated by social thinkers of classical antiquity, continued by medieval moralists, and taken over in modern times by both anthropologists and sociologists. The recognition of knowledge as a distinct cultural domain began with historians of philosophy and science, and many sociologists are now definitely considering science or knowledge in general as a distinct social institution. School education, viewed both historically and practically, has grown during the last hundred years into one of the major special fields of study; and nearly all recent sociological books classify it as an institution, either together with or apart from knowledge. Literature, art, and music, though they constitute the fields of such widely developed disciplines as philology, history and theory of art, and musicology, have received less attention from sociologists; we find them briefly discussed as subclasses of a more general class of institutions (*e. g.*, "recreational institutions").

The concept of institution thus serves as an intellectual instrument for a task which many, perhaps most sociologists have wished

SOCIAL ORGANIZATION

sociology to perform, that is, to synthetize all the special sciences of culture, if not all the specialized knowledge pertaining to "man," as has been attempted in some recent textbooks. This task has become more difficult since the concept of society can no longer serve as a center for the conceptual integration of institutions. Probably the most thorough and instructive attempt to achieve such a synthesis with the help of the concept of institution, but without referring all institutions to "society" in the old sense, is that of Constantine Panunzio. (37) The following extracts from his work express briefly, but clearly, the heuristic principles which seem to us most important for the present problem.

"There are at least eight fairly well integrated clusters or systems of human activities: the marital, familial, economic, educational, recreational, religious, scientific, and governmental systems. These we call the major institutions. Each performs a primary function . . . (p. 7).

". . . each of these systems consists of subsystems of concepts, usages and rules, associations, and instruments (p. 8).

". . . the master institutions are age-long systems (p. 19) . . . Likewise, the major social institutions have existed and do exist throughout the world . . . Actually they develop differently in various localities (p.20) . . . Institutions are further characterized by interpenetration; that is, they are interwoven in origins, development, structures, functioning, in concepts, usages, associations, instruments. (p. 21)"

In what sense is it possible to call any one of these institutions a "system"? Hardly in the realistic, concrete sense in which we think of the sun with its planets, of an engine, of a multicellular organism, or of a philosophic theory, as a system; in such cases we have in mind a particular, limited combination of interconnected elements which together constitute a single objectively integrated and orderly complex, behaving as a unit in certain relationships with other complexes. The institution, as defined by Panunzio, is a "system" in an ideational, abstract sense; the term "system" denotes here a type of order or, in the words of MacIver (who uses this term in a somewhat similar sense), a "mode of relations" (38) which an investigator finds when he compares many particular

---

37. *Major Social Institutions,* (New York: The Macmillan Co., 1939).
38. *Society,* (2nd ed., New York; Farrar and Rinehart, 1937), p. 144.

concrete systems and finds similar patterns in their inner structure and their relationships.

This is how, for instance, the term "capitalistic system" is used in economics, even though economists are aware that the distinctive character of the capitalistic order of economic relations is that it precludes a "unified economy," *i. e.*, the formation of a single real, concrete system integrating all smaller economic systems — farms, workshops, mines, factories, railroads, commercial enterprises, banks, etc. — into a functionally ordered whole.

Those multiple, real, concrete systems would come under Panunzio's category of "subsystems." For instance, if we take science as an institution, we find in this field a vast multiplicity and diversity of "subsystems": systems of concepts, *i. e.*, philosophic and scientific theories; "associations" for the common pursuit and transmission of knowledge; "subsystems of instruments," such as libraries, laboratories, observatories, experimental stations.

Now, why should a sociologist construct a systematic theory so comprehensive as to include under its leading concepts several fields of cultural phenomena on each of which many thousands of specialists are working and were already working long before sociology came into being? It obviously cannot be because he expects sociologists to supplant or to guide economists, political scientists, religionists, historians, and theorists of knowledge in carrying on inductive research within their several fields or in achieving a scientific systematization of their results — a very difficult task of scientific thought in any one of these fields and manifestly impossible for all fields taken together.

The significance of such a theory is not scientific, but philosophic. By applying the category of institution to all classes of cultural phenomena, a social philosopher implies that there is a common essence underlying their empirical diversity; by defining the specific "functions" of the several institutions, he tends to indicate that each of them is a part of a telic order which underlies the seemingly disorderly mass of human experiences and actions — in other words, that the historical human world is a cosmos, not a chaos.

Such a philosophy of culture can be more easily reconciled with the naturalistic metaphysics prevalent in modern thought than any of the older philosophies, such as Thomism or Hegelianism; and it seems particularly valuable for the educational purposes of broadening the intellectual horizon and organizing the thinking of college students. But the task of philosophy is entirely different from that of inductive science, though hardly less important; and we believe that the development of social thought is proceeding toward a clear differentiation between a general social philosophy of culture and sociology as an inductive science with a limited field of its own.

Will sociology drop the term "institution" and leave it to philosophy? Or will it keep this term, with its qualifying adjective "social," and give it the meaning of a heuristic scientific concept within its own special field?

This is not merely a question of terminological agreement. The conversion of an old term to a new usage symbolizes a challenge to all the theoretic implications of its previous meaning. Let us see what the consequences of such a challenge would be.

II

Empirical Approach. If the concepts symbolized by the terms social organization and social institution are to be effectively used for inductive studies, our fundamental heuristic premise must be that these terms denote general classes of empirical realities, each of which objectively exists. To prevent misunderstanding on the part of those who believe that data of sensory human experience differ from all other data of human experience in that through them and only through them do we learn what the truly objective reality is, *i. e.*, the world of "things-in-themselves" in contrast to everything else, which is "subjective," we had better define what we mean here by "reality" and "objectivity." From the scientific point of view, no datum of human experience is either objective or subjective in itself, for science does not study isolated data, only relations between data. Any datum is objectively real if it can be identified by several individuals who repeatedly experience it as *the same in its relations to other data* which they also experience, however different their repeated experiences of it.

A magical rite and a chemical experiment, David Copperfield and my neighbor's son, "la belle Héloïse" and "Miss America," "les neiges d'antan" and the falling snowflakes, the future association of nations and the battle which is just being fought are all objectively real, though each only within the frame of relationships in which it is identified.

And because nothing in the domain of social phenomena (or of cultural phenomena in general) really exists unless it has been produced and maintained in existence by conscious human agents, our next task is to find a way of solving the problem which arises whenever we want to study any phenomenon classified as "social organization" or as "social institution."

This problem is: Who are the agents who have produced and maintained this particular empirically identifiable instance of social *organization*, and how have they done it? Who are the agents who have produced and maintained in existence this particular, empirically identifiable *institution*, and how have they done it?

Social Organization as Organization of Social Groups. We must begin by defining more exactly the term "social organization." "Organization" generally means a dynamic system of human actions. These actions may be performed by one individual agent; e. g., a farmer or a craftsman, aiming to produce something, will organize his technical actions, and a philosopher or a scientist, trying to construct a theory, will organize his intellectual actions. "Social organization," however, is commonly used to denote the organization of actions of *several* agents who cooperate for the achievement of a common purpose. The organized actions may be social, i. e., bearing upon other people and purposing to influence the behavior of these people, as in a political campaign or in the functioning of a charitable agency. But they may be purely technical, as in an airplane factory; or religious, as in the collective cult of a divinity; or intellectual, as in group research. The organization itself, however, is always social, because it necessitates social interaction between the cooperative agents.

Furthermore, the term "social organization" is seldom applied by sociologists if the cooperation of the several agents is limited to one brief collective performance and ceases after a particular result has been achieved, as in a military attack, a hunt, a lynching. The use of this term is limited to cases where cooperation lasts for a lengthy period of time and each agent performs not one or a few sporadic actions but a regular "activity," i. e., a long series of actions, continuous or periodically recurring, coordinated with similar or different series of actions of other agents, as in a football team, a theatrical company, a governmental office, a workshop, a school.

Now, social organization in this sense can be realized only in a lasting "social group" or "association." Individuals belonging to such a group are aware that they are and will be regularly expect-

SOCIAL ORGANIZATION

ed to perform certain actions, and some of them act as organizers, leaders, coordinators of the regular activities of others with reference to the common purpose. Not all of these individuals need to be continuously active; indeed, in many groups a considerable proportion remain passive, acting only in reaction to the actions of others. The common purpose of the organized actions may be simple or complex. It may be a definite end, with the attainment of which the organization is expected to dissolve or to change its purpose, as in the case of the groups who carried on an organized campaign for women's suffrage. Or it may be an indefinite succession of recurrent aims which require permanent cooperation, as the successive production of a number of airplanes in a factory. It may also be an unattainable but approachable ideal, as in groups organized for the promotion of the universal brotherhood of men. Often the common purpose of the organized actions of group participants may be merely the perpetuation of the group itself, as in most gentes, clans, tribes, village communities, ancient city-states. The purpose does not have to be explicitly formulated or identically conceived by the agents; but at least those — be they many or few — who act as organizers, leaders, or coordinators must be aware of it, and others whose activities are integrated with reference to it must at least implicitly accept those parts or aspects of it which their activities help realize.

Social organization obviously implies interdependence between the effective achievements of participating agents: the contribution of every agent to the achievement of the common aim depends on the contributions of others. Mere interdependence between the achievements of social agents, however, does not imply social organization, for it may exist even if there is no common purpose for which the agents cooperate and each agent pursues a purpose of his own. Modern farmers depend for the attainment of their agricultural aims upon instruments produced by industrial agents; industrial agents depend for the effective achievement of their special technical purposes upon food produced by farmers, modern coal miners could not work steadily or effectively without railroad transportation, which is achieved by the activities of railroad men, while the latter could not run the trains without the coal produced by the miners. But except for a few cooperative associations, until recently no social organization integrated functionally for a common purpose the actions of farmers and those of industrial workers; apart from a few corporations, each owning some railroads and some mines, there was no organization which combined for a common purpose the activities of railroad men with those of miners. Only during the last few years certain groups, organized for the common purpose of "winning the war," initiated a certain degree of functional integration of interdependent, but not cooperatively organized systems of activities throughout the United States.

In thus redefining "social organization" with reference to particular "social groups" or "associations," instead of with reference to a "society," we are following the lead of many twentieth-century sociologists and anthropologists. Already Giddings (39) spoke of "the organization of . . . individual members (of a society) into specialized associations for achievement of various social ends. For example, a town has a municipal government, churches, schools, industrial corporations, labor organizations, literary and scientific societies, and social clubs . . . Associations . . . are purposive. Each association has a defined object in view, which its members are supposed to be aware of." He uses the term "constitution of a society" rather than "organization of a society" to denote all such associations "harmoniously correlated" (p. 171). Park and Burgess (40) definitely refer "organization and structure" to "social groups" (p. 51). Rivers in his work entitled *Social Organization* (41) explicitly states: "The primary aim of this book will be the study of social organization as a process by which individuals are associated in groups" (p.4). He classifies social groups, or "groupings," into domestic, political, occupational, religious, educational, clubs, secret societies (pp. 7-8). "All these different kinds of groupings are characterized by the feature of organization" (p. 9).

More recently, in such sociological theories as MacIver's, Hankins', (42) J. L. Gillin and J. P. Gillin's, (43) social organization is primarily, if not exclusively, conceived as group organization. Especially since the state has been defined not as a supreme and incomparable entity, but as a subclass of associations, political organ-

---

39. *The Principles of Sociology*, p. 171.

40. *Introduction to the Science of Sociology*, (1924), p. 42.

41. W.H.R. Rivers, *Social Organization*, ed. by W. J. Perry, (New York: Alfred A. Knopf, 1924).

42. Frank H. Hankins, *An Introduction to the Study of Society*, (New York: The Macmillan Co., 1938).

43. John Lewis Gillin and John Philip Gillin, *An Introduction to Sociology*, (New York: The Macmillan Co., 1942).

nization— the most complex and best known — becomes merely a specific variety of group organization. (44)

This does not mean, of course, that all social groups, or even all lasting social groups, are assumed to possess an organization. "Organized groups" are considered a subclass of social groups in general, and the term "association" is often used synonymously with "organized group."

However, this tendency to refer social organization to social groups is as yet neither general nor consistent. Earle Eubank stated in 1931: "Of recent years . . . the *group* concept has gradually supplanted that of *society* in our literature, and it may be regarded as the one about which all considerations of society forms revolve." (45) Even today, this statement must be considered as an anticipation of development to come rather than as a description of progress already achieved. We have seen that the core of the Spencerian theory of "society" still survives in the majority of textbooks. So far as we know, there are as yet only three books on social groups—one in English, one in French, one in German—and they are merely short essays. The fact that in the title of the section on social groups within this symposium the term "Sociography" instead of "Sociology" is used, indicates the present condition of inductive research in this field. The concept of social group has not yet become the main intellectual instrument for the study of institutions. Thus, considerations of those "societary forms" which are called institutions do not "revolve about" this concept, but are largely independent of it.

All textbooks of sociology have definitions of social groups in general, but most of them give only a few chapters (some only a few paragraphs) to a taxonomy of social groups, while devoting much more space to social institutions abstracted from social groups. In contrast with those sociologists who include States and churches within the general logical class of organized groups or associations, there are quite a few who speak of *the* State and *the* church as "social institutions." Even the concept of social organization is used in the Spencerian sense of an institutional organization, as something existing independently of organized groups.

The explanation of this situation lies in the slow and difficult

---

44. This is chiefly due to MacIver's theory, especially as expressed in *Society* (1937), p. 282 ff.
45. Earle Edward Eubank, *The Concepts of Sociology*, (Boston: D. C. Heath and Co., 1932), pp. 132-3.

development of the very concept of social group, which only in recent years has reached the stage where it can be used to redefine and solve the most important problems left unsolved by the concept of institution. Althought it is not our present task to discuss theories of social groups, still we must give a brief summary of this development, as without it the new trend in the theory of institutions would be incomprehensible.

What Are Social Groups? In nineteenth-century sociology, a group was conceived as an agglomeration of biopsychological individuals connected by relations of spacial proximity or genetic continuity or both. This is what Spencer meant by group. A group in this sense was a demographic part of the larger demographic whole — the territorial society. Sometimes the concept *group* was made coextensive with the term *society*, especially in speaking of a numerically small society. This implied that the group-society was a demographically separate and biologically self-sufficient whole in which individuals were integrally contained. This is why Sumner could speak of "in-group" and "out-group" — a distinction which would be meaningless unless the group were meant to include completely the human individuals belonging to it. If it were possible for an individual to belong simultaneously to several groups with overlapping memberships, every group would be to him an "in-group" with reference to all the other groups, and at the same time an "out-group" from the point of view of any one of the groups of which he was a member. But a human individual as a natural biopsychological entity cannot be at the same time a component of several separate, coherent aggregates of such entities, any more than an organic cell can at the same time be a component of several separate multicellular organisms. The concept of institution avoided this logical impasse, since the same biopsychological individual could perform many different activities separately and regularly in conjunction with different sets of other individuals, while being integrally contained together with all of them in the same natural aggregate.

It took many years of epistemological and methodological reflection to substitute a radically different heuristic conception of the social group and of the individual as group member. The first two leaders in this reflection, entirely independent of each other, were Cooley and Simmel. They approached the problem from different points of view, but their lines of reasoning converged. Cooley con-

SOCIAL ORGANIZATION

ceived the human individual not as a separate biopsychological entity, but as a participant in the social order in general; this opened the way to a logical solution of the problem how the same individual can participate in diverse social groups each with an order of its own. Simmel conceived the social group not as a natural complex, but as a general form of the cultural life of men; this made the coexistence of several social groups composed of the same individuals logically understandable, since in each group a different part of the total content of their cultural lives was included.

In later reflection, the theoretic development initiated by these thinkers became gradually synthetized. The final result of this synthesis is that both the social individual and the social group are scientifically treated as cultural products which have to be methodically approached not like trees and forests, animal organisms and animal herds, but like languages, religions, works of literature and art, philosophic and scientific theories. The investigator must apply to them what we have termed elsewhere the *humanistic coefficient*, that is, instead of taking them simply as data of his own direct experience and thought, he must consider them as somebody else's data and discover, by a rather difficult process of observation, symbolic communication, and social experimentation, how they appear and what they mean in the experience and thought of those conscious human agents who are producing them and participating in them. (46)

When approached by this method, an individual's membership in a social group has to be defined as a specific instance of that general class of social systems which is covered by the concept of *role*. The member of a group is a *person*, a socially standardized image and idea (or what Durkheim might have called a "collective representation") of an individual as experienced by other members and reflectively by himself. This person has a normatively regulated *function*, i.e., a set of "duties" which he is expected by other members to perform, and he is granted a regular *status*, *i. e.*, a set of "rights" which other members are expected to support. The same individual can perform during his life or any period of his life a

---

46. For a more systematic presentation if the following outline, cf. the author's "Social Groups as Products of Cooperating Individuals," *American Journal of Sociology*, 44: 799-811, May, 1939. The concept role, as here defined, has been used by the author for fourteen years; it represents an attempt to synthetize various contributions of his predecessors to the common problem of individual participation in a social order.

number of different roles and is a different person in every one of them.

What a social group means in the active experience of its participants can be discovered by studying well-developed groups which last for a lengthy period of time, include a relatively large number of persons, and have some degree of organization. Even though a lynching mob, a married couple, or a neighborhood is sometimes called a "group," such a combination lacks most of the essential characteristics of such social groups as a local church, a college, a scientific association, a trade union, an organized city, not to speak of a state.

Every fully developed social group is imagined, remembered, conceived by its participants as a super-individual, objective whole with a definite content and meaning. It is for them a complex social value composed of the persons of its members as elementary social values; and, of course, only those who are members belong to it. This experience of the group as a whole is usually expressed in symbols — name, flag, crest, memorial, songs, etc.

But the group is represented and conceived by its members not only as a value, but also as an agent. They ascribe to it a status in relation to individuals and other groups. They claim for it the right to possess, to use, and to control the use of various non-social values — "material," such as a portion of space, technical instruments, and economic goods, as well as "spiritual," such as myths, legends, traditions, mysteries, sacred objects and rites, sometimes a distinct language or dialect, aesthetic and intellectual products. They ascribe to it the right to claim certain services and values from individuals or other groups. They want for it recognition and prestige.

Moreover, according to the belief of its participants, the group — like a person — has a specific function or functions, a set of tasks which it "ought to" perform. These tasks may be social duties toward its own members, other groups, or even individual outsiders; or they may be such cultural tasks as technical production, the maintenance of a religious system, development of science or art, standardization of a language.

This composite view of the group as a value and as an agent is more than a system of beliefs. By regularly acting as if the social group were what they believe it to be, its human participants turn it from an idea into a reality within the human world, the very world where it is supposed to exist. As a dynamic system of individ-

SOCIAL ORGANIZATION

ual functions, it realistically uses and controls not only cultural, but natural, reality for collective purposes. To the system of functions which constitute its organization corresponds an orderly combination of individual statuses, which (in accordance with established usage) may be called its *structure*.

The reality of its structure can easily be ascertained by methodical observation. Take a social group organized for industrial production. The status of each member includes the right to occupy a certain ecological position in the area controlled by the group, the right to physical safety within this area, the right to use or to share in the use of certain instruments and materials possessed by the group, the right to such economic remuneration as will maintain him on a certain subsistence level, the right to technical aid from others when needed for the performance of his function, the right to obedience from his subordinates, the right to guidance from superordinates. Not only does recognition or non-recognition of the status of every member by others have observable consequences, but maintenance or non-maintenance of an orderly combination of all these statuses together by group members makes all the difference between the continued existence or non-existence of the industrial plant.

With the progress of comparative sociological investigation of social groups, great qualitative and quantitative differences between them are discovered. Moreover, they are found to be variously interconnected. Many smaller and simpler groups are combined into larger complexes which may or may not have a systematic order; in other cases, there may be a regular connection between groups, each of which nevertheless remains an entirely separate system.

We believe that the concept of social group can serve as a most effective intellectual instrument for an inductive, comparative study of institutions. But for that purpose it is necessary to take into consideration both the group, as an organized and structurally coherent system of the roles of its members, and the various combinations of interconnected groups.

Group Institutions. The idea that institutions ought to be conceived as parts of the organization of social groups in general is not new. Already Rivers said: "The various functions appertaining to social groups are usually known as customs. Certain customs . . . are so important . . . that the have been separated from other customs and called institutions" (op. cit. p. 5). Somehow, though, even sociologists who accept this idea do not use it fully as a leading heuristic principle in investigating institutions. This is well exemplified in the sociological theory of Hankins. He states clearly and explicitly: "Every association must . . . have an organization, that is, rules defining the relations and functions of its members and agents so that their common purposes can be carried out. These rules and agents constitute the group institutions. An institution may be defined as any prescribed usage or structure of relationships set up by an association or consciously approved thereby together with the means or agencies used in carrying out these relationships" (op. cit., p. 473).

From such a definition we would be justified in concluding that comparative studies of institutions ought to be carried on in connection with inductive comparative studies of those many and diverse organized groups or associations, small and large, simple and complex, which sociologists, historians, and anthropologists have discovered. Unfortunately, Hankins does not draw this conclusion, or at least does not use it, but returns to the concept of "society." He includes "society" as a subclass in the general class "group"; but this does not change its traditional conception. "We may define a society as any relatively permanent or continuing group of men, women and children, able to carry on independently the process of racial perpetuation and maintenance, on their own cultural level, and bound together by a tradition of common origin and common destiny" (p.468). The main institutions are referred to this group-society and classified into "the agencies of group adjustment to unseen powers; the agencies of group perpetuation; the agencies of group maintenance; and the agencies of group continuation" (p. 476).

Some of the leading sociologists even seem intentionally to avoid the methodical implications of the concept of social group as a general frame of reference for an inductive study of institutions. We may take as the most notable example F. Stuart Chapin's *Contemporary American Institutions*, precisely because it represents a strictly inductive, scientific approach to specific institutions as observable phenomena. Chapin's work is limited to what he terms "nucleated" institutions: "local government, local political organization, local business enterprise, the family, the school, the church and welfare agencies,", "to be contrasted with art, mythology, language, law, ethics, science, etc., which are general or diffused symbolic institutions. The term culture complex describes both types of institutions, but in the specific social institutions we rec-

SOCIAL ORGANIZATION

ognize the existence of a cultural nucleus or core complex. This nucleus is attached to a restricted locus through the agency of another type of social institution which is always part of the nucleated social institution . . . This culture trait is property" (p.13).

"The four main type parts that combine to produce the configuration or cultural connection known as the social institution are:

First, common reciprocating attitudes of individuals and their conventionalized behavior patterns.

Second, cultural objects of symbolic value . . .

Third, cultural objects, possessing utilitarian value . . .

Fourth, oral or written language symbols that preserve the descriptions and specifications of the pattern of interrelationships among the other three parts . . . When the formulation is compactly organized it is called a code" (p. 15).

Such a "culture complex," however, does not exist by itself. If we seek to discover the human agents who produce and maintain it, we find in certain cases that they are the cooperating agents who participate in the production and maintenance of an organized social group. For in every group the first three classes of phenomena listed by Chapin are included, besides those other phenomena called "persons" and the group as the complex social value composed of those persons. As to the "code," it is nothing but a symbolic expression, usually very incomplete and superficial, of those actively applied standards of valuation and norms of conduct on which the structure and organization of the group is really founded. Thus, when Chapin calls a local church an "institution," he means by it what some other sociologists mean by social group. (47)

But this is not all. We find a somewhat similar, though simpler and less coherent, culture complex maintained by a particular individual agent and a loose set or circle of other individual agents who by interacting with him help him play a certain role. For instance, the role of physician in a circle of patients or that of merchant in a circle of customers contains all those components which Chapin regards as necessary and sufficient to form an institution. However,

---

47. The difference between Chapin's conception of the relationship between "group" and "institution" and the conception here advocated is clearly shown by the fact that, after discussing "the family as a social group in interaction" (p. 90), he includes this group within "the family as an institution," as one of the four components of the latter (p. 100).

[209]

an individual physician's or merchant's role and a church as organized group are obviously very different social systems and cannot be included in the same logical class; just because they contain similar components.

Let us turn now to that specific "nucleated institution" of Chapin's which would unquestionably be termed a social institution by all sociologists, *viz.*, the local goverment. It manifestly differs both from the church as a group and from the role of a merchant. It can exist only as an integral part of a rather large, organized territorial group popularly called a "county" or a "city." This group has a well-defined membership: only persons with specific standardized qualifications belong to it. It is experienced by its members as a separate and united whole, and this experience is symbolically expressed in a name. Though the name of the county or the city designates primarily a territory with all the material objects permanently located therein, yet this territory itself is not experienced merely as a geographic area: it is a common value of the group — the most important of the common values — over which it exercises considerable control, and parts of it, *e. g.*, "public buildings," are considered its exclusive possession. As usual, all roles of members of the group include definite rights and duties.

The same individuals who belong to this group also perform various extraneous roles, either as members of other organized groups, *e.g.*, political parties, business associations, religious groups, or as "private" persons, *e. g.*, merchants, physicians, playboys. These extraneous roles may influence considerably their behavior as members of the city or the county group. But whatever they do in those other roles does not form a part of their standardized and regulated roles as "citizens" of their organized territorial group.

Now, some of the members of the "city" or the "county" are active in the "local government." How do their governmental roles differ from the roles of "ordinary citizens" which all members of their organized territorial group are performing? The difference is well known. A governmental role is "official," a term going back to the Roman "officium," as in Cicero's *De officiis*. The mayor or alderman, the chief of police or policeman, the city treasurer, the commissioner of public works, a member of the school board is a functionary who within the range of his duties represents the city group or the county group *as a whole* in its dynamic relations with individual members, non-members, and other groups. His function

SOCIAL ORGANIZATION

is supposed to be a part of the total functioning of his group as a super-individual agent, and other individuals are expected to react to his official actions as if they were the actions of this super-individual agent. The common idea of the members that their group as a whole is an agent becomes realized in the very measure in which their suppositions and expectations are fulfilled, *i. e.*, when and in so far as the functionaries really act as if the group acted through them and other members really react to these actions as if they were actions of the group. The official status that is granted to a functionary provides positive and negative sanctions intended to insure, on the one hand, that he will really act in accordance with his duties as a group agent, on the other hand, that others will really react to his actions as to those of a group agent. Both the functions and the statuses of such official roles are made independent of the persons of their individual performers, are patterned "impersonally." Various persons become mayors, aldermen, chiefs of police, and drop out after a time; but the patterned function and status of major, alderman, chief of police remain fundamentally similar components of the organization and structure of the city so long as its constitution is unchanged.

Now, we suggest that the term "group institution" be used to denote such official, impersonally patterned functions and statuses of members of any organized social group who act and are reacted to as if through them the group as a whole were acting. We see no reason for extending this term to all uniform patterns of thought and conduct with which group members are made to conform under sanctions. There are other terms—folkways, customs, mores, laws — which can be satisfactorily applied to such phenomena as celebration of holidays, established forms of gift giving or trading, private property rights, patterned relations between the sexes, called marriage, rules regulating automobile traffic, periodical examinations of school pupils.

Let us call "elementary group institution" the patterned function and status of an individual agent who is recognized as representing within a specific range of activity the group. The function and status of mayor, alderman, policeman is an elementary institution of the city; that of regent or trustee, president, provost, treasurer, registrar, dean, an elementary institution of a university; that of minister or elder an elementary institution of a church.

As we know, however, in a large and coherent social group, those tasks which the group as collective agent is supposed to perform require the participation and collaboration of many individual agents with different official roles. Thus, elementary institutions are combined into *compound institutions*, where not only the function and status of each individual, but their distribution and the connection between them is regulated. Compound institutions differ in complexity, and several less complex institutions can be integrated into a more complex one. The city government is a compound institution with a high degree of complexity and includes a number of diverse, less complex institutions.

Now, a compound group institution, including as it does a number of individuals functioning for a common purpose, is itself a social group with an inner organization and structure. However, its institutional character is primary, its group character secondary. Its members cannot maintain it in existence, apart from the larger group, and whatever inner order it may develop in addition to its institutional order is dependent upon the latter. The relation between it and the larger group on behalf of which it functions and of which it is an integral part differs essentially from the relation bebetween two distinct groups, one of which performs a specific function which the other does not perform but which it supports and controls.

Institutionalized Group. We use this term to denote groups which are essentially cooperative products of their own members, but whose collective functions and statuses are partly institutionalized by other social groups. This does not mean that the institutionalized group becomes a part of the organization and structure of the group which institutionalizes it; only that the latter recognizes the former as a group and subjects some of its functions to positive and negative sanctions.

A typical example of this process of institutionalization is recognition of an extracurricular student group by a university which grants it certain rights, under the condition that its functions will have a "desirable" educational influence, and subjects it to the control of faculty sponsors with negative sanctions for "undesirable" activities.

This concept of "institutionalized group" is meant to serve heuristic purposes different from those of the "institutional group" introduced by E. T. Hiller. (48) Hiller is concerned with relation-

---

48. "Institutions and Institutional Groups," *Social Forces,* 20: 297-306, March, 1942.

SOCIAL ORGANIZATION

ships between the group as a specifically social system which contains "interaction between, and valuation of, persons as necessary phases of its composition," and other nonpersonal cultural systems — linguistic, aesthetic, religious, technical — which have been commonly called institutions or institutional systems in sociological literature. An institutional group would then be a social system integrated with reference to one of these nonpersonal cultural systems which provides a common "value-orientation" for the participants of the group, "gives the basis for a distinctive organization of the group and the test of relevance of conduct by the participants."

The problem raised in the monograph quoted here is what influence does such a "collective value-orientation" have upon the group as a social system. We fully realize the importance of this problem for a sociological theory of social groups. We see also how it may be connected with an even wider problem: that of the influence which the groups termed "institutional" by Hiller have upon religious, aesthetic, technical and other non-social cultural systems. But for reasons discussed above, we believe that sociology should cease to refer to such fields of cultural phenomena as language, religion, art, technique, or knowledge by the name "institutions." We must, therefore, clearly distinguish our term "institutionalized group" from Hiller's term " institutional group."

The heuristic significance of the concept "institutionalized group" will be clear when we substitute it hypothetically for that of "institution" in studying such logical classes of social groups as the church, the school, the family. In every case we shall, first, limit our field of research to a subdivision of the general class; then analyze fully and realistically the composition, organization, and structure of particular churches, schools, or families selected as typical samples of this subdivision; next, ask ourselves by what social group, if any, these churches, schools, or families are institutionalized, and what this institutionalization consists in.

We shall find, for instance, that the abstract logical class "the church" contains social groups differing as widely in size and organized powers and structural complexity as the Roman Catholic Church and an independent Unitarian church of a few hundred members. We find that one territorial division of a widely extended church or a large and complex independent church within a state may be institutionalized by the state as a "state church," whereas the other churches or sects lack state sanction for their religious functions. No church is institutionalized as such by the United States or by any state in the Union; the religious functions of all of them are left to their own devices. Are there any other large and organized social groups besides states which institutionalize churches? We have been working on this problem recently and think that there may be some; but we have not yet proved it.

According to a current definition, "local" churches are "community institutions." We interpret this definition as a hypothesis that all local churches are groups institutionalized by communities, that is, that they are recognized as groups (not merely as agglomerations of individuals) and that their religious functions are subjected to positive and negative sanctions by those community groups within whose areas their centers are located. Such a hypothesis will have to be carefully tested by inductive research. Whether proved universally valid or universally invalid or — as seems probable — valid only for specific churches in specific communities under specific conditions, its testing will deepen our knowledge of churches, communities, and the very process of institutionalization.

Take schools. All schools are social groups with a definite composition and at least a rudimentary organization and structure. Their existence depends primarily and essentially on the combined activities of their members — teachers and learners. A few schools are materially independent. Quite a number depend on individual contributions from parents of learners for the economic status which both teachers and learners need to perform their respective functions; but the educational function of the school as a group is neither positively nor negatively sanctioned by any other group. Most schools, however, are institutionalized — in older times mainly by religious groups, in modern times mainly by organized territorial groups and also by national culture groups. The educational requirements which these two kinds of groups tend to impose upon schools sometimes harmonize, sometimes conflict. Professional groups, class groups, economic groups also institutionalize partly or completely certain schools. And, of course, many schools form a part of a larger school. With all that, a school as a social group maintains a certain degree of inner autonomy, a specific order of its own, similar to that of many other schools, but different from that of other types of group, since the roles of teachers and learners are essentially different from the roles of members of any other group, and the organization and structure of the school cannot be

SOCIAL ORGANIZATION

incorporated into the organization and structure of any other group. Until we discard our vague generalizations, normative rather than scientific, about schools as institutions and inductively study schools as groups and their various functional connections with the many, diverse larger groups which are more or less effectively institutionalizing them, we shall have no scientific sociology of schools.

The field of research now hidden under the veil of the doctrine that "the family is a social institution" is also wide and promising, though difficult. Fortunately, parental families as distinct social groups have been quite thoroughly investigated. But parental families have been throughout history and most of them are even now component groups of grandparental families or of unilateral perpetual families. They have been and are being institutionalized by religious groups, by territorial groups (ranging from a village to an empire), by culture groups (from a small tribe or folk group to a modern national culture group with millions of members), by class associations, by occupational associations, by technical groups, by economic corporations. Each of these groups tends to influence somewhat differently the functions of all the families which it tries to subject to its sanctions, and the process of institutionalization is somewhat different in each of them. We cannot fully understand the real, multiple, diverse, conflicting functioning of the many millions of parental families now in existence until we have investigated their functional relationship with those larger groups.

If now we turn from institutionalized groups to those groups which are institutionalizing other groups, we shall find that the study of the process of institutionalization helps us redefine the old and now useless concept of "society" in a way that will make it again heuristically useful. Let us conceive a society hypothetically as the total complex of social groups which are institutionalized by a large, united, and relatively independent social group. In accordance with the age-old tradition, we shall probably begin with the state. After investigating a state with its own institutional organization and structure, we shall extend our study to all those groups which, while not parts of the state, are institutionalized by the state. This will be easy, for the process of institutionalization assumes legal forms here. But eventually we shall find that many groups formed by individuals who are citizens of the state are not institutionalized by the state, but by some other large group or groups to which citizens of the state also belong and that, even among the groups which the state institutionalizes, there are some which another large group also subjects to its sanctions. Moreover, we shall discover that there are social groups which have members among the citizens of several states and institutionalize some of the groups to which these members belong. The best known among these are large religious groups. If we call the total complex of groups institutionalized by the same state a "society," we must therefore also apply this term to the total complex of groups institutionalized by the same large religious group. We find, thus, two types of "societies" — "political societies" and "religious societies" — and these frequently and considerably overlap.

A third type of society, different from political and from religious societies and not coextensive with either, is what we call "national culture society," a product of modern times, which we have been investigating lately. In certain historical periods with strong and coherent class groups, many groups are institutionalized by them; we shall be entitled to apply in such cases the term "class society," provided we do not dogmatically accept the doctrine that a class society is either the dominant society or coextensive with a political society.

We think that such a heuristic use of the concept "society" can be very helpful in investigating the collective life of mankind in any historical period, but particularly in the present period.

SELECTED BIBLIOGRAPHY

Allport, Floyd Henry, *Institutional Behavior*, (Chapel Hill: The University of North Carolina Press, 1933).

Ballard, Lloyd Vernon, *Social Institutions*, (New York: D. Appleton-Century Co., 1936).

Barnes, Harry Elmer, *Social Institutions in an Era of World Upheaval*, (New York: Prentice-Hall, 1943).

Chapin, F. Stuart, *Contemporary American Institutions*, (New York: Harper and Bros., 1935).

Cooley, Charles Horton, *Social Organization*, (New York: Charles Scribner's Sons, 1922).

Gillin, John Lewis, and John Philip Gillin, *An Introduction to Sociology*, (New York: The Macmillan Co., 1942).

Hertzler, Joyce, *Social Institutions*, (New York: McGraw-Hill Book Co., 1929).

Hiller, E. T., "Institutions and Institutional Groups," *Social Forces*, 20: 297-306, March, 1942.

SOCIAL ORGANIZATION

MacIver, Robert Morrison, *Society,* (New York: Farrar and Rinehart, 1937).
Panunzio, Constantine, *Major Social Institutions,* (New York: The Macmillan Co., 1939).
Rivers, W. H. R., *Social Organization,* (New York: Alfred A. Knopf, 1924).

Florian Witold Znaniecki (Ph. D., Cracow University) is Professor of Sociology at the University of Illinois. He lectured at the University of Chicago 1917-9. From 1920 to 1939, he was Professor of Sociology at the University of Poznan. He taught at Columbia University as Visiting Professor from 1931 to 1933, and again in 1939. He has published eight books and many articles in Polish (see section on Polish Sociology). Besides numerous articles in American periodicals, he is the author of the following books published in English: *The Polish Peasant,* in collaboration with W. I. Thomas, 5 vols., (Boston: Badger, 1918-20); *Cultural Reality,* (Chicago: University of Chicago Press, 1919); *The Laws of Social Psychology,* (Chicago: University of Chicago Press, 1925); *The Method of Sociology,* (New York: Farrar and Rinehart, 1934); *Social Actions,* (New York: Farrar and Rinehart, 1936); *The Social Role of the Man of Knowledge,* (New York: Columbia University Press, 1940).

CHAPTER IX

SOCIAL PSYCHOLOGY

by

JAMES W. WOODARD

We shall endeavor, in the first section of this chapter, to trace briefly the deveolpment of social psychology, chiefly with reference to the United States. For spatial reasons, fewer critical and evalutive remarks will be included than would otherwise be desirable. In the second section we shall discuss some selected aspects of an integral social-psychological theory, its requisite methodological tools and applied-science implications.

For spatial reasons, many good men, excellent books, and important areas will here fail of the attention they deserve. For that we are sorry. The contributions here footnoted (1) are excellent sum-

---

1. Kimball Young, "Social Psychology," in H. E. Barnes, ed., *History and Prospects of the Social Sciences,* (New York: Alfred A. Knopf, 1925); J. F. Markey, "Trends in Social Psychology," in G. A. Lundberg, Read Bain, and Nels Anderson, eds., *Trends in American Sociology,* (New York: Harper and Bros., 1929); F. B. Karpf, *American Social Psychology,* (New York: McGraw-Hill Book Co., 1932); L. L. Bernard, "Social Psychology," in *Encyclopedia of the Social Sciences,* 14:151-157; Jessie Bernard, "The Sources and Methods of Social Psychiatry" in L. L. Bernard, ed., *The Fields and Methods of Sociology,* (New York: Farrar and Rinehart, 1934); Herbert Blumer, "Social Psychology," in E. P. Schmidt, ed., *Man and Society,* (New York: Prentice-Hall, 1937); Kimball Young and Douglass W. Oberdorfer, "Psychological Studies of Social Processes," in H. E. Barnes, Howard Becker, and Frances Bennett Becker, eds., *Contemporary Social Theory,* (New York: D. Appleton-Century Co., 1940); and Leonard S. Cottrell, Jr., and Ruth Gallagher, *Developments in Social Psychology,* 1930-1940, Sociometry Monograph, No. 1 (1941).

maries and criticisms up to the point of, and in the background of, their successive times of publication. The reader is referred to them, and especially to the two most recent ones, to supplement the present paper. Or vice versa. For we shall touch briefly on or omit some areas and expand upon or include some others on that basis.

I

The dawn of the twentieth century of course carried impulses that had originated earlier. From adjacent fields, theories were still influential which carried social-psychological implications. In terms of the culture lag between scientific disciplines, some of these still appear in the work of historians and others. Such were the theories of the direct effects of the physical environment on the psychology of man and on his social institutions and civilizational level put forth a century or more before by Bodin, Montesquieu, Buckle, and others. And such were the theories of racial inequality put forth in the middle and latter nineteenth century by De Gobineau and Chamberlain. Mesmer, Bernheim, and Charcot had done work on hypnosis. And Sighele and Le Bon were applying their findings to mob behavior. Psychology itself was still largely atomistic, concerned with brass-instruments and structuralist description. But William James had written his momumental two volumes, giving impulse to the instinctive and functional approaches. And Binet and Freud were starting on what were later to appear as such important developments. In sociology, Bagehot, Spencer, and Comte had written; and Tarde was about to set forth a theory of society in terms of imitation and suggestion. Lester F. Ward had written his *Psychic Factors in Civilization;* F. H. Giddings had already set forth his "consciousness of kind" theory; and Ross was in process of writing his *Social Control.* Lazarus and Steinthal had started folk-psychology on its way. Wundt had carried it along. And, while William James was writting his *Varieties* in terms of individual religious experience, Durkheim had already written his *Les Règles.*

From this point, we can begin to pick out threads and follow them along. The psychological influence of the physical environment has been carried along by the anthropogeographers and some sociologists such as Le Play rather than by the social psychologists. Recently, Maurice Krout has included chapters and maps on environmental aspects in his social psychology text. And Clyde Kluckholn includes such a category in his formal classification of things affecting personality, one of the best systematic classifications of factors so far. (2)

Courses in racial psychology began to be offered in the 1900's but lapsed with the lapse of instinct and group mind and the impact of behaviorism. It was not until after the World War mental tests had been reshuffled and scrutinized, however, that the doctrine of important mental and personality differences among races was finally given over. The present emphasis in scientific circles (and only there unfortunately) is on the essential equality of races and the inadequacy of race as an explanation of social or cultural traits. Social psychology has turned from a study of race mentality as such to that of race prejudice. On that subject a great deal of work has been done, to the neglect of the study of other forms of prejudice. (3)

---

2. See *inter alia*, F. Thomas, *The Environmental Basis of Society*, (New York: The Century Co., 1925), the best general survey; C. O. Sauer, "Cultural Geography," in *Encyclopedia of the Social Sciences*, 6:621-624; H. Odum and H. E. Moore, *American Regionalism*, (New York: Henry Holt and Co., 1938); C. D. Forde, *Habitat, Economy and Society*, (New York: Harcourt, Brace and Co., 1934); I. Bowman, *Geography in Relation to the Social Sciences*, (New York: Charles Scribner's Sons, 1934); R. B. Vance *Human Geography of the South*, (Chapel Hill: University of North Carolina Press, 1932); E. Demolins, *Les grandes routes des peuples* (1901-1903); Fréderic Le Play, *Ouvriers européens;* Clyde Kluckhohn and O. H. Mowrer, "Culture and personality: A Conceptual Scheme," *American Anthropologist*, N. S. 46: 1-29, 1944; Maurice H. Krout, *Introduction to Social Psychology*, (New York, 1943).

3. Best treatments: (historical), F. H. Hankins, *The Racial Basis of Civilization*, (New York: Alfred a Knopf, 1926); (modern), O. Klineberg, *Race Differences*, (New York: Harper and Bros., 1935). Cf.: A. de Gobineau, *Inequality of Human Races* (Eng. trans. 1914); H. S. Chamberlain, *Foundations of the Nineteenth Century* (Eng. trans. 1911); M. Grant, *The Passing of the Great Race*, (New York: Charles Scribner's Sons, 1916); W. McDougall, *Is America Safe for Democracy?* (New York: Charles Scribner's Sons, 1921); C. C. Brigham, *A Study of American Intelligence*, (Princeton; Princeton University Press, 1923); T. R. Garth, *Race Psychology*, (New York: McGraw-Hill Book Co., 1931); E. Huntington, *The Character of Races*, (New York: Charles Scribner's Sons, 1924); F. Boas, *Anthropology and Modern Life*, (New York: W. W. Norton and Co., 1928); B. Lasker, *Race Attitudes in Children*, (New York: Henry Holt and Co., 1929); E. S. Bogardus, *Immigration and Race Attitudes*, (Boston: D. C. Heath and Co., 1928); J. Dollard, *Caste and Class in a Southern Town*, (New Haven: Yale University Press, 1937); W. D. Weatherford and C. S. Johnson, *Race Relations*, (Boston: D. C. Heath and Co., 1934); J. Dollard et al., *Frustration and Aggression*, (New Haven: Yale University Press, 1939); H. W. Odum, *Race and Rumors of Race*, (Chapel Hill: University of North Carolina Press, 1944).

SOCIAL PSYCHOLOGY

The handling of race confronts us with the same humanitarian interferences with objectivity which sociology knows so well. It is enough to remember that racial differences are slight and the overlappings great. Even if we could prove racial superiorities and inferiorities (which we cannot), individual selection rather than racial preferences and discriminations would be the functionally appropriate principle for the securing of either efficiency or justice. But because of the reaction against the absurd claims of the racial egotists; lest admission of *any* differences be misinterpreted; and because of the strong egalitarian bias of the non-racial egoist theorists; there is a strong compulsion to have findings come out on the dotted line of equal racial abilities. This is contrary to *a priori* expectations, since every other measurable trait shows differences, slight and overlapping as they may be, as do some of the empirical findings. The essence of science should be precise statement of its provable, probable, and plausible conclusions without bias, humanitarian or otherwise.

The gross anatomical relationships to subtle intellectual and personality characteristics — phrenology, head-shape, and the theories of Lombroso and Havelock Ellis, *e. g.* — have been discarded long since. The only survivor, running rather poorly, is Kretschmer's classification of morphological types. However, with the discovery of the importance of the glands of internal secretion, glandular explanations of personality had quite a vogue from about 1920 on. Their influence is more conservatively regarded now. But we have also become aware of the influence of basal metabolism, the alkalinity or acidity of the body chemistry, and the influence of certain disease states on personality. (4) The awareness of these is a healthy corrective for our tendency to social-cultural unilateralism in a *complete* theory of personality.

The work of Binet and Simon, coupled with that of Galton and

---

4. L. Berman, *The Glands Regulating Personality*, (New York: The Macmillan Co., 1921); E. Kretschmer, *Physique and Character*, (New York: Harcourt, Brace and Co., 1925); W. B. Cannon, *Bodily Changes in Pain, Fear, and Rage*, (New York: D. Appleton and Co., 1929); G. Draper, *The Human Constitution*. (Philadelphia: W. B. Saunders Co., 1924); E. M. L. Burchard, "Physique and Psychosis," *Comparative Psychology Monographs*, 13, 1936; O. Klineberg, S. E. Asch, and H. Block, "An Experimental Study of Constitutional Types, *Genetic Psychology Monographs*, 16, 1934; G. J. Rich, "A Biochemical Approach to the Study of Personality," *Journal of Abnormal and Social Psychology*, 23: 158-175, 1928.

TWENTIETH CENTURY SOCIOLOGY

Pearson, led to a movement toward eugenics which has never achieved much and which is now fairly neglected. But it led also to a prodigious development, under Thorndike, Cattell, Stern, Terman, and a host of others, of mental testing and measurement. The techniques devised came to be applied to the measurement of individual differences in native ability, educational placement and achievement, aptitude testing and vocational guidance, personality testing, the measurement of attitudes, and presently such large-scale things as public opinion, consumer demand, morale, and the like. Various correlations were run; and progressively from about 1914 on light was shed on the relation of individual ability to achievement, leadership, socio-economic status, industrial placement, genius, delinquency, and endless items of social psychological significance. Radical interpretations, such as the earlier Kallikak and Juke studies, bootless linking of ability with race and nationality, and the phase of interpreting delinquency too largely in such terms, got presently ironed out. A tremendously important development, with refinements and further contributions still accruing, its findings are still rather scattered, unintegrated as yet either into systematic theory or an integral practice. (5) Allport, *e. g.*, still maintains that innate differences in ability and personality factors are non-existent.

Democratic egalitarianism and moral-religious pietism affect our handling of individual differences. The radical environmentalism of the Allportians and the recondite character (to the layman) of some of the biological factors abet this. As excellent a book as Klineberg's *Social Psychology* has a *Conclusion* devoted to discounting biological factors and opposing eugenics in favor of education. This adoption of an either/or, rather than a both/and, approach to the treatment of two indispensables which cannot even be defined (as *effective* x or y) except in terms of each other betrays the social unilateralism which is our own occupational hazard (*Wissen-*

---

5. Good summaries: A. Anastasi, *Differential Psychology,* (New York: The Macmillan Co., 1937); F. S. Freeman, *Individual Differences,* (New York: Henry Holt and Co., 1934). Also, *inter alia,* A. H. Estabrook, *The Jukes in 1915,* (Dashington: Carnegie Institution, 1916); A. E. Wiggam, *The Fruit of the Family Tree,* (Indianapolis: Bobbs-Merrill Co., 1924); P. A. Sorokin, *Social Mobility,* (New York: Harper and Bros., 1927); L. M. Terman, *Genetic Studies of Genius,* (Stanford University: Stanford University Press, 1925-1926, 2 vols.); A. Myerson, et al., *Eugenical Sterilization,* (New York: The Macmillan Co., 1936).

sociologie please copy). That is one reason we should be encyclopaedic — to offset our own abstractive unilateralism.

Heredity and environment are both inextricably involved in developmental processes from the first cell division of the fertilized ovum on; in the learning process from fetal life on. The learning process is a cumulative and at least up to the point of arteriosclerosis, an accelerative process. Initial gains facilitate further gains, which not merely add on but also facilitate still further gains. Thus even insignificant initial differences compound into great eventual differences; just as initial 1 and 2 in a pair of Malthusian geometric series' grow further and further apart, becoming presently expressible in terms of vast differences. The fact that environment can be manipulated and heredity once given can not, should not mislead us into a *post hoc ergo propter hoc* error. Both are inextricably involved at very step. We have yet to learn the lessons the anthropogeographers have finally learned relative to man, physical environment, and the contained, cumulative, and accelerative cultural process — (1) that the indispensables are always actively present, inextricably intertwined at every point in the total process; (2) that "determinism" has to give way to "conditionism" and "possibilism"; (3) that *direct* entity-effects lose importance to *indirect* process-products; (4) that as a by-product of this, *specific* effects lose importance to the *general* processed achievements. But *both* indispensables are always reflected in *whatever* direct, indirect, specific, general, objectively measurable and manipulable, or obscurely intangible results. It is probably in this sense of setting initial tangents for processes which then dovetail into familial or other social interaction patterns to produce eventual marked differences in personality pattern, that innate differences will be more and more interpreted.

The whole matter of innate differences, however apparently trivial such differences may seem, is of such importance because the incapable stupid as well as the merely untutored furnish the material for mass exploitation, and the mass inertia in cultural lag. They are the most susceptible to prejudice, crowd psychology, propaganda, and rigidly stereotyped thinking. They gullibly follow demagogic leaders, accept the myths, legends, and fictions which support obsolescent or inappropriate social orders, and are raw material for practically every maladjustive social-psychological process. Consider the circularities of beneficial process that would result from an eugenical skewing of the curve of the distribution of abilities to give us an intelligent *mass*. That would eventually mean so much for education, democracy, industrial and military efficiency, and all the arts, sciences, and humanities, that an applied social psychology should be pretty strong in its recommendations. The problems of a global tomorrow, full of endless relativities and complexities, cannot be smoothly solved by stupid populational masses.

Social psychology proper is usually taken as starting with the founding in 1860 of the *Zeitschrift fuer Voelkerpsychologie und Sprachwissenschaft* by Lazarus and Steinthal. The Hegelian concept of "over-soul" and the organic view of society were carried along with varying emphases and lessening mysticism of causal efficacy successively by Lazarus and Steinthal, Wundt, Sighele and Le Bon, Durkheim, Lévy-Bruhl, McDougall, and possibly even Cooley, Mead, Lowie, and Benedict! (6) The group mind concept culminated in the work of Durkheim, however. Those following Durkheim in the above listing were more effective in modifying both the radical "group" theorists and the radical "individual" theorists (such as Allport and Schanck) in terms of the organic *interrelation* of individual *and* group. A very lively controversy in the twenties, the place of the individual *or* the group in a "hierarchy of reality" is now regarded as a dead issue by common consent. It still breathes a little, however. The same may be said for one of the off-shoots of the group mind theory, Lévy-Bruhl's "primitive mentality." An excellent corrective for the projected intellectualism and long-distance mind reading of Spencer, Tylor, Frazer and the earlier social theorists, it was at first over-accepted. It is now over-rejected. And

---

6. See, *inter alia*, Wilhelm Wundt, *Elements of Folk Psychology* (trans. by Schaub); Emile Durkheim, *Les règles de la méthode sociologique* (1895); *Elementary Forms of Religious Life* (1912; Eng. trans., 1915); C. E. Gehlke, *Emile Durkheim's Contribution to Sociological Theory* (1915); L. Levy-Bruhl, *La mentalité primitive;* also *Les fonctions mentales dans les sociétés inférieures;* F. Boas, *Mind of Primitive Man;* J. H. Robinson, *Mind in the Making;* Wm. McDougall, *The Group Mind* (1921); Floyd H. Allport, "Group' and 'Institution' as Concepts in a Natural Science of Social Phenomena," *Publications of the American Sociological Society,* 22: 83-99, 1927; also "The Group Fallacy in Relation to Social Science," *American Journal of Sociology,* 29:688-706, 1924; A. L. Kroeber, "The Superorganic," *American Anthropologist,* N. S. 19:163-213, 1917; Ruth Benedict, *Patterns of Culture,* (Boston Houghton Mifflin Co., 1934).

it cannot escape being brought presently into a more qualified and balanced acceptance.

Bagehot, Tarde, Ross, Ellwood, Bogardus, McDougall, and in some measure Giddings and the earlier work of W. I. Thomas attempted to interpret social phenomena in terms of psychological processes such as imitation, suggestion, habit, instinct, wishes, "consciousness of kind," etc., operative on the grand scale of the "psychic planes and currents" resulting from the association of men — hierarchies of prestige and suggestion, stellar points in social control, the crowd mind and mass movement, and large-scale action of individual mechanisms. (7) Their influence dwindled under the impact of behaviorism and the tracing out of the detailed processing (in terms of conditioned response and the like) of what they had depicted as the grand-scale action of rather vague factors. Thomas, making terms with the new tendencies, fared much better. In the years since, individual psychology, social psychology, sociology, and psychoanalysis have enriched, corrected, and given us a processed-out understanding of these hierarchies of control and psychic planes and currents. (8)

Stressed by Wm. James, elaborated by Thorndike and many others, and made the dominant concept of social psychology in

---

7. Walter Bagehot, *Physics and Politics* (1884); Gabriel Tarde, *The Laws of Imitation* 1903); S. Sighele, *La Foule Criminelle* (1901); Gustave Le Bon, *The Crowd* (1896); F. H. Giddings, *The Principles of Sociology* (1896); E. A. Ross, *Social Control* (1901) and *Social Psychology* (1908); Charles A. Ellwood, *Some Prolegomena to Social Psychology* (1901), *Sociology and its Psychological Aspects* (1914), and *Introduction to Social Psychology* (1917); Wm. McDougall, *An Introduction to Social Psychology* (1908).

8.See, *inter alia*, E. D. Martin, *The Behavior of Crowds*, (New York: Harper and Bros., 1920); F. H. Allport, *Social Psychology*, (Boston: Houghton Mifflin Co., 1924); S. Freud, *Group Psychology and the Analysis of the Ego* (1921); E. A. Strecker, *Beyond the Clinical Frontiers*, (New York: W. W. Norton and Co., 1940); Hadley Cantril, *The Psychology of Social Movements*, (New York: John Wiley and Sons, 1941); P. A. Sorokin, *Man and Society in Calamity*, (New York: E. P. Dutton and Co., 1942); Kimball Young, *Social Psychology*, (New York: F. S. Crofts and Co., 1944); R. T. LaPierre, *Collective Behavior*, (New York: McGraw-Hill Book Co., 1938); J. C. Fluegel, *The Psychology of Clothes*, (New York: Robert O. Ballou, 1930); E. B. Hurlock, *The Psychology of Dress*, (New York: Ronald Press Co., 1929); Thorstein Veblen, *Theory of the Leisure Class* (1915). (See later for public opinion, propaganda, morale, etc.).

the decade following 1908 by W. McDougall, the instinct theory, under the impact of behaviorism and the sharp attack of Dunlap, Faris, Allport, Kuo, Bernard, and others, all but completely succumbed in the space of five or six years. (9) Over-acceptance was followed by over-rejection in the form of a radical environmentalism, which only began subtantially to give way to synthesis after the mid-thirties. Preceded by *faculty*, instinct has been followed by *propensities* (McDougall) *prepotent reflexes* (Allport), *desires* (Dunlap), *drives* (Holt and Warden), *motives* (Gurnee), *viscerogenic needs* (Murray), *dependable motives* (Woodworth, Klineberg), *wishes* (Thomas), and *dynamic habit* (Dewey), among others. (10) The psychoanalysts, while lately rebelling considerably against the biological and instinctual foundations of Freudian theory, still yield ground slowly (*e. g.* Deutsch). Resemblances between twins, especially identical twins, wide variations in fetal behavior (Healy), evidence of personality differences from the very earliest days of life (Washburn), and indications of an hereditary

---

9. On instinct, see, *inter alia,* Wm. James, *Principles of Psychology* (1890); E. L. Thorndike, *Educational Psychology* (1913); Wm. McDougall, *Introduction to Social Psychology* (1908); W. Trotter, *Instincts of the Herd* (1916). On its criticism, see Knight Dunlap, "Are There Any Instincts?" *Journal of Abnormal Psychology,* 14: 307-11, 1919; J. R. Kantor, "A Functional View of Human Instincts," *Psychological Review,* 27: 50-72, 1920; W. S. Hunter, "The Modification of Instincts from the Standpoint of Social Psychology," *Psychological Review,* 27:247-269, 1920; L. L. Bernard, "The Misuse of Instinct in the Social Sciences," *Psychological Review,* 28:96-119, 1921; Z. Y. Kuo, "Giving Up Instinct in Psychology," *Journal of Philosophy* 18:645-64, 1921; Elsworth Faris, "Are Instincts Data or Hypotheses?" *American Journal of Sociology,* 27:184-196, 1921; C. C. Josey, *The Social Philosophy of Instinct,* (New York: Charles Scribner's Sons, 1922); F. H. Allport, *Social Psychology;* L. L. Bernard, *Instinct,* (New York: Henry Holt and Co., 1924).

10. Knight Dunlap, *Civilized Life,* (Baltimore: Williams and Wilkins Co., 1934); H. Gurnee, *Elements of Social Psychology,* (New York: Farrar and Rinehart, 1936); E. B. Holt, *Animal Drive and the Learning Process,* (New York: Henry Holt and Co., 1931); C. J. Warden, *Animal Motivation,* (New York: Columbia University Press, 1931); R. S. Woodworth, *Psychology,* rev. ed., (New York: Henry Holt and Co., 1929); O. Klineberg, *Social Psychology;* H. A. Murray, et al., *Explorations in Personality,* (New York: Oxford University Press, 1939); F. H. Allport, *Social Psychology;* W. I. Thomas, *The Unadjusted Girl,* (Boston: Little Brown and Co., 1923); John Dewey, *Human Nature and Conduct;* Helene Deutsch, *Psychology of Women,* (New York: Grune and Stratton, 1944).

SOCIAL PSYCHOLOGY

basis in the marked differences in social behavior of nursing children (Buehler) are modifying our earlier radical environmentalism. (11) The general problem of the occurrence and the degree of specificity of innate traits at the human level is not yet fully solved. We shall discuss some aspects of the problem in the second section of this chapter.

Behaviorism, improvement and extension of application of statistics and other objective-quantitative methods, trends in philosophy and in other sciences toward an indeterminate view of the universe, and stricter conceptual discipline as reflected in operationalism and semantics — the combined impact of these things greatly altered the "climate" of social psychology from about 1920 through the mid-thirties. Behaviorism, stemming from Pavlow, Watson, Lashley, and others, got its largest social-psychological reflection in the Allports, Weiss, Schanck, Bernard, and the extreme environmentalists, but modified the entire field more or less. (12)

The perfecting and extension of statistical methods marked all the sciences, and filtered into social psychology from all sides, perhaps especially from individual and educational testing and

---

11. H. H. Newman, et al., *Twins: A Study of Heredity and Environment*, (Chicago: University of Chicago Press, 1937); W. Healy, *Personality in Formation and Action*, (New York: W. W. Norton and Co., 1938); R. W. Washburn, "A Study of the Smiling and Laughing of Infants in the First Year of Life," *Genetic Psychology Monographs*, 6: 397-537, 1939; C. Buehler, "The Social Behavior of Children," in C. Murchison, ed., *Handbook of Child Psychology*, (Worcester: Clark University Press, 1933); L. T. Hogben, *Nature and Nurture*, (New York: W. W. Norton and Co., 1933); G. E. Schwesinger, *Heredity and Environment*, (New York: The Macmillan Co., 1933); R. S. Woodworth, *Heredity and Environment*, Social Science Research Bulletin 37, (New York: 1941).

12. See, inter alia, J. B. Watson, *Behaviorism*, (New York: W. W. Norton and Co., 1925); F. H. Allport, *Social Psychology*; A. P. Weiss, "A Set of Postulates for Social Psychology," *Journal of Abnormal and Social Psychology*, 21: 203-211, 1926; L. L. Bernard, *Instinct*; L. L. Bernard, *Introduction to Social Psychology*, (New York: Henry Holt and Co., 1926); D. Katz and R. L. Schanck, *Social Psychology*, (New York: John Wiley and Sons, 1938); F. H. Allport, *Institutional Behavior*, (Chapel Hill: University of North Carolina Press, 1933).

measuring. A listing of contributors would be endless (13). Terman, Thorndike, and Cattell among early contributors; Thurstone, with his least-perceptible-difference and equal-appearing interval techniques, vector analysis, etc., as perhaps the most eminent rationalizer and perfector of methods; a number of painstaking, balanced, and cautious users of and contributors to the method, of whom Clifford Kirkpatrick might be taken as an example, who, because of those very characteristics, made solid contributions but did not show the missionary zeal of, say, Stuart Rice, the inventive brilliancy of, say, Sam Stouffer, or the polemical fervor of say, Read Bain or George Lundberg; and finally a rather large number who had mastered the techniques but did not understand their limitations, hazards, or full-perspective meaning. This sometimes resulted in the futility of using fine tools on meaningless problems, inadequacy in interpretation, and a neglect of other methods amounting sometimes almost to taboo against their cultivation. The statistical emphasis led to a general objective emphasis, resulting also in such objective and quasi-objective methods as the sociometry and topology of Dodd, Lundberg, Moreno, Kurt Lewin, J. F. Brown, and others. (14)

---

13. See, *inter alia*, L. L. Thurstone, "Attitudes Can Be Measured," *American Journal of Sociology*, 33:529-554, 1928; L. L. Thurstone and E. J. Chave, *The Measurement of Attitudes*, (Chicago: University of Chicago Press, 1929); G. A. Lundberg, *Social Research*, (New York: Longmans, Green and Co., 1929), and *Foundations of Sociology*, (New York: The Macmillan Co., 1939); O. Klineberg, *Social Psychology*, Chap. XVI; G. Murphy, L. B. Murphy, and T. M. Newcomb, *Experimental Social Psychology*, 2nd ed., (New York: Harper and Bros., 1937), Chaps. XII and XIII; S. A. Rice *Statistics in Social Science*, (Philadelphia: University of Pennsylvania Press, 1930); E. W. Burgess and Leonard Cottrell, Jr., *Predicting Success or Failure in Marriage*, (New York: Prentice-Hall, 1939); L. L. Thurstone, *Vectors of the Mind*, (Chicago: University of Chicago Press, 1935), *Primary Mental Abilities*, (Chicago: University of Chicago Press, 1938), and "Current Issues in Factor Analysis," *Psychological Bulletin*, 37, No. 44, 1940.

14. See, *inter alia*, K. Lewin, *Principles of Topological Psychology*, (New York: MacGraw-Hill Book Co., 1936), and *A Dynamic Theory of Personality*, (New York: McGraw-Hill Book Co., 1935); J. F. Brown, "Individual, Group, and Social Field," *American Journal of Sociology*, 44-858-886, 1939, and *Psychology and the Social Order*, (New York: McGraw-Hill Book Co., 1936); J. L. Moreno, *Who Shall Survive?* (New York: Nervous and Mental Diseases Pub. Co., 1934); G. A. Lundberg, *Foundations of Sociology*; S. C. Dodd, *The Dimensions of Society*, (New York: The Macmillan Co., 1940); K. Lewin, "Field Theory and Experiment in Social Psychology: Concepts and Methods," *American Journal of Sociology*, 44:868-896, 1939; also issues of *Sociometry*.

SOCIAL PSYCHOLOGY

The rationale of the epistemological assumption of an indeterminate universe goes back at least to Hume, and traces through Karl Pearson and many others to Eddington, Jeans, Bridgeman, and other modern exponents. So does that of statistics and behaviorism. And (although part of the contemporary interest in symbolism derives from G. H. Mead, Markey, and others) so does the objectivity-strain and implicit skepticism of the semantics and operationalism of Ogden and Richards, Korzybski, Bridgeman, and others of that group. (15) The upward surge of all these viewpoints was in part a product of the pendulum-swings and tugging and pulling incident to the inner development of science and in part a reflection of the hard-boiled skepticism incident to the bewildered and disillusioned post-war world. The earlier concepts of instinct, race, group mind, and psychic planes and currents had derived from, been congenial with, and fed into each other. Now statistics, the indeterminate view of the universe, behaviorism, environmentalism, and semantics-operationalism did likewise. The result was a pretty thorough change of climate in social psychology.

It was not a complete change, however; and an incidental result was endless controversy in the journals and at the meetings. But these things buttressed each other, had a convincing underlying rationale worked out for them, and were congenial with the objective formalisms of research and thesis-writing. Their viewpoint was readily achievable and seemed easily defendable against the more subtle logic needed to modify them and set them in a fuller perspective. It is only in the last six or eight years that disputation has given way to tolerance, mutual modification, and calmer attempts at synthesis.

The concept of "attitude" was turned to as a "peaceful concept," the property of no school, escaping the nature-nurture controversy, useful to sociologist and psychologist alike, and susceptible of "measurement" and statistical manipulation both relative to the

---

15. See, *inter alia*, K. Pearson, *The Grammar of Science*, (1911); P. W. Bridgeman, *The Logic of Modern Physics*, (New York: The Macmilan Co., 1927); G. H. Mead, *Mind Self, and Society*, (Chicago: University of Chicago Press, 1934); J. F. Markey, *The Symbolic Process and Its Integration in Children*, (New York: Harcourt, Brace and Co., 1928); C. Wright Mills, "Language, Logic, and Culture," *American Sociological Review*, 4:670-680, October, 1939; Ogden and Richards, *The Meaning of Meaning*, (1923); Alfred Korzybski, *Science and Sanity*, (Lancaster: Science Press, 1933); C. W. Morris, "Foundations of the Theory of Signs," *Int. Encycl. of Unified Science*, (1938).

individual and on the larger scale of public opinion and the like. This peaceful concept was not without its controversies and varying definitions. (16) But it was useful; and, under the refined techniques of Thurstone and others, measurable in its simpler aspects. We came to know the pattern of attitudes on a great many things —from baking powder preferences to race, war, religion, sex, radicalism, etc. — and at least their rough relation to at least crudely defined positional points such as age, sex, economic level, educational level, national origin, religious affiliation, regional location, etc. (17) The investigation of attitudes became so important in the early thirties that some, such as Folsom and Bernard, thought for awhile that social psychology should be defined as the science of attitudes.

Large-scale attitude investigation laps over with the study of public opinion; and in the meantime the old straw-vote had matured into the disciplined public opinion poll as now carried out by the American Institute of Public Opinion, Fortune Magazine, the Crossley Corporation, etc. So we began to get empirical studies of at least the descriptive cross-sectional picture (and occasionally the trend picture) of those psychic planes and currents which were so interesting at the turn of the century.

But attitudes and public opinion lead out at once to prejudice, morale, mass movements, censorship and propaganda, prestige and leadership. And these things have their functional and processual sides, which kept clamoring for study also. Besides, the earlier psychic planes and currents people had said some things that hadn't been knocked out along with instinct and that couldn't be fully embraced in a mathematical figure. Psychoanalysis was beginning to make its contribution to social psychology. The anthropologists

---

16. See, e. g., Read Bain, "An Attitude on Attitude Research," *American Journal of Sociology*, 33:940-57, 1928; E. Faris, "Attitudes and Behavior," *American Journal of Sociology*, 34:271-281, 1928.

17. See, inter alia, L. L. Thurstone and E. J. Chave, *The Measurement of Attitudes;* G. W. Allport, "Attitudes," in Carl Murchison, ed., *A Handbook of Social Psychology*, (Worcester: Clark University Press, 1935); E. S. Bogardus, "A Social Distance Scale," *Sociology and Social Research*, 17:265-271, 1933; E. L. and R. E. Horowitz, "Development of Social Attitudes in Children," *Sociometry*, 1: 301-338, 1938; R. Stagner, "Fascist Attitudes," *Journal of Social Psychology*, 7: 309-319, 1936; D. Katz, "Attitude Measurement as a Method in Social Psychology," *Social Forces*, 15:479-482, 1937; Gardner Murphy and Rensis Likert, *Public Opinion and the Individual,* (New York: Harper and Bros, 1938).

SOCIAL PSYCHOLOGY

were presently to study such things as prejudice, leadership, and personality adjustment from the standpoint of ethnology. The Institute of Propaganda Analysis began to make its semi-sophisticated study of the less objective aspects of opinion manipulation. And so on. Thus the later works on crowds, public opinion, leadership, prejudice, propaganda, morale, and like by such people as Martin, Dollard, Du Bois, Lasswell, Arnold, Freeman, Doob, and others, profited by both the objective methods and materials and by the functional and processual insights. They represent the emerging strain toward synthesis — of methods and findings within the field, and between related scientific fields. They also represent the gain which the field as a whole was making — over the earlier planes and currents apeculations and the later sheerly-descriptive measurements. (18)

---

18. See e. g., E. D. Martin, *The Behavior of Crowds,* (New York: Harper and Bros., 1920); H. D. Lasswell, *Psychopathology and Politics,* (Chicago: University of Chicago Press, 1930); A. B. Wolfe, *Conservatism, Radicalism. and Scientific Method,* (New York: The Macmillan Co., 1933); A. H. Maslow, "Dominance-feeling, Behavior, and Status," *Psychological Review,* 64:404-29, 1937; "Dominance, Personality, and Social Behavior in Women," *Journal of Social Psychology,* 10: 3-39, 1939; S. Hofstra, "Personality and Differentiation in the Political Life of the Mendi," *Africa,* 1937, pp. 436-457; C. S. Ford, "The Role of a Fijian Chief," *American Sociological Review,* 3: 541-550, 1938; Dollard, *Caste and Class in a Southern Town;* Dollard et al., *Frustration and Aggression;* H. Cantril, *The Psychology of Social Movements,* (New York: John Wiley and Sons, 1941); Hortense Powdermaker, *After Freedom,* (New York: Viking Press, 1939); A. S. Gibb, *In Search of Sanity,* (New York: Farrar and Rinehart, 1942).

Also see on public opinion: F. H. Allport, "Toward a Science of Public Opinion," *Public Opinion Quartely,* 1: 7-23, 1937; Gardner Murphy and Rensis Likert, *Public Opinion and the Individual;* H. L. Childs, *A Reference Guide to the Study of Public Opinion,* (Princeton: Princeton University Press, 1934); W. Albig, *Public Opinion,* (New York: McGraw-Hill Book Co., 1939); Q. Wright, ed., *Public Opinion and World Politics,* (Chicago: University of Chicago Press, 1935); Paul F. Lazarsfeld, *Radio and the Printed Page,* (New York: Duell, Sloan, and Pearce, 1940); Walter Lippmann, *Public Opinion,* (New York: Harcourt, Brace and Co., 1922), and *The Phantom Public,* (New York: The Macmillan Co., 1925); H. L. Childs *Introduction to Public Opinion,* (New York; John Wiley and Sons, 1940); H. Cantril,*Gauging Public Opinion.* (Princeton: Princeton University Press, 1944).

Also see on censorship and propaganda: H. D. Lasswell, R. D. Casey, and B. L. Smith, *Propaganda and Promotional Activities: An annotated Bibliography,* (Minneapolis: University of Minnesota Press, 1935); George Creel, *How We Advertised America,* (New York: Harper and Bros., 1920); H. D. Lasswell,

TWENTIETH CENTURY SOCIOLOGY

The "peaceful concept" of attitude tended, like *wishes* before it, to become reified and used as stop-gap explanation and over-facile solution. Social problems being seen as due to the wrong attitudes, their solution was seen as a simple matter of changing those attitudes — as if free-will choices were to be influenced by admonitory verbalizations. (19) To overlook the disparity between the frame of reference for value involved in the attitude production and that of the one who wishes to alter them is like symptom-attacking in psychiatry. One cannot alter the functional alignment of the "positional point" by preachment, invective, force, or propaganda, but by altering the "field" with reference to which its position is functionally aligned.

Psychiatry, social work, sociology, social psychology, ethics, and cultural anthropology are discovering this all at once. So are progressive education, group work, conference leadership, industrial

---

Propaganda Technique in the World War, (New York: Alfred A. Knopf, 1927); L. W. Doob, *Propaganda,* (New York: Henry Holt and Co., 1935); F. E. Lumley, *The Propaganda Menace,* (New York D. Appleton-Century Co., 1933); E. Freeman, *Social Psychology,* (New York: Henry Holt and Co., 1936); L. W. Doob, *The Plans of Men,* (New Haven: Yale University Press, 1940); D. Waples, ed., *Print, Radio, and Film in a Democracy,* (Chicago: University of Chicago Press, 1942); H. Lavine and J. A. Wechsler, *War Propaganda and the United States,* (New Haven: Yale University Press, 1940); H. D. Lasswell, *Democracy through Public Opinion,* (Menasha, Wis.: George Banta Pub. Co., 1941); G. H. Gallup and S. F. Rae, *The Pulse of Democracy,* (New York: Simon and Schuster, 1940); Ladislas Farago and L. F. Gittler, eds., Germman *Psychological Warfare* (New York: G. P. Putnam's Sons, 1942); F. G. Bartlett, *Political Propaganda,* (New York: The Macmillan Co., 1940); publications of the Institute for Propaganda Analysis.

Also see on morale, etc.: Ray Abrams, *Preachers Present Arms,* (New York: Round Table Press, 1933); L. A. Pennington, *The Psychology of Military Leadership,* (New York: Prentice-Hall, 1943); Pitirim Sorokin, *Man and Society in Calamity,* (New York: E. P. Dutton and Co., 1942); M. A. May, *A Social Psychology of War and Peace,* (New Haven: Yale University Press, 1943); J. T. MacCurdy, *The Structure of Morale,* (Cambridge: Cambridge University Press, 1943); *Civilian Morale,* 2nd Yearbook, Society for the Psychological Study of Social Issues, (New York: Reynal and Hitchcock, 1942); Cantril *Gauging Public Opinion;* W. W. Waller, *The Veteran,* (New York: Dryden Press, 1944).

19. This was implicit, *e. g.,* in considerable portions of Elliott and Merrill's problems text.

management, and military morale officers. (20) The result may be a historical period in which social control, while still somewhat exploitative, is highly streamlined, a far cry from the lash and primitive ordering and forbidding, and steadily tending (by its contained pressures to smoother efficiency) also to meet society's technocratic-democratic and humanitarian-welfare imperatives.

When the psychoanalyst quits attacking the symptom and works with the meaning-giving context until the total field is realigned — the symptom disappears of itself. One of the important strides in psychiatry came with the recognition of the function of the neurotic symptom itself, vicious, haltingly accommodative, and blocking a fully integrating adjustment though it might be. So with social problems, including prejudice and bias, (racial and religious prejudice are rising steadily, thriving as does the hysterical symptom on direct attack). Like the neurotic symptom, although vicious and blocking full adjustment, prejudices also have their accommodative function from the center of reference of those who hold them. They persist until real changes are made in the complex of conditions that gives rise to them — freedom from insecurity, some real solution of conflicting interests, some genuine achievement of communal interests giving body to the verbalizations of idealized brotherly identifications, or some equitable, orderly, and effective mode of processing out irreducible conflicts. Then prejudice, no longer needed for tension release or as a folk-weapon of in-group solidarity, disappears. Thus the problem of changing attitudes, as a problem for applied social psychology, requires for its full solution the pooling of the resources of social psychology, psychiatry, economics, political science, etc., to change appropriately the total complex of their determination. And since those disciplines require the light of social psychology on the attitudinal and other psychological aspects of their own contributions in turn, this underlines the need for an integral theory to give sure-footedness to problems approaches.

---

20. See, e. g., J. M. Williams, *Principles of Social Psychology*, (1922); Thorstein Veblen, *Engineers and the Price System,* (1917); James Burnham, *The Managerial Revolution,* (New York: John Day Co., 1941); C. I. Barnard, *Functions of the Executive,* (Cambridge: Harvard University Press, 1939); F. J. Roethlisberger, *Management and Morale,* (Cambridge: Harvard University Press, 1941); Roethlisberger and William J. Dickson, *Management and the Worker,* (Cambridge: Harvard University Press, 1939); A. B. Wolfe, *Radicalism, Conservatism, and Scientific Method* (1923).

TWENTIETH CENTURY SOCIOLOGY

Consider the ("positional") attitudinal supports (and the "field" supports for the necessary attitudes in turn) of nationalism, a global organization, or the economic and political institutions of tomorrow — in an individuated age and a highly secularized society with exceedingly complex patterns of conflicting interests. Will over-reliance on propaganda, only verbalized brotherhoods, and merely pumped-up morale amount only to the suggestive production of symptoms, so to speak, eventually as ineffective as a merely suggestive therapy is in altering (the total field of) personality and character structure? Suggestive therapy too has a momentary but fleeting success. A naive, isolated, simple, and homogeneous folk accumulates myths and legends which through slow accretions and alterations come to have an organic relationship to their beliefs, values, and way of life. To think that unrealistic blueprinting, propaganda, or artificial morale techniques can construct new myths and fictions to support a social order of extraneous imposition in an individuated age similar to the organic folk buttressing of a simple people is something like mistaking a house of cards for a granite monolith. Do not the historical trends and types of society which occasion the recourse to, and momentary effectiveness of, censorship and propaganda also contain the seeds of their destruction again? Can the beliefs and loyalties of a more and more individuated age be regimented by spurious community-identifications and welfare *myths?* Or only by common-welfare *realities?* The implications of these social-psychological questions for the character which economic and political institutions may or may not take on in the future are obvious. Contrasting morale in different civilian, colonial, underground, and combatant groups begins to give us some answers. The post-war period will give us more. Is this possibly the last war that imperialist, laissez-faire, and non-welfare nations can successfully fight? Does the future belong to the welfare States — for social-psychological reasons When the application of the social sciences comes under the control of the possessors of economic and plitical power, as has the application of the other sciences, will the social sciences contain the ingredients of an enlightened statesmanship for them, or only the wherewithal for immediate exploitative manipulations?

These are questions we ask but do not answer. We put them vividly in order to underscore the need for social psychology to embrace its full task. The need of answers to them, whichever way the answers may lie, is evident enough. But we provide no answers,

SOCIAL PSYCHOLOGY

do no work on such problems. It is amazing that, with so much stress on *process* in sociology and social psychology (cross-sectional process, as in the ahistorical topological "field"), so little attention is paid to the processes of social-cultural evolution. Cooley, Mead, Freud, and Horney correct us on that at the individual level. But in our over-rejection of the stage and indefinite perfectibility theories, we leave the strategically important field of social evolution all but tabooed for respectable investigation. There lies in the work of Vico, Comte, Spencer, Morgan, Novicow, Vaccaro, Toennies, Marx, Durkheim, Lévy-Bruhl, Freud, Piaget, Cooley, Becker, Mannheim, Kohn, the present writer, and a number of others a great deal about the social psychological causes, results, and accompaniments of different types of societies at different points in social-cultural evolution. This material needs to be corrected, refined, added to, and put together in the perspective of our full relevant knowledge — and in the light of our growing awareness of contained processes, constant factors, contained strains, situational imperatives, situational emergents, and the like — and with our growing mastery of the subtler methods and disciplined functional theory building. What will be the conditions of the world of tomorrow? what possibilities and limitations? what inexorable imperatives. At this point of rapid, critical, revolutionary change in the intellectual-emotional climate and the attitudinal grounding of all our major institutions, no problem could be more strategic.

Slowly at first, but more rapidly after the mid-thirties, radical indeterminacy, radical behaviorism, radical environmentalism, and exclusive reliance on quantitative methods and "objectivated" concepts became progessively modified. This was due to still-vital survivals and also to new developments. Of survivals: (1) the functionalism of Wm. James, carried along by Woodworth and others in psychology; (2) still cogent elements in the psychic planes and currents contributions of Ross, Ellwood, and others; and (3) the cogency, variety, and importance of the contribution of the "Chicago school." This was exemplified, *e. g.*, (a) in the emphasis on *process* and the social-psychological procesing out of the social process itself which, stemming from Tarde, Wm. James, and Lester F. Ward, was carried on by Cooley, Park and Burgess, Dewey, and also by Waller, Becker, Dollard, Kimball Young, Warner, and others; (b) the eclecticism and proto-gestaltist, proto-psychoanalytic insights of Faris and Thomas; (c) the way in which Park and Thomas kept their doors open to new approaches, refused to become embroiled in mehodological disputation, but instead kept on studying their data, understanding it better and successfully *communicating* their *understandings;* and, perhaps most of all, (d) the importance and cogency of the "interactionalist" contribution, that "processing out" of the organic character of the individual-group relationship which, beginning with Wm. James and J. M. Baldwin, had been further developed by C. H. Cooley, G. H. Mead, John Dewey, and others. These things continually overflowed radical behaviorism and exclusive quantification as attempted containers of them. (21)

The work of Cooley and Mead had especial importance for the study of child development. Pestalozzi, Herbart, Preyer, Stern, Buehler, Piaget, Freud, Anna Freud, Melanie Klein, G. Stanley Hall, Wm. James, J. M. Baldwin, C. H. Cooley, G. H. Mead, Margaret Mead, W. I. and D. S. Thomas, Gardner and L. B. Murphy, J. S. Plant, and a host of others have studied child development from one approach or another, by one method or an-

---

21. For example, W. I. Thomas and F. Znaniecki, *The Polish Peasant,* (Boston: Richard G. Badger, 1918-1920, 5 vols.); W. I. Thomas, *Primitive Behavior,* (New York: McGraw-Hill Book Co., 1937); E. Faris, *The Nature of Human Nature,* (New York: McGraw-Hill Book Co., 1937); Park and Burgess, *Introduction to the Science of Sociology,* (Chicago: University of Chicago Press, 1921); John Dewey, *Human Nature and Conduct*; Dewey, *Freedom and Culture,* (New York: G. P. Putnam's Sons, 1939); G. H. Mead, *Mind, Self, and Society,* (Chicago: University of Chicago Press, 1934); Kimball Young, *Social Psychology,* rev. ed., (New York: F. S. Crofts and Co., 1944), and *Personality and Problems of Adjustment,* (New York: F. S. Crofts and Co., 1940); W. W. Waller, *The Old Love and the New,* (New York: Liveright Pub. Corp. 1929), *The Sociology of Teaching,* (New York: John Wiley and Sons, 1937), and *The Family, A Dynamic Interpretation,* (New York: Dryden Press, 1938); W. L. Warner and P. S. Lunt, *Social Life of a Modern Community,* (New Haven: Yale University Press, 1941); John Dollard, *Criteria for the Life History,* (New Haven: Yale University Press, 1935), *Caste and Class in a Southern Town,* and *Frustration and Aggression;* Leopard von Wiese and Howard Becker, *Systematic Sociology,* (New York: John Wiley and Sons, 1932); Becker, "Constructive Typology in the Social Sciences," Barnes, Becker, and Becker, *Contemporary Social Theory;* Krueger and Reckless, *Social Psychology,* (New York: Longmans, Green and Co., 1932); C. R. Shaw, *The Jack Roller,* (Chicago: University of Chicago Press, 1930); F. M. Thrasher, *The Gang,* 2nd ed., (Chicago: University of Chicago Press, 1937); A. Blumenthal, *Small Town Stuff,* (Chicago: University of Chicago Press, 1932); Nels Anderson, *The Hobo,* (Chicago: University of Chicago Press, 1931); etc.

other, and in one society or another. The study of child development gave impetus to, and provided a core for, experimental social psychology. All but non-existent in the twenties, the rapid growth of the latter, its devising of techniques of observation and validation of findings, and its steady inclusion of social and cultural frameworks can be traced in a comparison of the first and second edition of the Murphys' *Experimental Social Psychology*. Child guidance clinics, established as a part of the juvenile court movement, have been important not merely for the therapeutic treatment of juvenile delinquents but also for the study of child development. (22)

The achievements of psychology proper in understanding personality and its development, and the still-accruing result of per-

---

22. On child development, see J. Piaget, *The Language and Thought of the Child*, (New York: Harcourt, Brace and Co., 1926), *Judgment and Reasoning in the Child*, (New York: Harcourt, Brace and Co., 1928), *The Child's Conception of His World*, (New York: Harcourt Brace and Co., 1929), *The Moral Judgment of the Child*, (New York: Harcourt, Brace and Co., 1932); Anna Freud and Dorothy T. Buckingham, *War and Children*, (New York: Medical War Books, 1943). Also see Carl Murchison, ed., *Handbook of Child Psychology;* W.' I. Thomas and D. S. Thomas, *The Child in America*, (New York: Alfred A. Knopt, 1928); Gardner Murphy and Frederick Jensen, *Approaches to Personality*, (New York: Coward-McCann, 1932); J. S. Plant, *Personality and the Culture Pattern*, (New York: Commonwealth Fund, 1937); D. S. Thomas et al., *Some New Techniques for Studying Social Behavior*, (New York: Teachers College, Columbia University, 1929); H. M. Bott, *Method in Social Studies of Young Children*, (Toronto: University of Toronto Press, 1933); L. B. Murphy, *Social Behavior and Child Personality*, (New York: Columbia University Press, 1937); Murphy, Murphy, and Newcomb, *op. cit.;* W. Healy, *Personality in Formation and Action*, (New York: W. W. Norton and Co., 1938); M. Bayley, *Studies in the Development of Young Children*, (Berkeley: University of California Press, 1940); L. B. Murphy and R. E. Horowitz, "Projective Methods in the Psychological Study of Children," *Journal or Experimental Education*, 7: 133-140, 1938; L. K. Frank, "Projective Methods for the Study of Personality," *Journal of Psychology*, 8: 389-418, 1939; H. A. Murray et al., *Explorations in Personality*, J. Moreno, *Who Shall Survive?;* Dollard, *Criteria for the Life History;* Mead, *Coming of Age in Samoa* and *Growing Up in New Guinea*.

sonality testing and measurement deserve extended treatment. (23) We are most concerned at this point, however, with the understanding of the rise of the "Self" that came from the work of James, Baldwin, Cooley, and Mead, one of the "surviving" contributions above noted. (24) Among other things, James emphasized the extensions of the identification of the self, the multiplicity of selves, and the molding force of the group as expressed in what he termed 'club opinion,' More important perhaps was the functional character of his approach. Cooley's chief emphasis was on the organic relation between the individual and society as inseparable parts of a single whole, and the importance of primary face-to-face groups as the matrix of personal growth and the socialization of the individual. His kindly humanitarianism and Christian bias perhaps led Cooley to idealize this unity, and it is necessary to offset Cooley with Alfred Adler and then effect a new synthesis (somewhat as one offsets Prince Kropotkin with Marx or Sorel and then attempts to see the total picture again). Mead came a bit closer to synthesizing the paradox of (1) the skin-contained individual who is yet (2) organically related to a social-cultural matrix which necessarily has a

---

23. P. M. Symonds, *Diagnosing Personality and Conduct*, (New York: The Century Co., 1931); H. E. Garrett and M. R. Schenk, *Psychological Tests, Methods, and Results,* (New York: Harper and Bros., 1933); E. Mathews, "A Study of Emotional Stability in Children," *Juvenile Delinquency*, 8: 1-40, 1923; D. A. Laird, "Detecting Abnormal Behavior," *Journal of Abnormal and Social Psychology*, 20:128-141, 1925; S. D. House, "A Mental Hygiene Inventory," *Archives of Psychology*, No. 88, 1927; L. L. Thurstone and T. G. Thurstone, "A Neurotic Inventory," *Journal of Social Psychology*, 1:3-30, 1930; H. M. Bell. *The Adjustment Inventory* (1934); R. G. Bernreuter, *The Personality Inventory* (1931); C. Landis and S. E. Katz, "The Validity of Certain Questions which Purport to Measure Neurotic Tendencies," *Journal of Applied Psychology* 18: 343-356 1934; G. W., and F. H. Allport, *A-S Reaction Etudy: A Scale for Measuring Ascendence-Submission in Personality*, (Boston: Houghton Mifflin Co., 1929); S. L. Pressey, "A Group Scale for Investigating the Emotions," *Journal of Abnormal and Social Psychology*, 16:55-64, 1921; H. A. Murray et al., *Explorations in Personality;* J. E. Downey, *The Will Temperament and Its Testing* (1923); H. Rorschach, *Psychodiagnostik*, 2nd ed. (1932); M. and R. Bleuler, "Rorschach's Ink Blot Test and Racial Psychology," *Character and Personality*, 4: 97-114, 1935-1936; Andras Angyal, *The Foundation for the Science of Personality*, (New York: Commonwealth Fund, 1941).

24. James M. Baldwin, *Mental Development* (1895), *Social and Ethical Interpretations* (1897), *The Individual and Society* (1911); Charles Horton Cooley, *Human Nature and the Social Order* (1902), *Social Organization, A Study of the Larger Mind* (1909), *Social Process* (1918); George Herbert Mead, *Mind, Self, and Society*.

different center of reference for meaning and value than does the individual. And he traced in considerable and illuminating detail the rise of the self in conduct. In imagination, in play, and later on in the actual tasks of life, the individual must assume various roles. But the roles are delegated. They imply a disciping of the spontaneous self-centered impulses. Painful comparisons of how he did do and how he "ought" to do arise. Thus "the self arises in conduct, when the individual becomes a social object in experience to himself." The roles, the reflected self, and after a while the moral appraisals of those about one become internalized. But a distinction arises between the "me" thus compounded and the "I" which remains a relatively unpredictable, unobservable, and sometimes obstreperous element. It is not difficult to synthesize Mead's contribution with that of Freud, his "generalized other" becoming the "me" which becomes the conscience or super-ego in contrast to the "I" or "id." While the psychoanalysts have given us far more insights and more illuminating and detailed processing out of the further resulting complexities of adjustive and maladjustive processes, Cooley and Mead have probably given us a better description of the rise of the self and the initial stages of socialization than anything that the clinicians have so far offered.

Among new developments inducing a changed emphasis in the field were the following: (1) The rediscovery of the organism as a whole, and the integrative principle in biology. This was evidenced in the work on the integrative action of the nervous system, the metabolic gradient, vicarious functioning, and equipotentiality of Sherington, Child, Lashley, Loeb, and others. (25) (2) The application of the integrative principle to psychology in the Gestalt theories of Wertheimer, Koehler, Koffka, and others. (26) (3) Developments in social work, which needs a functional-processual approach

25. C. S. Sherrington, *The Integrative Action of the Nervous System* (1906); C. M. Child, *Physiological Foundations of Behavior*, (New York: Henry Holt and Co., 1924); Jaques Loeb, *The Organism as a Whole*, (1916); Karl Lashley, *Brain Mechanism and Intelligence*, (Chicago: University of Chicago Press, 1929).

26. W. Koehler, *The Mentality of Apes*, (New York: Harcourt, Brace and Co., 1926), *Gestalt Psychology*, New York: Liveright Pub. Corp., 1929), and *The Place of Value in a World of Facts*, (New York: Liveright Pub. Corp., 1938); Kurt Koffka, *The Graws of the Mind*, (New York: Harcourt, Brace and Co., 1924), and *Principles of Gestalt Psychology*, (New York: Harcourt, Brace and Co., 1935).

in studying the case-work client. For the client must be seen in his organic interrelations with his familial, community, and cultural milieu, and as a product of his life-history's "contained" and "interactive" developmental processes. (4) The establishment, stemming from the Juvenile Court movement, of child-guidance clinics and institutes for child study. (5) The slow admission (as one of the legitimate items entering into the mutual modifications and full-perspective synthesis of a respectable comprehensive theory) of the contribution of Karl Marx and his followers. This emphasized the organic interrelation between *ethos* or *Zeitgeist* and underlying social-structural and historical-processual imperatives. And it emphasized the consequent relativity of bias, attitude, and meaning to the "positional point" of the individual in the "status field" of his given society, itself to be considered in its relation to the underlying historical processes. (6) The elaboration, refinement, correction, and extension of application of psychoanalysis, the most functionally-processually oriented of all the sciences. This occurred under Freud, Adler, Jung, Rank, Horney, Sullivan, Burrow, Moreno, Fromm, and others. (7) The coming of age of anthropology. For anthropology shifted from the sheer historical descriptions of the early Boas school to the functionalism of Malinowski, Radcliffe Brown, Benedict, Mead, Hollowell, Powdermaker, Warner, Linton, G. Gordon Brown, and others. And it has lately developed interest in such social-psychological problems as personality, leadership, prejudice, acculturation, cultural *ethos*, and the cultural relativity of psychosis, neurosis, and personality adjustment. (27) (8)

---

27. B. Malinowski, "Culture," in *Encyclopedia of the Social Sciences*, 4: 621-646, *Sex and Repression in Savage Society*, (New York: Harcourt, Brace and Co., 1927), *Sexual Life of Savages*, (New York: Liveright Pub. Corp., 1929); P. Radin, *Crashing Thunder*, (New York: D. Appleton and Co., 1926); R. Linton, *The Study of Man*, (New York: D. Appleton-Century Co., 1936); Ruth Benedict, *Patterns of Culture*; M. Mead, *Coming of Age in Samoa*, (New York: William Morrow and Co., 1928), *Growing Up in New Guinea*, (New York: William Morrow and Co., 1930), and *Sex and Temperament in Three Primitive Societies*, (New York: William Morrow and Co., 1935); Warner and Lunt, *op. cit.*; H. Powdermaker, *Life in Lesu*, (New York: W. W. Norton and Co., 1933), and *After Freedom;* E. Beaglehole, *Property: A Study in Social Psychology*, (London: G. Allen and Unwin, 1931); M. Mead, et al., *Cooperation and Competition among Primitive Peoples*, (New York: McGraw-Hill Book Co., 1937); A. L. Hallowell, "Culture and Mental Disorder," *Journal of Abnormal and Social Psychology*, 29: 1-9, 1934; John Gillin, "Personality in Primitive Society," *American Sociological Review*, 4: 681-702, 1939 (good bibliography); Kluckholn and Mowrer, *loc. cit.*

SOCIAL PSYCHOLOGY

The functional-processualism of the "new history." (28) And finally, (9) the flow of contributions from peripheral sciences, such as those of Lasswell, Arnold, Frank, Fromm, Mannheim, Laski, and others. (29) These sometimes short-cut social psychology as such, carried an implicit contrast to our own methodological stultification, and indicated a task of comprehensive inclusion, critical eclecticism, and final synthesis that we were not doing.

Psychoanalysis began in the early work of Freud at the turn of the century. Using a functional approach, it makes delicate appraisals of needs, goals, distortions, displacements, adjustments, and maladjustments; and it uses the delicate methods of insight, processual analysis, a very active observer-subject interaction, and the piecing together of converging inferences for interpretation, explanation, understanding, and eventual wisdom. These things establish judgmental *plausibilities* in contrast to the more objective certitude of statistical *probabilities,* experimental *provabilities,* or geometric *demonstrabilities.* In this, they are at one with all the subtler non-quantitative methods, from the case history to systematic theory building. The prime characteristic in the use of these subtler, non-quantitative methods should be tentativeness in statement of findings and constant openness to new factors or angles that might indicate different conclusions, interpretative principles, or basic theoretical organization. Marx used this method too, as did Darwin in establishing evolution. All three showed the balance, suspended judgment, tentativeness of statement, and constant openness to new factors and angles of approach that must characterize the user of the plausibility-yielding methods. Darwin preeminently. But Marx and Freud also, given their own positional points, so to speak. For Marx and Freud needed a greater feel of certitude than their method would warrant the detached philosopher

---

28. Taking, say, C. J. H. Hayes' *Essays in Nationalism* as an example.

29. H. D. Lasswell, *World Politics and Personal Insecurity,* (New York: McGraw-Hill Book Co., 1935), *Psychopathology and Politics,* (Chicago: University of Chicago Press, 1930), *Democracy through Public Opinion,* (Menasha, Wis.: George Banta Pub. Co., 1941); Thurman Arnold, *Folklore of Capitalism,* (New Haven: Yale University Press, 1937); and *Symbols of Government,* (New Haven: Yale University Press, 1935); Jerome Frank, *Law and the Modern Mind,* (New York: Coward-McCann, 1930); E. Fromm, *Escape from Freedom,* (New York: Farrar and Rinehart, 1941); Karl Mannheim, *Man and Society in an Age of Reconstruction,* (New York: Harcourt, Brace and Co., 1940), and *Ideology and Utopia,* (New York: Harcourt, Brace and Co., 1936); Harold Laski, *The American Presidency,* (New York: Harper and Bros., 1940).

in admitting; the one for political action, the other for therapeutic application. And the storm of opposition to their too-incisive findings abetted this by driving them and their followers into what for a time approached dogmatic cultism. This is the opposite of what their delicate methods warrant. And as a result the first corrections and refinements could come only by the multiplication of dogmas and cults. Synthesis among clashing sub-schools and aceptance into and synthesis with the general body of scientific theory were (and still are) thus delayed for both Marxism and Freudianism. (30) It is in these terms that one reads the successive schools of Freud, Adler, Jung, the British school (Jones, Klein, etc.), and Rank (31). With Horney, we get the first notable attempt at (still self-conscious) synthesis. By the same token, good Marxians are now becoming willing to get rid of some of the excess baggage in Marxian theory; and "respectable" social theorists are beginning to take due notice of the import of both Freud and Marx.

The things that most interest us in psychoanalysis are its stressing of the goal-striving character of the psychic life; the hidden character of some of these strivings, repression producing distorted expression, displacements, symbolizations, rationalizations, over-protestations, defense mechanisms, and the like; the pervasive sexual and egotic elements; the rooting of adult tendencies in childhood; and the apparent conflict between the "instinctual" impulses and the social-cultural requirements. The import of these things

---

30. Waller has somewhere traced out this characteristic process of the isolation, defensive exaggeration, and eventual assimilation again of the radical contribution. There is thus a total-society as well as an individual-researcher aspect to scientific certitude, viewed as process.

31. See *inter alia*, S. Freud, *A General Introduction to Psychoanalysis* (1920), *New Introductory Lectures* (1933), *The Interpretation of Dreams* (1913), *Three Contributions to Sexual Theory* (1910), etc. (His *Selected Writings*, ed. by A. A. Brill, in the Modern Library series is a good selection). See also A. Adler, *The Neurotic Constitution* (1917), *The Practice and Theory of Individual Psychology*, (New York: Harcourt, Brace Co., 1924), *The Education of Children*, (New York: Greenberg, 1936), and *The Study of Organ Inferiority and Its Compensation* (1917); C. J. Jung, *Psychological Types* (1923); B. Hinkle, *The Re-creating of the Individual* (1923); C. J. Jung, "What Is Neurosis?" *International Journal of Individual Psychology*, 1, 1935; O. Rank, *Myth of the Birth of a Hero* (1914), *The Trauma of Birth*, (New York: Harcourt, Brace and Co., 1929), *Modern Education*, (New York: Alfred A. Knopf, 1932), *Technik der Psychoanalyse* (3 vols.); W. Healy and A. Bronner, *The Structure and Meaning of Psychoanalysis*, (New York: Alfred A. Knopf, 1930); J. T. MacCurdy, *Problems in Dynamic Psychology* (1922), a critique; etc.

SOCIAL PSYCHOLOGY

for social psychology in the interaction of individual, in the dovetailing of family or primary group milieux, and in certain institutions and aspects of the societal ethos is tremendous.

Psychoanalysis has undergone considerable corrections, refinements, and additions. Although yielding ground slowly, it has more and more modified the biological and instinctual basis of its theory. Forced constantly to see such trings as, *e. g.*, the inter-personal etiology of the neurosis and the inter-personal blockings to readjustment, it had to take account of the familial, personal, and social-cultural factors involved. There was much in Freud to that effect, inconsistent as it might be with the formal instinctual hypotheses; and these concessions were made at first implicitly, somewhat as religions change while keeping the letter of their creeds. But after Benedict's *Patterns of Culture* and in the works of Adler, Horney, Sullivan, Burrow, Moreno, Kardiner, and Fromm, it is made quite explicit. (32) In their several fashions, these take account of the social nature of the neurosis and also of the social nature of therapy and the therapeutic interaction.

Important as either self-analysis or group therapy would be, considering the time and expense of individual treatment, the main theoretical contribution here, especially with Horney, seems to be in their "processing out" of the etiology of neurosis. Neurosis is now seen as a process-product rather than the effect of some entity-cause. All the skin-contained and all the social-cultural factors are actively involved at all times in the vicious circle of causation, the self-feeding and self-accentuating process which eventuates in the neurosis. It is no longer a case of a trauma, buried for years under Vesuvian ashes, suddenly springing alive again and striking; nor

---

32. K. Horney, *The Neurotic Personality of Our Time*, (New York: W. W. Norton and Co., 1937), *New Ways of Psychoanalysis*, (New York: W. W. Norton and Co., 1938), and *Self-Analysis*, (New York: W. W. Norton and Co., 1942);A. Kardiner, *The Individual and His Society*. (New York: Columbia University Press, 1939); E. Fromm, *Autoritaet und Familie* (1936), *Escape from Freedom;* H. S. Sullivan, "Some Conceptions of Modern Psychiatry." *Psychiatry,* 3: 1-10, 1940, "A Note on Formulating the Relationship of the Individual and the Group," *American Journal of Sociology,* 44:932-937, 1939; Trigant Burrow, *The Biology of Human Conflict,* (New York: The Macmillan Co., 1937); W. Galt, "Phyloanalysis," *Journal of Abnormal and Social Psychology,* 27:411-429, 1937; J. L. Moreno, "Interpersonal Therapy and the Psychopathology of Inter-Relations," *Sociometry,* 1:9-76, 1937, "Psychodramatic Shock Therapy," *Sociometry,* 2: 1-30, 1939, "Psychodramatic Treatment of Marriage Problems," *Sociometry,* 3: 1-23, 1940.

a case of isolated causal chains; nor a case of full-blown, specific, and unswervable instinctual cravings in clash with a more and more repressive civilizational environment; nor yet a case of inner clash between biologically given *entities*; id and super-ego; or libido and death-wish. Growth and development involve contained processes within the organism, interactive processes with the environment, and a constant adjustment between these in turn. Since there are contained strains between the individual and the environment (especially his social-cultural milieu), sometimes vicious self-accentuating circles get set up leading to neurosis as an end-product or as an entrenched accommodative "way of life." Recent, as well as childhood things, have entered in, culturally fabricated strivings and thwarts as well as native impulses and urges. And therapy must not only uncover childhood traumas but also provide beneficent circles of adjustive realizational patterns to replace the vicious circles of the neurosis as a "way of life."

Since childhood conflicts and repressions have sometimes gained a life-long entrenchment, provided the vicious repetitive pattern, or had a life-long magnification within the subconscious, they are not thereby meaningless as some followers of Horney seem to think. Their uncovering and assimilation may still be especially strategic. The tendency to put Freud, Adler, Horney, etc., on an either/or basis derives from the dogmatic-cult period of analysis, as well as from a common-human tendency toward the simplicity of unilateralisms rather than the difficulties of complex synthesis. Horney did not refute Freud. She corrected and refined him. And she needs and will need correction and refinement in turn — both in terms of Freud and of our on-going knowledge. Analysis, starting with a vast over-emphasis on sex, must not renounce sex in favor of egotic inferiority when that is discovered but retain it in all its ramifications and set both in each other's perspective. And so with each new factor or angle until full inclusion, balanced emphasis, and solid synthesis are achieved. It is refreshing to observe the number of new angles and important factors — frustration, aggression, guilt, spontaneity, distrust, the cultural framework, etc. — that are beginning to be included into consideration by contemporary analytic theory. Horney, in her *Neurotic Personality*, in some measure synthesized Freud, Adler, sociology, and anthropology. And she gave us an example of the value of processual analysis as a method of scientific abstraction. Analysis is beginning to ap-

SOCIAL PSYCHOLOGY

proach the tentativeness and openness appropriate to the subtle complexity of its method.

Analysts themselves have made applications of their theories to social phenomena, as have others who are not professional psychiatrists; and social theorists, in turn, have helped correct and refine psychoanalytic theory. (33) There is at present a lively cross-fertilization between anthropology and psychiatry, raising among other things problems of the relation of neurosis to culture, the "absolute" and the "relative" definition of "normality," and the possibilities of an in-effect "neurotic culture" itself. The con-

---

33. B. Malinowsky, *The Father in Primitive Psychology*, (New York: W. W. Norton and Co., 1927), *The Myth in Primitive Society*, (New York: W. W. Norton and Co., 1926), *Sex and Repression in Savage Society;* Mead, *Coming of Age in Samoa, Growing Up in New Guinea,* and *Sex and Temperament in Three Primitive Societies;* Podermaker, *After Freedom;* Benedict, *Patterns of Culture;* M. J. Herskovits, "Freudian Mechanism in Negro Psychology," in *Essays Presented to C. G. Seligman,* (London: George Routledge and Sons, 1934); Kardiner, *op. cit.;* W. H. R. Rivers, *Psychology and Ethnology,* (New York: Harcourt, Brace and Co., 1926); Geza Roheim,, *Social Anthropology,* (London: Boni and Liveright, 1926); W. Sachs, *Black Hamlet,* (London: Geoffrey Bles, 1936); S. Freud, *Group Psychology and the Analysis of the Ego* (1922), *Totem and Taboo* (1918), *The Future of an Illusion,* (New York: Liveright Pub. Corp., 1928), and *Civilization and Its Discontents,* (New York: Robert O. Ballou, 1930); F. Alexander, "Psychoanalysis and Social Disorganization," *American Journal of Sociology* 42:781-813, 1937, *Our Age of Unreason,* (Philadelphia: J. B. Lippincott Co., 1942); E. B. Holt, *The Freudian Wish and Its Relation to Ethics* (1915); René Guyon, *Ethics of Sexual Acts,* (New York: Alfred A. Knopf, 1934); O. Rank, *Modern Education;* F. Alexander, "Psychiatric Aspects of War and Peace," *American Journal of Sociology,* 46:504-520, 1941; C. J. Jung, *Psychology and Religion,* (New Haven: Yale University Press, 1938); F. Alexander and Hugo Staub, *The Criminal, the Judge, and the Public,* (New York: The Macmillan Co., 1931); J. C. Fluegel, *Psychoanalytic Study of the Family,* (New York: G. E. Stechert and Co., 1921); J. S. Plant, *Personality and the Culture Pattern;* Kimball Young, *Personality and Problems of Adjustment;* L. K. Frank, "Society as Patient," *American Journal of Sociology,* 42:335-344, 1936, and "Cultural Coercion and Individual Distortion," *Psychiatry,* 2:11-27, 1939; H. D. Lasswell, *Psychopathology and Politics,* and *World Politics and Personal Insecurity;* M. E. Opler, "Personality and Culture," *Psychiatry,* 1:217-220, 1938; E. A. Strecker, *Beyond Clinical Frontiers,* (New York: W. W. Norton and Co., 1940); A. S. Gibb, *In Search of Sanity,* (New York: Farrar and Rinehart, 1942); etc.

tributions of Benedict and Kardiner and Linton are of pioneering significance here. (34)

There are numerous contributions, both early and recent, on the effects of familial, community, regional, and cultural frameworks, (35) of social role, class status, and occupation, (36) and of various critical impingements of the social process, such as un-

---

34. Anthropologists have taken their typological hazards rather badly. A designation of whole cultures as "Apollonian," "extravert," "ahistorical," etc., does not fit the whole culture with complete precision, any more than individual "types" fit the whole man precisely. Such descriptions will eventually need to be further processed out into their "sense in which" ramifications, specific adumbrations, and unique forms. This is said of the culture-as-a-whole, its "ethos," Zeitgeist, or Diltheyan integration. But, leaving its integral aspects, there is a further hazard poorly run. For, although the anthropologists have been at some pains to tell us that primitive peoples are not as alike as peas in a pod but do have some individuation, the emphasis on the general characteristics of cultures has tended to neglect the occurrence of exceptions and the tendency of individual behaviors to disperse along a range as well as to cluster about a norm. By failures of emphasis, they fall into the stereotyping fallacy. Still further, the constant reiteration that "all things are relative to the culture," while an excellent corrective provided by the functional approach against the hazards of over-straining for sheerly objective descriptions and for confusing of merely objective similarities, has led to a neglect of a study by anthropologists of the functional structures, processes, situational imperatives, etc., common to all cultures and societies. To correct this, a more active cross-fertilization between anthropology and sociology is needed, some synthesis of their findings, perhaps some eventual merging of their disciplines. Thus the anthropological work on culture types seems to have run all the hazards of typology rather badly. It is not, for all that, without its pioneering significance.

35. E. g., W. G. Summer, *Folkways* (1906); C. H. Cooley, *Human Nature and the Social Order*, (1902); W. I. Thomas, *The Unadjusted Girl*, (1923); R. M. and H. R. Lynd, *Middletown*, (New York: Harcourt, Brace and Co., 1929), and *Middletown in Transition*, (New York: Harcourt, Brace and Co., 1937); H. W. Odum and H. E. Moore, *American Regionalism*, (New York: Henry Holt and Co., 1938); Warner and Lunt, *op. cit.*

36. E. g., Niccollo Machiavelli, *The Prince* (c. 1520); Thorstein Veblen, *Theory of the Leisure Class* (1915); T. Parsons, *The Structure of Social Action*, (New York: McGraw-Hill Book Co.; 1937), "The Professions and Social Structure," *Social Forces*, 17: 457-467, 1939, and "The Motivation of Economic Activities," in C. W. M. Hart, ed., *Essays in Sociology*, (Toronto: University of Toronto Press, 1940); W. W. Waller, *The Sociology of Teaching;* E. C. Hughes, "Personality Types and the Division of Labor," *American Journal of Sociology*, 33:754-768, 1928; R. K. Merton, "Bureaucratic Structure and Personality," *Social Forces*, 18: 1-10, 1940; S. Ranulf, *Moral Indignation and Middle Class Psychology*, (New York: G. E. Stechert and Co., 1938); K. Davis, "Mental Hygiene and the Class Structure," *Psychiatry*, 1:55-65, 1938.

employment, divorce, war, demobilization, etc., (37) on individual and social-psychological adjustments and processes. Sociologists have never been really unaware of the relation of personality and other social-psychological matters to the socio-cultural framework. Such concepts as person, status, role, crisis, ethos, ethnocentrism, tribal morality, isolation, marginal man, assimilation, accommodation, and many others attest to that. From the *Folkways* and the *Polish Peasant* on down, sociology has carried implicitly and sometimes explicitly the relativities and syntheses now being rediscovered. The eclat with which their discovery is now greeted should teach us to render our understandings communicable: *i. e.*, measurable and quantitatively or experimentally manipulable; or else buttressed by full delineation of their converging inferences and "processed out" in the full detail of their origins and ramifications. It is no mean contribution that some of the recent work does these things.

Between the persisting factors and the new developments we have listed, the climate of social psychology is again undergoing change. This time, with somewhat less polemics and controversy. There is somewhat more of sober contemplation of three difficult problems: (1) that of setting the various methods in a common perspective; (2) that of weaving the various scattered findings, compartmented schools, and even human-social scientific disciplines themselves into a comprehensive and integral social theory; and (3) finding common ground for an integral and disciplined, but functionally incisive applied science.

II

Social psychology faces the same difficulty as sociology in defining its field. Shall it be an encyclopaedic science? A "pure" science

---

37. E. g., W. I. Thomas, "The Province of Social Psychology," *American Journal of Sociology*, 10, 1904 (his "crisis" concept); R. C. Angell, *The Family Encounters the Depression*, (New York: Charles Scribner's Sons, 1936); P. F. Lazarsfeld, "An Unemployed Village," *Character and Personality*, 1: 147-151, 1932; S. A. Stouffer and P. F. Lazarsfeld, *Research Memorandum on the Family in the Depression*, (New York: Social Science Research Council, 1937); W. W. Waller, *The Old Love and the New, War and the Family*, (New York: Dryden Press, 1942), and *The Veteran* (1944); Mark A. May, *A Social Psychology of War and Peace;* J. T. MacCurdy, *The Structure of Morale;* the sections on Psychology and War in current issues of the *Psychological Bulletin;* Anna Freud and Dorothy T. Buckingham, *War and Children.*

making its unique abstraction from the total universe of phenomena? A synthesizing bridge between the social sciences and their bio-psychological foundations? Or all three? The processual abstraction of the rise of the self, the structuration of personality, and the further adjustive, maladjustive, and readjustive processes which result, is a legitimate angle of abstraction for a "pure" social psychology. So is the classic "social process," when psychologically described. So would be an abstraction of the psychology of social organization (toward which we have some shreds and patches in myths, legends, leadership, etc.). And so would be abstractions of the psychology of cultural organization and of cultural processes (toward which, short of Summer and the recent studies of acculturation by anthropologists there is very little). (38) But there are comparative as well as universally-abstractable aspects. Further, both socieites and individuals are in process of growth or evolution. This necessitates also studying them as historical events. And the causal factors of an *event*, by contrast with those of a formal abstraction, ramify endlessly in all directions. Hence social psychology must be encyclopaedic. It must develop its unique universally-valid abstractions. And it must canvas thoroughly the typical temporal, spatial, individual, and cultural social-psychological actualities. That is a large task; but it has to be faced. Social psychology must also act as a bridge between all the social sciences and their bio-physical foundations, as bio-chemistry and bio-physics do for biology. Social psychology, the inseparable Siamese twin of sociology, must underlie all the various social science branches, pervade their broadest systematic theory, and accompany them in their most intimately intricate investigations.

There is needed a social theory that shall be integral, disciplinedly functional, and incisive to give sure-footedness, simplification, and common orientation to problems approaches. The treatment of social problems in most disciplines is inconsistent and bewildered — now from this unilateralism, now from that; now humanitarian and sentimental, now over-detached, cynical, or futile; now pietistic and aim-inhibited, and now revolutionary, dogmatic,

---

38. See James W. Woodard, "A New Classification of Culture and a Restatement of the Culture Lag Theory," *American Sociological Review*, 1:89-102, 1936, "The Relation of Personality Structure to the Structure of Culture," *American Sociological Review*, 3:637-651, 1938, "The Role of Fictions in Cultural Organization," forthcoming in *Transactions of the New York Academy of Science*.

SOCIAL PSYCHOLOGY

and wishful. And it is stop-gap and piece-meal. Lacking an integral functional-processual theoretical framework, it must necessarily remain "sympton attacking" rather than "field manipulation"; social tinkering rather than social engineering; confined to superficial and momentary "tactics" rather than incisive, long-run "strategy."

The strain toward synthesis in content, which might presently eventuate in the integral social theory so badly needed, is reflected in the many recent developments already noted. The strain toward synthesis in methodology is reflected in part by the attempt of the quantitative and objective methods to assimilate "organic relations" themselves. Vector analysis, topology, and sociometry represent this laudable but relatively unsuccessful attempt. To some, they seem to hinder communication by a barrage of jargon, rather than facilitating it. And to some they seem to mistake only heuristic or expositional value for proof value, amounting to mathematical realism. And *over-strained* operationalism seems wishful word magic all over again! (Somewhat as, with increased sophistication, the dream-work only becomes more elaborate in its disguises.)

The integral social theory needed to implement incisive social action must be a functional theory — functional in the sense of the organic sciences and not that of the mathematical sciences. It must deal with the functional aspects of structures and processes, and with resulting adjustments, accommodations, maladjustments, and potential readjustments. The very words "functional" and "adjustment" in this sense are meaningless at the level of chemistry and physics. They cannot be avoided at the level of organisms, persons, or societies. Hence we must not strain too hard to achieve "natural science" objectivity.

It is necessary for a functional science to develop an *autonomic nomenclature* and *autonomic criteria* in terms of which to state its functional appraisals. The strain toward a behavioristically objective, operational, or mathematical form of statement (which in the nature of the case cannot come to complete grips with a problem such as the functional *appropriateness* of an adjustment!), tends to substitute, for an answer to a difficult problem the answer to a related, but different one; to one that *is* solvable by the preferred approach. It is not easy *e. g.*, to determine what constitutes a well adjusted personality, to tell whether a given person has one, and to justify your interpretation. But it is easy to tell if those in the group about the subject think he is adjusted or not. Therefore, count the opposing vocalizations of inexpert judgment as to the reality involved. This will be objective, since it will yield a mathematical figure. Then submit the figure as the answer to the problem itself. To do this, however, you must first have adopted an objective, behavioristic, or "operational" definition in the first place. For example, "Personality adjustment *is* being regarded as adequate by the consensus of opinion of the group of which one is a part." (This sort or stop-gap operational circularity lurks in so much of our research, from personality and attitude testing to rating foster homes.) Thus the whole matter is rendered objective, measurable, and susceptible of mathematical statement. Is it beside the point that this answer has eluded the initial (difficult) problem and answered a different (easy) one? And that all it says, on critical scrutiny, is that personality adjustment is being regarded as have personality adjustment — *whatever* it *really* is!

But due account must be taken of the imperative on a science to develop its autonomic terminology and its own expertness in its own area. A physicist does not define mass in terms of the group's consensus of massiveness; nor a physiologist identify Brights disease in terms of those who think they have it. It is the business of a science, through thorough knowledge of the involved causal relationships (and, in the functional sciences, of the involved needs and structures and their functional processing), to set up its own expertness, its own (autonomic) conceptual tools and investigative procedures. Only then is the trained expert in the given field superior to the layman — so that, however much either the person or his group think he has Brights disease (or a maladjusted personality or an inappropriate set of social institutions) the physiologist (or the social psychiatrist or the sociologist) will be expert to tell whether they really have.

Thereby we must also note that 'normal,' as statistically (or culturally) defined and as functionally defined, has diverging connotations. Statistical 'normality' may, from the functional approach, mean only mediocrity or even a particulary widespread maladjustment. If everybody had Brights disease, it would be regarded as normal by the group consensus and it would be normal in the statistical definition. But an incisive functional science would presently still have to recognize it as a pathological condition (as it has with hook-worm, malaria, and other endemic diseases which are statistically normal for their regions), a failure of adjustive appropriateness from the *contained functional approach* of the physiologist. But it requires an autonomic terminology, an intimate knowledge of causal processings, a functional approach, and a sufficiently discrete differentiation of conceptual tools to enable one to state these things.

Only with the achievement of these can our complex functional sciences at the social level hope to fulfill their full task relative to the difficult problems that currently confront us at both the individual and the social level. Otherwise, these problems of diagnosis and correction will be eschewed by disciplined thinkers, who understandably prefer the *feel* of security in more objective but less incisive approaches. And the most significant problems will continue to be left to the moralizers, the undisciplined fanatics, and the contending embattled factions.

The method of demonstration, as in geometry, yields literally inescapable conclusions — *demonstrability*. The method of experiment, as in the physics laboratory, yields repeatable *provability*. Certitude is less than in demostration, however, since one is never absolutely certain that all the factors were known and controlled. The method of statistics yields only mathematical *probability*. Here certitude is still less and findings more tentative for one is never certain of the correctness of identification of the entities tabulated or the representativeness of the sampling. Likewise, the method of causal-processual analysis and the convergence of inference yields rational judgmental *plausibility*. Here certitude is still less and findings still more tenuous. For one is never sure that he has identified all the causes that were operative, or followed out the full intricacies of their processing, or taken account of all the situational imperatives, contained tendencies, constant factors, and integrational or configurative changes that have occurred. No more that, in each of the steps, all of the lines of converging inference have been known and correctly followed. But it would be as foolish for biology, psychology, and the social sciences to reject functional-processual analysis because its findings are so tenuous in character as it would have been for physics to reject statistics because its mere probabilities did not match the provabilities and demonstrabilities provided by the already established methods.

The plausibility-yielding methods are essentially the method used by all systematic theory building; by the grand strategy of induction as well as by much of the tactics of specific case investigations; by method as well as by technique. The social sciences have tended to lose sight of the grand strategy of induction, however, in their preoccupation with the tactical problems of local engagement. But we must not overlook the full sweep of science as a *process*. That there is no certain way in which to tell good insight from bad in the initial instance, or to distinguish instantly between correct and erroneous causal analyses, or to certify major theories or interpretations with unerring dispatch is insufficient reason for rejecting insight, processual analysis, convergence of inference, or systematic theory building as important scientific tools and methods.

And we do have criteria, perhaps themselves matters of verbalized plausibility, by which to judge their products. These criteria are: (1) the relative richness of factual material reduced to order by, or in harmony with, the interpretation or theoretical structure that has been built; (2) the relative absence of phenomena not in harmony therewith; (3) the breadth of inclusion and the wide range, both of data within the immediate field and of data and theory within adjacent and underlying sciences, from which implications are implicitly or explicitly drawn; (4) the many angles of convergence of implications upon any single item; (5) the internal rational consistency of the interpretation, configurational unit, or theoretical structure, as a whole; (6) the closely knit character of that internal consistency; (7) the minuteness with which the detailed causal processing has been followed or analyzed out; (8) the pragmatic test, in the more refined sense of the term. *i. e.*, the extent to which the conclusions are acceptable to the whole mind and seem to yield understandability to the phenomena studied. To these may be added, of course, certain criteria of all method, for example, the extent to which (9) predictability and (10) control are yielded.

This complex of criteria go together. In terms of just one of them, internal consistency for example, mediaeval theology might rate high. But internal consistency does not stand by itself as a criterion but as one of an integral complex of criteria, others of which are range of inclusion, the many angles of convergence, the detailed processing out, etc. A single case, or two or three, set down on a tabulation chart yields little statistical probability. No more do isolated insights or a few shreds of inference yield significant plausibility. But let the number of either increase, and certitude mounts, yielding, in the case of statistics a *summative* strength, like the similar and paralleling strands in a cable, in the plausibility-yielding methods a *configurative* strength, like the intermeshing strands in a fabric.

SOCIAL PSYCHOLOGY

In the nature of his method, the user of the plausibility-yielding methods cannot be a particularist or a unilateralist. The present strain for synthesis is his opportunity and the validation of his position. He may not limit himself to, say, behaviorism, or Gestalt, or Freudianism, or economic materialism, or diffusion, or independent origin, or even to non-quantitative or quantitative methods as exclusive of each other. He must set them all in the perspective of each other. Narrow identification with some single school of thought or limitation to a particular approach, method, or set of techniques are the logical opposite of his method and will be fatal to him. He will find that, by a diagnostic observation or experiment here; by invoking the side light of some other field or some conclusively established generalization there; by translating technical terms of one school into those of another; by changing an unqualified generalization to one couched in terms of the *sense in which* the relationships obtain, or the *conditions under which* now the relationships stressed by the one school and now those emphasized by the other obtain; here by accepting; there by rejecting; and again by the converging and buttressing of inferences; in these ways, starting out *sympathetically*, becoming progressively *critical* and *eclectic*, he presently becomes *synthetic* in his activity. He begins to emerge with range, depth, and consistency. For the functionalist, objective *knowledge* matures into *understanding*, even *wisdom!*

To the writer, functional analysis necessarily supplements causal-processual analysis when organic, psychological, or social phenomena are to be studied. The structures and processes of organisms must meet the situational imperative of continued existence or they will not survive. The mechanically causal nexus may not be such as to throw up such adaptive structures and processes in the first place, in which case no organic life ensues, as is presumably the case on the moon's surface. Or, throwing them up, the causal processes may not be such as to provide them the patterns for survival, in which case the individual or species dies or becomes extinct. That is, there is nothing mystical in the "situational imperative" or other functional concepts. But in life forms which do survive, not merely for an hour but with a continuity stretching over millions of years during which a long further-adaptive evolution has occurred, it must be evident that the imperatives of living have been fabricated with greater or less success into the essential nature of the living structures and processes themselves. In this area scientific investigation will need to reckon with that fact, over and above the scattered factual correlations and objective-causal processings. In the surviving species and the long socio-cultural evolution, a causal element that is *situational, integrative, configurative,* in a word, organic and *functionally selective* has been added to the sheer atomisms of the cause-effect sequences. This means that *the basic laws and principles governing biological, psychological and social phenomena will be functional in their very essence.* Their function often constitutes the *raison d'etre,* the reason for the very existence, as well as for the forms and characteristics of such phenomena. Realization of this has been reflected in the development already referred to (p. 240 ff.), from the metabolic gradient and equipotentiality to functional anthropology and psychoanalysis.

Functional concepts are difficult concepts, quite impervious to the so-called objective methods working alone. For between functioning identity and 'objective' identity there is no necessary relationship. The functional approach is thus couched in terms of needs, directional strivings, realizational potentialities, and structural or situational limitations, imperatives, or resources. Clear awareness of these requires a wealth of "clinically close" contact. It is this intimate tracing of the functional processes in their interrelationships with the organism's structures and needs which presently gives the functional expert his independence of morals, the group's opinion, or the subject's (individual or society) own beliefs — as already referred to *re* Bright's disease. For, like the method of causal-processual analysis and convergence of inference of which it is an extension, the method of functional analysis, with the further and further consistent fitting together of its analyses, constantly approaches (only) the ideal-goal of a *contained validation for its functional judgments.* (Just as the objective methods only approach the ideal goal of absolute descriptive accuracy).

Any criterion of adjustment, whether in physiology, psychiatry, or sociology, thus rests ultimately upon a *judgment* of functional appropriateness. Such a judgment depends in turn upon the full development of the given science, upon its development of autonomic nomenclature and an intimately-contacted independent expertness, upon the consistent interlacing of its causal and functional analyses with the findings of underlying, adjacent, and overarching functional disciplines, and upon the focusing of all this on a correct appraisal of the involved needs, the specialized organs or structures, the available energies or resources, and the confronting situational imperatives, limitations, and alternative possibilities in the particular case. A judgment of functional appropriateness is always made from an assumed angle of approach or point of view, that of the functioning entity, the going concern being considered. This is the only way in which a functional science can attack its central problem, that of function itself. For there certainly can be no such thing as function detached from reference to the functioning entity.

Science, through depersonalizing its instrumentation and its techniques, endeavors to approximate objective "truth." And since there is no such thing as objective "appropriateness" in the same sense, it has largely refused to deal with problems of functional appropriateness at all. This might be appropriate for the inorganic sciences, but would be fatal for the functional sciences. For the situation provides two ways for science to be "morally neutral". The first, not to try at all in that field, is an essentially defeatist position, as if the entirety of the universe were not open to inductive investigation. The second is to adapt the attack to the nature of the problem, *i. e.*, to assume one center of reference for value as readily as another! This, too, is a form of moral neutrality. One must assume that framework or "field" of inter-appropriateness whose 'center of reference' is the particular functioning entity under study. And he must pass with freedom and ease from one such framework to another as the exigencies of study require, or when the subject of study changes. If things begin to emerge after awhile which are common to all, or if overarching frameworks emerge, well and good. If they don't, likewise well and good. But the inductive method will have been extended to the entirety of the universe. And if we can arrive at inductive appraisals of functional appropriateness within those frameworks of interfunctioning whose centers of reference are the human person and human society, the result will be little short of revolutionary. It need only be remarked that biology, physiology, neurology, medicine, and psychiatry do this as a matter of course. And their results have been revolutionary.

We are now in a better position to undestand such terms as situational imperatives, situational emergents, processual products, and the like. It is evident, *e. g.*, (taking the group situation as the *functional "field"* relative to which all contained points are functionally aligned!) that the contained imperatives of group living will sooner or later throw up pervasive attitudes of dominance in some, submission in others, whether or not there were such instincts. Morals, too, are a group situational emergent, bound sooner or later to emerge as a result of the contained processes and contained imperatives of group living. They are not the result of a "moral sense" in man in contrast to the other animals. Again, the incest taboo is situationally necessitated by the imperatives contained in the family situation, not a result of an instinctive abhorrence. This replacement of causal explanation couched in terms of reified entities and isolated linear chains of sequence by explanation in terms of "situational emergents," "configurational" or "organic integrations," and "processual products" is one of the most important gains of the present century. It spells the difference between the older physic's (alchemy's) "virtues", geography's (all but astrological) "influences", biology's "entelechy", or psychology's "faculties," and our modern conceptions. Or betwen Tarde and contemporary social psychology; or Freud and Horney.

In *a priori* terms, there is a situational imperative for dynamic, ready-at-hand, adaptive action patterns in the very nature of biological organisms, if they are to survive. At the lower levels of evolutionary development, these ready-at-hand patterns may be in the nature of tropisms, rigid, irreversible, only crudely adaptive, and little incorporating the surrounding environment into themselves, the discrepancy being made up by the high birth and death rates. Successively up the scale of organic evolution plasticity intrudes and the close interweaving of innate and environmental factors becomes more marked.

When, as in the case of man the conditioned response or similar mechanisms are the main agents of producing the specificity of the behavior pattern, the possibility of culture arises. Whether born in the paleolithic, modern times, or a hundred thousand years in the future; whether born in central Africa, among the Greenland Eskimos, or among Parisians or Londoners; and into whatever social class or cultural area he is born, the human individual can form *whatever* specific patterns are required. In so doing, he introjects *whatever* socio-cultural environment into his behavioral equipment as specific dynamic-patterns. This fact (within the limits of due reciprocal appropriateness in return) permits the evolution of culture and social organization *as such*. Social-cultural evolution can occur at the superorganic level, reflecting (within the mentioned limits) whatever geographical, historical, or contained imperatives and evolutionary processes may be involved. Thus the super-organic becomes in some aspects a thing *sui generis*, in others an extension of the biological principle of adjustment in man. And human notivations and dynamic behavioral patterns reflect that fact. The specific dynamic motivations of man as they finally come to be formed weld together elements from three sources: the skin-contained needs, drives, appetites, and neural mechanisms; the modifications of these at the hands of sheerly individual experience; and the imperatives of the social-cultural milieu with which he is thus so organically related.

The prime movers of human motivation, then, are in considerable measure socially processed in their very genesis. Man, as a creature high in the evolutionary scale, is born with very few specific innate patterns of behavior. He has, and presently matures, quite a number of separate reflexes; and he has quite a number of appetitive, feeling, and emotional "dynamic cores" of behavior. But it remains for the conditioning of responses to give these their specific pattern and to tie the loose ends into larger patterns of behavior organically, and into time-and-space-bridging consistencies which will carry the organism through the clutter of merely adventitious stimuli (relative to survival or functioning) in its external adjustments. The factors of sheer conditioning, adience, canalization, and of sheer gestaltistic or configurational change are supplemented by the more dynamic appetitive, feeling, and emotional factors to make some of these larger patterns highly dynamic in character. Also, through the lowering and heightening of the thresh-holds of stimulation by emotion, feeling, appetite, and interests, they are highly selective, functionally. This is the dotted line on which Dewey's concept of dynamic habit, McDougall's concept of instinct in humans, psychoanalytic concepts of instinct and libido, Small's interests, Thomas' concept of the wishes, etc., etc., all have to come out in the case of human beings. By contrast with insects and lower animals, human drives are vastly more plastic and protean. They are equally driving, however, and concerned with the same general types of things functionally — danger, safety, survival, food, sex, etc.

These dynamic habits, complexes, drives, interests, or wishes (as you will) run all the way from the triviality and evanescence of a wish for an ice cream cone at a particular time to deep-lying, strong, insidiously permeative, and permanent motivations. Those that result from the contained imperatives of group living, whatever the specific culture, result in what we call human nature by contrast with merely animal nature. Further modifications or additions follow from particular types of cultural organization or levels of cultural development. These constitute cultural idiosyncrasies. Further modifications flow from the social role. And so on down to uniquely individual patternings. The inescapable situational emergence, in the group-living human animal, of the fundamental "wishes" for security, for response, and for recognition (status) is at once evident.

There will even be differences of emphasis in the total dynamic integration of the same person from time to time. Shifts in the dominance and subordination of various drives to each other within the total "value gradient" of the single personality thus occur from time to time in response to changing needs; following crises which have necessitated basic reorganization; or in response to alterations in the constellation of needs, the impingement of situational imperatives, and the flow of satisfactions and deprivations. Thus, despite certain underlying uniformities whose protean manifestation can still be observed through the further changes, the organization of personality in the child and the mature adult are often in many aspects quite different. Or in the same person before and after divorce, bereavement, or other crisis. Or in the same person after some years in a particular delegated or institutionalized role — as, say, parent, judge, army officer, teacher, salesman, night club entertainer, etc. Any single item has to be set in the perspective of this partly fixated and structured, partly protean and moving equilibrium — the "economy of the personality."

It must be seen that all degrees of specificity or generalization, of triviality or importance, of evanescence or permanence, and of segmentation or permeativeness will occur at the hands of the same underlying process. Except for an extremely important common core of 'human nature,' situationally emergent from the interplay of universal human needs and social-cultural living *as such*, one may expect various modifications and additions flowing from the culture type, the point in cultural evolution, the individual role and status, and various idiosyncratic factors. These may lead, *e. g.*, to such extreme idiosyncratic results as the stubborn compulsions, phobias, fetiches, etc., marking a specific patient. Thus does the relativity of human nature contrast with the fixity of the insect or the crustacean.

SOCIAL PSYCHOLOGY

Personality, in the psychiatric sense, is that a part of the psychic life organization which has been developed and structured in answer to the necessity to reconcile the conflicts between (1) the internal needs and impulses on the one hand with (2) the imposed demands and proffered satisfactions of the environing personal-social-cultural milieu on the other; and all this within the further limiting framework of (3) the world of reality in general. Since there are thus three somewhat conflicting, somewhat mutually supporting, but sometimes mutually exclusive sets of imperatives upon it, the personality tends to take on this three-fold structure in its organization, each segment tending to operate on different principles in accordance with the different imperatives, the diverging centers of reference for value and meaning. The super-ego is developed in response to the imperatives laid upon the individual by the surrounding persons, society, and culture. It is literally fabricated into the very structure of personality itself by the surrounding group because of the inescapable situational imperative to adjust or accommodate to the group's demands if one is to continue to live in the group. By contrast with the moral-principled super-ego, the id proceeds on the pleasure principle. Unrestricted by the other two segments of the personality, it would permit the wish so thoroughly to father thought and action as to carry the individual not merely against morals but against physical reality itself. The so-called ego proceeds on the reality principle. Much of the reactions to the merely physical world, eventually come relatively easily into its organization. (Objective science and objetive research, *e. g.*) Reactions to the social universe are much more complex, however, and long hinder even what would otherwise be comparatively simple. Thus the ego constitutes a rather narrow area of permissible or achievable rationality. It contains those rare syntheses of the conflicting imperatives derivative from the other two segments. It is thus almost interstitial between the super-ego and the id. But the ideal aim of psychotherapy is to enlarge its domain and, by getting repressed items and paradoxical considerations clearly into consciousness, to release the personality from the misery and strain if internal conflict and bestow freedom of form in appropriately handling all its adjustive problems, internal and external.

Such a structuration of personality cannot help but be fabricated in any human individual who grows up in a group. It is a situational emergent. (39) One's personality is well adjusted when these internal psychic factors are so smoothly integrated in their functioning as to permit and promote the fullest realization of a rich psychic life internally and the fullest realization of externally adjustive and creative potentialities. The *crux* of personality adjustment is thus internal .The practicing psychiatrist may in one case only have to adapt the individual to his culture as a "given constant." In another, he may have to help him live with his rebellion and rejection of obsolescent cultural forms. In a third case, he may have to help find a morale for instrumenting that very rebellion so that the client can go (but with no *internal* hindrances to the emergence of the fully appropriate responses) to the concentration camp, the marching battalion, or the political prison. At least the therapist has to face this dilema. He may not dodge it by "assuming" the *cultura qua* as a constant. Sometimes, especially, in periods of rapid cultural transition (or in metropolitan or transitional ecological areas), there simply does not exist a single, consistent, and unitary culture for the individual to adapt to. This fact not only sometimes makes the assumption of a cultural framework as a given constant impracticable. It is the very cause of some of our modern increase in neuroticism and personality maladjustment. The same is true of the marginal man whose internal organization has been worked out to fit a culture other than the one to which he must now adjust; even more so of the person of high social (or intellectual) mobility who was reared in one matrix and has to work out adaptations to several others successively or even simultaneously and still not get thrown out of internal adjustment.

In these circumstance, the 'reality principle' (with due regard for all the relativities of appropriateness) tends to displace the cultural frame of reference as the only available 'constant.' The synthesis of psychiatry and sociology thus has to go on to include the whole array of underlying and related disciplines for adequate guidance. The ideal goal of them all becomes the complete adjustment of all these areas to each other. And the practical aim of them all, including therapy, becomes not the achievement of a specific adjustment, but virtuosity in reaching *whatever* adjustment may be indicated. It becomes not adjustment but continuing adjustability.

---

39. See James W. Woodard, "The Relation of Personality Structure to the Structure of Culture," *loc. cit.*

SOCIAL PSYCHOLOGY

The relation of one's personality adjustment to his social adjustment and to the state of organization or chaos in the society of which he is a part may be subsumed in the following statements: (1) Adjustment within the personality is not necessarily identical with adjustment to one's social group. However, (2) long-run personality adjustment can scarcely be maintained, or the finest internal adjustment achieved in the absence of social adjustment. But (3) some personality maladjustment is even produced by the person's conformity into the group adjustment. In such cases inner maladjustment is a price paid for outer adjustment. And (4) sometimes, just as the internal solidarity of a group is heightened by the threat of an external enemy, a certain quality and duration of internal personality adjustment is fostered by tensions in one's social adjustment. (5) Social disorganization or cultural chaos and individual personality maladjustment often intensify each other reciprocally. Since the personality structure reflects in some measure the cultural structure in microcosm, its balance, smooth consistency, and functional appropriateness are strengthened if it functions in a social cultural milieu reflecting the same values, the same balance, inner consistency, and appropriateness. The adjustment difficulties of the marginal man are to this point. (6) Cultures differ in their favorability to individual personality adjustment and to various types both of personality and of adjustment patterns. (7) Full potentiality for intelligent *adjustability* (with due consideration of all these complex interrelationships) becomes the ultimate practical aim of all the human and social sciences including therapy.

Group adjustment may be defined in its turn, and in terms whose generalized form parallels those used to describe personality adjustment. A group is well adjusted when there exist smooth interfunctional relationships between constituent members and subgroups, yielding a total organization or integration which permits and promotes the fullest welfare-happiness and adjustment potentialities of the constituent units and the fullest realization of the total group's adjustive and creative potentialities relative to other groups and to the external world.

Since the individual personality and the social group are so organically if ambivalently united, their structures so interfabricated, and their adjustment destinies so intertwined, the integral character of all the functional sciences again becomes apparent. The way to individual freedom and fullness of realization at this point in history lies in the ultimate extension and perfection of social adjustment and organization rather than in its delimitation. Only smooth international, inter-class, inter-racial, inter-religious, and inter-cultural organization and adjustment can yield the permanent security and wide range of adjustive freedom necessary for the fullest personal realization and adjustment. Perhaps, at this point in history, full civilizational development and individual freedom alike wait on international organzation, with an inductive cultural foundation and a collective welfare slant.

By homologous contained imperatives, both the society and the individual, as units of functioning and survival, *must* have *an* integration, and there is a contained strain toward their achieving a homologous integration. But a rational, and thereby a complete, integration is not possible in early infancy or in the earliest primitive cultures — not until much experience has been accumulated. Hence, in both cases, the earliest attempts at integration cannot escape being incomplete, inconsistent, and emotional in character. (This, at the cultural level, gives the control culture initial dominance, resisting over millenia-long periods the freeing of the inductive and aesthetic-expressive cultures from its repressive control.) As emotional integrations, the earliest-formed organizations of personality, of social organization, and of culture tend to handle problems emotionally, repressing readily and resisting the necessary transitional break-ups incident to achieving mature and inclusive rational integration. The earliest occurring social organization thus overemphasizes status, caste, and the like; that of culture, the forms of repressive control. And the earliest (infantile) organization of personality thus tends to create fixations, regressive patterns and unassimilated nuclei through whose emotional pattern further experiences are filtered in a vicious circle whose cumulative working may carry on to neuroticism. As an incomplete and inconsistent pattern, the early attempts at integration achieve general workability of a sort by compartmentalization, rationalization, the development of split off segments, and the achievement of only accomodative mechanisms *between* these, rather than reaching the full adjustment of a single all-inclusive integration.

The contained process which forges the class-caste structure and the threefold structuration both of personality and of culture consists of: blocking at the hands of the dominant segment or subintegration; increased pressure from the blocked impulse; defensive over-protection on the part of the dominant segment and attempts

SOCIAL PSYCHOLOGY

actively to repress the antagonistic items; further exaggeration and consolidation of the repressed elements; still further overprotestation, consolidation, and protective severity on the part of the dominant segment; and so on in an accentuating process. Make it only a little more severe than usual and it is a vicious circle which will presently produce neuroticism and psychotic dissociation at the individual level, social disorganization and revolution at the social level, or civilizational collapse at the cultural.

Individual psychoanalysis consists in modifying the exaggeration in the demands of the extremes by getting the split-off segments, through cathartic awareness and functional analysis, into each other's perspective on the rational plane of the ego. This accomplished, as the excessively repressive demands of the one side die down, the excessive and overrebellious demands of the other also diminish. Full-perspectived, all-inclusive integration is approached. The same process happens at the cultural level as, down through time, the inductive culture slowly assimilates the dogmatic and repressive control culture into itself and the areas of rational behavior are expanded. Likewise at the social level as juridical, parliamentary, economic, political, expertized, and other modes of smoothly "processing out" conflicts come to replace arbitrary, forceful, and repressive modes of social control, and the areas of depersonalized and participatory control are expanded. Each gain in provability, representational balance, full-perspectived understandability, and interbuttressed security makes the next gain easier. For, as defensive dogmatism gives way, rebellious over-demands lessen also. This still further reduces the necessity for the first, etc.; until, as in individual analysis, the vicious circles are slowly reversed. Beneficent circles begin to yield creative and realizational adjustive patterns as a "way of life" for the whole personality, the total culture, the entire society. A consistently integrated, fully appropriate, and really civilized culture begins slowly to emerge.

But if the same "therapy" is indicated, quite parallel "resistances" to integration are offered by the contravalent segments of society. The vigor with which each segment claims freedom of speech and action for itself and its reluctance to grant the same access to the comumnity consensus to segments with antagonistic frames of meaning exemplifies this. An ephemeral social solidarity and morale may indeed be based on the dominance of a few segments, organizing action by propagandistic hoodwinking or forcefully repressing other segments. But for enduring social adjustment, all the factors must be brought into the focus of a common attention; they must be faced frankly; their diverse legitimacies must be admitted and set in a single framework of relativities; and modes of analyzing and processing out the conflicting elements must be found. In these ways there could finally be achieved an inclusive singleness of social meaning; and an uninhibited, undistorted, and consistent social action.

But none of the segments are "ethically neutral" in the sense required to achieve this integration successfully — as is, say, the analyst relative to the guidance of the conflict-torn individual patient. There exists no agency in the culture equipped to do it. Save one: the functional sciences! But certainly a pietistic rather than a truly functional science will be of little help. No more a dogmatically ethnocentric one like that of the totalitarians, at least not if enduringness in adjustment matters. Little more one which thinks that being ethically neutral means to avoid functional problems altogether and to stultify even factual description and measurement. The answer will not be found until the functional sciences succeed in validating an all-inclusive, consistent, and dynamically meaningful framework of functional reference within which all diverse imperatives and involved relativities have their due place. When the tools of the subtler methods and of the functional approach are perfected; when the total web of social theory is as incisive and as functional in approach as are the Marxian and Freudian strands in that web; when the corrective modifications, interbuttressings, and mutual enrichments have worked themselves out to set each entering strand in the perspective of all in such an integral synthesis; then the human and social science should begin to go from objective *knowledge* to causal-processual *understanding* and finally to functional *wisdom*. With such an integral theory giving sure-footedness, consistency, and strategic perspective to the application of the social sciences, social action might begin effectively to reinforce mankind's contained strain to replace sheer chaos-riddled survival with rich and consistent meaning resonance and full adjustive realization, personal, social, and cultural.

SOCIAL PSYCHOLOGY

SELECTED BIBLIOGRAPHY

Allport, F. H., *Social Psychology,* (Boston: Houghton Mifflin Co., 1924).
Cantril, Hadley, *Gauging Public Opinion,* (Princeton: Princeton University Press, 1944).
Cooley, C. H., *Human Nature and the Social Order,* (New York: Charles Scribner's Sons, 1902).
Dewey, John, *Human Naturse and Conduct,* (New York: Henry Holt and Co., 1922).
Durkheim, Emile, *Elementary Forms of the Religious Life,* (New York: The Macmillan Co., 1926).
Horney, Karen, *The Neurotic Personality of Our Time,* (New York: W. W. Norton and Co., 1937).
Kardiner, A., and Ralph Linton, *The Individual and His Society,* (New York: Columbia University Press, 1939).
Karpf, Fay B., *American Social Psychology,* (New York: McGraw-Hill Book Co., 1932).
Klineberg, Otto, *Social Psychology,* (New York: Henry Holt and Co., 1940).
Kohn, Hans, *The Idea of Nationalism,* (New York: The Macmillan Co., 1944).
Mannheim, Karl, *Man and Society in an Age of Reconstruction,* (London: Kegan Paul, 1940).
McDougall, William, *An Introduction to Social Psychology,* (Boston: J. W. Luce, 1926).
Mead, George H. *Mind, Self and Society,* (Chicago: University of Chicago Press, 1937).
Murchison, Carl, ed., *A Hand book of Social Psychology,* (Worcester: Clark University Press, 1935).
Murphy, Gardner, Lois B. Murphy, and Theodore M. Newcomb, *Experimental Social Psychology,* rev. ed., (New York: Harper and Bros., 1937).
Park, Robert E., and Ernest W. Burgess, *Introduction to the Science of Sociology,* (Chicago: University of Chicago Press, 1924).
Roethlisberger, F. J., *Managment and Morale,* (Cambridge: Harvard University Press, 1943).
Ross, E. A., *Social Control,* (New York: The Macmillan Co., 1901; republished, 1932).
Thomas, W. I., and Florian Znaniecki, *The Polish Peasant in Europe and America,* 2 vol. ed., (New York: Alfred A. Knopf, 1927).
Waller, Willard W., *The Family, A Dynamic Interpretation,* (New York: The Cordon Co., 1938).
Young, Kimball, *Introduction to Social Psychology,* rev. ed., (New York: F. S. Crofts Co., 1944).

James W. Woodard received his A. B. and his M. A. from Northwestern University, his Ph. D. from the University of Pennsylvania, his Phi Beta Kapa from Northwestern. He taught sociology at the University of Pennsylvania from 1924 to 1932, and at Temple University from 1932 on, being associate professor of sociology at the latter institution. He was visiting lecturer in sociology at University of Minnesota (1936), Swarthmore College (1935), and is at present visiting professor of sociology at Queens College. He was president of the Eastern Sociological Society (1936), and is president of the Philadelphia Anthropological Society (1943). Among his publications with relevance to social psychology are the following:

Intellectual Realism and Culture Change, Sociological Press, Hanover, 1935; "Psychological Aspects of the Problem of Moral Responsibility," *Jour of Crim. Law and Crim.,* 21, 2, 267-97; "The Biological Variate and Culture," *Soc. Forces,* 9, 1, 10-20; "Analysis of a Dream," *British Jour. of Med. Psych.,* 10, pt. 2, 186-207; "Five Levels of Description of Social Psychological Phenomena," *Sociologus,* 9, 1, 25-31; "Notes on the Nature of Sociology as a Science," *Soc. Forces,* 11, 1, 28-43; "The Socio-Psychology of Learning," *Jour. Ed. Soc.,* 6, 7, 387-400; "Critical Notes on the Culture Lag Concept," *Soc. Forces,* 12, 3, 388-398; "A New Classification of Culture and a Restatement of the Culture Lag Theory," *Amer. Soc. Rev.,* 1, 1, 89-102; "The Relation of Personality Structure to the Structure of Culture," *Amer. Soc. Rev.,* 3, 5; "Cultural Evolution and the Social Order," *Jour. Soc. Phil.,* 6. 7. 313-326; "The Role of Fictions in Cultural Organization," forthcoming in *Transactions of the New York Academy of Science.*

CHAPTER X

SOCIAL CONTROL

by

GEORGES GURVITCH

Introduction. The term "social control" and the problems involved, attracted much attention, especially in American sociology of the twentieth century, after E. A. Ross published in the *American Journal of Sociology* a series of papers under this title (1896-98) and united them in his book: *Social Control: A Survey of the Foundations of Order* (1901). Sociologists who represented positions very different from, if not opposed to, those of E. A. Ross, such as C. H. Cooley (*Social Process*, 1918), C. H. Ellwood (*The Social Problem*, 1915, and *The Psychology of Human Society*, 1925), R. E. Park and E. W. Burgess (*Introduction to the Science of Sociology*, 1921) and many others, adopted the term "social control" but gave it meanings corresponding to their respective sociological theories.

After the American Sociological Society devoted its *Proceedings* of 1917 to this topic (See Vol. XII) and until the present time, "social control" has become one of the main centers of American sociological interest and has inspired considerable literature. Some sociologists even believe that all sociological problems can be reduced to this one. This opinion, as we shall try to show, is an obvious and dangerous exaggeration.

Now what appears amazing and rather indisputable when one studies books and papers on social control, is the fact that various authors are not in agreement either about the definition of the term, about the field concerned, or about the boundaries of this new branch of sociology and its relationship to other branches.

This point was often recognized; for example, in 1921 Park and Burgess wrote (1): "Social control has been studied, but in the wide extension that sociology has given to the term it has not been defined." Four years later, F. E. Lumley wrote in his book: "A satisfactory definition of social control has not yet been made."(2) Fifteen years later in his book, Paul H. Landis again made the same complaint: "The term social control employed as a title has disadvantages because it has been given diverse meanings."(3) Thus, one might be anxious to know whether after fifty years of discussion some progress was made concerning the topic of "social control."

At the same time, neither the topic nor even the term appears entirely new. As far as sociology is concerned, Auguste Comte, being very much, if not too much, preoccupied with the problem of "order" and the role in it of specific forms of religion, morality, and knowledge, had already come very close to the problems of "social control." Emile Durkheim and his school, from the last decade of the nineteenth century on, devoted their main effort to the study of collective symbols, values, ideas, and ideals and their role in different types of society. Thus, they contributed to the development of new sociological disciplines, such as sociology of religion, of morals, of knowledge, of linguistics, of aesthetics, and of law. The Durkheimian school promoted greatly the study of "social control." However, the emphasis was placed more on the functional relationships of the forms studied to the types of society than to their practical action as types of "social engineering." This latter problem has attracted the main attention of American sociologists writing about "social control."

As to the term "social control," it was, as E. A. Ross noted, already employed by Herbert Spencer in his *Principles of Sociology* (vol. II, part 4, ed. 1893) in connection with his theory of "cere-

---

1. See *Introduction to the Science of Sociology,* (Chicago: University of Chicago Press, 1921), Chap. XII, pp. 785 ff.

2. F. E. Lumley, *Means of Social Control,* (New York: ihe Century Co., 1925), p. 12.

3. Paul H. Landis, *Social Control, Social Organization and Disorganization in Process,* (Philadelphia: J. B. Lippincott Co., 1939).

SOCIAL CONTROL

monial government" as the earliest form of government, without giving to this term any special prominence.

In a way independent from sociology and its development, several social sciences established long before the birth of sociology, such as political science, jurisprudence, education, social ethics, and even economics, so far as they included applied, practical or administrative sections, were occupied with problems close to different aspects of "social control." In this sense, Park and Burgess, on the one hand, and L. L. Bernard, on the other, are right when they state that social control may be studied: a) as a problem of "administration, policy and polity," and b) as a problem of sociology. (4) But it is only in this second and purely theoretical sense that it represents a specific field of scientific investigation. Social control as a problem of different administrative activities, or to put it in more modern and broader terms, as a problem of various types of "social engineering," can be handled seriously only on the basis of a sociological investigation combined with some frankly expressed and accepted evaluations.

The difficulties and the disagreements centering around the term and the problem of social control are intensified by the fact that "control" conveys in continental European languages (French, German, Russian, etc.) a much smaller degree of interference than in English. If in English the accepted meaning of "control" is power, might, domination, authority, in all other European languages "control" means supervision, inspection, surveillance, comptrollership. Now the most interesting thing about social control is that American sociologists of such different opinions as E. A. Ross and C. H. Cooley, and many others, gave to the term social "control" a sense distinctively closer to the European meaning of supervision, inspection, surveillance, and guidance than to the customary English one of power or domination. However, several America sociologists who have written about social control have remained rather true to the old English meaning of power, domination, or constraint as do F. H. Giddings and Kimball Young. (5) This perhaps forms a transition to the interpretation of the problem of social control, not in the sense of regulation,

---

4. Park and Burgess, *op. cit.*, p. 785; L. L. Bernard, *Social Control in Its Sociological Aspects*, (New York: The Macmillan Co., 1939), pp. 3-4.

5. See Franklin H. Giddings, *Studies in the Theory of Human Society*, (New York: The Macmillan Co., 1922), pp. 200 ff; Kimball Young, *Introductory Sociology*, (New York: American Book Co., 1934), pp. 520 ff.

evaluation, aspiration and formulation of social ideals, it as it was rightly conceived by earlier authors, but in a sense of all motivation and influencing of the fellowman's behavior or even of all "environmental-social stimuli" causing "reflex responses." This tendency to dissolve the problem of social control in that of social psychology, and even general psychology, in their different interpretations, was already clearly manifested in F. E. Lumley's book *Means of Social Control*, (1925) and received its most elaborate and radical expression by L. L. Bernard, especially in his book, *Social Control in its Sociological Aspects* (1939).

Finally, in the discussion about economic and social planning in the last decade, the term "social control" was employed in a new sense again. "Social control" in industry, labor relations, economy and so on, was understood by several authors as different degrees of nationalization, or socialization, or simply large scale organization of economic relations; and in addition, by some, as participation of workers in the ruling of planned economy, through shop committees and full development of collective bargaining. In this sense of an institution of industrial democracy the term "worker control" (but not "social control") was already very often employed in the period after the first World War. It seems to us obvious that "social control" in this new sense is very close to one of the particular aspects of "social engineering," and "administrative activity," and belongs to applied and practical considerations, combining judgments of reality and evaluations. It presupposes the sociological investigation already made about the problem of social control as a whole, and the description of a particular type of social structure where the economic planning applies.

This rather lengthy introduction appeared to us necessary in order to explain the purpose, the emphasis, and the manner of exposition in this chapter. Convinced that, despite all difficulties and confusions, investigations on "social control" represent a very important branch of contemporary sociology, having a specific object and performing a cardinal function, we shall try:

(1) In a first section, to set forth the most current conceptions and research in the field of social control, giving particular attention to its different definitions and interpretations;

(2) In a second section, to analyze critically the work done in this field, and to show why the problems involved are of such major interest for sociology;

(3) In a third section, to formulate our own position and to

SOCIAL CONTROL

develop a short outline of the principal topics which we consider as belonging to the field of social control, as a particular branch of sociology. Obviously, the shortage of space will force us to insist only upon the strictly indispensable, especially in the last two sections.

I

The conception of "social control" by its promoter — E. A. Ross — is not easy to sum up because of some ostensible fluctuations in his position. In the preface to his book Ross defines social control as *intended or purposeful social ascendency* as opposed to social influence, which is unconscious and spontaneous. (Cf. also p. 194.) He defines the task of his book as the separation of "the individual's contribution to social order from that of society." Thus the new field of research appears as *"the contribution to social order by society through the affirmation of its purposeful social ascendency."* Now the meaning of the term ascendency is understood by Ross in different ways: sometimes, in an ethical estimative, normative, or larger evaluational sense of superiority in a value-scale, sometimes in a purely psychological and largely factual sense of "pressure," "interference," "stimulation," "imposing of adjustment." "Intended social ascendency" taken in the first sense prompts Ross to speak of social control as *"regulative institutions"* (p. 42) of which "the offenses exasperate the group." (p. 49) He undertakes even to distinguish in "social control" the working of "social imperatives," of "social valuations," and of "social ideals." (p. 149) He shows the important role which belief in the supernatural, "social religion," ceremonies, personal ideals, public opinion (in the sense of diffused morality), morals, arts, education, knowledge, and law play in social control. He underlines the role of "ideals, beliefs, symbols or standards" in several kinds of social control (p. 40). But at the same time Ross is inclined to enlarge the sense of social control to the extreme limit, utilizing the second, purely psychological interpretation of ascendency; thus he includes all kinds of "social suggestions," independent of their "ethical element," "illusions," "persuasions," and "treats" in the domain of social control, underlining that it can be purely utilitarian, independent of ideals, founded on self-preservation (pp. 62-67), and representing "means deliberately chosen in order to reach certain ends." (p. 411)

TWENTIETH CENTURY SOCIOLOGY

In the first part of his book, entitled "The Grounds of Control," Ross tries to show that "social order" is neither instinctive nor spontaneous, but rests on and is the product of social control. Since society is impossible without order, social control is the indispensable element of social reality. This thesis is reinforced by Ross with two arguments of unequal value. Quite justified seems his insistence on the multiplicity of irreducible conflicts in social life which can be only provisionally stabilized by constantly renewed applications of social control, creating "better order." (p. 59). Quite controversial, however, seems his interpretation of "social order" as "a fabric rather than a growth" (p. 5), an artifice (p. 246) created unilaterally by social control; functional interdependence and integration in the entire social conjuncture are not analyzed. The "social reality" itself is seen in a nominalistic way, as rather an assemblage of isolated individuals, whose connection and emergence in a whole stems from social control (cf. the exaggeration in the criticism of sociability, solidarity, and sympathy theories, pp. 14 ff and pp. 296 ff).

In the second part of his book, entitled "The Means of Control," Ross describes several different kinds or forms of control, in the following order: public opinion, law, belief, social suggestion, education, custom, social religion, personal ideals, ceremony, art, enlightenment, illusion, social valuations, and ethical elements. He calls them "means of control" or "engines of control" (p. 320) probably in order to underline the fact that diferent kinds of control are integrated, in every type of society, in a specific whole; they are interconnected and complete each other. The main sociological interest of the problem of social control rests precisely in the study of different kinds of control as particular sectors of a unity, in which the hierarchy of particular controls varies according to the problems to be solved in a particular social conjuncture.

In the third part of his book, entitled "The System of Control," Ross, after having shown that the greater the "elasticity and sincerity" of control the more it is "truly social," describes the fluctuation of social control between "strong and weak," "more and less," "rigid and elastic." (pp. 395-406) The prominence in the "general system of control" of varieties founded on moral feelings or, on the contrary, on utility, depends itself upon the constitution of the society (pp. 411-416). "The limits of social control" consist in the fact that different kinds of control can compete, that their mutual importance and hierarchy varies, and that the "superior" (most efficient) forms of social control "are inward" (pp. 417-430). "The diffusion of control is, in fact, the chief security against its excess." (p. 431)

Ross seems to expect that diffused, inward forms of social control, such as instruction, suggestion, and social art (especially the last) will predominate over all others in creating order in future society (p. 416). But this does not prevent him from considering law (which he founds exclusively on utility) in the actual social structure as "the most progressive department of control" (pp. 74 ff, 106 ff). He accentuates this position in his *Principles of Sociology* (1921), dedicated to Dean Roscoe Pound, the famous sociologist of law, who constantly emphasized his acceptance of Ross' theory of social control (see below). Here, law is for Ross "the cornerstone of the edifice of order, the most specialized and highly finished engine of control employed in society" and it becomes doubtful if the future will bring a change in the predominance of law over other kinds of control.

W. G. Sumner's book *Folkways; A Study of the Sociological Importance of Usages, Manners, Customs and Morals* (1906) (as well as *The Science of Society*, 1927, 4 volumes in collaboration with A. G. Keller) contributed to the concentration of problems on social control around crystallized and standardized traditional patterns of different kinds. "Folkways are habits and customs of the society . . . ; then they become regulative and imperative for succeeding generations. While they are in vigor they very largely control individual and social undertaking." The regulative and imperative character of folkways is concentrated in the "mores": "including a judgment that they are conducive to social welfare and exercise coercion on the individual to conform to them, although they are not coordinated by any authority." "Institutions and laws are produced out of mores. An institution consists of a concept (idea) and a structure."

F. H. Giddings in his book, *The Scientific Study of Human Society* (1924) critized the author of *Folkways* for his utilitarian trend and for not having succeeded in distinguishing "the unappreciative and the appreciative, esteeming patterns," connected with "societal telesis" (pp. 74 ff, 143 ff, 69 ff). Thus Giddings prepared the way for the contrast between technical and symbolic-cultural patterns, which alone according to several authors play a real role in social control. In some ways, the writings of E. Westermarck on *The Origin and Growth of Moral Ideas* (1907, 2 vols.) and *Ethical Relativity* (1932) played the same role, so far as he founded "mores" upon emotions and not utility and was forced to contrast "disinterested and impartial emotions of approval and disapproval" with all others (*Ethical Relativity*, pp. 89-113). (6)

The meeting of the theories on "social control" with theories of folkways, mores and patterns did some good to both, enlarging their mutual perspectives. But at the same time, especially in so far as the earlier tendency to reduce the validity of all kinds of patterns to mere duration and sanctions was not transcended, several authors showed a dangerous inclination to reduce all kinds of social control to customary usages, and more or less traditional patterns. They did not seem to realize that in this way "social control" was in danger of becoming exclusively a device of social conservatism and traditionalism, a support of "order" as opposed to "progress," as if perpetual renewal of symbols, aspirations to values, creation of ideals, reforms, rebellions and revolutions, and so on, were not essential elements of social control, especially of such kinds of control as morality, education, art, knowledge. We can quote as an example *An Introduction to Sociology* by Jerome Davis, Harry Elmer Barnes and others (1927), where (pp. 467-483) all forms of social control are reduced to customs, folkways, mores, conventions, codes ("institutional control") and fads, fashion, crazes ("non-institutional control").

Obviously, the insistence on cultural, symbolic, valuational, ideal, creative, and spiritual ingredients in patterns organizing social control, can seriously limit if not entirely circumvent the dangers of transforming the folkways-control theory into a partisan "sociology of order," which from the start of the nineteenth century (De Bonald, De Maistre) clashed so often with the "sociology of progress" (Condorcet, Proudhon). (7) Thus L. T. Hobhouse (*Morals in Evolution*, 1908; *Mind In Evolution*, 1918; *The Rational Good*, 1921; *The Elements of Social Justice*, 1922) and follow-

---

6. Cf. for criticism of Westermarck's theories my paper, "Is the Antithesis of Moral Man and Immoral Society True?" *The Philosophical Review*, 52: 533-552, November, 1943.

7. The contrast between these two kinds of sociologies was developed by the late French philosopher, Léon Brunshvicg.

SOCIAL CONTROL

ing him, C. A. Ellwood (*The Social Problem*, 1915, 2nd ed. 1924; *The Psychology of Human Society*, 1925; *Methods in Sociology*, 1933) had the merit of insisting that even behind rigid mores and standards there "is the spirit in which they are conceived," the ideals that inspire them and that they have to express. C. A. Ellwood concluded from this that social control leans on "the social idealism" in "realizing the spiritual side of social life," which is represented "by higher cultural values, ideas and ideals." With Ellwood, all kinds of social control are reduced to social morality, law, religion and education as directly linked with realization of ideals in social life. At the same time Ellwood believes, as L. T. Hobhouse did, in continuous progress of society toward an ever-augmented spiritualization and rationalization, and aided by more conscious, more elevated, and more effective social control. It becomes obvious that the dangers of a partisan "sociology of order" are here opposed by a no less partisan "sociology of progress," which is just as questionable.

After E. A. Ross, the most significant contribution to the problem of social control was made in America by C. H. Cooley. It is only in his last book *Social Process* (1918, 2nd ed. 1927), that Cooley employed the term social control explicitly, but the problem, in connection with that of the structure of social reality, occupied him from the outset, i.e. in *Human Nature and Social Order* (1902), and especially in *Social Organization* (1909). Social control is for Cooley a *"self control" by society of its own process of organization and creation*, guiding not isolated individuals (as by Ross), who cannot be separated from and opposed to the living social whole, but *this whole itself, from within*.

Contrary to the social "nominalism" of Ross, but in accordance with Emile Durkheim's, and especially with G. H. Mead's and John Dewey's position, Cooley points out that "self" and "we," society and the individual are "twin-born" (*Social Organization*, p. 350) and represent only different directions, aspects or poles in the indissoluble unity of the concrete mental life. (8)

"The creativeness" of social life gives rise to collective symbols, patterns, and standards, behind which are collective values and ideals. In them social reality, which manifests itself equally in the "we" and in the "selves," constantly transcends itself. Collective symbols, values, and ideals, which are the results and the direc-

---

8. This point of view is called now the *reciprocity of perspectives*.

tives of this creative social process, are at the same time products and producers of social reality, in which order and change cannot be separated.

Social control, whose validity and action is based on and directed by collective symbols, values, and ideals, is thus a process immanent in the self-creation of society. It would be no less false to reduce the problems of social control to those of resolving conflicts among individuals or even groups (against Ross), than to reduce them to those of "mores of maintenance" and standardized patterns supporting an established order (against Sumner and his followers), (*Social Process*, pp. 35-49, 283 ff). "The social process is itself a rise of social ideals, a process of valuations." "Revolt against institutions" and against mores is as characteristic of social control as "the ethos of the mores." In fact, even the latter express in crystallized form values and ideals, which are the real foundation of social control (*Social Process*, pp. 283, 417, 420; *Social Organization*, pp. 13, 32, 320). In these conceptions Cooley meets his French colleague Durkheim, who wrote: "Society can neither create nor recreate itself without at the same time creating ideals. This creation is not supplementary to the formation of the society; it is an act by which the latter makes and remakes itself periodically." "From a certain aspect, society itself is a set of values and ideals." (E. Durkheim *Les formes élémentaires de la vie religieuse*, 1912, p. 604, English transl. 1926; *Philosophie et sociologie*, 1924, pp. 136, 141, 146).

Cooley's conception of social control allowed the introduction of the principles of dynamic spontaneity and creativeness, without sacrificing either the ideal value basis, or the paternal mode of expression of control. Thus the old discussion as to whether social control includes only purposeful (Ross, Giddings) or also unintentional action (followers of Sumner), was transcended by a *new* contrast formulated by Cooley, that between *unconscious or implicit* and *conscious* or *explicit* control; both imply value-aspirations, but neither of them necessarily imply purposefulness. The purposeful control which Cooley admits as but one kind of conscious or explicit control, is called by him "rational control," and is considered by him an aim to achieve (pp. 382 ff, 334 ff). These distinctions have been accepted by many sociologists, some of whom added, as we shall see, others such as between paternal and social, formal and informal, organized and unorganized, in-

SOCIAL CONTROL

stitutionalized and uninstitutionalized, symbolic and direct. These distinctions have certainly contributed to a greater clarity and richness in the study of the problem, for they have permitted the discovery and description of several superimposed levels of depth in each kind of social control, and in each type of society or group where it is acting.

The contrast between "primary" (or "face-to-face") and "secondary" groups and the recognition that social control manifests itself in particular groups, not less than in inclusive societies, is also due to Cooley, who revealed the plurality of agencies co-existing in each domain of control and underlined the important difference to be made between *kinds of control* and *agencies of control*. For instance in such agencies of control as the family, the church, the labor union, the State, and so on, different kinds of control (morality, law, art, education, knowledge, and so on) can compete, and conversely any one of these kinds of control can utilize any agency (group) for its action.

It is easy to see that it was unfortunate for the problem of social control that Cooley started to study it so late and stopped his work of deepening the analysis so early. Some absence of clarity about the main sociological-philosophical issue concerning the relationship between ideal values and social reality and the semi-vitalist, semi-mystical concept of creativeness, prevented perhaps the full realization in American sociology of all the promises and possibilities contained in Cooley's approach to the problem of social control.

Robert E. Park and Ernest W. Burgess, *Introduction to the Science of Sociology* (1921), Chapter XII, tried to sum up and to synthesize the results of previous research in the field. They defined "social control" briefly as *"interference with the social process,"* which seems to be a compromise between Ross and Cooley's interpretations. The same can be said about the following characteristics: "Social control and the mutual subordination of individual members to the community have their origin in conflict, assume definite organized forms in the process of accomodation and are consolidated and fixed in assimilation. Through the medium of these processes a community assumes the form of a society. (9) Certain quite spontaneous forms of social control are

---

9. Here we can observe the influence of the disputable and outmoded conceptions of the German sociologist, Toennies.

developed." (p. 785) Park and Burgess suggest the following classification under three heads: "a) elementary forms of social control; b) public opinion, c) institutions. This order . . . indicates the development of control from its spontaneous forms in ceremony, prestige and taboo; its more explicit expression in gossip, rumor, news and public opinion, to its more formal organization in law, dogma and in religious and political institutions." (p. 788) A careful distinction has to be made between "a) customs and folkways — residues of spontaneous past practices, b) mores — past practices combined with judgments such as they find expression in public opinion, c) public opinion itself as the most actual and mobile form." (p. 795) Thus mores occupy an intermediary position between the "elementary forms of social control" and "public opinion."

"From the point of view of corporate action, social control is the central fact and the central problem of sociology. Just as psychology may be regarded as an account of the manner in which the individual organism as a whole exercises control over its parts, . . . sociology, speaking strictly, is a point of view and a method for investigating the process by which individuals are induced to cooperate in some sort of permanent corporate existence which we call society." (p. 42) This characteristic seems to indicate, that Park and Burgess are inclined to underline the factual and psychological aspect of social control, rather than its link with norms, evaluations, values, spiritual meanings, ideals; this impression is confirmed by the fact that they consider the sociological problem of social control, as that "of *social forces and human nature*" (p. 785) and even do not mention morals, education, knowledge, art.

This trend toward dissolving the problem of social control in social psychology was considerably intensified in F. E. Lumley's book *Means of Social Control* (1925). Nothing would be more natural than the reduction of *means* (or, as the author says, *"instruments"*) of social control to questions of psychological pressure, so far as a clear-cut distinction between *kinds of control* and *means of realization for every kind* would be made. However, Ross and the greater part of authors following him did not make this distinction. What is interesting to notice is that Lumley came closer than any other author to this distinction, so far as he enumerates aspects of social control: a) *authority*, b) *program of action*, c) *adequate communication system*, d) *free and impressible persons or groups*

SOCIAL CONTROL

who respond. In his book he obviously deals with only two of these aspects, but unfortunately his general definitions and interpretations of the problem of social control are exclusively founded on those aspects. Thus despite his linking of social control with "imperative uniformities" (p. 6), he finally defines social control in a purely psychological way as *"effective will transference."* (p. 13) He even believes it possible to formulate the problem in terms of behavioristic psychology. "Here we have the familiar stimulus-response pattern; but it is an infinitely complicated pattern . . . We might speak of social control as the practice of putting forth directive stimuli or wish patterns, their accurate transmission to, and adoption by others whether voluntary or involuntary." (p. 13)

"Social control" consists in "mental devices" for psychological pressure which can be characterized as "human symbol method" in contrast to "physical force method." "Symbols are substitutes for other things in order to arouse feelings, create attitudes, convey ideas and promote activities in others." (p. 16) In other words they are identified with *signs*, in accordance with the positivistic interpretation, "There are thousands of such symbol organizations or mechanisms which the human race has developed consciously or unconsciously, for the purpose of applying pressure without physical contact," that is for social control.

Lumley suggests the classification of all social controls in two groups: a) "Those which are directed to the work of elicitation. These are applied to evoke from individuals and groups more of the same thing or something better in the same direction. As examples we might think of *rewards, praise, cajolery* (or *flattery*), *persuasion* (including advertising, slogans, and so on), *education.* b) On the other hand are numerous mechanisms calculated to restrain and repress the overly aggressive and to prod up the stupid and slow. In this category might be included *gossip, satire, calling names, laughter, criticism, threats* (commands), *propaganda* and *punishement."* (p. 19) The author's entire book is devoted to a valuable and interesting psychological analysis of these "instruments of pressure" of which the greatest part are, according to him, also "clear cases of mores." (p. 28) Whether these psychological analyses resolve the central problems of social control and whether they would not be, even from the psychological point of view, far more instructive if they were less general, and integrated in concrete frames (of *kinds of social control* and of *types of groups and inclusive societies*) where they work, are other questions that we shall discuss later (see second section of this paper).

Earle E. Eubank in his *Concepts of Sociology* (1932) seems also to favor a definition of social control excluding any intervention of ideal values and linking it with factual, especially psychological, influence as such. "Control in its broadest sense," he writes, "may be defined as anything that exercises a modifying influence on anything else." (p. 207) "Conceived in this extended way societary control is therefore defined as including any way in which a person or group exercises influence or constraint which modifies the behavior, thought or feeling of any other person or group." (p. 219) "Social self-control, then, is the group's constraint or pressure or influence directed toward non-conforming persons with the intent of bringing them into ways which are harmonious with that of the group as a whole."

Jerome Dowd takes the opposite stand to psychological and purely factual interpretations of social control. In his work *Control in Human Societies* (1936) he insists upon the exclusively "telic and conscious" meaning of social control (pp. 137, 7). He understands "control" as "guidance," "direction," ". . . . as to control an engine by a lever." (p. 6) "Any form of control necessitates the interaction of four distinct elements or factors: a) an authoritative person or group having the power to induce or compel group action; b) the existence of a formulated or understood purpose of the group action; c) the existence of formulated or understood standards, rules, or conventions, serving as the means of carrying out the purpose, and d) the existence of some kind of discipline, i.e. of some prescribed means of inducing or compelling obedience to the standards or convention." (pp. 347, 12-13)

The purposeful character of control involves social ideals, whose role in the field Dowd emphasized with energy (pp. 158 ff, 174-175, 369 ff). "Ceremonies, rituals, and symbols are important factors of discipline" as an ingredient of control (p. 174), but "the efficient discipline does not consist in getting everybody to confirm to fixed standards, but in getting everybody to motivate his acts through his devotion to some ideal or principle and to govern his acts thereby." (p. 175)

"Instruments" or means of control have to be, as Dowd rightly insists, distinguished from the control itself. Especially, with Dowd, *folkways, public opinion*, and *organizations* are neither kinds nor

SOCIAL CONTROL

agencies of control, but only instruments of it (pp. 7-11). Among them "organizations" are "the most efficient instruments of control." (p. 11)

As to the kinds of control there are principally only two: a) *paternal control* and b) *social control*. "For ten thousand years or more the form of control in human societies was paternal, that is, in the family, in industry, in the State, in religion, and in art, it was exercised by some authoritative person: the father in the family, the king in the State, the priest in the religious order and the master in the workshop." (pp. vii ff, 23 ff, 136 ff). "The democratic or social control appeared and started its development hardly more than a century ago." "Social or democratic control is a very recent thing in human history, and, as yet we have learned very little about it. It necessitates the development of higher ideals and better discipline in all our social institutions." (pp. vii ff, 137 ff, 292 ff, 400 ff) "The era of social conrol can be defined . . . as that epoch in the evolution of society when the diffused form of control began to predominate over the concentrated form, which has been defined as paternalism." (p. 137) Here the agencies of control are neither individuals with prestige nor privileged classes or circles, but each group and each society, viewed as "wholes." "Voluntary associations" supported by "social approval" and forming a "cooperative commonwealth" can be considered as the most efficient agencies of the "social control" to be fully developed in the coming centuries (pp. 400, 219).

Jerome Dowd's entire book is devoted to a historico-sociological description of "paternal control," rebellion against it, and the slow and uneven penetration of social control in the different spheres: *family, religion, State, education, art, industrial relations.*

With the voluminous textbook by L. L. Bernard, *Social Control in its Sociological Aspects* (1939), we return to an effort to dissolve the field of social control in that of social psychology. It is true that the author who wrote several studies on social control before publishing his textbook shows more moderation in his last writing and makes many concessions (cf. Part 1, pp. 3 ff, 25 ff, 30 ff). He recognizes that "both the *criteria* and the *techniques* of social control are basic for the analysis" (p. 30) and that in the evolution of society there is "a rise of ethical criteria of control." (pp. 25, 335 and 480 ff) However he continues to believe that the major portion of social control "properly belongs under the general category of Social Psychology" (p. 7); to concentrate all his attention on the "techniques of social control" (in its sociopsychological aspect) and to define social control in terms of behavioristic psychology. "Control itself is a process by which stimuli are brought to bear effectively upon some person or group of persons, thus producing responses that function in adjustment situations ... The essential fact which renders them controlled responses is that they function in some sort of adjustment situation which may or may not be the conscious objective of the controllers or of the controlled." But mostly it is "concerned with consciously directed adjustment. The subject matter of social control thus defined in terms of adjustment process necessarily refers mainly to means used in securing the adjustment and adaptation." (pp. 11-13) The "ethical criteria," limiting and replacing violence, "power of craft and cunning of the strong man" appear very late and are founded, according to the positivistic belief of Bernard, on knowledge which is brought by the development of social sciences (pp. 26, 336 ff).

After having dissolved the problems of social control in the "techniques" or methods of control, Bernard divides all "social controls" in *"the exploitive social controls"* and in *"the constructive social controls."* To the exploitive social controls belong: physical violence (of different kinds); physical and moral intimidations (including terror); use of fraud; punishments (tortures, third degree, imprisonment); reprisals; manipulations, intrigues, deceptions, confusions; intolerance, censorship, and repression (pp. 30-39, 56-334). To the constructive social controls belong: revolutions; non-violent coercion (positive assistance); regimentations, and standardizations of different kinds (from dictatorship to "democratic overall self-control"); supernaturalistic controls (magical and religious as expressed in taboos, miracles, visions, possessions, conversions and so on); ethical controls; custom and conventions; law, legislation; social reforms; education.

The effort of Bernard to make his treatment of the social control problem all-embracing, despite its exclusively psychological basis, is obvious, as it seems to us obvious that the discussions of means, instruments, or techniques of social control, without their connection with a peculiar kind of control, acting in a concrete social conjuncture and integrated as a constituent part in a specific unity of control processes, cannot advance our knowledge.

SOCIAL CONTROL

Paul H. Landis in his book *Social Control; Social Organization and Disorganization in Process* (1939) comes close to this critical conclusion. The author tries to develop and to elaborate in detailed form Cooley's views on the problem of control, combining them with more recent research and dropping the idealistic-spiritualistic ingredients of Cooley's theory. Social control is defined by Landis "as a *series of social processes by which the individual is made group responsible, by which social organization is built and maintained,*" by which human personality is formed through socialization, and "*a better social order*" can be attained, "for both an orderly society and an integrated personality can be built only on unquestioned values." (pp. viii, 47, 181) Social control implies "correction of some evils" (restraints), as well as regulations of different kinds, and "direction of social energy toward some more ideal goal." (pp. 7 ff, 13 ff, 33 ff) "Stereotypes," "patterns," "rules" are only one aspect of the social control process, which includes subtler ingredients of "group ethics," "social revolts," "cultural goals," scientific knowledge, values and ideals (pp. 15 ff, 68-146, 309 ff, 443-450).

Landis feels strongly that in every type of society the series of processes called social control represent a specific unity, a peculiar whole, the aspects of which have to be studied in their correlation and not in their isolation. Distinguishing more or less clearly between "goals," "*factors*" (kinds) *and "means"* of social control, the author insists upon the fact that goals and factors of control react differently according to the types of societies and groups, and that the "means" of control vary still more according to circumstances (pp. 95 ff, 157 ff, 465 ff, 331 ff, 4 ff). As to the "factors" (or kinds) of control, he studies them especially in their correlation with the "primary" and "secondary" groups following Cooley's distinction. The factors of control "of the primary group—*gossip, public opinion,* and *social expectancy*—largely disappear" in the secondary groups; the factors of control that actually predominate at the present time (*publicity, propaganda, law, government, science, technicways, mores, surnaturalisms,* and *education*) are intermediate between primary and secondary groups. But only education, more and more independent of the family, is not only maintaining but increasing its importance, becoming the "most subtle and ultimate form of social control," as Ellwood expresses it (pp. 151-325).

TWENTIETH CENTURY SOCIOLOGY

"Special means and devices of control are often isolated by the student from the general scheme of integrated patterns that characterizes a society, and discussed separately," but this always becomes a failure (pp. 4 ff, 331 ff).

After following the more or less clear distinctions maintained by Landis, the reader becomes somewhat concerned by seeing the author's integration of such classifications of kinds and forms of social control as *formal* (through official machinery of government) and *informal; conscious* and *unconcsious; socializing* and *sanctioning; establishing order* and *maintaining order; paternal* and *social*, among the "means of control" and putting them on the same level as the contrasts between "physical force and human symbol methods" or between "rewards and punishments." Here once again form and kinds of social control are confused with the means, instruments or techniques of their realization.

In order to complete this review of theories and books on social control, we have to sum up its interpretation by a prominent legal sociologist and philosopher, the "prince of jurisprudence" to whom E. A. Ross dedicated his *Principles of Sociology* (1921). Roscoe Pound, in several of his writings (*Introduction to Philosophy of Law*, 1928, *History and System of Common Law*, 1939, *Contemporary Juristic Theories*, 1941, but especially in his recent book *Social Control Through Law*, 1942) has insisted on the fact that law can be sociologicaly understood only in its quality of an "agency," "phase," or "form" of "social control" as a *"whole of processes"* and measures of "social engineering." The study of law as a part of a whole process of social control is the most essential point of the "sociological jurisprudence" of the twentieth century, whereas in the nineteenth century and earlier the "social sciences ignored each other" (pp. 124-125). Social control involves three elements: a) an "ideal element" of civilization and of the values implied; b) a real element of "power, influence, pressure"; c) an element of "social engineering and planning." (pp. 16 ff, 49 ff, 64 ff). Pound's definition of social control tends rather to limit it to restraint and regulation: "The pressure upon each man brought to bear by his fellowmen in order to constrain him to do his part upholding civilized society and to deter him from antisocial conduct, that is, conduct at variance with the postulates of social order." (pp. 17-18) At the same time he is convinced that "in the modern world law has become the paramount agency of

SOCIAL CONTROL

social control" (p. 20) and that today "social control is primarily the function of the State." (pp. 24-25, 49)

However, at the same time, Roscoe Pound insists strongly upon the fact that "we must not forget that law is not the only agency of sociol control." On the one hand the other "agencies" or "phases" of social control — *morals, religion,* and *education* — play in the whole process of social control a different role in diverse historical epochs and types of society (pp. 18 ff, 22 ff, 26 ff, 32 ff). Thus the hierarchy of kinds of social control is recognized as variable; each one can predominate over the others according to historical social conjunctures. On the other hand law has its "strength" and its "weakness" as an "agency" (kind) of social control, and it needs today "the backing of religion, morals, and education even the more if it can no longer have the backing of organized religion and of the home." (pp. 62, 21)

With Pound the kinds (or phases) of social control (morals, religion, law, education), differentiated according to values, are clearly distinguished from means or techniques of control; the decisive interest of the study of social control as *"whole process"* with several correlated aspects is well pointed out, but the actual role in it, not only of the State, but of the law-sphere as such, is tremendously exaggerated.

II

The study of "social control" as a special branch of sociology is indeed very characteristic of twentieth century sociology. But unfortunately most of the definitions and discussions concerning social control, which we tried to sum up in the first section, were too much impressed by the traditional points of view of nineteenth century sociology. In any case, they did not sufficiently succeed in freeing themselves from this influence. And that, we believe, is the main reason for difficulties and confusions in the field. The nineteenth century sociology had a marked tendency to reduce sociology to a philosophy of history or to a theory of evolution; to contrast or to reconcile "order" and "progress"; to insist upon the conflicts of the "society" and the "individual," either defending one, or the other; to overlook the fundamental pluralistic structure of every inclusive society and to speak of "Society" with a capital, as though it were possible to give a characteristic of a type of inclusive society without taking into consideration the varying hierarchy of particular groups and of combinations of groups in it; finally, to see in values, ideas, and ideals, and their symbolic expressions, either simple products of social reality, or on the contrary elements transcendent and entirely independent of it. All those simple contrasts, which were surpassed step by step and left behind by the developments of the twentieth century sociology, seem to reappear, in open or concealed form, in the discussion about "social control"; even in the most fruitful and profound analyses of it, such as by Cooley and Durkheim; Park, Burgess, and Ellwood; Dowd and Landis. We shall not try to give a critical analysis of every definition, interpretation, and theory separately, but shall sum up briefly the principal difficulties, as they appear to us.

The development of research into and discussions over social control is for us an impressive sign of growing consciousness that cultural patterns, rules, symbols, values, ideas, and ideals play a tremendous role in the structure of social reality as such. This role has to be impartially described and the place of "social control" in its different manifestations has to be accurately found among different aspects and depth-levels of social reality.

The *first prerequisite* for it, is to renounce the belief that "social control" is a result of "progress" or "evolution" of society, that it did not exist or was "deprived of ethical elements" at the early stages of human society. It is impossible to find or to imagine a *human society without social control* in it; "magical" and "religious" ethics are, no less than "rational" ethics today, important ingredients of earlier types of social control. Obviously the hierarchy of kinds and the intensity of social control change with each type of society, each concrete social conjuncture, and every type of particular group.

The *second prerequisite* for such an objective description is to free the problem of social control from every link with the outmoded contrast of "order" and "progress," both concepts being founded on a confusion of value-judgments and reality judgments. Social control is neither a "support of order," nor an engine of "progress," because both are our imaginative and unscientific constructions, and social control is a part of social reality. What is "order" from one point of view is "disorder" from another, and changes occur in the same society in different directions. Social reality is full of tensions of different kinds (organized super-structures and unorganized infra-structures; struggle between groups; competition between symbols, values, and ideas of different degrees of creativeness and crystallization, and so on), as well as of variable equilibria of different kinds. We can observe exactly the same situation within that part of social reality, which we shall call "social control."

The *third prerequisite* for a scientific analysis of social control is to realize that it is not specially linked with the so-called conflicts between "the society" and "the individuals."

It is neither an imposition of "social order" over "isolated individuals," nor an engine to combine these individuals into society, nor even finally an exclusive self-regulation or self-creation of society itself. Society and individuals have to be compared on the same level of depth, and both are characterized by several ones: thus, for instance, individual manifestations in the external world have to be compared with collective ones, individual habits to collective customs, inner-pressures within the individual to social pressures, personal aspirations to group aspirations and so on. Contrasts and conflicts, pressures and revolts occur among the depth levels of social reality as well as among the depth-levels "within" the individuals. Very often we take the conflicts between depth-levels that are parallel in the individual and in the society, for conflicts between the latter . . . On the other hand, "Self," "Alter Ego" and "We" are only three poles in the indissoluble unity of the conscious mental life. The direction toward self is considered as individual consciousness, the direction toward communication through signs and symbols between "selves" and "alter egos" as "inter-mental process," and the direction toward "we"—foundation of those signs and symbols—as "social or collective mentality." However, there is a constant interplay and tension among "we," "self," and "alter ego" that constitutes consciousness and mental life themselves. (10) *Social control* is certainly linked with tension-, conflict-, and revolt-situations characteristic of social as well as individual life; in view of the "reciprocity of perspectives" between both, these situations are characterized by a struggle among differ-

---

10. See Georges Gurvitch, *Essais de sociologie*, (Paris: 1938), pp. 1-169; "Mass, Community, Communion," *Journal of Philosophy*, 38: 485-495, 1941; "Is the Antithesis of Moral Man and Immoral Society True?" *loc. cit.*, and bibliography given there.

ent depth-levels, groups, patterns, rules, values, ideas, and ideals, and not by real conflicts between society and individuals.

The *fourth prerequisite* for research in the field of social control is the realization that every type of inclusive society is a *microcosm of groups* and every particular group a *microcosm of social bonds* (or forms of sociability). These social microcosms are arranged in various ways, according to the types of societies and groups, and to concrete historico-social conjunctures. "Social control" is a specific problem not only for the different types of inclusive societies, but also for each particular group and even, in many cases, for "social bonds" which constitute a group. Thus there is an inextricable pluralism of *agencies of social control,* in so far as we understand under those agencies real social bonds, groups and inclusive societies, each of which needs and applies another hierarchic unity of kinds of control, and is an active center of their realization. For instance, not only the uncivilized, the patriarchic, the feudal, the bourgeois, the capitalist, the socialist etc. societies, will have different systems of social control, but also such groups as the family, the church, the State, the labor unions, the schools, the clubs, etc., will apply distinct unities of control, and such different social bonds as mass, community, or communion will suppose different systems of control. To this it must be added that groups vary in character not only according to their types, but according to their integration in specific social conjunctures, which increases considerably the variations of corresponding systems of control (for example, family, State, church, economic activity groups etc. and their specific unities of controls being tremendously different according to types of inclusive societies in which they are integrated). Thus one has to be extremely cautious as to generalization concerning social control and tendencies in its development. Different systems of control subsist in the same society and their evolutional tendencies can go in opposite directions.

At the same time nothing would be more confusing than a failure to distinguish between *kinds of control* and *agencies of control.* The division of kinds of control is linked with the differentiation among cultural patterns, symbols, ideas, values, whereas the distinction of agencies of control is that of types of social bonds of groups and of inclusive societies. Every agency of social control in principle can serve as an active center for the realization of several kinds of social controls; *it is their particular combination in a system or*

SOCIAL CONTROL

whole corresponding to and applied by a specific agency (or social unity), which forms the central sociological interest of the problem of social control.

The *fifth prerequisite* of a sociological analysis in the field of social control is a clarification of the situation and role of values, ideas, and ideals, and their symbolic expressions in social reality, and their consideration as criteria of differentiation of kinds of control. Both the idealistic view (to which Max Weber, in a rationalistic way, and C. H. Cooley, in a vitalistic way, after all remain true) and the positivistic view (to which a large part of writers on social control continue to incline) have to be rejected. Cultural values, ideas, and ideals are not simple products of social reality, and they are not transcendent and isolated entities that can produce social reality. They are in *bilateral functional relationship with social life*, because they are particularized and singularized with reference to historical epochs, social types, and structures in which alone they can be grasped, tested, and experienced, and in so far as they are, they modify at the same time social reality. The inexhaustible richness of the infinite whole of values, ideas, ideals is never and can never be visible; social life, with its different types of bonds, groups, and societies renders visible limited sections of it, and through this limitation precisely gives them the opportunity to be experienced and to act. This transcending of the wrong contrast between *relativism* and *absolutism* (transcending which can be called *"functional relationism"*) permits us to base social control and the differentiation of its kinds on clear *criteria*, without separating them from social reality, and without dissolving them in simple techniques and means. Thus another confusion can here be avoided, namely, that of identification of kinds of control with the *means of their realization*, which can be identical for different kinds of control (for instance, propaganda) and which can be different for the same kind, according to circumstances.

Finally, only this conception permits the description of the exact role which "patterns" or "stereotypes" play in social control, and in its different kinds: (A) Not all patterns play a direct role in social control, that is, are expressions of one of its kinds. The *"technical patterns"* do not play this role and can serve only as means or instruments for realization of control. We understand under technical patterns standardized images of collective behavior, the ascendency of which is founded only on repetition and habitual routine. The main examples are the patterns of every day life and of economic activity, for instance the manner of preparing certain dishes, the fashioning of particular kinds of tools and their utilization, and so on. The greatest part of "means of social control" enumerated by F. E. Lumley and by L. L. Bernard belong to this category. There is no passage from technical patterns to *symbolic cultural patterns,* which are linked with cultural values, ideas, and ideals which they symbolize through sense expressions. These patterns presuppose the intervention in social life of spiritual meanings, values, ideas, and ideals, of which the symbols are the intermediaries adapted to concrete social situations. (11) They play an important role in *religion, morality, law, art, knowledge, education* which are the main kinds of social control and of which the cultural patterns can serve as direct expressions. (B) Cultural values, ideas, and ideals, and even symbols, do not necessarily have to be standardized, stereotyped, patternized in order to function as social controls. Their immediate, singularized action can be incomparably more effective, and the validity of cultural-symbolic patterns as forms of social control depends on the intensity of their link with the values, ideas, and ideals themselves. (C) The acts of experiencing, grasping, seeking, and creating new values, ideas, and ideals supercede in effectiveness as social control all other forms and must not be overlooked.

Thus our critical analysis guides us to the conclusion that *forms of control* have to be distinguished from *kinds of control,* which completes the result we reached before by contrasting *agencies of control, kinds of control,* and *means of control.* Every kind of control can take three different main forms: (a) symbolic-cultural patterns (rules included); (b) values, ideas, and ideals themselves; (c) experiencing, seeking, and creating new values, ideas, and ideals.

These forms of control represent, let us say, three depth levels in every kind of control, and the intensity of these strata varies according to social conjunctures, types of societies, and groups. This distinction seems to us to be more useful than not only those of "purposeful" and "unpurposeful," but also of "conscious" and "unconscious," "formal" and "informal," "explicit" and "impli-

---

11. With reference to these two main kinds of patterns, see my definitions in H. P. Fairchild, ed., *Dictionary of Sociology,* (New York: Philosophical Library 1944), p. 216, and my book, *Sociology of Law,* (New York: Philosophical Library, 1942), pp. 21-50.

SOCIAL CONTROL

cit," "institutionalized," "sanctioning," and "socializing" forms of social control. Those contrasts make rigid and artificial separations where in reality are only degrees in depth levels and continuous passages. Only the distinction of organized and spontaneous forms of social control, as well as that of paternal and democratic forms of it (which distinction, as we shall see is, when rightly understood, dependent on the first) have to be retained, in addition to the three forms we have described. But they too can be considered as depth levels and degres.

We believe that through all our critical remarks we have now prepared the ground for concluding this chapter with a summing up of our own position concerning social control.

III

Social control can be defined as the sum total or rather the whole of cultural patterns, social symbols, collective spiritual meanings, values, ideas and ideals, as well as acts and processes directly connected with them, whereby inclusive society, every particular group, and every participating individual member overcome tensions and conflicts within themselves through temporary equilibria and take steps for new creative efforts.

There can be found as many *kinds of social control*, as there can be established differentiated value-scales, ideals, and systems of ideas. *Religion* (in primitive society, also *magic* competing with religion), *morality, law, art, knowledge* and *education* are considered by us as the main kinds of social control. However, it must be borne in mind that each of these six kinds can be divided into several species or subkinds. In every type of society or group not only does the hierarchy among the six main social controls vary, but also the prominence within each of them of a particular species. For instance, as to knowledge, in different types of societies or groups there can predominate either perceptive or technical, or mystical or political, or scientific or philosophical knowledge, etc. Or as to law, there can be a prominence of "social law" or of "interindividual law," of organized or unorganized law, of law fixed in advance or of flexible law, or of intuitive law and so on.

Our definition of "social control" and our statement concerning the method by which the *kinds* of it have to be differentiated can provoke the following remark by an informed reader: "Social contiol," he would observe, "is in this interpretation only a different name for what was called '*cultural sociology*' or '*sociology of human spirit*'." It is only a common name for *sociology of religion; sociology of morality; siciolgy of law; sociology of knowledge; sociology of art; sociology of education*. These branches of sociology investigate different cultural patterns, social symbols, collective spiritual values, ideas and ideals in their functional relations with types of societies and groups, and concrete historico-social conjunctures.

Let us see what is right and what is wrong in this critical observation. There is no question for us that the subject-matter of "cultural sociology," or as we prefer to call it of "sociology of human spirit," coincides entirely with that of "social control" in our interpretation. But there are differences in the approach, in the point of view, in the method of study. These differences have a double aspect.

First, as already pointed out, the center of interest in the study of social control consist in the varying correlations between different kinds and forms of control, conceived as *ingredients*, as *integrated parts of a system*, or *a whole* of controls. (12) Different branches of the sociology of human spirit (which in themselves are only starting their scientific development) are here confronted one with the other, linked together, integrated in a unity, their results put in a melting pot. The development of the research in social control can thus provide the much required general introduction to the sociology of religion, of morality, of law, of art, of knowledge, and of education, preventing their isolation from each other and showing the variations of their respective importance in different types of societies and groups.

Second, whereas in different branches of the sociology of human spirit the emphasis is upon the functional relationships of the

---

12. Even in uncivilized societies where the kinds of control are undifferentiated or insufficiently differentiated, the problem is the same. There the competition and variable equilibria between two supernaturalistic subkinds of control, *magic* and *religion,* constitute the main issue of the social control system. See Marcel Mauss and H. Hubert, "Esquisse d'une théorie générale de la magie," *L'année sociologique,* vol. 7, 1904, and Marcel Mauss, "Essai sur le don, forme archaique de l'échange," *L'année sociologique,* N. S. vol. 1, 1923. For a critical appraisal, in connection with social control problems, see Georges Gurvitch, *Essais de sociologie,* (Paris: 1938), pp. 173-276, and "Magic and Law," *Social Research,* 9: 104-122, February, 1942.

SOCIAL CONTROL

ideational elements with the social conjunctures, their study *as parts of a whole, of a system of social control*, serves to accentuate their practical action upon these conjunctures and structures. In fact the hierarchy of kinds of control changes according to the effectiveness of their practical action in a type of society or group. The "social control approach" thus enriches the "sociology of human spirit" with the "social engineering problems," after having already contributed to the elimination of the danger of isolation and absolutization of the particular manifestations of culture.

From the kinds of social control must be distinguished the *forms of social control*, which can be characterized as depth-levels or strata in each kind of control as well as in the whole process of it. Thus "kinds of social control" and "forms of social control" crisscross, which multiplies sensibly the number of kinds and forms. We have in our critical analysis (Second Section) already distinguished: (a) the rather routine form of social control through cultural usages, patterns, rules and symbols; (b) the more spontaneous form of social control through values, ideas, and ideals themselves; (c) and the most spontaneous form of social control through direct collective experience of evaluation, of testing, of aspiration, and of collective creation. The first of these forms, while presupposing the two others as its inspiring sub-strata of different degrees of intensity, externally takes very often the expression of an "organization" or an "organized superstructure." An organization is a combination of more or less rigid and crystallized patterns which hierarchize and centralize collective conducts. It is these organized superstructures which exercise "constraint," which can become more or less remote or "distant" from spontaneous expressions of social life that manifest themselves in the infra-structures to these organizations. Thus *organized social control* is a particularly standardized, stereotyped and crystallized form of social control through patterns and rules. It is contrasted to *spontaneous social control* which starts with symbols of unpatterned character, takes then the more intensive form of control through values, ideas, and ideals, and gets its strongest expression in acts of collective experience, aspiration, and creation.

The contrast between "paternal" and "democratic" social control, on which Jerome Dowd insisted, is only a consequence of the factual relationship between organized and spontaneous forms of social control in a type of society or group. In so far as the organized social control is separated by an abyss from spontaneous social control and renders itself independent of it, it takes the form of an autocratic or paternal control. Insofar, on the contrary, as the organized social control is rooted in and penetrated by the spontaneous mobility of the subjacent spontaneous social controls, and a guarantee is given of this "open character" of organized control, it takes the form of a democratic control.*(13) Obviously, between both there are many intermediary forms.

To sum up, there are not less than *four main "forms" of social control*, criss-crossing the *six main "kinds"* of it:

1. *Organized social control* (which can be either autocratic or democratic according to its relationship with spontaneous forms of social control).

2. *Social control through cultural usages and symbols not crystallized in an organization*, and which are in various degrees more or less conected with routine, or on the contrary, more or less elastic and flexible (from rites and traditions, through daily practices to incessantly changing fashions and symbols renewing themselves).

3. *Spontaneous social control through values, ideas, and ideals.*

4. *Even more spontaneous social control through direct collective experiences, aspirations, and creations, including revolts and revolutions.*

In different types of societies, groups, and social bonds, and according to different social conjunctures, now one, now another of these four main forms plays a prominent role. *Thus not only the hierarchy of kinds in the whole process of social control varies, but also the role or intensity of different forms in each kind and in the whole process changes too.*

"*Agencies of social control*" as we have already said (Section II) have to be contrasted with *kinds* a well as with *forms* of social control. The agencies of social control are *inclusive societies, groups,* and *social bonds*, which give birth to kinds or whole systems of social control, need them, are controlled by them, and serve as active centers for their application. Generally speaking, every agency of social control is in principle able to produce and to apply any kind and form of social control, as well as any of their

---

13. See Georges Gurvitch, "Democracy as a Sociological Problem," *Journal of Legal and Political Sociology*, 1 (1-2): 46-71, October, 1942; *Essais de sociologie*, pp. 61 ff; *Expérience juridique et philosophie pluraliste du droit*, (Paris: 1935). pp. 235 ff; *Sociology of Law*, pp. 222 ff.

SOCIAL CONTROL

combinations in a whole process of control. But in reality empirical observations show us that different types of inclusive societies, groups, and social bonds favor different forms and kinds of control, and peculiar combinations of them as integrated parts of a whole. Conversely, different kinds, forms, and systems of social control exercise specific practical actions on peculiar agencies of control. The study of these specific functional relationships, as we stated already, represents the main topic of concrete sociological research in the field of social control.

Finally, the *means* or *techniques* or *instruments* of social control can not be considered as the direct subject-matter of the sociological study of social control. In view of the tremendous multiplicity of social controls and their combinations in wholes of controls, as well as in view of the infinite plurality of agencies of social control and specific social conjunctures in which they move, the means, techniques or instruments have such flexibility, variability, and relativity that they cannot be fixed and described without too much generalization and dogmatization of them. Furthermore, means of social control do not characterize either kinds or forms or agencies of control, because different kinds, forms, and agencies can utilize the same means, and the same kinds, forms, and agencies can utilize different means or instruments.

The sociological study of social control is only in its starting phases, and its further development, insofar as more clarity will be achieved, promises to become the much needed introductory and very important chapter of the "sociology of human spirit," conceived as a whole.

SELECTED BIBLIOGRAPHY

Bernard, L. L., *Social Control in its Sociological Aspects*, (New York. The Macmillan Co., 1939).

Bouglé, C., *The Evolution of Values*, trans. from the French, (New York: Henry Holt and Co., 1926).

Cooley, C. H., *Social Process*, (New York: Charles Scribner's Sons, 1918).

Dowd, Jerome, *Control in Human Societies*, (New York: D. Appleton, 1935).

Durkheim, Emile, *Philosophie et sociologie*, (Paris: Alcan, 1924).

Ellwood, C. H., *The Psychology of Human Societies*, (New York: D. Appleton, 1925).

Gidding, F. H., *The Scientific Study of Human Society*, (Chapel Hill: North Carolina University Press, 1924).

TWENTIETH CENTURY SOCIOLOGY

Gurvitch, Georges, *Sociology of Law,* (New York: Philosophical Library, 1942).
Gurvitch, Georges, *Morale théorique et Science des moeurs,* (Paris: Alcan, 1937).
Landis, Paul H., *Social Control; Social Organiaztion and Disorganization in Process,* (New York: J. B. Lippincott Co., 1939).
Lumley, F. E., *Means of Social Control,* (New York, The Century Co., 1925).
Mauss, Marcel, and H. Hubert, "Esquisse d'une théorie générale de la magie," *L'année sociologique,* 1904.
Mauss, M., "Essai sur le don, forme archaique de l'échange," *L'année sociologique,* 1923.
Park, Robert E. and Ernest W. Burgess, *Introduction to the Science of Sociology,* (Chicago: University of Chicago Press, 1921), Chap. XII.
Pound, Roscoe, *Social Control Through Law,* (New Haven: Yale University Press, 1942).
Ross, E. A., *Social Control: A Survey of the Foundations of Order,* (New York, The Macmillan Co., 1901; 2nd ed. 1912).
Summer, W. G., *Folkway: A Study of the Sociological Importance of Usages, Manners, Customs and Morals,* (New York, Boston: Ginn and Co., 1906).
Westermarck, E. A. *Ethical Relativity,* (New York: Harcourt, Brace and Co., 1932).

Georges D. Gurvitch was born November 2, 1894 in Russia. L. L. D. (1917) University of Petrograd; Magistrant of Public Law (1920), University of Petrograd; Assistant Professor, University of Petrograd (1919-1920). Associate Professor at The Russian Section of the University of Prague, Czechoslovakia (1921-1924). Magister of Social Philosophy, 1924. Lecturer at the Slavonic Institute of Paris, France (1925-1927). Lecturer at the Sorbonne, Paris (1928-1932). Naturalized French citizen, 1928. Docteur ès Lettres, Sorbonne, Paris University, 1932. Professor, Collège Sevigné, Paris (1932-1934). Associate Professor of Sociology, University of Bordeaux (1934-1935). Professor of Sociology, University of Strasbourg, France (1935).
Associate Professor of Sociology, New School for Social Research, New York City (1940-1943). Visiting Lecturer, Columbia University, New York (1942-1943). Professor of French Area Studies A. S. T. P., Rutgers University (1943). Research Associate, Harvard University, Department of Sociology (1944-1945). Director of the French Sociological Institute, Ecole Libre des Hautes Etudes, New York (1942).
Professor Gurvitch is author of numerous books including: *Rousseau and the Declaration of Rights,* 1918; *Fichte's System of Concrete Ethics* 1924; *Le Temps Présent et L'Idée du Droit Social,* 1932; *L'Idée du Droit Social,* 1932; *L'Expérience Juridique et la Philosophie Pluraliste du Droit,* 1935; *Morale Théorique et Science des Moeurs,* 1937; *Essais de Sociologie,* 1938; *Elements de Sociologie Juridique,* 1940; *Sociology of Law,* 1942; *La Déclaration des Droits Sociaux,* 1944.
He was Secretary General of the *International Institute of Sociology of Law* (Paris, 1931-1940) and editor of *Archives de Philosophie du Droit et de Sociologie Juridique.* (Paris, 1931-1940) He became in America the Editor-in-chief of the *Journal of Legal and Political Sociology.*

CHAPTER XI

SOCIOLOGY OF LAW

by

ROSCOE POUND

What is meant by the term sociology of law? That depends in part upon what we mean by the word "law."

From the time jurists began to organize and comment upon laws (*leges, lois, Gesetze*) for the purposes of teaching, law (*ius, droit, Recht*) in the sense of the body of authoritative guides to decision of controversies, has been a taught tradition. But from the Middle Ages there has been a significant difference between the Continental and the Anglo-American tradition. The one has been an academic tradition, a tradition of the universities. The other has been a practising lawyer's tradition, a tradition of the courts. On the Continent since the twelfth century law has been taught in the universities. In the beginning, legal education in England, except as to the law of the ecclesiastical courts, was under the direction of the practising lawyers and the supervision of the judges. It came to be in the control of the Inns of Court, self-governing societies of practitioners in the courts and students preparing to become such. The English universities taught the civil law (modern Roman law) and the canon law, but not the common law of England, the law of the King's courts. The universities taught law on the basis of Justinian's restatement of the Roman law and Justinian's legislation; the Inns of Court taught the remedies and procedure and resulting case law of the courts at Westminster. The universities taught a universal civil law and the law of a universal church. The Inns of Court taught the "law of the land," the statutes and customs of England — *leges et consuetudines Angliae*. The universities taught a law applicable throughout Christendom and, as men thought later, based upon reason and justice. The Inns of Court taught the common law of England, developed by experience of decision in the English courts and backed by the strong central government of the King.

Thus the words used in the one tradition for the regime of adjustment of relations and ordering of conduct through the force of a politically organized society, for the body of authoritative guides to determination in such a regime, and for the judical and administrative processes in such a society, diverged from the start from those used in the other tradition and have kept to different lines ever since. English lawyers did not pay much attention to Continental juristic writing till the end of the eighteenth and the nineteenth century. It was not until the present century that teaching of the law of the land in the United States passed definitely from practitioners in the courts to academic teachers, and in England it is in transition to the universities.

John Austin, the founder of English analytical jurisprudence, with whom the modern science of law begins in the English-speaking world, when after his training and experience as an English barrister he was appointed to teach jurisprudence, went to a German university and studied the German Pandectists by way of preparation. He saw that *Recht* and "law" did not translate with exactness. (1) Lightwood showed four meanings of "law" in English and five of *Recht* in German, and argued with much truth, that the course of juristic thought in the two countries had been influenced by the words jurists had been brought up to use. (2) Somló pointed out four juristic meanings of *Recht* in German and a lay usage to mean recognized claims arising from conventional norms — a usage of sociologists to which, perhaps he was referring. (3) Differences of content between *ius, droit, Recht,* on the one hand, and "law" and "right," and "a right," on the other hand, have led to mis-

---

1. John Austin, *The Province of Jurisprudence Determined,* (London: 1832), pp. 307-308n.

2. John M. Lightwood, *The Nature of Positive Law,* (London: 1883), pp. 68-71.

3. Felix Somló, *Juristische Grundlehre,* (Leipzig: 1917), p. 469.

leading translations, to misunderstanding of Continental books by Anglo-American jurists, and to misunderstanding of English and American books by Continental writers, even when translations were not used.

How the many meanings of "law" may embarrass Anglo-American juristic thought is illustrated by much recent realist writing in which ideas applicable to "law" as the judicial process are urged against "law" in the sense of the body of authoritative guides to determination of controversies. Duguit's argument as to rights in his lectures on the development of French law in the nineteenth century (4) is based in great part on use of *droit* as what in English we should call "law," as "what is right," and as "a right," as if one word, used for all three ideas, could be taken for one meaning containing them all. Perhaps the outstanding example, however, is to be seen in the English version of Duguit's lectures in the United States. (5) In spots they are made downright unintelligible to the American reader by rendering *droit subjectif* as "subjective law" and *droit objectif* as "objective law," as if there were two theories of two different kinds of what the American lawyer calls "law."

In the languages of Continental Europe the words used for the Latin *ius*, namely, *droit, derecho, diritto, Recht*, are entire equivalents. To take the French word as representative, neither "right" nor "law" exactly translates *droit*, which often can only be rendered in English by an awkward phrase. Sometimes, indeed, it means what we should call law, that is, the body of authoritative guides to determination of controversies. Sometimes, it is best rendered in English by "what is right." Sometime it means "a right." In juristic discussion it usually must be rendered as "what is right backed by politically organized society" or "right plus law." Often it means what an Anglo-American lawyer would have to express by "what we seek to bring about (or to maintain) through law." Scotch writers in the last century often translated *ius* and its equivalents in modern languages by "right" rather than by "law." (6) In Anglo-American juristic writing "law," as distinguished from "a law," usually

4. Léon Duguit, *Les transformations générales du droit privé depuis le Code Napoléon*, (Paris: 1912), pp. 1-22.
5. Léon Duguit, "Objective Law," *Columbia Law Review*, 20: 817; 21: 17, 126, 242, 1920-1921.
6. W. Hastie, *Outlines of Jurisprudence*, (Edinburgh: 1887) pp. 65-157; W. R. Herkless, *Jurisprudence or the Principles of Political Right*, (Edinburgh: 1901), Chap. 6.

means the system of authoritative materials for grounding or guiding judicial and administrative action recognized or established in a politically organized society. "A law" is the equivalent of *loi*.

To get away from words, jurists are considering three things: (A) What is better called the legal order, that is, the regime of adjusting relations and ordering conduct by the systematic application of the force of a politically organized society; (B) the authoritative grounds of or guides to determination of disputes in such a society — a body of authoritative precepts, developed and applied by an authoritative technique in the light or on the background of authoritative traditional ideals; and (C) what Cardozo has taught us to call the judicial process, to which we must add the administrative process. Each of these has been and still is called "law."

Until the present century, jurists confined their attention almost entirely to the second of the three, and commonly they looked only at the body of precepts. Vinogradoff used the term "law" to include, if not all social control, at any rate most of the processes of social control. (7) This broader usage is common with sociologists. (8) But certainly for jurists, and I suspect also for sociologists, it is expedient to avoid adding to the burdens of a term of too many meanings, and to use "law" for social control through the systematic application of the force of politically organized society. (9) I shall use the term in that sense.

I

Sociology applied to study of the legal order, of the body of authoritative grounds of or guides to decision in accordance with

---

7. Sir Paul Vinogradoff, *Outlines of Historical Jurisprudence*, (London: Oxford University Press, 1920) vol. I. It should be noted that Vinogradoff received his juristic training in Moscow and Berlin. The Russian *pravda* is an exact equivalent of *Recht*.

8. E. g. Eugen Ehrlich, *Grundlegung der Soziologie des Rechts*, (Muenchen und Leipzig: 1913), transl. by Walter L. Moll as *Fundamental Principles of the Sociology of Law*, (Cambridge: Harvard University Press, 1936); N. S. Timasheff, *An Introduction to the Sociology of Law*, (Cambridge: Harvard University Committee on Research in the Social Sciences, 1939); Georges Gurvitch, *Sociology of Law*, (New York: Philosophical Library, 1942).

9. See A. R. Radcliffe-Brown, "Law," in *Encyclopedia of the Social Sciences*, 9: 202, (1933).

which that regime is maintained by the judicial and the administrative process, and the relation of study of these to study of sociology, would seem to be the field of sociology of law. But as the standpoint of jurist and of sociologist are not wholly identical and the two are seldom united, a preliminary question might be raised as between sociology of law and sociological jurisprudence. Gurvitch considers that the two are not identical (10) and accuses sociological jurisprudence of an unscientific tendency to take up concrete problems of the legal order and of the judicial and administrative processes. If sociology is a pure theoretical science while jurisprudence, or at any rate sociological jurisprudence, is a practical science, the basis of the distinction is clear enough. Applied sociology, applied philosophy of law, applied historical method, brought to bear upon the legal order, the system of law, its technique and ideals, and the judicial and administrative processes, give us sociological jurisprudence, while a pure theoretical science applied to the phenomena of the legal order, the system of law, and the processes of the legal order, gives us a severely theoretical sociology of law. Yet it is a narrow view of science which denies that the one path is as legitimate as the other. The sociological jurist is studying law as a highly specialized social control in the developed State, in this respect following Austin in thinking of matured or developed law as his immediate province. He holds that legal institutions and doctrines are instruments of a specialized form of social control, capable of being improved with reference to their ends (pointed out or indicated in the other social sciences) by conscious intelligent effort. He thinks of a process of social engineering (using the term engineering in the sense with which industrial engineering has made us familiar) which in one way or another is a problem of all the social sciences. (11) In sociological jurisprudence we have a special and narrower problem of how to achieve this engineering task by means of the legal order, the body of established or recognized norms or precepts, technique of developing and applying them, and received ideals in the light of which they are developed and applied, and the judicial and administrative processes. It is treated as a problem of jurisprudence and so as a practical one, calling, if you will, for an applied science. Yet in its larger aspects sociological jurisprudence does not study the

---

10. Georges Gurvitch, *op. cit.,* P. 11.
11. *Ibid.* P. 11.

problem as simply one of its own. Law in all its senses is studied as a much specialized phase of what in a larger view is a science of society.

Bouglé has pointed out the convergence of two lines of development, one sociological and the other juristic, to give us what we now know as sociology of law. (12) Perhaps it is not so much that from different starting points they have converged to the point of uniting as that they have converged to close parallel. At any rate, the sociological line has had in the present century a strong influence upon the other which has brought the latter continually closer to it. On the whole, jurists have paid more attention to sociologists than sociologists have to law. Sociologists have for the most part looked only at penal codes and criminal law or at legislation.

To look first at the sociological line of approach, in a sense we must begin with Montesquieu. Ehrlich says truly that *L'Esprit des lois* "must be considered the first attempt to fashion a sociology of law." (13) Montesquieu wrote in the reign of the law of nature, a theory of a universal ideal system of legal precepts derived from reason, and, in one of its aspects, of a social compact demonstrated by reason. Reason was universal. There was one social compact. The nature of man, as revealed by reason, was one. Hence the law of nature discovered by reason from the nature of man, or from the corollary of the social compact discovered for us by reason, was the same in all places, at all times, and for all men. The positive law of any politically organized society was only declaratory of this natural law and was of no validity if it departed therefrom. Like every one else in his time, Montesquieu talks of the law of nature. But he gives the term a different meaning. To him law of nature meant the natural instincts of men to which laws must not run counter. In place of the doctrine of the law of nature school, he held that law was not of necessity the same throughout the world, but that it depended on a number of conditions which were not uniform everywhere. As he thought of law in terms of legislation, as an aggregate of enacted laws (a legacy of the academic study of the *Corpus Juris* as the legislation of Justinian) and was influenced by the current theory of his time that what ought to be law was law for that very reason, he did not distinguish how laws

---

12. *Ibid.,* P. 3.
13. Eugen Ehrlich, "Montesquieu and Sociological Jurisprudence," *Harvard Law Review,* 29:582, 583, 1916.

were to be made to fit the outward conditions in which they were to govern and how law grew out of and was shaped by those conditions. But he gives us a critical discussion of the ends of law and an explanation of law by its causes.

What today we call society, Montesquieu calls the general spirit. This is something not unlike the popular consciousness (*Volksbewustsein*) of the nineteenth-century historical jurists from which they derive the popular conviction as to what is right (*Volksueberzeugung*) based on experience but proceeding from a metaphysical conception. Montesquieu's "general spirit," on the other hand, has its origin in, is "the offshoot of" the "things which govern men." But he puts laws also among these things which govern men — "climate, religion, laws, principles of government, precedents, customs, morality." This, however, is not as confused as it seems at first glance. He means that law, one might say here social control, is a part of social life along with the other "things governing men" and each of these determines the others. Law is shaped by society and yet also shapes society. This is in sharp contrast to the idea of law as imposed on society by a lawmaker from without. There is an idea of the interdependence of the elements of social life. It is to be compared with the social consensus postulated by Comte and Spencer.

Montesquieu uses the term "society" to mean politically organized society, the state, as the law of nature school did. Yet he suggests more than once society as the product of natural forces and existing independent of the state instead of as an artificial product of a contract. He saw an intimate relation between laws and economic conditions, between laws and historical continuity of institutions, between laws and climatic and geographical conditions. Also he set out to gather materials as to what in the latter part of the nineteenth century was called ethnological jurisprudence. As Ehrlich says, "there is no topic of sociology of law for which *L'esprit des lois* does not contain a valuable suggestion." (14) He derived his principles not from theology or authority, as jurists of the Middle Ages, nor a priori from pure reason, as the jurists of the seventeenth and eighteenth centuries, nor metaphysically, as the philosophical and historical jurists of the nineteenth century, but from the facts which he collected and worked up during the two decades in which he was writing his book. But Montesquieu thought

---

14. *Ibid.* P. 587.

of laws, of *lois;* not of law, of *droit.* He thought in terms of legislation, as was not unnatural in a student of politics in the era of the codifying ordinances of Louis XIV. He thought of law as an aggregate of enactments as was general as to positive law in the eighteenth century.

Our real beginning, however, must be with Comte. Timasheff reminds us that sociology "was born in a state of hostility to law." (15) But it was more a hostility to laws than to law. Comte had only vague ideas as to law. He wrote after French law had been codified and French jurists of the time identified law with the Code Napoléon. (16) At the same time, the historical school of jurists was becoming the leading school in Continental Europe, and its influence on Comte and on Spencer, the leading English positivist, is manifest. The historical jurists did not believe in legislation. They held it an attempt to make what could not be made but must grow and develop. They held that social development was the realization of an idea which had an inherent power of unfolding or realizing itself. Comte rejected such metaphysical theories. But he conceived that there were laws of social development discoverable by observation, and that legislation was a futile attempt to replace or somehow affect these laws or their operation, and so as ineffectual as would be laws to alter the phases of the moon in the interest of calendar reform. So, thinking of law in terms of legislation, he prophesied the disappearance of law. The historical jurists held that law would develop itself and that artificial attempts to direct or change the course of its development by legislation were nugatory. To this doctrine of legislative futility the followers of Comte in what has been called the mechanical sociology added a doctrine of juristic futility. We could only observe the operation of the inexorable laws of social development. Juristic attempts to improve the law were idle, at least when carried beyond improvement in the form in which laws were expressed.

Comte's prophecy of the disappearance of law went on a different ground from the like prophecy made by Marx. Comte was prophesying the disappearance of law as a body of rules imposed by legislators. Marx was prophesying the disappearance of law in the sense of the regime of adjusting relations and ordering conduct by systematic application of the force of politically organized society.

---

15. N. S. Timasheff, *op. cit.,* P. 45.
16. See e. g. A. M. Demante, *Programme du cours de droit civil français,* (Paris: 1830), Vol. I, pp. 5-7.

SOCIOLOGY OF LAW

He thought that such a regime was only required for a class organized society; that when private property was abolished there would no longer be classes and so no longer need for law. Comte looked forward to a further development of the regime in which a complex system of precepts and of technique of developing and applying them would have evolved "naturally" from experience of life according to laws of social evolution found by observation. This attitude of sociologists toward law in the lawyer's sense lasted till the end of the last century.

Spencer treated of laws as what he called political institutions, that is, as developed or set up by a politically organized society. Laws as political institutions developed in a politically organized society was the theory of the historical jurist of his time, who adopted a political idealistic interpretation of legal history. Laws as political institutions set up by a politically organized society was the idea of the English analytical jurist of his time. If he thought at all of law, otherwise than as an aggregate of laws, he thought of it as hardened custom, "formulating the rule of the dead over the living." (17)

So far as Spencer's book on justice has to do with law, it is a survey and classification of "natural rights" (interests which the legal order ought to recognize and secure) derived logically from a social "law of equal freedom" which, we are told, is arrived at by observation of social phenomena and verified by further observation. (18) This law of social organization and development, as has often been pointed out, is in effect Kant's formula of justice, and the observation and verification, as to law, was done largely by reading the writings of Sir Henry Maine, and so in materials gathered and interpreted by the historical jurists. In consequence, his scheme of natural rights is substantially that of the nineteenth-century metaphysical jurists. (19)

Spencer tells us, no doubt truly, that he had never read Kant. (20) But those to whom Spencer turned for information about law had read him. The Table of References appended to Spencer's "Justice" shows that Maine's "Ancient Law" (1861) was the

---

17. Herbert Spencer, *Principles of Sociology,* (London: 1882), P. 514.
18. Spencer, "Justice," Part IV of *Principles of Ethics,* (London, 1891), Par. 27.
19. *Ibid.,* Chaps. 9-18.
20. *Ibid.,* App. A.

principal authority used. (21) It is hardly a mere coincidence that the idea of the function of law in maintaining the limits within which the freedom of each is to find the widest possible development (22) so closely resembles Savigny's formula — the "boundaries within which the existence and activity of each individual gains a secure free opportunity." (23)

Like the historical jurists, Spencer thought of liberty as the ideal relation among men. As Simkhovitch has put it, he conceived of Maine's theory of the progress from status to contract as the rational outcome of the universe. (24) Hence to him laws, which were a restraint on liberty, were presumably an evil. He considered that legal precepts had mostly come down from archaic organization of society and should be abrogated except as they were necessary to secure the liberty of each limited only by the like liberty of all. He wrote in the era of the legislative reform movement in England, when Parliament was busy repealing statutes and abrogating rules of law which had come down from the relationally organized society of the Middle Ages. This and the *laissez faire* economics of the time led him to think of laws made by and enforced in politically organized society as something which must disappear in the course of social evolution. Spencer had not a little influence in America in the time of the mechanical sociological jurisprudence.

Ward, too, thought only of legislation. He had very little to say about law. Much in the manner and probably under the influence of the contemporary American historical jurists, he took legislative lawmaking to be an attempt to affect the operation of the "real laws" which the positivist sociologist found behind the phenomena of social life. (25) Ward's influence on sociological jurisprudence in America was through his turning of sociology in the United States from biology toward psychology. (26)

---

21. *Ibid.*, American ed. pp. 287 ff.
22. Herbert Spencer, *Social Statics*, (London: 1850), Chap. 6, Par. 1; *Synthetic Philosophy, I, First Principles*, (London: 1862), Par. 2.
23. Friedrich Carl v. Savigny, *System des heutigen roemischen Rechts*, (Berlin: 1840), Vol. I, Par. 52. Savigny was the founder and leading representative of the historical school of jurists.
24. *Ex relatione.*
25. Lester F. Ward, *Dynamic Sociology*, (New York: D. Appleton and Co., 1883), Vol. I pp. 36 ff.
26. *Ibid.* pp. 468-472, 704-706; Vol. II, 11-17; Ward, *The Psychic Factors of Civilization*, (Boston: Ginn and Co., 1893, 2nd ed., 1906), p. 120; Ward, *Applied Sociology*, (Boston: Ginn and Co., 1906), p. 13.

SOCIOLOGY OF LAW

Durkheim (27) got away from the idea of law as legislation, as only an aggregate of laws, and sought to explain it as the expression of a basic social fact. But he got no further than a distinction between repressive law and restitutive law. By repressive law he refers to the sections of a penal code which seek to repress antisocial conduct by imposing penalties. As some would put it today, repressive law promulgates threats of punishment. By restitutive law he refers to the provisions of the civil code, which seek to prescribe remedies for wrongs. As it would be put by adherents of the threat theory of a law, restitutive law promulgates threats of enforced reparation of injuries. It is one of the staple phenomena of jurisprudence that jurists think and frame their theories largely with reference to the forms of the law in their time and place, and either they or their students and disciples put the theories universally. Durkheim's distinction was suggested by the form of French law at the time — a civil code and a penal code. He considered that repressive law corresponded to solidarity through similarity of interests while restitutive law corresponded to division of function. That is, he held that the criminal law corresponds to claims and demands which men assert founded on a likeness of the general claims we all make, while the civil side of the law corresponds to the specific claims each of us make growing out of his individual activities. But there is much more to the matter than this. It is true that social interests as such are primarily given effect by the criminal law, while individual interests as such are primarily secured by the civil side of the law. But the civil side of the law secures social interests in its selection of the individual interests it will recognize, in its delimitation of those which it recognizes, and in choosing means of securing them as delimited. For example, the social interest in political progress is not secured by provisions of the penal codes so much as by privileging publications with reference to free discussion of public affairs, the officials, and fair comment on matters of public interest. The social interest in the conservation of natural resources is not so much secured by prosecutions and penalties as by limitation of the enforceable liberties of use and of enjoyment of land which the civil side of the law recognizes in an owner of land. The social interest in the general morals is secured quite as much by limitations upon the recognized liberty of the individual to engage in legal transactions as by penal legislation.

---

27. Emile Durkheim, *De la division du travail social*, (Paris: 1893).

The social interest in the individual life is secured today largely by limitations on individual freedom of contract, making certain agreements unenforceable. Both Durkheim's repressive law and his restitutive law aim at maintaining the social interest in the general security.

Richard perceived this. He began with the idea that the social group has for its end to protect each of its members "against natural dangers and against the hostility of other groups." Hence, he said, "the whole reality of the group consists in the accord of individual efforts combined in view of this end." Conflict, strife, "a disaccord between the elements of the society" were inimical to this conception of social ends. Hence, he found in the contrast between the pursuit of social ends and "the minimum of vital competition even in the most united societies" the explanation of right and law. "The law itself," he said, "is a reaction of sociability" which tends to make the contrast between social and individual ends "disappear in reducing as far as possible the conflict of desires to the minimum." From this he drew the conclusion that association of the ideas of controversy over conflicting or overlapping interests is "the first defined element of right and law." (28) This was an important step forward in sociological theory of law.

Next, Ross took a great step forward in a series of articles published between 1896 and 1901 in the American Journal of Sociology, and reprinted in 1901 as a volume under the title of "Social Control." By "social control" he meant the control over the behavior of each of us exerted by his fellow men in groups and relations and societies, and this led to the idea of means or agencies of organized social control. He put law as the "most specialized and highly finished engine of social control employed by society." (29) Thus he gave us an idea which unifies the legal order, the body of authoritative guides to determination, and the judicial and administrative processes without requiring us continually to use the one word law for each of them and for all three thought of as somehow one. It will be noted that Ross used the term social control with reference to law in the lawyer's sense — the adjustment of relations and ordering of conduct through the systematic application of the force of a politically organized society. Economists have since been

---

28. Gaston Richard, *L'origine de l'idée de droit*, (Paris: 1892), p. 5.
29. Edward Alsworth Ross, *Social Control*, (New York: 1901, The Macmillan Co.), Chap. 11, p. 106.

giving the term a different meaning. They refer to a planned economy; an economy regulated by politically organized society to a plan.

Pareto had much vogue in the United States for a time, but seems to have had no effect upon jurisprudence. What he has to say as to law is incidental in illustration of his general theory. He considers the realities of legislative lawmaking, mostly in terms of penal legislation, and the realities of the judicial process, mostly in terms of administration of the criminal law, and French juries in criminal cases. What is most important for jurisprudence is his discussion of the conditions and theory of effective lawmaking and of ensuring obedience and enforcement. (30)

Max Weber had a better understanding of law than the sociologists who preceded him. He had a well grounded acquaintance with legal history and so with the juristic background of a sociological theory of law. His influence has been very marked both on contemporary sociology and on the sociologies of law which have appeared in the past two decades. His most significant contribution to jurisprudence is in connection with the fundamental juristic problem of the measure of value for recognition, delimiting, and securing of claims and demands, and the theory of interests. While, he tells us, the relation of historical phenomena to values is of great importance for civilization, yet he holds this to be beyond the province of a science. Universally valid scientific analysis must be kept separate from judgments of values. Nevertheless, we have to deal with values. One who pursues his own values necessarily interferes with the values of others. In the result, he tells us, there is a responsibility upon every human being. Herein we may find the task of the legal order (in the lawyer's sense — i. e. the ordering by the force of a politically organized society). There is a conflict of values to be organized and harmonized, where Kant saw a conflict of wills, Post a conflict of instincts, Jhering a conflict of interests, Stammler a conflict of ends or purposes, Marx a conflict or overlapping of material wants, and William James an overlapping of

---

30. Vilfredo Pareto, *Tratatto di sociologia generale*, Pars. 1863-1875, (1916, 2nd ed. 1923, French translation in 2 volumes as *Traité de sociologie générale*, 1919, English translation in 4 volumes as *The Mind and Society*, 1935). I use the paragraph numbers of the 1923 ed.

desires or demands. (31) But the question remains what is to be the measure of this harmonizing.

In sociological jurisprudence we may accept Max Weber's idea of sociology as having to do with the social activities of men — with activities "oriented to the activities of others." He finds the basis for the legal order in the responsibility cast upon every individual by the interference by each in the pursuit of his own values with the pursuit of their values by others. Here sociology connects with the theory of interests in jurisprudence. It connects with the juristic problem of adjusting relations and ordering conduct by the force of a politically organized society so as to give effect to the most that we may of the whole field of human values with the least friction and waste.

Sorokin has relatively little to say of law and that incidentally. But sociological jurisprudence, especially in its theory of interests, might build on his idea of culture as "the sum total of everything which is created or modified by the conscious or unconscious activity of two or more individuals interacting with one another or conditioning one another's behavior." (32) This idea of behavior conditioned by that of others bears on the question raised by certain realist jurists, whether claims and demands and desires precede legal recognition and securing of them or result from the threats promulgated by the legal order.

So much for the development of sociology since Comte as it has had to do (incidentally only, for the most part) with law or has affected juristic thought. Sociology of law is in this line of development. It proceeds from sociology toward law.

II

In 1911, Kelsen drew a sharp line of distinction between juristic and sociological method. (33) He argued that juristic method postulated the state, the constitution of the state as a source of norms, and a series of norms derivable from the highest norm. In this view jurisprudence had nothing to do with criticism of these

---

31. Max Weber, "Rechtssoziologie," in *Wirtschaft und Gesellschaft*, (Tuebingen: 2 ed. 1925), Part 2, Chap. 7.
32. Pitirim A. Sorokin, *Social and Cultural Dynamics*, (New York: American Book Co., 1937), Vol. III.
33. Hans Kelsen, *Ueber Grenzen zwischen juristischer und soziologischer Methode*, (Tuebingen: 1911).

norms except as to their logical derivation and consistency. It led to a pure theory of law by which to work out the logical interdependence of the norms of which a body of law (in the second of the lawyer's three senses) is made up, and the chief instrument is logical analysis. On the other hand, he argued that sociological method had to do with the needs of those who prescribe, as contrasted with those who apply the norms, and so with their content, as distinguished from their systematic arrangement, logical interdependence, and historical development. The vogue of Neo-Kantianism on the Continent, especially in central Europe after the first World War, and the influence of Kelsen have led to increased stress upon methodology and a tendency to set off separate domains of what had been coming to be regarded as a single science of law. This has gone far in some discussions of sociology of law, giving rise to disputes whether it is a "fact science" or a "normative science" or a "culture science," and a setting off of "positivist philosophy of law," "positivist theory of law," "sociology of law," and "applied science of legislation." (34) But such distinctions are not "fruitful. Each of the several distinct "sciences" no more than does a part, and often an indivisible part, for all but theoretical methodology, of a science of law. Excessive subdivision and limitation of fields is a reversion to the water-tight compartment learning of the nineteenth century. It lays out divisions to the exigencies of academic courses. I do not believe it worth while for sociology of law. But at any rate, whatever sociology of law may be, with the emphasis on sociology, sociological jurisprudence, with the emphasis on jurisprudence, is a science of law as a highly specialized form or agency of social control, approached from the standpoint of a science of society.

Of the sociologies of law which have appeared in increasing number in the present century, the most useful from the lawyer's standpoint is Ehrlich's *Grundlegung der Soziologie des Rechts*. (35) He uses "law" to mean all social control, following in this respect the historical school of jurists. The analytical jurists insist that

---

34. See N. S. Timasheff, "What is Sociology of Law" *American Journal of Sociology*, 43: 225, 1937; Barna Horváth, *Rechtssoziologie*, (Berlin: 1934), Pars. 27-32.

35. Eugen Ehrlich, *op. cit.* See review by Simpson, *Harvard Law Review*, 51: 190, 1937; by Timasheff in *American Sociological Review*, 2:120, 1937; and by Rheinstein, *International Journal of Ethics*, 48:232, 1938, and critique of the original by Vinogradoff, "The Crisis of Modern Jurisprudence," *Yale Law Journal*, 29:312 1920.

sanction is necessary to a law; that an enforcing agency — and since the sixteenth century in Europe and the lands settled from Europe that has meant a politically organized society putting force behind precepts — is essential to the existence of a law properly so-called. But Sir Henry Maine, looking at the beginnings of law, where sanction is at most feeble, and at social control in primitive societies, where sanctions are diffuse rather than organized, (36) and at international law, held that the significant feature was habit of obedience, and so sought to find a common element in all social control. (37) It must be noted, however, that the English analytical jurists and the English historical jurists are not talking about the same thing. The theory urged by the English historical school is rather a theory of the sanction of social control as a whole than of the sanction of particular laws or legal precepts, which is what the analytical jurists are talking about. Vinogradoff directs his preliminary discussion to social control as a whole and does not confine his use of the term "law" to that highly specialized form of institutional social control which analytical jurists and lawyers think of as law. (38)

Ehrlich, however, differs from the historical jurists of the last century in that while they, like the jurists of the past, were thinking of the body of authoritative materials in which tribunals feel bound to find the grounds of or guides to determinations, he, on the other hand, was looking functionally at the legal order, the regime of adjusting relations and ordering conduct in modern society, at the ordering of relations which makes up the legal order, and at particular legal precepts. In particular, Ehrlich stressed the limited function in social control of the norm for decision, that is, the relatively small part which it plays in everyday social control as a whole.

A law may be looked at from a number of different standpoints. From the standpoint of the legislator it may be regarded as a command to do or not do some particular thing or as a threat of some consequence if some particular thing is done or is not done. From the standpoint of the individual subject to it, a law may be regarded

---

36. I take these terms from A. R. Radcliffe-Brown, "Social Sanction," in *Encyclopedia of the Social Sciences*, 13:531-534 (1934).

37. Sir Henry Summer Maine, *International Law*, (American ed. New York, 1888), pp. 50-52.

38. Sir Paul Vinogradoff, *op. cit.*, Vol. I. Chap. 6.

as a rule of or a guide to conduct, or as a threat of some consequence if his behavior does not conform to the precept. From the standpoint of the judge, it is regarded as a rule of or guide to decision. Finally, from the standpoint of the counselor, it is a basis of prediction to his client of what courts or administrative officials will do on a given state of facts. Anglo-American jurists came to regard the third point of view as basic because judges and administrative officials feel bound to and normally do follow the precept as a rule of determination, and hence it may be relied on as a rule of conduct and as a basis of prediction. (39) Ehrlich rejects this, and in so doing he is followed by later writers on sociology of law. His method is to lay hold of the relation of law in the sense of the body of norms (authoritative models or patterns of decision) to the inner order of the groups and associations and relations which make up a society. He saw that, using "law" in the sense of the legal order, as the older historical jurists commonly did, this inner order of groups and associations and relations is the original and is still the basic form. The body of legal precepts and the technique of the judicial process are logically derivative forms. But in speaking of the inner order of groups and associations of every level as "law," just as in speaking of the inner order of a developed politically organized society as law, there is a confusion of (1) the regime maintained with (2) the processes that maintain it (in a developed society both a political process and a judicial and administrative process) and with (3) the body of authoritative guides and the received technique by which those processes are carried on. But this is a matter of terminology. It was a significant step in jurisprudence to think of the political organization of society as a group or association with an inner order and as such an agency of social control merely on a higher level than the rest but specifically rather than generically different.

Ehrlich had only the beginnings of a technique of getting at the relation of customs of popular action to the legal precepts in the books and the judicial and administrative processes in action. (40) But he set the example of studying such things and the technique

---

39. A. V. Dicey, "Private International Law as a Branch of the Law of England," *Law Quarterly Review*, 6:3; John C. Gray, *Definitions and Questions in Jurisprudence, Harvard Law Review*, 6:21, 1892; John W. Salmond, *Jurisprudence*, (1902), Par. 5.

40. Eugen Ehrlich, *Das lebende Recht der Voelker von Bukowina*, (Czernowitz: 1913).

is being developed. Fortunately, along with a sociological turn he had a competent juristic equipment. He was able to compare intelligently the legal and juristic thinking of Roman law, the English common law, the modern Roman law, and the law of Continental Europe of today as no one had done before him. His conception of a complex of social facts involved in the manifold associations and relations which make up human society should be compared with Duguit's "observed and verified fact" of social interdependence in an economic order. His idea of the inner order of groups and associations and relations as the basis of a legal order, giving us the "living law," should be compared with what the economic determinist sees as imposition of the will of the socially dominant class. His theory of the reaction of "living law" upon generalizations and formulas, and of precepts and formulas which no longer reflect the inner order of significant associations and relations, should be compared with the doctrine of the skeptical realists who can see nothing but individual behavior tendencies of individual judges. In each case he saw more and deeper than those whose views have had much vogue. He made a significant beginning of a comparative sociological jurisprudence. The value of his work for the relation of the judicial to the legislative process is obvious.

Next in order of time came Jerusalem's sociology of law. (41) He builds, as he tells us, on Max Weber in contrast with Kelsen. He proposes a method of "pure objectiveness." This method seeks to set forth right and law (the inner order of groups and associations and its phenomena) purely as an ingredient of social life, without regard to its worth as a concrete ordering of life for the individual observer. He calls this method of pure objectiveness the sociology of law. (42) Only one of the projected two parts was published.

In Horváth's sociology of law (43) a great part is taken up with terminological and methodological distinctions. He discussed right and law (*Recht*) as (1) a substitute for strife (this is what lawyer's law is historically), (2) as limitation of power, and (3) as organization of power. He used the term *Recht* partly in the sense of the legal order and partly in the sense of the judicial and adminis-

---

41. Franz W. Jerusalem, *Soziologie des Rechts*, (Jena: 1925).
42. *Ibid.* pp. iii-v
43. Barna Horváth, *Rechtssoziologie*, (Berlin: 1934). Review by Wilson, *Law Quarterly Review*, 52:138, 1936.

trative processes — in the latter respect like American realists. Limitation of power is the idea of Anglo-American public law. Organization of power is the Continental idea.

Horváth has made one important suggestion. One of the perennial and persistently difficult questions of jurisprudence is the relation of law and morals, of is and *ought-to-be*. The analytical jurist looks only at the precepts actually recognized and used as grounds of decision by the courts and as guides to determination by administrative agencies. The philosophical jurist has looked only, or at least chiefly, at what interests ought to be recognized and secured and what precepts ought to be established and enforced. Horváth considers that *Recht* (right and law — what law in the lawyer's sense is trying to maintain or bring about) is the relation between the two. Using the term "function" in the sense in which it is used in mathematics, he says that every *ought-to-be* is a function of an *is*, and every *is* is a function of an ought-to-be. That is, every legal precept which exists as an item of the positive law (that is, the body of precepts recognized and applied in the courts) is in its application an activity toward a model or pattern of what ought to be, and every *ought-to-be* pursues its purpose or end in the form of one or more positive precepts. Hence, he says, law relates facts of nature to norms. In this way he seeks to meet the current Neo-Kantian dogma of internal contradiction in the law; the proposition that the standpoints of a science having to do with facts and of one having to do with norms are antagonistic and exclusive; that natural phenomena and normative phenomena are not relatable. For example, in labor relations the give-it-up doctrine, much preached in jurisprudence today, tells us it is unscientific to consider anything but what the National Labor Relations Board actually does. When we look beyond that we indulge in unscientific subjective judgments. Horváth would say: The statute requiring collective bargaining with employees is an activity toward a model or pattern of security of tenure in jobs in industry and security in obtaining employment which it is considered ought to be. But the idea that these ought to be is carried out in the provisions of the Wagner Act and rules and determinations of the National Labor Relations Board. Thus there is something by which to measure the rules and determinations of the Board, which enables us to form judgments with respect to them.

In general, however, Horváth proceeds on the Neo-Kantian epistemology and so thinks of what he calls a "synoptic science," that is, one giving a general view, and considers that the significant feature is our point of view. Thus to him the scope of a sociology of law is relative to points of view, among which we may choose our own and have only to follow it out logically.

Timasheff (44) regards sociology as a theoretical science of generalizations as to social phenomena. As sociology is not a practical science, his sociology of law has nothing to do with the practical problems of the legal order. His main thesis is coordination of the ethical and the imperative, which seems a modern version of the idea of the classical Roman jurists, the idea of a body of moral precepts backed by the authority of politically organized society. But, as with all sociologists, he considers that law (that is, *droit*, right and law) exists wherever there is a group or association, so that a body of moral precepts involved in the existence of a group or association of any degree backed by the authority of that organization is to be called "law." There is in any such group or association a coordination of the ethical and the imperative, and that is law and there is a legal order. The difficulty which an Anglo-American lawyer has in understanding this comes from the translation of *rechtlich* as "legal" and *Rechtsordnung* as "legal" order.

He holds that a system of what he calls "legal rules" — *i. e.* precepts as to what is done and what is not done — "recognized and supported by the active center," corresponds to every "power structure." I take it such a power structure would be a pioneer mining district making rules as to location of mining claims, a trade union adopting rules, a bar association adopting a code of professional ethics, the bar in England recognizing the traditional ethics of the profession. Hence, he says, the hierarchy of power structures is paralleled by a hierarchy of legal orders (that is, regimes of control) those recognized by structures lower in the hierarchy giving way before the legal rules (as he considers them) supported by structures of higher degree. The State is the highest of these power structures and so the upper layer of law is to be found in "legal rules emanating directly from the state or indirectly recognized by it." But, he adds, other social groups have their "legal" rules also, and these are the lower level of law. He proposes to call the upper level "state law" and the lower level "social law." This use of "legal" is unusual in English. But the matter is not wholly

---

44. N. S. Timasheff, *op. cit.*

one of terminology. It could be wished that a word could be found for the lower level, using social control for the whole, law for his "state law," and finding a new adjective in place of "legal" for the precepts of Timasheff's "social law."

Gurvitch (45) regards sociology of law as "a kind of sociology of the human spirit" and insists upon "the mutual interdependence of this part of sociology and philosophy." His philosophy is "radical empiricism with an intuitional basis." That is, he finds reality in experience and in intuitions resulting from experience. His book is especially useful for the painstaking account of "the forerunners and founders of sociology of law" to which about half of its contents is devoted.(46)

He objects to the jurist's distinguishing of law in the lawyer's sense from other phases and agencies of social control. The jurist sets off law in the lawyer's sense, as a highly specialized phase and highly specialized instruments of social control in and by a politically organized society, from other phases and agencies of social control in such a society because he finds in legal history a gradual process of differentiation by which it is set off more and more definitely until in the maturity of legal systems the differentiation becomes complete. Gurvitch's objection to this is that each group or association of men has its own order, its own framework of order, its own jural values (*i. e.* values in terms of what is held "right") which it recognizes and seeks to maintain, and the State itself "is merely a particular group and a particular order." We may grant this, and it was one of the significant achievements of Duguit to bring it home to jurists, and yet be disinclined to stretch the term law to cover so much. What it means is that Anglo-American jurists look primarily at their special subject and set it off as such, and when like sociologists they look at social control as a whole, they prefer to speak of it by what to them is the broader term.

Take the case of the sit-down strike, much argued not long since. The claim to conduct such a strike was counted among the recognized jural values of important groups and associations. But it was not recognized by the body of authoritative precepts in our politically organized society. It was not counted among the jural values of that group. Hence it did not come to be received into the law in the lawyer's sense. It was not maintained and furthered by those who

---

45. Georges Gurvitch, *op. cit.*
46. Pp. 68-197.

exercised the power of politically organized society; it was suppressed by them. To the lawyer there are, on the one hand, the inner order and recognized jural values of groups and associations which are constrained to maintain that inner order and those jural values subject to the scrutiny of and in subordination to the precepts established and recognized by the organs of politically organized society. On the other hand, there are inner orders and recognized values which have behind them sanctions prescribed and made effective by the organs and officials of a politically organized society. To the lawyer this distinction is profound and generic. The sociological jurist is quite willing to agree that the State is a particular group with its own inner order. But he can for his purposes clearly distinguish, in modern, developed systems, the law of a politically organized society, paramount within and independent of legal control from without, from the inner order of groups and associations and relations which *legally* must operate in subordination to what the common-law lawyer would call the law of the land. For example, whatever the inner order of a household may be, or the framework of that order in a household coming to an American city from the Orient, or its jural values, that order and framework and those values are subject to be judged and controlled by a Juvenile Court or Domestic Relations Court.

Holding to an idea of sociology of the human spirit, Gurvitch finds that social phenomena exist in eight layers or levels. That is, they exist in the generalized mind in these layers. Without attempting to set them out in detail, let me seek to run a concrete example through these levels. In Magna Carta, one of the concrete grievances redressed was that the King was in the habit of commandeering the carts or wagons of his subjects without paying for them, and of taking fire wood for his castles without paying for it. He promised in Magna Carta not to do this without paying the "old price limited." Here there were values and ideas particularized with reference to the time. By the seventeenth century these have risen to his next level of collective ideas which serve as a spiritual basis for symbols and by the eighteenth century to the level of symbols and come into our constitutions in symbolic form in the proposition that private property is not to be taken for public use without compensation — a phase of the liberty and property symbol. In the meantime, on an intermediate level, along with the development of strong central governments in and after the sixteenth century, come nationalist ideas and ideas of collective claims as against indi-

SOCIOLOGY OF LAW

viduals, and out of these grow new patterns of subjecting individual property to the general good (not merely public use). Next on his fourth level are unorganized courses of conduct, such as resumptions of grants, forfeitures of franchises, confiscations of property, such as there were in the political contests in seventeenth-century England, in sixteenth and seventeenth-century Ireland, and in America during and after the Revolution. On the third level these become organized in the nineteenth-century idea of the police power, a standardized picture (idea) of subjecting liberty and property to collective benefit. On the second level we find organization giving effect to this picture.

Such is a possible concrete illustration of Gurvitch's scheme of levels of the collective mind in the development of social institutions. His elaborate scheme seems to me more one of logically laid out levels as a scheme of what logically must happen than of actually observed steps of development. Also, in the best illustration I could think of (Gurvitch gives none) one could see as well two ideas developing parallel, now one and now the other ahead for a time, as a series of levels one above the other. It will be noted that this scheme presupposes a collective mind looked at at different levels. Accordingly, he defines the aim of the "sociology of the human spirit or of the noetic mind" as "the study of cultural patterns, social symbols, and collective spiritual values and ideas in their functional relations with social structures and concrete historical situations of society." "Noetic mind" is a term taken from Edmund Husserl, the founder of phenomenology. We are told that "data which are non-sensuous and non-empirical (that is, are not *derived* from the senses nor from experience) but are conceived by pure intuition alone, are noetic." It is something postulated not something discovered. As applied in jurisprudence it reminds one of Savigny's *Volksueberzeugung* conviction on the part of a people as to what is right. Savigny held that experience of life led to discovery of the invisible boundaries, as he put it, within which in the conflict and overlapping of individual human demands and desires, the existence and activity of each individual gained a secure free opportunity. This experience led to a conviction on the part of the people as to what was right and just. The turning up of this idea in a new form in a sociology of law, is one of many indications that a type of philosophical school on the Continent is the successor of the historical jurisprudence of the last century.

TWENTIETH CENTURY SOCIOLOGY

So much for the sociological line, culminating in a number of recent books on sociology of law. We turn now to the juristic line, culminating in sociological jurisprudence.

III

In the last decade of the nineteenth century the historical school, founded by Savigny and reinforced by Sir Henry Maine was, on the whole, dominant in jurisprudence. On the Continent it had all but swallowed up the metaphysical school, the nineteenth-century successor of the dominant law-of-nature school of the seventeenth and eighteenth centuries. In the English-speaking world the historical and the analytical schools were contending, but for the time being the historical school seemed to be getting the better of the conflict. Philosophical jurisprudence was under a cloud which still casts a shadow of suspicion on the social philosophical jurists of today in England and in the United States in spite of their complete change of method. But some beginnings of what were to be the movements of the present century were then apparent and it is not hard to point out the forerunners of the science of law of today. Jhering's theory of rights as interests had appeared as far back as 1865, his discussion of the end of law and development of a social utilitarianism in 1877, and his attack on the "jurisprudence of conceptions" in 1884. But their effects were not to be felt in jurisprudence for a generation. Marx had formulated his economic interpretation of history in 1859 and it had begun to be taken up for history generally in 1885, but was still to be applied to legal history. The mechanical and biological sociology were doing something to clear the way for the sociological and the realist jurisprudence of the next century. As to the mechanical sociology, Spencer's *Justice* was just about to appear (it appeared in 1892) but when it did appear it reinforced the ideas of the metaphysical and historical jurists and of the later followers of Bentham. It had a belated effect in the United States in the economic determinism of Brooks Adams, who sought to combine analytical jurisprudence, mechanical positivist sociology, and Marxian socialism in an economic interpretation of legal history and of law. (47) Yet it was some gain to set jurists to relating the law more critically to other social phenomena. As to

---

47. Brooks Adams, Lectures I and II in *Centralization and the Law,* with an Introduction by M. M. Bigelow, (Boston: 1906).

the biological sociology, it began to affect jurisprudence with Post (48) and makes a start toward the unification of the social sciences a generation later. As far back as 1868, Gierke had published his epoch-making pronouncement that man owes what he is to the association of man with man and that the power of making associations gives the possibility of development of history. (49) In 1878, Jellinek had already suggested his theory of "social psychological guarantee" as sanction. (50) But Tarde's work for psychological theory was to come and a psychological sociology of law and psychological realism were far in the future.

Toward the end of the century, jurists began more and more to urge that none of the methods which had developed since the breakdown of the law-of-nature school was wholly sufficient. It was perceived that they sought to construct a science of law solely in terms of and on the basis of law in the sense of the body of authoritative grounds of or guides to judicial decision or law in the sense of the legal order or both, thought of as standing by themselves dissociated from other phenomena of social control or of civilization. On the one hand, there began to be a certain coming together of the nineteenth-century methods. On the other hand, there was quest of new methods. Out of this came three movements which led to three types of jurist characteristic of the present century. In one, the determining impetus came from revival of philosophy of law and the determining direction was philosophical, leading to a number of forms of social philosophical jurisprudence. In a second, the impetus came from the Marxian theory of history and the determining direction was economic, leading by way of an economic interpretation of legal history to a juristic economic determinism and thence to a number of types of realist jurisprudence. In the third, the determining direction came from positivism and the direction was sociological, leading to functional study of legal institutions in the light of all the social sciences and hence to consideration of the legal order as an agency of social control rather than exclusive consid-

---

48. Albrecht Hermann Post, *Der Ursprung des Rechts,* (Oldenburg: 1876); *Bausteine fuer eine allgemeine Rechtswissenschaft,* (Oldenburg: 1880); *Die Grundlagen des Rechts und die Grundzuege seiner Entwickelungsgeschichte,* (Oldenburg: 1884).

49. Otto Gierke, *Das deutsche Genossenschaftsrecht,* (Berlin: 1868), Vol. I, p. 1.

50. Georg Jellinek, *Die sozialethische Bedeutung von Recht, Unrecht, und Strafe,* (Wien: 1878). This theory was afterwards fully developed in his *Allgemeine Staatslehre,* (Berlin: 1900).

eration of the legal materials with which tribunals work in maintaining that order.

Of the different types of social philosophical school, the first in chronological order are the social utilitarians, the followers of Jhering. They were pioneers in social philosophical jurisprudence, and much of the thought of the present has built on Jhering who has been more and more an influence in the past twenty-five years. But today social utilitarianism is an element in the thought of other social philosophical schools rather than a subsisting school.

Rudolf Stammler (1856-1938), the leader of the Neo-Kantians, has been the strongest single influence in philosophical jurisprudence in the present century. In turning attention from the relation of morals and ethics to abstract rules and directing it to the relation of these matters to the administration of justice through rules, in his theory of the social ideal of the epoch as the criterion of justice through rules, and in giving us a theory of the application of legal precepts, he greatly broadened the field of jurisprudence and contributed much to what has been carried forward by others. In his first important book (51) he approached a sociological method. Later, however, he turned to logic relying on it much as the classical natural law relied on reason. His idea of natural law with a changing content (52) has done good service in recent thought.

While the Neo-Kantians connected the social philosophical school with the metaphysical jurisprudence of the nineteenth century, another type, the Neo-Hegelians, connected with the nineteenth-century historical school. In spite of its Hegelian philosophy, Savigny's school had ideas as to the origin and nature of law which might have led earlier than they did to a sociological method and theory. As it was, the attempt of the historical jurists to make a theory of laws fit the beginnings of law in the lawyer's sense, usage and custom, and international law as well as the law of the developed state, and their ideas of sanction, led to the use of the term "law" to cover all social control in which Vinogradoff agrees with Ehrlich and with all recent writers on sociology of law. Josef Kohler (1849-1919), (53) the leader of the Neo-Hegelians, thought

---

51. Rudolf Stammler, *Wirstchaft und Recht* (Berlin: 1895).
52. *Ibid.*, Par. 32.
53. Josef Kohler, "*Rechtsphilosophie und Universalrechtsgeschichte*" in *Holtzendorff Encyclopaedie. der Rechtswissenschaft* (6th ed., I, Leipzig, 1904); *Lehrbuch der Rechtsphilosophie,* (Berlin: 1908, 3rd ed., 1923), the first edition translated by Albrecht as *Kohler's Philosophy of Law,* (New York: The Macmillan Co., 1914); *Moderne Rechtsprobleme,* (Berlin: 1907, 2nd ed., 1913).

SOCIOLOGY OF LAW

of law as a product of the civilization of a people. It existed to maintain, further and transmit civilization, that is, the control over external nature or physical nature and the control over internal nature or human nature which has made it possible to attain the other. He called for a universal legal history which was to show "how the law has developed in the course of history, and in connection with the history of civilization; to show what results in the civilization of a people have been bound up in law, how the civilization of a people has been conditioned by law, and how law has furthered the progress of civilization." (54) He gave us a theory of sociological interpretation of legal precepts and a method of formulating the jural postulates of the civilization of the time and place which are of the first importance. His outlook was historical and sociological, although he was not in the positivist line of sociological thought.

In France, at the beginning of the century, the social philosophical movement took the form of a revived natural law. In part, this followed Stammler's idea of a natural law with a changing or growing content. In part, it turned to Neo-Scholasticism. But in one of its forms it connected with positivism and gave us a positivist sociological natural law. Léon Duguit (1859-1928) (55) found the foundation of his juristic thought in Durkheim and might be said to have used the law to illustrate Durkheim from the juristic side. This takes him back to Comte, and the older mechanical sociology appealed to him in his attacks upon the eighteenth-century natural rights, classical in French constitutional law, and the nineteenth-century metaphysical systems of rights. At the same time, he was attracted by Jhering's social utilitarianism which had much in common with positivism. But these two elements in Duguit's thought were at bottom discordant and as a result his writings are sometimes not clear and sometimes confused.

Duguit's system is one of natural law in that he conceives of everything in law as deriving its validity from and to be judged by a fundamental rule or principle of right and law. Following Comte he arrives at it by observation and verifies it by further observa-

---

54. Kohler, *"Rechtsphilosophie und Universalrechtsgeschichte,"* Par. 8.
55. Léon Duguit, *L'état, le droit objectif, et la loi positive,* (Paris: 1901), Chaps. 1-2 translated in *Modern French Legal Philosophy,* (New York: The Macmillan Co., 1916), pp. 258-259; *Les transformations générales du droit privé depuis le Code Napoléon,* (Paris 1912); *Le droit social, le droit individuel, et la transformation de l'Etat.* (Paris: 1908).

tion. But as Spencer arriving in the same way at his law of equal freedom in fact got it at second hand from Kant, so Duguit gets the content of his *règle de droit* from Durkheim. The principle gets a content of that from which it is supposed to be derived.

As a teacher of French constitutional law, Duguit had much to do with natural law and natural rights. Natural rights were the basis of the Declaration of the Rights of Man, fundamental in French constitutional theory. French constitutional law, since each department of government was the judge of its own powers and the constitution was not a legal document to be construed and applied in the courts, was obliged to draw heavily on juristic reasoning as to how the executive and the legislative powers could be made to work in harmony and was made up of customs of exercise of governmental powers and reasoning as to how on rational principles they ought to be exercised. He was in violent reaction from natural-law thinking, from the analytical thinking of the teachers of the French Civil Code, and from the metaphysical thinking of the dominant historical school. As he saw it, they were out of touch with observed and verified phenomena. Observation showed that there were no such things as rights. Hence, there were no natural rights. It showed there was no such thing as sovereign and subjects, and no reality in the distinction between public law and private law. (56) Accordingly, he held that all such things must be given up. A new start was to be made from the observed and verified fact of social interdependence through similarity of needs and diversity of functions, or, as it had become in the industrial society of his time, similarity of interest and division of labor. He derived from this the rule or principle of right-and-law binding all members of society to act so as to further this social interdependence and not to do anything which would impair it. This involves duties; it does not create or confer rights. In his doctrine there are no rights. (57)

He argues that legislation is an activity of individuals who exercise governmental powers. Hence, like all other human activity, it is subject to the rule or principle of right-and-law and so a legislatively enacted precept, although it may conform to the constitution, is not binding unless it tends to further rather than

---

56. *L'Etat, le droit objectif, et la loi positive*, Chaps. 4, 5; *Le droit social, le droit individual, et la transformation de l'Etat*, Lect. 2.
57. *Les transformations générales du droit privé depuis le Code Napoléon*, p. 24.

SOCIOLOGY OF LAW

impair or hinder social interdependence. Accordingly, he suggests a tribunal, composed of representatives of all social classes, to "judge of the legality of the law," that is, of whether a given precept or enacted rule conforms to the natural-law requirement of promoting social interdependence. (58) The decisions of such a tribunal would give us what might be called a positive natural law. But his natural law is not derived from reason but from observation. He observes social interdependence as a fact and also as a fact "the belief profoundly penetrating the mass of mankind at a given time and in a given country that such and such a rule is imperative and that such and such a change must be brought about." (59) These facts are taken to create the moral-legal duty which is the basis of his system.

In Duguit's view observation of society shows us not, as the nineteenth century thought, individual men endowed with rights and burdened with duties living among others likewise so endowed and burdened, but a society of men protected by that society so far as they perform their allotted functions therein, and restrained so far as their actions impede that function. On this basis he denies the proposition of the analytical jurist that law is something made consciously by lawmakers In this respect he is close to the historical jurists of the last century. Law, he tells, us, "is much less the work of the lawmaker than the constant and spontaneous product of the facts." (60) On the same basis he challenged the idea of liberty held by the metaphysical jurists. He denied the proposition of the French Civil Code that liberty is "the power of doing everything that does not injure another." (61) Liberty, he said, is a consequence of the obligation which the principle of right and law imposes on every one, namely, to develop his individuality as completely as possible in order to cooperate as effectively as possible toward social interdependence. (62) His ideal picture of the legal and social order is an idealization of a modern industrial city and the country dependent upon it in which everything is

---

58. *Le droit social, le droit individuel, et la transformation de l'Etat*, 2nd ed. (Paris: 1911), p. 58.
59. *Les transformations du droit public*, (Paris: 1913), p. 45.
60. *Les transformations générales du droit privé depuis le Code Napoléon*, p. 13.
61. French Civil Code, art. 6
62. *Les transformations générales du droit privé depuis le Code Napoléon*, p. 25.

taken to turn upon efficient production in the greatest possible quantity. Hence his idea of the end of law is in effect the Greek and Roman and medieval one of an orderly maintaining of an idealized status quo, applied to an industrial community. He had much vogue two decades ago. But his influence has been in politics rather than in jurisprudence. There has been no development of his ideas in contemporary jurisprudence.

While Duguit based a sociological natural law on Durkheim, Maurice Hauriou (1856-1929) (63) based a sociological-political and juristic theory on Neo-Scholasticism. It should be said, however, that the Neo-Thomism, which Hauriou accepts or assumes, might be replaced by the positivism to which he earlier adhered without affecting the institutional theory which is his chief contribution to the science of law. From either starting point he could arrive at the idea of institutions and systems without the state and of the state as only an institution. His point is that groups and associations organize certain of men's activities without merging their personality. As he uses the term, an institution is an idea of some work or enterprise realizing and persisting in some social milieu. An authority is set up and provides organs for itself in order to realize the idea, and the members of the group interested in realizing the idea bring about manifestations of common interest, directed by the organs of authority and governed by certain procedures developed or laid down for the conduct of the enterprise and the exercise of the authority. Examples of institutions in Hauriou's sense are: A business company, a trade union, a church society, a political party, the state. The same person may be more or less active in any number of these institutions, each organizing certain of his activities and yet not the rest. We speak of him as a member. But that means limb. He is not a member in the sense that his personality is swallowed up in the institution of which in consequence he is only a part. It is only as to certain of his activities that he is in the institution. This carries further the work begun by Gierke and developed by Ehrlich. It gives us a level

---

63. Maurice Hauriou, *"La théorie de l'institution et de la fondation,"* in *La cité moderne et les transformations du droit*, (Paris: 1925). See Renard, *La théorie de l'institution*, (Paris: 1930); Jennings, "The Institutional Theory," in *Modern Theories of Law*, (London: Oxford University Press, 1933); and the papers in (1931) *Archives de philosophie du droit et de sociologie juridique*, especially, Delos, "La théorie de l'institution," and Gurvitch, "Les idées-maitresses de Maurice Hauriou."

between, on the one hand, those groups and associations which are without organs or directing authority or certain procedures, and yet are in their way agencies of social control, and, on the other hand, the most highly developed type of institutional social control, namely, the legal order, control by the systematic employment of the force of a politically organized society.

Hauriou's is a sociological rather than a juristic theory. Neither Hauriou nor Renard, his chief exponent, has attempted to work out a system of jurisprudence nor any significant juristic doctrine on this basis. Perhaps, in the society of today, the multiplicity of such institutions, each carrying out or seeking to carry out its idea, might replace the crowd of individuals, each exerting his will in continual actual or potential conflict, which Kant sought to order. It may be significant that we have here a theory which finds the unit elsewhere than in the individual man and that this theory has become generally accepted by writers on public law at a time when that subject is crowding private law in the English-speaking world and is said to be swallowing it up on the Continent.

We are not concerned here with political features of the theory with relation to the corporative state.

A sociological school of jurists developed gradually parallel with the movement toward sociology from the historical and philosophical schools.

Sociology was founded by a mathematician. Moreover, in the first half of the nineteenth century the central point in scientific thinking was the mechanism of the physical universe. Laplace's *Mécanique céleste* attracted general attention to the idea of laws, mathematically demonstrable, controlling the operations of nature. There was a tendency to seek mathematical or mechanical laws according to which all things came into existence and by which they were governed in the course of their existence. As this was the type of thought of the first positive philosophers, it came to be that of the first positive philosophies of law and so of the beginnings of sociological jurisprudence. (64) It was especially congenial in jurisprudence and hung on there longer than elsewhere because of the influence of the historical school which was dominant in the science of law at that time. The ideas of the mechanical sociologists seemed to confirm the doctrine of the historical jurists. Many who

---

64. There is a good account of this in Giuseppe Carle, *La vita del diritto*, (Torino: 1890).

were beginning to be conscious that the metaphysical historical jurisprudence could not hold the ground much longer, were able to persuade themselves that they were moving forward by giving to their old views the new form of the mechanical sociology. (65) The achievements of the mechanical sociologists in jurisprudence were negative only. They helped clear away but they built little or nothing. They were of service in compelling jurists to relate law more critically to other social phenomena. They urged that the form of social phenomena was not an arbitrary and artificial fact, that society was not a mere human invention, that the development of society took place according to fixed principles and hence that systems of law and legal institutions developed in accordance with like principles. Thus they helped drive the other schools to seek a broader foundation and furnished not a little of the impetus which produced the social philosophical jurisprudence.

In sociology, the mechanical phase was succeeded by and overlapped by a biological phase. In sociological jurisprudence somewhat later there was the same succession. Darwin had made evolution the central idea in scientific thought. Attempts to work out a physical science of law were succeeded by a biological science of law. At first, the ideas were still those of the mechanical phase. Biology only affected the vocabulary. The biological phrase which appealed most to jurists was "natural selection." The "struggle for existence" appealed to them as a better way of putting the beliefs which they had formed under the influence of the historical school. As they put it, the end of law was to give play in an orderly maner to the "elimination of the unfit"; it was to further natural selection by a well ordered struggle for existence. (66)

In an ethnological type of this phase there was a further development of biological analogies. Under the influence of the idea of evolution, there was for a time an exaggerated reliance upon social control in primitive peoples. The embryology of law was to tell everything. Study of the social institutions of the most primitive peoples was expected to reveal the fundamental data of jurisprudence. The essential idea of a legal institution could be found and understood if one could only get at the institution in its most

---

65. See J. Charmont, *La renaissance du droit naturel,* (Montpelier: 1910) p. 117. Good examples may be seen in Melville M. Bigelow and others, *Centralization and the Law*, (Boston: 1906), Lect. 4.

66. There is a good discussion of this type of juristic thought in L. Tanon, *L'évolution du droit et la conscience sociale,* (3rd. ed., Paris: 1911), pp. 116 ff.

primitive form. The chief result was the ethnological interpretation of law and of legal history. (67)

A third type was philosophical. Where the metaphysical jurists had sought to work out a complete system from some philosophical conception, such as personality or liberty or will, jurists of this type of the biological phase tried in the same way to work out a complete system from some biological principle. A principle of struggle and survival and of adaptation of institutions and precepts through struggle was put in various forms. The best example is Vaccaro. (68) He starts from a conception of law (in the sense of the body of authoritative grounds of or guides to determination) as the outcome of class conflict. It has grown and grows out of the struggle of social classes for supremacy. His method is very like that of the metaphysical jurists. They usually deduced everything from a principle of harmonious co-existence of the individual with the whole. He makes it the co-existence of social classes. The function of law is to adapt men to a social environment of class conflict by determining the conditions of class co-existence. (69) Where he differs from the metaphysical jurists is in his emphasis on relativity. He regards law as resulting from conflict at particular times and places; as he puts it, "from the action and reaction of men as they are at a given historical moment." (70) His failure to discriminate social control, the legal order, and the system of authoritative legal precepts, makes his discussion of little value today.

Three successive influences turned the attention of sociological jurists toward psychology and led to a more significant development. First, was the study of group psychology leading to a psychological movement in jurisprudence from which it spread to politics. This was due to the work of the great Germanist, Otto von Gierke (1841-1921). Second, there was a complete change of method in the social sciences generally resulting from the work of the American sociologist, Lester F. Ward (1841-1913). Third came Tarde (1843-1904) working out the psychological or sociological laws of imitation and showing the extent to which imitation governs in the development of legal institutions.

---

67. See Roscoe Pound, *Interpretations of Legal History*, (Cambridge: The University Press, 1923), Lect. 4.

68. Michel-Ange Vaccaro, *Lesbases sociologiques du droit et de l'Etat*, (Paris: 1898), translation of *Le basi del diritto e dello stato*, (1893).

69. *Ibid.* p. 452.

70. *Ibid.*

Gierke struck a sociological note in the first sentence of his great work. (71) It led to a new way of thinking of the idea of the historical school that identified law with all social control. As Wundt put it, the State is not necessary to law. What is necessary is an association or society which is capable of producing a collective will because of correspondence of ideas and interests. (72) We have seen what Ehrlich and Hauriou and contemporary sociologists have made of it. Gierke's theory of associations became as strong an attack upon the abstract individualist jurisprudence of the nineteenth century upon one side as Jhering's theory of interests was upon another side.

Ward did not affect jurisprudence directly. But his contention that social forces were "essentially psychic," and hence that the foundations of sociology were to be found in psychology, led to a change of front which took away the supports of the mechanical and biological sociological jurisprudence. His phrase "efficacy of effort" contrasting with the doctrine of the historical school and the earlier sociological jurists that effort to improve the law was futile, had much to do with attracting American jurists to the sociological school in its formative era in the United States.

Tarde (73) refused to follow the biological sociologists who spoke of evolution of law and used instead "transformation," a term which French jurists have since employed very generally. He was a trained lawyer as well as a sociologist and was the first sociologist to give us a theory of what is the most significant part of legal systems, namely, the taught tradition which lawyers call "law" as distinguished from enacted rules or laws. As a practical lawyer he knew the importance of the traditional element, of doctrinal writing and of judicial decision. He knew the significance of the modes of juristic thinking which give continuity to legal systems. These modes of thinking and mental habits as to the development and application of legal precepts are the most enduring element in the law.

Today social psychology has an important place both in philosophical and in sociological jurisprudence.

71. Otto Gierke, *Deutche Genossenschaftsrecht*, (Berlin, 1868), Vol. I, p. 1. It is a striking testimony to the dominance of the metaphysical historical jurisprudence that it took more than a decade for Gierke's sociological pronouncement to begin to affect juristic thought.

72. Wilhelm Wundt, *Logik*, (2nd ed., Stuttgart: 1895) Vol. II (2), p. 543.

73. Gabriel Tarde, *Les transformations du droit*, (Paris: 1903).

SOCIOLOGY OF LAW

Psychology seems to me to have been making clear that the control of individual aggressiveness which organized society exercises is not merely something set up by a ruling class or socially or economically dominant group to hold in check a restless group of have-nots or even a relatively small criminal class. Although the criminal law commonly stands to the layman for the whole, it is by no means all or even the most significant part of the law. The civil side adjusts the everyday relations and orders the everyday conduct of normal men and in a highly developed society is the significant part. The social group as a condition of its existence requires peace and order. But it is a chief need of social man as an individual to have organized social control to hold back his aggressive urge and adjust it to the exigencies of his social urge. The word instinct has been overworked and made to cover so many things that one hesitates to use it. If, however, we use it to mean certain fundamental tendencies of human behavior, appearing in childhood and manifest throughout life, there are two kinds of these tendencies, one which may be called the aggressive or self-assertive instinct, and another which may be called the social instinct. The aggressive or self-assertive instinct leads man to think only of his own desires and demands and to seek to satisfy them at the expense of others and overcome all resistance to them. Bringing up and education seek to teach control of the tendencies referred to this instinct. But it is deep-seated and a reserve of force is needed to hold it in. The exercise of that force, however, is something which itself requires control, since the aggressive instinct of those who wield it may govern its application. Thus we get a problem of balance of force and control of force which is at the root of internal contradiction in criminal law and criminal procedure from which we have thus far found no escape and is in the background of most of the difficulties of government and the legal order. Aggressive self-assertion even to the point of violence is potential in almost all men. It runs counter to the social instinct of the individual and he usually repudiates it or conjures up explanations after the event to give it color of reason. But its potential existence and frequent manifestations require a reserve of force somewhere to keep it in control. A task of social control, and so of the highly specialized social control which we call law, is to check this individual tendency to aggressive self-assertion to satisfy individual desires, as is abundantly shown whenever the reserve of force is withdrawn or suspended as, for example, in a revolution, or a police strike, or some sudden catastrophe. When the coercive agencies of politically organized society are for a time in abeyance, violence seems to break out spontaneously.

In jurisprudence we express this in what is called the theory of interests. We define an interest as a desire or demand which human beings either individually or in groups seek to satisfy, of which, therefore, the adjustment of relations and ordering of conduct must take account. Such desires and demands of human beings to have or do things become significant whenever a number of human beings come in contact. There is a conflict or overlapping of these desires and demands. The aggressive self-assertion of individuals to satisfy them requires restraint, and the legal order has the task of determining which of them are to be recognized and secured and within what limits, and to order their satisfaction with a minimum of friction and waste. But we must bear in mind that this restraint of aggressive self-assertion, achieved by social control with a reserve of force, is not only a need of society, it is a need of the individual himself.

On the other hand, all normal men show an aptitude for some sort of life in groups and associations and relations, and the tendency toward this is as fundamental, as deep-seated, as that toward aggressive self-assertion. Human behavior goes on normally as if in general this social instinct prevails over the instinct of self-assertion. The universality of groups and associations, the existence of society, and the history of civilization show this. What McDougall calls the instinct of gregariousness and loyalty and veracity as tendencies connected with it is one way of putting this. Aristotle saw it when he said that man was a political animal, meaning that men naturally associated themselves in organized societies. Indeed, Aristotle pointed out that otherwise man was the fiercest of beasts. Without organized social control, his aggressive self-assertion would prevail over his cooperative social tendency and civilization would come to an end. This is what is meant when we say that one side of civilization is conquest of internal nature. It is conquest of one side of internal nature to keep it in balance with another side. It is this normal condition of development of the social instinct or tendency to keep in restraint the aggressive, self-assertive instinct or tendency which marks civilization. This is what certain philosophers have in mind when they say that the task of the legal order is to maintain, further, and transmit civilization. It is what has made possible the conditions under which men have been able to gain continually increasing control over external nature and harness it to the use of mankind and so to inherit the earth and to maintain and increase that inheritance.

In another direction, study of the world view of courts, of judges, of doctrinal writers and study of the psychology of legal and juristic thinking have come to be prominent activities of jurists. On the Continent, a considerable literature has sprung up on this subject,(74) and there is a beginning of such literature in America.(75).

Ward, in 1902, urged that none of the lines of sociological study thus far pursued could be relied on to do the whole work of a social science. (76) There was no one all-sufficient method. (77) Later, it was felt that not only was it needful to combine the several methods which had been employed in sociology and to unify that science, but that it was also needful to put sociology into relation with the other social sciences. The social sciences were to be unified by recognizing that in a large view they were departments or phases of a science of civilization. (78) Both of these ideas came into sociological jurisprudence. It was recognized that each of the directions which had been taken had something for the science of law as a whole, and that no one was to be pursued exclusively. (79) It was recognized that the entire separation from the other social

---

74. E. g. *Les méthodes juridiques*, (Paris: 1910), lectures by French jurists; Karl Georg Wurzel, *Das juristische Denken* (Wien: 1904) translated in *Science of Legal Method* in Modern Legal Philosophy Series, Vol. 9; Alfred Bozi, Die *Weltanschauung der Jurisprudenz*, (2nd ed., Hannover: 1911).

75. *Science of Legal Method*, Modern Legal Philosophy Series, Vol. 9; Benjamin N. Cardozo, *The Nature of the Judicial Process*, (New Haven: Yale University Press, 1921); Jerome Frank, *Law and the Modern Mind*, (New York: Brentano's, 1930); Edward Stevens Robinson, *Law and the Lawyers*, (New York: The Macmillan Co., 1935); Clarence Morris, *How Lawyers Think* (Cambridge: Harvard University Press, 1937).

76. "Contemporary Sociology," a reprint of three papers published in *American Journal of Sociology*, 7:475, 620, 749.

77. Ward enumerated twelve "leading sociological conceptions or unitary principles," each of which had been "put forward with large claims to being in and of itself the science of sociology" and said that they were "so many minor streams, all tending in a given direction and converging." *Pure Sociology*, p. 14. It is noteworthy that all but two of the twelve had been put forward in the same way in sociological jurisprudence.

78. This was well put in Albion W. Small, *The Meaning of Social Science*, (Chicago: University of Chicago Press, 1910), p. 87.

79. See Raoul Brugeilles, *Le droit et la sociologie*, (Paris: 1910), pp. 160ff.

sciences in the nineteenth century was unfortunate. On the one hand, the leaving of jurisprudence to itself and ignoring its problems by the other social sciences was a mistake. On the other hand, the jurist's conviction of the self-sufficiency of jurisprudence was unfortunate. It was chargeable in large part with the backwardness of the law in meeting social ends, the tardiness of lawyers in admitting or even perceiving such ends, and the gulf between legal thought and popular thought on matters of social reform which was so marked in the first decade of the present century. (80) Much of the world-wide discontent with the legal order, which was so marked before the first World War and now is reappearing, was due to modes of juristic thought and to juridical and juristic methods that were the result of want of "team play" between jurisprudence and the other social sciences. (81) Sociological jurists came to insist on the impossibility of a wholly detached, self-centered, self-sufficing science of law. (82) They insisted that the legal order was a phase of social control (83) and that it could not be undestood unless taken in its whole setting among social phenomena.

Such was the environment in which sociological jurisprudence developed in the United States. It begins with Mr. Justice Holmes. (84) In his juristic thinking he went through an analytical stage, as shown by his earlier writings in the American Law Review be-

---

80. See Gabriel Tarde, *Les transformations du droit*, (Paris: 1903), "Introduction."

81. See Edward A. Ross, *Social Psychology*, (New York: The Macmillan Co., 1908), pp. 223-224; Bruce, "Laissez Faire and the Supreme Court of the United States," *Green Bag*, 20:546, 1908.

82. "The error of the classical conception was in looking upon law as a science isolated from the others, self-sufficient, furnishing a certain number of propositions the combination whereof ought to provide for all needs. In reality, the law is only a resultant. Its explanation is outside of itself. Its sources must be sought elsewhere." Paul Van der Eycken, *Méthode positive de l'interprétation*, (Brussels and Paris: 1907), p. 112. "Nothing is more fallacious than to believe that one may give an account of the law by means of itself." Ernest Roguin, *La règle de droit*, (Lausanne: 1889), p. 8.

83. Roscoe Pound, *Social Control Through Law*, (New Haven: Yale University Press, 1942), Lecture I.

84. Oliver Wendell Holmes (1841-1935) lecturer and instructor, 1870-1873, Professor of Law, 1882, at Harvard; Associate Justice of the Supreme Court of Massachusetts, 1882-1899, Chief Justice, 1899-1902; Associate Justice of the Supreme Court of the United States, 1902-1932.

SOCIOLOGY OF LAW

tween 1870 and 1880. (85) Next, he went through a historical stage, as might have been expected in the last quarter of the nineteenth century. (86) Experience upon the bench and wide reading of and deep reflection upon the juristic writing of the time, led him at the end of the century to the sociological position. (87) In significant departures from the legal science of the last century he anticipated American thinkers and teachers of the present century from ten to twenty years. In the definite break with the method of the historical school, in the study of methods of judicial thinking and understanding of the scope and nature of judicial logic; in recognition of the relation between the law finding element in judicial decision and the policies that must govern lawmaking; in faith in the efficacy of effort to make the law more effective for its ends; in giving up the idea of jurisprudence as a self-sufficient science; in a functional point of view, in contrast with the purely anatomical or morphological standpoint of the last century — in each of these respects he foreshadowed, if he did not develop, the characteristic methods and ideas of a sociological science of law.

At this point I may refer briefly to my own work. I was brought up in analytical jurisprudence (Austin, Holland, Gray), turned to historical jurisprudence (Savigny, Maine), passed next to the social philosophical schools (Jhering, Stammler, Kohler) (88) and then under the influence of Ross and Small to sociological jurisprudence.

---

85. The more important of these are reprinted with a bibliography in *Harvard Law Review*, 44:725-798.

86. *The Common Law* (Boston: 1882). This stage of his thinking is brought out strikingly in his dissenting opinion in Miller v. Hyde, 161 Mass. 472, 478 (1894).

87. "The Path of the Law," *Harvard Law Review*, 10:467, 1897, reprinted in Oliver Wendell Holmes, *Collected Legal Papers*, (New York: Harcourt, Brace and Co.), pp. 167-202; "Law in Science and Science in Law," *Harvard Law Review*, 12:442 1899, reprinted in *Collected Legal Papers*, pp. 210-243. See Roscoe Pound, "Judge Holmes's Contributions to the Science of Law," *Harvard Law Review*, 34:449, 1921.

88. "A New School of Jurists," *University Studies*, University of Nebraska, (Lincoln, Nebraska: 1904), pp. 249-266; "Do We Need a Philosophy of Law," *Columbia Law Review*, 5:339, 1905.

TWENTIETH CENTURY SOCIOLOGY

(89) I have worked specially on the nature of law, (90) the development of ideas as to the end of law, (91) law and morals, (92) the theory of interests, (93) and the judicial and administrative processes. (94)

---

89. "The Need of a Sociological Jurisprudence," *Green Bag*, 19:607, 1907; "Law in Books and Law in Action," Report of the 14th Annual Meeting of the Maryland State Bar Association, p. 298, (1909), reprinted in *American Law Review*, 44:12, 1910; "The Scope and Purpose of Sociological Jurisprudence," *Harvard Law Review*, 24:591; 25:440, 489, 516; *The Spirit of the Common Law*, (Boston: Marshall Jones Co., 1921); *Interpretations of Legal History* (1923); "Fifty Years of Jurisprudence," *Harvard Law Review*, 50:557; 51:444, 777; *Social Control Through Law*, (1942); *Outlines of Lectures on Jurisprudence*, (5th ed., Cambridge: Harvard University Press, 1943).

90. "Theories of Law," *Yale Law Journal*, 22: 114, 1912; "Juristic Science and Law," *Harvard Law Review*, 31:1047, 1918; "The Administrative Application of Legal Standards," *Reports of American Bar Association*, 44:445, 1919; "The Progress of the Law—Analytical Jurisprudence," *Harvard Law Review*, 41: 174, 1927; "The Ideal Element in American Judicial Decision," *Harvard Law Review*, 45:136, 1931; "Hierarchy of Sources and Forms in Different Systems of Law," *Tulane Law Review*, 7:475, 1933; "A Comparison of Ideals of Law," *Harvard Law Review*, 47: 1, 1933; "More About the Nature of Law," in *Legal Essays in Tribute to Orrin Kip MacMurray*, (Berkeley: University of California Press, 1935); "What is Law?" *West Virginia Law Quarterly*, 47:1, 1940; *Social Control Through Law*, pp. 35-62.

91. "The End of Law as Developed in Legal Rules and Doctrines," *Harvard Law Review*, 27: 195, 1914; "The End of Law as Developed in Juristic Thought," Harvard Law Review, 27:605, 1914; 30:201, 1917; "Twentieth Century Ideas as to the End of Law," in *Harvard Legal Essays in Honor of Joseph Henry Beale and Samuel Williston*, (Cambridge: Harvard University Press, 1934), pp. 357-375.

92. "The Limits of Effective Legal Action," Report of the 22nd Annual Meeting of the Pennsylvania Bar Association, p. 221, (1916), reprinted in *International Journal of Ethics*, 27:150, 1917; *Law and Morals*, (Chapel Hill: University of North Carolina Press, 1924; 2nd ed., 1926).

93. "Interests of Personality," *Harvard Law Review*, 28: 343, 445, 1915; "Individual Interests in the Domestic Relations," *Michigan Law Review*, 14: 177, 1916; "A Theory of Social Interests," *Papers and Proceedings of the American Sociological Society*, 15: 1, 1921; "A Survey of Social Interests," *Harvard Law Review*, 57:1, 1943.

94. "Executive Justice," *American Law Register*, 55:137, 1907; "Justice According to Law," *Columbia Law Review*, 13:696, 1914; 14:1, 103, 1915; "The Theory of Judicial Decision," *Harvard Law Review*, 36: 641, 802, 940, 1923; *Administrative Law: Its Growth, Procedure, and Significance*, (Pittsburgh: University of Pittsburgh Press, 1942).

SOCIOLOGY OF LAW

Mr. Justice Cardozo (95) began in social utilitarianism but turned to sociological jurisprudence. (96) His setting off of the judicial process from the other meanings to which the term law had been applied, yielding an idea applicable also to the administrative process, and not only giving us a very useful term but obviating confusion between the regime, the process by which it is maintained and the body of authoritative precepts governing or guiding the process, has made much of the older discussion of the nature of law obsolete and is making for a better understanding of that fundamental subject.

Two recent American books deserve mention, the one behaviorist-sociological, (97) the other functionalist-sociological. (98)

But the outstanding recent contributions from a juristic sociological standpoint are those of Llewellyn. (99) After a notable beginning in skeptical realism he turned to the sociological approach. In his paper on the Problem of Juristic Method he gives us much the best outline of the task of a sociology of law and of the way of going about performance of it which has appeared. His striking terminology has at any rate the merit of presenting a vivid impression of the exact meaning sought to be conveyed. "Law-job," "law-ways," "law-stuff," the "trouble-case," the "cleaning up of messes," all but explain themselves.

He begins with the entirety or group. Next, we see that "diver-

---

95. Benjamin Nathan Cardozo (1870-1938) Justice of the Supreme Court of New York, 1913-1917; Judge of the Court of Appeals of New York, 1917-1927, and Chief Judge, 1927-1932; Associate Justice of the Supreme Court of the United States, 1932-1938.
96. *The Nature of the Judicial Process*, (New Haven: Yale University Press, 1921); *The Growth of the Law*, (New Haven: Yale University Press, 1924); *Paradoxes of Legal Science*, (New Haven: Yale University Press, 1928).
97. Huntington Cairns, *The Theory of Legal Science*, (Chapel Hill: University of North Carolina Press, 1941).
98. Ruby R. Vale, *Some Legal Foundations of Society*, (San Francisco: C. W. Taylor, 1941, 3 vols.). The volumes are respectively entitled, *Understanding, Conciliation,* and *Purpose*. They have to do with politics as well as jurisprudence.
99. Karl Nickerson Llewellyn, "On Reading and Using the New Jurisprudence," *Columbia Law Review*, 40:581, 1940; "The Normative, the Legal, and the Law Jobs: The Problem of Juristic Method," *Yale Law Journal*, 49:1355, 1940; K. N. Llewellyn and E. Adamson Hoebel, *"The Cheyenne Way: Conflict and Case Law in Primitive Jurisprudence,* (Norman: University of Oklahoma Press, 1941), Part. I, Chap. 3 (Primitive Law and Modern) and Part 3 (The Law-Jobs and Juristic Method—Chap. 10, Claims and Law-Ways, Chap. 11, The Law-Jobs).

gent urges or desires" arise among members of the group which "tend to friction and disunity." Here is a "constituent of law life as fundamental as the group order which it may disturb." Third, there is the "claim made by some member or members upon or against others and the relation of those claims to the order of the whole." Claims are generated either by expectation or by wish, but there is an "inveterate drive" for them to be asserted in title of the whole, as involved in the working of the whole and so justified and rightful. The handling of the claims goes to the very heart of group existence. Unless the resulting law-jobs get done, the group breaks up, dwindles away, or dies. This fundamental sociological exposition goes to the root of such questions as the nature of law, the basis of legal recognition and securing of interests, the end of law, and whether rights have some reality behind them or are merely inferences from threats or laws and are asserted only because a legal order has taught men to do so. Any group or any society is "subject occasionally or insistently to the annoyance or even disruption of members at odds or outs with one another over expectations and demands disappointed or resisted." There is need of some kind of settlement unless the group is ultimately to be dissolved. There is, therefore, a continuing strong pressure for instances of settlement and settlement procedure to become institutional.

This leads him to make a sound distinction as to the term "legal." The legal in the order of a group or culture is, he tells us, "more than mere norm, more than mere normative standard. The legal has teeth." It is true, he points out, that the legal has normative aspects. There is a more or less normative purpose, but the "heart of the legal lies in this character of being imperative rather than merely normative." As Jhering put it, "a legal proposition without legal compulsion behind it is a contradiction in itself; a fire that burns not, a light that shines not." (100) Taken in connection with Radcliffe-Brown's distinction between "diffuse" and "organized" sanctions (101) we get a use of the term "legal" more satisfactory to the Anglo-American, to whom "legal" does not have the double meaning involved in *droit, recht, ius*. But, as Llewellyn makes clear the legal is not merely successful force. The legal is part of an order.

---

100. Rudolf von Ihering, *Der Zweck in Recht,* (3rd ed., Leipzig: 1893), Vol. I. p. 332.
101. A. R. Radcliffe-Brown, "Social Sanction," *Encyclopedia of the Social Sciences,* 13:531-534.

TWENTIETH CENTURY SOCIOLOGY

Violence outside of the order is extra-legal or contra-legal. In other words, there is an institutional social control backed by organized sanctions. The case for regarding law as social control through the systematic application of force by an organized society could not be put better. His discussion of authority and regularity as involved in the "legal" (102) clears up an old subject of debate in jurisprudence.

Sir Henry Maine had laid down that the judge precedes the law; that judgments precede "customary law." (103) In this he was followed by Richard. (104) Ehrlich, however, had taken a contrary view (105) and he was followed by Vinogradoff, (106) Malinowski, (107) and Allen. (108) The soundness of Maine's proposition and the way in which the term "custom" has befogged the discussion is well brought out by Llewellyn. (109) Malinowski (110) distinguishes rules of conduct which refer to relations between individuals and groups, delimit divergent interests, and curtail disruptive tendencies, on the one hand, and, on the other hand, a specific mechanism which is brought into existence when a conflict of claims arises or a rule of social conduct is broken. He calls the former law (3) and the latter law (4) and criticizes Llewellyn and Hoebel for "an almost exclusive stress on the study of law (4)." (111) But the common-law-lawyer cannot but be aware of the role of Malinowski's law (4) in the development of our system and the jurist will not forget how the Roman law grew through the case law of the praetor's edict. *The Cheyenne Way* shows how this operates

---

102. *The Cheyenne Way*, 283-289.
103. *Ancient Law*, (London: 1861), Chap. I.
104. *L'origine de l'idée de droit*, p. 5.
105. *Fundamental Principles of the Sociology of Law*, translated by Moll, pp. 37-38.
106. *Historical Jurisprudence*, Vol. I, pp. 368-369; *Collected Papers*, pp. 465-478.
107. *Crime and Custom in Savage Society*, (New York: Harcourt, Brace and Co., 1926), pp. 1-68.
108. Carleton Kemp Allen, *Law in the Making*, (3rd ed., London: Oxford University Press, 1939), pp. 115-119.
109. *The Cheyenne Way*, pp. 274 ff
110. Bronislaw Malinowski, "A New Instrument for the Interpretation of Law," *Lawyers Guild Review*, 2: 1, 4-7, 1942.
111. *Ibid.* p. 11. I have discussed this fully in a paper "Sociology of Law and Sociological Jurisprudence," *University of Toronto Law Journal*, 5: 1, 12-18, 1943.

SOCIOLOGY OF LAW

from the beginning. Llewellyn has taken the right course in finding law in the "cleaning up of messes" and experience of how they may be cleaned up with the least friction and waste.

No abridged statement of the salient points in Llewellyn's exposition can do justice to what is the most basic and thoroughly thought out sociological theory of law which has yet appeared.

As affected by sociology and sociological jurisprudence, the characteristics of the science of law today may be said to be:

(1) A functional attitude.
(2) Study of law (in all three meanings) in relation to and as a part of the whole process of social control.
(3) A movement for preventive justice.
(4) A movement for individualization.
(5) A movement for team play with the other social sciences.
(6) Study of the limits of effective legal action. (112)

All of this is not sociology of law. But it is sociological jurisprudence.

---

112. For full references under each head see Roscoe Pound, *Outlines of Lectures on Jurisprudence*, 5th ed., pp. 32-36.

SELECTED BIBLIOGRAPHY

Cairns, Huntington, *The Theory of Legal Science*, Chapel Hill: University of North Carolina Press, 1941.

Cardozo, Benjamin N., *Nature of the Judicial Process*, (New Haven: Yale University Press, 1921).

Cardozo, Benjamin N., *The Growth of the Law*, (New Haven: Yale University Press, 1924).

Ehrlich, Eugen, *Grundlegung der Soziologie des Rechts*, (Muenchen und Leipzig: Duncker and Humblot, 1913).

Gurvitch, Georges, *Sociology of Law*, (New York: Philosophical Library, 1942)

Gurvitch, Georges, *L'idée du droit social*, (Paris: Recueil Sirey, 1932).

Gurvitch, Georges, *Essais de sociologie*, (Paris: Recueil Sirey, 1938).

Holmes, Oliver Wendell, *Collected Legal Papers*, (New York: Harcourt, Brace and Co., 1921).

Horváth, Barna, *Rechtssoziologie*, (Berlin: Verlag fuer Staatswissenschaften und Geschichte, 1934).

Jerusalem, Franz W., *Soziologie des Rechts*, (Jena: Gustav Fischer, 1925).

Llewellyn, K. N., "The Normative, the Legal, and the Law Jobs: The Problem of Justice Method," *Yale Law Journal*, 49:1355, 1940).

Llewellyn, K. N. and E. Adamson Hoebel, *The Cheyenne Way: Conflict and Case Law in Primitive Jurisprudence*, (Norman: University of Oklahoma Press, 1941).

SOCIOLOGY OF LAW

Malinowski, Bronislaw, "Introduction," in *Law and Order in Polynesia* by H. Ian Hogbin, (New York: Harcourt, Brace and Co., 1934).

Pound, Roscoe, "The Scope and Purpose of Sociological Jurisprudence," *Harvard Law Review*, 24:591; 25:440, 489, 516, 1911, 1912.

Pound, Roscoe, *Social Control Through Law*, (New Haven: Yale University Press, 1942).

Radcliffe-Brown, A. R., "Social Sanction," *Encyclopedia of the Social Sciences*, 13:531.

Timasheff, N. S., *An Introduction to the Sociology of Law*, (Cambridge: Harvard University Committee on Research in the Social Sciences, 1939).

Weber, Max, "Rechtssoziologie," in *Wirtschaft und Gessellschaft*, (2nd ed., Tuebingen: J. B. C. Mohr, 1925), Part 2, Chap. 7.

Pound, Roscoe, born at Lincoln, Nebraska, 1870. Educated, University of Nebraska, A. B. 1888, A. M. 1889, Ph. D. 1897, and at Harvard Law School. Commissioner of Appeals, Supreme Court of Nebraska, 1901-1903; Dean of the College of Law, University of Nebraska, 1903-1907; Professor of Law, Northwestern University, 1907-1909; Professor of Law, University of Chicago, 1909-1910, Harvard University, 1910-1936; Dean of the Faculty of Law, Harvard, 1916-1936, University Professor, Harvard, 1937—. LL. D. Michigan, 1913, Chicago, 1916, Harvard, 1920, Cambridge (England) 1922, California, 1929; J. U. D Berlin, 1934. Honorary Fellow, Stanford, 1941. Director, Survey of Criminal Justice, Cleveland, 1922; President, American Academy of Arts and Sciences, 1935-1936; awarded gold medal of American Bar Association, 1940. Corresponding Fellow of the British Academy; Foreign Fellow, Royal Society of Naples; Honorary Fellow, Royal Academy of Palermo; Corresponding Member of Argentine Institute of Juridical and Social Philosophy; Member, Académie internationale de droit comparé, and of Institut International de droit public. In addition to writings cited in notes 88-94, author of *Introduction to the Philosophy of Law*, 1922; *Criminal Justice in America*, 1930; *The Formative Era of American Law*, 1938; *The Task of Law*, 1944.

CHAPTER XII

CRIMINOLOGY

by

JEROME HALL

I

Introduction. Criminology is only loosely described as an "application" of social science. The relationship is one of interdependence — social science providing general theories, whereas criminology explores the incidence of these theories in distinctive, specific configurations of fact, with consequent illumination of the theories themselves, and modification of them accordingly. A discussion of 20th Century Criminology is, therefore, necessarily concerned with special aspects of social science, whose significance is accentuated by the drama of harmful, frequently violent behavior, deliberate adjudication on matters involving major interests, high questions of morality, and the solemn infliction of penalties, even death, on fellow beings. Moreover, in this century more than any other in modern times, criminologists have seen such a fanatical implementation of "respectable" and long avowed theories by dictators who professed to take Scientific Criminology seriously, indeed, with such diabolical literalness as to impel fresh and searching reexamination of the entire field. It has become painfully apparent that sound "social action" in this context calls for rather more than sophistication in research techniques and scientific methods if the relevant problems are to be even vaguely apprehended.

CRIMINOLOGY

But recent History (1), while stimulating the most thoroughgoing criticism of contemporary criminology, cannot be accepted as a fair measure of the available knowledge, however suggestive as an index of prevalent error in this field. For if we repudiate the claims of Scientific Sociology and also that renewed evangelism that exhorts the abandonment of general social science and the development only of the special disciplines, in the sublime conceit that social scientists can solve all conflicts to everyone's satisfaction if only they will put their minds to work on the solution of practical problems (the obvious fact is that we frequently have much more knowledge than we are willing or able to apply) — if we dismiss both these vagaries, an appraisal of 20th Century Criminology can begin to be circumspect. Thus if we examine the 20th century literature, explicitly designated "Criminology," what must be said by way of adverse criticism is not the hardly relevant observation that criminology is not Science. Nor shall we discuss the specific points or sound criticism that have been stressed in recent years — the diversity of subjects and problems dealt with, ranging from studies of practical administration to arguments on free will, for which no integrating theory has been provided; failure to provide control groups; failure to observe or allow for any check on subjective classification; uncritical manipulation of statistics; the triviality of a great portion of the literature due to the lack of any thought for the theoretical import of the study. These criticisms have been voiced repeatedly and at length. (2) What is now required is a more fundamental and challenging analysis. But before attempting to supply that it is necessary to take note of some of the more important accomplishments of 20th Century Criminology.

Some Achievements of 20th Century Criminology. Despite the validity of much of the above noted criticism, it is also true that considerable progress has been made in criminology during the present century and especially in the United States. For many reasons, perhaps not least because of the pressing nature of conditions that provide unusual, if not enviable, opportunities for research in this country, American criminology in the present century repre-

---

1. Jerome Hall, "Nulla Poena Sine Lege," *Yale Law Journal*, 47:165-193, December, 1937.
2. See Jerome Michael and Mortime Adler, *Crime, Law and Social Science*, (New York: Harcourt, Brace and Co., 1933); and Walter C. Reckless, *The Etiology of Delinquent and Criminal Behavior*, (New York: Social Science Research Council, 1943).

sents a substantial advance over that previously attained. It is important to stress this, partly because most of what follows is necessarily, through lack of space, confined to adverse cristicism, but chiefly because current derogation, posited on the premise that criminology is not but can be an exact science, though unsound, and therefore posing false criteria of evaluation, nonetheless so haunts the consciousness of many criminologists as to constitute a major bar to further discovery. Undeniably 20th Century Criminology has made considerable progress in many directions — especially in relatively precise formulation of relevant sociological theories, in study of case histories, in criminal psychiatry and in the use of psychoanalytic methods. Beginnings have been made in the institutional study of crime (especially in the fields of theft and juvenile delinquency) by a synthesis of methods and an integration of various types of data. Very extensive studies of administration have been contributed through collaboration of various groups, sometimes supported by generous governmental subsidies. Throughout there has been improvement in the required skills and methods. (3) Yet, despite these advances, the most salient fact about 20th Century Criminology is that it is a congeries of unresolved conflicts.

The Basic Unresolved Conflict. The basic inner-contradiction

---

3. Notwithstanding its avowed predilection for the ideal of rigorous science, 20th Century Criminology has neglected a major aspect of scientific method— its purely formal side. A logician who examined the best criminological researches would find numerous generalizations, resting on determinate data and extending beyond statements of statistical averages or descriptions of the particular facts examined. These generalizations may not satisfy all of the formal tests of physical science, rigorously determined, but they approximate them, and they can frequently be restated appropriately to that end. It is possible to classify these propositions as descriptions, minor generalizations, scientific laws, and theories; in any event the attempt to provide some such classification would seem highly desirable. The end-product of such endeavors might fall far short of expectation; it might, at times, seem little more than a labored formalization of much that is exceedingly simple, if not obvious. But there would nonetheless be considerable gain in such linguistic and logical enterprise if carried on in strict awareness of the nature of the data involved. For it would necessitate frequent surveys of criminological researches, discussion of the meanings of terms and of the best mode of definition; it would entail careful criticism of results claimed. It would require constant comparison with related researches. In each of these procedures, many gains should be attainable: in methods of research, in elimination of ambiguity, in precision of results, in appreciation of the nature of scientific inquiry and of organized knowledge, as well as the auxiliary advantages arising from close collaboration.

results from the pervasive failure to integrate those diverse streams of thought that have come to be known as Classical and Positivist Criminology. We may come to grips with this problem most directly by brief comparison of the two major representatives of these Schools — Beccaria and Ferri. Beccaria wrote in 1764, Ferri's most important work appeared in 1884 (*Criminal Sociology*). Beccaria's essay is an avowed polemic, a criticism of the prevailing criminal law and its administration, a plea for mitigation, for rational corrrespondence between the magnitude of the crime and the severity of punishment, a vehement denunciation of torture, secret accusation, and an indiscriminate capital penalty. All of this the 20th century criminologist is wont to dismiss as "politics" or "ethics" — a facile but hardly satisfactory disposition. Beccaria was also interested in the prevention of crimes: "It is better to prevent crimes, than to punish them. That is the fundamental principle of good legislation . . ." He stressed the importance of science to that end. "Would you prevent crimes? Let liberty be attended with knowledge." After noting various methods of prevention, he concludes that "the most certain method of preventing crimes is, to perfect the system of education." Before one summarily dismisses Beccaria from the domain of the criminologist, one had better recall, also, that his little essay led not only to the greatest penal reforms in modern history but also stimulated the production of "a moral science" based on the mathematical formulas implicit in the pain and pleasure principle and in "the greatest good to the greatest number." Many questions of fact and knowledge, relevant to criminology, were undoubtedly little articulated by Beccaria, but they are frequently implied in his argument. 20th Century Criminology, especially in the United States, is so largely a mere application of the European Positivist School, that Ferri, its chief theoretician, needs no summarization. (4) The emphasis

---

4. It is an interesting fact, noted by a number of Europeans, that Positivist Criminology has had a far greater vogue in America that on the continent of its origin. In 1893, in his Introduction to Arthur MacDonald's, *Criminology*, Lombroso noted that "our school has taken such deep root" in America, which consoled him for "the neglect" of the "old world." The author of the book acknowledged "his indebtedness first, and most of all, to Lombroso." Lombroso also wrote the Introduction to Draehm's, *The Criminal—A Scientific Study* (1900). A book of major importance, Parsons, *Responsability for Crime*, (New York: Columbia University Press, 1909) adopted and presented the ideas of the Positivist School in detail. From that time until the beginning of World War II, this School attained its maximum influence in the United States.

on biology, physical anthropology, statistics, climate, economic conditions, etc. are the familiar concerns of contemporary criminologists. What has escaped adequate notice is that the Positivists no less than the Classicalists built their theories on a definite philosophical foundation, with the difference that their "ideologies" are both invalid and, also, dangerous to democratic values.

Certainly any historian of criminology, indeed of social ideas generally, would stress the diverse cultures in which Beccaria and Ferri wrote. He would note that any 18th century criminologist would be deeply concerned in the arbitrary regime that was distinguished by barbaric corporal punishment, in the broad judicial discretion that meant not equity but punishment according to rank and status, and especially in the general, ill-defined laws which provided ample range for indiscriminate death sentences. In a broaded configuration, he would note the rising tide of rationalism, of the Encyclopaedists, of the intellectual revolt against unrestrained government that shortly had its practical incidence in the American and French revolutions. In contrast, Ferri wrote in the halcyon days of Liberalism, the issue of individual protection against political tyranny apparently resolved forever. He wrote well after Comte and in the heyday of Evolution. He wrote after Socialism had made an auspicious beginning. The rather obvious interrelations between criminological theories and contemporaneous culture raise serious questions regarding the possibility of constructing any valid criminology, indeed any social science. These issues cannot be elaborated here, but it is apparent that any sound criminology must at least resolve the conflicts implicit in any attempted integration of the Classical and Positivist Schools. The most serious criticism of 20th Century Criminology is that it has hardly become aware of the existence of this major problem; far from trying to rise above the inhibiting restrictions of the Schools, it has gone whole-hog positivistic.

Some Major Doctrines of Positivist Criminology. Because this has been the dominant influence, the chief avenue to the required resolution of the principal contradictions must be by way of criticism of positivistic criminology. The writer has elsewhere discussed in detail the positivists' efforts to define "crime" in terms of nonlegal criteria (5) and has argued that not only the errors com-

---

5."Prolegomena to a Science of Criminal Law," *University of Pennsylvania Law Review,* 89: 570-575, March, 1941.

CRIMINOLOGY

mitted there but, also, the attempt itself constitute the most important and most typical of positivistic fallacies. Of almost equal importance are the positivistic dogma of determinism stated in terms of the denial of "free-will" (thus injecting metaphysics while asserting the indifference of Science thereto), the assertion, nonetheless, of "social accountability" (with thinly disguised anti-individual bias) and the consequent repudiation of punishment, together with the espousal of "social-defense," characterized by unquestioning adherence to the thesis that any measure *necessary* to "protect Society" (the accused and, of course, the convicted, individual is automatically excluded therefrom) is justifiable. A corollary of these doctrines is that criminology must be confined to external, observable phenomena — a thesis which, it will be noted, is itself unverifiable. It would be possible to document the above very general description in great detail, especially by references to 20th Century Criminology in this country, for the major trends have been so pervasive and so uncritical of the guiding premises that the dominating and distinctive imprint of Positivist Criminology is unmistakable.

II

Critiscism of Positivist Criminology. It is necessary to appraise the influence of positivism on 20th Century Criminology more closely, and thus to describe the chief aspects of the major current problem as precisely as possible in a brief survey such as this. Firstly, and by way of qualifying what follows, it is apparent that "Positivism" is as ambiguous a term as might be imagined to designate the diversity of viewpoints represented by certain writers. This is not the place for detailed refinement of the term, and its meaning will be implied in the following criticism, without any suggestion that it is entirely without merit, or that the only alternative is a return to pre-Copernican methods of studying social problems. Secondly, some correction in perspective may be achieved by recalling that while modern sociology usually acknowledges Comte as its creator, actually Hume and even Hobbes are more significant as regards the theoretical foundations of Positivism. Thirdly, attention must be directed to a central ambiguity in "Positivism," itself, relevant particularly to criminology. For this discipline, as will appear, "law" is of crucial importance; and in modern thought, the "positivistic" interpretation of "law" is of major significance. Specifically, in the Anglo-American culture, John Austin serves most importantly in the development of this (Imperative) theory of law, which insists on the essential difference between "positive" law and morality and on their rigorous separation. The point here is not that this theory thus originated (actually it goes back at least to the Greeks) nor is it that the Imperative School, being preeminently logicians, were almost solely interested in the forms of "positive" law. It is rather that the term "positive" was used by them to distinguish rules sanctioned by the state from ethics. But, it is apparent, from the viewpoint of Positivism, sociological and logical, laws enforced by the state are anything but "positive." They had little place in Comte's work, and, for the logical positivists, they represent a form of assertion, not any reality. Patently, if they have any existence at all, it is not that of any sensible realm. Thus a curious linguistic coincidence has introduced a confusion in criminology that goes to the root of the problem of laying any valid theoretical foundation of the discipline, an inner-contradiction that is not mitigated by the fact that legal positivists share common dogmas with sociological positivists concerning ethics. In short, as regards criminology, Positivism has been dominant in analysis of the central concept, "crime," and, accordingly, in obscuring the nature and range of data denoted by that term. It has confined efforts to comprehend the causes of crime within narrow, superficial limits. It has been equally potent in penology and in reform programs generally. It has helped, one might even say compelled, the exclusion of systematic ethical appraisal. Thus it has fostered difficulties in the way of unifying the field of criminology and has, instead, produced a hopeless diversity in subject-matter. In all of these regards, the influence of Positivism has been a major disaster and it is necessary to understand why this is so.

Generally, it may be said that in each of these effects Positivism has erred as half-truth and as exaggeration. While making vast pretensions to scientific originality and objectivity (the Lombrosian myth has been thoroughly exploded) it has actually adhered to more or less emotional, and therefore, unquestioned preferences, notably, its tenets on "determinism" and its restriction to sensible phenomena, that have impeded significant explanations of the causes of criminal behavior. Its dogmas (Ferri, a lifelong Socialist became an ardent Fascist and hailed Mussolini as God's gift to Italy) biased not only theories concerning prevention, but, also;

combined with its determinism, stigmatized punishment as vengeance — at the same time opening the door to unmitigated cruelty in the name of "measures of safety." Its greatest strength lay in its emphasis on facts and on their careful study, but here its exaggeration led to a thoroughgoing repudiation of criminal law as fortuitous, arbitrary and non-factual — and thus rendered it impossible to erect any theoretical structure, essential to the support of criminology as a distinctive discipline. It is possible to implement this criticism by a constructive outline of the present theoretical requirements of criminology.

The Paramount Need — A Theory of the Subject-Matter of Criminology. The major problem confronting 20th century criminologists is the theoretical determination of the subject-matter of their discipline. As the writer has elsewhere argued, (6) the "actual" rules of criminal law provide the essential framework. Because of its paramount importance and in order to remove the inhibiting influence of Positivism, especialy on this crucial inquiry, some elaboration of this thesis is required.

The literature on the problem is considerable since it constitutes the basic theoretical question not only of legal sociology but even, for some, notably Durkheim, who regarded all social facts as "coercive," of all of sociology. In any event, any theoretical inquiry pointed at the demarcation of a distinctive subject-matter of criminology must, in the first instance, segregate the normative from the non-normative social data ("social" is thus assumed to include both types); secondly, it must explore the differences among the norms with a view to distinguishing legal from non-legal rules; and finally, it must determine whether there is any sound basis for differentiating some legal rules from others, specifically, criminal from private law. It is the writer's position that all of the above steps are defensible and necessary regardless of the fact that at the periphery of the various relevant data, there are fusion and interconnections. It is possible here merely to indicate a few of the criteria that constitute the chief support of the above position.

No elaboration is required of the commonly accepted fact that all groups exhibit behavior under pressure, that they reveal not merely habitual patterns but, also, and more significantly, conduct more or less consciously directed towards socially approved goals, and, in this goal-orientation are guided by numerous influences

---

6. *Ibid.,* pp. 575-579.

that can be explicity stated in terms of normative propositions, which never merely describe what actually happens, but, on the contrary, imply a minimal tension between the significance of the imperatives and the actual relevant patterns of behavior.

Law and Other Social Norms. What must be confronted next is an increasing tendency to equate the norms of all groups, and to designate all of them as "law." In this country we have been rather wont to speak of customs, usages, mores, regulations, etc. not very discriminately and on the assumption that they are quite different from "law." Hence, at least the initial effects of the above emphasis are salutary in the Anglo-American culture where the strict reservation of the term "law" for politically enforced rules has obscured essential similarities of all norms. On the other hand, however, it is necessary to question the validity of employing "law" to include the norms of various groups as well as those of the State (community). As to the prevailing tendency, what needs to be stressed is that little, if any, illumination is provided by differentiation in terms of "political" organization or of rules enforced by "courts" since this merely alters the focus of inquiry, and, indeed, complicates matters by making knowledge of primitive society the condition of any sound judgment. Moreover, if we exclude territoriality, as we must (*e.g.*, Gypsies, Japanese groups in this country) and consider that all societies have appropriate, if very crude, institutions (a loose council, a group of elders, a sole chieftain, arbitrators, etc.) and modes of procedure for the adjudication of conflicts that are rational in their terms, it is apparent that these criteria, "politicality" and "courts," are arbitrarily chosen, that they do not supply essential differences. The alternative, or at least, a supplementary method is comparison of current norms with a view to discovering important factual differences. Although no simple test is available to decide whether any differences that may be noted are "sufficiently" important to support the thesis that criminology must center on social phenomena relevant to rules of criminal law, it is submitted that the norms constituting criminal law are distinguishable from all others, and that consequently the above position is the most defensible one available. The first necessary step (after distinguishing normative from non-normative data) is to distinguish "law" from other social norms in terms of criteria that are socially more significant than those noted above.

As regards various familiar groups — family, club, union, corporation, university, army, etc, — it is agreed that all exhibit "normative facts." It is possible to segregate certain norms as relational, relatively specific, sanctioned, and effective to some appreciable degree, and to designate these as "law". But it is rather apparent that such a demarcation is very inclusive; certainly within this broad category it is possible and important to note various distinctions. The central issues concern the nature of the interests protected and that of the sanctions, but we must also take note of several preliminary criteria. Some norms (of the "State") are all-inclusive, *i. e.*, they apply to all persons within the society, whereas others apply only to members of a narrower group. The former tend to be general, the latter to be specific. In the event of conflict, the former must prevail — they are the supreme rules in the authoritative hierarchy of norms. The former do not depend for their enforcement on the volition of those subject to the rules; the latter do. The distinctive sanction of the former is physical force, of the latter various other "evils." Finally, to render explicit what has been already implied, the interests protected by the former are social in the sense of being inclusive of the entire society; those of the latter are more or less restricted to particular groups within the society.

Each of the above differentiae bristle with moot issues. Thus. *e. g.*, a single religion can be common to an entire society — but its sanction is not force (unless, as did the mediaeval church, it exercises "worldly powers"). Again, we are born into families no less than into society and our subjection to the familial norms seems, at first sight, to be as involuntary as that regarding those of the State. But there are limits on what parents can do, as is evidenced daily in domestic and juvenile courts, *i. e.*, the familial norms are subordinate. Moreover, the sanctions are corrective, disciplinary rather than punitive, although the two are necessarily more or less intermingled. But the crucial difference is that subjection to familial norms terminates at maturity; in a deeper sense, subjection to these rules is not, therefore, aptly termed "involuntary." It is neither that nor voluntary, but rather non-voluntary, and hence does not controvert the general distinction drawn above. Next, as regards characterization of the legal sanction as "force," the chief issues inhere in the nature and divisibility (*i. e.*, ambiguity) of "coercion." Thus churches "impose" penance and excommunication, unions expel or fine and they prevent or threaten livelihood. But there is an essential difference. In the former there is always at least a theoretical area of choice, whereas, as regards "law," as here restricted, it is otherwise; this colors the meaning of even outwardly identical overt sanctions. It is true, of course, that many persons would rather suffer any extent of physical pain than be excommunicated, and, also, that they are so conditioned that they can hardly be said to submit themselves to the ecclesiastical sanctions "voluntarily." So, too, of the laborer who faces great hardships if he rejects the terms offered him. Unquestionably not only these controls but also much more amorphous ones such as public opinion, self-respect and deep-seated loyalties are frequently more effective than the cruder sanctions of the State. Nonetheless it must be recognized that force from which there is no possible escape, where, once the decision is rendered, the sanction operates in utter disregard of any desire, thought or possible choice of the violator, must be contrasted, first with forms of coercion that operate chiefly on the mind, and, secondly, with the enforcement of sanctions where some degree of consent exists even though submission is the only decision apparently available to a rational being; even an apparently unwise or a very cruel alternative still leaves room for choice — witness the martyrs. Coercion in such situations is surely different from that wholly one-sided, inexorable operation of legal sanctions, and this basic fact is rather vaguely signified in the assertion that the State has a "monopoly" of force. It is noteworthy, also, that the force thus employed is approved by the society generally, and that the conditions of its exercise require that it be deferred until after a more or less standardized procedure, necessitating some degree of deliberation, has been employed. Accordingly, it may be concluded that those norms that symbolize social interests, whose sanction is force that operates rather specifically as prescribed, and in total disregard of the offender's volition can be distinguished from other norms, and may properly be designated "rules of law." These rules, viewed as social facts, constitute the data of legal soclogy, which this writer has defined as "a theoretical social science consisting of generalizations regarding social phenomena insofar as they refer to the contents, purposes, applications, and effects of legal rules." (7)

Penal and Civil Law. The final inquiry, in this connection, is whether penal law can be distinguished from "private" (civil) law.

---

7. "Criminology and a Modern Penal Code," *Journal of Criminal Law and Criminology*, 27:4, May-June, 1936.

This problem has recently been discussed in detail by the writer, (8) and it is possible here to give only the barest outline of the considerations which led him to answer the above question affirmatively. The problem is complicated by the common origin of torts (the most relevant branch of private law for the instant problem) and criminal law, by the fact that all law presupposes social interests in some sense, by the lack of complete correspondence between the divisions of positive law and the principles induced from their respective major functions, and by the difficulty of sharply differentiating the sanctions that are actually employed.

If we qualify our inferences accordingly, the following generalizations are defensible concerning the crucial points of comparison: civil law is concerned with individual damage whereas penal law deals with social harms that are not measurable pecuniarily. Civil law is concerned with distribution of economic losses, *i. e.*, with reparation, whereas penal law is confined to punishment for conduct that is morally culpable. The most troublesome questions are provided by harms that are both damaging to individuals and also morally culpable, hence directly violative of social interests. But the correct deduction is not that the two fields "overlap." The immorality of such misconduct is the essence of the criminal harm whereas it is merely incidental to the private damage, and this is the chief avenue to differentiation of the values respectively implemented by the two types of legal rules. The differences drawn in terms of values that are social because violative of general moral principles and those that run in terms of the "individual" as a separate, though social, being are supported by the differences between punishment and other legal sanctions. Penal law is much more frequently integrated in the mores, and it is, also, usually defensible ethically. (The writer's position is that the criminal law should be confined to rules which are ethically defensible, and, also, for the most part, that are integrated in the mores.) The rules of private law are much less frequently defensible on ethical grounds. They represent largely an adaptation to the prevailing economic system, and as such become integrated in the mores, but to a lesser extent than do the penal laws.

The differentiation of normative facts from non-normative ones, of legal norms from other social norms, of penal law from other

---

8. "Interrelations of Criminal Law and Torts," *Columbia Law Review*, 43: 753-779, 967-1001, September and December, 1943.

legal rules provides the distinctive structure of criminology, that which denotes specific social data and establishes their significance for criminology. Clearly this theoretical position does not disparage the importance of social phenomena other than the norms, especially of those that determine the meanings of the penal rules and their changes in the dynamism of a varying social configuration. On the contrary, a corollary of the present thesis is that the meanings of the penal rules must be determined by their relationship to other normative facts, and, generally, in contexts in which language (including technicality), social and economic conditions, public opinion and the forensic conditions that influence the judical process must all receive careful attention. But the major accomplishment is that Sociology of Law is unified by its ultimate reference to "actual" legal rules. Sociology of Criminal Law is, accordingly, that division of legal sociology which deals primarily with social phenomena relevant to the norms of penal law; hence Criminology, in this view, is synonymous with Sociology of Criminal Law.

Legal Rules as Social Facts. In order to diminish the ambiguity hardly avoidable in a very succinct statement, it is important to stress that interpretation of legal rules which treats them as social data. For rules of law are commonly interpreted formally in terms of presriptions, each of which is composed of a description of behavior-circumstances (hypotheses) and a description of treatment-consequences (sanctions), the two descriptions being joined by a verb meaning "must" or "shall be" (imperative). It is only when rules of law are viewed as facts, *i. e.*, as integrated in the mores (the writer has suggested the term "actual law" to distinguish such norms from "formal law") that they constitute phenomena of primary sociological significance. In addition, rules of law usually embody social values, and may be criticized with reference to ethical principles. There are, of course, many rules of law that are not integrated in the mores. This does not mean that these rules are unwarranted or useless since frequently they represent one of several rational solutions, or they cover a very specialized area, concerning which the public is uninformed and indifferent, or they have lost their former actuality and have become mere words. Obviously the status of any rule with reference to moral attitudes and as regards its effectiveness generally is of paramount interest to the legal sociologist. Finally, it is clear that many rules of law are both integrated in the mores and embody social values. This is a phase of the general theory that norms which from one viewpoint are social facts are, from another viewpoint, ethical principles; or more directly, that the mores can usually be defended as ethical. As stated, the criminologist's concern is with criminal law as "facts" and with social data that are significantly related to the rules of penal law; but, as will be argued shortly, this scientific interest is inseparable from, indeed includes, that of evaluation.

The norms of the criminal law have been stressed, not only because they have been dismissed as insignificant by the cruder positivism but, also, because they are essential if the sustaining theory of criminology as a distinctive social discipline is to be formulated. If the primacy of the norms of criminal law is admitted then various other questions, such as that concerning norms other than those of the penal law, of penal laws that are not integrated in the mores, etc., fall into a logical, subordinate position. The foregoing emphasis on legal norms obviously carries certain implications as regards the general body of sociological theory that provides the ultimate theoretical support. Although the irrelevance of "behaviorism" and indeed, of any crude positivism is clearly indicated, it must not be imagined that such stress on non-sensible entities minimizes the importance of any relevant facts, of observation, or of employment of all available skills and techniques of research. It would be superfluous to touch on this, were not the bias so potently restricted to observable phenomena. Thus the generalization that criminology is concerned with "anti-social behavior and the reactions of the group thereto" is correct so far as it goes. But if we wish to plumb the import of such processes, it is necessary to take full cognizance of the essential role of legal norms. They provide criteria necessary for determination of the meaning of the behavioral processes, *i. e.*, of the immediate phenomena of aggression and social reaction; and as urged, they also supply the distinctive framework for the discipline concerned with behavior that is significantly referable to them.

The determination of this major theoretical issue suggests the general boundaries of criminology. It must be concerned, firstly, with the meanings of the rules of criminal law — and this requires investigation of their origins, the legislative history, the relevant preceding and accompanying social problems with emphasis on the opinions and attitudes of various groups, marked out from the more or less passive "majority," and, of course, the authoritative interpretations of the courts and other official organs are essential to this inquiry. Against this background of the social meanings of the various prescriptions under scrutiny it is necessary to study intensively the penetration of the various symbols, relevant affective states, opinions, attitudes, etc., into the particular groups whose behavior is of special interest. This requires an elaboration of the various modes of activity that emphasize correspondence with or divergence from the general social "ideology." Since it may be assumed that there will always be both correspondence and divergence in any given society, the need, as regards "culture conflict," is accordingly, two-fold: firstly, to supplement studies pointed in that direction with others on "culture correspondence" and, secondly, to carry on the most detailed investigations possible into the various relevant social forces — religions, educational institutions, newspapers read, local traditions including the comeraderie of gangs, local leadership, etc. — until the point is reached where a vivid, realistic insight into the local meanings of the general social normative systems, especially those embodied in the criminal law, can be secured. The goals of the above two sorts of investigation are quite definite ones — determination of the meanings of the prevailing criminal norms in the society generally, and their specific interpretation by the particular group under study.

Etiology of Criminal Behavior. The next major step in the "explanation" of criminal behavior brings us directly to the problem that is most often discussed: the etiology of such behavior. One purpose of the above discussion of the meaning of the norms and their interpretations by the groups studied has been to insist that criminal behavior cannot be understood without the detailed investigations indicated; that it is futile to probe for causes before there is clear understanding of the nature of the external phenomena (individual behavior and social reactions) whose occurrence it is sought to explain. (Criminologists have frequently fashioned better than they deserved so that many extant studies can be placed in a theoretically significant frame-work, *e. g.*, even when they have argued that criminal laws are merely fortuitous or arbitrary, they have usually nonetheless devoted their energies to study the etiology of violations of criminal laws — in fact, in the writer's opinion, they have overdone this to the exclusion of other essential study.) If this primary theoretical requirement is recognized, it is possible to discuss "causation" profitably.

CRIMINOLOGY

The etiology of criminal behavior obviously raises all of the difficult general problems of social causation in the special contexts of phenomena relevant to criminal law. As regards the etiology of crime, such utter diversity of opinion exists as to include the narrowest particularisms, *e. g.*, defective glands, and the broadest of generalities, such as "culture conflict." The one becomes irrelevant when its probability all but disappears, and the other, highly suggestive in the general direction of research, is too vague to function as a theory of causation. The problem is obviously a major concern of all theorists in this field. Since the etiology of criminal behavior is merely a phase of the general problem of social causation, this is assuredly not the place for elaboration of the fundamental issues. That they are of prime importance for criminology is a further indication of the superficiality of those who would abolish general social science and restrict the field to special disciplines that would be more than ever centered on the solution of practical social problems. (Indeed a major defect of 20th Century Criminology is the acceptance by many researchers of the above limitation on their inquiries, in effect, of a ban on their theorizing — with the result that the articulation of assumptions and hypotheses is conspicuous by its absence, and the end-product is much too frequently a description of immediate data rather than generalization regarding phenomena included in carefully defined concepts, with due attention to the requirements of any "objective" methods of investigation and to the possibility of corroboration.)

Because the reaction from the simplistic mechanics of the social positivists is frequently, and understandably, extreme, it is necessary to emphasize that the alternative is by no means pure subjectivism that permits no possible verification. For, concerning the etiology of criminal behavior, what must be stressed is that the substitution of "motivation" for "cause" does not imply that 'explanation" is wholly different as regards social phenomena. Not only does human behavior run in habits, usages and institutions, *i. e.*, in regular patterns that are describable in general terms, but also, motives, once they begin to operate, may defensibly be regarded as functioning with as great certainty as causes. Hence it is clearly necessary for adequate explanation of criminal behavior to discover and to describe generally the pertinent conditions of such conduct — and the premises and hypotheses, so far as that objective is concerned, are precisely those of physical science. In this viewpoint the differences in the discoverable knowledge inhering in degrees of precision result from inability to segregate the operative variables rather than from the presence of fortuitous or spontaneous forces that are distinctive.

The major question, however, concerns the adequacy of explanation if the criminologist stops short with generalized description of the patterns and conditions of criminal behavior. Certainly it is a fact that except when the criminologist tries out his hand at epistemology, he is anything but the "objective" scientist portrayed in exhortations on methods. His common strictures on punishment should make this sufficiently obvious, but the like is apparent also in his assessment of the causes of criminal behavior. Thus, actually, the patent inadequacy of explanation of criminal behavior that is supposed to be rigorously scientific is increased by the unavowed employment of hypotheses that are evidently not "causal" in this sense. The prized, purely scientific explanations (if they existed) would be grossly inadequate because they would not account for enormously important segments of criminal conduct. For in our efforts to "really" understand criminal behavior, we leave the role of observer and "assimilate" the personality of the offender. From this perspective "conditions" merely set the scene; they limit or encourage, and they transform the expression of human desire. It is not that the conditions are mere "occasions" rather than true causes, but that fuller understanding requires participating in the personality as an acting force after the physical and social conditions are known. Logically there may be a basic antithesis between causal explanation proceeding on premises of universal determinism, and that derived from sympathetic participation in the dynamic functioning of the human personality. Actually, however, these two types of explanation supplement each other, and both are regularly relied upon unless barred by arbitrary sophistication. We want to know the general conditions, physical, biological and social, that influence the specific problem-solving and media of expression exemplified in criminal behavior; and we want, also, to know the inner processes of reasoning and evaluation that precede and accompany the various modes of activity. Hence the rising interest in the psychoanalytic technique, not only as a description of psychologically significant conditions supplementing external ones, but, also, as coming to close grips with the inner mental processes. Ultimately, whatever the terminology, this essential complement to

CRIMINOLOGY

the scientific causal explanations must deal with conduct designated in traditional metaphysics as manifestations of "free will," and the importance of this phase of criminal behavior is attested not only by the work of great novelists and dramatists but, also, as noted, by psychoanalysis (not as therapy but as method of investigation). It will not do simply to assert that science must be restricted to external conditions that "cause"; for, whatever the direction of the dialectics, whether we view "freedom of will" as an essential fact to be described in terms and on hypotheses that are relevant to the distinctive phenomena of personality, or whether we view "freedom" simply as an inevitable limitation on the precision of existing scientific methods and knowledge, and hence as a mere margin of error, the fact is that we remain unsatisfied with explanation that leaves untouched the inner states, the reasonings and rationalizations, the form in which the problems were presented, and in which various motives came into being, in short, the dynamism of the thinking, aspiring, problem-solving personality. We cannot apprehend this "process," by rigorous scientific explanation, alone, because such knowledge of it as we have, clearly indicates that the process is not limited by preceding or accompanying conditions — else we could not intelligently say that anyone ever *solved* any problem. If it offends one's scientific sensibilities to probe sympathetically into this inner realm of personal experience for further insight into criminal behavior, then we can only conclude that the major source of such knowledge will continue to be the imaginative portayals of the novelist and playwrite. But literature, however suggestive, is not social science. However valuable as penetrating insight and as a repository of possible theories concerning criminality, its limitations, aside from dramatization of the facts, are those of many avowed criminological researches — the theories employed are not expressed or they are not tested; no serious efforts are made to generalize from the particulars examined, and, of course, there is hardly any occasion for any summation that can even remotely be called a "systematization" of knowledge.

Although exploration into the inner processes of social and individual action indicate a reliance on art rather than on scientific method, this does not mean that such explanation is necessarily subjective and beyond criticism. There is always the appeal to common sense, to trained imagination and to experience, *i. e.*, to the same tribunals that arbitrate the claims of "truth" in any field. The theories employed can be articulated, the terms and concepts clearly defined and uniformly employed, and the evidence relied on can be described in detail. In addition, if it be granted that the various "solutions" reached by offenders, manifested in their criminal behavior, can be criticized by reference to other possible ones, it becomes both relevant and necessary to make such appraisals. The underlying premises are that more or less "correct" answers to human problems are discoverable, that human minds are rational, *i. e.*, able to discover such answers. Thus explanation of criminal behavior moves from the sphere of general description to that of criticism on the basis of objective standards of truth and morality, or, more precisely, the generalized description is itself largely influenced by the latter criticism.

The Role of Values in Criminology. Even more egregiously than as regards the significance of legal rules, 20th Century Criminology has erred in its handling of the value problem, correct solution of which is essential not only for any adequate explanation of criminal behavior, but, also, for sound criticism of practically every other criminological problem. Not mere misinterpretation confronts us here, but either complete indifference to morality or out-and-out repudiation of its relevance for criminology. The net products have been a stress on irrationality posited solely on the affective phases of human nature, and a crude utilitarianism, restated in terms of pursuit of interests or dominance of ruling classes, and signifying ultimately the primacy of brute force. The conflicts between the criminologist's professed scientific predilections and his common sense are plain. As "scientist" the contemporary criminologist is not concerned with ethics — yet as an ardent proponent of positivistic sociology, he embraces determinism. He is interested only in mores (not ethics) and since these vary temporally and spatially, the criminologist is a relativist but in the spirit of Carpenter, Darrow and Ross, he becomes a vehement evangelist when he appraises the misconduct of the rich and powerful, even when, admittedly, they have violated neither mores nor penal law. He pretends reliance on verifiable data in his complete repudiation of "punishment." but in his espousal of rehabilitation and "protection to society," he exhibits a strange combination of "humanitarianism" and stark calculated cruelty. The net result is self-deception and a degree of inconsistency patent to any one except the devotees of the cult. In fear of ancient superstitions, impenetrable mysticisms and dogmatic theologies, many contemporary criminologists have taken refuge in dogmas that are equally indefensible.

CRIMINOLOGY

Admittedly, dogma cannot be refuted by counter-dogma. Anyone who advances the thesis that moral values comprise a central portion of any sound criminology must therefore recognize that the prevalent bias against this position is far from groundless. The recourse of the critic of contemporary criminology as well as that of any other social theorist can only be defense of that position which is least vulnerable rather than of one that is scientifically demonstrable. Hence it should not be thought presumptuous to ask the criminologist to consider himself a representative sample of the "data" he studies. In his research he reveals qualities that cannot be described in terms that denote bare physical movements or physiological functioning. In his efforts to discover laws of criminal behavior and to predict the probabilities of conduct consequent on release, he exemplifies processes that are quite unlike those described as tropisms or as mechanical adjustments to the drives for self-preservation and growth. Much of human behavior that seems superficially remote from instinctual gratification is, of course, fairly accountable for as satisfaction of "higher" desires. So, too, as regards a large part of bizarre professional vocabulary whose least function is not implementation of status and prestige. But when all such allowances are made there remain the roles of truth-seeker and reformer, as well as methods whose fair characterization summon such adjectives as "humane," "rehabilitative." There remain the words each thoughtful person addresses to himself to distinguish what he wants from what is "good," and the actions stimulated by his own interests from what is "right." If these matters constitute an essential part of any explanation of the criminologist's conduct, which he would regard as necessary though not sufficient, perhaps he can be persuaded in increasing number that his "analysis of criminal behavior" should be concerned with beings who are essentially like himself. If the hypotheses that human nature is distinctive, that personality implies rationality, that human conduct embodies degrees of autonomy and self-control, that we deal with beings who, like the social scientist, are problem-solvers, generalizers, and prone to effort that becomes understandable only in terms of value-experience — if these hypotheses fit the realities more closely than do the prevalent ones, the criminologist's job becomes more difficult than the elaboration of positivistic formulas, and it probably does not lead to the Science of Man dreamed of since Hume; but it does promise greater actual accomplishment both in undestanding and in reform. The prevalent preoccupation with scientific method and the consequent neglect of man as a problem-solving, value-experiencing person means that some of the most significant data have been consistently ignored. The inadequacy of explanation derived solely from the use of scientific methods would be obvious, but where decent contributions have been made they have resulted from disregard of rigorous scientific limitations. Indeed it is not insignificant in this connection, that the basic tenet of positivism — that only what can be verified by observation is true — is itself unverifiable. In any event it should be evident to common sense, if not to sophisticated sociologism, that somehow we have got to get at the conduct that is distinctively human, and that any discipline which ignores these social facts is grossly inadequate. There can be no question that the approach indicated above will lead to a new sort of criminology, that many problems, hitherto completely neglected, would move into the very center of scholarly interest, and that explanation would be required that, though lacking the current insignia of the discoveries of "scientific research" would nonetheless or even because of that very fact, reveal deeper layers of motivation and human adaptation than any that have thus far been discovered. The tendencies in this direction already exist; what is required is their unabashed pursuit, freed from the inhibitions of positivistic criminology, and implemented by refinement in techniques, much closer attention to the description of the data relied upon, and detailed reporting of diagnoses and results.

The type of analysis indicated suggests an additional major division of criminology. This has been variously designated as "criminal policy," "legislation," etc. The point to be urged is not so much that, as regards legislation, treatment, etc., criminologists should be among those who are most competent to formulate correct policies, and hence could render a valuable service — that much is plain. Rather it is that the failure to deal explicitly with the data of criminology as problems of ethics has resulted inevitably in crude and unavowed indulgence in such criticism. For the stubborn refusal to deal with problems of policy, as such, has confused these questions with those concerning fact. Since it is more apparent in criminology than in most other social disciplines that questions of policy are constantly agitated, no claim of scientific restriction can be persuasive. What is required is explicit recognition that criminologists have always been and are now deeply interested in criminal policy, *i. e.*, in ethical criticism of accepted

CRIMINOLOGY

policies and in the discovery of better ones. If this should be frankly recognized and acted upon, there would be a concomitant awareness of the patent fact that philosophy is an essential adjunct to an adequate criminology. The challenge to the 20th century criminologist is to articulate his philosophical position in so far as it is relevant to the data and theories of his discipline. The least increment will be a keen awareness of the differences between a philosophical interpretation and generalized description of behavior.

Penology. This need is most readily apparent in 20th century penology. The prevalent academic attitude — it is hardly more — is that punishment is a useless relic of barbarism, a mere symbol of man's lust for vengeance, hence lacking in any rational support. The plain fact is that no such conclusion is established; the vehemence of the assertion is accompanied by fast and loose play with history and statistics. The issue is important especially because of the appeal to altruism, but no show of sentiment, however deeply felt, can keep the bald assertions from being more than sheer pretensions to scientific knowledge. The usual, perfunctory resort to history stresses past torture and the continuance of criminality. But it is obviously fallacious to confuse punishment with cruelty. And, passing over that elementary matter, it is not improbable that past rigorous methods did diminish criminality. (9) Indeed, it is widely believed that crimes of violence have diminished while nonviolent ones may have increased. But the question is enormously complicated by increase in population, in penal laws, in changes in efficiency of police, by invention and a whole complex web of cultural forces that render precise determinations highly dubious, if not utterly impossible. When the focus of proof is shifted to relatively contemporary data, the emphasis is on recidivism. But here, too, the sweeping repudiation of punishment rests on similar shifting devious sands. If the record of the total number of persons convicted of crimes, even serious ones, is examined, only a small percentage is found to be repeaters. The bulk of offenders are from 17 to 22 years old, and they have been infrequently or not at all penalized. As they get older their criminality diminishes, and since they are still relatively young men in their thirties when it drops off quite sharply, it is fair to conclude that their later law-abidingness

---

9. Giddings, at least, was consistent in this regard. See F. H. Giddings, "The Relation of the Criminal to Society," in *Proceedings of the Academy of Political Science,* (New York: Columbia University, 1911), 1:561.

is not due to the onset of arterial sclerosis. It is even permissible to think that many of them have learned their lesson, that it is not pleasant or profitable to spend years in a penal institution.

Of all the palpable falsehoods of positivistic penology none is so perverse as the dogma that "crime is a disease," that all criminals are sick persons who must be treated in hospitals. The notion wears a superficial cloak of humanity since it abjures the infliction of punishment as senseless, explainable only by reference to the brute nature of impassioned animals bent on vengeance. (10) This grain of merit, the appeal to magnanimity and to the utopian instincts of reformers, is the very thing that renders the dogma dangerous. But even the slightest skepticism must raise serious doubts concerning the validity of the current penology. The recently increasing awareness that criminal behavior is not at all confined to the poor or otherwise unfortunate excludes this simplistic particularism. Especially in the past few years and on an international scale, some of the ablest people have been the greatest criminals, and it is not insignificant that criminologists who have long advocated the positivist penology, reveal no inclination to view the "international gangsters" as diseased, to state it mildly.

The whole problem of treatment is so plainly related to ethics that one would expect at least a clear articulation of the particular philosophical position maintained. The level of thinking on this problem is indicated by the fact that those who espouse only "deterrence" refuse to confront their actual assumption of the "guilt" of those punished, whereas those who cling exclusively to reformation not only indulge in this same assumption, but also pretend that scientific knowledge on rehabilitation exists. Nor do the latter consider the consequence of their position regarding the cases of the one-time murderer and of the inveterate petty offender. It is not possible within the limits of this paper to provide the constructive outlines of a defensible philosophy of punishment. The major point, for the present, must be not to establish the efficacy of punishment or to justify it on moral grounds, but rather to stress what should be almost self-evident, namely, that as regards the entire problem of "treatment," 20th Century Criminology is so limited by unexpressed and deeply-held emotional preferences

---

10. *Cf.* "'Punishment' has been restored to the code to replace the term, 'measure of social defense' which had been used formerly." J. N. Hazard, "Soviet Textbooks on Law," *Slavonic and East European Review*, 31:215-16, 1943.

CRIMINOLOGY

as to preclude any possibility of sound investigation. This is particularly unfortunate because the treatment of offenders provides exceptional opportunities for research. But, just as in other divisions of criminology, the essential condition of significant discovery is sound theory.

SELECTED BIBLIOGRAPHY

Alexander, F., and H. Staub, *The Criminal, the Judge and the Public*, (New York: The Macmillan Co., 1931).

Barnes, Harry Elmer, and J. P. Shalloo, "Modern Theories of Criminology and Penology," Harry Elmer Barnes, Howard Becker, and Frances B. Becker, eds., *Contemporary Social Theory*, (New York: Appleton-Century Co., 1940), pp. 688-753.

Dostoevsky, F., *Crime and Punishment*, (New York: The Macmillan Co., 1937).

Ewing, A. C., *The Morality of Punishment*, (London: 1929).

Glueck, Sheldon and Eleanor, *One Thousand Juvenile Delinquents*, (Cambridge: Harvard University Press, 1934).

Hall, Jerome, *Theft, Law and Society*, (Boston: Little, Brown and Co., 1935).

Hall, Jerome, "Prolegomena to a Science of Criminal Law," *University of Pennsylvania Law Review*, 89: 549-580, March, 1941.

Hall, Jerome, "Crime as social Reality," *Annals of the American Academy of Political and Social Science*, 217: 1-11, September, 1941.

Oppenheimer, Heinrich, *The Rationale of Punishment*, (London: 1913).

Reckless, Walter C., *The Etiology of Delinquent and Criminal Behavior*, (New York: Social Science Research Council, 1943).

Sellin, Thorsten, *Culture Conflict and Crime*, (New York: Social Science Research Council, 1938).

Shaw, Clifford R., et al., *Brothers in Crime*, (Chicago: University of Chicago Press, 1938).

Sutherland, Edwin H. *Principles of Criminology*, (Philadelphia J. B. Lippincott Co., 1939).

Jerome Hall, Jur. Sc. D. (Columbia), S. J. D. (Harvard) is Professor of Law at Indiana University, and was formerly Professor of Criminal Law and Criminology at Louisiana State University. He is U. S. Secretary of the Criminal Law Section of the International Society of Comparative Law, a Member of the Special Committee on Civil Liberties of the Social Science Research Council, and Chairman of the Committee on a 20th Century Legal Philosophy Series of the Association of American Law Schools.

Dr. Hall is author of *Theft, Law and Society* (1935), editor of *Readings in Jurisprudence* (1938), and has published numerous monographs and articles in legal and social science periodicals, the most recent of which is "Interrelations of Criminal Law and Torts," *Columbia Law Review*, 43: 753-779, 967-1001, September and December, 1943.

CHAPTER XIII

THE SOCIOLOGY OF KNOWLEDGE

by

ROBERT K. MERTON

I

The last generation has witnessed the emergence of a special field of sociological inquiry: the sociology of knowledge (*Wissenssoziologie*). The term "knowledge" must be interpreted very broadly indeed, since studies in this area have dealt with virtually the entire gamut of cultural products (ideas, ideologies, juristic and ethical beliefs, philosophy, science, technology). But whatever the conception of "knowledge," the central orientation of this discipline remains largely the same: it is primarily concerned with the relations between knowledge and other existential factors in the society or culture. General and even vague as this formulation of the central focus may be, a more specific statement will not

SOCIOLOGY OF KNOWLEDGE

serve to include the diverse approaches which have been developed.

Manifestly, then, the sociology of knowledge is concerned with problems which have had a long prehistory. So much is this the case, that this discipline has found its first historian, Ernst Gruenwald. (1) But our primary concern is not with the many antecedents of current theories. There are indeed few present-day observations which have not found previous expression in suggestive apercus. King Henry IV was being reminded that "Thy wish was father, Harry, to that thought" only a few years before Bacon was writing that "The human understanding is no dry light but receives an infusion from the will and affections; whence proceed sciences which may be called 'sciences as one would'." And Nietzsche had set down a host of aphorisms on the ways in which "needs" determined the "perspectives" through which we interpret the world so that even sense perceptions are permeated with value-preferences. The prehistory of Wissenssoziologie only goes to support Whitehead's observation that "to come very near to a true theory, and to grasp its precise application, are two very different things, as the history of science teaches us. Everything of importance has been said before by somebody who did not discover it."

Quite apart from its historical and intellectual origins, there is the further question of the basis of contemporary interest in the sociology of knowledge. As is well known, the sociology of knowledge, as a distinct discipline, has been especially cultivated in Germany and France. Only within the last decades, have American sociologists come to devote rapidly increasing attention to problems in this area. The growth of publications and, as a decisive test of its academic respectability, the increasing number of doctoral dissertations in the field partly testify to this sharp rise of interest.

An immediate, and obviously inadequate, explanation of this development would point to the recent transfer of European sociological thought by sociologists who have lately come to this country. To be sure, these scholars were among the culture-bearers of *Wissenssoziologie*. But this merely provided availability of these

---

1. Nothing will be said of this prehistory in this paper. Ernst Gruenwald provides a sketch of the early developments, at least from the so-called era of Enlightenment in *Das Problem der Soziologie des Wissens*, (Wien-Leipzig: Wilhelm Braumueller, 1934). For a recent survey, see H. Otto Dahlke, "The Sociology of Knowledge," H. E. Barnes, Howard and F. B. Becker, eds., *Contemporary Social Theory*, (New York: Appleton-Century, 1940), pp. 64-89.

conceptions and no more accounts for their actual acceptance than it would in any other instance of culture diffusion. American thought proved receptive to the sociology of knowledge largely because it dealt with problems, concepts, and theories which are increasingly pertinent to our contemporary social situation, because our society has come to have certain characteristics of those European societies in which the discipline was initially developed.

The sociology of knowledge takes on pertinence under a definite complex of social and cultural conditions. (2) With increasing social conflict, differences in the values, attitudes and modes of thought of groups develop to the point where the orientation which these groups previously had in common is overshadowed by incompatible differences. Not only do there develop different universes of discourse, but the existence of any one universe challenges the validity and legitimacy of the others. The coexistence of these conflicting perspectives and interpretations within the same society leads to an active and reciprocal *distrust* between groups. Within a context of distrust, one no longer inquires into the content of beliefs and assertions to determine whether they are valid or not, one no longer confronts the assertions with relevant evidence, but introduces an entirely new question: how does it happen that these views are maintained? Thought becomes functionalized; it is interpreted in terms of its psychological or economic or social or racial sources and functions. In general, this type of functionalizing occurs when statements are doubted, when they appear so palpably implausible or absurd or biased that one need no longer examine the evidence for or against the statement but only the grounds for it being asserted at all. (3) Such alien statements are "explained by" or "imputed to" special interests, unwitting motives, distorted perspectives, so-

---

2. See Karl Mannheim, *Ideology and Utopia*, (New York: Harcourt, Brace, 1936), pp. 5-12; 45; P. A. Sorokin, *Social and Cultural Dynamics*, (New York: American Book Co., 1937), II, pp. 412-413.

3. Freud had observed this tendency to seek out the "origins" rather than to test the validity of statements which seem palpably absurd to us. Thus, suppose someone maintains that the center of the earth is made of jam. "The result of our intellectual objection will be a *diversion of our interests; instead of their being directed on to the investigation itself*, as to whether the interior of the earth is really made of jam or not, *we shall wonder what kind of man it must be who can get such an idea into his head . . .*" Sigmund Freud, *New Introductory Lectures*, (New York: W. W. Norton, 1933), p. 49. On the social level, a radical difference of outlook of various social groups leads not only to ad hominem attacks, but also to "functionalized explanations."

cial position, etc. In folk thought, this involves reciprocal attacks on the integrity of opponents; in more systematic thought, it leads to reciprocal "ideological analyses." On both levels, it feeds upon and nourishes collective insecurities.

Within this social context, an array of interpretations of man and culture which share certain common presuppositions finds widespread currency. Not only ideological analysis and Wissenssoziologie, but also psycho-analysis, Marxism, semanticism, propaganda analysis, Paretanism and, to some extent, functional analysis have, despite their other differences, a similar outlook on the role of ideas. On the one hand, there is the realm of verbalization and ideas (ideologies, rationalizations, emotive expressions, distortions, "folklore," derivations), all of which are viewed as expressive or derivative or deceptive (of self and others), all of which are functionally related to some substratum. On the other hand, are the variously conceived substrata (relations of production, social position, basic impulses, psychological conflict, interests and sentiments, interpersonal relations, and residues). And throughout runs the basic theme of the unwitting determination of ideas by the substrata; the emphasis on the distinction between the real and the illusory, between reality and appearance in the sphere of human thought, belief, and conduct. And whatever the intention of the analysts, their analyses tend to have an acrid quality: they tend to indict, secularize, ironicize, satirize, alienate, devalue the intrinsic content of the avowed belief or point of view. Consider only the overtones of terms chosen in these contexts to refer to beliefs, ideas and thought: vital lies, myths, illusions, derivations, folklore, rationalizations, ideologies, verbal facade, pseudo-reasons, etc.

What these schemes of analysis have in common is the practice of discounting the *face value* of statements, beliefs, idea-systems by re-examining them within a new context which supplies the "real meaning." Statements ordinarily viewed in terms of their manifest content are "debunked," whatever the intention of the analyst, by relating this content to attributes of the speaker or the society in which he lives. The professional iconoclast, the trained debunker, the ideological analyst and their respective systems of thought thrive in a society where large groups of people have already become alienated from common values; where separate universes of discourse are linked with reciprocal distrust. Ideological analysis systematizes the lack of faith in reigning symbols which has become widespread;

hence its pertinence and popularity. The ideological analyst does not so much create a following as he "speaks for" a following to whom his analyses "make sense," i.e. conform to their previously unanalyzed experience. (4)

In a society where reciprocal distrust finds such folk-expression as "what's in it for him?"; where "buncombe" and "bunk" have been idiom for nearly a century and "debunk" for some 17 years; where advertising and propaganda have generated active resistance to the acceptance of statements at face-value; where pseudo- Gemeinschaft behavior as a device for improving one's economic and political position is documented in a best-seller on how to win "friends" who may be influenced; where social relationships are increasingly instrumentalized so that the individual comes to view others as seeking primarily to control, manipulate and exploit him; where growing cynicism involves a progressive detachment from significant group relationships and a considerable degree of self-estrangement; where uncertainty about one's own motives is voiced in the indecisive phrase, "I may be rationalizing, but..."; where defenses against traumatic disillusionment may consist in remaining permanently disillusioned by reducing expectations about the integrity of others through discounting their motives and abilities in advance; — in such a society, systematic ideological analysis and a derived sociology of knowledge take on a socially grounded pertinence and cogency. And American academicians, presented with schemes of analysis which appear to order the chaos of cultural conflict, contending values and points of view, have promptly seized upon and assimilated these analytical schemes.

The "Copernican revolution" in this area of inquiry consisted of the hypothesis that not only error or illusion or unauthenticated belief but also the discovery of truth was socially (historically) conditioned. So long as attention was focussed on the social determinants of ideology, illusion, myth, and moral norms, the sociology

---

4. The concept of *pertinence* was assumed by the Marxist harbingers of *Wissenssoziologie*. "The theoretical conclusions of the Communists are in no way based on ideas or principles that have been invented, or discovered, by this or that would-be universal reformer. *They merely express, in general terms, the actual relations* springing from an existing class struggle, from a historical movement going on under our very eyes..." Karl Marx and Friedrich Engels, *The Communist Manifesto*, in *Karl Marx, Selected Works*, (Moscow: Cooperative Publishing Society, 1935), I, p. 219.

SOCIOLOGY OF KNOWLEDGE

of knowledge could not emerge. It was abundantly clear that in accounting for error or uncertified opinion, some extra-theoretic factors were involved, that some special explanation was needed, since the reality of the object could not account for error. In the case of confirmed or certified knowledge, however, it was long assumed that this could be adequately accounted for in terms of a direct object-interpreter relation. The sociology of knowledge came into being with the signal hypothesis that even "truths" were to be held socially accountable, were to be related to the historical society in which they emerged.

To outline even the main currents of the sociology of knowledge in brief compass is to present none adequately and to do violence to all. The diversity of formulations — of a Marx or Scheler or Durkheim; the varying problems — from the social determination of categorial systems to that of class-bound political ideologies; the enormous differences in scope — from the all-encompassing categorizing of intellectual history to the social location of the thought of Negro scholars in the last decades; the various limits assigned to the discipline — from a comprehensive sociological epistemology to the empirical relations of particular social structures and ideas; the proliferation of concepts — ideas, belief-systems, positive knowledge, thought, systems of truth, superstructure, etc.; the diverse methods of validation — from plausible but undocumented imputations to meticulous historical and statistical analysis — in the light of all this, an effort to deal with both analytical apparatus and empirical studies in a few pages must sacrifice detail to scope.

To introduce a basis of comparability among the welter of studies which have appeared in this field, we must adopt some scheme of analysis. The following paradigm is intended as a step in this direction. It is, undoubtedly, a partial and, it is to be hoped, a temporary, classification which will soon disappear as it gives way to an improved and more exacting analytical model. But it does provide a basis for taking an inventory of extant findings in the field; for indicating contradictory, contrary and consistent results; setting forth the conceptual apparatus now in use; determining the nature of problems which have occupied workers in this field; assessing the character of the evidence which they have brought to bear upon these problems; ferreting out the characteristic lacunae and weaknesses in current types of interpretation. Full-fledged theory in the sociology of knowledge lends itself to classification in terms of the following paradigm.

TWENTIETH CENTURY SOCIOLOGY

PARADIGM FOR THE SOCIOLOGY OF KNOWLEDGE

1. *WHERE is the existential basis of mental productions located?*
   a. *social bases*: social position, class, generation, occupational role, mode of production, group structures (university, bureaucracy, academies, sect, political party), "historical situation," interests, society, ethnic affiliation, social mobility, power structure, social processes, (competition, conflict, etc.).
   b. *cultural bases*: values, ethos, "climate of opinion," Volksgeist, Zeitgeist, type of culture, culture mentality, Weltanschauungen, etc.
2. *WHAT mental productions are being sociologically analyzed?*
   a. *spheres of*: moral beliefs, ideologies, ideas, the categories of thought, philosophy, religious beliefs, social norms, positive science, technology, etc.
   b. *which aspects are analyzed*:
   their selection (foci of attention), level of abstraction, presuppositions (what is taken as "data" and what as "problematical"), conceptual content, models of verification, objectives of intellectual activity, etc.
3. *HOW are mental productions related to the existential basis?*
   a. *Causal or functional relations*: determination, cause, correspondence, necessary condition, conditioning, functional interdependence, interaction, dependence, etc.
   b. *Symbolic or organismic or meaningful relations*:
   consistency, harmony, coherence, unity, congruence, compatibility (and antonyms); expression, realization, symbolic expression, *Strukturzusammenhang*, structural identities, inner connection, stylistic analogies, logicomeaningful integration, identity of meaning, etc.
   c. *Ambiguous terms to designate relations*:
   correspondence, reflection, bound up with, in close connection with, etc.
4. *WHY? manifest and latent functions imputed to these existentially conditioned mental productions.*
   a. to maintain power, promote stability, orientation, exploitation, obscure actual social relationships, provide motivation, canalize behavior, divert criticism, deflect hostility, reassurance, control nature, coordinate social relationships, etc.
5. *WHEN do the imputed relations of the existential base and knowledge obtain?*
   a. historicist theories (confined to particular societies or cultures).
   b. general analytical theories.

There are, of course, additional categories for classifying and analyzing studies in the sociology of knowledge, which cannot be fully explored in this paper. Thus, the perennial problem of the implications of existential influences upon knowledge for the epistemological status of that knowledge has been, from the very outset, hotly debated. "Solutions" to this problem, which assume that a sociology of knowledge is necessarily a sociological theory of knowledge, range from the claim that the "genesis of thought has no necessary relation to its validity" to the extreme relativist position that truth is "merely" a function of a social or cultural basis, that it rests solely upon a social consensus and, consequently, that any culturally accepted theory of truth has a claim to validity equal to that of any other.

But the foregoing paradigm serves to organize the distinctive approaches and conclusions in this field sufficiently for our purposes.

The chief approaches to be considered here are those of Marx, Scheler, Mannheim, Durkheim and Sorokin. Current work in this area is largely oriented toward one or another of these theorists, either through a modified application of their conceptions or through counter-developments. Other sources of studies in this field indigenous to American thought, such as pragmatism, will be advisedly omitted, since they have not yet been formulated with specific reference to the sociology of knowledge nor have they been embodied in research to any notable extent.

Where is the Existential Basis Located? A central point of agreement in all approaches to the sociology of knowledge is the thesis that thought has an existential basis insofar as it is not immanently determined and insofar as one or another of its aspects can be derived from extra-cognitive factors. But this is merely a formal consensus, which gives away to a wide variety of theories concerning the nature of the existential basis.

In this respect, as in others, Marxism is the storm-center of Wissenssoziologie. Without entering into the exegetic problem of closely identifying "Marxism" — we have only to recall Marx' "je ne suis pas un marxiste" — we can trace out its formulations primarily in the writings of Marx and Engels. Whatever other changes may have occurred in the development of their theory during the half-century of their work, they consistently held fast to the thesis that "relations of production" constitute the "real foundation" for the superstructure of ideas. "The mode of production in material life determines the general character of the social, political and intellectual processes of life. It is not the consciousness of men that determines their existence, but on the contrary, their social existence determines their consciousness." (5) In seeking to functionalize ideas, i.e., to relate the ideas of individuals to their sociological bases

---

5. Karl Marx, *A Contribution to the Critique of Political Economy*, (Chicago: C. H. Kerr, 1904), pp. 11-12.

Marx locates them within the class structure. He assumes, not so much that other influences are not at all operative, but that class is a primary determinant and, as such, the single most fruitful point of departure for analysis. This he makes explicit in his first preface to *Capital*: "... here individuals are dealt with *only in so far* as they are the personifications of economic categories, embodiments of particular class-relations and class-interests." (6) In abstracting from other variables and in regarding men in their economic and class roles, Marx hypothesizes that these roles are primary determinants and thus leaves as an open question *the extent to which they adequately account for thought and behavior in any given case.* In point of fact, one line of development of Marxism, from the early *German Ideology* to the latter writings of Engels, consists in a progressive definition (and delimitation) of the extent to which the relations of production do in fact condition knowledge and forms of thought.

However, both Marx and Engels, repeatedly, and with increasing insistence, emphasized that ideologies of a given social stratum need not stem only from persons who are *objectively* located in that stratum. As early as the *Communist Manifesto,* Marx and Engels had indicated that as the ruling class approaches dissolution, "a small section ...joins the revolutionary class ...Just as therefore, at an earlier period, a section of the nobility went over to the bourgeoisie, so now a portion of the bourgeoisie goes over to the proletariat, and in particular, a portion of *the bourgeois ideologists,* who have *raised themselves* to the level of comprehending theoretically the historical movement as a whole." (7)

Ideologies are socially located by analyzing their perspectives and presuppositions and determining how problems are construed: from the standpoint of one or another class. Thought is not mechanistically located by merely establishing the class position of the thinker. It is attributed to that class for which it is "appropriate," to the class whose social situation with its class conflicts, aspirations, fears, restraints and objective possibilities within the given socio-

---

6. Karl Marx, *Capital,* (Chicago: C. H. Kerr, 1906), I, p. 15; *cf.* Marx and Engels, *The German Ideology,* (New York: International Publishers, 1939), p. 76; *cf.* Max Weber, *Gesammelte Aufsaetze zur Wissenschaftslehre,* (Tuebingen: J. C. B. Mohr, 1922), p. 205.

7. Marx and Engels, *The Communist Manifesto,* in *Karl Marx, Selected Works,* I, p. 216.

historical context is being expressed. Marx' most explicit formulation holds:

> One must not form the narrow-minded idea that the petty bourgeoisie wants on principle to enforce an egoistic class interest. It believes, rather, that the *special* conditions of its emancipation are the *general* conditions through which alone modern society can be saved and the class struggle avoided. Just as little must one imagine that the democratic representatives are all shopkeepers or are full of enthusiasm for them. *So far as their education and their individual position are concerned,* they may be as widely separated from them as heaven from earth. *What makes them representatives of the petty bourgeosie is the fact that in their minds* (im Kopfe) *they do not exceed the limits which the latter do not exceed in their life activities,* that they are consequently driven to the same problems and solutions in theory to which material interest and social position drive the latter in practice. *This is ueberhaupt the relationship of the political and literary representatives of a class to the class which they represent.* (8).

But if we cannot derive ideas from the objective class position of their exponents, this leaves a wide margin of indeterminacy. It then becomes a further problem to discover why some identify with and express the characteristic outlook of the class stratum in which they objectively find themselves whereas others adopt the presuppositions of a class stratum other than "their own." An empirical description of the fact is no adequate substitute for its theoretical explanation.

In dealing with existential bases, Max Scheler characteristically places his own hypothesis in opposition to other prevalent theories. (9) He draws a distinction between cultural sociology and what he call the sociology of real factors (*Realsoziologie*). Cultural data are "ideal," in the realm of ideas and values: "real factors" are oriented toward effecting changes in the reality of nature or society. The former are defined by ideal goals or intentions; the latter derive

---

8. Karl Marx, *Der Achtzehnte Brumaire des Louis Bonaparte,* (Hamburg: 1885), p. 36 (italics inserted).

9. This account is based upon Scheler's most elaborate discussion, "Probleme einer Soziologie des Wissens," in his *Die Wissensformen und die Gesellschaft* (Leipzig: Der Neue-Geist Verlag, 1926), pp. 1-229. This essay is an extended and improved version of an essay in his *Versuche zu einer Soziologie des Wissens,* (Muenchen: Duncker und Humblot, 1924), pp. 5-146. For further discussions of Scheler, see P. A. Schillp, "The Formal Problems of Scheler's Sociology of Knowledge," *The Philosophical Review,* 36: pp. 101-120, March, 1927; Howard Becker and H. O. Dahlke, "Max Scheler's Sociology of Knowledge," *Philosophy and Phenomenological Research,* 2: pp. 310-322, March, 1942.

from an "impulse structure" (*Triebstruktur*, e.g. sex, hunger, power). It is a basic error, he holds, of all naturalistic theories to maintain that real factors — whether race, geopolitics, political power structure, or the relations of economic production — unequivocally determine the realm of meaningful ideas. He also rejects all ideological, spiritualistic, and personalistic conceptions which err in viewing the history of existential conditions as a unilinear unfolding of the history of mind. He ascribes complete autonomy and a determinate sequence to these real factors, though he inconsistently holds that value-laden ideas serve to guide and direct their development. Ideas as such initially have no social effectiveness. The "purer" the idea, the greater its impotence, so far as dynamic effect on society is concerned. Ideas do not become actualized, embodied in cultural developments, unless they are bound up in some fashion with interests, impulses, emotions or collective tendencies and their incorporation in institutional structures. (10) Only then — and in this limited respect, naturalistic theories (e.g. Marxism) are justified — do they exercise some definite influence. Should ideas not be grounded in the immanent development of real factors, they are doomed to become sterile Utopias.

Naturalistic theories are further in error, Scheler holds, in tacitly assuming the *independent variable* to be one and the same throughout history. There is no constant independent variable but there is, in the course of history, a definite sequence in which the primary factors prevail, a sequence which can be summed up in a "law of three phases." In the initial phase, blood-ties and associated kinship institutions constitute the independent variable; later, political power and finally, economic factors. There is, then, no constancy in the effective primacy of existential factors but rather an ordered variability. Thus, Scheler sought to relativize the very notion of historical determinants. (11) He claims not only to have confirmed his "law of the three phases" inductively but to have derived it from a theory of human impulses.

Scheler's conception of *Realfaktoren* — race and kinship, the structure of power, factors of production, qualitative and quantita-

---

10. Scheler, *Die Wissensformen* . . ., pp. 7, 32.
11. *Ibid.*, pp. 25-45. It should be noted that Marx had long since rejected out of hand a similar conception of shifts in independent variables which was made the basis for an attack on his *Critique of Political Economy;* see *Capital,* I, p. 94n.

tive aspects of population, geographical and geopolitical factors — hardly constitutes a usefully defined category. It is of small value to subsume such divers elements under one rubric, and, indeed, his own empirical studies and those of his disciples do not profit from this array of "factors." But in suggesting a variation of significant existential factors, though not in the ordered sequence which he failed to establish, he moves in the direction which subsequent research has followed.

Thus, Mannheim derives from Marx primarily by extending his conception of existential bases. Given the *fact* of multiple group affiliation, the problem becomes one of determining *which* of these affiliations are decisive in fixing perspectives, models of thought, definition of the given, etc. Unlike "a dogmatic Marxism," he does not assume that class position is alone ultimately determinant. He finds, for example, that an organically integrated group conceives of history as a continuous movement toward the realization of its goals, whereas socially uprooted and loosely integrated groups espouse an historical intuition which stresses the fortuitous and imponderable. It is only through exploring the variety of group formations — generations, status groups, sects, occupational groups — and their characteristic modes of thought that there can be found an existential basis corresponding to the great variety of perspectives and knowledge which actually obtain. (12)

Though representing a different tradition, this is substantially the position taken by Durkheim. In an early study with Mauss of primitive forms of classification, he maintained that the genesis of the categories of thought is to be found in the group structure and relations and that they vary with changes in the social organization. (13) In seeking to account for the social origins of the categories, Durkheim postulates that individuals are more directly and in-

---

12. Karl Mannheim, *Ideology and Utopia*, (New York: Harcourt Brace, 1936), pp. 247-8. In view of the recent extensive discussions of Mannheim's work, it will not be treated at any length in this essay. For the writer's appraisal, see R. K. Merton, "Karl Mannheim and the Sociology of Knowledge," *Journal of Liberal Religion*, 2: 125-147, 1941.

13. Emile Durkheim and Marcel Mauss, "De quelques formes primitives de classification," *L'Année Sociologique*, 6: 1-72, 1901-02. ". . . even ideas as abstract as those of time and space are, at each moment of their history, in close relation with the corresponding social organization." As Marcel Granet has indicated, this paper contains some pages on Chinese thought which have been held by specialists to mark a new era in the field of sinological studies.

clusively oriented toward the groups in which they live than they are toward nature. The primarily significant experiences are mediated through social relationships, which leave their impress on the character of thought and knowledge. (14) Thus, in his study of primitive forms of thought, he deals with the periodic recurrence of social activities (ceremonies, feasts, rites), the clan structure and the spatial configurations of group meetings as among the existential bases of thought. And, applying Durkheim's formulations to ancient Chinese thought, Granet attributes their typical conceptions of time and space to such bases as the feudal organization and the rhythmic alternation of concentrated and dispersed group life. (15)

In sharp distinction from the foregoing conceptions of existential bases is Sorokin's idealistic and emanationist theory, which seeks to derive every aspect of knowledge, not from an existential social basis, but from varying "culture mentalities." These mentalities are constructed of "major premises": thus, the ideational mentality conceives of reality as "non-material, ever-lasting Being"; its needs as primarily spiritual and their full satisfaction through "self imposed minimization or elimination of most physical needs." (16) Contrariwise, the sensate mentality limits reality to what can be perceived through the senses, it is primarily concerned with physical needs which it seeks to satisfy to a maximum, not through self-modification, but through change of the external world. The chief intermediate type of mentality is the idealistic, which represents a virtual balance of the foregoing types. It is these "mentalities," *i.e.* the major premises of each culture, from which systems of truth and knowledge are derived. And here we come to the self-contained emanationism of an idealistic position: it appears plainly tautological to say, as Sorokin does, that "in a sensate society and culture the Sensate system of truth based upon the testimony of the organs of senses has to be dominant." (17) For sensate mentality has already

---

14. Emile Durkheim, *The Elementary Forms of the Religious Life,* (London: Allen and Unwin, 1915), pp. 443-4; see also Hans Kelsen, *Society and Nature,* (University of Chicago Press, 1943), p. 30.

15. Marcel Granet, *La pensée chinoise,* (Paris: La Renaissance du Livre, 1934), *e.g.* pp. 84-104.

16. Pitirim A. Sorokin, *Social and Cultural Dynamics,* (New York: American Book Co., 1937-41, 4 vols.), I, pp. 72-73.

17. *Ibid.,* II, p. 5.

been *defined* as one conceiving of "reality as only that which is presented to the sense organs." (18)

Moreover, an emanationist phrasing such as this by-passes some of the basic questions raised by other approaches to the analysis of existential conditions. Thus, Sorokin considers the failure of the sensate "system of truth" (empiricism) to monopolize a sensate culture as evidence that this culture is not "fully integrated." But this surrenders inquiry into the bases of those very differences of thought with which our contemporary world is concerned. This is true of other categories and "principles" of knowledge for which he seeks to apply a sociological accounting. For example, in our present "sensate" culture, he finds that "materialism" is less prevalent than "idealism"; "temporalism" and "eternalism" are almost equally current; so, too, with "realism" and "nominalism," "singularism" and "universalism," etc. Since there are these diversities within a culture, the overall characterization of the culture as sensate provides no basis for indicating which groups subscribe to one mode of thought, and which to another. Sorokin does not systematically explore varying existential bases *within* a society or culture; he looks to the "dominant" tendencies and imputes these to the culture as a whole. (19) Our contemporary society, quite apart from the *differences* of intellectual outlook of divers classes and groups, is viewed as an integral exemplification of "sensate culture." On its own premises, Sorokin's approach is primarily suited for an overall characterization of cultures, not for analyzing connections between varied existential conditions and thought within a given society.

What Mental Productions Are Being Sociologically Analyzed? Even a cursory survey is enough to show that the term "knowledge" has been so broadly conceived as to refer to every type of assertion and every mode of thought ranging from folk belief to positive science. "Knowledge" has often come to be assimilated to the term "culture" so that not only the exact sciences but ethical convictions, epistemological postulates, material predications, synthetic judgments, political beliefs, the categories of thought, eschatological

---

18. *Ibid.*, I, p. 73.
19. One "exception" to this practice is found in his contrast between the prevalent tendency of the "clergy and religious landed aristocracy to become the leading and organizing classes in the Ideational, and the capitalistic bourgeoisie, intelligentsia, professionals, and secular officials in the Sensate culture . . ." III, pp. 250. And see his account of the diffusion of culture among social classes, IV, p. 221 ff.

doxies, moral norms, ontological assumptions, and observations of empirical fact are more or less indiscriminately held to be "existentially conditioned." (20) The question is, of course, whether these diverse "ideas" stand in the same relationship to their sociological basis, or whether it is necessary to discriminate between spheres of knowledge precisely because this relationship differs for the various types of "ideas." For the most part, there has been a systematic ambiguity concerning this problem.

Only in his later writings, did Engels come to recognize that the concept of ideological superstructure included a variety of "ideological forms" which differ *significantly*, *i.e.* are not equally and similarly conditioned by the material basis. Marx' failure to take up this problem systematically (21) accounts for much of the initial vagueness about *what* is comprised by the superstructure and how these several "ideological" spheres are related to the modes of production. It was largely the task of Engels to attempt this clarification. In differentiating the blanket term "ideology," Engels granted a degree of autonomy to law.

> "As soon as the new division of labour which creates professional lawyers becomes necessary, another new and independent sphere is opened up which, for all its general dependence on production and trade, still has its own capacity for reacting upon these spheres as well. In a modern state, law must not only correspond to the general economic position and be its expression, but must also be an expression which is *consistent in itself*, and which does not, owing to inner contradictions, look glaringly inconsistent. And in order to achieve this, the faithful reflection of economic conditions is more and more infringed upon. All the more so the more rarely it happens that a code of law is the blunt, unmitigated, unadulterated expression of the domination of a class—this in itself would already offend the "conception of justice." (22)

If this is true of law, with its close connection with economic pressures, it is all the more true of other spheres of the "ideological superstructure." Philosophy, religion, science are particularly cons-

---

20. *Cf.* Merton, *op cit.*, 133-135; Kurt H. Wolff, "The Sociology of Knowledge: Emphasis on an Epirical Attitude," *Philosophy of Science*, 10: 104-123, 1943; Talcott Parsons, "The Role of Ideas in Social Action," *American Sociological Review*, 3: 652-64, 1938.

21. This is presumably the ground for Scheler's remark: "A specific thesis of the economic conception of history is the subsumption of the laws of development of *all* knowledge under the laws of development of ideologies." *Die Wissensformen* . . ., 21.

22. Engels, letter to Conrad Schmidt, 27 October, 1890, in *Marx, Selected Works*, I, p. 385.

SOCIOLOGY OF KNOWLEDGE

trained by the pre-existing stock of knowledge and belief, and only indirectly and "ultimately" influenced by economic factors. (23) In these fields, it is not possible to "derive" the content and development of belief and knowledge merely from an analysis of the historical situation:

> Political, juridical, philosophical, religious, literary, artistic, etc., development is based on economic development. But all these react upon one another and also upon the economic base. It is not that the economic position is the *cause and alone active,* while everything else only has a passive effect. There is, rather, interaction on the basis of the economic necessity, which *ultimately* always asserts itself. (24).

But to say that the economic basis "ultimately" asserts itself is to say that the ideological spheres exhibit some degree of independent development, as indeed Engels goes on to observe:

> The further the particular sphere which we are investigating is removed from the economic sphere and approaches that of pure abstract ideology, the more shall we find it exhibiting accidents (i.e., deviations from the 'expected' development) in its development, the more will its curve run in a zig-zag. (25).

Finally, there is an even more restricted conception of the sociological status of natural science. In one well-known passage, Marx expressly distinguishes natural science from "ideological" spheres.

> With the change of the economic foundation the entire immense superstructure is more or less rapidly transformed. In considering such transformations the distinction should always be made between the material transformation of the economic conditions of production *which can be determined with the precision of natural science,* and the legal, political, religious, aesthetic or philosophic—in short, ideological forms in which men become conscious of this conflict and fight it out. (26).

Thus, natural science and political economy, which can match its precision, are granted a status quite distinct from that of ideology. The conceptual content of natural science is not imputed to an economic base: merely its "aims" and "material":

> Where would natural science be without industry and commerce? Even this "pure" natural science is provided with an aim, as with its material,

---

23. *Ibid.,* I, p. 386.
24. Engels, letter to Heinz Starkenburg, 25 January, 1894, *ibid.,* I, p. 392.
25. *Ibid.,* I, 393; *cf.* Engels, *Feuerbach,* (Chicago: C. H. Kerr, 1903) pp. 117 ff. "It is well known that certain periods of highest development of art stand in *no direct connection* with the general development of society, nor with the material basis and the skeleton structure of its organization." Marx, Introduction, *A Contribution to the Critique of Political Economy,* pp. 309-10.
26. Marx, *A Contribution to the Critique of Political Economy,* p. 12.

only through trade and industry, through the sensuous activity of men. (27).

Along the same lines, Engels asserts that the appearance of Marx' materialistic conception of history was itself determined by "necessity," as is indicated by similar views appearing among English and French historians at the time and by Morgan's independent discovery of the same conception. (28)

He goes even further to maintain that socialist theory is itself a proletarian "reflection" of modern class conflict, so that here, at least, the very content of "scientific thought" is held to be socially determined, (29) without vitiating its validity.

There was an incipient tendency in Marxism, then, to consider natural science as standing in a relation to the economic base different from that of other spheres of knowledge and belief. In science, the focus of attention may be socially determined but not, presumably, its conceptual apparatus. In this respect, the social sciences were sometimes held to differ significantly from the natural sciences. Social science tended to be assimilated to the sphere of ideology, a tendency developed by later Marxists into the questionable thesis of a class-bound social science which is inevitably tendentious (30) and

---

27. Marx and Engels, *The German Ideology*, p. 36 (italics inserted). See also Engels, *Socialism: Utopian and Scientific*, (Chicago: C. H. Kerr, 1910) pp. pp. 24-25, where the needs of a rising middle class are held to account for the revival of science. The assertion that "only" trade and industry provide the aims is typical of the extreme, and untested, statements of relationships which prevail especially in the early Marxist writings. Such terms as "determination" cannot be taken at their face value; they are characteristically used very loosely. The actual *extent* of such relationships between intellectual activity and the material foundations were not investigated by either Marx or Engels.

28. Engels, in *Marx, Selected Works*, I, p. 393. The occurrence of parallel independent discoveries and inventions as "proof" of the social determination of knowledge was a repeated theme throughout the nineteenth century. As early as 1828, Macaulay in his essay on Dryden had noted concerning Newton's and Leibniz' invention of the calculus: "Mathematical science, indeed, had reached such a point, that if neither of them had existed, the principle must inevitably have occurred to some person within a few years." He cites other cases in point. Victorian manufacturers shared the same view with Marx and Engels. In our own day, this thesis, based on independent duplicate inventions, has been especially emphasized by Dorothy Thomas, Ogburn, and Vierkandt.

29. Engels, *Socialism: Utopian and Scientific*, p. 97.

30. V. I. Lenin, "The Three Sources and Three Component Parts of Marxism," in *Marx, Selected Works*, I. p. 54.

into the claim that only "proletarian science" has valid insight into certain aspects of social reality. (31).

Mannheim follows in the Marxist tradition to the extent of exempting the "exact sciences" and "formal knowledge" from existential determination but not "historical, political and social science thinking as well as the thought of everyday life." (32) Social position determines the "perspective," i.e. "the manner in which one views an object, what one perceives in it, and how one construes it in his thinking." The situational determination of thought does not render it invalid; it does, however, particularize the scope of the inquiry and the limits of its validity. (33).

If Marx did not sharply differentiate the superstructure, Scheler goes to the other extreme. He distinguishes a variety of forms of "knowledge." To begin with, there are the "relatively natural Weltanschauungen": that which is accepted as given, as neither requiring nor being capable of justification. These are, so to speak, the cultural axioms of groups; what Joseph Glanvill, some three hundred years ago, called a "climate of opinion." A primary task of the sociology of knowledge is to discover the laws of transformation of these Weltanchauungen. And since these are by no means necessarily valid, it follows that the sociology of knowledge is not concerned merely with tracing the existential bases of truth but also of "social illusion, superstition and socially conditioned errors and forms of deception." (34).

These Weltanschauungen constitute organic growths and develop only in large time-spans. They are scarcely affected by theories. Without adequate evidence, Scheler claims that they can be changed in any fundamental sense only through race-mixture or conceivably through the "mixture" of language and culture. Building upon these very slowly changing Weltanschauungen are the more "artificial"

---

31. Nikolai Bukharin, *Historical Materialism*, (New York: International Publishers, 1925) pp. xi-xii; B. Hessen in *Society at the Cross-Roads*, (London: Kniga, 1932) p. 154; A. I. Timeniev in *Marxism and Modern Thought*, (New York: Harcourt, Brace, 1935), p. 310; "Only Marxism, only the ideology of the advanced revolutionary class is scientific."

32. Mannheim, *Ideology and Utopia*, pp. 150, 243; Mannheim, "Die Bedeutung der Konkurrenz im Gebiete des Geistigen," *Verhandlungen des 6. deutschen Soziologentages*, (Tuebingen: 1929), p. 41.

33. Mannheim, *Ideology and Utopia*, pp. 256, 264; cf. Merton, "Karl Mannheim . . .," p 143.

34. Scheler, *Die Wissensformen* . . ., pp. 59-61.

forms of knowledge which may be ordered in seven classes, according to degree of artificiality: 1. myth and legend; 2. knowledge implicit in the natural folk-language; 3. religious knowledge (ranging from the vague emotional intuition to the fixed dogma of a church); 4. the basic types of mystical knowledge; 5. philosophical-metaphysical knowledge; 6. positive knowledge of mathematics, the natural and cultural sciences; 7. technological knowledge. (35). The more artificial these types of knowledge, the more rapidly they change. It is evident, says Scheler, that religions change far more slowly than the various metaphysics, and the latter persist for much longer periods than the results of positive science, which change from hour to hour.

This hypothesis of rates of change bears some points of similarity to Alfred Weber's thesis that "civilizational change" outruns "cultural" change and to the Ogburn hypothesis that "material" factors change more rapidly than the "non-material." Scheler's hypothesis shares the limitations of these others as well as several additional shortcomings. He nowhere indicates with any clarity what his principle of classification of types of knowledge—so-called "artificiality"—actually denotes. Why, for example, is "mystical knowledge" conceived as more "artificial" than religious dogmas? He does not at all consider what is entailed by saying that one type of knowledge "changes more rapidly" than another. Consider his curious equating of new scientific "results" with metaphysical systems; how does one compare the degree of change implied in neo-Kantian philosophy with, say, change in biological theory during the corresponding period? Scheler boldly asserts a seven-fold variation in rates of change and, of course, does not empirically confirm this elaborate claim. In view of the difficulties encountered in testing much simpler hypotheses, it is not at all clear what is gained by setting forth an elaborate hypothesis of this type.

Yet only certain aspects of this knowledge are held to be sociologically determined. On the basis of certain postulates, which need not be considered here, Scheler goes on to assert:

> The sociological character of all knowledge, of all forms of thought, intuition and cognition is unquestionable. Although the *content* and even less the objective validity of all knowledge is not determined by the

---

35. *Ibid.*, P. 62.

controlling perspectives of social interests, nevertheless this is the case with the *selection* of the objects of knowledge. Moreover, the 'forms' of the mental processes by means of which knowledge is acquired are always and necessarily co-determined sociologically, i.e. by the social structure. (36).

Since explanation consists in tracing the relatively new to the familiar and known and since society is "better known" than anything else, (37) it is to be expected that the modes of thought and intuition and the classification of knowable things generally, are co-determined (mitbedingt) by the division and classification of groups which comprise the society.

Scheler flatly repudiates all forms of sociologism. He seeks to escape a radical relativism by resorting to a metaphysical dualism. He posits a realm of "timeless essences" which in varying degrees enter into the *content* of judgments; a realm utterly distinct from that of historical and social reality which determines the *act* of judgments. As Mandelbaum has aptly summarized this view:

> The realm of essences is to Scheler a real of possibilities out of which we, bound to time and our interest first select one set and then another for consideration. Where we as historians turn the spotlight of our attention depends upon our own sociologically determined valuations; what we see there is determined by the set of absolute and timeless values which are implicit in the past with which we are dealing. (38).

This is indeed counter-relativism by fiat. Merely asserting the distinction between essences and existences avoids the incubus of relativism by exorcising it. The concept of internal essences may be congenial to the metaphysician; it is wholly foreign to empirical inquiry. It is noteworthy that these conceptions play no significant part in Scheler's empirical efforts to establish relations between knowledge and society.

Scheler indicates that different types of knowledge are bound up with particular forms of groups. The content of Plato's theory of ideas required the form and organization of the platonic academy; so, too, the organization of Protestant churches and sects was determined by the content of their beliefs which could exist only in this and no other type of social organization, as Troeltsch has shown. And,

---

36 *Ibid.*, p. 55.
37. See the same assumption of Durkheim, cited in fn. 14 of this paper.
38. Maurice Mandelbaum, *The Problem of Historical Knowledge*, (New York: Liveright, 1938), p. 150; Sorokin posits a similar sphere of "timeless ideas," e.g. in his *Sociocultural Causality, Space, Time*, (Durham: Duke University Press, 1943), p. 215, *passim.*

similarly, *Gemeinschaft* types of society have a traditionally defined fund of knowledge which is handed down as conclusive; they are not concerned with discovering or extending knowledge. The very effort to test the traditional knowledge, insofar as it implies doubt, is ruled out as virtually blasphemous. In such a group, the prevailing logic and mode of thought is that of an "ars demonstrandi" not an "ars inveniendi." Its methods are prevailingly ontological and dogmatic, not epistemologic and critical; its mode of thought is that of conceptual realism, not nominalistic as in the Gesellschaft type of organization; its system of categories, organismic not mechanistic. (39)

Durkheim extends sociological inquiry into the social genesis of the categories of thought, basing his hypothesis on three types of presumptive evidence. (A) The fact of cultural variation in the categories and the rules of logic "proves that they depend upon factors that are historical and consequently social."(40) (B) Since concepts are imbedded in the very language the individual acquires (and this holds as well for the special terminology of the scientist) and since some of these conceptual terms refer to things which we, as individuals, have never experienced, it is clear that they are a product of the society. (41) And (C), the acceptance or rejection of concepts is not determined *merely* by their "objective" validity but also by their consistency with other prevailing beliefs. (42)

Yet Durkheim does not subscribe to a type of relativism in which there are merely competing criteria of validity. The social origin of the categories does not render them wholly arbitrary so far as their applicability to nature is concerned. They are, in varying degrees, adequate to their object. But since social structures vary (and with them, the categorical apparatus) there are inescapable "subjective" elements in the particular logical constructions current in a society. These subjective elements "must be progressively rooted out, if we are to approach reality more closely." And this occurs under determinate social conditions. With the extension of intercultural contacts, with the spread of inter-communication between persons drawn from different societies, with the enlargement of the

---

39. Scheler, *Die Wissensformen* . . . , pp. 22-23; compare a similar characterization of "sacred schools" of thought by Florian Znaniecki, *The Social Role of the Man of Knowledge*, (New York: Columbia University Press, 1940), Chap. 3.
40. Durkheim, *Elementary Forms* . . . , 12, 18,439.
41. *Ibid.*, pp. 433-435.
42. *Ibid.*, p. 438.

society, the local frame of reference becomes disrupted. "Things can no longer be contained in the social moulds according to which they were primitively classified; they must be organized according to principles which are their own. So logical organization differentiates itself from the social organization and becomes autonomous. Genuinely human thought is not a primitive fact; it is the product of history..." (43) Particularly, those conceptions which are subjected to scientifically methodical criticism come to have a greater objective adequacy. Objectivity is itself viewed as a social emergent.

Throughout, Durkheim's dubious epistemology is intertwined with his substantive account of the social roots of concrete designations of temporal, spatial and other units. We need not indulge in the traditional exaltation of "the categories" as a thing set apart and foreknown, to note that Durkheim was dealing not with them but with conventional divisions of time and space. He observed, in passing, that differences in these respects should not lead us to "neglect the similarities, which are no less essential." If he pioneered in relating variations in systems of concepts to variations in social organization, he did not succeed in establishing the social origin of "the categories."

Like Durkheim, Granet attaches great significance to language as constraining and fixing prevalent concepts and modes of thought. He has shown how the Chinese language is not equipped to note concepts, analyze ideas, or to present doctrines discursively. It has remained intractable to formal precision. The Chinese word does not fix a notion with a definite degree of abstraction and generality, but evokes an indefinite complex of particular images. Thus, there is no word which simply signifies "old man." Rather, a considerable number of words "paint different aspects of old age": *k'i*, those who need a richer diet; *k'ao*, those who have difficulty in breathing, and so on. These concrete evocations entail a multitude of other similarly concrete images of every detail of the mode of life of the aged: those who should be exempt from military service; those for whom funerary material should be held in readiness; those who have a right to carry a staff through the town, etc. These are but a few of the images evoked by *k'i* which, in general, corresponds to the quasi-singular notion of old persons, some 60 to 70 years of age.

---

43. *Ibid.*, pp. 444-445; 437.

Words and sentences thus have an entirely concrete, emblematic character. (44)

Just as the language is concrete and evocative, so the most general ideas of ancient Chinese thought were unalterably concrete, none of them comparable to our abstract ideas. Neither time nor space were abstractly conceived. Time proceeds by cycles and is round; space is square. The earth which is square is divided into squares; the wall of towns, fields and camps should form a square. Camps, buildings and towns must be oriented and the selection of the proper orientation is in the hands of a ritual leader. Techniques of the division and management of space — surveying, town development, architecture, political geography — and the geometrical speculations which they presuppose are all linked with a set of social regulations. Particularly as these pertain to periodic assemblies, they reaffirm and reinforce in every detail the symbols which represent space. They account for its square form, its heterogeneous and hierarchic character, a conception of space which could only have arisen in a feudal society. (45)

Though Granet has established the social grounds of concrete designations of time and space, it is not at all clear that he deals with data comparable to Western conceptions. He considers traditionalized, or ritualized or magical conceptions and implicitly compares these with our matter-of-fact, technical or scientific notions. But in a wide range of actual *practices*, the Chinese did not *act* on the assumption that "time is round" and "space, square." When comparable spheres of activity and thought are considered it is questionable that this radical cleavage of "categorial systems" occurs, in the sense that there are no common denominators of thought and conception. Granet has demonstrated qualitative differences of concepts in *certain contexts*, but not within such comparable contexts as, say, that of technical practice. His work testifies to different foci of intellectual interests in the two spheres and within the ritualistic sphere, basic differences of outlook, but not unbridgeable gaps in other spheres. The fallacy which is most prominent in Levy-Bruhl's concept of the "prelogicality" of the primitive mind thus appears in the work of Granet as well. As Malinowski and Rivers have shown, when comparable spheres of thought and

---

44 Granet, *La Pensée Chinoise*, pp. 37-38, 82 and the whole of chapter I.
45. *Ibid.*, pp. 87-95.

activity are considered, no such irreconcilable differences are found. (46)

Sorokin shares in this same tendency to ascribe entirely disparate criteria of "truth" to his different culture types. He has cast into a distinctive idiom the fact of shifts of attention on the part of intellectual elites in different historical societies. In certain societies, religious conceptions and particular types of metaphysics are at the focus of attention, whereas in other societies, empirical science becomes the center of interest. But the several "systems of truth" coexist in each of these societies within given spheres; the Catholic church has not abandoned its "ideational" criteria even in this sensate age.

Insofar as Sorokin adopts the position of radically different and disparate criteria of truth, he must locate his own work within this context. It may be said, though an extensive discussion would be needed to document it, that he never resolves this problem. His various efforts to cope with a radically relativistic impasse differ considerably. Thus, at the very outset, he states that his constructions must be tested in the same way "as any scientific law. First of all the principle must by nature be logical: second, it must successfully meet the test of the 'relevant facts,' that is, it must fit and represent the facts." (47) In Sorokin's own terminology, he has thus adopted a scientific position characteristic of a "sensate system of truth." When he confronts his own epistemologic position directly, however, he adopts an "integralist" conception of truth which seeks to assimilate empirical and logical criteria as well as a "supersensory, super-rational, metalogical act of 'intuition' or 'mystical experience'." (48) He thus posits an integration of these diverse systems. In order to justify the "truth of faith" — the only item which would remove him from the ordinary criteria used in current scientific work — he indicates that "intuition" plays an important role as a *source* of scientific discovery. But does this meet the issue? The question is not one of the psychological *sources* of

---

46. *Cf.* B. Malinowski in Joseph Needham ed., *Science, Religion and Reality*, (New York: The Macmillan Co., 1925), p. 28. "Every primitive community is in possession of a considerable store of knowledge, based on experience and fashioned by reason." See also Emile Benoit-Smullyan, "Granet's La Pensée Chinoise," *American Sociological Review*, 1: 487-492, 1936, and for a contrary view, the unpublished acount of Granet's work by C. Wright Mills.

47. Sorokin, *Social and Cultural Dynamics*, I, p. 36; *cf.* II, pp. 11-12n.

48. *Ibid.*, IV, Chap. 16, *Sociocultural Causality* . . ., Chap. 5.

valid conclusions, but of the *criteria* and *methods of validation*. Which criteria would Sorokin adopt when "supersensory" intuitions are not consistent with empirical observation? In such cases, presumably, so far as we can judge from his work rather than his comments about his work, he accepts the facts and rejects the intuition. All this suggests that Sorokin is discussing under the generic label of "truth" quite distinct and not comparable types of judgments: just as the chemist's analysis of an oil painting is neither consistent nor inconsistent with its aesthetic evaluation, so Sorokin's "systems of truth" refer to quite different kinds of judgments. And, indeed, he is finally led to say as much, when he remarks that "each of the systems of truth, within its legitimate field of competency, gives us genuine cognition of the respective aspects of reality." (49) But whatever his private opinion of intuition he cannot draw it into his sociology as a *criterion* (rather than a source) of valid conclusions.

How are Mental Productions Related to the Existential Basis? Though this problem is obviously the nucleus of every theory in the sociology of knowledge, it has often been treated by implication rather than directly. Yet each type of imputed relation between knowledge and society presupposes an entire theory of sociological method and social causation. The prevailing theories in this field have dealt with one or both of two major types of relation: causal or functional, and the symbolic or organismic or meaningful. (50)

Marx and Engels, of course, dealt solely with some kind of causal relation between the economic basis and ideas, variously terming this relation as "determination, correspondence, reflection, outgrowth, dependence," etc. In addition, there is an "interest" or "need" relation; when strata have (imputed) needs at a given stage of historical development, there is held to be a definite pressure for appropiate ideas and knowledge to develop. The inadequacies of these divers formulations have risen up to plague those who derive from the Marxist tradition in the present day. (51)

Since Marx held that thought is not a mere "reflection" of objec-

---

49. *Sociocultural Causality* . . . , pp. 230-1n.
50. The distinctions between these have long been considered in European sociological thought. The most elaborate discussion in this country is that of Sorokin, *Social and Cultural Dynamics*, e.g. I, chapters 1-2.
51. *Cf.* the comments of Hans Speier, "The Social Determination of Ideas," *Social Research*, 5: 182-205, 1938; C. Wright Mills, "Language, Logic and Culture," *American Sociological Review* 4: 670-680, 1939.

tive class position, as we have seen, this raises anew the problem of its imputation to a determinate basis. The prevailing Marxist hypotheses for coping with this problem involve a theory of history which is the ground for determining whether the ideology is "situationally adequate" for a given stratum in the society: this requires a hypothetical construction of what men *would think and perceive* if they were able to comprehend the historical situation adequately. (52) But such insight into the situation need not *actually* be widely current within given strata. This, then, leads to the further problem of "false consciousness," of how ideologies which are neither in conformity with the interests of a class nor situationally adequate come to prevail.

A partial empirical explanation of "false consciousness" implied in the *Manifesto* rests on the view that the bourgeoisie control the content of culture and thus diffuse doctrines and standards alien to the interests of the proletariat. (53) Or, in more general terms, "the ruling ideas of each age have ever been the ideas of its ruling class." But, this is only a partial account; at most it deals with the false consciousness of the subordinated class. It might, for example, partly explain the fact noted by Marx that even where the peasant proprietor "does belong to the proletariat by his position he does not believe that he does." It would not, however, be pertinent in seeking to account for the false consciousness of the ruling class itself.

Another, though not clearly formulated, theme which bears upon the problem of false consciousness runs throughout Marxist theory. This is the conception of ideology as being an *unwitting, unconscious* expression of "real motives," these being in turn construed in terms of the objective interests of social classes. Thus, there is repeated stress on the unwitting nature of ideologies:

Ideology is a process accomplished by the so-called thinker consciously indeed but with a false consciousness. The real motives impelling him

---

52. *Cf.* the formulation by Mannheim, *Ideology and Utopia*, pp. 175 ff; Georg Lukács, *Geschichte und Klassenbewusstsein* (Berlin: 1923), pp. 61 ff; Arthur Child, "The Problem of Imputation in the Sociology of Knowledge," *Ethics*, 51: 200-219, 1941.

53. Marx and Engels, *The German Ideology*, p. 39. "In so far as they rule as a class and determine the extent and compass of an epoch, it is self-evident that they do this in their whole range, hence among other things rule also as thinkers, as producers of ideas, and regulate the production and distribution of the ideas of their age . . ."

remain unknown to him, otherwise it would not be an ideological process at all. Hence he imagines false or apparent motives. (54).

The ambiguity of the term "correspondence" to refer to the connection between the material basis and the idea can only be overlooked by the polemical enthusiast. Ideologies are construed as "distortions of the social situation"; (55) as merely "expressive" of the material conditions; (56) and, whether "distorted" or not, as motivational support for carrying through real changes in the society. (57) It is at this last point, when "illusory" beliefs are conceded to provide motivation for action, that Marxism ascribes a measure of independence to ideologies in the historical process. They are no longer merely epiphenomenal. They enjoy a measure of autonomy. From this develops the notion of interacting factors in which the superstructure, though interdependent with the material basis, is also assumed to have some degree of independence. Engels explicitly recognized that earlier formulations were inadequate in at least two respects: (A) that both he and Marx had previously over-emphasized the economic factor and understated the role of reciprocal interaction; (58) and (B) that they had "neglected" the formal side — the way in which these ideas develop. (59)

The Marx-Engels views on the connectives of ideas and economic substructure hold, then, that the economic structure constitutes the framework which limits the range of ideas which will prove socially effective; ideas which do not have pertinence for one or another of the conflicting classes may arise, but will be of little consequence. Economic conditions are necessary, but not sufficient, for the emergence and spread of ideas which express either the interests or outlook, or both, of distinct social strata. There is no strict determinism

---

54. Engels' letter to Mehring, 14 July 1893, in *Marx, Selected Works*, I, pp. 388-9; cf. Marx, *Der Achtzehnte Brumaire*, p. 33; *Critique of Political Economy*, p. 12.

55. Marx, *Der Achtzehnte Brumaire*, p. 39, where the democratic Montagnards indulge in self-deception.

56. Engels, *Socialism: Utopian and Scientific*, pp. 26-27. Cf. Engels, *Feuerbach*, pp. 122-23. "The failure to exterminate the Protestant heresy *corresponded* to the invincibility of the rising bourgeoisie . . . Here Calvinism proved itself to be the true religious disguise of the interests of the bourgeoisie of that time . . ."

57. Marx grants motivational significance to the "illusions" of the burgeoning bourgeoisie, *Der Achtzehnte Brumaire*, p. 8.

58. Engels, letter to Joseph Bloch, 21 September 1890, in *Marx, Selected Works*, I, p. 383.

59. Engels, letter to Mehring, 14 July 1893, *ibid.*, I, 390.

of ideas by economic conditions, but a definite predisposition. Knowing the economic conditions, we can predict the kinds of ideas which can exercise a controlling influence in a direction which can be effective. "Men make their own history, but they do not make it just as they please; they do not make it under circumstances chosen by themselves, but under circumstances directly found, given and transmitted from the past." And in the making of history, ideas and ideologies play a definite role: consider only the view of religion as "the opiate of the masses"; consider further the importance attached by Marx and Engels to making those in the proletariat "aware" of their "own interests." Since there is no fatality in the development of the total social structure, but only a development of economic conditions which make certain lines of change *possible* and probable, idea-systems may play a decisive role in the selection of one alternative which "corresponds" to the real balance of power rather than another alternative which runs counter to the existing power-situation and is therefore destined to be unstable, precarious and temporary. There is an ultimate compulsive which derives from economic development, but this compulsive does not operate with such detailed finality that no variation of ideas can occur at all.

The Marxist theory of history assumes that, *sooner or later*, idea-systems which are inconsistent with the actually prevailing and incipient power-structure will be rejected in favor of those which more nearly express the actual alignment of power. It is this view that Engels expresses in his metaphor of the "zig-zag course" of abstract ideology: ideologies may temporarily deviate from what is compatible with the current social relations of production, but they are ultimately brought back in line. For this reason, the Marxist analysis of ideology is always bound to be concerned with the "total" concrete historical situation, in order to account both for the temporary deviations and the later accommodation of ideas to the economic compulsives. But for this same reason, Marxist analyses are apt to have an excessive degree of "flexibility," almost to the point where *any* development can be "explained away" as a temporary aberration or deviation; where "anachronisms" and "lags" become labels for the explaining away of existing beliefs which do not correspond to theoretical expectations; where the concept of "accident" provides a ready means of "saving" the theory from facts which seem to challenge its validity. (60) Once a theory

---

60. *Cf.* Max Weber, *Gesammelte Aufsaetze zur Wissenschaftslehre*, pp. 166-170.

includes concepts such as "lags," "thrusts," "anachronisms," "accidents," "partial independence" and "ultimate dependence," it becomes so labile and so indistinct, that it can be reconciled with virtually any configuration of data. Here, as in several other theories in the sociology of knowledge, a decisive question must be raised in order to determine whether we have a genuine theory: how can the theory be invalidated? In any given historical situation, which data will contradict and invalidate the theory? Unless this can be answered directly, unless the theory involves statements which can be controverted by definite types of data, then it remains merely a pseudo-theory which will be compatible with any array of data.

Though Mannheim has gone far toward developing actual research procedures in the substantive sociology of knowledge, he has not appreciably clarified the connectives of thought and society. (61) As he indicates, once a given thought-structure has been analyzed, there arises the problem of imputing it to definite groups. This requires not only an empirical investigation of the groups or strata who prevalently think in these terms, but also an interpretation of why these groups, and not others, manifest this type of thought. This latter question implies a social psychology which Mannheim has not systematically developed.

The most serious shortcoming of Durkheim's analysis lies precisely in his uncritical acceptance of a naive theory of correspondence in which the categories of thought are held to "reflect" certain features of the group organization. Thus "there are societies in Australia and North America where space is conceived in the form of an immense circle, *because* the camp has a circular form... the social organization has been the model for the spatial organization and a reproduction of it." (62) In similar fashion, the general notion of time is derived from the specific units of time differentiated in social activities (ceremonies, feasts, rites). (63) The category of class and the modes of classification, which involve the notion of a hierarchy, are derived from social grouping and stratification. These social categories are then "projected into our conception of the world." (64)

---

61. This aspect of Mannheim's work cannot be treated in detail here; *cf.* Merton, "Karl Mannheim and the Sociology of Knowledge," *loc. cit.*, pp. 135-139; also Mills, "Language, Logic and Culture," *loc. cit.*
62. Durkheim, *Elementary Forms* . . ., pp. 11-12.
63. *Ibid.*, pp. 10-11
64. *Ibid.*, p. 148.

In summary, then, categories "express" the different aspects of the social order. (65) Durkheim's sociology of knowledge suffers from his avoidance of a social psychology.

The central relation between ideas and existential factors for Scheler is interaction. Ideas interact with existential factors which serve as selective agencies, releasing or checking the extent to which potential ideas find actual expression. Existential factors do not "create" or "determine" the content of ideas; they merely account for the *difference* between potentiality and actuality; they hinder, retard or quicken the actualization of potential ideas. In a figure reminiscent of Clerk Maxwell's hypothetical daemon, Scheler states: "in a definite fashion and order, existential factors open and close the sluice-gates to the flood of ideas." This formulation, which ascribes to existential factors the function of selection from a self contained realm of ideas is, according to Scheler, a basic point of agreement between such otherwise divergent theorists as Dilthey, Troeltsch, Max Weber and himself. (66)

Scheler operates as well with the concept of "structural identities" which refers to common presuppositions of knowledge or belief, on the one hand, and of social, economic or political structure on the other. (67) Thus, the rise of mechanistic thought in the sixteenth century, which came to dominate prior organismic thought is inseparable from the new individualism, the incipient dominance of the power-driven machine over the hand-tool, the incipient dissolution of *Gemeinschaft* into *Gesellschaft*, production for a commodity market, rise of the principle of competition in the ethos of western society, etc. The notion of scientific research as an endless process through which a store of knowledge can be accumulated for practical application as the occasion demands and the total divorce of this science from theology and philosophy was not possible without the simultaneous destruction of the economy of needs and without the rise of a new principle of infinite acquisition characteristic of modern capitalism. (68)

In discussing such structural identities, Scheler does not ascribe primacy either to the socio-economic sphere or to the sphere of knowledge. Rather, and this Scheler regards as one of the most sig-

---

65. *Ibid.*, p. 440.
66. Scheler, *Die Wissensformen* ..., p. 32.
67. *Ibid.*, p. 56.
68. *Ibid.*, p. 25; *cf.* pp. 482-84.

nificant propositions in the field, both are determined by the impulse-structure of the elite which is closely bound up with the prevailing ethos. Thus, modern technology is not merely the application of a pure science based on observation, logic and mathematics. It is far more the product of an orientation toward the control of nature which defined the purposes as well as the conceptual structure of scientific thought. This orientation is largely implicit and is not to be confused with the personal motives of scientists.

With the concept of structural identity, Scheler verges on the concept of cultural integration or Sinnzusammenhang. It corresponds to Sorokin's conception of a "meaningful cultural system" involving "the identity of the fundamental principles and values that permeate all its parts," which is distinguished from a "causal system" involving interdependence of parts. (69)

Having constructed his types of culture, Sorokin's survey of criteria of truth, ontology, metaphysics, scientific and technologic output, etc. finds a marked tendency toward the meaningful integration of these with the prevailing culture.

Sorokin has boldly confronted the problem of how to determine the *extent* to which such integration occurs, recognizing, despite his vitriolic comments on the statisticians of our sensate age, that to deal with the "extent" or "degree" of integration necessary implies some statistical measure. Accordingly, he developed numerical indexes of the various writings and authors in each period, classified these in their appropriate category, and thus assessed the comparative frequency (and influence) of the various systems of thought. Whatever the technical evaluation of the validity and reliability of these cultural statistics, he has directly acknowledged the problem overlooked by many investigators of "integrated cultures" or *Sinnzusammenhaengen*, namely, the approximate degree or extent of such integration. Moreover, he plainly bases his empirical conclusions very largely upon these statistics. (70) And these conclusions again

---

69. Sorokin, *Social and Cultural Dynamics*, IV, Chap. 1: I, Chap. 1.

70. Despite the basic place of these statistics in his empirical findings, Sorokin adopts a curiously ambivalent attitude toward them, an attitude similar to the attitude toward experiment imputed to Newton: a device to make his prior conclusions "intelligible and to convince the vulgar." Note Sorokin's approval of Park's remark that his statistics are merely a concession to the prevailing sensate mentality and that "if they want 'em, let 'em have 'em." Sorokin, *Sociocultural Causality, Space, Time*, p. 95n. Sorokin's ambivalence arises from his effort to integrate quite disparate "systems of truth."

testify that his approach leads to a statement of the problem of connections between existential bases and knowledge, rather than to its solution. Thus, to take a case in point. "Empiricism" is defined as the typical sensate system of truth. The last five centuries, and more particularly, the last century represent "Sensate culture par excellence!" (71) Yet, even in this flood-tide of sensate culture, Sorokin's statistical indices show only some 53% of influential writings in the field of "empiricism." And in earlier centuries of this sensate culture, — from the late 16th to the mid-18th — the indices of empiricism are consistently lower than those for rationalism, (which is associated, presumably, with an idealistic rather than a sensate culture). (72) The object of these observations is not to raise the question whether Sorokin's conclusions coincide with his statistical data: it is not to ask why the 16th and 17th centuries are said to have a dominant "sensate sysem of truth" in view of these data. Rather, it is to indicate that even on Sorokin's own premises, overall characterizations of historical cultures constitute merely a first step, which must be followed by analyses of deviations from the "central tendencies" of the culture. Once the notion of *extent* of integration is introduced, the existence of types of knowledge which are not integrated with the dominant tendencies cannot be viewed merely as "congeries" or as "contingent." Their *social* bases must be ascertained in a fashion for which an emanationist theory does not provide.

A basic concept which serves to differentiate generalizations about the thought and knowledge of an entire society or culture is that of the "audience" or "public" or what Znaniecki calls "the social circle." Men of knowledge do not orient themselves exclusively toward their data nor toward the total society, but to special segments of that society with their special demands, criteria of validity, of "significant" knowledge, of pertinent problems, etc. It is through anticipation of these demands and expectations of particular audiences, which can be effectively located in the social structure, that men of knowledge organize their own work, define their data, seize upon problems. Hence, the more differentiated the society, the greater the range of such effective audiences, the greater the variation in the foci of scientific attention, of conceptual formulations and of procedures for certifying claims to knowledge. By linking each of these

---

71. Sorokin, *Social and Cultural Dynamics,* II, p. 51.
72. *Ibid.,* II, p. 30.

typologically defined audiences to their distinctive social position, it becomes possible to provide a wissenssoziologische account of variations and conflicts of thought within the society, a problem which is necessarily by-passed by any emanationist theory. Thus, the scientists in seventeenth century England and France who were organized in newly established scientific societies addressed themselves to audiences very different from those of the savants who remained exclusively in the traditional universities. The direction of their efforts, toward a "plain, sober, empirical" exploration of specific technical and scientific problems differed considerably from the speculative, unexperimental work of those in the universities. Searching out such variations in effective audiences, exploring their distinctive criteria of significant and valid knowledge, (73) relating these to their position within the society and examining the socio-psychological processes through which these operate to constrain certain modes of thought constitutes a procedure which promises to take research in the sociology of knowledge from the plane of general imputation to testable empirical inquiry. (74)

The foregoing account deals with the main substance of prevailing theories in this field. Limitations of space permit only the briefest consideration of one other aspect of these theories singled out in our paradigm: functions imputed to various types of mental productions. (75)

Functions Imputed to Existentially Conditioned Mental Pro-

---

73. The Rickert-Weber concept of "Wertbeziehung" (relevance to value) is but a first step in this direction; there remains the further task of differentiating the various sets of values and relating these to distinctive groups or strata within the society.

74. This is perhaps the most distinctive variation in the sociology of knowledge now developing in American sociological circles, and may almost be viewed as an American acculturation of European approaches. This development characteristically derives from the social psychology of G. H. Mead. Its pertinence in this connection is being indicated by C. W. Mills, Gerard de Gré, and others. See Znaniecki's conception of the "social circle," *op. cit.* See, also, the beginnings of empirical findings along these lines in the more general field of public communications: Paul F. Lazarsfeld and R. K. Merton, "Studies in Radio and Film Propaganda," *Transactions of the New York Academy of Sciences*, 6: 58-79, 1943.

75. An appraisal of historicist and ahistorical approaches is necessarily omitted. It may be remarked that this controversy definitely admits of a middle ground.

ductions. In addition to providing "causal explanations" of knowledge, theories ascribe "social functions" to this knowledge, functions which presumably serve to account for their persistence or change. These cannot be examined in any detail here, though a detailed study of these functional analyses would undoubtedly prove rewarding.

The most distinctive feature of the Marxist imputation of function is its ascription, not to the society as a whole, but to distinct strata within the society. Not only does this hold true of "ideological thinking," but also of natural science. In capitalist society, science and derivative technology become a further instrument of control by the dominant class. (76) Along these same lines, in ferreting out the "economic determinants" of scientific development, it has often been thought sufficient to show that the scientific results enabled the solution of some economic or technological "need." But the application of science does not necessarily testify that the need has been significantly involved in leading to the result. Hyperbolic functions were discovered two centuries before they had any practical significance and the study of conic sections had a broken history of two millennia before being applied in science and technology. Can we infer, then, that the "needs" which were ultimately satisfied through such applications served to direct the attention of mathematicians to these fields, that there was, so to speak, a retroactive influence of some two to twenty centuries? Detailed inquiry into the relations between the emergence of "needs," recognition of these needs by scientists or by those who direct their selection of problems and the consequences of such recognition is required before the role of needs in determining the thematics of scientific research can be established. (77)

In addition to his claim that the categories are social emergents,

---

76. For example, Marx quotes from the 19th century apologist of capitalism, Ure, who, speaking of the invention of the self-acting mule, says: "A creation destined to restore order among the industrious classes . . . This invention confirms the great doctrine already propounded, that when capital enlists science into her service, the refractory hand of labor will always be taught docility." *Capital*, I, p. 477.

77. Compare B. Hessen, *op. cit.*, R. K. Merton, *Science, Technology and Society in 17th Century England*, (Bruges: "Osiris History of Science Monographs," 1938), chapters 7-10; J. D. Bernal, *The Social Function of Science* (New York: The Macmillan Co., 1939); J. G. Crowther, *The Social Relations of Science,* (New York: The Macmillan Co., 1941).

Durkheim also indicates their social functions. The functional analysis, however, is intended to account not for the particular categorial system in a society but for the existence of some system common to the society. For purposes of inter-communication and for coordinating men's activities, a common set of categories is indispensable. What the apriorist mistakes for the constraint of an inevitable, native form of understanding is actually "the very authority of society, transferring itself to a certain manner of thought which is the indispensable condition of all common action." (78) There must be a certain minimum of "logical conformity" if joint social activities are to be maintained at all; a common set of categories is a functional necessity. This view is further developed by Sorokin who indicates the several functions served by different systems of social space and time. (79)

II

Further Problems and Recent Studies. From the foregoing discussion, it becomes evident that a wide diversity of problems in this field require further investigation. (80)

Scheler had indicated that the social organization of intellectual activity is significantly related to the character of the knowledge which develops under its auspices. One of the earliest studies of the problem in this country was Veblen's caustic, impressionistic and often perceptive account of the pressures shaping American university life. (81) In more systematic fashion, Wilson has dealt with the methods and criteria of recruitment, the assignment of status and the mechanisms of control of the academic man, thus providing a substantial basis for comparative studies. (82) Setting forth a typology of the roles of men of knowledge, Znaniecki developed a

---

78. Durkheim, *Elementary Forms* . . ., p. 17, 10-11, 443.
79. Sorokin, *Sociocultural Causality, Space, Time, passim.*
80. For further summaries, see Louis Wirth's preface to Mannheim, *Ideology and Utopia*, pp. xxviii-xxxi; J. B. Gittler, "Possibilities of a Sociology of Science," *Social Forces*, 18: 350-359, 1940.
81. Thorstein Veblen, *The Higher Learning in America*, (New York: Huebsch, 1918).
82. Logan Wilson, *The Academic Man*, (New York: Oxford University Press, 1942); *cf.* E. Y. Hartshorne, *The German Universities and National Socialism*, (Harvard University Press, 1937).

series of hypotheses concerning the relations between these roles and the types of knowledge cultivated; between types of knowledge and the bases of appraisal of the scientist by members of the society; between role-definitions and attitudes toward practical and theoretical knowledge; etc. (83) Much remains to be investigated concerning the bases of class identifications by intellectuals, their alienation from dominant or subordinate strata in the population, their avoidance of or indulgence in researches which have immediate value-implications challenging current institutional arrangements inimical to the attainment of culturally approved goals, (84) the pressures toward technicism and away from "dangerous thought," the bureaucratization of intellectuals as a process whereby problems of policy are converted into problems of administration, the areas of social life in which expertise and positive knowledge are deemed appropriate and those in which the wisdom of the plain man is alone considered necessary — in short, the shifting role of the intellectual and the relation of these changes to the structure, content and influence of his work require growing attention, as changes in the social organization increasingly subject the intellectual to conflicting demands. (85)

Increasingly, it has been assumed that the social structure does not influence science merely by focusing the attention of scientists upon certain problems for research. In addition to the studies to which we have already referred, others have dealt with the ways in which the cultural and social context enters into the conceptual phrasing of scientific problems. Darwin's theory of selection was modeled after the prevailing notion of a competitive economic order; a notion which in turn has been assigned an ideological function

---

83. Florian Znaniecki, *Social Role of the Man of Knowledge*, (New York: Columbia University Press, 1940).

84. Gunnar Myrdal in his treatise, *An American Dilemma*, (New York: Harper and Bros., 1944), repeatedly indicates the "concealed valuations" of American social scientists studying the American Negro and the effect of these valuations on the formulation of "scientific problems" in this area of research. See especially II, pp. 1027-1064.

85. Mannheim refers to an unpublished monograph on the intellectual; general bibliographies are to be found in his books and in Roberto Michel's article on "Intellectuals," *Encyclopedia of the Social Sciences*. Recent papers include C. W. Mills, "The Social Role of the Intellectual," *Politics*, I, April 1944; R. K. Merton, "Role of the Intellectual in Public Policy," presented at the annual meeting of the American Sociological Society, Dec. 4, 1943; Arthur Koestler, "The Intelligentsia," *Horizon*, 9: 162-175, 1944.

through its assumption of a "natural identity of interests." (86) Russell's half-serious observation on the national characteristics of research in animal learning points to a further type of inquiry into the relations between national culture and conceptual formulations. (87) So, too, Fromm has attempted to show that Freud's "conscious liberalism" tacitly involved a rejection of impulses tabooed by bourgeois society and that Freud himself was in his patricentric character, a typical representative of a society which demands obedience and subjection. (88)

In much the same fashion, it has been indicated that the conception of multiple causation is especially congenial to the academician, who has relative security, is loyal to the status quo from which he derives dignity and sustenance, who leans toward conciliation and sees something valuable in all viewpoints, thus tending toward a taxonomy which enables him to avoid taking sides by stressing the

---

86. Keynes observed that "The Principle of the Survival of the Fittest could be regarded as one vast generalization of the Ricardian economics." Quoted by Talcott Parsons, *The Structure of Social Action*, (New York: McGraw-Hill Book Co., 1937), 113; *cf.* Alexander Sandow, "Social Factors in the Origin of Darwinism," *Quarterly Review of Biology*, 13: 316-26, 1938.

87. Bertrand Russell, *Philosophy*, (New York: W. W. Norton and Co., 1927), pp. 29-30, Russell remarks that the animals used in psychological research "have all displayed the national characteristics of the observer. Animals studied by Americans rush about frantically, with an incredible display of hustle and pep, and at last achieve the desired result by chance. Animals observed by Germans sit still and think, and at last evolve the solution out of their inner consciousness." Witticism need not be mistaken for irrelevance; the possibility of national differences in the choice and formulation of scientific problems has been repeatedly noted, though not studied systematically. *Cf.* Richard Mueller-Freienfels, *Psychologie der Wissenschaft*, (Leipzig: J. A. Barth, 1936), Chap. 8, which deals with national, as well as class, differences in the choice of problems, 'styles of thought,' etc., without fully acquiescing in the echt-deutsch requirements of a Krieck. This type of interpretation, however, can be carried to a polemical and ungrounded extreme, as in Max Scheler's debunking 'analysis' of English cant. He concludes that, in science, as in all other spheres, the English are incorrigible 'cantians.' Hume's conception of the ego, substance, and continuity as biologically useful self-deceptions was merely purposive cant; so, too, was the characteristic English conception of working hypotheses (Maxwell, Kelvin) as aiding the progress of science but not as truth—a conception which is nothing but a shrewd maneuver to provide momentary control and ordering of the data. All pragmatism implies this opportunistic cant, says Scheler, *Génius des Krieges*, (Leipzig: Verlag der Weissenbuecher, 1915).

88. Erich Fromm, "Die gesellschaftliche Bendingtheit der psychoanalytischen Therapie," *Zeitschrift fuer Sozialforschung*, 4: 365-97, 1935.

SOCIOLOGY OF KNOWLEDGE

multiplicity of factors and the complexity of problems. (89) Emphases on "nature" or "nurture" as prime determinants of human nature have been linked with opposing political orientations. Those who emphasizes heredity are political conservatives whereas the environmentalists are prevalently democrats or radicals seeking social change. (90) But even "environmentalists" among contemporary American writers on social pathology adopt conceptions of "social adjustment" which implicitly assume the standards of small communities as norms and characteristically fail to assess the possibility of certain groups achieving their objectives under the given institutional conditions. (91) The imputations of perspectives such as these require more systematic study before they can be accepted, but they indicate recent tendencies to seek out the perspectives of scholars and to relate these to the framework of experience and interests constituted by their respective social positions. The questionable character of imputations which are not based on adequate *comparative* material is illustrated by a recent account of the writings of Negro scholars. The selection of analytical rather than morphological categories, of environmental rather than biological determinants of behavior, of exceptional rather than typical data is ascribed to the caste-like resentment of Negro writers, without any effort being made to compare the frequency of similar tendencies among white writers. (92)

Vestiges of any tendency to regard the development of science and technology as self-contained and advancing irrespective of the social structure are being dissipated by the actual course of historical events. An increasingly visible control and, often, restraint of scientific research and invention has been repeatedly documented, notably in a series of studies by Stern, (93) who has also traced the

89. Lewis S. Feuer, "The Economic Factor in History," *Science and Society*, 4: 174-175, 1940.

90. N. Pastore, "The Nature-Nurture Controversy: a Sociological Approach," *School and Society*, 57: 373-377, 1943.

91. C. Wright Mills, "The Professional Ideology of Social Pathologists," *American Journal of Sociology*, 49: 165-190, 1943.

92. William T. Fontaine, "'Social Determination' in the Writings of Negro Scholars," *American Journal of Sociology*, 49: 302-315, 1944.

93. Bernhard J. Stern, "Resistances to the Adoption of Technological Innovations," in National Resources Committee, *Technological Trends and National Policy*, (Washington U. S. Government Printing Office, 1937), pp. 39-66; "Restraints upon the Utilization of Inventions," *The Annals*, 200: 1-19, 1938, and further references therein; Walton Hamilton, *Patents and Free Enterprise*, (TNEC Monograph No. 31, 1941).

bases of resistance to change in medicine. (94) The basic change in the social organization of Germany has provided a virtual experimental test of the close dependence of the direction and extent of scientific work upon the prevailing power structure and the associated cultural outlook. (95) And the limitations of any unqualified assumption that science or technology represent "the basis" to which the social structure must "adjust" become evident in the light of studies showing how science and technology have been put in the service of social or economic demands. (96)

To develop any further the formidable list of problems which require and are receiving empirical investigation would outrun the space limits of this paper. There is only this to be said: the sociology of knowledge is fast outgrowing a prior tendency to confuse provisional hypothesis with unimpeachable dogma; the plenitude of speculative insights which marked its early stages are now being subjected to increasingly rigorous test. Though Toynbee and Sorokin may be correct in speaking of an alternation of periods of fact-finding and generalization in the history of science, it seems that the sociology of knowledge has wedded these two tendencies in what promises to be a fruitful union. Above all, it focusses on those problems which are at the very center of contemporary intellectual interest.

---

94. Bernhard J. Stern, *Social Factors in Medical Progress*, (New York: Columbia University Press, 1927); *Society and Medical Progress*, (Princeton: Princeton University Press, 1941); cf. Richard H. Shryock, *The Development of Modern Medicine*, (Philadelphia: University of Pennsylvania Press, 1936); Henry E. Sigerist, *Man and Medicine*, (New York: W. W. Norton and Co., 1932).

95. Hartshorne, *German Universities and National Socialism;* R .K. Merton, "Science and the Social Order," *Philosophy of Science*, 5: 321-337, 1938.

96. Only most conspicuously in time of war; see Sorokin's observation that centers of military power tend to be the centers of scientific and technologic development (*Dynamics*, IV, 249-51); cf. I. B. Cohen and Bernard Barber, *Science and War* (ms.); R. K. Merton, "Science and Military Technique," *Scientific Monthly*, 41: 542-545, 1935; Bernal, *op. cit.;* Julian Huxley, *Science and Social Needs*, (New York: Harper and Bros., 1935).

SELECTED BIBLIOGRAPHY*

DeGré, Gerard L., *Society and Ideology: an Inquiry into the Sociology of Knowledge*, (New York: Columbia University Bookstore, 1943).

Durkheim, Emile, *The Elementary Forms of the Religious Life*, (London: Allen and Unwin, 1915).

SOCIOLOGY OF KNOWLEDGE

Engels, Friedrich, *Ludwig Feuerbach,* (Chicago: C. H. Kerr and Co., 1903).
Granet, Marcel, *La pensée chinoise,* (Paris: La Renaissance du Livre, 1934).
Gruenwald, Ernest, *Das Problem der Soziologie des Wissens,* (Wien-Leipzig: Wilhelm Braumueller, 1934).
Mannheim, Karl, *Ideology and Utopia,* trans. by Louis Wirth and Edward Shils, (New York: Harcourt, Brace and Co., 1936).
Mannheim, Karl, *Man and Society in an Age of Reconstruction,* trans. by Edward Shils, (New York: Harcourt, Brace and Co., 1940).
Marx, Karl, and Friedrich Engels, *The German Ideology,* (New York: International Publishers, 1939).
Scheler, Max, *Versuche einer Soziologie des Wissens,* (Muenchen und Leipzig: Duncker und Humblot, 1924).
Scheler, Max, *Die Wissensformen und die Gesellschaft,* (Leipzig: Der Neue-Geist Verlag, 1926).
Sorokin, Pitirim A., *Social and Cultural Dynamics,* (New York: American Book Co., 1937-1941, 4 vols.).
Wilson, Logan, *The Academic Man,* (New York: Oxford University Press, 1942).
Znaniecki, Florian, *The Social Role of the Man of Knowledge,* (New York: Columbia University Press, 1940).

* For extensive bibliographies, see Mannheim, *Ideology and Utopia*; Harry E. Barnes, Howard Becker, and Frances B. Becker,, eds., *Contemporary Social Theory,* (New York: D. Appleton-Century Co., 1940).

Robert K. Merton, Ph. D. (Harvard), is Assistant Professor of Sociology, Columbia University and Associate Director, Bureau of Applied Social Research, Columbia University. He has previously taught at Harvard and Tulane Universities. Professor Merton is the author of *Science, Technology and Society in Seventeenth Century England,* and of numerous papers in scientific journals.

CHAPTER XIV

SOCIOLOGY OF RELIGION

by

JOACHIM WACH

I

The Nature and Aims of a Sociology of Religion. (1) Like other sociological disciplines — the sociology of art or of law — the sociology of religion is the offspring of two different scholarly pursuits, the study of *society* and the study of *religion*. Its character, methods, and aims reflect this parentage. In addition to the problems which the sociology of religion inherits from the two parental disciplines, it has its own peculiar difficulties and tasks. That is to say: sociology of religion shares with the sociology of other activities of man certain problems and, in addition, has its own which are due to the peculiar nature of *religious* experience and its *expression*. (The theory of religious experience is to be

---

1. For a broader exposition of the concept of the sociology of religion, as advocated here, and for illustrations from different religious faiths and groups, and more inclusive bibliography, see Joachim Wach, *Sociology of Religion,* (Chicago: University of Chicago Press, 1944).

worked out by the philosopher, theologian, and psychologist in cooperation with the student of religion.

Like other sociological disciplines, the sociology of religion is a young branch of study, not more than half a century old. That does not mean that major contributions toward an inquiry into the nature of socio-religious phenomena have not been made long before, but as an organized systematical discipline (emancipated from the older disciplines in and from which it developed) the sociology of religion is of recent date. Earlier contributions were made by students in widely different fields: theology, philosophy, and philology, jurisprudence and the social sciences, and later archaeology and anthropology. A great deal of material was thus gathered, particularly in the course of the nineteenth century, and periodically grouped and reviewed from theological and philosophical, psychological and sociological viewpoints. What was lacking, at least until the beginning of the twentieth century, was finally evolved by the cooperation of a group of outstanding scholars of different nationalities: *categories* with which to organize the vast material assembled. The sociology of religion had to develop its own methodology based on an unbiased examination of the nature of its subject matter.

Before we can survey attempts in this direction we have to trace briefly some of the major trends in the development of studies to be integrated into a systematic sociology of religion. It is perhaps significant that exchange of ideas and mutual interdependence between the scholars of various nations — American, English, Dutch, French, German, Scandinavian — has been in this dislipline as strong as, if not stronger than, in other fields of sociological research.

The Emergence of Sociology of Religion by Cooperative International Efforts of Different Schools.

A. French Sociology of Religion. (2) French Sociology of Religion is characterized all through the nineteenth century by the dominance of the tenets of the philosophy of history as sociology, as developed by Auguste Comte and his successors. Its course, methodology, and aims were determined by students of sociology, not by those of religion. It was conceived in a broad, encyclopedic at-

---

2. Cf. Henri Pinard de la Boullaye, S. J., *L'étude comparée des religions*, (Paris: Gabriel Beauchesne, 1922, 1929, 2 Vols.); Simon Deploige, *The Conflict between Ethics and Sociology*, (Saint Louis, Mo. and London: B. Herder Book Co., 1938).

tempt to review the life and growth of society; it was determined by the interest in an application of "scientific" methods ("laws") to socio-historical phenomena including religious ideas and institutions (theory of stages of development), and finally by the endeavour to include the material gathered in anthropological and ethnological research. Theological and metaphysical norms were to be replaced by positivistic principles. That is, positive philosophy was to set the norms for the organization of life and society. According to this conception, mankind is not only the subject but also the object of religion.

The first trend of modern French sociology of religion is marked by the well-known works of Emile Durkheim (3) and other contemporary writers: Lucien Lévy Bruhl, Marcel Mauss, etc. Durkheim's concept of sociology is characterized by a marked emancipation from the tenets of Comte's philosophy of history as sociology (sociology as a method) and by a corresponding tendency toward construction of a typology of social groupings, in which he included religious communities. In his concept of the nature of religion he agrees with *Comte*. His chef-d'oeuvre, *Les formes élémentaires de la vie religieuse*, applies the categories of a typological sociology to the data of primitive religious communities. *Lévy-Bruhl* (4) concentrates his attention upon the psychological investigation of the group-consciousness in primitive society. *L'année sociologique* formed for over a decade the center of studies in the sociology of religion.

A second trend is indicated by the synthetic studies of a number of French scholars, such as Numa Denis Fustel de Coulanges (1830-1889), and E. F. A. Count Goblet d'Alviella, and then more recently

---

3. Emile Durkheim, *The Rules of Sociological Method*, 8th ed. tr., edited by G. E. G. Catlin, (Chicago: University of Chicago Press, 1938); Talcott Parsons, *The Structure of Social Action*, (New York: McGraw-Hill Book Co., 1937), Part II, Chaps. X-XII and "Theoretical Development of the Sociology of Religion" *Journal of History of Ideas*, 5: 176 ff., 1944.

4. Lucien Lévy-Bruhl, *L'expérience mystique et les symboles chez les primitifs*, (Paris: Félix Alcan, 1938); *Les foactions mentales dans les sociétés inférieures*, (Paris: Félix Alcan, 1928); *La mentalité primitive*, (Oxford: The Clarendon Press, 1931); transl. by L. A. Clare, (London: Allen and Unwin; New York: The Macmillan Co., 1923); *The 'Soul' of the Primitive*, transl. by A. Clare, (New York: The Macmillan Co., 1928); *Le surnaturel et la nature dans la mentalité primitive*, (Paris: A. F. Alcan, 1931).

SOCIOLOGY OF RELIGION

Arnold Van Gennep and Paul Foucart. (5) In their writings certain concepts, rites, and institutions fundamental to religious group life are analyzed and compared. Inasmuch as these authors did not limit themselves to a discussion of primitive society, though they concentrate on non-Christian religion, a rapproachement between sociological and sociopsychological studies, on the one hand, and the efforts of the school of "comparative religions" (F. Max Mueller, C. P. Tiele, W. Robertson Smith) on the other, was affected. The latter investigations were carried on by a school of students of religion who aspired at emancipation from theological conceptions, working for the establishment of a science of religion on the basis of the critical (historical and philological) and comparative method.

The *third* trend is characterized by (a) a clearer methodological consciousness concerning the field, purpose, and method of the sociology of religion; (b) a profounder understanding of the nature of religious communion; (c) a rapproachement between students of *religion* from theological and philosophical points of view, and of students of *society*. (6) Outstanding are the works of Raoul de la Grasserie and P. Pinard de la Boullaye, S. J., of Roger Bastide and Robert Will. The last phase reflects to a considerable extent the influence of the German sociology of religion of Max Weber and Ernst Troeltsch (particularly the studies of Robert Will).

To Pinard de la Boullaye we owe the best existing history of the study of religion and a thorough discussion of its methods including the sociological approach. He gives attention to the social

---

5. Arnold Van Gennep, *La formation des legendes*, (Paris: E. Feauncarion, 1910); Eugene Comte Goblet d' Alviella, *Introduction à l'histoire générale des religions*, (Bruxelles: Mozbach and Falk, 1887); *Croyances, rites, institutions*, (Paris: 1911); Numa Dennis Fustel de Coulanges, *La cité antique*, 20 ed., (Paris: Hachette et Cie, 1908); Paul Faucourt, *Les mystères d'Eleusis*, (Paris: A. Picart, 1914).

6. Raoul de la Grasserie, *Des religions comparées au point de vue sociologique*, (Paris: V. Girard et., E. Briere, 1899); Roger Bastide, *Eléments de sociologie religieuse*, (Paris: Armand Colin, 1935); Robert Will, *Le culte*, (Paris: Félix Alcan, 1925-1929); cf. also *Annales Sociologiques B. Sociologie Religieuse*, (ed. by Marcel Mauss and M. Granet, Paris: F. Alcan, 1939); Pinard de la Boullaye, *op. cit*. The author of this report did not have occasion to do full justice to the modern French school of sociology of religion in his own recent contribution (note 1), because some woks were not available to him.

Cf. also Robert K. Merton, "Recent French Sociology," *Social Forces*, 12: 537 ff., 1933.

organization of religion and to the problem of authority. The work of de la Grasserie is more important than often realized. It is characterized by a keen systematic interest, by relative absence of the preconceptions of the positivistic school, and by comprehensiveness of material. Though he presses the analogy of the religious body with the physical organism and though his concept of the "divine society" is open to criticism, he does offer very helpful categories for the understanding of "external religious society," and particularly of the "societies to the second power," as created by prophets and saints. The relations between religious and civil societies receive his attention. Bastide's brief summary extends the field of the sociology of religion too widely; only one chapter ("L'organisation religieuse") deals with its tasks as we will have to define it. The most comprehensive treatment of the subject in French is now Robert Will's volumes on the nature and forms of cults with which this reviewer, whose outline in German was known to the author, agrees on many important points. The study makes the threefold assumption that man, in his cultic functions, faces (1) God, (2) the world of cultic forms, (3) the religious community. It presents first an analysis of man's communion with God ("communion in God"), including a review of the main types of cultic activity (sacrifice, mystery, prayer) and of religious attitudes (mystery and revelation on the divine side, adoration and edification on the human side). Secondly, it offers an inquiry into the principles (causes, laws, values), the forms (media, personnel, action and atmosphere), and finally the general sociological categories of religions communality, in virtual if not conscious agreement with the theories of Scheler, Litt and Mead. This exposition is followed by an analysis of the cultic group, its milieu and symbols. Lack of space precludes a detailed discussion of Will's system in this context.

B. *German Sociology of Religion.* (7) In Germany (a) *philoso-*

---

7. Cf. Wach, *Sociology of Religion;* Max Weber, *Gesammelte Aufsaetze zur Religionssoziologie,* (Tuebingen: J. C. B. Mohr, 1920-1921); Weber, *Wirtschaft und Gesellschaft,* (Tuebingen: J. C. B. Mohr, 1921), Sec. III, Chap. IV, "Religionssoziologie"; Ernst Troeltsch, *The Social Teaching of the Christian Churches,* (New York: The Macmillan Co., 1931); Leopold von Wiese and Howard Becker, *Systematic Sociology,* (New York: John Wiley and Sons; London: Chapman and Hall, 1932); Erich Rothacker, *Einleitung in die Geisteswissenschaften;* (Tuebingen, J. C. B. Mohr, 1920); Joachim Wach, *Einleitung in die Religionssoziologie,* (Tuebingen J. C. B. Mohr, 1930); Theodore Abel, *Systematic Sociology in Germany,* (New York: Columbia University Press, 1929); Talcott Parsons, *op. cit.,* Part III.

SOCIOLOGY OF RELIGION

phical preoccupation with the various types of cultural activities on an idealistic basis (Johann Gottfried Herder, G. W. F. Hegel, Johann Gustav Droysen, Herrmann Steinthal, Wilhelm Wundt); (b) legal studies (Aemiluis Ludwig, Ritcher, Rudolf Sohm, Otto Gierke); (c) *philology* and *archaeology*, both stimulated by the romantic movement of the first decades of the 19th century; (d) *economic theory* and *history* (Karl Marx, Lorenz von Stein, Heinrich von Treitschke, Wilhelm Roscher, Adolf Wagner, Gustav Schmoller, Ferdinad Toennies); (e) *ethnological* research (Friedrich Ratzel, Adolf Bastian, Rudolf Steinmetz, Johann Jakob Bachofen, Hermann Steinthal, Richard Thurnwald, Alfred Vierkandt, P. Wilhelm Schmidt), on the one hand; and historical and systematical work in *theology* (Church history, Canonical Law — "Kirchenrecht") Systematic theology (Fr. E. D. Schleiermacher, Richard Rothe) and in *philosophy of religion*, on the other, prepared the way during the nineteenth century for the following era to define the task of a sociology of religion and to organize the material gathered by these pursuits. The names of Max Weber, Ernst Troeltsch, Werner Sombart and Georg Simmel — all pupils of the above mentioned older scholars — stand out. The first named has fostered more than anybody else the investigation of the relation between economics and society on one side and religion on the other — typologically and historically in *Gesammelte Aufsaetze zur Religionssoziologie* and systematically in *Wirtschaft und Gesellschaft*. Troeltsch, concentrating on the Christian world, presented his comprehensive studies of Christian groups and their social and moral concepts (*Soziallehren der Christlichen Kirchen*). To Sombart we owe extensive treatment of the development of forms of economical and correlative social and religious concepts. (8) In Georg Simmel's *Soziologie* the first consistent attempt at a purely formal sociology was made; in his sociology of religion Simmel follows Durkheim. (9) After the first World War a new generation of sociologists (Karl Dunkmann, Leopold von Wiese, (10) Alfred Vierkandt Ottmar Spann), and of students of religion, both Protestant and

---

8. *Der moderne Kapitalismus,* Muenchen and Leipzig: Duncker und Humblot, 1928); transl., by Nussbaum, *A History of Economic Institutions of Modern Europe,* (New York: F. S. Crofts, 1933).

9. *Soziologie,* (Berlin: Duncker und Humbolt 1925); Nicholas J. Spykman, *The Social Theory of Georg Simmel,* (Chicago: University of Chicago Press, 1925).

10. Wiese and Becker; *op. cit.;* Wiese, *Sociology,* ed. by Franz H. Mueller, (New York: Oscar Piest, 1941).

Catholic (Romano Guardini, G. Gundlach, Johann Baptist Kraus) — the most outstanding of which was Max Scheler (11) — followed the lead of the older generation (cf. "Erinnerungsgabe fuer Max Weber"), joined by Scandinavian and Dutch scholars (especially Gerardus Van der Leeuw, whose work is one of the most important contributions to the comparative study of religions between the two wars, and Hendrik Kraemer). The philosophical and historical work of Wilhem Dilthey, himself averse to establishing an independent sociological discipline, proved to be important systematically and epistomologically (Theodor Litt, Joachim Wach).

With the advent of National Socialism the official philosophical and racial teachings of the Third Reich, prepared by its ideological forerunners, began to make themselves felt in all disciplines concerned with the study of religion and of society. (Cf. the later volumes of *the Archiv fuer Religionswissenschaft*). No significant contribution in our field can be listed. (13)

C. *English Sociology of Religion*. (14) In England the development of legal and historical studies (Henry Sumner Maine, Frederic William Maitland, Paul Vinogradoff, Ernest Barker) coalesced with anthropological (Edward Burnett Tylor, John Lubbock, Andrew Lang, John George Frazer) and psychological research (Robert Randolph Marett, Graham Wallace, A. R. Radcliffe-Brown). In philosophy the empirical and naturalistic school (John Stuart Mill, Herbert Spencer) as well as the idealistic (Thomas Hill Green, Bernard Bosanquet) focussed their attention on the problems of the nature and development of society. The con-

---

11. Unfortunately Scheler's books are not translated. Cf. bibliography and discussion by H. Otto Dalke, *"The Sociology and Knowledge"* in Harry E. Barnes and Howard Becker, eds., *Contemporary Social Theory*, (New York: D. Appleton-Century Book Co., 1940) Chap. IV.

12. Cf. Alexander Goldenweiser, "The Relation of the Natural Science to the Social Sciences," in *ibid.*, Chap. V.

13. Cf. for a survey: Alfred Krauskopf, *Die Religion und die Gemeinschaftsmaechte*, (Leipgiz: B. C. Teubner, 1935); Eva Hirschmann, *Phaenomenologie der Religion*, (Wuerzburg: Konrad Triltsch, 1940). Gustav Mensching, *Vergleichende Religionswissenschaft*, (Leipzig: Hochschulwissen, 1938) was not available to the author.

14. Robert M. McIver, "Sociology," in *Encyclopedia of the Social Sciences*, 14: 232-247; Ernest Barker, *The Citizen's Choice*, (Cambridge, Eng.: Cambridge University Press, 1937); R. R. Marett, *Taylor*, (London: Chapman and Hall, 1936); Ernest B. Harper, "Sociology in England," *Social Forces*, 11: 325 ff., 1932.

SOCIOLOGY OF RELIGION

cept of evolution (Charles Darwin, Herber Spencer, Walter Bagehot, Edward Westermarck) and the metholodogy of positivism (Thomas Buckle) had far-reaching influence. Though the task of a sociology of religion has never been as clearly and systematically defined as in France and Germany, great contributions were made in England through the cooperation of the students of the gradually emerging sociology (Leonard T. Hodhouse, Morris Ginsberg, Robert M. MacIver) and of the study of history (Charles H. MacIlvain and John N. Figgis) and of economics (C. C. J. Webb, Richard Tawney) with students of religion interested in the problems of social theology. Anglican and non-conformist theologians, philosophers, and writers (Thomas Carlyle, John Ruskin, Frederic Dennis Maurice, Charles Kingsley), especially the Christian Socialists, were interested in the normative aspect of the problems of religion and society. (15) In the younger generation several of these trends are blended: William Temple, John MacMurray, Maurice B. Rickett, Vigo A. Demant. (16) Max Weber's influence in England never reached as deep as in France or the United States; it remained limited to his theories on economics. On the other hand, the studies in "comparative religion," stimulated by the untiring efforts of Max Mueller, were cultivated at Oxford and Cambridge in close contact with continental archaeological, philological, and historical investigations (Ernest Crawley, Gilbert Murray, Jane Harrison, Frank Byron Jevons, E. O. James) (17)

D. North American Sociology of Religion (18) In the United

---

15. Cyril K. Gloyn, *The Church and the Social Order (from Coleridge to Maurice)*, (Forest Grove, Oregon: Pacific University, 1942); William Peck, *The Social Implications of the Oxford Movement*, (New York: Chas. Scribner's Sons, 1932).

16. John MacMurray, *Creative Society*, (New York: Assosiation Press, 1936) and *The Structure of Religious Experience*, (New Haven: Yale University Press, 1936); Maurice B. Reckitt, *Faith and Society*, (New York and London: Longmans, Green and Co., 1932); Vigo A. Demant, *God, Man, Society*, (London: Morehouse, 1934).

17. Floyd N. House, *The Range of Social Theory*, (New York: Henry Holt and Co., 1929), Chap. XVIII, "The Sociology of Religion."

18. William F. Ogburn and Alexander Goldenweiser, *The Social Sciences and Their Interrelation*, (Boston, etc.: Houghton, Mifflin Co., 1927); Floyd N. House, *op. cit.;* Earle E. Eubank, "The Field and Problems of the Sociology of Religion," and Arthur E. Holt, "The Sources and Methods of the Sociology of Religion" in L. L. Bernard, ed., *The Fields and Methods of Sociology*, (New York: Ray Long' and R. R. Smith, 1934); Barnes and Becker, *Contemporary Social Theory*, especially Chap. XXIII; Barnes and Becker, *Social Thought from Lore to Science*, (Boston, etc.: D. C. Health and Co., 1938).

States interest in the sociology of religion was stimulated by the encyclopedic tendencies of the earlier sociologists (William Graham Sumner, Albert G. Keller, Edward A. Ross) (19) and by the work of historical and systematical social theology (Francis G. Peabody, Charles A. Ellwood, Shailer Mathews, Shirley J. Case). The movement of the Social Gospel (20) focussed the attention of students of religion on social phenomena from a normative point of view. The peculiar problems of American denominationalism (Heinrich H. Maurer, H. Richard Niebuhr, William Warren Sweet, Paul Douglass) (21) are reflected in the interest in socio-religious statistics (William F. Ogburn) and urban-rural studies (Robert E. Park, Ernest W. Burgess, Carle C. Zimmermann and H. P. Douglass, Edward de S. Brunner, John H. Kolb,). (22) Catholic scholars have shown their interest by critical and positive investigations supplemented by philosophical reflection. (23) Cultural anthropol-

---

19. Howard W. Odum, *American Masters of Social Sciences*, (New York: Henry Holt and Co., 1927).

20. Shailer Matthews, "The Development of Social Christianity in America." in *Religious Thought in the Last Quarter Century*, (Chicago: University of Chicago Press, 1927); James Dombrowski, *The Early Development of Christian Socialism in America*, (New York: Columbia University Press, 1936); Charles H. Hopkins, *The Rise of the Social Gospel in American Protestantism*, (New Haven: Yale University Press, 1940); Aaron I. Abell, *The Urban Impact on American Protestantism*, 1865-1900, (Cambridge: Harvard University Press; London: Oxford University Press, 1943).

21. William W. Sweet, *Religion in Colonial America*, (New York: Chas. Scribner's Sons, 1942); J. L. Neve, *Churches and Sects in Christendom*, (Burlington, Ia.: Lutheran Library Board, 1940); H. Richard Niebuhr, *The Social Sources of Denominationalism*, (New York: Henry Holt and Co., 1929). See also works cited in following note.

22. Publications of the Institute for Social and Religious Research, especially those of Harlan Paul Douglass, Edward de S. Brunner and J. H. Kolb. Cf. also above Note 15; F. Ernst Johnson, *Christianity and Society*, (Nashville: Arlington Press, 1935); E. W. Burgess, *The Urban Community*, (Chicago: University of Chicago Press, 1925); Robert E. Park, E. W. Burgess, and R. D. McKenzie, *The City*, (Chicago: University of Chicago Press, 1925); Ezra Dwight Sanderson, *Rural Sociology and Rural Social Organization*, (New York: John Wiley and Sons, 1942); S. C. Kincheloe, *The American City and Its Church*, (New York: Missionary Education Movement, 1938).

23. *The Catholic Univ. of America Studies in Sociology*, especially nos. II, VI, and VII: Edward J. Kiernan, *Arthur J. Penty, His contribution to Social Thought*, No. II, 1941; Roberta Snell, *The Nature of Man in St. Thomas Compared with the Nature of Man in American Sociology*, No. VI, 1942; W. T. O'Connor, *Naturalism and the Pioneers of American Sociology*, No. VII, 1942.

ogy, experiencing an unprecedented development in the United States, contributed immense and valuable material on ideas, customs, and institutions of primitive peoples, and, to a considerable extent, categories with which to order it (Daniel Brinton, Franz Boas, Alfred Kroeber, Clark Wissler, Paul Radin, Bronislaw Malinowski, Robert H. Lowie, Ralph Linton). (24) Social psychology began to form a bridge between sociological and psychological studies (James Mark Balwin, Wm. McDougall, R. E. Park, George H. Mead, Ellsworth Faris, Charles A. Ellwood). (25) Philosophical (John Dewey, George H. Mead, Olaf Boodin, William E. Hocking, Edgar Brightman) (26) and sociological theory and analysis (Mark Baldwin, Charles H. Cooley, Ellsworth Faris, R. M. MacIver, Howard Becker, Talcott Parsons) prepared the way for an understanding of socio-religious organization, while detailed sociological analysis of relevant phenomena (27) was carried on

---

24. Robert H. Lowie, *An Introduction to Cultural Anthropology*, (New York: Farrar and Rinehart, 1941); Ralph Linton, *The Study of Man*, (New York, D. Appleton-Century Co., 1936); Franz Boas, *General Anthropology*, (Boston, etc.: D. C. Heath and Co., 1938); Alexander Goldenweiser, *Anthropology*, (New York: F. S. Crofts, 1937); Wilson Wallis, *An Introduction to Anthropology*, (New York: Harpers, 1926); Eliot D. Chapple and Carleton S. Coon, *Principles of Anthropology*, (New York: Henry Holt and Co., 1942); Catholic: Albert Muntsch, *Cultural Anthropology*, (New York: Bruce Publishing Co., 1936).
25. Otto Klineberg, *Social Psychology*, (New York, Henry Holt and Co., 1940); R. T. La Pierre and P. R. Farnsworth, *Social Psychology*, 2nd ed., (New York: McGraw-Hill Book Co., 1942). Excellent criticism is given by Herbert Blumer, "Social Psychology" in Emerson P. Smith, ed., *Man and Society*, (New York: Prentice Hall, 1937), Chap. IV.
26. Edgar S. Brightman, *A Philosophy of Religion*, (New York: Prentice-Hall, 1940).
27. William I. Thomas and Florian Znaniecki, *The Polish Peasant in Europe and America*, (Boston: Gorham Press, 1918-20); Cf. Herbert Blumer, *An Appraisal of Thomas' "The Polish Peasant in Europe and America,"* (New York: Social Science Research Council, 1939); Ellsworth Faris, "The Sect and the Sectarian" in *The Nature of Human Nature*, (Chicago: University of Chicago Press, 1938); Liston Pope, *Millhands and Preachers, A Study of Gastonia*, (New Haven: Yale University Press, 1940); Raymond J. Jones, *A Comparative Study of Civil Behavior Among Negroes*, (Washington: Howard University, 1939); Arthur H. Fauset, *Back Gods of the Metropolis*, (Philadelphia: University of Pennsylvania Press, 1944); J. F. C. Wright, *Slava Bohu, The Story of the Dukhobors*, (New York: Farrar and Rinehart, 1940); Ephrain Ericksen, *The Psychological and Ethical Aspects of Mormon Group Life*, (Chicago: University of Chicago Press, 1922); Edward Jones Allen, *The Second United Order among Mormons*, (New York: Columbia University Press, 1936); Robert Henry Murray, *Group Movements through the Ages*, (New York: Harper and Bros., 1935);

TWENTIETH CENTURY SOCIOLOGY

by William I. Thomas, Florian Znaniecki, M. E. Gaddis, Arthur E. Holt, Samuel Kincheloe, W. Lloyd Warner and others. (8) Max Weber's influence is felt in the synthetic studies of William F. Albright (*From Stone Age to Monotheism*). (29) A systematic treatment of the problems of the sociology of religion has been undertaken more recently with broad perspective by Pitirim Sorokin and influenced by Weber, Troeltsch, and Dilthey, by Joachim Wach.

Sociology of Religion and Allied Fields. (30) As with other fields of sociological research the question has been asked if there is good enough reason to treat socio-religious phenomena separately instead of handling them in the traditional disciplines, (theology, philosophy, anthropology, etc.). Yet, as against such doubts the work done by modern scholarship has proved the right to an independent existence of "sociology of religion." The interdependence of this branch of studies with others, however, is not only historically Conditioned but has its *raison d'être* in nature of its subject matter. There has been much discussion whether the sociologist of religion is right in viewing his material from a special point of view and handling it according to a special method, or whether he has a more or less well-circumscribed field which he can call his own. The first concept seems to lead to unending controversies, and it is indeed doubtful if the application of just a viewpoint or method could justify the setting up of a separate discipline of studies. Though the sociologist of religion makes use of a specific method — paralleled by that employed in other branches of applied sociology — he is in the position to claim a distinct group of phenomena as his own. Although religious group life, the very subject he attempts to study. can also be examined from theological and historical, philosophical and psychological, anthropological and juridical viewpoints, it can be shown that when the work of all these disciplines is accomplished, there still remains a task to be done.

David Ludlum *Social Ferment in Vermont,* Columbia Studies in American Culture, No. 5, (New York: Columbia University Press, 1939).

Perry Miller, *The New England Mind,* (New York: The Macmillan Co., 1939);

28. Cf. above, Note 21, and William Lloyd Warner and Paul S. Lunt, *The Social Life of a Modern Community* and *The Status System of a Modern Community,* (New Haven: Yale University Press, 1941, 1942); for the non-Christian world: John F. Embree, *Sure Mura, A Japanese Village,* (Chicago University of Chicago Press, 1939), Chap. VII.

29. W. F. Albright, *Archaelogy and The Religion of Israel,* (Baltimore: Johns Hopkins University, 1942); See also Pitirim A. Sorokin, *Social and Cultural Dynamics,* (New York: American Book Co., 1937-1941.

30. See, for the following paragraphs, the references in Notes 17 and 27.

SOCIOLOGY OF RELIGION

II

Controversial Issues and Criticism. In the definition of aims, methods and limits of the new discipline there is still, in spite of growing unification and concentration, disagreement on a number of major points.

A. Norms. Opinion is divided as to whether sociology of religion should be a normative or descriptive science, and, if the latter, to what extent sociology of religion can and ought to be descriptive. Historically, sociology of religion — as general sociology — originated from both the growing social consciousness in the wake of the industrial development in the modern western world and of its social consequences, and the failure of the official academic philosophy and theology to take this development into account. The situation in Catholicism differed from that in Protestantism. So it is not surprising that considerable confusion prevailed at first, which was partly due to terminological difficulties and partly to a dissensus on the question of aim and method. As sociology came to mean a weapon of aggression for some, others, bent on the defensive, wanted a "religious," "Christian," or "Protestant" sociology. They all agreed that the aim of sociology of religion was to establish norms. As previously indicated, it took considerable time for the development of the concept of a descriptive sociology of religion, implying that the establishment of norms was the concern of the theologian, philosopher, and social theoretician. In the meantime, the newly emerging descipline was suspected by many — and not without reason — to be guided by ulterior motives and by intentions hostile or at least indifferent to religious claims. This problem will be discussed below. Even among scholars who conceive of the study of the interrelation of religion and society as primarily a descriptive task, there are quite a few who do not deny the normative interest which ultimately (originally and finally) dictates the inquiry. But they feel that in order to make the results more than subjective impressions, preferences, or evaluations, chances for verification of the results must be given. That implies abstinence — at least methodical — and temporal — from all subjective evaluation and the use of all the methodological and critical tools which have been developed in the humanities in the course of the nineteenth century. Yet they would feel not justified in regarding their result as the last world of wisdom but would very definitely expect an appreciation and evaluation which puts these results in the proper perspective of a unified system of knowledge, philosophy, or theology; and it is irrelevant whether the latter task is performed in personal union with that of description so long as the integrity of the latter is guaranteed. The question is not so much if it is possible, justifiable, or advisable to have a viewpoint or standpoint from which to pass such judgment but rather where the proper place for introducing it ought to be.

As long as the topics to be dealt with are removed from the investigator's immediate interest and concern, the difficulties seem to be not so great. There is no reason why a Roman Catholic, a Protestant and, say, a Marxist student should not concur in their study of Americn Indian ceremonial, Babylonian mythology, or Buddhist ethics. But the difficulties are greater if the topic were the causes of the Reformation or the nature of the sect. Yet we like to believe that, though there is a Catholic and a Marxian philosophy of society, there can be only *one* sociology of religion which we may approach from different angles and realize to a different degree but which would use but one set of criteria. Divergence of opinion is caused not so much by the variety and difference of the views on society as by those on religion. Though it seems by no means necessary to have identical concepts of the nature and function of religion, it is desirable not to be determined by antipathy or sympathy to the degree which would make an objective investigation impossible. Objectivity does not presuppose indifference, just as sympathy or antipathy does not necessarily disqualify for an unbiased examination according to the historical or critical method. Once the possibility of understanding a religion different from our own in time and space is admitted, there is no reason why the student can not try to apply the principles of investigation in all instances.

B. Comparison. A few words might be said about the role of the *comparative* method in the study of socio-religious phenomena. In the second half of the nineteenth century the importance of comparison as a help to the understanding of the subject of humanistic studies became recognized. The science of religion was no exception. For a while the unlucky term "comparative religion" (for comparative study of religion) was extremely popular. Everything was compared to everything else, superficial similiarity passing frequently for identity. Now there can be no doubt that analogies can be very helpful for the interpretation not only of religious concepts and rites, but also of forms of religious organization. Yet it must be undestood that individual features have to be interpreted as part of the configuration they form and that it is dangerous to isolate them from the context in which they occur.

C. Meaning. This leads us to another methodological problem which we have had occasion to touch upon previously. The hermeneutical principle to understand configurations as meaningful wholes warrants a further conclusion. Religious ideas, rites, and forms of organization have a *meaning* to which the sociologist of religion has to do justice, just as has the historian or psychologist of religion. In other words, concepts like *Communion of Saints, Familia Dei,* etc. want to be understood with their full *intention.* We will realize it in paying attention to the interpretation which is given these terms in the group which acknowledges them. This realization does by no means imply assent, for the normative quest is excluded; rather it enables the interpreter to understand the phenomenon in the context in which it belongs. The sociologist of religion must give his most serious consideration to the *self-interpretation* of any religious group he studies.

D. Value and Validity. We come now to one of the most difficult and delicate problems of the methodology of our field which has caused a great deal of discussion and misunderstanding. The failure to find an adequate solution has more than anything else prevented for a long time a fruitful cooperation between students of sociology and of religion. (There is little comfort in the observation that a very similar situation prevails in the relation of psychology to the science of religion).

It is understandable that the idealistic emphasis on the efficacy of spiritual motives and forces, ideas, and energies in the philosophy and history of the early nineteenth century led to a reaction which urged students of social life and development to concentrate on the opposite viewpoint according to which spiritual developments have to be regarded as products of material conditions. (Feuerbach, Marx, Engels, against Hegel). There was definitely some justification for correcting a one-sided interpretation of the social "roots" and conditions out of which in the history of man religions concepts and institutions have grown and are growing. The mistake begins when this relation is interpreted in deterministic terms and when the conclusion is drawn that a statement on the (social) origins and conditions of an idea or phenomenon means or implies an answer to the question of its value or validity. It continues and gets worse when the reverse, the shaping of social factors, conditions, and orders by spiritual (religious) forces is overlooked or denied, as we find it in a legion of modern studies more or less dedicated to economic determinism.

The crucial term which is of the greatest importance in this context is "ideology." What is meant by designating certain religious concept of a cult group ("brotherhood," "communion of saints") as "ideology"? The Marxian understanding is that they are, thus labeled, "debunked," shorn of any claim to validity, that they are, psychologically speaking, illusions. Others would not go so far but feel inclined to interpret ideologies as ideas originated from and hence in their validity limited to a certain sociological sphere. Max Scheler, the creator of the modern "sociology of knowledge," has coined the term *relationism* — as distinct from *relativism* — for this theory. It certainly will appeal more than the former interpretation to anyone who identifies himself, traditionally or on his own decision, with any one religious value or a system of religious values. Yet this theory seems also to conflict with the claims of universal validity which is characteristic certainly not of all but of a great part of religous messages, interpretations, and systems. This contradiction is, however, more apparent than real. Does the teaching of a Isaiah or a Luther, even if "explained" sociologically, really lose any of its validity? It does not seem so. Even if it could be shown that economic or general social conditions in a given society have prompted a desire for deliverance, the ideas of redemption that may be included in a religious message are not invalidated by an inquiry into their social "background," provided we do not conceive of the relation in deterministic terms but consider conditions as a framework which may include a variety of contents. We feel that an understanding of the origins, the development, and the meaning of the teachings, practices, and organization of a religous group to which the sociologist of religion tries to contribute, would not only not interfere with but would actually intensify the loyalty of the members of the group. Once the suspicion is removed that the sociologist has an axe to grind and that he is bent on demonstrating the illusionary character of religious ideas and concepts when inquiring into their sociological background, the cooperation of science of religion and sociology of religion will be more fruitful. The interpretation of the meaning of concepts, acts, and behavior given by devout individuals or groups may or may not agree with the findings of the historian, psychologist, or sociologist. The members of a group may deceive themselves as to the primary motives prompting them to think, act, or feel as they do. The case is simple where the ideological, philosophical, or theological justification for a type of rule e.g. is a front behind which lust for domination and ambition for power hide. Here the official ideology and the actual state of things obviously do not coincide. But the problem is frequently much more difficult, as psychologists (Jung) and social philosophers (Nietzsche, Sorel, Pareto, Spengler) have pointed out. The inaugurators of the modern sociology of knowledge (Scheler, Karl Mannheim) have shown that the analysis of the social conditioning of ideas and convictions, though in itself not entitling to decisions as to their validity or invalidity, may contribute to the realization of the partial character of views or intentions expressed in them. "The function of the findings of sociology of knowledge lies somewhere in a fashion hitherto not clearly understood, between irrelevance to the establishment of truth on the one hand, and entire adequacy for determining truth on the other." (31) The idea of the particularization of the validity of expressions of religious experience will have to be followed out in epistomology and in the theory of religious experience.

E. Empiricism vs. Apriorism. Another point on which opinions are divided is the question of which of two approaches should be used by the sociologist of religion, the *empirical* or the *aprioristic*. One group of scholars advocates the first, gathering data without regard to any scheme or any preconceived idea of the phenomenon in question. An extreme example is the statistical school. The other extreme is represented by students who like to start with a given, "intuited," or deduced concept of, for example, the nature of prayer and sacrifice or of sin and grace. It is easy to see that we are here not really confronted with an alternative because the empiricist can not wholly dispense with categories with which to organize his facts, nor can his opponent forego documentation and illustration of ideas by empirical (historical) facts. Flesh and bones — both are indispensible, neither an unorganized mass nor a more skeleton would be satisfactory. The typological method, which has been advocated by a number of sociologists of religion, serves the function of bridging the gap between the two extremes: the richer and

---

31. Karl Mannheim, *Ideology and Utopia*, p. 256.

finer it is developed the more it will serve to combine wealth of detailed information with keen structural analysis.

F. Individualism vs. Collectivism. A disagreement exists also between the advocates of an *individualistic* and those of a *collectivistic* view of society and of religion. More than in the case of the previously mentioned alternatives, questions of principles are involved here. While some are inclined to view the process of civilization and of religious growth as a progressive realization of the infinite value of the individual, others are inclined to give priority to the whole before its parts and to consider as central in religion acts constituted by communal worship. Again we are not really faced by an alternative. The sociologist of religion will realize that it is rather a question of emphasis; individual expression and pecularity being present already on the level of so-called primitive civilization and communal worship playing a most important part in the highest forms of religion and culture.

G. Identity of Influence. In anthropology, one of the neighboring sciences, a long controversy developed between the advocates of seemingly alternative attempts to explain *similarities* of thought and behaviour patterns in less advanced cultures and societies. One school — both sides are represented in each, French, English, German and American research — is inclined to interpret all such similarities as the result of historical influences. The other sees in them the indication of an identical constitution and endowment of man. Inasmuch as the sociologist of religion is confronted with the necessity of accounting for apparently identical or similar patterns in religious behavior, ideas, and forms of organizations on different cultural levels, he is interested in a constructive solution of this apparent dilemma. Observation and reflection, however, will tell him that he is not faced with a true alternative. He will distrust all hasty assumption of equality as long as there is a change of historical derivation from other sources while not refusing to allow for independent growth and development of religious concepts and institutions under analogous conditions and circumstance. (Not enough attention has been paid to Rudolf Otto's paper "Das Gesetz der Parallelen in der Religionsgeschichte," which outlines his theory on the "convergence of types").

H. The Place of Statistics. Though there can be hardly any doubt that a full yet cautious use of statistics can be of great use to the sociologist of religion, there has been, at least until recently, a difference in practice between continental and American students.

SOCIOLOGY OF RELIGION

The former have been and are more reluctant to make extensive use of the statistical method; the latter have placed during the earliest decades of the tweentieth century a not quite justifiable overemphasis on this approach. Whereas some authors of the former groups arrive at a priori-constructions lacking the broad basis of verifiable facts, the latter school seems to be too reluctant to give that interpretation to their findings which alone can make them really meaningful.

I. Doctrine and Cult. In the science of religion as it began to take shape since the middle of the nineteenth century a controversy developed regarding the significance and the primacy of different types of expressions of religious experience. The problem of chronological and axiological *priority* of theory (myths, beliefs, ideas, concepts, doctrines, dogmata) and practice (worship, rites, ritual) in religion was discussed by students of different religions and civilizations (W. Robertson Smith, Andrew Lang, Wilhelm Schwartz, Otto Gruppe). The sociologist of religion is vitally interested in striking the right balance and placing adequate emphasis on the various types of expression. As against intellectualism he will insist on the central nature and function of *worship* in its various aspects, named by some the very core of religion; to any neglect and underestimation of the *rational* expression of religious experience he will have to protest by demonstrating its significance as vehicle of the self-interpretation of the religious community. He does not see any necessity to argue for chronological priority of either of the two aspects, bearing in mind their interrelation and mutual stimulation.

III

Inter-Relation of Religion and Society. Sociological studies in religion will have to include the whole width and breadth of mankind's religious experience. For practical purposes, the individual sociologist, who has special intents in mind, may have to concentrate on a problem of problems of a given period of the history of civilization and religion, in a specific area or group. In principle, however, no type of devotion or phenomenon of religious significance should be excluded. If the system of the sociology of religion is not broad enough to include them all, something must be wrong with it.

The student of religion must acquaint himself with the research of the *sociologist*. The latter examines the foundations of society,

— that is, the total and specific environment of the social being in both its positive and negative effect —. and psychologically and sociologically meaningful attitudes, as manifested in communality. He analyzes all forms of societal organization and association (typology of communities). He studies the constructive and destructive social forces which determine the dynamics of social life and the patterns of social change, transformation, and revolution in relation to the physical, mental, cultural, and technical environment. Research in abstracto and in concreto supplement each other: general categories are verified in historical and empirical documentation, and individual phenomena are interpreted in the light of such categories.

The student of *religion* can be expected to supply the sociologist with a working theory of religious life and its manifestations. He is concerned with the theologico-philosophical, epistemological, psychological, phenomenological and historical analysis of the nature and meaning of religion and with the forms of expression of religious experience and the dynamics of religious life. Systematic inquiry into the forms and contents of belief, worship, and rites will be based on the study of the religious act and its motivation and meaning. It will be focused on the problem of religious communion and will do justice to the wide variety of types of communal religious life and activity.

The historical and systematical analysis of the inter-relation between religion and general as well as specific environmental factors and conditions (physical, cultural, social) can be successfully undertaken only by close cooperation of the student of religion with the student of society. The former will have to avail himself of the categories worked out in sociological research; the latter will have to give careful attention to the meaning of religious language and terminology. A threefold meaning will have to be recognized: first, the actual meaning of any word and concept, sometimes obscured by tradition and age; secondly, the religious implications of terms like sin, repentance, grace, redemption, etc.; thirdly, the concrete, individual "theological" interpretation given to the term in a religious community (by individual religious leaders). On this basis religious acts like adoration, prayer, and the conduct and attitudes of a cult group will have to be interpreted. There is no hope of grasping the spirit and of understanding the life, symbolism, and behavior of religious group so long as no serious attempt is made to correlate the isolated traits (concepts, rites, customs) observed with a notion of the central experience which produces them.

As indicated above, *systematic and historical approaches* are both necessary for the study of the religious group, the former aiming at the construction of types of sacred communion, the latter attempting to embrace all the variegated forms religious fellowships have shown under different ethnic, historical, cultural, and social conditions. Worship in the *home* may serve as a simple example. Irrespective of profound differences in general and special environment, cultural niveau and religious level, the rites conducted in the "homes" of the American Indian, the Egyptian, the Chinese, or the German or Englishman of the sixteenth century have certain features in common, as compared with public congregational ceremonies. Further proof of the fruitfulness of combined systematic and historical inquiries can be found in the discovery of many similarities in the religious implications of the beliefs and ceremonials at all times surrounding the *sacred* ruler in vastly different societies, as well as in a parallel disinclination to corporate rites with *mystics* in practically all great civilizations.

We shall now list the main tasks of a sociology of religion:

I. The study of the *interrelation* of religion and society.

What are the main points of contact? Analysis of the nature and structure of society as well as of religion is carried out in the disciplines dedicated to this purpose (general sociology, theology, and philosophy of religion). Inasmuch as it is an interaction which is examined, justice must be done to the influence both of society on religion, and of religion on society.

(a) "Religion" means both experience and its expression in thought and action — in concepts, forms of worship, and organization. It is essential to correlate the expression with the experience to which it testifies. The influences of social forces, structures, and movements on the expression of religious experience is more easily ascertained than their effect upon the experience itself. While some conceive of it in terms of determinism, others are inclined to emphasize the autonomy and independent dynamics of religious life.

A wide field is open for the sociologist of religion in the examination of the sociological roots and functions of myths, doctrines and dogmas, of cultus and association in general and in particular (*hic et nunc*). To what extent are the different types of the expression of religious experience in different societies and cultures socially conditioned (technological, moral, cultural level)? What is

TWENTIETH CENTURY SOCIOLOGY

the contribution of social forces to the differentiation of religious life and its forms? To what extent does the latter reflect social stratification, mobility, and differentiation (division of society according to sex, age, occupation, property, rank and prestige)? What of the social background and origins of religious movements and of the leaders and their congregations? What does religion contribute to the integration and disintegration of social groups? How do ecological factors influence the religious community?

Through the ages different ethnic groups have developed in the different geographical areas of the world. Societies have been formed in these areas by these groups. Their activities resulted in the formation of cultures. With the development of culture, differentiation within the different societies increased; hence the sociologist of religion has to take into account the temporal, regional, ethnic, cultural and social factors. The research of the archeologist, historian and philologist supplies him with material for the study of religious grouping from the beginnings of history to the present day. He is aware of the difference of the anthropogeographical milieu (climate) in which these groups evolved. He learns from physical and cultural anthropology about the variety of physical, mental and spiritual endowment and development of the different ethnic groups. Again the historian, the sociologist, and political scientist lend him material for the examination of historical societies and civilizations from the point of view of his interest.

The five continents are broken down into smaller regional, cultural and social areas, down to village, house, and family units. The periods of world history are divided into epochs, each of which is accentuated by the growth and decline of historical cultures and societies; in each of these shortlived tribal units have succeeded each other in the domination of a given region or section of the populated earth, either simply co-existing or vying with each other for temporary or semi-permanent superiority.

What has been the role of religion in these narrowly defined units? Again it is not the historical question of sequence and development, of motive and effect which the sociologist of religion is called upon to answer. He is interested in cross sections and in the analysis of structures, in extracting the typical from the empirical details.

He will not omit considering any primitive society, the study of which may contribute to his knowledge of the sociology of primitive religion in whatever period or area or ethnic context it may be found. He will include all that is known of ancient and medieval and modern Oriental cultures and societies (Near, Middle and Far East) and extend his examination of Western society and cultures back beyond the classical world finally to include the successive types developed in the various great periods of the Christian era down to this day. Registering the rise and growth of religious groups, he will proceed to analyze their nature, structure, and constitution and will thus contribute to the typological understanding of religiously motivated grouping. He will compare instances where religious concepts, forces, and personalities effected subtle or far-reaching changes and transformations in the cultural and social context in which they occurred. He will study the activities of religious leaders and groups, forms of action and response, and with the help of the psychologist will ascertain their meaning and motivation. He will be arrested by the similarity, though not the identity, of patterns of behavior, thought, and reaction under often widely different conditions and circumstances, and he will untiringly contribute to a more comprehensive and profound knowledge of the typology of religious thought and feeling, religious ideas institutions, religious theory and practice.

(b) The *sociologist* is interested in the sociologically significant function and effect of *religion* upon *society*. Granted that religious forms and institutions, like other fields of human and cultural activity, are conditioned by the nature, atmosphere, and dynamics of a given society, to what extent does religion contribute to the cohesion of a social group and to the dynamics of its development and history? It should be borne in mind that because religion conceived of as a vital force transcends its expression, it cannot be unreservedly regarded as one among many spheres of cultural activity. Some are inclined to look upon it as the fountainhead or the matrix of all cultural and social activity of a group of human beings. The theory of the identity of religion with the sum total of man's cultural and social life does not do justice to its peculiar nature. Careful analysis of causes of cultural and social changes reveal the part religion plays in the fomentation of the revolutionary and evolutionary development of society. Of all varieties of social life and grouping within a given society, religious associations of a peculiar and not of the traditional type will arrest the attention of the student. The growth and decline of *specifically* religious organizations and groups is a theme of the greatest importance to the sociologist as well as to the historian of religion.

He will investigate the nature and typology of these groups, their structure, and their constitution. Size, character, purpose, relation to the other groups, leadership of the specifically religious group will have to be investigated. What is the function of the different expressions of religious experienece in integrating it? Why do these groups present a variety of different forms of organization, and how is the latter related to the self-interpretation of the group?

II. *The Religious Group*. The religious group is characterized by the nature and order of the basic relationships of its members: in the first place, that of each member to the *numen*; in the second place that of the members to each other. The sociologist of religion will have to examine the character of this twofold relationship in the case af each individual group because the nature, intensity, duration, and organization of a religious group depends upon the way in which its members experience God, conceive of, and communicate with Him, and upon the way they experience fellowship, conceive of, and practice it. Inasmuch as religious communion conversely strengthens religious faith and action, we find a circle — however, not of a vicious nature. The sociologist of religion, interested in the study of a cultic group, cannot be satisfied with reviewing its theology as the foundation of the theory and practice of fellowship among its members. He must probe further, studying the religious experience on which theology and other modes of expression (behavior, rites, language) are based. More than other types of association, a religious group presents itself as a *microcosm* with its own laws, outlook on life, attitude and atmosphere. Wherever political, artistic, scientific, or other groups exhibit comparable cohesion and comprehensiveness, they usually can be shown to be of a semi-religious nature. Altogether too frequently students of religious communities have been satisfied to juxtapose findings as to beliefs, customs, and patterns of organization regarded as representative, without correlating them to the central attitudes and the norms characteristic of the group. Yet it is essential to realize that religious communities are constituted by loyalty to an ideal or set of values which is the basis of their communion. In other words, a religious group should not be regarded as just a fellowship of persons drawn together by mutual sympathy of common interest, or even by common ideas and customs. While these factors enter in they are not basic.

Certain religious communities have been described as units in which parallelism of spontaneity rules. They are not really *typical*, but rather exhibit a minimum of what it takes to form a religious community.

Next to loyalty to an ideal or values postulated by the central religious experience from which the group springs, the degree of *intensity* of its religious life is decisive. That, too, is at times overlooked by those who are inclined to evaluate the significance of a religious group exclusively by its size and structure. Intensity is a dynamic quality; it will frequently change, it will rise and fall. It is characteristic of some religious groups to sustain a certain, perhaps high, degree of intensity developed early in their history and maintained at an even level, while others pass through varying phases. The intensity of religious experience may find special expression in some one doctrine or practice, or occasionally in several.

In the earlier stages of the study of religious psychology, French, German and American scholars unfortunately concerned themselves primarily with marginal cases of pathologically developed religious temperament. The sociologist of religion must beware of falling into the same error in overemphasizing random phenomena (eccentric forms of sectarianism, etc.). The historical beginnings of religious and sectarian communities, however, are important fields of investigation of the mediums through which religious experience finds expression. The size of a religious group deserves the attention not only of the statistician, but also of al those who believe that a very different psychology typifies the masses on the one hand and intimate circles on the other. The size of the group, however, may be determined entirely by chance and circumstance.

Within the group there is a distinction between those members who will engage in religious activity from personal choice or in deference to tradition such as converts and parishoners of a local congregation, and those who are actively religious — temporarily or consistently — such as lay-deacons or the participants in a procession. Interest can be both passive and active, the latter being exceedingly diversified in form, purpose, means, and duration.

The *ideals and values* uniting the group may be considered in the first place as the formulation of desires and aspirations, derived from a basic religious experience. As such they have expressive significance. Secondly, they serve as symbols or standards for the religious community. Thirdly, they render expansion, missionary propaganda, and conversion possible by their communicative value. Finally, they serve to integrate the religious community which binds itself to them. They may be either spontaneously formulated, or acknowledged as tradition (successions of waves of conversions and of generations of followers).

More concretely, all religious groups are united by certain convictions — the acknowledgment of the ideals and values just mentioned — formulated loosely or concisely in statements of faith or doctrinal *creeds*, by certain *cultic* acts which tend to develop and strengthen their communion with the deity (rites, sacraments), and by a cultivation of a *fellowship* in the spirit of the ideals professed. The larger the group, the more the need for a renewed and possibly more intimate grouping may be felt. The sociology of the religious group of the second power, to use de Grasserie's terminology (collegia, associations, brotherhoods, oratories and the like), offers a wide open field and should be developed much more than it has been hitherto. Inasmuch as the growth of religious fervor in élite religious groups may lead to hierarchical development (order, sect), the sociologist of religion may combine his study of intensity and size with that of the structure of the group. For this task the criteria elaborated in general sociology will prove helpful. Yet a warning should be voiced against too unguarded an application of terms and viewpoints derived from the sociological study of other human activities.

Two examples will illustrate this point. Observing the practice of a cultic group, the outsider may be inclined to compare the "control" exercised by a religious leader to that in political or economic organizations without realizing that obedience may in each case be very differently motivated, and that it hence may not be really the same thing. Again the term "behavior" is often enough made to cover a variety of forms of conduct, without regard for the intention distinguishing them. Both paying taxes and sharing out of religious motives with one's brother are ways of handing out money, but how differently the acts are motivated and how different the "value"!

The greatest differences and varieties can be found in the *structures* of religious groups.

Though we possess many excellent monographs on the historical development of an infinite number of cults, there is room for much more extensive and intensive study of the typology of the constitutions of religious communities. Corresponding to the twofold level of religious organization, the natural and the specifically religious bases, the order of cultic communities varies. In the first instance and frequently in the second, it is patterned after "secular" models (the father as leader of a cult-group, tribal organization paralleled by cultic set-up). But it may also develop it own forms (monasticism, egalitarianism). The study of the structures of religious groups should be caried on without prejudice in favor of one or the other principle of organization, *e. g.* the charismatic as against the hierarchical, or vice versa, — and application of the general methodological requirement discussed above. Historical orientation should be supplemented by typological investigation.

Constitution may refer to a loose, temporary, undifferentiated set-up, or — with many intermediate stages — to a highly stratified and comprehensive order. The structure of the religious as of most other groups is determined by the division of functions. Such a division is practically ubiquitous from the simplest to the most complex cultic associations. It may consist in an individual occasionally or permanently taking over functions, duties, and responsibilities, with or without corresponding rights, honors, and privileges (prestige).

The degree of differentiation of functions does not necessarily depend upon the general cultural level. Elaborate specialization is found in less advanced societies (West African, Polynesian,) and in higher cultures (even in non-conformist Protestant and certain sectarian groups). The process of differentiation of functions within the group may involve specifically religious activities exclusively or may have a broader scope. It may be initiated, recognized, and justified on a pragmatic basis ("useful," "necessary") or on grounds of principle (metaphysical basis, theological explanation). A wide and little cultivated field is open to the investigator in the comparative study of the differentiation of functions, especially in the narrow sense (function in the cultus). Another is the study of the social background and situation of the members composing the group, these factors having a bearing on its nature and structure particularly in the case of transitory phenomena (meeting, festival). The social origin of the group and the composition of its constituency pose two different problems.

Still another is the analysis of the "atmosphere" and the spirit prevailing. There is a sociological basis for the Christian teachings on the "Holy Spirit" and its communication. (32) The atmosphere can be determined by a careful investigation of the central values

---

32. Edwin E. Aubrey, "The Holy Spirit in Relation to the Religious Community," *Journal of Theological* Studies, 45, 1940.

acknowledged, the attitudes prescribed and practiced in the community, and the development through which it has gone.

What constitutes a church, a denomination, a sect, a society, a confraternity? What is the significance of gradation, authority, order in a religious community? The sociologist of religion will have to answer that question on the basis of broad theological and juridical, historical, psychological, and sociological information. What is the (theological) self-interpretation of the nature and significance of its fellowship, is the first question. The second concerns the historical origin and development, the third, the prevailing spirit (intensivity, exclusivity, broadness, compromise) and the general attitude toward the world (identification, withdrawal, critical acceptance, consecreation). The student will take into account the immanent development within the cult-community and the impact of outside influences and outside patterns and examples. He wil examine the role of intimacy to the first, second, and third power (examples: the circle of Jesus' followers, the renewed intimacy on the basis of the experience of the sixteenth century Reformers, the Pictist group of the seventeenth century. etc.). As far as the constitution of religious groups is concerned we find a variety of principles. There is a subjective and an objective viewpoint. That is, in principle, a community may be universal; actually it may be limited to a certain social, racial or local group of people. There are furthermore universal and selective groups. Changes occur in which nationally or racially limited groups — this limitation may be objective or subjective — are transformed into universal communities. Conversely a universal orientation may be qualified by national, social, or other criteria, as in the case of the national religious bodies in Eastern and Western Christianity, in Islam, and in Buddhism. Various degrees of this "qualification" can be observed (relative isolation, language, youth-problem). The sociologist will be interested in exploring the relationship prevailing between the different subgroups.

Differentiation within the religious group can be conditioned in two ways: by religious and by extra-religious factors. As far as the former is concerned we find a considerable amount of variability in the nature, intensity, and color of the unifying, basic religious experience, shades or differences in theoretical (belief, myth, doctrine) and practical (worship, activities) expression. They make for differentiation within the practice, tradition, and organization of a religious community in certain periods, locally and otherwise, particularly if combined with the second factor. Extra-religious

SOCIOLOGY OF RELIGION

influences making for differentiation are represented by technical, cultural, social, economic developments, resulting in social stratification according to differences of sex and age, property, occupation and status. Sociologists have here a very important and rewarding task in exploring the effects of these differences upon the religious group. The transformation of devotional attitudes, of concepts, rites and institutions, rise of new and decline of old ideas and practices under the impact of these factors with respect to the different religious bodies has not been sufficiently investigated.

The problem of *authority*, with all its implications, has to be discussed. More comparative study of the foundation upon which authority is supposed to rest, the forms which it may take, the methods by which it works, its execution and its delegation, are necessary. Typologies of religious charisma (founder; prophet, priest, etc.) as outlined by Max Weber, A. Causse, G. Vander Leeuw and J. Wach, should be worked out in much greater detail. The theory of personal and official charisma will prove very fruitful; it has recently, been applied to the study of primitive society, Indo-European and Hebrew religion, and medieval Christianity.

General and Specific Sociology of Religious Groups. In contrasting origin and development, nature and purpose, structure and attitudes of the religiously motivated group with that of other types of grouping, the sociologist will attempt to define its general characteristics. Although there is room for doubt if such procedure would do justice to the individuality of the historical phenomenon, that is, of the group *hic et nunc*, it must be pointed out that parallelisms and similarities exist which call for investigation. The following examples will illustrate what we mean by such *similarities*: (1) the general motivation of sharing certain common religious experiences, the differences in content in the latter notwithstanding; (2) the nature of the acts whereby they are expressed; (3) the process of crystallization of religious fellowships around charismatic leadership; (4) the general pattern of the development from simple into complex structures; (5) comparable types of religious authority and of attitudes in religious audiences; (6) parallelism in the reaction of types of cult groups to their environment; (7) differentiation of functions within the group according to general criteria (age, sex, property, occupation, rank).

These parallelisms and resemblances might pertain to a limited number of groups, to be defined by these very similarities (from two to any number), or they may extend from a large number to practically all groups of a special type, or to religious groups in general. *Types* may be defined geographically, chronologically, ethically, culturally, or religiously. Thus, the motive of the urge to spread the faith may identify one religious group with many others, while its absence (limitation or rejection of propaganda) distinguishes it from other. Some cult-communities owe their existence primarily to missionary societies, orders, etc. in different religions. Some are of a militant character manifested in the means employed and in their "ideology" in general; others are quieter, more contemplative in nature. In both cases the religious motive is decisive. A great number of Hindu religious groups have some general convictions in common, notwithstanding divergences in theology and cultus; some share forms of devotion, which, however, my be addressed to different deities, and so forth. Christian sects exhibit attitudes which, if contrasted to those of other religious organizations, offer striking parallels. Some use rites not known to others within the some brotherhood of faith, such as the washing of feet, unction, the kiss of peace.

A satisfactory and distinctive *nomenclature* will have to be worked out by the student of the general sociology of religious groups. Terms and categories should preferably be familiar, rather than fanciful new creations ("hierology," "hierosophy," etc.). Yet mistakes must be avoided which may arise from the application of a technical term developed in a distinctive historical, social, cultural, or religious context to a wider range of phenomena.

It is the task of *general sociology* to investigate the sociological significance of the various forms of intellectual and practical expression of religious experience (myth, doctrine; prayer, sacrifice, rites; organization, constitution, authority); it falls to the *specific sociological study* to cover sociologically concrete, historical examples: a Sioux (Omaha) Indian myth, an Egyptian doctrine of the Middle Kingdom, Murngin or Mohammedan prayer, the Yoruba practice of sacrifice, the constitution of the earliest Buddhist Samgha, Samoyed priesthood, etc. Such studies should be carried out for the smallest conceivable units (one family or clan, a local group at a given period of time, the occasional following of one cult leader, etc.). There is no danger of this task turning into a historical, psychological, anthropological, theological undertaking, because the sociological viewpoint will be the decisive one. Thus the philologist would ascertain the meaning of a passage of the Indian Atharva-Veda; the historian would assign it to a period in the cultural, political, and religious development of the Hindu, the psychologist would concentrate on its origin and significance as an expression of feeling and thought; and the anthropologist would deal with it from a folkloristic point of view. The sociologist is interested in its origin and formation, in the structure and meaning of the Hindu community of faith. There can be some doubt as to how the work of the special sociologist of religion should be organized, that is, in which order he would proceed best. Inasmuch as research is carried on in a number of related disciplines, there is no hope that what is most needed always will be taken up first. However, the angles which ought to be of paramount concern to those interested in the systematic development of our field are the temporal, the spatial, the ethnic and cultural, and the religious viewpoint.

(a) The sociologist is interested in religious groups of the past and the present. Though contemporary conditions may claim his attention from the pragmatic point of view, the investigation of phenomena of even the remote past ought not to be neglected (sociology of ancient cults everywhere). In this emphasis normative philosophy or theology of society on the one hand, and descriptive sociology on the other, differ.

(b) Notwithstanding his interest in the socio-religious situation of the society of which he is a member, the student of religious groups cannot afford to exclude from his range of effort a concern with religious grouping in all parts of the populated earth. Because everything that exists is worth knowing — though not to the same extent — no religious group established anywhere should be omitted in these studies.

(c) The same is equally true of ethnic divisions, cultures and societies. Within a chronoligical and spatial framework, each tribe and people, each culture and society will find its place. Naturally not all can claim the interest of the student to the same extent as those which stand in a closer or looser relation to the culture or society under investigation. But as long as socio-religious conditions in a major cultural context remain unexplored, the work is not done.

(d) It is understandable that in a Christian society Christian groups will appear the major, though certainly not the exclusive, subject of interest to the sociologist of religion. As he is obliged to include all forms of Christian communities, so he will have to extend his studies over the whole field of non-Christian religious grouping in all its varieties. It may be advisable to proceed, if the special viewpoint warrants it, from the nuclear topic interest to wider and wider contexts; to include the study of religious groups, historically or phenomenologically related to Christianity (Greek, Roman, Hebrew), to those typologically similar (Mystery religions, Buddhism), and finally to those of a radically different character. As far as Christian groups are concerned, a great deal remains to be done to bring the investigation of the "lesser" groups up to date. Attention has for a long time been concentrated on all forms of "official" religion, while religiously and sociologically important and interesting grouping within or without has been neglected. Of the non-Conformist groups only the "spectacular" one have attracted attention. The study of creeds and rites must be supplemented by a thorough examination of organization and constitution, in theory and practice. In this context we have to repeat that the exploration of historical origin and development is no substitute for systematic and typological study.

SELECTED BIBLIOGRAPHY

James, E. O., *The Social Function of Religion*, (Nashville: Cokesbury Press, 1940).

Linton, Ralph, *The Study of Man*, (New York: D. Appleton-Century Co., 1936).

Niebuhr, H. Richard, *The Social Sources of Denominationalism*, (New York: Henry Holt and Co., 1929).

Pinard de la Boullaye, Henri, S. J., *L'étude comparée des religions*, (Paris: Gabriel Beauchesne, 1922, 1929, 2 vols.).

Sorokin, Pitirim A., *Social and Cultural Dynamics*, (New York: American Book Co., 1937-1941, 4 vols.).

Troeltsch, Ernst, *The Social Teaching of the Christian Churches*, (New York: The Macmillan Co., 1931).

Van der Leeuw, Gerardus, *Religion in Essence and Manifestation*, (London: G. Allen and Unwin, 1938), Sec. II, B.

Wach, Joachim, *Sociology of Religion*, (Chicago: University of Chicago Press, 1944).

Wallis, Wilson D., *Religion in Primitive Society*, (New York: F. S. Crofts and Co., 1939).

Weber, Max, *Gesammelte Aufsaetze zur Religionssoziologie*, (Tuebingen: J. C. B. Mohr, 1920-1921, 3 vols.).

Weber, Marx, *Wirtschaft und Gesellschaft*, (Tuebingen: J. C. B. Mohr, 1921), Sec. III, Chap. IV, "Religionssoziologie."

Wiese, Leopold von, and Howard Becker, *Systematic Sociology*, (New York: John Wiley and Sons; London: Chapman and Hall, 1932).

Will, Robert, *Le culte*, (Paris: Félix Alcan, 1925-1929).

SOCIOLOGY OF RELIGION

Joachim Wach, born January 25, 1898 at Chemnitz (Germany), studied at the Universities of Munich, Berlin, Freiburg in Br., Leipzig, received degree of Doctor of Philosophy (Leipzig) 1922. Privatdozent at Leipzig 1924, Professor Extraordinarius 1927-1935, Doctor of Theology (Heidelberg) 1929. Since 1935 Visiting, since 1939 Associate, Professor at Brown University, Providence, R. I., Honorary Member of Phi Beta Kappa. Author of *Religionswissenschaft,* (Leipzig: J. B. Hinrichs, 1924); *Typen der religioesen Anthropologie,* (Tuebingen: J. C. B. Mohr, 1932); *Das Verstehen, Geschichte der hermeneutischen Theorie,* (Tuebingen, J. C. Mohr, 1926-1932, 3 vols.); *Einleitung in die Religionssoziologie,* (Tuebingen, J. C. B. Mohr, 1931); article, "Religionssoziologie" and others in *Die Religion in Geschichte und Gegenwart* (ed. by Hermann Gunkel and Leopold Zscharnack) and article "Religion" in *Handwoerterbuch der Soziologie* ed. by Alfred Vierkandt.

CHAPTER XV

SOCIOLOGY OF ECONOMIC ORGANIZATION

by

WILBERT E. MOORE

A sociology of economic organization is only incidentally an analysis of the social origins of economic science, or a treatise on the social organization of professional economists. In this chapter we are concerned with an assessment of the facts and principles in sociology which impinge on the subject matter studied by economists, and more particularly in appraising the development of a sociological theory of economic action and economic organization.

The relations between the sciences of economics and sociology vary with the levels of abstraction and analysis under consideration. (1) As a preface to our brief review of contemporary develop-

---

1. Most of the discussions of these inter-scientific relations have chiefly stressed the contribution of sociology to the problems of motivation, and to the analysis of the institutional framework of economic organization. See for example, C. Bouglé, "La sociologie économique en France," *Zeitschrift fuer Sozialforschung*, 3 (3): 383-408, 1934. Eduard Heimann, "Sociological Preconceptions of Economic Theory," *Social Research*, 1: 23-44, February, 1934; Adolf Loewe, *Economics and Sociology, A Plea for Co-operation in the Social Sciences*, (London: George Allen and Unwin, 1935); A. B. Wolfe, "Sociology and Economics," in William Fielding Ogburn and Alexander Goldenweiser, eds., *The Social Sciences and Their Interrelations*, (Boston etc.: Houghton Mifflin Co., 1927), pp. 299-310. Parsons deals with these sociological preconditions for economic action on the one hand and economic theory in the other, but gives a much more comprehensive analysis of the role of the normative order in economic organization, and of the role of abstraction in scientific theory (whereby the sting is removed from the criticism that economics is insufficiently or incorrectly descriptive). See especially Talcott Parsons, "Sociological Elements in Economics," in Harry Elmer Barnes, Howard Becker, and Frances Bennett Becker, eds., *Contemporary Social Theory*, (New York: D. Appleton-Century Co., 1940), pp. 601-646. See also Parsons, *The Structure of Social Action*, (New York: McGraw-Hill Book Co., 1937), *passim*.

ments in this field, we may note some of the more salient problems of theoretical development in the social sciences. With some oversimplification, the diverging views of scientific propriety may be reduced to a set of alternatives.

(A) The social sciences may attempt to mark off concrete areas as special domains, claiming to describe and analyze those areas "completely," and viewing as criminal trespass all investigation in the field by scholars not of the brotherhood. In the present century sociology and economics have both been afflicted with this view. The economist has claimed all areas remotely relating to the production, financing, distribution, and even consumption of goods and services including the social organization required for these activities. By this view industrial organization and management, labor relations, the institutional control of economic action, the buying behavior of consumers, and so on, have been the appropriate data for "realistic" economic analysis. To the sociologist was left certain of the "social problems" deriving from economic dislocations. The sociologist has frequently accepted and even insisted upon this division of labor, since he was engaged in the detailed description of communities or criminals or the American family.

(B) The social sciences may recognize the role of analytical abstraction, giving up the hopeless (and bootless) task of describing reality in its totality in favor of the development of a theoretical system. This theoretical system would be made up of principles — stated within the limits to which they apply — and the empirical and logical relations between principles. By this view the economist would study, for example, the principles of economic action and the behavior of the market under various conditions, whereas the sociologist would formulate the principles of social organization and the normative order in society.

The former view has led to a stupendous bulk of investigation, frequently duplicated, and often directed toward problems having small practical and no theoretical significance. It has also produced numerous border skirmishes, disputed jurisdictions, and stridently sectarian gospels. The latter view sacrifices some immediate practicality, although possibly contributing a greater degree of long-range practicality through the development of fundamental principles. It seems on the whole to offer the greater chance of genuinely scientific development. It is this view which is here assumed, as indeed the other position would seem to offer little support for the type of studies with which we are here concerned.

Although for most of the present century some European scholars have been analyzing certain phenomena in economic activity in terms of genuinely sociological conceptual schemes, a comparable development in American scholarship is very recent. The greater part of the descriptive data, some of which are utilizable for sociological analysis, has been developed by those outside the formal ranks of sociologists. And it is on the descriptive level that we yet must seek many of the ingredients of what we may call a sociology of economic organization.

I

A review of contemporary developments in those branches of sociology having the greatest significance for analysis of productive and commercial organization may perhaps be most conveniently approached by the expedient of indirection. That is, we may first note those aspects of analysis left untouched or inadequately formulated by economic theory and amenable to sociological investigation. This indirect procedure is indicated for at least two reasons: (a) economic theory has been developed to a considerably more advanced point than have the interrelated principles of the other social sciences, and this allows a relatively greater ease in marking off the limits of competence or adequacy in existing theory; (b) correlatively, sociological theory in this as in other aspects is poorly developed, and is thus difficult to summarize directly and positively. The procedure does not imply the intentional relegation of sociological analysis to those residual categories neglected by the so-called more specialized sciences, but is rather adopted as a preface to subsequent positive statement of principles clearly established.(2)

Although subject to violent and somewhat unjustified attack, the main body of economic theory is still "classical" economics together with continued refinements of the central principles; viewed broadly and in retrospect such heresies as those of the Austrian School are refinement and shifts of emphasis rather than major changes. That

---

2. Any classificatory principle as applied to scientific developments is likely to cut across others which might be useful for other purposes. We do not adopt a chronological, biographical, or geographical review precisely because the pressent interest is in an assessment of subject matter and principles.

SOCIOLOGY OF ECONOMIC ORGANIZATION

main body of theory has developed along fairly definite lines. Postulating economic ends or "wants" as unlimited and random — although with a marked tendency to biologize them in one way or another — and a rational orientation of the actor (familiar *homo oeconomicus*) to those ends, the economist has derived the principles of maximizing utility, the calculation of alternative courses of action, and ultimately the behavior of the market. For the latter, however, certain further assumptions need to be made: the individuals act separately and not in combination, competition is (relatively) unrestricted, and the market itself is subject to no direct controls other than those imposed by the "automatic" operation of the pricing mechanism. Although the extreme position would assume a complete absence of "external" control, realization that the formulation is not only abstract but inherently unstable has generally led to assumption of sufficient control to keep the competition "fair."

Our present interest is not simply in the undoubted fact that this formulation is not concretely descriptive of economic affairs, or even that it could not be. Rather, the more important questions concern the points at which sociology has a bearing on the general analysis of economic behavior. The foregoing drastically abbreviated statement of the subject matter of economics is sufficient to indicate the several important difficulties once this type of behavior is related to the social order as a whole. These difficulties, briefly enumerated below, provide a convenient approach to the sociological contributions to their resolution.

(A) The "liberal" economic order assumed by the classical economists, or any other economic order, can only operate within certain social conditions. Those conditions include at least the minimum control necessary to regulate competition, to reduce the otherwise efficient use of force and fraud, and in general to determine and enforce those rules of conduct which give predictability to social relations. As we shall note below, this set of conditions is customarily called the institutional framework, and as such has received a great deal of attention.

(B) A critical problem in classical economic theory which has received very little acceptable amendment in modern economics is the question of ends and motives. The assumption of rationality itself has been subject to strong and somewhat irrelevant attack, as we shall note below. A greater difficulty rises in the explanation of the nature and sources of ends pursued in economic affairs. The observable facts that ends are not random, wants not unlimited, and so on point to further investigation concerning the character of value systems and the ways in which the individual is induced to comply with the normative order of society.

(C) A consideration of a different order concerns the role of groups and combinations in economic affairs. Since combinations did not meet the assumptions of a completely competitive order in the older economics, only recently have economists begun to study economic principles wich take into account the very extensive *organization* of industry and trade. The role of power and authority in the contemporary organization of labor unions and industrial enterprises tends still to be minimized in economic theory and in the dogma of individualism. What must interest the sociologist in this situation, however, is rather the application of general principles of organization to a concrete area, although leaving open the possibility of secondary principles applying peculiarly to economic organizations.

(D) An additional and not entirely homogeneous group of problems cuts across the foregoing considerations to a certain extent, but is most closely related to problems of "institutional conditions," which, when viewed sociologically also become problems of functional relationships.

The areas for investigation include: the deliberate social controls of the economic order, including economic planning in its various forms, and the effects of these controls not only on the economic organization but upon the entire social structure; the significance of occupation and division of labor for general social status; the sources of labor supply and factors affecting its quantity, quality, and mobility; the relations among economic interest groups and between these groups and other types of organizations; the role of technology and economic organization in molding the social structure and effecting social change.

The possible fields for sociological investigation naturally increase with the specificity of the problem. We shall briefly note below the state of the science with respect to principles established at various levels of generalization.

Institutional Conditions for Economic Action. A great deal of work of sociologists and economists alike in the study of the way in which a society operates has taken the form of attacks on the abstract principles of the older economics. Some of the attacks, notably those made by the American "institutionalists" as noted below, have simply attempted to dismiss classical theory on the grounds that it was insufficiently descriptive or erroneous altogether. Others have atempted to state a little more clearly the nature of the assumptions made in "liberal" economics and to discover if such conditions could exist. A very few have proceeded to positive statement of economic principles under different conditions, or to a positive statement of the principles of social order which define or at least limit the sphere of production and trade. As a whole, the studies direct attention to what may be called the "institutional preconditions" for economic organization.

As a minimum statement of the types of institutional controls (3) within which any economic system must operate, it may be noted that some well-understood principles must govern the division of labor, the disposition of property rights, and the methods of distribution. Stated less austerely, the social order must provide answers to the questions: who does what, who controls what (and whom), and who get what? The recongnition of the cogency of these questions has become increasingly widespread, and considerable research has been devoted to an examination of the influence of variations in these institutions on the economic framework in particular and on the social order in general.

The importance of the division of labor has long been recognized in economic theory, and indeed formed one of the principal points of interest of Adam Smith and Ricardo. The way in which specialization increases labor productivity is well understood by economists. The questions of sociological interest revolve around the social conditions which facilitate or impede a free (or any other) labor system, the mobility in response to economic demand, and the integration of the specialized workman into the broader structure of the economy and the society.

The assumption of the free and competitive labor market, with few if any restrictions on the ready response of labor supply to market demand, is a basic tenet of classical wage theory. Recent modifictions of wage theory made in view of other conditions do not answer the need for an analysis of the circumstances in which various types of labor systems develop. A limited number or studies have investigated specific labor systems or particular aspects of

---

3. An "institution" is here regarded as a system of norms (that is, rules of conduct) referring to a major aspect of social life.

labor under a capitalistic economy. Nieboer's work on slavery, with materials drawn almost entirely from primitive societies, suggested that forced labor is developed under conditions of open resources and relative ease of subsistence. (4) Marx, as we shall note below, observed the close relationship between control of rights in valuable things (that is, property) and control over labor; which leads by implication not fully developed by Marx to the hypothetically intimate connection between variations in property arrangements and variations in division of labor. Weber noted the relationship between the system of exchange in a capitalist order and the "rational" division of labor, and suggested that a system of free labor is dependent on a free market. (5) Very little attention has been devoted to the relations betwen the division of labor and other bases of distinction and stratification, the political order, kinship systems, and the like. (6) The significance of familial institutions and of methods of affixing status for occupational specialization has, however, been given some attention with reference to human society in general, (7) especially with regard to the minimum limitation on status (and therefore occupational) competition. Weber's work may be regarded as having conclusively demonstrated the role of religious and ethical conceptions in the competitive individualism and extensive division of labor characteristic of early capitalism. (8)

Many of the foregoing developments await integration within the framework of general principles. The minimum division of labor for a social order to function (chiefly the differentiation deriving from the ascribed statuses on the basis of age, sex, and kinship afliliation)

---

4. H. J. Nieboer, *Slavery as an Industrial System,* 2nd ed., (The Hague: Martinus Nijhoff, 1910), pp. 417-437.

5. Max Weber, *Wirtschaft and Gesellschaft,* (Tuebingen: J. C. B. Mohr, 1922), pp. 31-121.

6. Frederic Le Play in the last century attempted to link types of labor relationships with type of family systems; see his *Les ouvriers européens,* (Paris: Imprimerie Impèriale, 1855). Aside from acute over-simplification, Le Play's work is most marred by special pleading for what would now be called a peasant society.

7. See especially Ralph Linton, *The Study of Man,* (New York: D. Appleton-Century Co., 1936), Chap. VIII, "Status and Role."

8. See especially Max Weber, *The Protestant Ethic and the Spirit of Capitalism,* tr. by Talcott Parsons, (London: G. Allen and Unwin, 1930). The role of ethical and religious ideologies in the institutional modifications of American Negro slavery has been analyzed by Wilbert E. Moore, "Slave Law and the Social Structure," *Journal of Negro History,* 26: 171-202, April, 1941.

is more exactly fixed than is the point of maximum specialization under various conditions. Since modern industrial society has developed along lines of ever-increasing specialization, the societal organization necessary to allow extreme differentiation and interdependence warrants attention. This was the problem posed and partially resolved by Durkheim, who demonstrated that interdependence alone does not guarantee "social soildarity," and implied that a normative system in which the individual directly participates is a minimum condition for extensive occupational specialization. (9) Althought this problem has received very little further attention the obverse problem of the significance of specialization for the character of societal organization has been studied widely with respect to occupational differentiation and social stratification, as noted below. Only a very limited number of studies have been devoted to the characteristics of group participation, conformity with regulatory principles, lines of distinction and mobility, and so on, within specific occupations or groups of occupation. (10) Even more limited is work on a genuinely sociological classification of occupations, with identification of the significant elements in occupational categorization.

The control over scarce values, and especially over productive wealth (capital), is an additional institutional arrangement of the

---

9. See Emile Durkheim, *On the Division of Labor in Society*, tr., by George Simpson, (New York: The Macmillan Co., 1933), especially Preface to the Second Edition. See also Talcott Parsons, *The Structure of Social Action*, pp. 301-375. An interesting parellel to Durkheim's analysis from the point of view of economic theory is provided by John Maurice Clark, *Preface to Social Economics*, (New York: Farrar and Rinehart, 1936), Chap. III, "The Changing Basis of Economic Responsibility."

10. See W. Fred Cottrell, *The Railroader*, (Stanford University, Calif.: Stanford University Press, 1940); Frances R. Donovan, *The Saleslady*, (Chicago: University of Chicago Press, 1929). Extensive studies of industrial workers, particularly "operatives" in mass-production industries, have been made with some attention to occupational characteristics. See especially F. J. Roethlisberger and William J. Dickson, *Management and the Worker*, (Cambridge: Harvard University Press, 1939). Some suggestive comments on industrial technologists are made by Roethlisberger in *Management and Morale*, (Cambridge: Harvard University Press, 1941), Chap. V; and at least one profesional group has been brought under sociological observation: Logan Wilson, *The Academic Man*, (New York: Oxford University Press, 1942). Studies of deviant occupations are also available: Kingsley Davis, "Sociology of Prostitution," *American Sociological Review*, 2: 744-755, October, 1937; E. H. Sutherland, ed., *The Professional Thief*, (Chicago: University of Chicago Press, 1937).

highest significance for the ordering of economic production and exchange. Here, as in the case of division of labor, the assumptions made by classical economics were partly wrong in principle (in the sense that they could not exist) and partly and increasingly wrong in fact (in the sense that they no longer exist). The assumptions, usually summarized as "private property," involved at least two principles: that of unlimited rights under unitary control, and that of individual as opposed to group ownership. The former assumption is intrinsically impossible in view of the necessities of social order that require the reservation of rights by the political authority, and is subject to further modification through the division of property rights in the same locus of value exemplified in the modern corporation. The latter assumption is violated to some extent in all societies and widely negated in some. (11) The significance of these limitations and modifications has been widely noted by the American "institutional" economists, naturally with primary emphasis on their implications for economic theory. (12) Somewhat less attention has been devoted to the general types of property institutions in relation to systems of production on exchange. (13) Although this lack of extensive comparative analysis seriously limits the adequacy of the generalizations applicable to the rapidly changing and somewhat amorphous institutional controls on the use of wealth in modern society, the significance of the subject-matter is at least widely recognized.

The institutional conditions which define and limit the system of economic exchange and distribution have perhaps received less direct attention than in the case of any other aspect of the relevant institutional framework. Since the recognition of the significance of institutions has, at least in Anglo-American social scientific develop-

---

11. For a more complete statement of the principles of private property and their modifications, see Wilbert E. Moore, "The Emergence of New Property Conceptions in America," *Journal of Legal and Political Sociology*, 1 (3-4): 34-58, April, 1943.

12. See especially John R. Commons, *Legal Foundations of Capitalism*, (New York: The Macmillan Co., 1924); Richard T. Ely, *Property and Contract in Their Relations to the Distribution of Wealth*, (New York: The Macmillan Co., 1914, 2 vols.). See also Adolf A. Berle, Jr., and Gardiner C. Means, *The Modern Corporation and Private Property*, (New York: The Macmillan Co., 1933).

13. For a concise review of developments, with special regard to property systems in primitive societies, see A. Irving Hallowell, "The Nature and Function of Property as a Social Institution," *Journal of Legal and Political Sociology*, 1 (3-4): 115-138, April, 1943.

ment, come more often from economists than from sociologists, the general neglect of distribution in economic theory may partly explain the neglect of the circumstances regulating the distributive system. By the principles of the older economics distribution was effected through the system of exchange, beyond which it was unnecessary to go. Under the assumptions of competition and useful specialization, the impersonal market affixed rewards and punishments according to merit. To the extent that the rewards were converted to property rights they were of possible further importance as capital; to the extent that the rewards were converted to consumers' goods they tended to lose all economic significance. In general, the direct and important factor in distribution was *demand*, which provided part of the dynamic element in the exchange system and together with supply fixed the market price. Now although the demand side of the market equilibrium has been given casual or intensive consideration by economists of various persuasions, the emphasis has been placed on the satisfaction of various "wants." The assumption of distribution according to merit in the productive organization has consistently obscured both the exact nature of the wants to be satisfied, and the significance of familial and other organizational patterns for the allocation of goods among consumers. Sociologists have long understood the function of the family as the consuming unit, but have generally failed to apply this knowledge rigorously in interpreting economic behavior. Yet the application is so clear that it may be taken as established that the behavior of the exchange system is directly affected by the fact that each claim upon the wealth of the society subject to exchange, whether originating in proprietary rights or in claims for services, is likely to represent the claims of a plurality of persons for support. The latter claims rarely rest on merit as economically defined. By a slight extension of this principle the rationale for some of the modifications imposed on the "free" market becomes understandable: the necessity in an integrated social order of ensuring not only that the market remain genuinely open to those who have recognizable rights to buy or sell but also that values other than the reward for narrowly defined merit be served. These values include the protection of health and stability of the family. (14)

The system of exchange itself, especially the function of money in providing a measure of the individual's standing as well as a convinient means for carrying on the relationships of producers and consumers, is of course an eminently social creation, as insistently pointed out by Simiand. (15) No work of comparable proportions has been devoted to other specific aspects of exchange systems, although some ethnological research adds emphasis to the integration of any exchange system into the social order of which it is a part. (16)

In summary, the theoretical foundations for the analysis of the institutional preconditions of economic organization are soundly laid, although the actual principles governing various modes of relationship are unequally developed. The interest of economists in taking into account new conditions may in the future be matched on the part of sociologists seeking the principles of institutional variation and integration. (17)

The Status of Ends and Motives. A question of fundamental importance in the analysis of economic activity is that of the motives which prompt the participation of the actors, or the ends which are to be pursued. It is at this point that the older economics has been subject to attack perhaps even more severe than in the case of the role of institutions. The assumption of the rational, self-interested individual devoted to the efficient pursuit of unspecified ends, that is, *homo oeconomicus,* has created a deal of trouble for

---

14. The "economics of consumption" is a small but recognized field in contemporary scholarship; it is, however, largely confined to descriptive studies of family budgets and to attempts to account for consumers' choices. Some systematization has taken place with respect to the relative order of choices according to level of living. See Maurice Halbwachs, *Recherches sur la hiérarchie des besoins dans les sociétés industrielles contemporaines,* (Paris: Alcan, 1912); Carle C. Zimmerman, *Consumption and Standards of Living,* (New York: D. Van Nostrand Co., 1936).

15. François Simiand, "Le monnaie réalité sociale," *Annales sociologiques,* Série D, Fasc. 1: 1-86, 1934; *Le salaire, l'évolution sociale et le monnaie,* (Paris: Alcan, 1932, 3 vols.).

16. See, for example, Bronislaw Malinowski, *Crime and Custom in Savage Society,* (New York: Harcourt, Brace and Co., 1926).

17. Perhaps the most complete statement of the principles established and the area awaiting investigation is to be found in Parsons, *The Structure of Social Action.*

economic theory. On the one hand, the theory itself has been internally unstable, since in the situation of a plurality of actors it required either a factually untenable assumption of a "natural identity of interests" or some equally untenable denial of the independent character of ends. (18) On the other hand, the formula has been subjected to an increasing barrage of evidence pointing the irrational and non-rational orientation of the human individual to his circumstances and goals.

Without a review-in detail of the extensive literature, it is now clear (a) that the behavior of the "economic man" may in fact be approximated within fairly narrow sectors of the social order, and oriented toward ends that *by definition in the particular social order are self-interested*; (b) that the concrete behavior of the social individual, including that of the business man or laborer in an economic context, is likely to include elements of irrational and non-rational behavior, capable of being understood within the broader framework of the normative order of society (19); (c) that motives are in fact of primarily social origin, inculcated through socialization of the young, and at least roughly consistent with the ultimate values held in the society (20); (d) that the approved and market-sanctioned acquisitiveness characteristic of individual capitalism has had in fact its greatest extension in that economic order, and far from being a universal principle of human motivation, was developed in a very special set of ideological and institutional circumstances. (21)

---

18. This whole problem is cogently treated by Parsons in *ibid.*, Chap. II. Much of the remainder of Parsons' book deals with the solution provided to this and kindred problems by a group of sociologists (especially Durkheim, Pareto, and Weber). The present brief review constitutes only an inadequate summary of the developments in this field. See also Ferdinand Toennies, *Gemeinchaft und Gesselschaft*, tr. by Charles P. Loomis as *Fundamental Concepts of Sociology*, (New York: American Book Co., 1940), and Parsons' discussion, *op. cit.*, pp. 686-694.

19. See Clark, *op. cit.*, Chap. IV; Frank H. Knight, *The Ethics of Competition*, (New York: Harper and Bros., 1935); Vilfredo Pareto, *The Mind and Society*, (New York: Harcourt, Brace and Co., 1935, 4 Vols.); Parsons, *The Structure of Social Action*, passim.

20. See especially Emile Durkheim, *L'éducation morale*, (Paris: Alcan, 1925); Parsons, *The Structure of Social Action*, pp. 376-408.

21. See Werner Sombart, *Der moderne Kapitalismus*, 2nd ed., (Leipzig: Duncker und Humblot, 1913, 3 Vols.); Weber, *The Protestant Ethic*. For a

TWENTIETH CENTURY SOCIOLOGY

The importance of the "institutional conditions" now becomes more evident: they function to integrate the isolated economic act or the particular economic organization into the fabric of the normative order of society; that is, the institutions so "define the situation" that self-interested action also fulfills the expectations of society.

It is to be noted that the foregoing summary of developments is highly selective, since the social psychology underlaying much of modern economic theory is that of uncritical hedonism, whereas the main body of American sociologists have followed a behaviorism scarcely mitigated by the recognition of the phenomenon of moral conformity. (22)

Social Organization. The role of authority and power in economic relationships, and the importance of organizations in productive enterprise, provide eminently sociological elements in the interpretation of industrial and commercial affairs. Anglo-American economic theory has until very recently neglected these aspects of economic affairs, and the support by the older legal structure of the abstract conception of a community of independent producers and traders tended to force the hard and uncomfortably negative facts into the mold of abstract theory. On the other hand, Marx and his

---

broader extension of the relation between normative systems and economic developments, see Pitirim A. Sorokin, *Social and Cultural Dynamics,* Vol. III, *Fluctuation of Social Relationships, War, and Revolution,* (New York: American Book Co., 1937), Chap. VIII.

22. The selectivity seems appropriate since our concern is not with a review of doctrinal controversies which persist beyond the establishment of principles encompassing within a single body of theory those phenomena cited in contending doctrines. That many sociologists deny either the existance or the importance of well-established facts (such as the denial of ends as an independent factor in action, or the insistence that no principles exist which cannot be counted or measured) is regrettable, but not decisive within the canons of science.

The applicability of the principles noted is already widely established. Among recent works, see Elton Mayo, *The Human Problems of an Industrial Civilization,* (New York: The Macmillan Co., 1933); Roethhlisberger and Dickson, *op. cit.*

followers, as well as a number of other German economists, (23) have made the social structure of the productive enterprise a cardinal principle in economic theory. It should be noted that the formulations of the classical and neo-classical economists are not wrong under the conditions noted or assumed, but only wrong in the concrete sense that the conditions do not obtain.

Recent developments in economic theory take into account various modern tendencies toward combination in economic relations: the effects of industrial corporations and cartels on a nominally competitive market, the determination of wages under conditions of collective bargaining, and so on. (24) On the other hand, both sociologists and "management engineers" have recognized in the industrial organization a highly specialized form of social organization, which formally belongs to the general category "bureaucracy." Indeed, the principles of formal organization have been more highly developed by experts in management than by professional sociologists, although the necessary emendations of the principles (especially in terms of the inevitable collateral appearance of informal organization) have been worked out by observers with a sociological orientation. (25) A great deal of empirical research is taking

---

23. See, for example, Gustav Schmoller, *Ueber einige Grundfragen der Socialpolitik und der Volkswirtschaftslehre,* (Leipzig: Duncker und Humblot, 1898); Sombart, *op. cit.* Marx especially had the merit of insistence upon the authoritarian relationship deriving from (Marx tended to say, symbolized in) property, that is, differential access to capital. Although the thesis is presented at numerous junctures in *Kapital,* the most succinct statement is to be found in *A Contribution to the Critique of Political Economy,* (New York: International Library Publishing Co., 1904), especially in the "Author's Preface." See also Paul M. Sweezy, *The Theory of Capitalist Development,* (New York: Oxford University Press, 1942).

24. See Edward Chamberlin, *A Theory of Monopolistic Competition,* (Cambridge: Harvard University Press, 1933); J. M. Clark, "Toward a Theory of Workable Competition," in American Economic Association, *Readings in the Social Control of Industry,* (Philadelphia: The Blakiston Co., 1942), pp. 452-457; John T. Dunlop, *Wage Determination under Trade Unions,* (New York: The Macmillan Co., 1944).

25. The classic work on bureaucracy is of course Weber's. See his *Wirtschaft und Gesellschaft,* pp. 650-679. For an example of the principles of formal organization as applied to an industrial bureaucracy, see Elmore Petersen and E. Grosvenor Plowman, *Business Organization and Management,* (Chicago: Richard D. Irwin, 1941). The juxtaposition of formal and informal organization is analyzed by Chester I. Barnard, *The Functions of the Executive,* (Cambridge: Harvard University Press, 1938); Roethlisberger and Dickson, *op. cit.*

place in this field, much of it sociologically naive, but capable of interpretation and extension with theoretical as well as practical importance.

Economy and Society. A final group of problems, which partially comprise some of the preceding ones from a slightly different point of view, center around the position of production and trade in the general structure of society. The emphasis at this juncture is on organizational and institutional interdependence and the functioning of society as a whole. Thus, the regulatory devices that are normally called the "social controls of industry" may be properly regarded as an elaboration of the "institutional conditions" which we have already discussed from the point of view of economic theory. The significance of these controls in sociological theory is, however, more than simply as conditions for economic action. They not only limit but also in the broadest sense define economic action. The "conditions" from the point of view of economic theory are actually central structural elements in the cohesiveness of society. For in the process of limiting economic action they determine the ends which the economy should serve, and the additional values with which it should be consistent. The modern deliberate controls of industry simply provide new conditions for the economist, and these conditions may either be taken into account and new principles formulated for those circumstances, or neglected at the expense of increasing "unreality" (that is, abstractness) of existing theory. (26) For the sociologist the controls raise a series of problems barely touched upon in contemporary theory. For example, to what extent is it possible to plan a society? Given a particular set of values, what organizational structure is most effectively designed to achieve part of them at the least possible sacrifice of others? These are questions only recently noted in sociological analysis and to which the answers are available only in limited terms. (27)

---

26. The significance of social controls for economic theory is illustrated by a recent collection of economic essays. See American Economic Association, *Readings in the Social Control of Industry*. One may search this volume in vain for any reference to the ends toward which the controls are oriented.

27. The questions have been approched for the most part with respect to problems of planning in a democratic political and social order. See Georges Gurvitch, "Democracy as a Sociological Problem," *Journal of Legal and Political Sociology*, 1 (1-2): 46-71, October, 1942, and other papers in the same issue; Karl Mannheim, *Man and Society in an Age of Reconstruction*, (New York: Harcourt, Brace and Co., 1940).

The elaborate development of economic "interest groups" raises many other questions not treated here, including that of the distribution of power among these groups and as between any particular power group and the political order. For an excellent study in this field, see Robert A. Brady, *Business as a System of Power*, (New York: Columbia University Press, 1943).

SOCIOLOGY OF ECONOMIC ORGANIZATION

A quite different range of problems arises with regard to a field long recognized as on the borderline between economics and sociology: the size, characteristics, growth, and distribution of population. Demography touches economic analysis at two outstanding points: the supply of labor, and demand for goods. These relations are most frequently viewed with respect to the dynamics of population, and there has been a notable tendency to consider population as an empirically independent and even extra-social variable. One standard interpretation has followed the teachings of Malthus. Thus, population growth has been viewed as limiting levels of living, over-running labor demand, and providing a source of "pressures" released through war, migration, or economic imperialism. More recent work, however, emphasizes the impossibility of a human population without social organization, and the intimate relation of the latter to variations in the former. Social institutions control fertility and mortality, and changing technological and economic patterns have direct and indirect consequences for the size and the age-sex composition of the population. (28) The recognition of divergent patterns of population growth under different conditions allows the prediction of future population size and composition under varying assumptions, and the analysis of the implications of the projected demographic situations for the economy and society in question. (29) Moreover an accumulating wealth of data and a perfection of techniques may allow fairly rapid expansion of significant generalizations in the future.

Closely related to the strictly demographic questions are those regarding the size, mobility, and quality of the labor force. We have already noted that the division of labor constitutes a fundamental institutional condition making impossible an occupational specialization based purely on grounds of "maximum utilization." Although traditional economic theory, and particulary wage theory, assumed the existence of a large, mobile, and presumably qualified supply of labor, various limitations are apparent on each of these counts. Demography, as already noted, has given some attention to size of the labor force, and has also developed some

---

28. Some of these relationships are treated by E. F. Penrose, *Population Theories and Their Application*, (Stanford University, Calif.: Food Research Institute, 1934).

29. See Frank W. Notestein, Irene B. Taeuber, Dudley Kirk, Ansley J. Coale, and Louise K. Kiser, *The Future Population of Europe and the Soviet Union; Population Projections;* 1940-1970, (Geneva: League of Nations, 1944).

rather poorly interpreted data on spatial mobility. Very little attention has been devoted directly to the question of institutional and organizational provisions for occupational trainning and placement, or the limits to "maximum utilization" of labor deriving from the specific character of the social order. A considerable amount of work has been done, however, on occupational mobility as it relates to social stratification. (30)

The analysis of occupational position and social status is in fact about as comprehensive as any sociological work in the field of the relations of economy and society. Much of the interest in this field is attributable to the work of Marx and numerous followers of various shades of political opinion and sociological persuasion. A large and on the whole sound literature has developed on the alternative principles of stratification and modes of differential valuation. (31) It seems clear that within a modern industrial society occupation is the largest single (although by no means sole) determinant of general social position. (32)

The Marxian thesis that occupation *directly determines* a class-oriented ideology is amply disproved. It especially neglects the dynamic element of socialization, which is, however, class-differentiated and thus certainly provides an indirect basis for occupational determination of ideology. The latter factor also serves to explain the often-demonstrated departures in practice from the open-class ideology of equal opportunity and free mobility. The comparative literature is reasonable abundant, but is inadequately grounded in theory and therefore often provides no answers to questions concerning occupational specialization and the differential social valuation of occupational roles. It may, however, be maintained that occupation is never irrelevant for social status, although the dynamic relationship appears to be reversed under a

---

30. See, for example, Percy E. Davidson and H. Dewey Anderson, *Occupational Mobility in an American Community*, (Stanford University, Calif.: Stanford University Press, 1937); Pitirim Sorokin, *Social Mobility*, (New York: Harper and Bros., 1927). The latter reference remains about the best summary of the factors facilitating and impeding social (including occupational) mobility.

31. The schematic summary given by Weber (*Wirtschaft und Gesellschaft*, pp. 177-180, 631-640) retains its general utility as a classificatory scheme.

32. See, for example, H. Dewey Anderson and Percy E. Davidson, *Ballots and the Democratic Class Struggle*, (Stanford University, Calif.: Stanford University Press, 1934).

SOCIOLOGY OF ECONOMIC ORGANIZATION

caste situation. Indeed, it would appear, and not surprisingly, that the independent importance of occupation is in direct ratio to the emphasis upon economic production in the social order.

The modern facts of organization and combination in industrial enterprises and commercial establishments leads to still another field for sociological inquiry: the principles governing the relations of groups within the economic order. In general, the sociologist may perhaps safely neglect the relations between industrial enterprises so long as these are primarily market phenomena, although even here the problems of new controls for the benefit of unrepresented but legitimate "interests" require the type of functional analysis increasingly prevalent in sociological research. But the relations between managers and laborers, particularly in the development of collective bargaining, are even less amenable to market analysis. It is evident that new principles of social organization are being worked out, mostly on a sheerly empirical basis, but offering opportunities for both application and expansion of sociological theory. Thus, economists and sociologists alike have observed the development of a kind of "industrial jurisprudence" or common law, largely outside the framework of the formal statutes and decisions, but obviously ultimately accountable to the fundamental legal principles. (33)

Finally, a great many scholars, impressed by the extreme rapidity of social change, have sought solutions to the dynamic relations between economy and society. The most widely held views, unfortunately often unsupported either by fact or logic, attribute primary causal significance to "economic factors" in social change. The varying emphases may be conveniently reduced to three: the primacy of economic (roughly, hedonistic) motives, the inherent dynamics of economic organization and institutions, and the independent expansion of (largely industrial) technology. The first of these positions is least often supported as an explicit principle of causation, but implicity assumed in a vast range of economic literature. Knowledge of extensive cultural variability with respect to values and motives has sufficed to prevent most sociologists from subscribing to the view directly.

---

33. See John R. Commons and Associates, *Industrial Government*, (New York: The Macmillan Co., 1921); Georges Gurvitch, *Le temps présent et l'idée du droit social*, (Paris: J. Vrin, 1931); Sumner H. Slichter, *Union Policies and Industrial Managment*, (Washington: The Brookings Institution, 1941).

The thesis that the character of the economic organization shapes the main contours of the social order, and provides the initial impetus to societal changes, has received more elaborated development. Perhaps the clearest exposition, which at the the same time is the most tenable when stated within rigidly defined conditions, is still that of Marx and his interpreters. (34) For the most part the predictions of Marx have miscarried because the conditions assumed did not in fact remain constant, and not because the theory was bad. But as we shall note in the following section, the difficulty with this position in general, and this applies equally to the Marxian theory, is that the "economic factor" is poorly identified and indeed upon close examination is found to include elements perfectly capable of variation quite independently of productive or market organization. Such, for example, is the case with property, as already noted. The work of Weber and Sombart has served the useful purpose of leading once more to a functional interpretation of dynamic relations. (35)

A particular variety of economic interpretation has gained wide currency in sociology. This is the interpretation of social change in terms of resistance and adaptations to expanding technology, the latter regarded as inherently accumulative or dynamic. Veblen's maintence of this position was largely confined to economic developments in recent times, and did not entirely neglect the independent significance of non-technological values — which Veblen, however, was inclined to lump under the heading of "vested interests." (36)

---

34. See Joseph A. Schumpeter, *Capitalism, Socialism, and Democracy*, (New York and London: Harper and Bros., 1942); Sweazy, *op. cit.*

35. See the works of Weber and Sombart previously cited. Professor Schumpeter maintains that "The whole of Max Weber's facts and arguments fits perfectly into Marx's system." (See *op. cit.*, p. 11) If this be so, it is the best possible demonstration of a conception of "economic determinism" on the part of Marx so broad as to be meaningless. A more accurate appraisal would seem to indicate: (a) that Marx overstated his case, for whatever reasons, and did so partly by including in his principal dynamic factor (forms and conditions of production) many of the attendant and independently variable conditions; and (b) that Marx left some conditions, necessary for the accuracy of his formulation, implicit, or rather denied their relevance at all. This latter was especially the case with ideas, values, and "ideologies," which are precisely those elements emphasized by Weber.

36. See especially the following works of Thorstein Veblen: *The Engineers and the Price System*, (New York: Viking Press, 1933); *The Vested Interests and the State of the Industrial Arts*, (New York: B. W. Huebsch, 1919); *Absentee Ownership and Business Enterprise in Recent Times*, (New York: B. W. Huebsch, 1923).

SOCIOLOGY OF ECONOMIC ORGANIZATION

More recent adaptations of the position, particularly as exemplified in the "culture lag" hypothesis, have been less restrained in claims made, and, as we shall note in the following section, have done considerably more violence to fact and logic.

The developments here reviewed leave a great many significant questions unanswered. We shall return to a summary of the more important of these lacunae in the concluding section of this chapter. To the extent that the lines of scientific interest have simply stopped short of an ideally conceived goal of complete knowledge there is no cause for grave alarm; at most, it might be argued, although on uncertain grounds, that sociologists should have devoted more attention to this field and less to others. But to the extent that the developments appear inimical to a sound theoretical conception of available evidence, more positive criticism seems indicated. To that criticism we turn in the following section.

II

Most of the incidental criticisms of modern developments in the sociology of economics have already been indicated in the previous section, while additional criticism has been implicit in the selection and rejection of points to be stressed. (37) There is therefore no intention of reviewing the literature here in critical detail. Rather, we have selected one extensive development that seems most subject to criticism. That development is the wide acceptance of economic and technological primacy in social change.

Perhaps the greatest difficulty in the assessment of the accuracy of the various forms of "economic interpretation" is the definition and identification of the variables. As previously noted, few sociologists have subscribed to the patently erroneous view that all human behavior may be reduced to the struggle for existence, the "acquisitive instinct," or the satisfaction of economic wants expressed in mainly physiological terms. It is rather in the conditions, forms, and organization of productive enterprise that most adherents to the doctrine of economic primacy find their prime mover. Marx and his followers, for example, have emphasized technology and "relationships of production" as providing the dynamic factors

---

37. Some of the selectiveness is bound to be somewhat arbitrary in view of the uncertain state of sociological theory. Thus, some developments neglected as "minor" may ultimately have considerable theoretical significance.

which lead to the gradual or sudden transition from one productive system to another. As previously implied, two difficulties are encountered in this interpretation: (a) The "economic factor" so defined includes a number of distinct elements, at least some of which are independently variable. It thus becomes difficult to assess precisely what dynamic role is to be assigned to each of the elements. The fact of independent variability has an even further significance, for some of the elements are economically relevant, but are far from being "determined" by the other elements. Thus, property arrangements may be modified to give more or less power to an employer, or profits may be taxed away to provide unemployment relief or finance an international war. The exploitative power of the owner of capital may be regulated by law, and the terms of the wage contract limited by legislation designed to protect the health of children. These are changes in the conditions and relationships of production; but the dynamic lies outside the economic organization and not the other way around. Actually, of course, a functional relationship holds, and its interpretation may be conveniently appoached by primary attention to changes in productive organization. The difficulty lies in claiming that this matter of convenience is something more — that it represents the true basis of societal organization. It is perhaps equally convenient to examine the functional relationships from any other starting point.

(b) Above all, however, it is necessary to go further and examine the character of the conditions actually not included as elements in the "economic factor" but which are in fact necessary for the supposed course of economic developments actually to take place. Notable in this respect is the constancy of ends. The explicit denial by various "economic determinists" that any assumption is made concerning the primacy of economic motives, and the partially accurate insistence that the behavior of specific individuals is rather a function of their position in the system, do not eliminate the relevance of ends. One form of productive enterprise will lead to a more efficient or highly organized form only so long as and to the extent that the value system remains reasonably favorable to the change. When conflicts of interests, economic and otherwise, arise, as they inevitably must in a dynamic situation, the victory of certain interests depends on the whole normative and structural situation. There is no *a priori* reason for supposing that "economic" interests will prevail; equally there is no *a priori* reason for supposing that the economic structure is any more immanently dynamic than any other. The analysis must be made for each particular case, until such time as general principles have sufficient predictive range to reduce the cases to types. The evidence has been so exclusively confined to the development of capitalism that comparative analysis is diffcult. However, even in this limited case the evidence previously reviewed supports the general validity of the foregoing observations.

A current and very popular mode of interpretation of social change places primary or exclusive emphasis on an inherently expanding technology. Its popularity seems to be partly a mathematical function of its simplicity, and partly a fortuitous result of its being superficially correct for some of the data arrayed under its aegis. In its crudest form this interpretation attempts to draw a distinction between accumulative "material" culture (machines, tools, artifacts), and non-material or adaptive culture (ideas, knowledge and values). (38) This view makes the initial error of failing to see that culture objects are only part of the culture in so far as they embody ideas and values. The attention to the "material culture" has left the impression that machines are self-inventing, self-perpetuating, and self-expanding, and that non-material culture tends to "lag" behind the existing pile of culture objects.

A more tenable formulation makes of technology (which is a system of ideas, principles, and interests) a segment of culture more subject to change than other aspects of culture, and therefore possibly of causal significance in social change. Under certain conditions this is likely to be a correct interpretation, precisely because of the instrumental character of technology. That is, the elaboration of techniques for the achievement of some societal values is likely to require modification of other practices and possibly beliefs. Thus, changes in the design and performance of automobiles have certainly "caused" modification of American recreational customs, and have been relevant to changes in courtship ideals and practices. Likewise, the increased mechanization of industry has in-

---

38. See William F. Ogburn, *Social Change,* (New York: Viking Press 1936), Part IV, "Social Maladjustments." See also William F. Ogburn and Meyer F. Nimkoff, *Sociology,* (Boston, etc.: Houghton Mifflin Co., 1940), Chap. XXIV, "The Social Effects of Inventions." Sorokin indicates the shortcomings of the thesis under review with detailed analytical and empirical criticism. See his *Social and Cultural Dynamics.* Vol. IV, *Basic Problems, Principles, and Methods,* (New York: American Book Co., 1941), pp. 155-196, 302-321, where also the principal literature is cited.

creased the competitive advantages of large industries and "caused" considerable industrial transformations.

The error of attributing sole or primary causal importance to an expanding techonology has consisted in the neglect of the important qualification, "under certain conditions." These conditions may be briefly stated.

(A) For technological change to be "primary" the end or goal of technological "progress" must be assumed, and must remain constant. A change in ends makes previous technology wasteful, and creates a temporary lag in development of a new technology. Thus a nation at war finds its peace-time industrial technology oriented toward ends which are no longer primary (such as refrigerators and automobiles) and its wartime production limited by an inadequate technology. In this case it is obviously the goal which is of causal significance in the change, and not the technology. (39).

---

39. Although not attributing to technology a primary causal importance, MacIver has attempted a distinction between technology (or civilization) and culture, the former being accumulative and the latter not. He meets the problem of constancy of ends in two ways.

(1) He emphasizes correctly the constancy of certain societal problems, such as the control and use of nature, control of production, and control of power and authority. In these realms he claims technology is accumulative. However, it must be noted that these are very general problems, and that for concrete societal goals the appropriate technology may reach a perfectly adequate plane for the *existing* problem of control. It is true that the goals themselves tend to be moving ones, as for example under conditions of expanding population. In this case, however, the end is changing, not constant, and primary importance in that change certainly cannot be attributed to expanding technology. It is perhaps unnecessary to add that an expanding technology for the achievement of certain ends may create or make possible other changes incidentally.

(2) MacIver also emphasizes, particularly with reference to economic or political goals, the lack of intimate relationship between techniques and the social values to be served. Thus he notes that the same techniques of political control may be used for the most widely different values, such as democracy and fascism. On these grounds he is justly criticized by Merton for attempting to separate means and ends. (See Robert K. Merton, "Civilization and Culture," *Sociology and Social Research,* 21: 103-113, 1936). Although it is true that there are generalized techniques which may be used for a variety of ends, it must be insisted that the ends limit the choice of means, and that with reference to very concrete ends the relationship is very close. Thus the techniques which can be used for the achievement of very general ends are themselves not only general, but few in number.

See R. M. MacIver, *Social Causation,* (Boston: Ginn and Co., 1942), Chap. X; and *Society: A Textbook of Sociology,* (New York: Farrar and Rinehart, 1937), Chaps. XIV, XXIV-XXVI.

SOCIOLOGY OF ECONOMIC ORGANIZATION

The doctrine of technological primacy has had some validity as an interpretation of industrial transformation, precisely because the goal of economic productivity has been more or less correctly assumed, and has remained reasonably constant. Other scientific principles could be applied to other practical (that is, socially approved) ends, and to a considerable degree they have been in such fields as medicine, public health, and even propaganda and social control. As in the case of the culture of capitalism, much of the original impetus to the acquisition of useful knowledge was grounded in religious ideology. (40).

As a universally valid principle the technological interpretation of social change is forced to find some source of the ends to be achieved. Thus, there is a marked tendency for this view to become a watered-down version of the doctrine of economic causation, and fall heir to the difficulties of that doctrine as well.

(B) Not only must this variety of causal imputation assume the ends, but the relation between various societal values must be subject to variation. That is, since the most efficient achievement of one end may intrude upon or destroy other social values, any technology is only capable of expansion to the degree that the consequences in modification of other values can and will be absorbed and accepted by the society. Thus the introduction of new productive machinery may cause technological unemployment. This in turn results in a series of intrusions upon such values as the "right to work." Likewise, concentration of time and energy in one direction may remove these scarce resources from the achievement of other values (such as widespread participation in the arts, development of low-cost housing, or perfection of the machinery of government). In general, expanding industrial technology has continued to be a causal factor precisely because the society has been willing to make the necessary adjustments. That is, the original goal of more economical production has retained precedence over other values.

Inventions, then, do have social results; they also have social causes, and their acceptance or rejection depends upon the social framework. Some of the results may, and likely will, be unanticipated. This gives rise to a "culture lag" if those unanticipated results are changes which the existing structure is poorly designed to accept or incorporate. But the "culture lag" is certainly not a predestined

---

40. See Robert K. Merton, *Science, Technology, and Society in Seventeenth Century England*, in the series Osiris, Vol. IV, Part 2, pp. 360-632, (Bruges, Belgium: The Saint Catherine Press, 1938).

result of the slowness of adaptive culture in "catching up" with the inevitably changing material culture; the lag is in fact capable of purposive solution. It is possible to adjust to the machine (thus preserving the dominance of the original goal, but modifying others), or it is possible to change, modify, regulate, or abandon the machine in view of other values. Even in the modern industrial world the dictum that "You can't fight social (that is, technological) trends" is discounted by the fact that inventions *are* controlled when their results would be contrary to business interests. (41).

The analysis of long-range social change is perhaps the weakest point in modern sociological theory. In any event, it is certainly the weakest point in the sociological analysis of the dynamic relations between economy and society.

III

Developments during the Twentieth Century in the field of sociology of economics appear on the whole to be auspicious for the future. Despite a seeming reluctance of many sociologists, particulary in the United States, to devote attention to the scientific problems at hand, substantial strides have been taken. It should be noted, however, that there is no good reason for maintaining that all aspects of economic behavior not included in "classical" economics is sociological by default. Economic principles may be formulated under numerous conditions besides those of a "liberal" economic order. Although not immediately germane to this review, it is noteworthy that "comparative economics" is little developed, and that a considerable area for economic research remains open both in modern Western societies and in other types of social orders. Even were such an expansion in economic theory to take place, however, there would remain large questions for sociological inquiry. The development of

---

41. See United States Congress, Temporary National Economic Committee, *Investigation of Concentration of Economic Power, Hearings ...*, (Washington: U. S. Government Printing Office, 1939-1941), Part 3, *Patents—Proposals for Changes in Law and Procedures* (1939); Part 30, *Technology and Concentration of Economic Power* (1940). See also Walton Hamilton, *Patents and Free Enterprise*, United States Congress, Temporary National Economic Committee, *Investigation of Concentration of Economic Power*, Monograph No. 31, (Washington: U. S. Government Printing Office, 1941). Veblen dealt at some length with the practice of business interests sabotaging industrial (productive) interests. See the works cited in note 36 above.

SOCIOLOGY OF ECONOMIC ORGANIZATION

new economic principles under changing social conditions and the extensive sociological analysis of those conditions combine to document what should have been evident all along, as emanating from the logic of science: namely, that economic laws like any others are universal only in abstraction and will operate only within the conditions upon which they are based. Only much more comparative investigation will reveal how many of the relevant conditions are empirically universal, and why.

With respect to the values and regulatory principles which provide the social setting for economic behavior, sociological development has been substantial. Beyond the establishment of the general importance of these structural elements in society, there has been achieved an approximate indentification of the necessary limits to variability in some economic relations and behavior: the limits to economic rationality as a scheme for social behavior, the limits of "private" property, and the limits of occupational specialization. Short of these limits, knowledge is understandably most extensive concerning Western industrial society. Thus, the importance of a particular value system in the developments of industrial capitalism has been demonstrated. Similarly, extensive research has indicated in some detail the relations between income and occupation on the one hand and general social position on the other. In both of these cases, however, lack of familiarity with the results, or the ease of maintaining less adequate conceptions (such as the common three-class differentiation) stand in the way of advanced reesarch.

Future research needs to be turned particularly to much more extensive comparative and functional analysis of institutions, with particular regard to specific relationships in institutional and organizational forms. This even applies to modern Western society. For example, to what extent can "free institutions" be incorporated within a social order exercising extensive control over production and distribution? Does a system of collective bargaining in labor relations necessarily lead to an increasing emphasis on stability of status, and the reintroduction of the "estate" principle of stratification? Answers of these questions may have a bearing on public policy as well as on the general body of scientic theory.

In the present century we have witnessed a slow but steady reaffirmation of the distinctly human data of social life, especially the categorically demonstrable fact that ends and ideas make a difference. With respect to economic behavior, the necessity has been not so much the emphasis on the subjective orientation of the actor (which is generally assumed in economic theory) but upon the character of the ends and their approximate consistency with the normative expectations of society. We are not yet in a position to assess the relative "effectiveness" of various normative systems in relation to such matters as the production of economic goods and services. Moreover, the significance of the increasing use of money as a "universal means" is perhaps not fully understood. For a example, to what extent does "pecuniary emulation" tend to break down occupational ethics that have traditionally emphasized disinterested behavior as in medicine? These questions of course must remain unanswered by those sociologists whose conceptual framework is limited by a naive environmentalism.

The application of sociological principles to the analysis of industrial and other economic organizations has proceeded rather far, although carried on for the most part tangentially to the main body of sociological research. The principles of bureaucratic organization, applicable to industrial enterprises, are fairly certain. Preliminary research has undertaken the study of the to-be-expected "informal" organization in highly specialized structures. Yet much of the work of specialists in industrial management is limited to the discovery, but not the analysis, of the "human factor" as a residual category. The field remains open for the development of principles which will determine the limits to segmentation of roles in formal structure, and provide systematic formulation of the social conditions for the operation of specialized organizations.

Finally, we need an entire restatement of the theory of social change and of the methodological problems in the analysis of social change. With reference to the role of economic organization and industrially oriented technology, much time and labor have been wasted in demonstrating the obvious and completely misinterpreting its significance. This is especially evident in the "culture lag" hypothesis. Yet we actually know little of the necessary conditions for industrialization in societies outside the main lines of Western development; or the effects of industrialization on institutional structures under various circumstances. The evidence is accumulating, but the analysis is not. It is suggested that the conception of a "moving equilibrium" will be a more useful and more accurate tool for analysis of interdepence and change than the use of economic organization or some other partial aspect of social structure. The equilibrium approach has the added advantage of dovetailing with

SOCIOLOGY OF ECONOMIC ORGANIZATION

a functional approach for the analysis of interpendence and short-term variation.

There is, of course, no requirement within the scientific ethic that research should be practical in the sense of immediately applicable for the achievement of ends other than advanced knowledge. It is, however, at least politic for a body of scientists to attempt to provide the facts relevant to the determination of public policy. Whatever may be said for the merit of the field under review with respect to the advancement of the science, the growing importanc of economic problems in the modern world suggests that sociologists may find it appropriate to devote renewed attention to the social behavior of economic men.

SELECTED BIBLIOGRAPHY

Clark, John Maurice, *Preface to Social Economics,* (New York: Farrar and Rinehart, 1936).

Commons, John R., *Legal Foundations of Capitalism,* (New York: The Macmillan Co., 1924).

Durkheim, Emile, *On the Division of Labor in Society,* tr. by George Simpson, (New York: The Macmillan Co., 1933).

Ely, Richard T., *Property and Contract in Their Relation to the Distribution of Wealth,* (New York: The Macmillan Co., 1914).

Mannheim, Karl, *Man and Society in an Age of Reconstruction,* (New York: Harcourt, Brace and Co., 1940).

Mayo, Elton, *The Human Problems of an Industrial Civilization,* (New York: The Macmillan Co., 1933).

Parsons, Talcott, *The Structure of Social Action,* (New York: McGraw-Hill Book Co., 1937).

Roethlisberger, F. J., and William J. Dickson, *Management and the Worker,* (Cambridge: Harvard University Press, 1939).

Simiand, François, *Le salaire; l'évolution sociale et la monnaie,* (Paris: Alcan, 1932, 3 vols.).

Slichter, Summer H., *Modern Economic Society,* (New York: Henry Holt and Co., 1931).

Sombart, Werner, *Der moderne Kapitalismus,* 2nd ed., (Leipzig: Duncker und Humblot, 1913, 3 vols.).

Weber, Max, *Wirtschaft und Gesellschaft,* (Tuebingen: J. C. B. Mohr 1922).

Wilbert E. Moore, Ph. D. (Harvard), is Research Associate at the Office of Population Research, Princeton University, on leave of absence from The Pennsylvania State College where he is Assistant Professor of Sociology. In addition to articles published in professional journals on slavery, social stratification, property, and economic planning, he has written *Industrial Relations and the Social Order,* to be published by The Macmillan Company in 1945; At the present time Professor Moore is continuing work on comparative studies of social stratification and labor systems.

CHAPTER XVI

HUMAN ECOLOGY*

by

EMMA C. LLEWELLYN

and

AUDREY HAWTHORN

The Scope of Human Ecology. In presenting theories about Human Ecology, we are outlining the notions of a particular group, known in America as The School of Human Ecology. They are by no means the only group of thinkers who concern themselves with the word Ecology. Their interpretations of the field are not coincident with the interpretations of others and vary considerably among themselves. All have one point of general agreement, that human ecology studies man and his environment. What aspects of man, what aspects of environment, and with what concepts it shall be approached find no common denominator.

There are human ecologists who regard the field as synonymous with the human organism, its environment, and the relations between the two, a synthesis of the natural and social science, almost always geographically oriented. Bews, (1) a botanist, is an out-

---

* In this paper only American literature in the field is taken into consideration.
1. J. W. Bews, *Human Ecology*, (London: Oxford University Press, 1935).

standing advocate of this school. He regards all sciences, natural and social, as contributing to the study of man, the center for the application of knowledge.

There are many separate disciplines, each of which, in a narrower sense regards human ecology as an aspect of itself. Botanists, (2) biologists, (3) geographers, (4) ethnographers, (5) demographers, (6) and economists (7) see it as an auxiliary discipline.

Among sociologists themselves, the word differs in scope. (8)

---

2. F. E. Clements, *Plant Succession: an Analysis of the Development of Vegetation,* (Washington: Carnegie Institution of Washington, 1916); F. E. Clements, *Research Methods in Ecology,* (Lincoln: University of Nebraska Press, 1905); William M. Wheeler, "Symbiosis," in R. E. Park and E. W. Burgess, *Introduction to the Science of Sociology,* (Chicago: University of Chicago Press, 1921), p. 169 ff.; also "Ant Society," p. 182 ff.

3. Warder Clyde Allee, *Animal Aggregations, a Study in General Sociology,* (Chicago: University of Chicago Press, 1931); G. C. Adams, "The Relation of General Ecology to Human Ecology," *Ecology,* 16: 316-335, July, 1935; Friedrich Alverdes, *Social Life in the Animal World,* (New York: Harcourt, Brace and Company, 1927).

4. H. H. Barrows, "Geography as Human Ecology," Association of American Geographers, *Annals,* 13: March, 1923; Charles Langdon White and George T. Renner, *Geography: an Introduction to Human Ecology,* (New York: D. Appleton-Century Company, 1936).

5. Robert Redfield, "The Regional Aspect of Culture," American Sociological Society, *Publications,* 24: 33-41, 1930.

6. Harold F. Dorn, "Migration and the Growth of Cities," *Social Forces,* 16: 328-337, March, 1938.

7. Harland Bartholomew, *Urban Land Uses,* (Cambridge: Harvard University Press, 1932); Stanley L. McMichael and Robert F. Bingham. *City Growth and Values,* (Cleveland: Stanley McMichael Publishing Organization, 1923).

8. R. D. McKenzie, "The Field and Problems of Demography, Human Geography, and Human Ecology," in L. I. Bernard, ed., *The Fields and Methods of Sociology,* (New York: Ray Long and Richard Smith, 1934), pp. 52-66; James A. Quin, "Topical Summary of Current Literature on Human Ecology," *American Journal of Sociology,* 46: 191-226, September, 1940.

McKenzie makes a particular distinction between geography, demography, and human ecology: geography is concerned with place, ecology with process. Location in geography is position on the earth's surface, in ecology is position in a spatial grouping of interacting human beings or interrelated human institutions. Economics and ecology differ mainly in the direction of attention . . . A simple study of the community as a population aggregate is demography, a study of population groups and physical habitat is geography, a study of the relation of population groups as a symbiotic unity is human ecology; that is, the center of attention is the relation of man to man. R. D. McKenzie, "The Field and Problems of Demography, Human Geography, and Human Ecology," *loc cit.* p. 52.

TWENTIETH CENTURY SOCIOLOGY

Many of them regard ecology as identical with any study of natural areas, (9) or with any study of man regionally based. (10) Lundberg, admiring the achievements of the "school" and lamenting its narrowness, also regards it as properly an inclusive study of man, particularly as a synthesis of all social science. (11) Quinn considers it a special and abstract science delimited by a strict concern with the "sub-social" interactions of man, and segmenting biology, geography and sociology, while yet retaining an exclusive center of its own preoccupation. (12) The official ecological school, however, predominantly accepts the definition of McKenzie, one of its leaders. "Human Ecology deals with the spatial aspects of the symbiotic relations of human beings and institutions. It aims to discover the principles and factors involved in the changing patterns of spatial arrangements of population and institutions resulting from the interplay of human beings in a continuously changing culture." (13)

---

9. R. M. McIver, *Society: a Textbook of Sociology*, (New York: Farrar and Rinehart, 1937).

10. Howard W. Odum, *Southern Regions of the United States*, (Chapel Hill: University of North Carolina Press, 1936); Rupert B. Vance, "But Is It Human Ecology?" *Social Forces*, 10: 456-457, March, 1932; Rupert B. Vance, *Human Geography of the South*, (Chapel Hill: University of North Carolina Press, 1932).

11. G. A. Lundberg, *Foundations of Sociology;* (New York: The Macmillan Co., 1939), particularly pp. 493-494.

12. James A. Quinn, "Human Ecology and Interactional Ecology," *American Sociological Review,* 5: 713-723, October, 1940; James A. Quinn, "The Nature of Human Ecology: Re-examination and Re-definition," *Social Forces*, 18: 161-168, December, 1939.

13. R. D. McKenzie, "Ecology, Human," *Encyclopedia of the Social Sciences*, 5: 314.

The limitation of the scope of human ecology to symbiotic relations to the exclusion of the cultural has yielded much explanatory literature which it is not fruitful to repeat here. This distinction is fundamental to the thinking of most members of the school. Park, one of the founders of the school of human ecology, refers to ecology as an attempt to investigate the processes of biotic balances and equilibrium, distribution and transition, this symbiotic society to be clearly distinguished from the cultural. (R. E. Park, "Human Ecology," *American Journal of Sociology,* 42: 1-15, July, 1936). Mukerjee emphasizes the close relationship of ecology to *Gemeinschaft,* with its fractional, rational and impersonal contacts, as opposed to the cultural, integrated and personal groups of *Gesellschaft.* (In: "Ecological and Cultural Patterns of Social Organization," *American Sociological Review,* 8: 643-649, December, 1943). Quinn adds: "Eco-

HUMAN ECOLOGY

The special set of theories to which we turn have been conditioned by the historical circumstance of their development. The University of Chicago has been the dominant center of studies of human ecology. Park and Burgess, (14) the founders of the field, turned to plant and animal ecology as providing useful analogies for a more exact study of human aggregates. These concepts were applied to materials derived from social surveys, particularly urban surveys. Human ecology was, then, modified from its inception by the fact that its interest in applying concepts of the biotic aggregate found material in the complex urban society.

The development of ecology in America was given an indigenous turn by the special conditions of American life. Its concepts were

---

logy as a branch of sociological theory investigates the processes and the results of impersonal, sub-social interactions between human beings, the ways in which human beings or human groups interact through dependence upon limited supplies of their environment to produce (a) typical space distributions and subsistence chains, and (b) typical successions of these phenomena." (James A. Quinn, "The Development of Human Ecology in Sociology," in Harry Elmer Barnes and Howard Becker, eds., *Contemporary Social Theory*, (New York: D. Appleton-Century Company, 1940), p. 212.

None of these writers denies the importance of the cultural factor within society, but they generally assume, as does Park, that human society is organized on two levels, the biotic and the cultural, with the cultural resting upon the biotic, which is basic. (R. E. Park, "Human Ecology," *American Journal of Sociology*, 42: 1-15, July, 1936; and "Succession, an Ecological Concept," *American Sociological Review*, 1: 171-179, April, 1936).

14. See R. E. Park and E. W. Burgess, *Introduction to the Science of Sociology*, (Chicago: University of Chicago Press, 1921); R. E. Park, "Dominance: the Concept, its Origin and Natural History," in R. D. McKenzie, *Readings in Human Ecology*, rev. ed. (Ann Arbor: George Wahr, 1934), pp. 381-385; R. E. Park, "Succession: an Ecological Concept," *American Sociological Review*, 1: 171-179, April, 1936; R. E. Park, "Symbiosis and Socialization: a Frame of Reference for the Study of Society," *American Journal of Sociology*, 45: 1-25, July, 1939.

No architecture comes out of a void, nor does any set of concepts. The concepts of the ecological theorists began taking articulate form about 1915 and were set by the end of the 1920's. Material was already available in descriptive surveys of communities, in such analyses as Hurd's *Principles of City Land Values*, (New York: Real Estate Record and Guide, 1924) first written in 1911; and Charles J. Galpin's *Social Anatomy of an Agricultural Community*, (Wisconsin Agricultural Experiment Station Research Bulletin 34: May, 1915). To such works as these, ecologists applied the analogies drawn from plant and animal communities.

related to the locus of its inception. It saw community life as a rapidly growing organism, with expanding area, with increasing land values, and with an increasing number and complexity of institutions. Affected by the theories of laissez faire and free enterprise, ecologists saw an ever-competing and expanding business center as the dominant center of the community. This dominant business center influenced the structure of the whole community, as the increase in communication, transportation and technology increased the division of labor and mobility. In short, the ecologist reflected many of the beliefs and attributions of modern technological life particularly salient on the American scene.

I

The underlying concepts of the ecological theorists vary, and have been subject to sharp criticism for these variations, although it is not clear that in this they are unique in the social sciences. (15) The general picture which follows, therefore, would present accurately no one ecologist.

Human ecology attempts to describe the factors that influence

---

15. Milla A. Alihan, *Social Ecology: a Critical Analysis,* (New York: Columbia University Press, 1938) concerns herself almost exclusively with the ecologists' expression of theories, rather than with method and researches. She is distressed not only by differing interpretations of members of the school, but also by confusion arising from contradictory statements of the same person. We have tried to take later rather than earlier expressions of writers, assuming that in the process of further thinking, modifications and changes occur. There has been no systematic presentation of this body of ecological theories. McKenzie's *Readings in Human Ecology* (published in mimeographed form, revised, in 1934, and largely unavailable) and Hollingshead's "Human Ecology," in R. E. Park, ed., *Outline of the Principles of Sociology,* (New York: Barnes and Noble, 1939), pp. 63-170, cover the ground only in a general way.

Authors vary in emphasis as well as in theory. For instance, Park emphasizes community, McKenzie process. Quinn tends to severely curtailed description, while Mukerjee embeds his theories in rich description of specific regions, often using them as a guide points in presenting a *gestalt.*

Normatives also find no place in present theories. This does not appear to be out of indifference as to what should be, for many, especially early, writings emphasize social work or planning as essential in urban life, but probably out of a belief that knowledge must precede wise community action. See E. W. Burgess, "Can Neighborhood Work Have a Scientific Basis?" in R. E. Park, *The City,* (Chicago: University of Chicago Press, 1925), pp. 142 ff., and ecological papers presented at the Russell Sage Foundation Conference on Regional Planning, in 1925.

HUMAN ECOLOGY

the location, size, and physical organization of the community. It distinguishes *community* from *society*, and accepts an organic interpretation of the dynamics of community (an aggregate of individuals, groups or institutions) as a series of interdependant *natural areas*, one within the other, each area controlled by a center of *dominance*, and varying in its characteristics (physical and the correlated social) according to the distance from the center of dominance. *Competition* is the driving force, both for determining relative position, and for changes in spatial relations over time, when *equilibrium* or balance, is disturbed. Changes take place through the locomotive powers of man (mobility being the means of survival and readjustment), through *invasion* and *succession*. This change is evidenced in *concentration, segregation* and *centralization*. The discussion which follows divides ecological theories into those on STRUCTURE and PROCESS, a division artificial but useful.

A. *Structure and Organization: Community.* Basic to ecology is the idea of community, referring both to a selection of attention within the area of study, and to the geographical extent of the area itself. In selecting the area of attention, a distinction has already been made, cutting off Society from the scope of ecological concern. (16) Community, then, represents the relationship of symbiosis or factors involved in living together in a defined space, independant of the social factors of concensus and communication investigated by other sociologists. Human ecology is a study of the community as a natural result of the competitive process, and the form to be examined is the location of people and institutions.

Park, who turned to plant and animal communities as providing analogies and terms, still pointed, in 1936, to Darwinian theories of struggle for existence as the underlying community structure of plants, animal, and humans. (17) From plant ecology were taken certain concepts which have remained central to the human ecological approach. (18)

1. *Community* as an aggregate of individuals spatially located.

2. *Competition* as one of the fundamental conditions of their need to obtain sustenance, and *cooperation* as one of the means of mutually adjusting to this common need. This *competitive-cooperation* for the basic physical resources has been summed up by ecologists in the word *symbiosis*.

---

16. R. E. McKenzie, "Ecology, Human," *loc. cit.*
17. R. E. Park, "Human Ecology," *American Journal of Sociology*, 42: 1-15, July, 1936.
18. F. E. Clements, *Plant Succession*, and *Research Methods in Ecology*.

3. All of the sub-social or basic physical adjustments made by individuals to each other on a non-thoughtful level are called *biotic*.

4. The series of relations and mutual adjustments of individuals to each other in the acquisition and distribution of sustenance is the "web-of-life."

5. The role played by each individual in the acquisition and distribution of sustenance determines his *niche* in the *division of labor* or function.

6. This community of individuals achieves an *equilibrium* with the environment, wherein needs are adjusted to natural resources.

7. When this equilibrium between community and environment is upset, and when new factors enter in to disturb the status quo, then a state of disequilibrium, or unbalance, involves new processes of adjustment and reassertion.

When these concepts are applied to the human aggregate, this competitive-cooperation takes the form, in a modern, evolved community of division of labor, and mutual, non-conscious benefits of exchange.

Competition involves a struggle for space and for ecological position. It is the free natural order of the community as against the restraints imposed by society. It is an aspect of life common to all organisms, on which society is superimposed to control its members. Community, therefore, based on competition, is a more fundamental and universal organization than society, and one of its causal determinants. There is a relation of interaction, but ecology sets out to interpret society and its changes in terms of the more fundamental manifestations of community. Among aggregations of humans, when biotic struggle is interfered with by custom, it approaches economic competition, though ties are still vital and physical rather than customary and moral. (19) The concept of the competitive nature of the community was influenced by the Adam Smith school of economists long before Park turned to the natural sciences. The inclusion of economic competition with its intertwining of social forces makes particularly difficult the separation of the threads of the purely biotic community.

According to Park the essentials of a human community are (1) a population territorially based, (2) more or less completely rooted in the soil it occupies, and (3) individuals living in a relation of mutual interdependence which is symbiotic rather than social. (20)

Quinn adopts a broader definition of the term community. (21) According to him, the ecological structure is only a part of the

---

19. R. E. Park, "Succession: an Ecological Concept," *loc. cit.*
20. R. E. Park, "Human Ecology," *loc. cit.*
21. J. A. Quinn, "Culture and Ecological Phenomena," *Sociology and Social Research*, 25: 313-320, March, 1941.

community, one important abstraction from reality, aiding the simplification of complex community life. McKenzie, who emphasises community less than he does position, sometimes seems to take this view. But, whatever their definition of the term community, the focus of ecologists' attention remains on that level described as the biotic community.

The Geographic and Spatial Aspect of Community. This emphasis on a special aspect of attention within the community might be called the intensive aspect of community. There is another, an extensive aspect of attention, which has been the subject of a great deal of ecological study: namely, the physical delimitations of community. Its unit is the "natural" area of geographic and measurable surface of the ground. It is natural because it came into being without design and as a result of natural competition. It is viewed from a functional standpoint. Zorbaugh says of the natural area in relation to the city: (22) "A natural area is a geographical area, characterized both by physical individuality and by the cultural character of the people who live in it. They are atoms of city growth. Natural areas of the city are real units. They can be accurately defined."

Natural areas differ in size. The smallest is the neighborhood. (23) In an ascending order of magnitude, ecologists have studied, as natural areas, divisions within the city, the city as an entity without its hinterland, the city with its hinterland (the metropolitan area), and the broader ecological units of regions. Though these units have been the limits of investigation, they are not the limits of geographic thinking, which includes the possibility of states, nations and the world. (24)

The region is becoming increasingly important as a focus of ecological investigation. "Perhaps the most important contribution of ecology is the idea of the region as an intricate network of interrelations. The region exhibits a complex pattern of adaptations between the environmental factors . . . in human societies the mutuality of adaptations, which are endless and ever shifting, gives to us the picture of the total situation as a configuration like the *gestalt*

---

22. H. W. Zorbaugh, "The Natural Areas of the City," American Sociological Society, *Publications*, 20: 188-197, July, 1926.

23. Many ecologists do not, however, regard the neighborhood as a natural area, but as a constituent part of a natural area.

24. R. D. McKenzie, "The Concept of Dominance and World Organization," *American Journal of Sociology*, 33: 28-42, July, 1927.

of Wertheimer, Kohler and Kofka. The change of any factor of the environment... brings about a complete change... in which plants, animals and humans find a new equilibrium." (25)

There is another definition of natural area employed by ecologists, particularly in the study of service institutions in relation to population distribution and its limits. Galpin, concerned with finding natural political units in Wisconsin rural communities, set a precedent for this type of definition. (26) Through a study of the contacts of population and service institutions, he found natural areas of interfunctioning of the populace with their specialized services. He distinguished a variety of natural areas of which one population may be an active part.

The most developed theories on natural areas have come through studies of the city, particularly in Chicago, although applied in other cities and regions. Burgess has made famous the concept of the ideal city pattern of five concentric circles to which American cities and probably non-American modern cities are said to conform. (27) The first and interior zone is the central and business district, retail and banking. The second zone is one of transition, containing business, light industry, and low rent residences. Third is the zone of working men's homes, fourth the zones of better residences, and fifth, the suburban or commuters' zone. Each of these zones is distinguished not only by physical traits, but by accompanying social conditions and behavior which have great significance for the sociologist.

This descriptive generality, the circular zone, has been subject to considerable criticism. (28) Tests in many other cities do not seem to conform to the pattern, and Chicago itself forms only a semi-circle, intersected by the lake. Quinn states that certainly circular zones, geometrically accurate, do not exist, but the probable existance of a significant tendency toward the formation of zones seems to have merit, and is worth further testing, (29) especially if

---

25 R. Mukerjee, "The Regional Balance of Man," *American Journal of Sociology*, 36: 455 ff., November, 1930.

26. Charles J. Galpin, *The Social Anatomy of an Agricultural Community*, (Madison: Wisconsin Agricultural Experiment Station, Research Bulletin 34, May 1915).

27. E. W. Burgess, "The Growth of the City: an Introduction to a Research Project," in American Sociological Society, *Publications*, 18: 85-97, 1924. See also in R. E. Park, *The City*, (Chicago: University of Chicago Press, 1925).

28. J. A. Quinn, "The Burgess Zonal Hypothesis and its Critics," *American Sociological Review*, 5: 210-218, April, 1940.

29. *Ibid.*

zones are to be regarded, not as a distance from a center, but in terms of time-cost.(30) A variation in zonal patterns is presented by other ecologists as a distributive pattern of the community in an axiatic shape, that is, the city develops like a star, according to the radiation outward of communication facilities from the center. (31) Others assume the city to be a mosaic of natural areas fitting or not into a zonal structure. (32)

Dominance. All spatially fixed aspects of communal structure: (roads, factories, homes, etc.) become integrated into a rather definite pattern with relation to dominance and subordination as the dynamic organizing factor. Ecologists have drawn on Child's theory of organic growth, (33) and see in the complex modern community two aspects: the increasing differentiation of units and the concentration of an area of dominance. The primitive community lives on the periphery and has no center of dominance. But modern communities, with their transportation and communication facilities, making possible the development of specializing institutions, become increasingly dominated by a center. This center which acts as a sort of central cortex of the city is the business and banking area, and it tends to be the geographic center as well. (34)

The pressure of increasing competition for place in the business area results in expansion radially outward from the center. Populations area shifted to the various areas of the community in terms of economic status and racial sentiments. (35) Land values are the

---

30. R. D. McKenzie, "The Scope of Human Ecology," in American Sociological Society, *Publications,* 20: 14, 1925 (Papers and Proceedings).

31. R. D. McKenzie, "The Field and Problems of Demography, Human Geography, and Human Ecology," *loc. cit.,* p. 64. Hurd sees both principles of city growth apparently equally important. R. Hurd, *Principles of City Land Values,* (New York: 1911), pp., 58-59.

32. R. E. Park, "Sociology," in Wilson P. Gee, ed., *Research in the Social Sciences,* (New York: The Macmillan Co., 1929) Calvin F. Schmid, *Social Saga of Two Cities: an Ecological and Statistical Study of Social Trends in Minneapolis and St. Paul,* (Minneapolis: Minneapolis Council of Social Agencies, 1937).

33. C. M. Child, *The Physiological Foundations of Behavior,* (New York: Henry Holt and Co., 1924).

34. Carl A. Dawson, "Sources and Methods of Human Ecology," in L. L. Bernard, ed., *The Fields and Methods of Sociology* (New York: 1934), p. 295.

35. R. D. McKenzie, "The Ecological Approach to the Study of the Human Community," in R. E. Park, *The City,* (Chicago: University of Chicago Press, 1925), p. 74.

surface indicator of rate and direction of change of the population and institutions. (36) Thus dominance is an inseparable part of the theory of zones, its dynamic counterpart. The business district conditions the growth and differentiations of satellite zones by the strength of the influence of the central zone, as measured either by physical distance or by time-cost. (37)

The *Gradient*, (38) a corollary of dominance, is a concept also taken from physiology. (39) The gradient is the measurement or the rate of change of a variable condition, such as poverty or home ownership, according to its distance from the center of dominance. The phenomena measured by the gradient are supposed to be related in orderly fashion to each other and to the center of dominance. Burgess expressed an early hope that the measurement of gradients in urban organization and growth might acquire an accuracy measurable in mathematical terms. (40) Though many studies have been made of social organization with the gradient as the frame of reference, this important theory is not well developed.

B. *Process: Dynamics of Change.* "Human ecology is not concerned only with presenting the patterns of ecological organization at a given moment," says McKenzie. "Spatial and sustenance relations in which human beings are organized are ever in process of change in response to the operation of a complex environment and cultural factors. The task of ecology is to study these processes of change in order to get principles of operation and the nature of forces producing them." (41) Organization and structure may

---

36. R. Hurd, *Principles of City Land Values*, (New York: Real Estate Record and Guide, 1911 (reprinted 1924).

37. A. B. Hollingshead, "Human Ecology," in R. E. Park, *Principles of Sociology*, (New York: Barnes and Noble, 1939), pp. 117-124; E. W. Burgess, "The Growth of the City: an Introduction to a Research Project," in R. E. Park, *The City*, (Chicago: University of Chicago Press, 1925) pp. 47-61; Milla A. Alihan, *op. cit.*, p. 114.

38. Dawson speaks of the gradient as the notion used to measure the degree of dominance which a center exercises in successive zones out toward its periphery. Carl A. Dawson, "Sources and Methods of Human Ecology," in L. L. Bernard, ed., *The Fields and Methods of Sociology*, p. 295.

39. C. M. Child, "Biological Foundations of Social Integration," American Sociological Society, *Publications*, 22, June, 1928 (Papers and Proceedings). See also F. E. Clements, *Plant Succession*.

40. E. W. Burgess, "The Determination of Gradients in the Growth of the City," American Sociological Society, *Publications*, 20: 141. 1925, (Papers and Proceedings).

41. R. D. McKenzie, "The Scope of Human Ecology," *loc. cit.*

be regarded as frozen as of a given instant, in an equilibrium which is a natural balance between numbers and resources. But when some factor disturbs the balance it is dominated by process, until a new equilibrium is established. The result is repatterning of natural areas, particularly in the city where constant growth is assumed to take place and radial expansion gives direction to processes. Processes represent mainly physical movements, external indices in time and space.

Process is said to be a direct expression of the constant competition of persons, goods, and institutions for position, so that, in fact, the underlying process is assumed to be competition. (42) McKenzie names the major processes (43) as centralization, concentration, segregation, invasion, and succession. To these should be added *mobility*, a process interlinked and precedent to the other processes. *Dominance*, too, is a process of great importance; but it has been primarily presented by ecologists as a device for explaining the pattern of the city, rather than its repatterning.

It is important to bear in mind one more point, that the processes most frequently applied to an analysis of the city, are assumed to be applicable to natural areas of all sorts, and to both people and institutions.

Concentration. Concentration seems to be both a pattern and a process. It is a tendency for an increased number of people to settle in a given area or region, a tendency common to plants and animals as well as human aggregations, and is measured by density of population. It is a consequent of dominance and results in modern society from successful competition of industry and modern forms of transportation and communication. It is used in its quantitative aspects as a term of distinction between rural and urban regions. Since specialization and division of labor lead to concentration, the term is used in its qualitatives aspect as a means of distinguishing types of community into primary service, commercial, industrial, and specialized, such as resorts and colleges.(44) Thus density and specialization are two separate aspects of concentration. Dispersion is the opposite of concentration and both have been

---

42. R. E. Park, "Human Ecology," *loc cit.*
43. R. D. McKenzie, *ubi cit.*, note 41.
44. R. D. McKenzie, "The Ecological Approach to the Study of the Community," in R. E. Park, *The City*, (Chicago: 1925), pp. 66-68.

noted frequently by ecologists as tendencies resulting from modern increase in mobility. (45)

Centralization is a temporary form of concentration. It is a congregation of people in a locality for a definite purpose for the satisfaction of particular interests. It is a temporary stage of unstable equilibrium and said to be a process of community formation. (46) Apparently this is because the coming together of population around the market or shopping place, even though it be temporary, forms the opening wedge for the development of a relatively permanent aggregation, both of people and institutions. Of itself, this temporary aggregation takes on many aspects of community. A good deal of description has occurred of specialized centralization and the relation of communication, transportation, and population reservoir to the degree and type of centralization. (47) Yet there has been little integrating of theories of centralization, dominance, or concentration. Concentration appears to be more permanent than centralization, more diverse in its community relations and less confined to one or more specific aspects of interdependance; but distinctions are not clear. (48)

A further aspect of concentration is *segregation*. This is an important process for ecology, really underlying the assumption that ecological description may represent social correlatives. It is

---

45. R. D. McKenzie, "The Scope of Human Ecology," *loc. cit.* "Steam transportation, by increasing the fluidity of commodities, ushered in a new epoch in regional concentration: motor and electric transportation, by increasing the fluidity of people, is now producing a new era in dispersion. Whatever retards the movement of commodities limits concentration, and whatever facilitates the movement of people leads to dispersion. The forces at work during the last few years have been favorable to dispersion. High freight rates, high taxes, and labor costs are forcing many industries to disperse or relocate. On the other hand, the automobile and rapid transit lines are permitting the concentrated urban populations to spread over adjacent territory."

46. R. D. McKenzie, "The Scope of Human Ecology," in E. W. Burgess, ed. *The Urban Community*, (Chicago: University of Chicago Press, 1926), p. 175.

47. For example, Paul H. Landis, *The Growth and Decline of South Dakota Trade Centers*, (Brookings, S. D.: State College of Agriculture and Mechanical Arts, Dept. of Rural Sociology, April, 1933); Charles J. Galpin, *The Social Anatomy of an Agricultural Community*, Wisconsin Agricultural Experiment Station, Research Bulletin 34: 1915. R. W. O' Brien, "Beale Street, Memphis: a Study in Ecological Succession," *Sociology and Social Research*, 26: 430-436, May, 1942; C. R. Hoffer, "Services of Rural Trade Centers," *Social Forces*, 10: 66-71, October, 1931.

48. Milla A. Alihan, *op. cit.*, pp. 155-156.

the concentration of type of population, physical structure, and utilities within a natural area. (49) In the symbiotic society which comprises the ecological community, each person as well as each institution struggles for position. Bound to others by the interdependence of division of labor, the person's sustenance relations, his "niche" in the interwoven aggregate of people, is evidenced by his occupation, his income, his social standing. His degree of success determines where he takes his place in the community. Land values and rents are the primary determinants in limiting his choice. (50) In this sense, the area selects and segregates. The factors of selection include physical, social, geographic, economic, and psychological, but the economic factor is regarded as basic. (51) Though the implication is that the area determines the type of distribution, McKenzie makes some distinction between economic levels. He finds that ecological segregation decreases in homogeniety as income level rises and choice has more play. Given choice, then, it may be the individual who selects the area. (52) Occupation, race, age, sex, and nationality are attractive forces of selection which work to differentiate one area from another. The natural area, then, selecting and selected, is a product of the sorting and shifting process of segragation and as a result of this segregation there is a tendency toward homogeniety. Distinct types appear. The assumption is that ecological natural areas become cultural areas as well, (53) that location determines the type of the institution and the relative frequency of a type of person or behavior. This is one of the assumptions on which is built the validity of ecological patterns as indices.

These terms, half pattern and half process, are the result of man's power of locomotion, which has been heightened by conditions of modern living. *Mobility* is the center key to the interpretation of

---

49. R. D. McKenzie, "The Scope of Human Ecology," in E. W. Burgess, ed., *The Urban Community*, p. 179.

50. Zorbaugh, H. W. "Natural Areas of the City," Americal Sociological Society, *Publications*, 20: 188-197, July, 1926.

51. R. D. McKenzie, "The Scope of Human Ecology," in E. W. Burgess, ed., *The Urban Community*, p. 180. Burgess gives less emphasis to the economic and more to the physical. See E. W. Burgess, "Can Neighborhood Work Have a Scientific Basis?" in R. E. Park, *The City*, p. 144.

52. R. D. McKenzie, "The Scope of Human Ecology," in E. W. Burgess, ed., *The Urban Community*, p. 180.

53. R. E. Park, "Sociology," *loc. cit.*, p. 33.

modern civilization. (54) According to Mukerjee, mobility has various levels and is both social and ecological, the latter concerning itself with spatial distributions brought about as a result of the process of competition and selection, brought into operation by differential opportunities of living conditions in the habitat. (55) Changes in the arts, in technology, in natural environment stimulate mobility through their effects on competition. In primitive groups ecological mobility may exist together with social immobility; but not so in modern society, where movement and migration are not only an incident but also a cause of almost every form of social change. (56) Thus, ecological mobility has come to be a measure of change of ecological position and also an index of expansion and metabolism. (57)

Contrasted with mobility is fluidity, often called movement without necessary change of ecologic position (58) (the slums are called mobile but not fluid because inhabitants move in and out at a high rate but move little, while within the area). Yet fluidity, differing in intensity with age, sex, and other differentials, is an important factor, according to McKenzie, in the processes of segregation and centralization. (59)

Migration as a relatively permanent change of geographic position of persons or groups, a form of change subject to quantitative consideration, and by its very nature spatially oriented, has been subject recently to study increasingly oriented to an ecological field of reference. But ecology theories tend to identify and merge migration with concepts of invasion and succession.

Invasion is another ecological process, made possible through mobility. This is the encroachment of one area of segregation upon another, usually an adjoining area. (60) The term is used for group displacement only, and usually, though not always, the dis-

---

54. R. Mukerjee, "Mobility, Ecological and Social," *Social Forces,* 21: 154-159, December, 1942.
55. *Ibid.*
56. R. E. Park, "Sociology," *loc. cit.,* p. 15. See also R. E. Park, "Succession," *loc. cit.,* p. 179.
57. E. W. Burgess, "The Growth of the City; an Introduction to a Research Project," in R. E. Park, *The City,* p. 59.
58. R. D. McKenzie, "The Scope of Human Ecology," *American Journal of Sociology,* 32 (no. 1, pt. 2) July, 1926. p. 144.
59. *Ibid.*
60. R. D. McKenzie, *ubi cit.,* note 46, p. 180.

placement of a higher by a lower cultural group. In the city it is an expression of growth, zone to zone, area to area (61) Invasion results in change of use of land and change in type of occupant. When invasion reaches a point of complete change in population type or use of structures it becomes *succession*. (62)

According to Park, there is no sound reason why the word "succession" should not be applied to any orderly and irreversible series of events, if they can be used as indices of less obvious and more fundamental changes. (63) McKenzie sees succession as a cyclical change in communities. Regions within a city pass through different stages of use and occupancy in a regular and eventually precisely predictable fashion. Succession takes place radially from the center outward. Obsolescence and deterioration of buildings makes for a change in type of occupancy, operating as a downward trend in rentals, with lower and lower income levels of the population until a complete change in use of territory occurs (as from residence to business) or a new development of the old use. The entire community may pass through a series of successions due to mutations of its economic base and the population type usually changes with the economic base. The processes leading towards succession are generally stated as initiation, invasion-and-reaction, development and finally the climax of replacement, with a new type emerging. (64)

Some ecologists have recently pointed out that the definition of human ecology as the temporal as well as the spatial distribution of population is but inadequately fulfilled if it be assumed, as it is generally, that the temporal aspect means spatial succession, which is mere description of ecological processes in terms of the history of the area and which omits the community process by which physical redistribution is brought about. Engel-Frisch,

---

61. Some writers regard it as a sub-process of succession, though one need not lead to the other. See E. W. Burgess, "Residential Segregation in American Cities," American Academy of Political and Social Science, *Annals*, 140: 105-110, November, 1928.

62. There is considerable confusion in the use of these two terms, especially since, according to McKenzie, these stages of invasion appear to be duplicated in succession. Perhaps if invasion were regarded as the dynamic process and succession as the resulting pattern, thinking might be clearer.

63. R.E. Park, "Succession, an Ecological Concept," *loc. cit.*, p. 172.

64. R. D. McKenzie, "The Scope of Human Ecology," *American Journal of Sociology*, 32: (no. 1, pt. 2) p. 153-154. July, 1926.

a pupil of McKenzie, says: "Temporal succession may be the basis of spatial succession. That is, spatial succession is usually brought about by daily movements of people." (65) It is suggested by the same author that by studying temporal succession one may be able to see more dynamically the processes involved in ecological change. This includes the temporal aspects of rhythm (recurrent fluctuations or movement in accommodation to physical, psychical and cultural environment); *timing* (the synchronization of the rhythms of individuals and groups) and *tempo* (the number of events occuring per unit of time). Since it is the daily movements of people through space which, increment by increment, bring about change in that space these daily movements may be the means of furthering understanding of ecological processes and change. (66)

The ecology of man, says Park, differs from that of other living things in that he is not so dependent on physical enviroment; exchange of goods and services help to emancipate him, and the communal structure assumes an institutional character. (67) Thus, institutions become an extension of the food chains of animal ecology. Usually these are identified as "sustenance chains" or at least commercial institutions; but non-commercial enterprises, particularly the church, have come under ecologial purview. The theories just discussed, both of structure and process, are applied simultaneously to population units and institutions. This results in some confusion in the rather scanty theoretical consideration of institutions alone. It is said that concentration is the tendency of basic types of institutions to locate at focal points of transportation and communication and that focal points attract persons from an area of participation. (68) It is also said that part of ecology's task is to measure the dispersive and integrative influence of typical communal institutions on various elements of population (69) and that institutional development follows closely the patterning of population. (70) There is some consideration of relative

---

65. G. Engel-Frisch, "Some Neglected Temporal Aspects of Human Ecology," *Social Forces,* 22: 43-47, September, 1943.

66. *Ibid.* p. 46. See also R. W. O'Brien, "Beale Street, Memphis, a Study in Ecological Succession," *loc. cit.*

67. R. E. Park, *ubi. cit.* note 42, p. 12.

68. Carl A. Dawson and W. E. Gettys, *An Introduction to Sociology,* (New York: Ronald Press Co., 1935).

69. R. D. McKenzie, *ubi. cit.,* note 46, p. 172.

70. R. D. McKenzie, *The Metropolitan Community,* (New York: McGraw-Hill, 1937), p. 190.

mobility of institutions of different type or differing fixed structure, of the relation of trade and industry type to population and of an invasion process differing from that of population, which would lead to the belief that ecologists may no longer consider institutions entirely identical to populations as units of study. (71)

II

The ecological shool has given impetus to a large body of research. The freshness of its aproach, its vivid concern with the facts of community life have resulted in studies as important to consider as the theories themselves.

A. *Investigations.* Some of these studies are designed to test or amplify a specific hypothesis of the ecological school. Many of them are devoted to technical considerations, such as determination of the natural area. Some are really studies of sociological problems, keener and more precise versions of traditional social surveys on an ecological basis. Some are studies of distributive aspects of sustenance chains which approximate the economic approach. The publications considered here are all concrete collections of facts gathered within an ecological frame of reference.

1. *Natural areas and their Structural Patterns.* The concept of dominance provided an impetus to investigation of the growth of the city in relation to its dominant or business center. McKenzie first studied the neighborhood in 1923, when he classified into types according to occupation, the functional relation of neighborhood in Columbus, Ohio. (72) The neighborhood was seen early by Burgess as an important functional unit for study by social workers. (73) But the point of view of the ecologist was primarily

---

71. For instance, R. D. Martin, "The Church and Changing Ecological Dominance," *Sociology and Social Research,* 25: 246-257, January, 1941. Quinn gives an interesting turn to the study of institutions in presenting for testing a theory to help explain why men and institutions locate where they do. He refers to it as an hypothesis about "a mobile ecological unit," but appears to consider this in the light of schools, factories, etc. J. A. Quinn, "Hypothesis of Median Location," *American Sociological Review,* 8: 148-156, April 1943.

72. R. D. McKenzie, "The Neighborhood," *American Journal of Sociology,* 27, September-November, 1921, January, March, May, 1922.

73. E. W. Burgess, "Can Neighborhood Work Have a Scientific Basis?" *loc. cit.;* E. W. Burgess, "The Natural Area as the Basis for Social Work in the Large City," in National Conference of Social Work, *Proceedings,* 53: 504-510, 1926. See also F. E. Frazier, "Negro Harlem: an Ecological Study," *American Journal of Sociology,* 43: 72-88.

investigative, realizing that intelligent administration and planning were impossible without accurate and concrete knowledge. Since the time of McKenzie and Burgess, many studies of neighborhoods have been made, investigating the characteristics of spatial distribution of the population.

The city, as an intricate interrelationship of distributive activities of greater or less dominance, has been a useful concept for seeing the city as a whole. Literature on the city has been complex, produced by students of many fields over a period of years. Strictly within an ecological frame of reference, a study of the city would entail only those aspects of the city which revolved around the distributive aspects of human activity on a biotic level. Even on this level, however, there are other aspects of the city which are new emphases, contributed by the researchers of ecology. Burgess's interpretation of concentric circular zones has been the dominant hypothesis on the organization of cities. Many studies have been directed to his theories of zonal pattern, (74) some confirming his general hypothesis, some modifying it or questioning its validity. Davies, (75) for instance, after a test in New Haven, dismisses the present hypothesis of zones as being incompatible with the actual facts of distribution in American cities.

The measurement of zones has been accomplished mainly through the gradient. Mowrer, (76) through studying the organization and disorganization of the family in Chicago, arrived at a zonal distribution characterized by diverse behavior in families and family type. Other studies found patterns of behavior in felony, delinquency,

---

74. Calvin F. Schmid, *Social Saga of Two Cities: an Ecological and Statistical Study of Social Trends in Minneapolis and St. Paul;* Raymond Bowers, "Ecological Patterning of Rochester, New York," *American Sociological Review*, 4: 180-189, April, 1939.

75. M. R. Davie, "The Pattern of Urban Growth," in G. P. Murdock, ed., *Studies in the Science of Society,* (New Haven: Yale University Press, 1937), pp. 133-161.

76. E. R. Mowrer, "The Trend and Ecology of Family Disintegration in Chicago," *American Sociological Review,* 3: 344-353, June, 1938.

There have been few studies concentrating on the gradient as a technique. The studies which have been made, involving measuring the rates of such variable factors as home ownership, divorce, juvenile delinquency, have used the gradient as the conceptual approach. Burgess devised the gradient used by cutting an axial radiant line across the five zones of the city and dividing the line into intersections based on geographical measurement of distance, 1/4 mile units, (later combined to make mile square averages) using materials summarised from U. S. census tract reports.

home ownership and other variable social phenomena differing in quantitative frequency in the various zones. (77) This may be regarded as a modification of the hypothesis of zones by the gradient, which states that desirable factors increase and undesirable factors decrease according to distance from center.

Other studies have been made of frequency of types of behavior associated with zonal areas. The correlated behavior is social, and the different patterns of social behavior seem to be related to the characteristics of the ecological areas in which they occur. Studies have been made of the incidence of juvenile delinquency, family dependancy, housing suicide, divorce, and combinations of these according to natural areas of the city. (78) Types of associated behavior occurring with special frequency within a given type of ecological area indicate both the selective and segregative influence of that area. Some studies have intensively studied one natural area, including its function and population type and the whole culture which is manifested within it. (79) Faris's study of types of in-

---

77. Clifford R. Shaw, "Correlation of Rate of Juvenile Delinquency with Certain Indexes of Community Organization and Disorganization," *American Sociological Society, Publications,* 22: 174-179, 1928; H. W. Zorbaugh, *The Gold Coast and the Slum,* (Chicago: University of Chicago Press, 1929); James H. S. Bossard, "Ecological Areas and Marriage Rates," *American Journal of Sociology,* 44: 70-85, July, 1938; James H. S. Bossard, and Thelma Dillon, "The Spatial Distribution of Divorced Women,—a Philadelphia Study," *American Journal of Sociology,* 40: January 1935.

Elsa Longmoor, and Erle F. Young, "Ecological Interrelationships of Juvenile Delinquency, Dependency and Population Mobility: a Cartographic Analysis of Data from Long Beach, California," *American Journal of Sociology,* 41: 598-610, March, 1936; Mapheus Smith, "Relief Intensity Gradients," *Social Forces,* 16: 208-223, December, 1937; A. W. Lind, "Some Ecological Patterns of Community Disorganization in Honolulu," *American Journal of Sociology,* 36: 206-220, September, 1930.

78. Robert E. L. Faris, and H. W. Dunham, *Mental Disorders in Urban Areas,* (Chicago: University of Chicago Press, 1939).

79. Howard H. Harlan, *Zion Town: a Study in Human Ecology,* (Charlottesville: University of Virginia, 1935); Norman S. Hayner, "Hotel Life and Personality," *American Journal of Sociology,* 33: 784-795, March, 1928; E. H. Shideler, "The Business Center as an Institution," *Journal of Applied Sociology,* 9: 269-275. March-April, 1925; H. W. Zorbaugh, "The Dweller in Furnished Rooms: an Urban Type," American Sociological Society, *Publications,* 20: 83-89, 1926; Nels Anderson, *The Hobo: the Sociology of the Homeless Man,* (Chicago: University of Chicago Press, 1923); Frederic M. Thrasher, *The Gang,* (Chicago: University of Chicago Press, 1927; revised edition 1936); H. W. Green, "Composition and Characteristics of a Typical City Analyzed by Census Tracts," American Statistical Association, *Journal,* 27: 80-91, March, 1932 (supplement) Proceedings.

sanity which are likely to be reported within various ecological zones offers possibilities for future research in the analysis of personality potentialities.

There have been some ecological studies of the city as an entity, and an increasing number of surveys both of small towns and of rural communities. (80)

There metropolis and its outlying area have received attention. Work done has centered around the points: how far does the Metropolitan region extend, and what are the measures and types of influence of the city on its hinterland? Several methods for determining the extent of influence of the city have been devised: (1) measures of distributive activity (of buying in and selling to the city and its degree of economic dominance over other local trade centers); (2) inter-communication by various transportation routes, by telephone, mail, etc. as measures of the degree of influence of the city's dominance over its hinterland. Park and McKenzie have used newspaper circulation as an index of the degree of metropolitan influence. (81)

Concern with the region as an area of research has been increasing among human ecologists (82) as well as among the social planners,

---

80. Asael T. Hansen, "The Ecology of a Latin American City," in E. B. Reuter, ed., *Race and Culture Contacts*, (New York: McGraw-Hill Book Co., 1934), pp. 124-142; E. E. Eubank, "A New Census Tract Map for Cincinnati," American Sociological Society, *Publications*, 24: 156-158, 1930.
81. R. E. Park, "Urbanization as Measured by Newspaper Circulation," *American Journal of Sociology*, 35: 60-79, July, 1929; John A. Kinneman, "Urbanization as Measured by Hospitalization," *American Sociological Review*, 5: 723-730, October, 1940; Selden C. Menefee, "Newspaper Circulation and Urban Regions," *Sociology and Social Research*, 21: 63-66, September-October, 1936; E. E. Eubank, "The Base Map as a Device for Community Study," *Social Forces*, 6: 602-605, June, 1928; R.D. McKenzie, "The Rise of Metropolitan Communities," in President's Research Committee on Social Trends, *Recent Social Trends in the United States*, (New York: McGraw-Hill Book Co., 1933), 1: 443-496.
82. Selden C. Menefee, "A Plan for Regional Administrative Districts in the State of Washington; an Ecological Study," Seattle: University of Washington, *Publications in the Social Sciences*, 8, No. 2, 29-80, December 1935; R. Mukerjee, "The Regional Balance of Man," *American Journal of Sociology*, 26: 455-456, November, 1930; R. Mukerjee, "The Processes of Regional Balance," *Sociological Review*, 33: 173-181, October, 1931.

administrators, (83) and sociologists. (84) The need for increased knowledge of the nature of an area as large as the region has made for the development of new techniques for determining a functional definition. Most ecological studies have centered about rural regions, considered as relatively homogeneous. The techniques used to determine the boundaries of an area have included the devising of indices for the measure of homogeniety of land use, population, common activity, and extent of distributive activities. Thus many of the studies have dealt with buying and selling as an index of the boundaries of a rural area, while others have used the sharing of common services and institutions as one of the criteria for delimitation. (85) But the region has not yet received an exact formula for definition. Ecologists have not only been concerned with the geographical distribution, but with shifts in distribution, their description and their consequences.

(2) *Mobility*. This is becoming an important area of investigation. There has been some distinction made in the word mobility; one phenomenon is the physical movement to or away from an area. This can be measured by the ratio of vehicular use to total population, (86) by the estimating of city or business address as against

---

83. U. S. National Resources Committee, *Regional Factors in National Planning and Development*, (Washington: U. S. Government Printing Office, 1935); also Regional Planning Series, 1936; Shelby M. Harrison, Round Table Discussion on "The Implications of the Regional Concept," American Sociological Society, *Publications*, 24: 357-258, May, 1930.

84. W. Russell Tylor, "The Process of Change from Neighborhood to Regional Organization and its Effect on Rural Life," *Social Forces*, 16: 530-542, May, 1938; Rupert B. Vance, "Implications of the Concepts 'Region' and 'Regional Planning'," American Sociological Society, *Publications*, 29:85-93, 1935.

85. C. E. Lively, "Spatial Mobility of the Rural Population with Respect to Local Areas," *American Journal of Sociology*, 43: 89-102, July, 1937; Perry P. Denune, *The Social and Economic Relationships of Farmers with Towns in Pickway County, Ohio*, (Columbus: Ohio State University, Bureau of Business Research, 1927; Monograph No. 9); C. R. Hoffer, "*A Study of Town-County Relationships*, (East Lansing, Michigan: Michigan Agricultural Experiment Station, 1928)', Special Bulletin 181; C. R. Hoffer, "Services of Rural Trade Centers," *Social Forces*, 10: 66-71, October, 1931; Bruce L. Melvin, *Village Service Agencies in New York*, 1925, (Ithaca: Cornell University Agricultural Experiment Station, 1929), Bulletin 493; C. E. Lively, "The Appearance and Disappearance of Minor Trade Centers in Minnesota, 1905-1930," *Social Forces*, 10: 71-75, October, 1931.

86. E. W. Burgess," The Growth of the City: an Introduction to a Research Project," in R. E. Park, *The City*, pp. 59-61.

the distance of the home etc. The other use of the word mobility pertains to the mental susceptibility to new experience, and may be used eventually as an index to test degrees of intellectual sophistication. (87) Physical mobility has been considered as a possible index of social disorganization. Ecologists hold the theory that succession, accompanied by a high rate of mobility, results in social disorganization. Consequently special emphasis has been put upon the changing zone, called the zone in transition or the interstitial area, where mobility is the encroachment of one zone of land use or population type on another area. "Where mobility is the greatest and where, in consequence, primary controls break down completely, there develop areas of promiscuity and vice." The increase of factors of disorganization has been found to be particularly apparent in the interstitial area. (88)

Succession. Within this category fall all the studies of natural areas in relation to the change of land use. These studies involve the passage of time as well as of spatial arrangement. (89) Studies of succession have been made in many geographic areas. Lind studied the ecological organization of Hawaii, and the process of succession as represented by a change in land use. (90) McKenzie studied succession in the Puget Sound area of Washington. (90) Other

---

87. Howard Becker, "Forms of Population Movement: Prolegomena to a Study of Mental Mobility," *Social Forces,* 9: 147-160; 351-361.

88. E. W. Burgess, "The Growth of the City; an Introduction to a Research Project," in R. E. Park, *The City,* p. 59; See also Frederic M. Thrasher, *"The Gang,* (Chicago: University of Chicago Press, 1927; revised edition, 1936); H. W. Zorbaugh, *The Gold Coast and the Slum.*

89. C. E. Lively, "Spatial and Occupational Changes of Particular Significance for the Student of Population Mobility," *Social Forces,* 15: 351-355, March, 1937; Mapheus Smith, "The Mobility of Eminent Men," *Sociology and Social Research,* 22: 452-461, May-June 1938; Thomas Earl Sullenger, "A Study in Intra-Urban Mobility," *Sociology and Social Research,* 17: 16-24, September-October, 1932; A. H. Hobbs, "Specificity and Selective Migration," *American Sociological Review,* 7: 772-81, December, 1942; Lyonel C. Florant, "Negro Internal Migration," *American Sociological Review,* 7: 782-791, December, 1942; Lowry Nelson, "Distribution, Age and Mobility of Minnesota Physicians, 1912-1936," *American Sociological Review,* 7: 792-801. December, 1942.

90. A. W. Lind, *An Island Community: Ecological Succession in Hawaii,* Chicago: University of Chicago Press, 1938); R. D. McKenzie, "Ecological Succession in the Puget Sound Region," American Sociological Society, *Publications,* 23: 60-80, 1929; A. B. Hollingshead, "Changes in Land Ownership as an index of Succession in Rural Communities," *American Journal of Sociology,* 43: 764-777, March, 1938.

HUMAN ECOLOGY

studies have been made limiting the factors involved to such enquiries as the characteristics of succession in professional family residence, occupational succession, and status factors involved in change of residence. (91) The study of succession, or change in type of function over a period of time, involves the problem of a shifting population, and here human ecology has borrowed from the field of demography, and studied migration in and out of regions as a manifestation of the equilibrium of the distributive aspects of an area, its division of labor, and its opportunities.

Concentration and centralization from a dynamic point of view, that is, the process of increasing aggregation, have been neglected in concrete study, a conspicuous gap between ecological theory and investigation.

In the study of institutional concentration there has been increasing investigation of sustenance chains and services, confined, however, to a static picture of community as population serviced by these institutions and to the degree of specialized services offered in relation to density of population. (92)

B. *Methods.* Many people regard the greatest contribution of ecologists to be their methodological approach rather than their theories. Despite the fact that many theories have been developed without checking, the general intent has been empirical: to investigate the actual phenomena which comes within the scope of human ecology and to generalize on the basis of an objective knowledge of the frequency of occurrence. This leads them to rely on quantitative methods, designed to eliminate as far as possible subjective conclusions. Presentation of material employs the technique of maps, of frequency distributions and, to an increasing degree, correlations. Accuracy is an earnest consideration, as is evidenced by the desire to gain exact determination of gradients, indices, and area delimitations.

---

91. Aryness Joy, "Note on the Changes of Residence of Families of American Business and Professional Men," *American Journal of Sociology,* 33; 614-621, January, 1928; H. A. Gibbard, "The Status·Factor in Residential Succession," *American Journal of Socioloy,* 48: 835; E. R. Mowrer, "Family Disorganization and Mobility," American Sociological Society, *Publications,* 23: 134-152, 1929.

92. Inez K. Rolph. "The Population Pattern in Relation to Retail Buying, (Baltimore)," *American Journal of Sociology,* 38: 368-376, November, 1932; Bruce L. Melvin, "Village Service Agencies in New York, 1925," (Ithaca: Cornell University Agricultural Experiment Station. *Bulletin* 493, August, 1929).

Because they are interested in the spatial distribution of human phenomena, human ecologists have turned their attention to the making of maps for the discovery and presentation of patterns of occurrence of human phenomena. (93)

Base maps are useful to anyone interested in spatial relations, since these give basic data regarding the contours and topography of the area in a relevant but modified form, so that it is possible to superimpose the specific data to be used. A series of these superimpositions may be made, revealing relationships between variables and the environment on which they are located.

Isometric Maps are being developed. The most involved use of this map was employed by Elsa Longmoor and E. F. Young at Long Beach, California. The isometric map appears roughly like those issued by the weather bureau, showing high and low preasure areas, charted by lines connecting the variables in the specific study mentioned, that is, juvenile deliquency, dependency and mobility.

Other maps in use by ecologists include the census tract map, which shows the topography and land use of a designated census area, and the cross-hatch map.

Indices are another device employed extensively. One of these is the population pyramid, a pictorial presentation of age and sex distribution, with children at the base and old people at the top, the whole divided vertically according to sex. Perfect symmetry is never achieved, but the distinctive skewness of different areas (the small proportions of children and females in the business district and the large proportions of them at the city's periphery; the large proportion of older men in the interstitial areas, etc) leads to its use as an index of type of natural area. Another index, also usually presented in pictorial or map form, shows in rank order the incidence of social factors in each area of a city and, as a composite, represents an index of degree of urbanization and of influence exerted by city over the hinterland. Burgess also devised an

---

93. Calvin F. Schmid, "Graphic Representation," in Pauline Young, *Scientific Social Surveys and Research*, (New York: Prentice-Hall, 1939), Ch. XIV; Elsa Longmoor and E. F. Young, "Ecological Interrelationships of Juvenile Delinquency, Dependency and Population Mobility: a Cartographic Analysis of Data from Long Beach, California," *American Journal of Sociology*, 41: 598-610, March, 1936; E. R. Mowrer, "The Isometric Map as a Technique of Social Research," *American Journal of Sociology*, 44: 86-89, July, 1938.

index of social disintegration based on mobility. Ogburn has made a needed effort to open the way to testing the assumption that ecological findings are indices of social conditions. (94)

The use of quantitative statistics in the revealing of relationships has been implicit in many investigations already cited.

Pitfalls of the statistical method are many, including the dangers of too small sample, too narrow time span for adequate comparison, and the doubtful utility of low correlations. (95) But it is to be expected that with the growth of control over the statistical technique the increased advantages of quantitative analysis of large spatial distributions will become apparent.

C. *Sources.* Ecologists have taken advantage of every type of material which may be useful in their studies. Geographical materials; demographical data, such as census and census tract tables; (96) sociological sources, such as welfare agency data, divorce statistics; legal materials such as court records, land and deed records; gas and telephone files—all have been drawn upon. Medical, health, and welfare data, and educational materials have also been used.

Of these sources the census has probably been the most useful. The process of large scale fact accumulation is difficult, expensive and time consuming. One of the problems ecologists face, by virtue of their predilection for quantitative data, is the fact that only government organizations and occasional foundations have the resources to collect such material. Since no amount of careful manipulation will make inaccurate raw materials accurate, there is the beginning of a feeling among ecologists that their technique must involve correct evaluation. Reckless suggests the next step to be an actuarial study of the extent of allowance which must be made for variations in categories of people reported. (97)

---

94. W. F. Ogburn and L. C. Coombs, "An Economic Interpretation of the Social Characteristics of Cities." *American Journal of Sociology*, 46: 305-315, November, 1940.

95. F. A. Ross, "Ecology and the Statistical Method," *American Journal of Sociology*, 38: 507-522, January, 1933.

96. Calvin F. Schmid. "The Theory and Practice of Planning Census Tracts," *Sociology and Social Research,* 22: 228-238, January-February, 1938; Walter C. Reckless, "The Initial Experience with Census Tracts in a Southern City," *Social Forces,* 15: 47-54; E. E. Eubank, "A New Census Tract Map for Cincinnati," American Sociological Society, *Publications,* 24: 136-138.

97. Walter C. Reckless, "Implications of Prediction in Sociology," *American Sociological Review,* 6: 471-477, August, 1941.

TWENTIETH CENTURY SOCIOLOGY

III

The decade of the 1920's saw the growth of a feeling of restlessness among all the social sciences and the growth of reaction against the "arm chair philosophers." The desire grew for empirical development, analogous to that in the natural sciences, and was strongly evidenced in the development of institutional economics legal realism, behavioral psychology. This development took two divergent forms: the study of the situation as a whole and the attempt to devise severely limited techniques so that generalization could be based on accurately acquired data. The first leads to *gestalt* and "integration of social science"; the second to concentration on "objective segments," selected as significant indices of the complex whole. Human ecologists, like other social scientists, present this dichotomy, at least in attitude. But ecologists, though not unconcerned with the total situation, have developed their theories chiefly around segmental aspects of man, his relations to environment and to other men.

A set of ideas has been presented which represents in a rough way what is known as the "ecological school." They might be summarized as follows: Competition is the basic process in human as in plant communities, which form themselves into natural areas of various sizes, produced by geographic and other conditions. The nature of competition among humans, however, shows more prominently the interdependence, the division of function, of the symbiotic order. This competitive-cooperation is a determinant in locating the members of the aggregation, in their spatial distribution. Social organization and cultural forces exist and modify the biotic, but the symbiotic is basic to the cultural which rests upon it, though it influences the symbiotic. People and institutions, in this symbiotic organization, are held together by and distributed through the principles of dominance; that is, there is a center in the community, which is the business district; diversification of areas occurs because of the relative pull or dominance of the center as measured by distance from it. The ecological and social "gradients" are so related that the former may serve as indices of the more subtle and less measurable social. When anything occurs to disturb the balance or equilibrium of the community, competitive forces increase and may lead to change in the area of dominance and, with it, in the natural areas related to it. Centralization and concentration are both processes and patterns that occur by way of competition and dominance. Mobility is the process which makes possible the subsequent adjustments. It also makes possible, again through competition, the processes of segregation, of invasion and succession.

It will be noted that this is not one theory but a set of theories, that they refer equally to people and to institutions, that some are unrelated to others, that the manner of interrelation is not clear and finally, that probably no one ecologist holds all of them in the form stated. Dominated by Park, Burgess and McKenzie, seconded by Mukerjee, Wirth, Quinn and others, no systematic treatment has been attempted of the whole or of relationships between the fragmentary individual theories. According to Park, it is possible that the writers responsible for this "school" and its doctrine were not even aware that they were creating a school. (98)

Perhaps these early ecologists intended only to guide the Chicago graduate school students with some tentative hypotheses in surveying their own city. But these generalizations became set and have controleld theory since, producing unfortunate rigidity. (99)

Many of the ecological concepts appear to be useful. The emphasis on the biotic aspects of human society can be valuable at this stage of knowledge in the social sciences, provided that other factors, though not yet measurable, be in some way taken into account, as modifying forces. Such concepts as Dominance, Competition, Succession seem shrewd beginnings, but they have not really been subjected to the test of materials collected, of "fact finding." Consequently, they remain fuzzy, indefinite, and such elaborations as have occurred, as the extension of dominance to wide regions, are purely speculative. However concrete they may seem on the surface, one of the dangers of ecological theories is that, sounding concrete and like common sense, they appear both more inclusive and more definite than they prove to be in application. This is because the concepts did not grow logically from factual studies and because a discipline, to be vital and representative of realities, cannot emerge from an arm chair background, even though it represents a revolt against arm chair philosophizing. Consequently, when examined in detail, concepts too often fall apart. "Competition" is unclear; the hasty inclusion of institutions and population units

---

98. R. E. Park, Review of *Social Ecology,* by M. A. Alihan, in American Academy of Political and Social Science, *Annals,* 202: 264, March, 1939.

99. Warner E. Gettys, "Human Ecology and Social Theory, *Social Forces,* 18: 469-476.

as subject to the same laws causes confusion; "centralization" and "concentration," "invasion" and "succession" are sometimes used interchangeably, even by the same author; "mobility" concepts remain unclear. "Community" and "society," though formally distinguished, are yet interchanged (as in the "gradient") because the ecologists, being honest men, cannot, in facing their data, fail to recognize the weight of cultural factors, so that the cultural, though unprovided for by explicit concept, slips in anyway. "Process" does not yet explain change but merely describes, a description useful in itself and valuable, but leaving out as yet the dynamic factors that lead to change. And, finally, the interrelationships of the various ecological theories have not been thought through or faced, tending to result in a sense of mutual reinforcement which is deceptive.

This is not intended as a condemnation of the human ecological school. They have possibly achieved one of the most hopeful approaches in modern sociological thought. (100) They have produced a distinguished body of research for so new a discipline and need now to recognize that the empirical approach they sponsored must itself be utilized to make sounder their very interesting leads.

To confine the word ecology to the work of those who have professed an explicit set of theories about it would be to negate the principles of the school itself, that it is not what people think about location that counts; it is where they live. A great deal of valuable work has been done in producing immediate wisdom and fact material about people, institutions and their habitat, and an increasing literature is aimed towards objective and scientific knowledge. This work may or may not use the terminology of the school, but the influence is apparent. Perhaps the school developed

---

100. The problem of combining generalization with fact materials is not limited to human ecology; other sociologists, economists, psychologists, lawyers, face the same difficulties in the progress of knowledge. Llewellyn says, after expressing the value of speculative hypotheses, "What I am trying to say is that broad synthesis (at the present stage), and the philosophy of method, are areas of limited possibility until we get more of reliable data, more reliably gathered, arranged in terms of meaningful hypotheses. A half dozen men on Cairns' work, and a dozen on Gurvitch's will be adequate, for a while. But we need six hundred, and can use six hundred dozen, in intelligent labor on increase of the area of the significantly known, or indeed of the significantly better-than merely-suspected . . . Data fertilize theory even more, if possible, than theory fertilizes data." K. N. Llewellyn, "The Theory of Legal 'Science'," *The North Carolina Law Review*, v. 20, No. 1. p. 16. December, 1941.

its theories too early, and too much *ad hoc;* certainly it did not sufficiently wait upon material and pore over it to face the inevitable drastic revision of hypotheses in terms of actual life. But it did move towards measurable data, and towards techniques of objective generalization on the basis of actual facts. In recent years discussion about ecological theories has been somewhat neglected, but much work goes on within its frame of reference.

An example of the kind of work which is building up exact and detailed information for ecology may be taken from the field of migration. Migration is not a new topic; it has been of concern to States as well as to anthropologists, demographers, historians, and sociologists. It has a large literature, much of it speculative and contradictory. Says Dorothy Thomas: (101) "There is abundant evidence that internal migration has had a marked effect in redistributing population. How far this spatial re-arrangement has resulted in a qualitative sifting has, up to the present, been less clearly demonstrated. Lack of clear-cut evidence has not, however, operated as a check on speculation. Examination of the literature reveals four apparently conflicting hypotheses as to the direction of this selection, in so far as it involves cityward migration from rural areas:

1. Cityward migrants are selected from the superior elements of the parent population.
2. Cityward migrants are selected from the inferior elements.
3. Cityward migrants are selected from the extremes: i.e. both the superior and inferior elements, and
4. Cityward migrants represent a random sample of the population...

"We have, then, evidence of a sort that migration selects the better elements, the worse elements, both the better and the worse, and also that it is unselective. Even though we may decide that the evidence is tenuous, it is not improbable that the selection does operate positively, negatively, and randomly, at different times, depending on a variety of factors, that, up to the present, have not been adequately investigated." She suggests, then, six factors for further investigation, one of them that the distance spanned in migration be viewed as a possible modifier of the strength of selection. This was in 1938.

101. Dorothy S. Thomas, "Selective Migration," *The Milbank Memorial Fund Quarterly,* 16: 403-407, October, 1938.

TWENTIETH CENTURY SOCIOLOGY

In 1940, Samuel A. Stouffer published a study on mobility (102) stating: "Whether one is seeking to explain why persons go to a particular place to get jobs, "why" they go to trade at a particular store, "why" they go to a particular neighborhood to commit a crime, or "why" they marry the particular spouse they choose, the factor of spatial distance is of obvious significance." He presented the hypothesis that: "The number of persons going a given distance is directly proportional to the number of opportunities at that distance, and inversely proportional to the number of intervening opportunities." He proceeded, by comparing expected and observed figures, to test his hypothesis. A year later, Margaret L. Bright and Dorothy S. Thomas published in the same journal the results of a study of interstate migration, following Stouffer's methods, designed to test further his hypothesis and resulting in both confirmation and modification. (103)

This small series is presented in detail as an excellent example of studies going on within the ecological field of reference. A careful search of what is known and what is guessed, a memo on next steps of research, the framing of a hypothesis both definite and testable, a specific testing of it, a further testing and modification of it, the opening consideration of other modifying factors. Such work is a long way from proposing or accepting a system; it proceeds on the assumption that more verified knowledge is needed before broad generalizations can be made, and that social, like natural, science, must move forward by small segments. In this sense, ecology has spread far beyond the confines of those who accept, as orthodoxy, its tenets. Many other studies, though not directed specifically to a hypothesis and its testing, have added to our immediate knowledge of service institutions, of types of people and where they live, of types of conduct and the places of its most frequent occurence. There is need of more of this and need to put together what has been done and to evaluate it.

Whether as a body of hypotheses or as a field of inquiry, ecology is not the only road to knowledge concerning men in groups. What it has done is to point out that, in spite of his complex modern

---

102. S. A. Stouffer, "Intervening Opportunities: a Theory Relating Mobility and Distance," *American Sociological Review*, 5: 845-867, December, 1940.

103. Margaret L. Bright, and Dorothy S. Thomas, "Interstate Migration and Intervening Opportunities," *American Sociological Review*, 6: 773-783, December, 1941.

way of living, man is still related to the earth. Further, that with the complications and specializations of modern life, the interdependence of man increases. Human Ecology has aimed both to describe the results of this interrelationship and to put them into testable form.

If Human Ecology is to remain an abstract and specialized science, it must make its peace with culture. If it is to continue to claim to be a simplified interpreter of subtler cultural aspects of society, it must test further its hypotheses of relationship, and see to what degree this holds. McKenzie divided ecological problems into four: the ecological classification of communities, the determination of ecological factors in growth and decline of the community, the investigation of the effect of ecological changes on the social organization, and the study of ecological processes in determining internal structure of the community. (104) These problems are specialized ones, indicating that as a discipline Human Ecology may remain fragmentary, one approach to the many faceted study of human relationships, though its methods continue to spread.

Yet possibly ecology would gain more at present by not expending so much energy in trying to define its scope, but by a frankly exploratory attitude, to see where intertwined problems will lead it. In this it is hoped that the ecology of the future will not be too eclectic. Its early concern with definition of scope reminds one of the childhood fascinator: "When is a door not a door? When it is ajar." Theoreticians may long for the security of a closed system, but a young discipline cannot afford it. Not only should it gather into its thinking what ethnography, geography, and general ecology has to offer, but it should look to the vital life of the community for its feeder cases, not neglect a clinical relation to going situations. The fully controlled study is difficult and expensive in this field unless the ecologist limits himself to census tracts or similar material. Valuable leads can be gained by contact with local surveys, planning commissions, from the Tolan Committee on Migration or the National Resources Planning Board. Far too much had been expended in seeking to keep ecological theory "pure," and this despite its origins in real estate speculation and social surveys. George Washington Carver did much of his research on the weeds around his college. Statistics, when it turned to advertis-

---

104. R. D. McKenzie, "The Ecological Approach to the Study of the Human Community," *American Journal of Sociology*, 30: 287-301, November, 1924.

ing, learned something more about sampling than it had known as a "pure" discipline.

With its interest in spatial patterns and processes of change, it seems logical that Human Ecology should concern itself with local or regional planning and control. This is a subject which individual ecologists have considered important, yet which, in theorizing about the discipline, they have been extremely reluctant to approach. On the surface, social planning represents a direct contradiction to ecology's assumption that it deals solely with the "natural." Competition as a determiner of space relations of man is seen as "natural." Division of labor with all its concomitant occupational, institutional, and residential distribution is natural because it stems from competition, which is natural. But why should service institutions be more natural, in that sense, than other evidence of collective action: the fixed price retail store more than the County Agent's office? It is not improbable that Human Ecology will have to face this dilemma in the future. Its units are geographical: so are those of politics. It is true that the two units are not identical, the natural area is more functional than the political, but the latter tends to turn its attention more and more to the former, witness metropolitan area planning and the T. V. A. For control, prediction is needed, and for prediction, accuracy. But accuracy does not of necessity come with exclusion. The same revolt which led to Ecology leads also to integration; and there are no God-given divisions of the social disciplines.

SELECTED BIBLIOGRAPHY

Alihan, Milla Aissa, *Social Ecology; A. Critical Analysis*, (New York: Columbia University Press, 1938).

Allen, W. C., *Animal Aggregations, a Study in General Sociology*, (Chicago: University of Chicago Press, 1921).

Bernard, L. L., *Fields and Methods of Sociology*, (New York: Farrar and Rinehart, 1934).

Dawson, C. A. and W. D. Gettys, *An Introduction to Sociology*, 2nd ed., (New York: The Ronald Pres, 1935).

Halbwachs, Maurice, *La Morphologie Sociale* (Paris: Armand Colin, 1938).

Hollingshead, A. B., in R. E. Park, ed., *An Outline of the Principles of Sociology*, (New York: Barnes and Noble, 1939), pp. 63-168.

Hurd, Richard M., *Principles of City Land Values*, (New York: Real Estate Record and Guide, 1911).

McKenzie, R. D., *Readings in Human Ecology*, rev. ed., (Ann Arbor: George Wahr, 1934).

HUMAN ECOLOGY

Mukerjee, R., *Regional Sociology*, (New York: The Century Co., 1926).
Park, R. E., E. W. Burgess, and R. D. McKenzie, *The City*, (Chicago: University of Chicago Press, 1925).
Park, R. E., and E. W. Burgess, *Introduction to the Science of Sociology*, (Chicago: University of Chicago Press, 1921).
Quinn, James A., "The Development of Human Ecology in Sociology," in Harry Elmer Barnes and Howard Becker, eds., *Contemporary Social Theory*, (New York: D. Appleton Century Co., 1940).

Emma C. Llewellyn. Member of Faculty, Sarah Lawrence College, formerly Assistant Professor, Institute of Human Relations, Yale University. B. A., Wisconsin University, graduate work Bryn Mawr College, London School of Economics, L'Ecole de Droit (Paris), Yale. Publications and researches in borderline fields of sociology, economics, and law.

Audrey Engle Hawthorn majored in rural sociology at New College of Columbia, being associated with regional studies of the South, and took an M. A. in sociology at Columbia. After graduate work in social anthropology at Columbia and Yale, travelled in Latin America on a fellowship from the Institute of Human Relations and the Office of the Coordinator of Inter-American Affairs. With her husband, anthropologist Harry B. Hawthorn, she observed aspects of the culture of a modern Latin American city, and is currently engaged in writing on the Latin American woman and family.

PART II

CHAPTER XVII

FRENCH SOCIOLOGY

by

CLAUDE LEVI-STRAUSS

To Marcel Mauss, in the constant thought of his seventieth anniversary spent under a double oppression.

I

French sociology was born early, and it still suffers from the gap which existed, at the time of its birth, between the boldness of its theoretical premonitions and the lack, or insufficiency, of concrete data. Sociology — both word and thing — was created by Auguste Comte; he conceived it, not only as a new science, but as the supreme human science intended to embrace and to crown the work of all other disciplines. Unfortunately, at that time, they did not have much to offer, and Comte's sociology remained in suspense between its overwhelming ambitions and the frailty of its positive basis. To some extent, this difficult situation continued during the first part of the 20th century. That it has largely been overcome may be seen from the recent renewal of interest toward the aims and methods of French sociology shown everywhere in the world, especially among the English-speaking groups. While Malinowski's tumultuous rallying can rather appear, we believe, doubtful, Radcliffe-Brown's faithfulness is more significant: from *The Andaman Islanders* starting with a quotation of Henri Hubert's preface to the *Manuel d'histoir*, *des religions* by Chantepie de la Saussaye, to his 1935 paper "On the Concept of Function in Social Science," (1) he always acknowledged the paramount contribution of Durkheim and his companions to the methodology of the social sciences. The strong interest in Durkheim awakened among young American sociologists and anthropologists as a result of Radcliffe-Brown's stay at the University of Chicago is well known. (2) One of its many consequences was the translation of *Les règles de la méthode sociologique* (3), forty years after first publication. It is only fair to say that men like Redfield did not wait that long to express their keen interest; in the latter's last book, Durkheim is once more referred to as one of his main inspirations. (4) The interest in Durkheim and the Durkheimian school has not subsided in the past few years; on the contrary. It will be enough to mention Lowie's (5) and Parsons's (6) attentive commentaries, and the recent publication of articles (7) and even of a book (8) on the subject. Although the main contributions of the French school appeared during the first quarter of the 20th century — and even during the last years of the nineties — they definitely do not belong to the past.

The main reason for this renewed interest will be made clear later in this article. It comes essentially from the fact that French sociology foresaw long ago that sociology is a science of the same type as the other sciences, and that its ultimate end lies in the discovery of general relations between phenomena. But there is another reason which — although less important — should be pointed out from

---

1. *American Anthropologist*, N. S., 37: 394, 1935.
2. Fred Eggan, ed., *Social Anthropology of North American Tribes*, (Chicago: University of Chicago Press, 1937).
3. *The Rules of Sociological Method*, (Chicago: University of Chicago Press, 1938).
4. R. Redfield, *The Folk Culture of Yucatan*, (Chicago: University of Chicago Press, 1941), Preface, p. x; and p. 343.
5. Robert H. Lowie, *The History of Ethnological Theory*, (New York: Farrar and Rinehart, 1937).
6. Talcott Parsons, *The Structure of Social Action*, (New York: McGraw-Hill Book Co., 1937).
7. J. Sholtz, "Durkheim's Theory of Culture," *Reflex*, 1935. Harry Alpert, "Emile Durkheim and the Theory of Social Integration," *Journal of Social Philosophy*, 6: 172-184, January, 1941.
8. Alpert, *Emile Durkheim and his Sociology*, (New York: Columbia University Press, 1939).

FRENCH SOCIOLOGY

the beginning. In other countries, especially Great Britain and the United States, sociology has long suffered from the existence of bulkheads between it and anthropology. Such outstanding examples as Linton, Redfield and Warner show that this is no more true; but the fact itself, as well as its inconveniences, was still pointed out a few years ago by Kroeber: "The persistence with which these two theoretically allied disciplines, born nearly at the same time in western Europe, have in general kept separate from each other, is in itself an interesting problem in cultural history. It suggests that they spring from different sets of impulses and aim at different ends." (9) As Kroeber also shows, this never existed with French sociology. Should these "different sets of impulses" be referred to the fact that sociology, considered as a technique at the disposal of the group to improve its strength and facilitate its working, calls for people accepting the social order, while anthropology has often provided a haven for individuals poorly integrated in their own surroundings? It may be. In this case, we find easily the answer to the problem raised by the French case. In France, from Montaigne on, social philosophy was nearly always linked to social criticism. The gathering of social data was to provide arguments against the social order. It is true that modern sociology was born for the purpose of rebuilding French society after the destruction wrought, first by the French Revolution, and later by the Prussian War. But behind Comte and Durkheim, there are Diderot, Rousseau and Montaigne. In France, sociology will remain the offspring of these first attempts at anthropological thinking. (10)

Some other differential characteristics of French sociology should be made clear in order to avoid misunderstandings. French sociology does not consider itself as an isolated discipline, working in its own specific field, but rather as a method, or as a specific attitude toward human phenomena. Therefore one does not need to be a sociologist in order to do sociology. Many types of studies which, elsewhere, would be referred to sociology are, in France, successfully performed under other disciplines. This is especially the case for the French school of "human geography" whose members, although trained only as geographers, have nevertheless achieved outstanding sociological work,

---

9. A. L. Kroeber, "History and Science in Anthropology," *American Anthropologist*, N. S. 37: 1935, p. 559, n. 14.

10. Cf. on this point: René Hubert, *Les sciences sociales dans l'Encyclopédie*, (1923), and René Maunier, *Introduction à la sociologie*, (1929).

usually monographs dedicated to the human, as well as to the ecological aspects of a region or a country. Works by geographers deeply impregnated with a sociological spirit, and which can be said to be, in a way, truly sociological, are, for instance: J. Sion, *Les paysans de la Normandie Orientale.* (Paris: 1909) ; R. Dion, *Essai sur la formation du paysage rural français,* (Tours: 1934) ; Pierre Gourou, *Esquisse d'une étude de l'habitation annamite* and *Les paysans du Delta Tonkinois,* (Paris: 1936). The same tendency is still more marked among the geographers of the younger generation: Pierre Monbeig, Jean Gottmann, and others.

This universalism of French sociology has allowed it to contribute to the renewal of several human sciences. More will be said later in this chapter of Simiand's contribution to economics. But even disciplines apparently far removed have benefited from the sociological impulse: first of all, linguistics, whose modern European masters Ferdinand de Saussure (*Cours de linguistique générale,* 1916) and Antoine Meillet (*Introduction à l'étude comparative des langues indo-européennes,* Paris: 1903; *La méthode comparative en linguistique historique,* Oslo: Oct. 1925; *Linguistique historique et linguistique générale,* Paris: 1921-1936, 2 vols.) have repeatedly confessed their agreement with, and their indebtedness to, Durkheim's teaching.

Hence, there is an occasional smugness on the part of French sociology, which did not pass unnoticed by the representatives of the others social sciences, provoking among them some irritation. Because French sociology was able to grasp early the whole width of its theoretical scope (11) — long before becoming able to fulfill it —, it could not be avoided that other disciplines, starting with their own methods, would meet it halfway. This process of getting together would have been helpful to everybody (and in many cases it actually was) if, from time to time, sociologists had not assumed the attitude of a conceited mother witnessing the first paces of her young children and helping them with advice. This was not always welcomed by the hard working people of the other branches who were fully aware of achieving something of their own. Their impatience was sometimes expressed bitterly, for instance, in the case of historians and geographers, in the brilliant but somewhat confused book by L. Febvre and L. Bataillon, *La terre et l'évolu-*

---

11. Cf. on this point M. Mauss, "Division et proportions des divisions de la sociologie,"*Année sociologique,* N. S., 1924-25.

FRENCH SOCIOLOGY

lution humaine, (Paris: 1922) (12); in the more recent discussions between M. Halbwachs, a disciple of Durkheim, and A. Demangeon, at the same time a great sociologist and a great geographer, although refractory to the occasional imperialism of the Durkheim school (13); and in M. Bloch's criticism of Simiand's work, which did not prevent the former from achieving, in the field of history, an outstanding work, truly sociological in character. (14)

In two cases at least — beside that of the linguists — the cooperation and mutual indebtedness was accepted unreservedly by both sides. The first is Henri Hubert who worked simultaneously in sociology of religion (in cooperation with Mauss) and in history and archaeology with his two books: *Le Celtes et l'expansion celtique jusqu'à l'époque de la Tène*, and *Les Celtes depuis l'époque de la Tène et la civilisation celtique*, (Paris: 1932). (15) The second is Marcel Granet, the head of French sinological studies, whose books are a direct emanation of the Durkheim school. (16) The adventurous character of his last reconstructions (17) cannot allow one to forget his illuminating earlier contributions to the study of Chinese social structure. Thus not only linguistics and geography, but European archaeology and Chinese early history, have been fecundated by the sociological influence. This influence was so wide that it reached even the "avant-garde" in art and literature. In the years immediately preceding World War II, the "Collège de

---

12. *A Geographical Introduction to History*, English translation, (New York: Alfred A. Knopf, 1925). See also the article "History," by H. Berr and L. Febvre, in *Encyclopedia of the Social Sciences*, 7: 357-368.

13. A. Demangeon, *La plaine picarde;* and (in collaboration with L: Febvre) *Le Rhin*, (Paris: 1935).

14. M. Bloch, in *Revue historique*, January-February, 1934, and the books by the same: *Les rois thaumaturges*, (Strasbourg: 1924); *Les caractères originaux de l'histoire rurale française*, (Oslo: 1931); *La société féodale*, (Paris: 1939). The review edited by M. Bloch since 1929: *Annales d'histoire économique et sociale* is sociological as well as historical.

15. English translation: *The Rise of the Celts*, (New York: Alfred A. Knopf, 1934), and *The Greatness and Decline of the Celts*, (London: George Routledge and Sons, 1934).

16. M. Granet, *Fêtes et chansons anciennes de la Chine*, (Paris: 1919); *La polygynie sororale . . .* , (Paris: 1920); *La religion des chinois*, (Paris: 1922); *Danses et légendes de la Chine ancienne*, (Paris: 1926, 2 vols.); *La civilisation chinoise*, (Paris: 1929); *La pensée chinoise*, (Paris: 1934). Most of them are translated.

17. M. Granet, *Catégories matrimoniales et relations de proximité dans la Chine ancienne*, (Paris: 1939).

TWENTIETH CENTURY SOCIOLOGY

Sociologie" directed by Roger Caillois, became a meeting place for sociologists on one hand, and surrealist painters and poets on the other. The experience was a sucess. This close connection between sociology and every tendency or current having Man, and the study of Man, as its center, is one of the more significant traits of the French school. (18)

It is in this light that the contribution of French sociology to psychology, ethnology, law, and economics should be understood. Without dissociating itself from these pre-existing disciplines, sociology has defined, for each of them, a specific approach. It does not pay a great attention to who is carrying on this approach, whether independant scholars or sociologists *stricto sensu*. As a result, it is somewhat difficult, in a summary account, to disentangle what belongs to sociology proper from the contribution of the other branches. The reader interested in a more complete study will find some help in C. Bouglé's useful little book: *Bilan de la sociologie française contemporaine*, (Paris: 1935), and in G. Davy's work: *Sociologues d'hier et d'aujourd'hui*, (Paris: 1931). (19)

If there was no place for psychology in Comte's system, on the contrary, Durkheim and Mauss have constantly insisted on the psychic nature of social phenomena. This is apparent as early as 1898, in Durkheim's article in the *Revue de métaphysique et de morale*, "Représentations individuelles et représentations collectives." This difference comes from the fact that Durkheim perceived the possibility of a new psychology, objective and experimental, permitting the reconciliation of the two characters of social facts, at the same time "things" and "representations." As was shown by Charles Blondel (*Introduction à la psychologie collective*, Paris: 1928) Comte's opposition was directed less against psychology itself than against the introspective and metaphysical psychology of his time. But Durkheim was not satisfied with stressing the mental side of

---

18. See all the work of the "Centre International de Synthèse" directed by H. Berr with the cooperation of many sociologists, and: *Les sciences sociales en France*, by R. Aron, A. Demangeon, J. Meuvret, and others, (Paris: Centre d'études de politique étrangère, 1937). Also the earlier article by E. Durkheim and P. Fauconnet: "Sociologie et Sciences Sociales," *Revue Philosophique*, Mai 1903.

19. See also P. Fauconnet: "The Durkheim School in France," *Sociological Review*, 19: 15-20, January, 1927.

FRENCH SOCIOLOGY

social processes. (20) He progressively reached the conclusion that they belong to the realm of ideals, and consist essentially in values. (21)

If Durkheim considers sociology as a kind of psychology, it is, however, a psychology of a special nature, irreducible to individual psychology. This is the meaning of his fight against Tarde (22) who contends that all social phenomena can be explained through individual psychological processes, *i. e.* imitation and fashion. Although Durkheim's criticism of Tarde in *Le suicide*, (Paris: 1897) is devastating, it will probably appear, in the light of the approximation, closer every day, between sociology and psychology, that Tarde was at least holding some clues to the problem, and it would be interesting to proceed to a reappraisal of his almost forgotten work in the light of modern ideas on the diffusion of cultures. As pointed out by Blondel (*loc. cit.*) the opposition between Durkheim and Tarde was not so great as both of them thought it was.

During the last years, psychology (with psycho-analysis, the Gestalt and the study of conditioned reflexes) has contributed more to sociology than it has received from it. In France, however, the opposite trend predominated. While D. Essertier was trying to put together the results of Bergsonian psychology and of sociology (*Les formes inférieures de l'explication; Psychologie et sociologie*, both published in 1927; *La sociologie*, 1930), a logist like Halbwachs, a psychologist like Blondel, did not hesitate to renew psychological problems in the light of sociological data. (23)

The clash occured on the ground which Durkheim had himself chosen: the problem of suicide. Against A. Bayet (*Le suicide et la morale*, Paris: 1923) and M. Halbwachs (*Les causes du suicide*,

---

20. E. Durkheim, *Les règles de la méthode sociologique*, Preface to the 2nd edition.

21. E. Durkheim, "Jugements de valeur et jugements 'de réalité," *Revue de métaphysique et de morale*, 1911; C. Bouglé, *Leçons de sociologie sur l'évolution des valeurs*, (1922).

22. G. Tarde, *Les lois de l'imitation; Essais et mélanges sociologiques; La logique sociale*, (1895); *Etudes de psychologie sociale; Les lois sociales*, (1898); *L'opinion et la foule*, (1901).

23. M. Halbwachs, *Les cadres sociaux de la mémoire*, (Paris: 1925); Charles Blondel, *La conscience morbide*, (Paris: 1914); "Les Volitions," in *Nouveau traité de psychologie*, ed. by G. Dumas.

Paris: 1930) who were following Durkheim's path and extending his analysis in the field of the history of morals and social motivation, respectively, psychiatrists such as A. Delmas and M. de Fleury claimed for suicide a strictly psychological and individualistic explanation. It is significant that the synthesis was undertaken by a sociologically-minded psychologist, Blondel, in his book *Le suicide* (1933).

We already know that in France, sociology and anthropology work together. This cooperation finds an organic expression in the *Institut d'Ethnologie de l'Université de Paris* jointly directed — until 1938 — by M. Mauss, L. Lévy-Bruhl, and Dr. Paul Rivet, the latter also curator of the *Musée de l'Homme* (Anthropological Museum). The same cooperative spirit inspires the teaching — directed towards more practical ends — of the *Ecole Coloniale*. (24) Several tendencies should be distinguished, however.

There are first the free-lance writers, belonging to a tradition anterior to the constitution of the Durkheim school, and who preferred to follow an independent line than to rally to the new orthodoxy. Among those, E. Nourry (Saintyves) can only be mentioned here as his work, strictly folklorical in character, can be linked, if indirectly, to sociology. The case of A. van Gennep is different: also a folklorist (25) he published several books with a wider scope. The best known are: *Tabou et totémisme à Madagascar* (1904), *Les rites de passage* (1909), *Religions, moeurs et légendes* (1908-12) *L'état actuel du problème totémique* (1920). René Maunier, a jurist mainly interested in North African law and customs, works closer to the Rivet-Mauss group. He edits the *Etudes de sociologie et*

---

24. In French colonial possessions, specialized Institutes carry on sociological, as well as linguistic, archaeological and ethnological research. The more important are the *Ecole Française d'Extrême Orient,* the *Institut de l'Afrique Noire,* the *Institut des Hautes Etudes Marocaines* and the *Institut des Hautes Etudes Sahariennes.* In connection with socio-anthropological research in the French colonial possessions, the following may be quoted: A. Grandidier, *Histoire . . . de Madagascar* (1875-1917); M. Delafosse, *Haut-Sénégal Niger,* (1912, 3 vols.); *The Negroes of Africa,* trans. by F. Fligelman, (Washington: Associated Publishers, 1931); H. Labouret, *Les tribus du Rameau Lobi* (1931); *Les Manding* (1934); *Les pêcheurs de Guet N'dar* (1935); R. Montagne, *Les Berbères et le Makhzen* (1930); *Villages et kasbas berbères* (1930).

25. A. van Gennep, Le folklore (1920); *Le folklore de la Bourgogne* (1934); *Le folklore du Dauphiné,* (1932-33, 2 vols.); *Le folklore de la Flandre et du Hainaut* (1935-36, 2 vols.); *Manuel de folklore français contemporain,* vols. 3 and 4 (the first two published), 1937-38.

d'ethnologie juridique (since 1931) and his published works include general treatises: *Essai sur les groupements sociaux* (1929); *Introduction au folklore juridique* (1938), *Sociologie coloniale* (1932-36, 2 vols.) as well as monographs: *La construction collective de la maison en Kabylie* (1926); "Recherches sur les échanges rituels en Afrique du Nord," *Année Sociologique*, N. S. 2, 1927; *Mélanges de sociologie nord-africaine* (1930). His is a challenging and highly original mind.

Closely associated with the Durkheim school was Lévy-Bruhl, one of the directors of the *Institut d'Ethnologie*, although both have explained their theoretical disagreements. (26) His first books on Jacobi and Comte still belong to the philosophical field. The shift in interest took place with *La morale et la science des moeurs* (1903) where he tried to lay out the foundation for an inductive study of morals. From 1910 on (with *Les fonctions mentales dans les sociétés inférieures*), he dedicated himself to the description and analysis of the primitive mind: *La mentalité primitive* (1922); *L'âme primitive* (1927); *Le surnaturel et la nature dans la mentalité primitive* (1931); *La mythologie primitive* (1935); *L'expérience mystique et les symboles chez les primitifs* (1938). His work, the meaning of which will be analyzed later in this chapter, was received by many as a challenge. While Georges Gurvitch (*Morale théorique et science des moeurs*, 1937) claimed for moral values the same experimental reality as belongs to customs and rules, P. Rivet, R. Allier, asserted that the distinctive features of the primitive mind, according to Lévy-Bruhl, can be found also among the civilized. On the other hand, Olivier Leroy (*Essai d'introduction critique à l'étude de l'économie primitive*, 1925) emphasized the positive side in the primitive mind.

In Durkheim's and Mauss' work, sociology and anthropology cannot be separated. The connection is particularly obvious in Durkheim's article "La prohibition de l'inceste," published in the *Année sociologique*'s first volume, and in his books *De la division du travail social* (1893; American translation by G. S. Simpson, New York, 1933) and *Les formes élémentaires de la vie religieuse* (1912; English translation, London, 1915). In collaboration, Durkheim and Mauss published a pioneer essay, "De quelques formes primitives de classification" (*Année sociologique*, vol. 6, 1901-2) which, al-

---

26. See G. Gurvitch, "The Sociological Legacy of Lucien Lévy-Bruhl," *Journal of Social Philosophy*, 5: 61-70, 1939.

though suffering from over-simplification, makes one regret that others did not follow the same direction. With Mauss, anthropological influence becomes predominant. His first publications, in collaboration with H. Hubert, are dedicated to problems in religious sociology ("Essai sur le sacrifice," *Année sociologique*, vol. 2, 1897-98; "Esquisse d'une théorie générale de la magie," *ibid.* vol. 7, 1902-3; *Mélanges d'histoire des religions*, 1909). Three essays by Mauss have exerted an outstanding influence both on his contemporaries and on the sociologists of the younger generation, and they may well be considered as the gems of French socio-anthropological thinking. These are: "Les variations saisonnières dans les sociétés eskimo" (*Année sociologique*, vol. 9, 1904-5); "Essai sur le don, form archaique de l'échange" *ibid.* N. S. vol. I, 1932-24); "Une catégorie de l'espirit humain: celle de personne . . ." (Huxely Memorial Lecture, *Journal of the Royal Anthropological Institute*, 68, 1938). A jurist, P. Huvelin, has also contributed to the problem of magic with: "La magie et le droit individuel," (*Année sociologique*, vol. 10, 1906) and "Les tablettes magiques et le droit romain," in *Etudes d'histoire du droit commercial romain* (ed. by H. Lévy Bruhl, 1929).

Mauss's influence extends to theorists as well as to field-workers. Among the first, G. Gurvitch's "La magie et le droit" (in *Essais de sociologie*, 1938), R. Bastide's *Sociologie religieuse* (1935), and — in a slightly different field — R. Caillois's essays on myth and the sacred (*Le mythe et l'homme*, 1938, *L'homme et le sacré*, 1939) may be quoted. Among the second, mention should be made of A. Métraux, *La religion des Tupinamba* (1928); M. Leenhart, *Notes d'ethnologie néo-calédonnienne* (1930) and *Documents néo-calédoniens* (1932); and M. Griaule, *Masques dogons* and *Jeux dogons* (1938).

Although Durkheim and Mauss have always proclaimed their diffidence in respect to cultural history, they inspired historians of civilizations, especially as regards the history of ideas. To Granet's work on Chinese thought and culture, already mentioned, M. Schuhl's *Essai sur la formation de la pensée grecque* (1934) may be added. In another field, there are the learned but simplistic works of G. H. Luquet: *L'art néo-calédonien* (1926); *L'art et la religion des hommes fossiles* (1926); *L'art primitif* (1930). Beyond primitive art, the sociological inspiration also reached general esthetics, for instance in Ch. Lalo's books: *L'art et la vie sociale* (1921) and *L'expression de la vie dans l'art* (1933).

FRENCH SOCIOLOGY

Durkheim was convinced that the anthropological analysis of social phenomena should, and could, lead to an explanatory synthesis showing how modern forms have grown out of more simple ones. He laid out the methodological principles, both of analysis and synthesis, in his capital book: *Les règles de la méthode sociologique* (1894; American translation, 1938). His other early book *De la division du travail social* (1893) was, in his mind, a first sample of this synthetic reconstruction; it is also — for this very reason perhaps—his weakest work. Some of his disciples have chosen to follow the same direction; see G. Davy, *La foi jurée* (1922) and G. Davy and A. Moret, *Des clans aux empires* (1923). In this respect, Mauss has shown more caution: see "La civilisation: le mot, l'idée (in: *Centre International de Synthèse*, Ire Semaine, fasc. 2, 1930).

Finally, Durkheim's synthesis was to be achieved in moral conclusions. This aspect of his thought may be found in several books and articles: *Éducation et sociologie* (1922); *L'éducation morale* (1925); "La détermination du fait moral" (*Bulletin, Sociéte Française de Philosophie*, 1906, reprinted in: *Sociologie et philosophie*, 1924); "Introduction à la morale" (*Revue philosophique*, 1920); "La morale professionnelle" (posthumously published in *Revue de métaphysique et de morale*, 1937). Durkheim's morals were discussed by G. Gurvitch, "La morale de Durkheim" (in: *Essais de sociologie*, 1938). (27)

Sociology of law was given special attention by Durkheim and his fellow-workers. In "Deux lois de l'évolution pénale" (*Année sociologique*, vol. 4) Durkheim suggested an approach which was to be followed by two of his disciples: P. Fauconnet, with *La responsabilité* (1920) dedicated to a study of the evolution of the notion of responsibility, from its early objective forms to its modern individualization, and G. Davy, with *La foi jurée* (1922) where he tried to discover in the *potlatch* the origins of contractual law. In another direction A. Bayet (*La science des faits moraux*, 1935; *La morale des Gaulois*, 1930) emphasized the conflicts and overlappings between codified law and the non-crystallized morals of the group. In a similar way, Jean Ray (*Essai sur la structure logique du Code Civil français*) showed in written law, not the work of an abstract reason, but the concrete translation of the group's life and needs. In *Le droit, l'idéalisme et l'expérience* (1922) G. Davy offered a discussions of the relations between sociology and modern

---

27. See also R. Lacombe, *La méthode sociologique de Durkheim* (1926).

juridical thinking. To the progress of the latter a highly original mind, E. Lévy, made a fruitful contribution with his sociological interpretation of such juridical notions as credit and contract: Emmanuel Lévy, *L'affirmation du droit collectif* (1903); *Le fondement du droit* (1929); *La vision socialiste du droit* (1926).

However, the main contribution to the sociology of law was that of Georges Gurvitch, both the editor of the *Archives de philosophie de droit et de sociologie juridique* and the author of many books where he analyzed and followed the historical development of the idea of social rights. Such are: *L'idée du droit social* (1932); *Le temps présent et l'idée du droit social* (1932); *L'expérience juridique* (1936); *Sociology of Law*, (New York: Philosophical Library, 1942); *La décalration des droits sociaux* (1944).

In the field of economic sociology, the outstanding name is François Simiand's. He fought against the conception of economics as an abstract, rational science, and showed that it cannot be isolated from other disciplines devoted to the study of man, particularly sociology and history. (28) With modern society as a field, this truly great mind's approach was not unlike to Mauss's analysis of primitive groups. In his early book *La méthode positive en science économique* (1912), Simiand made a thorough criticism of deductive economics and pointed out the fallacy of the notion of *homo oeconomicus*. His mimeographed lectures at the Conservatoire National des Arts et Métiers (*Cours d'économie politique . . . professé en 1928-29 et 1930-31*, 3 vols.) introduce a basic classification; he distinguished, in economics, "species" (industry, agriculture, trade...), "regimes" (cooperation, artisanry...) and "forms" (concentration, dispersion...). On this basis, the problems of economics are presented in an entirely new light. In two books published at a twenty-five years' interval, *Le salaire des ouvriers des mines de charbon en France* (1907) and *Le salaire, l'évolution sociale et la monnaie* (1932, 3 vols.), he defined an interpretation of economic changes which received the name of "social monetarism": he put the emphasis on the group will, showing how capitalists and workers try to maintain their standard of life, and how, accordingly, the general movement of prices depends upon the volume of currency. Finally all fluctuations are linked to variations in gold production. This is made more precise and developed in *Recherches sur le mouvement*

---

28. C. Bouglé, "La méthodologie de François Simiand et la sociologie," *Annales sociologiques*, Ser. A., fasc. 2, 1936.

générale des prix (1932) and *Les fluctuations économiques à longue période et la crise mondiale* (1932). Historians (29) have ironically pointed out what they called sociology's acceptance of the most contingent type of explanation. But behind gold production, there is the social group and the entire Western culture. Thus, like Mauss, Simiand seeks the explanation in "total facts," not in historical accidents.

An important part of M. Halbwachs's work may be considered as being astride economics and social morphology. By the latter, Durkheim used to designate the study of the group's concrete basis (geographic, demographic and structural). This notion was developed by Halbwachs in his book *Morphologie sociale* (1938), a useful summary of what has been done in this direction in other countries. A first attempt in social morphology was C. Bouglé's *Essai sur le régime des castes* (1908), while G. Gurvitch tried to discover the basis of a qualitative morphology in "Les formes de la sociabilité" (in *Essais de sociologie*). In two books, *La classe ouvrière et les niveaux de vie* (1913) and *L'évolution des besoins dans les classes ouvrières* (1933), Halbwachs offered a sociological method to determine what is a social class, using wider criteria than those of the economist. Here too, we find an attempt at reaching the "total facts," in the direction shown by Mauss in his early essay in social morphology: "Les variations saisonnières dans les sociétés eskimo" (*loc. cit.*).

From the above summary of the main trends in French sociology, it may be seen that the approach set up by Durkheim and Mauss still exerts a considerable influence at the present time. Therefore an appraisal of French sociology cannot be made without a closer analysis of their principles and methods. To this task the second part of this article is devoted.

II

All that makes the greatness and the weakness of Durkheim's work is found in *Les formes élémentaires de la vie religieuse*. First, the fundamental principle of his method, which is, at the same time, the fundamental principle of all sociological method: "When a law has been proved by a well done experiment, this proof becomes univer-

---

29. Marc Bloch, *loc. cit.*

sally valid." (30) Therefrom all the pitfalls of the comparative method are eliminated. But there are also the contradictions: "Simple as it is, the system which we studied offers all the great ideas, and all the main ritual attitudes which provide the basis of all religions, even the more advanced: distinction of all things between sacred and profane; notion of soul, spirit, mystic personality; national and even international deity; negative cult together with the ascetic practices which are but its exasperated forms; rituals of oblation and communion; imitative rites, commemorative rites, piacular rites, nothing essential is lacking." (31) Henceforth, precisely, this religion (i.e. the Australian one) may be a *simple* religion; it is not an *elementary* one. This may be implied in the opening phrase of *Les formes*: "In this book. we propose to study the most primitive and simple religion among those now known . . . found in societies the organization of which is surpassed by none in simplicity," a religion which may be explained "without calling upon any element borrowed from an anterior religion." (32) Obviously we find here a confusion between the historical and the logical points of view; between the quest for origins and the discovery of functions. If, as Durkheim himself says, in a somewhat ambiguous way, every religion, while being "a kind of delirium," (33) cannot be "a pure illusion" (34); if although the objects of religious thought are "imaginary," (35) "no human institution can be established upon a ground made of errors and lies," (36) then the direct study and analysis of any religion, should suffice to bring out its explanation, i.e. the function it fulfills in the society where it is found. If, on the other hand, the study of "anterior" forms is requested, it can only be because the considered phenomenon cannot be explained anymore on a functional basis, a point which Durkheim — although called the father of functionalism by Malinowski — could have well accepted: "a cultural trait may exist without being of any use, either because it was never adjusted to any vital aim, or because, while having been formerly useful, all its usefulness is now lost and it persists through the sheer strength of custom.

30. P. 593.
31. P. 593.
32. P. 1.
33. P. 124.
34. P. 596.
35. P. 600.
36. P. 3.

Indeed, there are still more survivals in society than in the organism." (37)

If this were true, the historical method should be predominant in sociology: "every society was born from other societies" (38); however it is an entirely different principle of explanation which Durkheim finally accepts: "the primary origin of every social process of importance must be looked for in the internal structure of the social group." (39) This oscillation between what would be called today the functional and the historical approaches is particularly striking in Durkheim's important article "La prohibition de l'inceste" where anthropologists may find a remarkably clear interpretation of the genesis of the Australian eight-class systems through the cross-cutting of a matrilineal dichotomy based on filiation, and a patrilineal fourfold division based on residence. (40) From a sociological point of view, however, the general thesis is less satisfactory. It is well known that Durkheim, while formulating a devastating criticism of the theory which was, later on, to become Malinowski's, explains the incest taboo through the horror for menstrual blood, itself based on totemic beliefs. If this theory were to be accepted, the only conclusion would be that incest taboos are, among us, mere survivals and void of any actual sociological significance. But Durkheim cannot accept this conclusion; then it becomes easy to understand how he was led to the fundamental principles of *Les règles*: "Organ is independent from function; the causes which bring the former to being are independent from the aims it fulfills." (41) The historical and the functional approaches are equally important, but must be used independently. At least this is the first inference which comes to mind. But before inquiring how Durkheim tries to reestablish the unity of his system, it it worth looking for the underlying structure of this dualism.

No social phenomenon may be explained, and the existence of

---

37. *Les règles de la méthode sociologique*, p. 112.
38. *Ibid.*, p. 129.
39. *Ibid.*, p. 138.
40. *Année sociologique*, vol. 1.
41. *Les règles*, p. 113; and further, the basic distinction (borrowed by A. R. Radcliffe-Brown) between *cause* and *function*, together with the first sociological definition of the idea of *function*: "The function is the correspondence between the considered fact and the general needs of the social organism"(*ibid.*, p. 117). Thus Durkheim hoped to eliminate the very search of *intention* in the interpretation of social processes.

culture itself is unintelligible, if symbolism is not set up as an *a priori* requirement of sociological thought. Durkheim was strongly aware of the importance of symbolism, but probably not enough: "Without symbols, social feelings could have but a precarious existence." (42) He could have said: no existence at all. But his hesitation, however slight, is highly revealing: it shows that this Kantian (for no other philosophical influence was stronger on his mind) is reluctant to think dialectically on the very occasion when an *a priori* form is inescapably required: sociology cannot explain the genesis of symbolic thought, but has just to take it for granted in man. On the contrary, when the functional method is needed, Durkheim suddenly shifts to the genetic: he tries to deduce symbol from representation, and emblem from experience. For him, the objectivity of the symbol is only a translation, or an expression of this "outwardness" which is an inherent property of social facts. (43) Society cannot exist without symbolism, but instead of showing how the appearance of symbolic thought makes social life altogether possible and necessary, Durkheim tries the reverse, i.e. to make symbolism grow out of society. He does it with an ingenious theory of tattooing's origins where he finds the missing link between nature and culture. As a matter of fact, he sees it as nearly instinctive, as shown by the large part it plays among the lower classes of our society. (44) But either tattooing must be considered in man as a true instinct, and the whole argument breaks down, or it is a product of culture and we fall in a vicious circle.

Modern sociologists and psychologists solve such problems by calling upon the activity of the unconscious mind; but at the time when Durkheim was writing the main results of modern psychology and linguistics were lacking. This explained why Durkheim struggled between what he conceived — and this was already a considerable progress upon the thinking of the late 19th century as illustrated, for instance, by Spencer — as an irreducible antinomy: the blindness of history, and the finalism of conscience. Between the two, there is of course the unconscious teleology of the mind. Strangely enough, Durkheim, who saw with the utmost clarity the necessity of intermediary levels of collective reality to provide the specific object of sociological studies, refused to take the same step

---

42. *Les formes élémentaires*, p. 330.
43. *Ibid.*, p. 331.
44. *Ibid.*, pp. 331-333.

in respect to individual reality. Yet it is on those intermediary levels that the apparent opposition between individuals and society disappears and that it becomes possible to pass from the one to the other. Here lies perhaps the explanation for the stubborness of this opposition throughout his system. On the first point, and when defining the principles of classification in sociology he writes: "between the confusing mass of all historical societies and the concept, unique but ideal, of Humanity, there are intermediaries: those are the social species." (45) He adds that the laws of social processes should be drawn, not from the study of the "historical societies" as Comte and Spencer wrongly tried, but from that of the "species" or types. This, he says, shows the impossibility of any theory of unilinear evolution of mankind. (46)

One may criticize the methodological principles on which Durkheim built his social typology: "Societies are made up of parts put together... which themselves are simpler societies." (47) One may doubt the validity of any genetic morphology making it possible to follow the way in which a society "composes itself with itself, and its components together." (48) Even in the simplest society we may find each and every element of the more complex. But if Durkheim did not succeed in discovering the foundations of a sound social morphology, he was at least the first one to undertake, with a clear conception of its paramount importance, the basic task of formulating one.

Thus Durkheim fully acknowledges the existence of intermediary levels which sociology claims as its specific object, in contradistinction with history on one hand, and social philosophy on the other. However, he is quite unwilling to accept, for the individual, analogous levels which could provide the link between the psychological and the sociological approaches. Beyond the meaningless diversity of historical processes, he sees nothing except "human tendencies, needs and desires." (49) Then "unless we postulate a preestablished harmony, providential indeed, we cannot admit that, from the beginning, man has carried within himself, in a virtual state but ready to awaken on the call of circumstances, every

---

45. *Les règles*, p. 95.
46. *Ibid.*, p. 96.
47. *Ibid.*, p. 100.
48. *Ibid.*, p. 100.
49. *Ibid.*, p. 113.

tendency the opportunity of which will be realized in the course of evolution." (50) This is because "a tendency, too, is a thing; it can neither appear, nor become modified, just because we deem it useful." (51) And he concludes: "There is no aim, and still less means, which impose themselves necessarily upon all men." (52) "Therefore, if it were true that historical development was carried on for the realization of aims, clearly or confusedly felt, then social facts should offer the most infinite diversity, and almost any comparison would prove to be impossible." (53)

All this argument is based on the assumption that there can be, in psychological and social life, only one kind of finality, i.e. conscious finality. But the theoretical implications of Durkheim's position are none the less striking. According to these pages, social evolution, if teleologic, could only bring disorder and an innumerable multiplicity of unconnected achievements. On the other hand, it is on the assumption of the purposelessness of social processes that he explains the "amazing regularity" with which "social phenomena reproduce themselves under the same circumstances." (54) He adds: "This generality of the collective forms would become unintelligible had final causes, in sociology, the preponderance which they are supposed to possess." (55) All this argument is directed against Comte and Spencer, and the service that Durkheim thereby does to sociology can hardly be overestimated: without getting rid of finalistic interpretation, sociology cannot pretend to become a science. If finalism is to be abandoned, however, it has to be replaced by something else making possible an understanding of how social phenomena may present the character of meaningful wholes, of structuralized ensembles. Durkheim felt strongly the paramount importance of this problem, and it can be said that all his work is an attempt to discover its solution. He did not fail because of a lack of insight, but because the more advanced human sciences, psychology and linguistics, had not yet succeeded at the time when he was thinking in bringing forward, with the Gestalt and with phonemics, the methodological instruments by the help of which alone sociology can lay its own path.

50. *Ibid.*, p. 114.
51. *Ibid.*
52. *Ibid.*, p. 116.
53. *Ibid.*
54. *Ibid.*, p. 117.
55. *Ibid.*

FRENCH SOCIOLOGY

But he saw the direction of that path, and he was showing it firmly to his fellow scholars when making his way between these two pitfalls of sociological thinking: social philosophy on one hand, and cultural history on the other. Cultural analysis never reaches the social species, but only historical phases. (56) And while the monographic method is useful to gather facts, it should not make us forget that "the aim of every science never is to add facts together, but to reach scientific facts under the level of the unscientific." (57)

We may now measure the way which French sociology travelled from Emile Durkheim to Marcel Mauss. The latter, a relative of the former, was first associated with his work and contributed to the preparation of the book which — from a methodological point of view at least — may well be considered Durkheim's masterpiece: *Le suicide*. Curiously enough, it is precisely in *Le suicide* that Durkheim answered beforehand the criticism that Kroeber was to address, forty years later, to the French school as represented by Marcel Mauss. (58)

One can hardly disagree with Kroeber when he finds an expression of the "philosophic ancestry" of the "Année Sociologique" group in their "reluctance... to embark actively in field studies." (59) Two remarks should be made in this respect, however. There is first the fact that, at the beginning of the 20th century, the British and the American schools had already accumulated such a vast material of factual information, without attempting to use it for scientific purposes, that it was not illegitimate for the French school to undertake the task of working out that material, instead of joining into a gathering work which would have soon become blind and meaningless. Practical and theoretical work can never be dissociated; on the contrary, they help and enlighten each other. The proof is brought forward in the best specialists' testimony: "although Professor Warner does not blindly follow Durkheim, his work shows that the latter's original interpretation of aboriginal ceremonial life... was sound. I have long been convinced of this, and ever since it has been my good fortune to get to understand native life in Australia,

---

56. *Ibid.*, p. 109, n. I.
57. *Ibid.*, pp. 97-98.
58. A. L. Kroeber, "History and Science in Anthropology," *American Anthropologist*, N. S., 37, 1935.
59. *Ibid.*, p. 560.

TWENTIETH CENTURY SOCIOLOGY

I have been amazed at the remarkable manner in which Durkheim was able to penetrate that life through the medium of Spencer and Gillen, Strehlow and a few others. Durkheim's position cannot be completely held, but his work is an inspiration." (60)

That *Les formes élémentaires de la vie religieuse*, twenty-five years after the time when it was written by a man who never went in the field, might remain an inspiration to the distinguished Australian field-worker, is, one should confess, no mean achievement, and one seldom occuring in the history of sociological science.

Besides, when dealing with French sociology, one must never forget that the first generation of Durkheim's disciples was decimated during the first world war, and that the gap has not yet been filled. No doubt men such as Robert Hertz, (61) had they lived, would have accomplished brilliant field-work. The younger generation of French sociologists, who reached maturity around 1930, has, during the last fifteen years, almost entirely — but no doubt temporarily — relinquished theoretical work in order to make up for this default. (62)

Kroeber's appreciation of Mauss's work, properly speaking, is more surprising. He reproaches him for what he calls his "categorizing," i.e. "the grouping of phenomena under such concepts as Gifts or Sacrifice." (63) This is, he says, not profitable any more "because these concepts are derived from common, unscientific experience, and not specifically from the cultural data under investigation." (64) And he adds: "No physicist or biologist would approach his data from the angle of the categories 'long' and 'flat' and 'round,'

---

60. A. P. Elkin, review of W. Lloyd Warner, *A Black Civilization*, in: *Oceania*, I, 1937-38, p. 119.

61. Robert Hertz, *Mélanges de sociologie religieuse et de folklore*, (ed. by Marcel Mauss), (Paris: 1928).

62. Africanists, such as Marcel Griaule, B. Maupoil, Michel Leiris, Denise Paulme, Roger Bastide; Americanists such as Jacques and Georgette Soustelle, Claude Lévi-Strauss, Henri Lehmann, Alfred Métraux and George Devereux—the latter two Americans but schooled in Paris—, and many others, have resolutely connected themselves, almost all of them, with the "Musée de l'Homme" and the "Institut d'Ethnologie" of Paris University, both directed by Professor Paul Rivet. For that reason, their work is mainly anthropological in character and cannot be considered here. But none of them would disclaim his indebtedness to the Année Sociologique school, and especially to their master, Marcel Mauss.

63. A. L. Kroeber, *loc. cit.*

64. *Ibid.*, p. 560.

useful and real enough as these concepts are in daily life." (65) This criticism implies so many misunderstandings, and it raises questions so fundamental to the comprehension of the French point of view that its discussion deserves some care.

No other sociological school has ever dedicated so much application to the problem of definition, and of distinction bewteen scientific and unscientific facts than the French school. In *Les règles* Durkheim criticizes Spencer, pricisely on the ground that the latter has confused, under the general category of "monogamy" two institutions which are entirely different, *de facto* monogamy such as found on the lower cultural levels, and *de jure* monogamy, featured by modern society. He says: "an opportune definition would have prevented this error." (66) The fundamental requirement of an objective definition, on the other hand, is that it should express phenomena by an integrative element belonging to their nature, not through their conformity with a more or less ideal notion. (67) This is exactly the problem raised by Kroeber. And here is the answer: "At the time when the work is to be started, when facts have not yet been submitted to any elaboration, they can only be approached from the angle of those traits external enough to become immediately visible." (68) Those are not the more important; however, the deeper strata, endowed with a greater explanatory value, are still unknown, and these external characters must be used as a starting point. (69)

Have Durkheim and Mauss been unfaithful to their methodological program, as suggested by Kroeber? Indeed, if behind such broad categories as Sacrifice, or Gifts, or Suicide, there are not at least *some* characters which are common to all forms — among, of course, many others, which are different — , and if this does not allow the use of those categories as starting points for the analysis, then sociology may as well abandon every pretention to become scientific, and the sociologist must be resigned to pile up descriptions of individual groups, without any hope that the pile shall ever become of any use, except, perhaps, to cultural history.

But the point lies elsewhere. For neither Durkheim nor Mauss

---

65. *Ibid.*
66. Durkheim, *Les règles*, pp. 48-49.
67. *Ibid.*, p. 163.
68. *Ibid.*, p. 163.
69. *Ibid.* pp. 163 ff.

have ever maintained those categories as expressing the ultimate nature of their data. Quite the contrary, they have attempted — and sometimes succeeded — to reach, behind them, these hidden, fundamental elements which are the true components of the phenomena. The conclusion of Durkheim's *Le suicide* is well known: "There is not one suicide, but suicides." (70) All the book is intended to achieve this dissociation of the broad, superficial category of suicide into several irreducible types: egoistic suicide, altruistic suicide, anomic suicide. These categories cannot be considered entirely valid; since 1897, many new data have appeared, especially on suicide among primitive peoples, and we could not, now, maintain the clear-cut distinction suggested by Durkheim betweeen suicide in primitive and in modern societies. The inadequacies of Durkheim's work, mostly due to the lack or insufficiency of data, have been acknowledged by his disciples to the extent that one of them, Maurice Halbwachs, wrote a new book on the same question (*Les causes du suicide*). But Kroeber's criticisms are methodological, and here, obviously, they cannot find support.

The same answers may be given in Mauss's behalf. It is true that he wrote on Sacrifice (H. Hubert and M. Mauss, *Mélanges d'histoire des religions*, 1909). But to what result? Let us hear his comments on his work: "It (sociology) shall discover true coalescences of social phenomena; for instance, the widespread notion of the sacrifice of the God may be explained through a kind of fusion occuring between certain sacrificial rites and certain mythical ideas." (71) And also: "A serious research work leads to unite what the unscientific mind distinguishes, and to distinguish what it confuses." (72) For, as he said in the same article, sociology should not be satisfied with the discovery of correlations: the pointing out of the cases when the correlations do not take place is not less important than its positive counterpart. A good sociological explanation must "account for differences as well as similarities." (73) Indeed, one could say that the entire purpose of the French school lies in an attempt to break up the categories of the layman, and to group the data into a deeper, sounder classification. As was emphasized by Durkheim, the true and only basis of sociology is social

---

70. Durkheim, *Le suicide*, p. 312.
71. M. Mauss and P. Fauconnet, article "Sociologie" in *La grande encyclopédie*.
72. *Ibid.*
73. *Ibid.*

morphology, i.e. this part of sociology the task of which is "to constitute and to classify the social types." (74)

Let us open a parenthesis. This analytical work, trying to reduce the concrete complexity of the data (and of which Lewis H. Morgan shall forever remain the great forerunner) into more simple and elementary structures is still the fundamental task of sociology; Mauss's *Essai sur le don* and *Les variations saisonnières dans les sociétés eskimo* may be considered, in this respect, as models. It should be confessed however that, on account of its philosophical ancestry (behind Durkheim is Comte, and behind Comte, Condorcet) the French school has sometimes felt a strong temptation to follow its methodologically impeccable analytical work with a less satisfactory attempt toward synthesis. After having reduced the concrete into more simple types, they have tried to rearrange these types into one or more series. Durkheim consistently fought against the theory of unilinear evolution, but not so much because it is unilinear or because it is an evolution, as because he was not satisfied with the kind of data which Comte or Spencer had arranged serially. For the historical data they have used, he substitutes social types or species; but even a superficial reading of *Les règles* makes it clear that these are to be classfied along the line of one or several genetic series. This tendency, which Durkheim never succeeded in overcoming entirely, is especially apparent in Fauconnet's *La responsabilité* or in Davy's *La foi jurée*. The important point is that it is far less conspicuous in recent works (such as Mauss's) than in the earlier ones.

We may now come back to Kroeber's argument. When Durkheim studies division of labor, it is in order to reach such abstract, hidden categories as "organic solidarity" and "mechanical solidarity"; when he analyzes suicide, he formulates the notion of integration of the individual to the group; when Mauss undertakes a comparison between the different types of gifts, it is to discover, behind the more diversified types, the fundamental idea of reciprocity; when he follows the transformation of the psychological conceptions of the "Ego," it is in order to establish a relation between social forms and the concept of personality. These categories may be good or bad; they may prove useful or be wrongly chosen

---

74. *Les règles,* p. 100.

(75); but if they do not belong to the kind of categories which it is the aim of sociology to define and to analyze, then let us say that sociology must abandon every pretense of becoming a scientific study. They do not resemble the cateogries of "long," "flat," or "round," but rather such categories as "dilatation," "ondulation," or "viscosity," of which the physicist has precisely made his study. (76). Physics finds its object in the study of the abstract properties of gases, for instance, not in monographic descriptions of the smell of rose, violet, turpentine or methyl phenyl acetate, and their historical relation in the process of differentiation of organic life.

In that respect, Mauss follows Durkheim. Mauss himself has always made clear that he considers himself as the keeper of Durkheimian tradition. There are many differences however, not the outcome of any disagreement between them, but due, rather, to the fact that ten or twenty years make a big difference in the evolution of a young science.

In the first place, both minds are different. Durkheim always remained a teacher of the old school. His conclusions are toilsomely reached and dogmatically asserted. He was brought up as a philosopher; and notwithstanding his wide sociological and anthropological information, he always approached it from the outside, as a man accustomed to different topics and different methods of thinking. Also, at the time when he gathered his material, the great efflorescence of anthropological field-work had not yet started, and in many respects, the data he had to use may now seem insufficient. While Mauss's intellectual training — as in the case

---

75. For instance, Mauss discusses the validity of the opposition drawn by Durkheim in *De la division du travail social* between "organic" and "mechanical" solidarity. (M. Mauss, "Fragment d'un plan de sociologie générale," *Annales sociologiques*, ser. A, fasc. 1, 1934).

76. To make things clear I shall quote Mauss again: "What makes, for us, the unity of the sacrificial system may now be seen. It does not come, as Smith thought, from the fact that all kinds of sacrifices are the offspring of a more primitive and simple form. Such a sacrifice does not exist ... all the sacrificial rituals known to us already possess a high degree of complexity" ... But, "if it is true that sacrifice is so complex, whence does its unity come from? Indeed, while assuming the utmost diversity of forms, it always consists in the same process which may be used to the most different ends. This process consists in the establishment of a communication between the sacred and profane worlds through the intermediary of a victim, i. e. **of a thing destroyed during the** ceremonial." (Hubert and M. Mauss, "Essai sur le sacrifice,"*Année sociologique*, vol. 2, 1897-8, pp. 132-33). This treatment may hardly be called "categorizing unscientific experience."

of the great majority of French sociologists — was also in philosophy, he had the benefit of Durkheim's pioneer work; furthermore he had access to a newer, better, and richer material. Durkheim belongs definitely to the past, while Mauss is, still now, on the level of the more modern anthropological thought and research. Besides, his fabulous memory, his untiring intellectual curiosity, have allowed him to build up a world-wide — and, if one may say so, a time-wide — erudition: *"Mauss sait tout"* his students used to say half-humorously, half-admiringly, but, always, respectfully. Not only does he "know everything," but a bold imagination, a genius-like feeling of the social stuff urge him to make a highly original use of his unlimited knowledge. In his work, and still more in his teaching, unthought-of comparisons flourish. While he is often obscure by the constant use of antitheses, short-cuts and apparent paradoxes which, later on, prove to be the result of a deeper insight, he gratifies his listener, suddenly, with fulgurating intuitions, providing the substance for months of fruitful thinking. In such cases, one feels that one has reached the bottom of the social phenomenon, and has, as he says somewhere "hit the bed-rock." This constant striving toward the fundamental, this willingness to sift, over and over again, a huge mass of data until the purest material only remains, explains Mauss's preference for the essay over the book, and the limited size of his published work.

These intellectual differences — a more productive and systematical mind for Durkheim, but also heavier and more pedantic, a less "athletic" and organized mind, but more intuitive, and, one could even say, more esthetic for Mauss — do not exhaust the parallel. In many respects, Mauss's method is more satisfactory than his master's. We have already pointed out that he escapes almost completely the temptation for synthetic reconstruction. When he follows Durkheim in refusing to dissociate sociology and anthropology, it is not because he sees in primitive societies early stages of social evolution. They are needed, not because they are earlier, but because they exhibit social phenomena under simpler forms. As he once told this writer, it is easier to study the digestive process in the oyster than in man; but this does not mean that the higher vertebrates were formely shell-fishes. He also overcame another shortcoming of Durkheim's method. The latter had consistently criticized the comparative method, such as it was used by the British school, especially by Frazer and Westermarck, (77) but he was, in turn, severely attacked for having (in *Les formes élémentaires*) drawn universal conclusions from the analysis of a privileged case. Mauss's method keeps equally distant from those dangers. He always considers a small number of cases, judiciously chosen as representing clearly defined types. He studies each type as a whole, always considering it as an integrative cultural complex; the kind of relation he aims at discovering is never between two or more elements arbitrarily isolated from the culture, but between all the components: this is what he calls *"faits sociaux totaux,"* a particularly happy formulation for the type of study called elsewhere — and later — functionalist.

We saw how Durkheim struggled between his methodological attitude, which makes him consider social facts as "things," and his philosophical formation which uses those "things" as a ground on which the fundamental Kantian ideas can be firmly seated. Hence he oscillates between a dull empiricism and an aprioristic frenzy. This antinomy is obvious in the following text: "If sociological phenomena are just objectivated systems of ideas, to explain them is to re-think them in their logical order and this explanation finds in itself its own proof; at most, a few examples could be added as confirmation. While, on the contrary, only methodical experiments can extract from things their secret." (78) Durkheim has consistently repeated, however, that those things, i.e. social facts, are "collective representations," and what does this mean, if not "objectivated systems of ideas"? If, on the other hand, social facts are psychic in nature, nothing precludes an attempt to "re-think them in their logical order," although this order is not immmediately given to the individual consciousness. The solution of Durkheim's facticious antinomy lies in the awareness that these objectivated systems of ideas are unconscious, or that unconscious psychical structures underlie them, and make them possible. Hence their character of "things"; and, at the same time, the dialectic — I mean un-mechanical — character of their explanation.

More than Durkheim, Mauss is aware of this basic problem of the relationship between sociological and psychological phenomena. Although the latter never wrote a word inconsistent with the

---

77. See his enlightening reviews of the contemporary publications in the *Année sociologique*. Most of them could be written nowdays.
78. *Les règles*, p. 177.

former's teaching, (79) he listens more carefully to the echoes of modern psychology and keeps on the alert, so that the bridges between the two sciences may never be cut. In his early article on *Sociology*, (80) Mauss states that although sociology is a kind of psychology specifically distinct from individual psychology, "it is nevertheless true that one may pass from the facts of individual consciousness to collective representations through a continuous series of intermediaries." More recently, he insisted on the necessary cooperation between sociology on one hand, and, on the other, psycho-analysis and the theory of symbolism. Durkheim's hesitations in respect to the theory of symbolism have definitely disappeared: "The activity of the collective mind is still more symbolic than that of the individual mind, but in the same direction." (81) And if he remains faithful to Durkheim when he writes: "The notion of symbol is entirely ours, an outcome of Religion and Law," (82) he reestablishes immediately the contact with psychology by concluding his analysis with this remark about Pavlov: "The musical sound which induces salivation in the dog is, at the same time, the condition and the symbol of its response." (83)

Lévy-Bruhl's opposition to Durkheim has the meaning of a protest against the latter's thesis that social representations, and social activities, are syntheses more complex, and morally higher, than individual achievements. This conflict is not new in French sociology. The individualistic point of view of the 18th century philosophers had been criticized by the theoreticians of reactionary thought, especially by de Bonald, on the ground that social phenomena, having a reality *sui generis*, are not simply a combination of individual ones. There is a tradition linking individualism to humanism, while the assumption of the specificity of the collective in relation to the individual seems, also traditionally, to imply the higher value of the former over the latter. To what extent this dilemma should be considered irreducible cannot be discussed here. But the passage from the objective to the normative is almost as apparent in Durkheim as among his predecessors. Durkheim was undoubtedly

---

79. E. Durkheim, "Représentations individuelles et représentations collectives," *Revue de métaphysique et de morale*, 1898.
80. *Loc. cit.*
81. "Rapports réels et pratiques de la psychologie et de la sociologie," *Journal de psychologie*, 1924, p. 904.
82. *Ibid.*, p. 903.
83. *Ibid.*, p. 920.

a democrat, a liberal and a rationalist. However the Preface to the second edition of *De la division du travail social*, written in 1901, rouses disturbing echoes when one reads it now. In *Les formes élémentaires*, he identifies somewhere the social order, evil and unjust, with Satan. (84) However, in a system which finds in social life the aim and the origin of every high spiritual activity, it is difficult to keep constantly separated Society, considered as the universal form of human life, and the concrete cultures of each individual group, which are its only visible expressions. A group where the collective feelings are strong is "superior" to another one where individualism predominates: "We are living a phase of moral mediocrity." (85) The trend toward normative conclusions is still more obvious in *Les règles*: "Our method is not revolutionary; in a way, it is essentially conservative since it considers social phenomena as things, the nature of which, however flexible and malleable they might be, cannot be changed at will." (86) The opposite method is "dangerous." The following passage of *Les formes* starts as a refutation of Lévy-Bruhl, and ends in a glorification of the social group: "Society is definitely not the illogical or alogical being, incoherent and whimsical, as which it has been too often described. On the contrary, collective consciousness is the highest form of psychological life; it is a consciousness of consciousnesses... It sees things from their permanent and essential side... It sees from above, it sees from far away... It grasps the whole known reality." (87) Obviously, any social order could take pretense of such a doctrine to crush individual thought and spontaneity. Every moral, social, or intellectual progress made its first appearance as a revolt of the individual against the group.

Lévy-Bruhl's conception of the primitive mind as "pre-logical" may now appear queer and outmoded; but it cannot be rightly understood without placing it in this background. Durkheim describes social life as the mother and eternal nurse of moral thought and logical thinking, of science as well as faith. On the contrary, Lévy-Bruhl believes that whatever was ever achieved by man, this was not done under, but against the group; that the individual mind may be in advance over the group mind. But while he is

---

84. *Les formes élémentaires de la vie religieuse*, pp. 601-2.
85. *Ibid.*, p. 610.
86. *Les règles*, Preface, p. vii.
87. *Les formes*, p. 633.

basically opposed to Durkheim, he commits the same methodological mistake, *i. e.* to "hypostasize" a function. His society, illogical, mystical, dominated by the "participation" principle, is the counterpart of that Society conceived by Durkheim as the everlasting spring of science and morality. The only difference is that the individual, from society's obedient pupil in one conception, becomes its revolted son in the other. The analysis of the pre-logical mind of the primitive, wholly dominated by the group, allows us to measure the paramount importance of the gain realized when the individual started to think independently from the group: this gain, says Lévy-Bruhl, is rational thought.

Thus Lévy-Bruhl, while missing what was really important in Durkheim's teaching, *i. e.* his methodology, was kept fascinated by its weaker part: the philosophical residues. The first half of his work at least is dedicated, almost entirely, to the building of a different interpretation; but this is equally residual. He certainly intended to work in a direction opposite to the Bonald-Comte-Durkheim type of synthesis; he only succeeded in shifting the synthesis backward: but it is not more acceptable as the starting point of the evolution of human thought than as its point of arrival. Against Lévy-Bruhl, Mauss rightly points out that, if the study of "participations" (not only in primitive mind but also in modern) is important, the study of "oppositions" is not less important. (88) There is no such thing as a primitive state of syncretism and confusion.

During the last part of his life, however, Lévy-Bruhl became more and more aware of his theory's inadequacies. He progressively relinquished his first attempts to describe the primitive mind as specifically and objectively different from the civilized (*Les fonctions mentales dans les sociétés inféricures*, 1910; *La mentalité primitive*, 1922), and came to a more prudent and negative attitude: that the categories of the civilized mind *cannot* be used in the study of the primitive.

In this respect, his belated fight against Tylor and Frazer would have been more successful if, by that time, field-anthropologists had not already abandoned the vicious intellectual habits of the old school. However his last books (from *L'âme primitive*, 1927, up to *L'expérience mystique et les symboles chez les primitifs*, 1938) still make a challenging and fruitful reading. The information is

---

88. M. Mauss, *loc. cit.* pp. 910-911.

wide, and the way it is put to use reveals a subtle feeling for the suggestive and the significant. An exceptionally clear mind and a delightful style makes it easy to assimilate the material. Not often has the reading of compilations been made so pleasurable. The integrity, charm and generosity of his soul may still be felt in his work after his early conclusions have been criticized and discarded.

It is difficult to pass a definite judgment on Georges Gurvitch's work as this author is still in the full swing of production, and there is no doubt that many problems raised in his previous books will be answered by him in the future. Like Lévy-Bruhl, he belongs to the group of independent thinkers who, while working in close cooperation with the "Année Sociologique" people, made no mystery of their dissent from Durkheimian orthodoxy. In Gurvitch, we find a meeting point for two different currents: on one hand a philosophical heritage coming directly from Bergson and Phenomenology; on the other hand, a keen feeling of certain aspects of sociological experience in modern society, sharpened by a wide familiarity with Proudhon, and with the daily life and fight of labor unions. On the one hand, an intuitionist philosophy; on the other, the intuitive apprehension of determinate aspects of social reality. In Gurvitch's system, theory and practice always support each other and converge toward the same interpretation. This interpretation, in turn, is altogether ontological and methodological: we have, first, the assertion that the division of human reality, between the individual on one hand and society on the other, is entirely ficticious; and next, the idea that the traditional debate between sociologists as regards the ultimate nature of social phenomena is meaningless, since every type of approach is but a specific point of view on a reality, in itself complex and diversified.

The inspiration of Gurvitch's sociology is juridical; his material comes mainly from the analysis of the transformations of law — especially the status of property and labor — in modern society. These transformations show that the 18th and early 19th centuries' conception of an abstract State, depositary of all right and power superseding the isolated citizen, could not stand the impact of concrete needs and tendencies. Instead of the jurists' attempts to systematize an abstraction, he offers a fluid picture of what has really taken place: the formation of a multiplicity of groups, each generating its own law, and the progressive establishment of an antagonistic equilibrium between them. Thus, according to Gurvitch, social life should be considered as the gushing forth of a constantly renewed multiplicity of social forms. This is the basis of his ontological pluralism.

But this pluralism is also methodological; it does not consist only in the thesis that society reduces itself, ultimately, into groups never yielding to the dissociation of the collective and the individual. It says also that the nature of those groups is expressed, phenomenologically, on a multiplicity of levels: the geographic and demographic basis of social life, the social system of symbols, the organizations, the behavior—fixed and non-cristallized—, the world of ideas and values, finally the collective consciousness. Between all these levels of reality there is no opposition, still less exclusion. Therefore Gurvitch's method aims at integrating into a structuralized whole all these approaches that sociologists have usually considered incompatible. His plural realism supports a consequent relativism which in turn, serves as a basis to a positive empiricism.

Whether Gurvitch's many-sided construction will be able to stand up durably without fissures is difficult to say in advance, not knowing how he intends to finish the structure. But his attempt is significant: while the "Année Sociologique" group has felt more and more the urge to travel away from its philosophical origins and to keep up with an increasing interest in anthropology, it is, on the contrary, in the open confrontation between a clear-cut philosophical position and a lively sociological experience that Gurvitch finds a chance to overcome the traditional conflicts of sociological thought. One is allowed to believe that this concrete experience represents the truer foundation of his contribution, and what gives it its original value, together with its deep significance. It is to be hoped that the new and rich notions that Gurvitch has predominantly applied, so far, to the history of ideas, will soon find their expression in the analysis of some concrete aspects of social reality. (89)

III

What future may be foreseen for French sociology? During the last forty years, its progress has been mainly in the shift which has taken place, under Mauss's influence, from the method of the concomitant variations to the method of residues. For Durkheim, the former was the fundamental method of the social sciences. (90)

---

89. A different approach to Gurvitch's thought may be found in the excellent essay by Roger Bastide: "A sociologia de Georges Gurvitch," *Revista do Arquivo Municipal de São Paulo*, lviii, 1940.

90. *Les règles*, pp. 159-166.

He overlooked the fact that, all the components of a given culture being necessarily connected, the method of concomitant variations will always give a positive answer: two series of variations being given, some kind of correlation will appear between them. Thus Durkheim discovered, in western societies, a correlation between progress in the division of labor and the increase of population, both in volume and in density. C. Bouglé worked along the same line in his book on *Les idées égalitaires* (1899). Undoubtedly correlations of this type exist; but they do not offer — as Durkheim thought — the explanation of the phenomenon under consideration. Should the series be chosen differently, other correlations would appear, probably *ad infinitum*.

Mauss's usage of the method of concomitant variations is different. He needs it, less to achieve an integrative synthesis, as was the case with Durkheim, than to dissociate the series under consideration according to the requirements of a critical analysis. But when this analysis is achieved, there is something which remains, and which furnishes the true nature of the phenomenon: "The different explanations which could be offered to show the motive of the belief in magic, leave a residue, which we shall now describe... Therein... lie the deep reasons of this belief." (91) This method does not contradict Durkheim's, but it limits and deepens it. From now on, the interest will be directed toward analysis, not synthesis.

There is another landmark which should help French sociology to keep the right direction. We saw how Durkheim hesitated between an outward, empiricist approach to social facts considered as "things" mechanically and atomistically conceived, and a method which, while equally experimental, is better aware of the dialectical character of social processes. This confused attitude may be held responsible, at least partly, for Malinowski's misinterpretation of Durkheim's best teaching when he tries to draw it toward behaviorism: "the whole substance of my theory of culture... consists in reducing Durkheimian theory to terms of behavioristic psychology." (92) Nothing could be farther from a true understanding of the basic French point of view. But French sociology must keep away from an opposite danger, *i. e.* to try to save the rights of rational thinking at the price of accumulating an external mysticism which

---

91. Hubert et Mauss, "Esquisse d'une théorie générale de la magie," *Année sociologique,* vol. 7, 1902-3, p. 106.

92. B. Malinowski, "Culture" in *Encyclopedia of the Social Sciences,* 4: 236.

FRENCH SOCIOLOGY

shall later turn back against rational thought itself. This is Lévy-Bruhl's story. We saw how, from a systematic theory of the "prelogical" character of primitive thought, he progressively came to a purely critical point of view, avoiding any hypothesis on how primitives actually think. But one does not accumulate "prelogism" with impunity. From his original dogmatism, Lévy-Bruhl turned toward a complete agnosticism: of primitive thought, nothing can be known except that it is wholly and utterly different, that it belongs to the realm of another "experience," totally heterogeneous to our own. But this mystery which surrounds primitive thought surreptitiously contaminates modern thought: "What needs an explanation is not that many societies more or less primitive show a frank belief in the truth of these tales (he is referring to folk tales), but rather that in our society this belief disappeared long ago." (93) Thus, at the beginning of his work, we find civilized thought, studying and appraising from its safe position the heterogeneous characters of primitive thought. But here, modern thought discovers in itself the same mystery which was supposed to differentiate the primitive mind from the civilized. First a dogmatic interpretation, later an agnosticist attitude in relation to the primitive mind, were supposedly required to save rational thinking and individual freedom. Finally, it is the modern mind which appears altogether unable to understand primitive mind, while reducing itself to a mere extension of the former.

Lévy-Bruhl's setback will undoubtedly caution French sociology against the dangers of general theories. As a matter of fact, the time for theorizing seems definitely past. In one of his last publications before the outbreak of the war, Mauss presented French sociology with the most elaborate and illuminating program of concrete research ever devised in his country. (94) And its conclusions leave no doubt as to the clear understanding, by French sociologists, of the causes of some of their predecessors' misadventures: "the supreme achievement of all those observations, — biological, psychological and sociological, — of individuals' life inside the social group, is the seldom made observation of what must be the principle and the end of sociological observation: the birth, life and death of a given society, made from three approaches: purely so-

---

93. *La mythologie primitive,* p. 317.
94. M. Mauss, "Fragment d'un plan de sociologie générale descriptive," *Annales sociologiques,* Ser. A, fasc. 1, 1934.

ciological, socio-psychological, bio-sociological... It would be useless to philosophize about general sociology when everything needs to be taken cognizance of, then known, and finally understood." (95) Elsewhere he says: "There is no need to discuss; just observe, and dose." (96)

Confronted with these new tasks, modern French sociologists will undoubtedly keep before the eyes Durkheim's great and significant example. Durkheim, who was well trained in philosophy and the history of religions, but was not a field-anthropologist, wrote a book to build up a new theory of the origin of religion on the ground provided by contemporary field-work. It is generally acknowledged that, as a theory of religion, his book is inacceptable, while the best Australian field-workers hailed it as the forerunner of the discoveries they made only several years later. What reason may be found for this apparent paradox? First, that the time is not ripe for drawing up general hypotheses about the origin of human institutions; next, that it is precisely because Durkheim was well acquainted with the principles and classifications of the religious sciences that he was able to perceive, in data gathered by others, significant traits and hidden meanings that the field-worker could not grasp without thoretical training. And now, what are the conclusions? The first is obviously that sociology should relinquish every attempt at discovering origins, and laws of evolution. This is what we learn from the part where Durkheim failed. But his success teaches something different: sociologists cannot satisfy themselves with being craftsmen, exclusively trained in the study of a particular group, or of a particular type of social phenomena. They need, even for the most limited study, to be familiar with the principles, methods and results of other branches of the study of man: philosophy, psychology, history, etc. They must, indeed, turn more and more toward concrete studies; but they cannot hope to be successful if they are not constantly helped and supported with a general, humanist culture back of them. The philosophical ancestry of French sociology has played it some tricks in the past; it may well prove, in the end, to be its best asset.

95. *Ibid.*, p. 56.
96. *Ibid.*, p. 34.

FRENCH SOCIOLOGY

SELECTED BIBLIOGRAPHY

Durkheim, Emile, *The Elementary Forms of the Religious Life,* (London: 1915).
Durkheim, Emile, *The Rules of Sociological Method,* (Chicago: University of Chicago Press, 1938).
Durkheim, Emile, *Le suicide,* (Paris: 1897).
Granet, Marcel, *La civilisation chinoise,* (Paris: 1929).
Granet, Marcel, *La pensée chinoise,* (Paris: 1934).
Gurvitch, Georges, *Essais de sociologie,* (Paris: 1938).
Gurvitch, Georges, *Sociology of Law,* (New York: Philosophical Library, 1942).
Halbwachs, Maurice, *Les causes du suicide,* (Paris: 1930).
Halbwachs, Maurice, *L'évolution des besoins dans les classes ouvrières,* (Paris: 1933).
Hubert, Henri, *The Greatness and Decline of the Celts,* (London: George Routledge and Sons, 1934).
Lévy-Bruhl, Lucien, *L'expérience mystique et les symboles chez les primitifs,* (Paris: 1938).
Lévy-Bruhl, Lucien, *Morceaux choisis,* (Paris: 1936).
Maunier, René, *Essai sur les groupements sociaux,* (Paris: 1929).
Mauss, Marcel, "Une catégorie de l'esprit humain, celle de personne," *Journal of the Royal Anthropological Institute,* vol. 68, 1938.
Mauss, Marcel, "Essai sur le don, forme archaique de l'échange," *Année sociologique,* N. S. vol. I, 1923-1924.
Mauss, Marcel, "Les variations saisonnières dans les sociétés eskimo," *Année sociologique,* N. S. vol. I, 1923-1924.
Simiand, François, *Le salaire, l'évolution sociale et la monnaie,* (Paris: 1932, 3 vols.).
Tarde, Gabriel, *The Laws of Imitation,* (New York: 1903).

Claude Lévi-Strauss, Licencié en Droit, Agrégé de Philosophie, Paris. Formerly Professor of Sociology, University of São Paulo, Brazil, and Research Associate, Service National de la Recherche Scientifique, France. Member, Directory Council, Société des Américanistes de Paris. Chief of the French Mission to Central Mato Grosso, Brazil (1935-36); of the Franco-Brazilian Expedition to Western and Northern Mato Grosso and Amazonas, Brazil (1938-39). Since 1941: Visiting Professor in Anthropology, The Graduate Faculty of the New School for Social Research (New York); member of the Directory Board and Professor of Anthropology, Ecole Libre des Hautes Etudes (New York). Taught at Barnard College (Summer Session, 1944). Author of articles in: *Journal de la Société des Americanists de Paris; American Anthropologist; America Indigena; Renaissance; La Terre et la Vie; Revista do Arquivo Municipal de São Paulo; Revista Contemporanea,* etc. Contributor, *Handbook of South American Indians,* Smithsonian Institution (in print); books in preparation.

CHAPTER XVIII

AMERICAN SOCIOLOGY

by

ROBERT E. L. FARIS

I.

Development of the Major Characteristics of American Sociology. Sociology in the United States of America is unique in a number of respects. It reflects the peculiar conditions of the nation in much the same way as do the skyscraper buildings, the Hollywood photoplays, the football spectacles, and other characteristic products of this land. In comparison with other countries, the United States has a large number of persons producing an enormous amount of sociological publication. There are efforts which are psychologically similar to the aims of the builders of the Empire State Building or the Grand Coulee Dam. There is also a practicality in the empiricism of American methods of sociological research which contrasts with the lofty and dignified sociology of, for example, nineteenth century Germany as the American politician contrasts with the European Emperors.

These characteristics did not come into being suddenly, nor were they present in all stages of the American preoccupation with so-

AMERICAN SOCIOLOGY

ciology. They evolved in the daily efforts of men who were seeking to deal with certain problems of human behavior. These men worked in cooperation with one another, were influenced by foreign scholars, and were also guided by circumstances of life in the United States. The process of building a sociology was not completely within the control of human intentions, nor were the directions of achievements foreseen to any impressive extent. Sociology developed here in a sympodial process — a tentative, vine-like groping in which a tendril which reaches blindly may find a sucessful hold and develop into a twig, which may in turn become the main trunk if the extensions find further encouragement ahead. In this fashion the imaginative and experimental efforts of men are selected and controlled by the fundamental conditions of the society in which they are working. In the following sections the outstanding incidents and forces in this process are suggested.

Pre-Sociological Thought in the United States. During the latter part of the eighteenth century and through most of the nineteenth century, the only sociology offered in American colleges was that offered in courses in "Moral Philosophy." The content was for the most part topics of reform and welfare and ethical questions as they bore on society. The courses were frequently under the control of theology and had the purpose of indoctrination. In the southern states this sometimes included the moral justification of slavery.

There were connections between this development and philosophy as it was taught in Europe, and there was also something of a trend toward an orientation of this knowledge which could be recognized as sociological. The word "sociology" began to appear before the Civil War, although it did not come into general use until much later. "Social science," however, became a popular term about the time of the Civil War, and courses designated by this name were presented at several colleges. The subject matter was largely the list of topics which would now be referred to as "social problems." There was little science or system involved, except that part that came from theology and philosophy. Perhaps the most important result of this effort was to create a hunger for a sociology which could not yet exist. Albion Small once characterized this phase of development as an expression of the theme: *Up from Amateurism.* It was a struggle on the part of the thinkers on philantropy and reform to become intelligent.

House credits this social science movement with the greatest direct influence in getting something that was eventually called "sociology" accepted by American colleges and universities as a proper subject for the curriculum. (1) This was, of course, a crucial stage in its development, as House further suggests. The establishment of sociology in the universities was an influence toward systematization and standardization, as classroom presentation and cooperation with other institutions necessitated these improvements. Also the acceptance of this body of subject matter by the universities made sociology a recognized profession and gave encouragement to research and writing in the field. Crude as the early social science was, it played its part in getting the camel's nose in the tent. (2)

The Importation of Sociology from Europe. During this period several active traditions were in the course of development abroad. Auguste Comte had been writing on the subject and had introduced the word "sociology" and had attempted to indicate its place in the scheme of knowledge. A lively group in Germany was at work on a tradition which was to a considerable extent imported by American scholars of importance who studied in Germany. Albion W. Small, who was one of these latter, gives an impressive list of outstanding American scholars known to him, who studied in Germany during the decade of the seventies, which he considers to be the most stimulating decade in German social science. (3) These scholars brought back not pure systems of thought to be loyally followed, but impulse, ambition, dissatisfaction with previous knowledge, and a yearning for an independent science of society.

The giants of European sociology did not all become famous in the United States. Many of them did not remain giants for long, but either by forming a link in a successful chain of tradition or by showing the futility of a particular method or system of conceptualization, they made their contributions to the advancement of American sociology.

One European who did become famous in this country was Herbert Spencer. His method was not sound, nor all of his information adequate, but he did work out a system of principles which was widely read in the United States and which gave further currency

---

1. Floyd Nelson House, *The Development of Sociology*, (New York: McGraw-Hill Book Co., 1936), pp. 224, 249, and 251.
2. An extensive account of the "social science" movement is given by L. L. Bernard and Jessie Bernard, *Origins of American Sociology*. (New York: Thomas Y. Crowell Co., 1943).
3. Albion W. Small, *Origins of Sociology*, pp. 325-326.

and prestige to the word "sociology." He may be given credit for being a part of the influence which turned the attention of sociology somewhat away from social problems and reform and directed the movement toward science. His interests in biology and ethnology were partly responsible for the attention American sociologists, particularly Sumner and Giddings, gave to to these subjects.

Sociology as the "Queen of the Sciences." Although there is little of Lester Ward's theory, method, or terminology that has been retained in contemporary sociology, he was a man of importance in the American sociological movement and has made, in a way he did not intend, a significant contribution. Comte had previously formulated the hierarchy of the sciences, with sociology as a culmination, and Spencer had handled sociology as if the universe was its subject matter, but the conception of sociology as the "science of sciences" reached its height with Ward and then almost imediately withered away. It was a grandiose thought, but the reaction against it established once for all that this was not to be the direction of a successful sociology.

Ward's conception speaks for itself:

> It is not quite enough to say that it is a synthesis of them all. It is the new compound which their synthesis creates. It is not any of them, and it is not all of them. It is that science which they spontaneously generate. It is a genetic product, the last term in the genesis of science. The special social sciences are the units of aggregation that organically combine to create sociology, but they lose their individuality as completely as do chemical units, and the resultant product is wholly unlike any of them and is of a higher order. All this is true of any of the complex sciences, but sociology, standing at the head of the entire series, is enriched by all the truths of nature and embraces all truth. It is the *scientia scientiarum*. (4).

With this policy as his guide, Ward worked out his cosmic system which had organization and range, even if its scope doomed it. For one thing, few persons would have the breadth of education which would qualify them to handle it. Ward did teach courses expounding his system at Brown University, but scarcely anywhere else could his lectures be handled. After his death his sucessors at Brown made some attempt to carry on the tradition, but within fifteen years it became extinct even there.

The United States, since the days of the Revolution, have not found conceptions of monarchy congenial, and a science which would play the role of "queen" could not endear itself to the scien-

---

4. Lester Ward, *Pure Sociology*, (New York: The Macmillan Co., 1909), p.91.

tist in other fields. The royal aspect was not entirely a figure of speech. Ward's successors at Brown at one time advanced seriously a proposal that the University be reorganized in accordance with his description of the proper relations of the fields of knowledge, with sociology at the top as a sort of central desk to which the other sciences would pass their findings and have them integrated and ruled upon. Of all the states Rhode Island has the most stubborn record and reputation for individual liberty, from the time of its founding to the present day. The resentment in the faculty of the University at the above proposal will disappear only when the last surviving member from this period has retired. At the time of this move and its defeat, the candle flame of sociology at Brown University sputtered and came close to extinction. Less than twenty years after his death, Ward, the "Father of American Sociology," lost all importance even within the department in which he had expounded his system. His name is rarely mentioned in the sociology courses there.

Small wrote:
> Yet in principle *Dynamic Sociology* had better chance for permanent influence the day it appeared than ever after. It was as though a duplicate of the Tower of London had been created in Philadelphia on July 4, 1776. *Dynamic Sociology* affected the few who valued it most highly, and the present writer was of the number, as a pillar of fire. But the currents of the world's thought were already moving so fast that its leadership was bound presently to be overtaken and passed. (5).

Ward may be said to have given benefit to sociology in other ways, however. His influence further reduced the theological and humanitarian emphasis and encouraged the scientific spirit. He not only insisted on sociology as a science but was concerned with the quest for method and made special recommendation of statistical method. Through his publications and correspondence with the sociologists of his day, he stimulated thought and encouraged men to seek for a sociology that would work. Although the modern generations know little of his contributions, they owe an appreciable debt to him for this stimulation.

The Search for a Field and Methods. The emergence of an American sociology was gradual, and any selection of a date would be arbitrary. There were sociologists before the turn of the twentieth century, and even a department of sociology in 1893 at the

---

5. Albion W. Small, *Origins of Sociology*, p. 342.

AMERICAN SOCIOLOGY

University of Chicago. Small, who was head of this department and an important figure for several decades, stated that there was not yet an American sociology, but a state of confusion, a dissatisfaction, and a hope and intention to have a sociology:

> Unsatisfied bewilderment was the original state of the American sociologists, if they may be referred to as a group before they arrived at visibility or self-consciousness as a group. Thus when the present writer published his syllabus, *Introduction to the Science of Sociology,* in 1890, his Thesis I read:
>
> Sociology is the science which has for its subject matter the phenomena of human society, viz., the varieties of groups in which individuals are associated, with the organization, relations, functions, and tendencies of these various associations.
>
> In other words, Sociology is the science which combines and correlates all the special social sciences.
>
> It would require a high voltage of imagination to invent a more cheerful *non sequitur* unafraid. The first sentence contains an explicit premonition of the conclusion about the group center of attention toward which the sociologists converged during the following thirty years. The second sentence affirms a judgment which the sociologists have meanwhile become more and more inclined to disclaim, which at best is not involved in the first.(6).

Looking backward from the present, one may see the progress of this new science as logical enough and the course that it took as virtually inevitable, but the experience of the pioneers at the time was more of the nature of blind, if determined and hopeful, groping. For a time they were groping to find the nature of the entity "society," but, as Small wrote, "society" steadily resisted expression as a thing at all and gradually resolved itself into a near-infinity of group relationships and processes. The task altered from defining an entity to devising mental tools for detecting and interpreting all sorts of group phenomena. This was a major change of direction and meant the abandonment of seven-league boots and the undertaking of many smaller steps. A sociology of this kind was not to be created by the exertions of one man but could only grow as a result of many years of cooperative drudgery. As this stage developed, there was less tendency for one man to dominate the science in the sense that Spencer, and later Ward, did, but there were a number of leading scholars who pointed out directions, undertook studies, and encouraged students to go further along these lines.

William Graham Sumner was one of the earliest of those whose

---

6. *Ibid.,* pp. 344-345.

specific concepts and conclusions proved so fruitful that they are still in use and in the process of further development in research. Although in his political views Sumner was not the detached and objective person his writings appear to reflect, his sociology did complete the break with the humanitarian tradition. In studying folkways, mores, and institutions, he showed that these develop in social interaction, that the processes have laws of their own and are not controlled by the principles of biology or other sciences. In doing this, he gave sociologists something to take hold of and started a train of interest and investigation that has ever since remained vigorous. The value of this empirical and inductive approach was immediately visible. As much as any other study, *The Folkways* may be said to have given American sociology its start along the way of empirical research, thus giving it one of its distinctive characteristics.

Franklin H. Giddings evolved an original and somewhat systematic conceptual system which has not survived as well as the contributions of Sumner, but in another fashion he has been a significant part of the process which made American sociology what it is. Through his interest in science he stimulated the development and application of research methods, particularly statistical methods. His students and their students in turn have made impressive progress in the application of statistics to sociology. The movement shows no sign of weakening, and it is likely that the future of sociology may show far more influence of these techniques of measurement than we have yet seen. There has been cross-fertilization from other sciences, and from other countries, as well as other statistical workers within sociology; but if Giddings and his followers were all removed from the history, the loss to method in sociological research would be notable.

Edward A. Ross expended his impressive vigor in so many directions that he resists ready classification and evaluation. He never accepted the pure research aim that became prevalent in American sociology during his lifetime but continued to emphasize the "duty" of the sociologist to insist on reform. His enormous list of publications operated as a force to further sociology in several ways. By their readability they stimulated interest both among students and the general public. Ross had a flair for publicity which kept his name, and the subject of sociology, in a conspicuous place in the public mind. Another effect of his efforts was to point out fields of investigation, and if his own researches did not always stand up under critical examination, he had at least indicated pathways as well as blind alleys. It is not suggested that all of Ross' publication was futile, but rather that all of it, including that part which is no longer in general use, operated to further the progress of American sociology.

A major event in this history was the research study by William I. Thomas and Florian Znaniecki which was published following the first world war. *The Polish Peasant in Europe and America*, a five-volume publication in its first edition, was the first large-scale sociological study in which the entire method and body of data were reported. Sumner's *Folkways* had to be based on observations made by other persons, but Thomas and Znaniecki published the original materials which they had gathered themselves, so that a reader could see the complete set of data on which the conclusions were based. Verbatim statements, life-histories, letters written by the peasants, and such materials constituted a large portion of the publication. Sociologists after this study could never again be content with the easy and broad generalization based on meager and second-hand data.

Not all of the concepts used during this study have remained in currency, not even in the later publications of either Thomas or Znaniecki. The classification of personal motives has not yet reached stability in sociological thought, twenty-five years later. It is difficult to say to what extent the concepts of the *Polish Peasant* study grew out of the research and to what extent it reflected the training and ability of the authors. Certain of the concepts have remained useful, however. The idea of social disorganization was expressed in this study about as soundly as it has been at any later time. The idea of the "definition of the situation," which is known in other terms in psychology, allows the psychological characteristics of the persons to enter into the social interaction as factors. The notion of external conditions as "environments" of persons was of limited use until we could recognize that persons react differently in these conditions according to what aspects they perceive and what meaning these aspects have to their possibilities of action. In short, it is the "definition of the situation" that gives the direction to behavior, not the environment of physical conditions.

The post-war prosperity of the 1920's left little of American life unaffected, and sociology shared in it by expansion in every respect. More departments were established in colleges and universities, more students were enrolled, more advanced degree were granted, and a great expansion in research and publication took place. It was no longer the fashion for each sociologist to build a system and thus become the father of a school of thought. Research efforts were rather more and more directed toward intensive study of a restricted subject, along the lines of the *Polish Peasant* study of Thomas and Znaniecki. Minor investigations were encouraged which covered questions not necessarily of great importance in themselves, but which produced modest links required in the organization of knowledge. From time to time whole new avenues of inquiry were opened up, some of which have endured and expanded, others of which have become forgotten.

This was the period in which American sociology began to find itself. Its course was no longer governed by the logic of classification of sciences or by any individual's decision but was established by tentative and exploratory efforts in many directions, some of which were rewarded by success. Schools of thought do not survive well in this stage of development, and such schools as were once characteristic of American sociology have been steadily withering away, or perhaps it would be better to say the differences have been dissolving.

The size of the research field and the number of persons involved in the activity make cooperation necessary. In this respect sociology inevitably lags behind other sciences, but the change is always in the direction of greater cooperation in research, with interchange of methods and findings, research teamwork involving borderline disciplines, and, recently, large enterprises in which the parts of a problem are assigned to various researchers in the fashion that is followed in the physical and biological sciences. It is also necessary that there be some standardization of terminology and organization. The processes of language growth will take care of some of this whether or not it is guided by the conscious control of human beings, but in recent years there have been organized efforts to speed the process. This is done by committees working within the American Sociological Society, by the effect of the Encyclopedia of the Social Sciences and by glossaries in works of general sociology and recently by a Dictionary of Sociology. (7)

The large undergraduate enrollment in sociology courses not

---

7. Henry Pratt Fairchild, ed., *Dictionary of Sociology*, (New York: The Philosophical Library, 1943).

AMERICAN SOCIOLOGY

only made it necessary to have well organized textbooks for instruction, but the number of transfers of students from one college to another and from college to another university for graduate work brought out the importance of some standardization of at least the introductory course, and since this course usually expresses the general content of sociology, the effect is toward the standardization of the field. An author may have his own theoretical objections to the use of certain concepts, but if they are in wide currency, he may find it advisable to include them in his textbook. Thus concepts, ideas, conclusions, are put in a kind of market place and emerge out of a process of interaction with some sort of price or value attached. In this process schools of thought do not easily persist.

This process of standardization of the field of sociology in the United States has been going on for a quarter of a century and is still under way. It is gradual and continual, but there is at least one major event in this history which requires mention. It is the publication in 1921 of the *Introduction to the Science of Sociology,* by Robert E. Park and Ernest W. Burgess. Barnes and Becker pronounce it the "... most influential texbook in the history of American sociology." (8) Although generally held to be difficult for undergraduate use, the book was widely studied by graduate students and by sociologists, and it virtually standardized certain of the fundamental conceptions of sociology. (9) Such concepts as social interaction, communication, social process, competition, conflict, assimilation, accommodation, personality, and collective behavior have taken their standard sociological meaning primarily from this work. Most subsequent textbooks in sociology, even those written by authors from different sociological traditions, have been much influenced by this book. Furthermore, the suggestions for research included in the organization of each chapter in the Park and Burgess text have given direction to many investigations. In the production of this work sociology in the United States reached a sort of maturity. From this point onward, as at no time previosly,

---

8. Harry Elmer Barnes and Howard Becker, *Social Thought from Lore to Science,* p. 982.

9. Its virtues were immediately apparent to one of Ward's successors at Brown University, and the Park and Burgess system was transplanted here, utterly replacing Ward's tradition, before there was any direct relation between the Brown and Chicago departments.

it was possible to see ahead to a certain extent the way in which sociology would grow.

Objectivity, Empiricism, and Scientific Method. The emphasis on empirical study is generally regarded as a distinguishing characteristic of American sociology. It is not unknown elsewhere —Geddes in England made concrete studies of housing and city planning; Le Play, Durkheim, and Halbwachs in France conducted studies of family budgets and of suicide; and elsewhere such studies have been undertaken. But in general throughout Europe there appears to be more of the welfare and political emphasis, and also a philosophical approach.

The tradition is strongly developed in the United States that sociology should be developed in much the same spirit as a "pure science." This does not mean that it must be a useless science or that it must have no known connection with practical matters, but rather that the research itself should be done in a mood of detachment with the conclusions following from the study and not necessarily answering to any political party line or necessarily resulting in an immediate reform or welfare program.

In the field of race relations, for example, the antipathies are strong enough to destroy objectivity unless care is taken. Yet there is much research done by both Negroes and whites in the relations between these two groups, and with a few unimportant exceptions the research is little affected by the attitudes or the race memberships of the sociologists involved. In much of the published research it is difficult or impossible to infer from the writing itself whether the author is Negro or white. A Negro author in one instance was accused by a critic, ignorant of his racial membership, of belonging to the highly prejudiced lower-class southern white group.

Although the political attitudes of sociologists in the United States probably cover about the same range as those of the American public, there is no cleavage of sociology into radical and conservative wings, or into communist and fascist sociologies. The political attitudes of a scholar are generally considered irrelevant to his research, and in most cases are not widely known, even among colleagues who are personally acquainted with him. The American Sociological Society contains a small group of enthusiasts who make constant attempts to commit the Society to political resolutions, but these notions are invariably and decisively rejected, even though the political sympathies of the membership as persons and citizens may often be with the resolution. The adopted policy is to keep separate the roles of sociologist and citizen, of research specialist and political advocate.

This point of view may have several explanations. Although it is not quite true that the American people do not take politics seriously, there is a certain national practice of applying some of the detachment which is also characteristic of so many American sport activities. The game is played hard, and played to win, but the opponent is not an enemy, and no grudges are to be held. Friendships are not to be made or broken along the lines of this form of conflict. To the majority of Americans the intensity of political sentiment in some European regions looks unsportsmanlike and ridiculous.

The interaction of American sociology with other sciences, through the influence of Ward, Giddings, various social psychologists, and statisticians, has had the effect of bringing into the field of sociology some of the scientific temper. This willingness to take the longer and surer road, and to disregard for the time being the urgencies of a suffering humanity, incurs the impatience of humanitarians. It is a general sentiment among representatives of the profession of social work that the objectivity of the sociologist reflects an indifference to human welfare. It would be more accurate to regard the sociologist's attitude as analogous to the patient, long-run view of the medical research scientist who does not engage in medical practice, but undertakes basic study which may eventually save many lives.

The empiricism of American sociology is often contrasted with the philosophic character of European, particularly German, sociology. It is natural that where the numbers of investigators are small, and facilities for research meager, that scholars should apply their energies to the task that can best be done alone: the task of organization. But it is not true that in the United States, where opportunities for so much factual research have been rich, the work of generalization and interpretation has been entirely neglected. In fact a constant contact has been maintained with the work of European scholars. A number of American sociologists undertook graduate study in European Universities. Many have maintained contacts through travel abroad, and a number of prominent foreign sociologists have taught as visiting professors in

American universities. The coming to power of the Fascist regimes in Germany and Italy, and the outbreak of the second World War has resulted in the permanent migration of a number of distinguished scholars to this country.

Contact with Europe is also maintained through professional literature. Graduate students are expected to make themselves familiar with the history of sociology, and are encouraged to learn to read the original French and German writings. Many outstanding sociologists of these countries have had their important books translated into English, so that even one who does not read the foreign languages may become familiar with such authors as Simmel, Lippert, Weber, Toennies, Von Wiese, Comte, Durkheim, LeBon, Tarde, and others.

Among the influences which have been particularly strong in America are the German sociologists, the French group known as the Durkheim school, and Westermark in England. Park at Chicago, Sorokin and Parsons at Harvard, MacIver at Columbia, and other leading American sociologists have continued to build on these traditions. Although there does take place a certain amount of investigation with little or no conscious theory underlying it, for the most part the empirical research in the United States is part of the same effort to construct an organized and tested body of useful knowledge.

Financial Support for Sociology. An important factor in the success of American sociology has been the wealth of facilities available. This is to a considerable extent an aspect of the relatively high standard of living in this country. The large number of persons who attend the colleges produces a requirement for a large number of teachers of sociology. Although not all of the colleges and universities have sociology courses in the curriculum, and though some of those that do have sociology allow it to be taught by unqualified persons working primarily in some other field of knowledge, there still are probably over two hundred regular full-time teaching positions in sociology in the colleges and universities in the United States. As House points out, this is undoubtedly several times the total in the rest of the world. (10) There are in addition an unknown number of professional sociologists working for governmental agencies, for private business organizations, and many engaged in full-time research.

---

10. Floyd N. House, *The Development of Sociology*, p. 244.

AMERICAN SOCIOLOGY

The size of this force alone would account for a great deal of productivity. But in other ways the relative abundance of available funds has contributed to the output. A number of the notable studies have been made possible only by large provisions of money. The Polish Peasant study, for example, was financed by a generous grant from Helen Culver, who made other notable donations to educational causes. The large and important cooperative research project under the direction of William F. Ogburn, published in 1933 under the title of *Recent Social Trends*, was made possible by an enormous grant from the Rockefeller Foundation. Many smaller studies have been made possible by financial support from individuals, foundations, and in some cases, from governmental agencies. In the field of rural sociology, particularly, the federal government subsidizes a large amount of sociological research. Since there is no distinct borderline between sociology and rural sociology, the entire field is enriched by this special support.

A number of the larger universities provide funds for research. and many furnish facilities that aid in the gathering, tabulating, and preparing of materials. There are a number of sociological or social science research laboratories well equipped with calculating, card sorting and punching machines, map-making equipment, and other working aids. The provision of research assistants, stenographic aid, and other assistance is also a part of this abundance.

The Social Science Research Council plays an important role in stimulating and guiding research, by several means. It aids the preparation of young scholars by the granting of pre-doctoral and post-doctoral fellowships for special study and experience. It providess grants to aid in research projects, and organizes research on matters of importance. For a time it supported the Social Science Abstracts, and it encouraged and aided the production of the Encyclopedia of the Social Sciences. Its abundant resources, and strategic use of them, have been important in stimulating research in all the social science for more than two decades.

This prosperity that did so much to promote sociology and sociological research came perhaps too suddenly in the decade following the first World War; and the abruptness of the process of expansion produced some undesirable conditions. The demand for professors in colleges that were adding to their sociology offerings rose more swiftly than the supply of adequately trained persons. The result was that many poorly qualified persons came into the field, and some who were scarcely qualified in any way. Graduate students in unmanageable numbers flooded some of the larger universities, and many found employment on college faculties before their training was completed. Thus a heterogeneous and somewhat undigestible mass was taken into the profession of sociology. The result is the teaching and research became necessarily uneven in quality, and that the progress toward standardization and cooperation in the field is likely to be for several decades behind where it might have otherwise been.

II

American Specialties in Sociology. While American sociology in general was developing its characteristic features, there were also emerging particular developments within the field, each of which is in certain respects unique, and in some essential way connected with the conditions of life in the United States. Their importance varies, as does the duration of scholarly interest in them. A few have had such vigorous and sucessful growth that they require special mention.

Urban Ecological Studies. The growth of the large industrial cities in the United States, particularly west of the Atlantic states, was a more rapid process than in other regions of the world. Chicago, for example, grew to three million within the first century of its existence. The growth of American cities was also less complicated by the matters of tradition and sacredness, and the patterns of settlement were therefore more nearly determined by secular processes, particularly competition for space with comm_rcial value. It is therefore easier to conceive of laws of urban growth in such circumstances where the aspects that make each city unique are at a minimum, and the aspects which are relatively standard are also relatively visible. It is natural, then, that the examination of the nature of the city, and of the effect of urban conditions on the life of the people should be of particular interest here.

About a century ago, a German scholar, Crystaller, speculated on the pattern a city would assume if it were located in the middle of a flat plain, with no waterways or any other features that would interfere with an "ideal type" of urban pattern. Since cities of size never are located in such a situation, the pattern was necessarily imaginary. The great mid-western cities, however, particularly Chicago and Cleveland, are about as free as a metropolis can be from such interfering features, and it is in such cities that the urban ecological studies have been most enthusiastically and successfully undertaken. Chicago, particularly, has been exploited in this respect. The sociology department, and to some extent the other social science departments at the University of Chicago, have accumulated a large amount of basic data which have made possible useful studies of many aspects of urban life. Among the phenomena of behavior that are illuminated by the techniques of urban ecological study are delinquency and crime, family disorganization, suicide, mental disorders, political disorganization, and matters connected with vital statistics.

This urban ecology is not a school of thought, nor for the most part a unique method, but rather a field of particular interest, which is interconnected in various ways with the rest of the sociological field. The civilized world is in the process of transition from rural to urban forms of social organization. By study of the nature of the cities, and their effects on people, it is possible not only to understand what has been happening, but also, since the process is not yet finished, to have the basis for a more accurate view of the future.

Race and Culture Contacts. Other nations have had the experience of receiving large numbers of alien people, through invasion, importation of slaves, and other forms of migration, but none have had quite the same experience as the United States, which brought over so many different racial and national groups, and at such rapid immigration rates, that assimilation became and still remains a major national problem. As a practical and political problem it could not be, and was not, ignored. Welfare organizations, patriotic societies, the governmental agencies of the country, all became concerned in one way or another. It remained for the sociologist to take the detached point of view necessary for objective research. At the time Thomas and Znaniecki undertook their study of the Polish peasant, the population of the city of Chicago, in which much of the research was carried on, was about three quarters foreign born or of foreign-born parentage. Boston, New York, Philadelphia, and other great cities had large proportions of foreign population, and the cities of the far west had large settlements of Oriental peoples. The southeastern group of states contain such high proportions of Negro population that in some districts they outnumber the dominant white population.

Sociological research on the questions of race and cultural contacts has been a set of painstaking efforts to describe and explain the processes of migration, of accommodation and assimilation, of hostility and conflict, and to study the socio-psychological aspects of these developments. The general and scientific character of this interest is shown in the range of investigations, which include studies of race relations not only in local regions and in areas of such proximity as Hawaii and Canada, but of other parts of the world in which the United States has no particular responsibility or interest. The range of these studies would be even greater were it not for obstructions that are often placed in the way of objective research in cultural matters by governments of many countries. In some countries this amounts to flat refusal to permit American scientists to undertake investigations of this type within their borders.

Social Psychology. The course of development of the science of psychology was such as to be, in the early period of the development of sociology, of limited use to sociologists. Scientific methods in psychology were for decades applied mainly to aspects of human reactions which are essentially physiological. The social behavior of human beings was studied and interpreted on a different basis, with very little actual research or science involved. There was an extensive practice of speculating on the number and type of instincts possessed by humans, and of the way in which institutions grew from these innate motives. There was also a popular explanation of the life cycles of the behavior traits of persons in terms of the recapitulation of the history of the species. These and other aspects of early twentieth century psychology, though not then rejected by all sociologists, did not fill the demand for a theory of human behavior which would be consistent with the knowledge the sociologits and anthropologists were accumulating.

The Pragmatic Movement in philosophy was itself a characteristic American development, and from it there descended a tradition of social psychology which has remained on the whole the most influential in the field of sociology. The names most centrally identified with this contribution are those of John Dewey, George H. Mead, Charles Horton Cooley, and Ellsworth Faris. These men all bridged the disciplines of philosophy, psychology, and sociology. In the body of thought which they collectively, and with the cooperation of others, developed, the break with earlier attempts to account for human behavior on the basis of a biological determinism became complete. Beginning with the observed plasticity and versatility of the human infant, they showed how the traits of mind and personality arise in the processes of social interaction, so that man becomes a social being because he lives in social groups. Although Cooley insisted that the person and the society were but the distributive and collective aspects of a same thing, there is, in the life time of each person, a priority of the group, since the group is always there before the person, and imposes strong influences on his development.

In this body of thought, action is the primary datum of human behavior. Imagination and emotion occur as part of the crisis when the ongoing action is blocked. When a successful means of continuing the action is found, the automatic character of action is re-established and imagination is free to be applied to other incomplete acts. During the crisis the person may work out a solution by means of the trial-and-error process carried on in his imagination, or he may be aided by suggestions from other persons. Culture contains standard means of dealing with the situations which recur frequently in the experiences of its members, so that it is not necessary for each person to find his own solutions for those situations which are culturally defined. Wishes are not instinctive, but are generated in social life, and are therefore of almost limitless variety, as the data of ethnology demonstrate. In this social psychology there is no conception of an essential conflict between the culture and the biological nature of the individual. Mental conflict does, however, take place when conflicting cultural influences meet within one person.

This social psychology answered the need of sociologists more than any other available. While this knowledge was being worked into the systematic thought of American sociology, various other well-publicized schools of thought were competing for attention. Psychoanalysis, particularly of the Freudian variety, built up a strong following especially among members of the social work profession. Behaviorism, Gestalt psychology, and academic social psychology all found some disciples in America, but the sociologists had adopted a useful tradition and were therefore relatively immune to the sweep of fashion in psychology.

Folk Sociology. With the advance of knowledge it was virtually inevitable that the close relation of sociology to anthropology should be somewhat affected by the trend toward specialization. A number of departments which formerly contained both subjects have split apart and the divisions have taken somewhat independent courses. The branch of anthropology which is concerned with the study of cultures, however, is logically inseparable from sociology, and so in this field the two disciplines remain in contact and have an indistinct borderline.

The comparisons made between urban and rural society can be studied in greater relief if the larger range, which includes the preliterate folk cultures, is examined. Within or near the borders of the United States there are a number of regions which for one reason or another are so isolated that the people inhabiting them have this extremely simple form of culture. Among the regions that have been successfully studied are the Appalachian and Ozark Mountain regions, rural Quebec province, sea island Negro communities along the south Atlantic coast, and the interior regions of Yucatan in Mexico. A notable leader in this field is Robert Redfield, who is qualified both as a sociologist and an anthropologist, and who through his own research and that of his students, has successfully blended the systematic knowledge of the two fields.

The Sociology of Regionalism. At the University of North Carolina, under the vigorous leadership of Howard W. Odum, there has been developed a considerable interest in what is known as "regionalism." This is the study of divisions of the country which are larger than states, and which have distinctive geographical, economic, and cultural features which set them apart from one another. The interest in this topic has spread to other universities, mostly those located in southern states, and a considerable body of publications is emerging from their studies.

The south is the most distinctive region within the United States, and is the only one in which there was a serious threat of secession. In economic organizations, cultural life, and political behavior this section preserves many conspicuous differences from the rest of the country. It is therefore somewhat to be expected that southern sociologists should be most conscious of regionalism and most interested in developing it.

In the literature of this movement there are reflections of an attitude which is not solely that of objective research. There is a general reform aspect visible, and to some extent political thoughts of altering the administrative aspects of government to fit in with conceptions of regionalism. It is not always clear whether the aim is to *unify* groups of similar states, or to *divide* the nation along regional lines. Whatever the purpose of the political proposals, they would be controversial not only among sociologists but among citizens anywhere. The mobility and fluidity of the United States population, the diffusion and standardization of culture, and other influences of the sort, are having the effect of reducing the regional basis of differences in American culture. If this trend continues, as it appears likely to do, the interest in regionalism may become a historical subject.

Rural Sociology. As has been indicated in Part I of this chapter, rural sociology is not a development that emerged spontaneously from the scientific investigation of society. It is rather a highly cultivated and subsidized effort to benefit farmers. The support from Congress is undoubtedly motivated to a considerable extent by the desire to appeal to the rural voter. As a result, the "land-grant," or agricultural colleges are provided with funds for the developing of teaching, and of research, in matters of sociology connected with welfare of farm life. This provides for the United States more professorships in rural sociology than in any other branch of sociology.

The contributions to sociology from this field have not been proportionate to the funds expended and the number of sociologists employed. There have been useful additions to the general literature on selective migration, on the nature of folk society, on secularization and change, and other subjects, but there is also a considerable amount of practical investigation with local application, or of advocacy of changes and reforms, which make no contribution to a general body of knowledge. It is likely, however, that the difficulty of making a logical separation of rural sociology from general sociology, and the awareness of the greater long-run value of fundamental research, may in time cause the difference to diminish or disappear.

The Sociology of Change. The study of social change is by no means an exclusive possession of American sociologists, but there has been an emphasis on the study of technological change and its consequences to society that is so extensive that it is something of an American specialty. The largest amount of research has been done by, or stimulated by, William F. Ogburn, whose book *Social Change* has remained a subject of lively discussion since its publication in 1922.

Although it is not held that all social change is the consequence of new inventions and discoveries, the research supports the great importance of this source of change. Through revolutionizing the standard of living, through making possible improvements in transportation and migration, and extensive and instantaneous communication, and in other fundamental ways, technological developments alter the entire framework of a society, and thus necessarily deeply affect human behavior. Ogburn has pointed out in many publications the fact that the adjustments to technological changes do not all come at the same time, and that there occurs in a changing society the phenomena of *cultural lag*, in which social conditions which in one period are adapted to the technology of the society do not change as soon as the technology changes, and hence for a time are out of adjustment. It may be the speed of the process of mechanization of life in America, and perhaps also the extent to which the mechanization has developed in the large cities that account for the strong interest in this subject.

Future Developments in American Sociology. The course of the sociological tradition in the United States, up to the present time, has been determined by the groping process described in the preceding sections. For several decades sociologists have been attempting to define the precise limits of the subject, and although the conception has become much clearer than it was in the days of Ward, it is likely that this process is not yet over.

Before sociology achieves a stable and a clearly delimited field of investigation, it is possible or likely that some of the old interests may be shared with other sciences, that more fresh research leads may be imported from other countries, and that new ground may be broken from time to time, as it has been frequently in the past. There is something of a trend now visible for the investigation of family life not only to be shared with researchers in other fields, but to become something of a field itself. The social psychology, on the other hand, which has been worked out within the ranks of the sociologists may be retained, but it is also conceivable that the development of more relevant and satisfactory knowledge within departments of psychology may eventually make this duplication of effort unnecessary. It is difficult to conceive of a borderline between sociology and social psychology which is ever anything but indistinct and fluid.

Among the interests which have had earlier developments abroad before American sociologists gave major attention to them have been the questions of social classes and caste organization, labor conflict, and the sociology of knowledge. Except for the Negro-white caste-like situation in the southern states, about which objectivity was for some time not easily achieved, the social organization in the United States has not until recently provided subject matter for these topics, at least as clearly as has been the case

AMERICAN SOCIOLOGY

in other countries. It may be that there have been the elements of a class system in the United States all along, but if so it was a loose and unformulated system, and the traditional belief has been that this is a nation without classes and of unlimited opportunity for all. Membership in a lower occupational class was for the most part considered to be temporary, so that class loyalty did not easily develop. The thoroughgoing, permanent cultural adjustment of the members of each class, visible in many European countries, did not become established in this country. Hence the Marxian conceptions of class morality, class beliefs, and class policies have not appeared to be applicable to the American scene, until in recent years when careful attempts have been made to see to what extent subtle examination will reveal the traces of traditions which have been more distinctly visible elsewhere.

Among the matters which seem to call for more intensive investigation is the general subject of conflict. Beside the matter of war, now the greatest menace to mankind and never adequately investigated, there are the disputes within nations that have the possibility of becoming dangerous. There are foreshadowings of intense labor conflict to come when the nation is no longer occupied with waging a war, and many indications of outbreaks of racial strife to come in the same period. The kind of fundamental research that sociologists are equipped to undertake is not likely to bring solutions in time to avoid any such trouble, but the imminence of such conflict will probably be a stimulus to this kind of research.

Although under some constant pressure to do so, it is not probable that sociology will abandon the policy of devoting the major part of research effort to the construction of a general and fundamental body of knowledge. During the depression of the 1930's, and the second World War, a number of sociologists were called upon to make available such of their knowledge and skills as might be helpful. The response was willing, and the experience undoubtedly helpful to those who took part, but in many cases it was found that whatever quick service could be given by a sociologist might also be done by other well-educated and skillful persons, and that the incomplete state of the systematic sociological knowledge limits its value in an immediate crisis. In the present stage it is probably fair to say that the sociologist has little to offer in an emergency beside skill and perhaps refined judgment, and that the practical value of the knowledge will only be evident in a later stage of its scientific development.

TWENTIETH CENTURY SOCIOLOGY

The achievement of a superior science will depend on the discovery of more satisfactory research methods. An increasing amount of attention is being given to the development of methodology, and progress is continually made. Methods of many kinds are being devised and improved, but the most vigorous, and in the judgment of an increasing number of sociologists, the most promising field is that of quantitative methods. The past twenty years has seen, in this country and abroad, the development of new and valuable techniques, and of means of making available adequate data to analyze by the new processes. This development is, of course, neither peculiarly American nor sociological, as it it being carried on in other countries, notably England, and in other fields of study, including biology, psychology, education, economics, and political science.

The time may not yet be ripe for the development of a quantitative systematic science of sociology, but there is an enthusiastic group which believes that it is, and the first attept to outline snch a system was made by Stuart C. Dodd, in *Dimensions of Society*, published in 1942. Dodd attempts to express the characteristics and environment of people by symbols, mathematical in character, so that they can be handled by methods analogous to mathematics. The work is too new and controversial to be judged at this time, but it is of interest as the spearhead of one vigorous direction of movement in the methodology of sociological research.

It it to be expected that research will continue a trend that has been present during most of the history of modern sociology — a trend away from individual system-building efforts and toward teamwork among researchers, as is characteristic in the older sciences. There should consequently be fewer great leaders with followings of loyal disciples, and less spectacular formulations of new conceptions. The steady and solid progress, however, of a worthy science will bring its own justification.

SELECTED BIBLIOGRAPHY

Barnes, Harry Elmer, and Howard Becker, *Social Thought from Lore to Science*, (New York: D. C. Heath and Co., 1938).

Bernard, L. L., ed., *Fields and Methods of Sociology*, (New York: Farrar and Rinehart, 1934).

Bernard, L. L., and Jessie Bernard, *Origins of American Sociology*, (New York: Thomas Y. Crowell, 1943).

AMERICAN SOCIOLOGY

Eubank, Earle E., *The Concepts of Sociology*, (New York: The Macmillan Co., 1931).

House, Floyd N., *The Development of Sociology*, (New York: McGraw-Hill Book Co., 1936).

Karpf, Fay B., *American Social Psychology*, (New York: McGraw-Hill Book Co., 1933)

Lichtenberger, J. P., *The Development of Social Theory*, (New York: The Century Co., 1923).

Lundberg, George, Read Bain, and Nels Anderson, *Trends in American Sociology*. (New York: Harper and Brothers, 1929).

Rice, Stuart A., ed., *Methods in Social Science—a Case Book*, (Chicago: The University of Chicago Press, 1931).

Small, Albion W., *Origins of Sociology*, (Chicago: The University of Chicago Press, 1924).

Sorokin, Pitirim A., *Contemporary Sociological Theories*, (New York: Harpers and Brothers, 1928).

Robert E. L. Faris received the Ph. D. from the University of Chicago. He has taught sociology at Brown University, McGill University, Bryn Mawr College, and is at present Associate Professor of Sociology at Syracuse University. He is co-author, with H. Warren Dunham, of *Mental Disorders in Urban Areas*, and author of "Cultural Isolation and the Schizophrenic Personality," "The Sociological Causes of Genius," and other articles. His present research interests are in urban ecological studies, the social psychology of ability, and in the selection of ability in social classes.

CHAPTER XIX

BRITISH SOCIOLOGY

by

J. RUMNEY

I

Sociology as an independent discipline is still not too firmly established in England, although, what may be called a sociological approach has been long in existence, going as far back at least as the eighteenth century. Perhaps the reason lies in the fact that sociology is essentially the product of rapid social change and crisis. But England has been the country of stability and gradual change, of reform and evolution rather than of crisis and revolution. This meant that at no time were the foundations of social life closely scrutinized. What analysis there was, was piece-meal, haphazard and unsystematic. It is not surprising therefore that England excelled in philanthropy and social service, but not in systematic thought or planning. It excelled in the local survey but that is simply "the collection of facts relating to social problems, and conditions in order to assist directly or indirectly the formulation of practical measures with reference to such problems. That is to say it does not, as a rule, itself put forward any specific scheme of action, nor on the other hand, is it concerned with evolving any comprehensive sociological theory. It collects facts, which others may use as they please." (1)

The circumstances too, in which sociology was born, have an important bearing on its development in England. If from the theoretical point of view, it arose as an attempt to unify the knowledge of the different social sciences, and to get a "vue d'ensemble" of society which had become imperative owing to the increasing interconnectedness of social life, from the practical point of view it arose as a criticism of all partial schemes, nostrums and panaceas of social regeneration that were urged upon society as a result of the Industrial and French revolutions. This practical aspect is clearly evident in Comte's sociology. He wanted to criticize the validity of the conflicting ideas that sprang up to reorganize society, and to preserve whatever he could of the social order. He sought to establish principles of an "ordered progress" and his sociological formula became "Neither restoration nor revolution." He became a conservative, and in his laters years turned his energies to the founding of a religion of humanity which was nothing more than a form of Catholicism minus God. Moreover, his sociology was essentially a theory of society in which action has no part. What is the use, it may be asked, of understanding society without changing it?

These social implications of Comte's sociology, and their utilization by the dominant social thought to buttress the status quo, made sociology suspect in the eyes of more radical thinkers. The fact that most of the sociologists following Comte were conservative minded on fundamental social issues, apart from religion, increased this suspicion. Under the guise of scientific objectivity and detachment, their sociology was frequently a rationalization for their prejudices, and especially a weapon for fighting socialism. In attempting to preserve an extant social order, there was little need to examine the foundations of society, nor again to develop a comprehensive theory of society. Even in the case of Herbert Spencer, the comprehensiveness is either cosmic or ethnographic but not "societal." Considered as a subject for university study, additional difficulties beset sociology in England. Spencer, who more than anybody else had introduced and developed the subject, was regarded by the universities as naturalistic and materialistic, a dangerous solvent to ancient beliefs and traditions. This perhaps may have

---

1. A. F. Wells, *The Local Survey in Great Britain*, (London: Allen and Unwin, 1935), p. 18.

been forgiven him, but not the fact that like many other eminent Englishmen he was not a university man and held no academic position. Moreover, sociology as a newcomer had to fight the vested interests firmly established in university chairs, curricula, examinations — a battle that is by no means over. (2) It is barely forty years ago that sociology was first taught in the University of London by L. T. Hobhouse and Edward Westermarck.

The Background of English Sociology: Eighteenth Century Social Thought. With the profound economic and political transformations of the eighteenth century there began to be felt in England, as elsewhere on the continent, a conscious recognition of social development and the possibility of mankind guiding and controling it. Thinkers became intensely interested in everything that concerns man on earth — not man in heaven. They eagerly discussed the rise and fall of empires, the stages in social evolution, the growth of population, poverty and the wealth of nations. Since it is not possible to discuss all of them here, a few words might be said of the more important ones, for the problems they discussed and their social insights have influenced later thought. Had English sociology folowed these more intensively, rather than the thinkers of the nineteenth century, its progress would undoubtedly have been much more rapid.

As early as 1714 Mandeville in his *Fable of the Bees* suggests that civil society might have its origin in the dangers savages faced from wild animals, or from each other, or from a variety of man's wants. On the influence of custom he has a passage which it would be difficult to improve upon. He writes, "What Men have learned from their Infancy, enslaves them, and the Force of Custom warps Nature, and at the same time imitates her in such a manner, that it is often difficult to know which of the two we are influenced by." (3) David Hume's sociological essays are among his best and his penetrating analysis of the social contract theory, a model of its kind. John Brown in *An Estimate of the Manners and Principles of the Times* in 1758 criticizes the organismic conception of society which a century later Spencer revived with harmful consequences to sociology. "In Societies of whatever kind," he writes, "there seems no such necessary or essential Tendency to Dissolution. The human

---

2. See E. M. Burns, "Great Britain," in "Introduction II, The Social Sciences as Disciplines," *Encyclopedia of the Social Sciences,* 1: 231-247.

3. Bernard Mandeville, *Fable of the Bees,* ed. by F. B. Kaye, (London: Oxford University Press, 1924), vol. 1, p. 330.

BRITISH SOCIOLOGY

Body is naturally mortal; the political only so by Accident; Internal Disorders or Diseases may arise: External violence may attack or overpower....." (4) Ferguson, discarding the theories of primitive man, elaborated by Hobbes and Rousseau, make a systematic attempt to study human society by means of inductive investigations. He is more concerned with groups such as the Arab clan or the American Indian than with humanity, and his writings admirably reflect a modern scientific temper. He claims that in "in respect to what men have actually done or exhibited, human nature is a subject of history and physical science." (5) Millar followed Ferguson's method and approach, and cleverly anticipated Bachofen's theory of *Das Muetterrecht*. In his *Origin of the Distinction of Ranks or an Inquiry into the Circumstances which Give Rise to Influence and Authority in the Different Members of Society*, he discusses such matters as the condition of women in different societies, the jurisdiction and authority of a father over his children, and he authority of a chief over the members of a tribe. He classifies the stages of social evolution into Hunters and Fishers, Pastoral, Agricultural, and Commercial, and in each of these stages he examines the location of authority resulting from the distinction of ranks, and distribution of property and power. (6) Dunbar, another contemporary, discusses the "Primeval Form of Society," 'Language as an Universal Accomplishment," and many other matters. (7) Lord Monboddo anticipates future theories as to the origin of man, and like a modern anthropologist studies primitive societies for the light they may throw on problems of civilization. (8) And still another forerunner of anthropology is Lord Kames in his *Sketches of the History of Man*. (9)

What distinguishes all these precursors of modern English sociol-

---

4. John Brown, *An Estimate of the Manners and Principles of the Times*, 7th ed. (1758), p. 107.

5. Adam Ferguson, in his Introduction to *The Principles of Moral and Political Science*, (1792, 2 vols.).

6. John Millar, *The Origin of the Distinction of Ranks* etc., (4th ed., "to which is prefixed an account of the Life and writings of the author by John Craig, Esq.," 1806).

7. James Dunbar, *Essays on the History of Mankind in Rude and Uncultivated Ages*, (London: 1780).

8. James Burnett, Lord Monbaddo, *of the Origin and Progress of Language*, (London: 1773-1792, 6 vols.).

9. Henry Home, Lord Kames, *Sketches of the History of Man*, (Edinburgh: 1774).

ogy is their emphasis on social institutions — a characteristic of present-day sociology — and their attempt to study society objectively and as a whole. This attitude is also evident in Adam Smith, who never isolates his economics from the rest of society, and who in his *Theory of Moral Sentiments* promises to give "an account of the general principles of law and government, and of the different revolutions they have undergone in different ages and periods of society, not only in what concerns justice, but in what concerns police, revenue, arms and whatever else is the subject of Law." Here we have an anticipation, Ingram claims, "of general Sociology, both statical and dynamical, an anticipation which becomes still more remarkable when we learn from his literary executors that he had formed the plan of a connected history of the liberal sciences and elegant arts, which must have added to the branches of study already enumerated a view of the intellectual progress of society." (10)

Although these works were widely known and widely translated into French and German, they did not lead to a systematic study of society. The reason lies partly in the growing concentration of English thought on economics and economic problems, reflecting England's role as the workshop of the world, and partly in the French revolution which frightened many thinkers, and which undoubtedly arrested critical and scientific thought for two generations. Ferguson, for instance, held extreme views in 1759, but after the Revolution gave them up and argued for the necessity of inequality in rank and the expediency of hereditary distinctions. The next stimulating stage in English sociological thought was to come with the challenge of socialism.

Socialism and Sociology. It is significant that the two words sociology and socialism arose about the same time, and were often used interchangeably as referring to the science of society or the science of social change. (11) Since the crticism of society is the first step in sociology, and the second, that the object of criticism is society itself, *i. e.* social relations and not human nature, the challenge of socialism was vital. Robert Owen, for instance, re-

---

10. J. K. Ingram, *A History of Political Economy*, (New York: The Macmillan Co., 1915), p. 89.

11. "Sociology" was coined by Auguste Comte in 1839, and used by J. S. Mill in 1842. "Socialists" was first used in England in Owen's *New Moral World* on December 19, 1835, and "Socialism" in 1841 by T. R. Edmonds in an "Address to the Socialists."

garded the family, property and religion as the satanic devices which enslave mankind. Earlier, Charles Hall in *The Effects of Civilization*, 1805, had attacked the system of private property, and william Thompson in 1824 urged the abolition of all sinecures, standing armies, State churches and all the disqualifications imposed upon women. (12) Other severe attacks were made by Thomas Hodgskin, John Gray, Francis John Bray, and the philosophical anarchist William Godwin. Gradually a conception of the socialist society developed, based on scientific laws. Thus J. N. Bailey, (13) a socialist writer in 1840, declares that "The Science of Society treats of the laws by which the formation of human character is determined; of the mode in which scientific knowledge schould be applied to the production of wealth; and of the way in which societies of men should be governed..." Mary Hennel in expounding Owen's philosophy sets down the laws governing human society in *The Elements of the Science of Society*. (14) Still later Dr. Travis uses as synonymous socialism, Social Science, and the Science of Society. (15)

Comte himself had been a pupil of Saint Simon, one of the greatest of socialist thinkers, but as we pointed out before, antagonized by his master's revolutionary views, had become a conservative. Sociology in a sense is thus an intellectual reaction to the socialist movement. But it has also been stimulated by it. The socialist criticism of society imposed upon sociology the task of clarifying its basic ideas, of testing its scientific objectivity and impartiality, and of analyzing the relationship between the theory and the practice of society. This problem has not yet been solved.

The English Positivists. The group of Comte's disciples in England known as the English Positivists never achieved any great

---

12. William Thompson, *An Inquiry into the Principles of the Distribution of Wealth*, (London: 1824).

13. J. N. Bailey, *Preliminary Discourse on the Objects, Pleasures and Advantages of the Science of Society*, (London: 1840), p. 29.

14. Mary Hennel, *An Outline of the Various Social Systems and Communities . . .*, (London: 1844).

15. Some of the more specifically sociological, but not socialist, works that appeared in England during this period are: Hugh Murray, *Enquiries Historical and Moral Reflecting the Character of Nations and the Progress of Society*, (Edinburgh: 1808); A. H. Moreton, M. P., *Civilization or a Brief Analysis of the Natural Laws that Regulate the Numbers and the Condition of Mankind*, (London: 1836); Charles Bray, *The Science of Man: A Birdseye View of the Wide and Fertile Field of Anthropology*, (London: 1868); Hugh Doherty, M. D., *The Philosophy of History and Social Evolution*, (London: 1874).

measure of success, and it was unfortunate that they concentrated on the Polity or the worship of Humanity, and neglected the scientific aspects of his sociology. Moreover, "by maintaining a middle stand in an age of conflict, they aroused the enmity of all factions, *e. g.* struggles between religious devotees and their opponents, employers and workmen, socialists and the supporters of private property rights, feminists and those who championed the traditional views concerning the proper position of women..."(16) And finally their religious views provoked the hostility of some of the acutest minds of the time. Mill referred to the Polity as a system of spiritual and temporal despotism unequalled since the time of Ignatius Loyola, and other sharp critics were Ruskin, Huxley, Spencer and Sir James Stephen.

Indirectly, however, the Positivists certainly influenced the mental climate of the time. They were all zealous crusaders and able men, and deserving of mention are Richard Congreve, Frederic Harrison, John Henry Bridges and Edward Spencer Beesley. Bridges undoubtedly was an influence in the philosophy of L. T. Hobhouse. In 1893, *The Positivist Review* was started and lasted until 1924, when its name was changed to *Humanity*. Then after one year it was discontinued. Some of the Positivists eventually found peace in the Catholic Church and among them were Philip Thomas, Kegan Paul and Malcolm Quinn. Even more indirectly, the Positivists stimulated a great deal of social thought by attracting to the study of society men such as John Morley, Lord Houghton, Lord Arthur Russel, John Ingram, Benjamin Kidd, George Eliot, G. H. Lewes, Patrick Geddes, Havelock Ellis and J. A. Hobson. (17)

Mill, Buckle, and Spencer. There is a direct line of continuity from Comte by way of Mill, Buckle, and Spencer to the English sociology of to-day. There is the same emphasis on the study of social institutions, on problems of social evolution, and the study of society as a whole. Under the influence of Comte, J. S. Mill adopted the use of the word "Sociology" in 1842, and in discussing the "Logic of the Moral Sciences," he suggests that the backward state of the social sciences can only be remedied by applying to them the methods of the physical sciences, and more specifically the historical

---

16. John Edwin McGee, *A Crusade for Humanity; The History of Organized Positivism in England,* (London: Watts and Co., 1931), pp. 229-230.

17. Gladys Bryson, "Early English Positivists and the Religion of Humanity," *American Sociological Review.* 1: 343-362, June, 1936.

method. (18) The function of sociology is to discover the laws according to which any state of society produces the state which succeeds it. But the laws of history, he goes on to argue, are empirical and cannot be extended beyond the particular time and place they were manifested, unless they grow from human nature, and would follow in the new circumstances. One of his biographers, Bain, tells us that Mill contemplated a book on Ethology to deal with the laws of human character, regarding it as the foundation and cornerstone of Sociology, and that in 1847 he wrote "I do not know when I shall be ripe for beginning Ethology. The scheme has not assumed any definite shape with me yet." Bain goes on to say, "His failure with Ethology fatally interfered with the larger project, which I have no doubt he entertained, of executing a work on Sociology as a whole." (19)

In spite of the many crudities exhibited by H. T. Buckle, his works constitute a definite advance in establishing a science of society. It was no mean achievement to attempt to determine the statistical regularity of moral actions, and to show that marriage depends upon such external conditions as the price of grain, or suicide upon wages, and religion upon scenery, climate, and soil. If he exaggerated the pressure of the physical environment, or the growing power of ideas, or the unimportance of the individual, he at the same time drew attention to the preponderance of society and culture, and to the necessity of knowing the laws governing social life if man is to be happy. Of his own book *The History of Civilization in England* he has this to say: "The fundamental ideas are: 1st That the history of every country is marked by peculiarities which distinguish it from other countries, and which being unaffected, or slightly affected by individual men, admit of being generalized. 2nd. That an essential preliminary to such generalization is an enquiry into the relation between the condition of society and the condition of the material world surrounding such society. 3rd. That the history of a single country (such as England) can only be understood by a previous investigation of history generally." (20)

The greatest influence upon modern sociology has been exerted

---

18. J. S. Mill, *A System of Logic*, (London: 1843).
19. Alexander Bain, *J. S. Mill*, (London: 1882), pp. 78-79; see also Mill's book, *Auguste Comte and Positivism*, (London: 1865).
20. See the Introduction in the *Miscellaneous and Posthumous Work of H. T. Buckle*, ed. by Helen Taylor, (1872, 3vols.). The best book on Buckle is entitled *Buckle and his Critics* by J. M. Robertson, (London: 1875).

TWENTIETH CENTURY SOCIOLOGY

by Herbert Spencer. His influence is evident not only in England on L. T. Hobhouse, but on Durkheim in France, Small, Giddings and Sumner, in the United States, and von Wiese, Oppenheimer, Schmoller and Mueller-Lyer in Germany. His use and application of ethnological data and the comparative method are clearly stamped upon his English successors. They all followed him in his emphasis upon the superorganic character of society, and the close dependence of sociology on biology, psychology, history and ethics. He thus went further than Comte, to whom sociology was the science of human action in its broadest sense, and which excluded all specialisms from its scope. To Spencer all these specialisms were necessary if sociology were to become a truly generalizing science. He was one of the first to point out the need for a comparative psychology, a path that was more fully explored by Hobhouse, and Spencer's classification of societies — social morphology — marks a great advance upon Comte. His discussions of social evolution and social progress need qualification, but he recognized that only upon their careful analysis will prevision become possible in sociology.

The comparative method which in essence compares, analyzes, and sifts the relevant from the irrelevant by varying the circumstances when examining any social phenomenon, is one of the main legacies of Spencer to modern sociology. Hobhouse, Ginsberg, and Wheeler used this method to obtain a series of valuable correlations among the institutions of the simpler peoples, and to find out what changes in any one institution are functionally correlated with changes in other institutions. (21) Spencer himself, using this method, compiled with the help of assistants a number of important works entitled *Descriptive Sociology* which unfortunately are not widely known, considering the vast storehouses of facts they are, and which few sociologists have as yet utilized. Of these works Spencer himself writes, "The classified compilations and digests of materials to be thus brought together under the title of Descriptive Sociology, are intended to supply the student of Social Science with data standing towards his conclusions in a relation like that in which accounts of the structures and functions of different types of animals stand to the conclusions of the biologist. Until there had been such systematic descriptions of different kinds of organisms,

---

21. L. T. Hobhouse, M. Ginsberg, and S. C. Wheeler, *The Material Culture and Social Institutions of the Simpler Peoples*, (London: Chapman and Hall, 1915).

as made it possible to compare the connexions, forms and actions and modes of origin of their parts, the science of life could make no progress. And in like manner before there can be reached in Sociology, generalizations having a certainty, making them worthy to be scientific there must be definite accounts of the institutionalized actions of societies of various types, and in various stages of evoution, so aranged as to furnish the means of readily ascertaining what social phenomena are historically associated." (22)

The application of the comparative method is beset with difficulties, and it is not surprising that Rivers and other diffusionists challenged its use. But the dangers in the method do not lie in its neglect of the phenomenon of diffusion, for the determination of the sources of cultural elements is not incompatible with the comparative method. They lie in abstracting an institution or element of behavior from its context, in assuming that the unit of comparison is the same and has the same functional value in different societies, and in confusing the comparative method with the evolutionary method or hypothesis. As to the last point, the comparative method may suggest evolution, but the two processes must be kept distinct. Even if evolution is shown to apply it need not necessarily be unilinear evolution with a fixed and unvarying number of stages such as Spencer assumed. Hobhouse, who more than anybody else kept distinct morphology and development, is not altogether free from the other pitfalls in the method.

The Institute of Sociology. In 1903, the year Herbert Spencer died, a paper by M. Victor Branford entitled "Origin and Use of the Word Sociology" was printed for private circulation to accompany a circular prepared by a group of scholars and men of affairs interested, and addressed to various representatives of philosophical, scientific and practical interests, asking their opinions as to the advisability of forming a Sociological Society." (23) In response to the overwhelming body of affirmative opinion the Society was instituted. The Rt. Hon. James Bryce, in his first presidential address gave "a few reasons why a new society may be needed which will add something to the agencies that exist for the purpose of devising and conducting inquiries into the various functions, or

---

22. Herbert Spencer in the Preface to first volume of the *Descriptive Sociology*, vol. I. *Lowest Races*, (London: 1874). See also J. Rumney, *Herbert Spencer's Sociology*, (London: Williams and Norgate, 1934).

23. From a memorandum submitted to me by Mr. A. Farquharson, General Secretary of the Institute of Sociology, some years ago in London.

let us say, the various spheres of activity which characterize human society." The reasons given are:

1. That the ever-expanding ramifications of social investigation had created the need for a society or association to survey with the eye of science the whole field of human activity and to "father" the many incipient branches of social study beginning to emerge.

2. That there is a need for a single society to bring the many diverse, interlacing, but as yet unconnected, branches of scientific social investigation already developed into systematic co-operation, and to bring the specialists in the different groups together to meet and compare notes more often.

3. That the backwardness in this country as compared with other countries in scientific social investigation on the theoretical side, except in the field of Political Economy, is in contrast to our great practical advancement in the sphere of philanthropy, and that it should be of enormous benefit to practical philanthropists to have the aid of men of theory. (24)

If the Institute of Sociology as the Sociological Society later became, has been successful as it undoubtedly has been in promoting sociology as a separate discipline and as an academic subject, it has also given sociology that variegated character of its own membership, which represents numerous specialisms as well as "philosophical, scientific and practical interests," and the complex structure of English society in general. Thus it is illuminating to examine the discussion on the scope of sociology in the first volume of the *Sociological Papers* issued in 1904. The theme of the discussion was "On the Relation of Sociology to the Social Sciences and to Philohophy" and the participants included Durkheim, Victor Branford, J. H. Bridges, Dr. Emil Reich, J. A. Hobson, J. M. Robertson, and L. T. Hobhouse. Written communications were submitted by Paul Barth, Marcel Bernes, Lévy-Bruhl, James Bryce, J. Bury, S. J. Chapman, Alfred Fouillée, Bertrand Russell, J. H. Muirhead, J. S. Nicholson and many others. On the whole, Durkheim's arguments urging a synoptic approach won acceptance. L. T. Houbhouse adopted a similar view. "General Sociology," he maintained, "is neither a separate science complete in itself before specialism begins, nor is it a mere synthesis of the social sciences consisting in the mechanical juxtaposition of their results. It is rather a vitalizing principle that runs through all social investiga-

---

24. *Ibid.*

tion, nourishing and nourished by it in turn, stimulating inquiry, correlating results, exhibiting the life of the whole in the parts and returning from a study of the parts to a fuller comprehension of the whole." (25) Regarding the controversy whether sociology is a mere co-ordination of the separate sciences or whether it is itself a particular science dealing with all social relations not considered under other social sciences, Professor Bosanquet shrewdly refers to "that false antithesis, that sociology was either a number of sciences which had no central science as their connection or a single science, which was not a part of a number of sciences." (26)

Since the lines between sociology and the social sciences are rather fluid, one may be apt to get a false picture of English intellectual development by discussing only professional sociologists. So before we turn to an examination of Hobhouse, Westermarck and Ginsberg who are known as England's most noted sociologists of the present time, the contributions of other social scientists will be briefly mentioned, even though they be a mere catalogue of names.

II

The Contributions of the Social Sciences. The catholicity of views and the wide range of interests that mark English sociology are confirmed by a glance at the membership of the Institute of Sociology. On its Council, there have served among others Lord Bryce, Victor Branford, A. C. Haddon, Sir Patrick Geddes, James Sully, E. J. Urwick, G. P. Geoch, L. T. Hobhouse, J. A. Hobson, Benjamin Kidd, J. M. Robertson, Alexander Shand, Graham Wallas, E. Westermarck, G. L. Gomme, H. J. Mackinder and C. W. Saleeby. Recent presidents of the Institute include R. R. Marett, E. Barker, G. P. Gooch, A. M. Carr-Saunders, M. Ginsberg and K. Mannheim. All these are outstanding names in one or other of the social sciences. Since the lines of demarcation have never been clear or sharp in England, the social sciences are fluid, and have a tendency to coalesce and become concrete, unlike their highly abstract and separate continental counterparts. And since isolation and compartmentalization are rather rare, the social scientist in England is not merely an economist and nothing else, or a historian and nothing else, but

---

25. L. T. Hobhouse, in *The Sociological Review*, 1: 8, January, 1908.
26. B. Bosanquet, in *Sociological Papers*, (London: Macmillan and Co., for the Sociological Society), vol. 1, 1905, p. 206.

TWENTIETH CENTURY SOCIOLOGY

a little bit of everything. And this should be borne in mind in the following classification acording to subject matter.

In anthropology the most noted names of past and recent years are those of Maine, Lubbock, MacLennan, Tylor, Lang, G. Lane-Fox, Sir James Frazer, G. H. L. F. Pitt-Rivers, R. R. Marett, Sir Arthur Keith, W. H. R. Rivers, Robert Briffault, B. Malinowski, E. Westermarck, W. J. Perry and Lord Raglan. In social biology the names of Francis Galton, W. Bateson, J. B. S. Haldane, J. Huxley, L. Hogben and C. P. Blacker come to mind. Human geography is represented by H. J. Mackinder, Victor Branford, Patrick Geddes, A. J. Herbertson, A. R. Cowan, J. Fairgrieve, M. I. Newbigin, C. P. Lucas, G. G. Chisholm, J. McFarlane, and H. J. Fleure. Statistics and biometry are associated with the names of G. U. Yule, K. Pearson and A. Bowley. The field of population has been studied by A. M. Carr-Saunders, Enid Charles, L. Hogben and Sir William Beveridge, and that of sex by Havelock Ellis and E. Westermarck. In social psychology there have been important contributions by W. Bagehot, W. Troter, W. McDougall, G. Wallas, A. Shand, H. G. Tansley, B. Hart, M. Ginsberg, F. C. Bartlett, T. H. Pear, J. T. MacCurdy, J. Bowlby, R. H. Thouless, E. Glover, Ian Suttie, E. Miller, and Sir Martin Conway. Historians and social historians, and historians of societies and social institutions, are represented by A. Toynbee, J. H. Clapham, R. H. Tawney, Sidney and Beatrice Webb, J. B. Bury, Sir Flinders Petrie, Sir W. J. Ashley, the Hammonds, G. Slater, L. Knowles, G. P. Gooch, G. L. Gomme, F. F. C. Fuller, John Morley, and J. K. Ingram; and on the periphery, closer to sociology than history, are J. M. Robertson, G. Spiller and F. S. Marvin. Economics has been refined by J. M. Keynes, L. Robbins, John Strachey, E. F. M. Durbin, and P. Sargant-Florence, and politics by H. J. Laski, E. Barker, J. L. Stocks, G. Catlin, R. H. S. Crossman and H. W. Brogan. The study of international relations and international problems has been pursued by D. Mitrany, A. Zimmern, H. N. Brailsford, J. A. Hobson, C. D. Burns, Leonard Woolf and James Bryce. Social philosophers and others who have influenced contemporary thought include T. H. Green, B. Bosanquet, F. H. Bradley, J. S. Mackenzie, E. J. Urwick, S. Alexander, C. D. Broad, A. S. Eddington, F. C. S. Shiller, B. Russel and A. N. Whitehead — and we should also mention H. G. Wells and G. B. Shaw.

In many cases, as we have already pointed out, the contributions are not limited to one field. A good example is Patrick Geddes who was equaly at home in biology, human geography, eugenics, city-planning, and social work, and who together with Victor Branford initiated regional and local surveys. J. M. Robertson also comes to mind, as one who ranged widely in literature, history, religion, and rationalism. He is perhaps not as well known as he should be. His *Essays in Sociology* (1904) are full of keen insight and his study of Buckle a masterly analysis. And recently we have Arnold Toynbee who in the monumental *A Study of History* ranges over many civilizations and skillfully dissects the causes of their growth and decay.

Some excellent social surveys have also been made. A social survey may be said to consist of the collecting of data concerning the living and working conditions of people in a given locality, in order to assist the formulation of practical social measures — and it is perhaps this emphasis that distinguishes the work of Booth and others from that of the followers of Le Play such as Branford, Geddes, and Farquharson who emphasize much more the action of the environment on the inhabitants. (27) Some of the best known surveys are those of Charles Booth entitled *Life and Labour of the People in London* (1889-1903) and the *New Survey of London Life and Labour*, completed only a few years ago under the direction of Sir Llewellyn Smith and Sir William Beveridge. Another very important survey is *The Social Survey of Merseyside* (3 vols., 1934), carried out by A. M. Carr-Saunders and D. Caradog Jones, which includes among other things a comprehensive analysis of the population and of working class expenditure, a study of the localization of industry, occupational mobility between generations from one social class to another and from one occupation to another, infant mortality, differential fertility, local government, leisure-time activity, and the services of church, school and social agencies. On a smaller scale are the surveys of Henry Mess on the Tyneside, Owen in Sheffield, Hilda Jennings in Brynmawr, Richard Evans in Hull, Percy Ford in Southampton, Terence Young Becontree in Dagenham, and Herbert Tout in Bristol.

A new development in England is the Mass Observation movement which, beginning in 1937, has now firmly established itself as a form of collective research. The object of Mass-Observation is to study the social institutions of the British people, their habits and beliefs, in the same way that anthropology studies primitive peoples.

---

27. D. Caradog Jones, "Evolution of The Social Survey in England since Booth," *American Journal of Sociology*, 46: 818-825, May, 1941.

TWENTIETH CENTURY SOCIOLOGY

By means of volunteer field workers who keep detailed accounts of important events, and trained investigators who record public opinion by reliable sampling methods, a vast amount of information has been accumulated on pubs, politics, religion, the human side of industry, the effects of the war on these, and on the behavior and attitudes of the public. Although it is still too early to evaluate the final usefulness of this movement — it may easily become a tool of government to "snoop" on people and politics — it has already produced a number of interesting studies. (28) "Though still in a highly experimental stage, it has the only available machinery for recording social change in Britain at these deeper and more significant levels, and all its efforts are devoted to keeping this record as objectively and in as great detail as time and technique allow." (29)

Hobhouse, Westermarck, and Ginsberg. L. T. Hobhouse stands out as the great English sociologist of recent years — and not only as a sociologist but as a great man and a great teacher. All who studied under him will always remember his inspiration, kindliness and understanding. Hobhouse synthesizes in a new creative pattern the formative influences of Spencer, Comte, Bridges, Mill, and Green. Like Spencer, he too constructed a system of sociology, but his system was widely different from that of his predecessor. His function, as Barker points out, was "to deepen liberal thought; to reconcile its old conceptions with new social demands and a new social philosophy: to turn Liberalism from Laissez-Faire to a genuine sympathy with labor." (30)

His conception of the scope of sociology, to which we have already referred, helps to explain the many fields of thought such as philosophy and psychology he ventured in and made his own. To Hobhouse, sociology was not a specialism, nor simply a synthesis of specialisms, but the interpretation of social life as a whole. Like Comte, he points to the inter-connection of social phenomena and

---

28. See the following publications issued by Mass-Observation: *First Year's Work*, (London: Lindsay Drummond, 1938); *Britain*, (London: Penguin Press, 1938); *War Begins at Home*, (London: Faber, 1940); *Home Propaganda*, (London: Advertising Service Guild, 1941); *People in Production*, (London: Advertising Service Guild, 1942).

29. H. D. Willcock, "Mass-Observation," *American Journal of Sociology*, 48: 445-456, January, 1943. See also Raymond Firth, "An Anthropologist's View of Mass-Observation," *Sociological Review*, 31: 166-193, January, 1939.

30. E. Barker, on L. T. Hobhouse, *Proceedings of the British Academy*, 1929, p. 536; see also *L. T. Hobhouse: His Life and Work*, (London: G. Allen and Unwin, 1931), by Morris Ginsberg and J. A. Hobson.

the need for a discipline that will give a *vue d'ensemble* of social life. In search of such a view he specialized in comparative psychology, the fruit of which is *Mind in Evolution* (1901, rev. ed., 1926) which has influenced Watson, Yerkes, Kohler and other students of primate behavior. He turned to comparative ethics and formulated his conclusions in *Morals in Evolution* (1901, rev. ed., 1915). These conclusions were tested in a monograph he wrote with Ginsberg and Wheeler entitled *The Material Culture and Social Institutions of the Simpler Peoples* (1915), an essay on the correlation between culture and social institutions. He then examined the field of social psychology (*Mind in Evolution, Development and Purpose*, 1913, rev. ed., 1927, and also *Social Development*, 1924), and showed the part played by impulse and rational purpose in social life. To epistemology and philosophy he contributed *The Theory of Knowledge* (1896, rev. ed., 1921) and developed an organic view of rationality that was to be basic in his sociological thought. Indeed his sociological system incorporates his wide researches, and exhibits a skilful blend of the scientific and philosophic temper. Four books really constitute his system and together they are entitled *The Principles of Sociology*. The first is *The Metaphysical Theory of the State* (1918) which demolishes the Hegelian theory of the State and paves the way for a philosophy based on individual development and the common good. The second is the *Rational Good* (1921) which works out a comprehensive ethical theory wherein the good is a harmony of mind with objects, and of purposes with each other. The third, entitled *Elements of Social Justice* (1922), applies his ethical theory to concrete political and economic problems and comes out in favor of the positive State. And his final volume, *Social Development* (1924), examines the extent to which social and ethical development have occurred together.

Social development is indeed the central idea of Hobhouse's sociology. But development not in terms of the unfolding of some spiritual principle as with the idealist philosophers, and not in terms of biological evolution as with Spencer, who equated evolution with progress, but in terms of a harmony based on the free and rational cooperation of men. But can such development be demonstrated, can it be measured? To do this, Hobhouse sets up certain non-ethical criteria, such as scale, efficiency, freedom, and mutuality, and then sees whether they correlate with intellectual development, so that certain types of institutions predominate in certain stage of culture. His next problem was to inquire whether there has been ethical advance, that is, advance in a certain direction and in accordance with rational standards he had developed in his ethics. On the whole, Hobhouse finds coincidence of social development with ethical development. Progress has occured, and can occur — but only in so far as the rational mind of each individual links up with that of others and recognizes that the fulfillment of needs and purposes of each requires the fulfillment of all.

A number of difficulties suggest themselves in Hobhouse's scheme of correlation. In the first place, it may be questioned whether his non-ethical criteria avoid ethical implication. Hobhouse took his criteria from the nature of organic development and as such they are ethically neutral. But applied to social development can they retain their neutrality? In the second place there is the difficulty of obtaining a satisfactory morphology considering that the units required for comparison must be carefully determined. And finally there is the difficulty of passing morphology to development.

Nevertheless Hobhouse's treatment of social development is the most thorough ever undertaken. In opposition to Spencer he shows that progress is not an automatic process but one that rests on human energy, and that there can be no real test of the possibility of progress until the effort is made. The rational ideal will conquer in the long run, he thinks, because it is based on harmonious fulfilment. Nor does Hobhouse believe that such progress requires a different human nature or new qualities in man. It only needs an intensification of those qualities such as courage, devotion, sacrifice and loyalty manifested in everyday life. And finally, as regards methodology, Hobhouse offers the hope that the problem of progress is not altogether beyond solution.

Although Westermarck is not an Englishman by birth he embodies in himself so much of the social thought of Adam Smith, Darwin, Buckle and Spencer, and their emphasis on the inductive and comparative study of social institutions, that his place in English sociology is assured. Indeed, for many years he taught at the University of London together with Houbhouse, and he followed Hobhouse in regarding sociology as the general science of social phenomena and synthesizing such disciplines as economics politics, history, and law. Not a systematic sociologist, he is primarily concerned with social institutions defined as forms of social relationships regulated and sanctioned by society. His masterly studies on marriage and the family, *The Origin of Human Marriage* (1889) and *The History of Human Marriage* (1898, 1921), have received international acclaim. In addition, his studies of beliefs, customs, rituals, and the growth of moral ideas provide an inexhaustible treasure-house to the sociologist. Some of his more important works in these fields are *The Origin and Development of Moral Ideas* (1906, 1912), *Ethical Relativity* (1932), *Christianity and Morals* (1937), *Ritual and Belief in Morocco* (1926) and *Pagan Survivals in Mohammedan Civilization* (1933).

The chief problem with which Westermarck is concerned is the relationship between the growth of morals and the growth of social institutions. His ethical theory stems from Adam Smith, and he makes his starting point the retributive emotions such as resentment and gratitude. As such these emotions are not moral emotions, and they only become so when they are infused with sympathy which enable the individual to experience emotions on behalf of others. This brings about the impartiality and generality of moral judgments which thus reflect the emotions felt by society. His comparative study of social institutions leads him to the conclusion that on the whole moral judgments have become more enlightened—a conclusion at which Hobhouse also arrived although by a different route. Into the question of ethical relativity with which his name is associated and which according to him "implies that there is no objective standard of morality, and objective presupposes universality" we cannot enter here. The whole question appears to be partly one of definition. Westermarck's *Origin and Development of Moral Ideas* is conclusive proof that some actions such as himicide and theft are forbidden, and that generosity and mutual aid are everywhere commended. If this be the case there is universality and an objective standard of morality. Westermarck himself shows that where differences do obtain in moral rules as in suicide or infanticide among differenet people, they may be accounted for by variations in internal conditions, by differences in knowledge as to the nature and consequences of an act due to magical and religious notions, and by differences in the size of the group among whom moral rules are held to apply.

The wide acceptance of his views on the monogamic origin of the family are undoubtedly due to some extent to the "cultural compulsives" of the time. And Robert Briffault's *The Mothers* had a most salutary effect therefore in bringing up the whole problem for reexamination. But it should be noted that the attempt to obtain data in favor of or against original promiscuity by pointing to the sexual relations existing among the apes is not an admissible procedure, and both Briffault and Westermarck are guilty of the error of applying biological categories relevant in the study of animal behavior to complex sociological phenomena. It is oversimplifications of this kind, a rather facile use of the comparative method, and the ready appeal to instincts or similar psychological postulates as causes of social institutions that detract from Westermarck's magnificent labors over half a century.

Like his predecessor Hobhouse in the chair of sociology at the London School of Economics, Morris Ginsberg conceives of sociology as a synoptic science. "The important thing," he maintains, "is to resist the tendency of the social sciences to become isolated from one another, and from general sociology which can surely only flourish by their systematization." (31) His work is the best exemplification of his position, and his wide training in philosophy, biology, and psychology is reflected in it. With Hobhouse and Wheeler he is co-author of the previously noted monograph "The Simpler Peoples" and he is also the author of a critical study of the philosopher Malebranche (*Dialogues on Metaphysics*). In 1921 he published *The Psychology of Society*, a penetrating analysis of social psychology. Here he discusses the concept of instinct, the nature of will and reason, the theory of the social mind, tradition, custom, public opinion, the unity that belongs to different groups such as community and association, and the meaning of racial and national characteristics. Following Hobhouse, he finds that both intellectualists and anti-intellectualists are guilty of a false separation between emotion and intellect which is responsible for the minimization of the role of reason in social life.

If his work, so far, has essentially been a continuation of Hobhouse's sociology, he is critical of its weaknesses in the handling of the comparative method, and the tendency for generalizations based on insufficient data. What is needed now, he suggests, is the employment of the comparative method in a larger and more careful way than was atempted by either Durkheim or Hobhouse, and with greater care in the determination of the units for comparison. He goes on to say, "The extension of the comparative method is of the greatest, importance in any effort to determine the relative role of the economic, political and cultural factors in the history of civilization, and it may well turn out that this problem will receive a

---

31. M. Ginsberg "On the Place of Sociology," *Conference on the Social Sciences*, 1935, p. 12.

BRITISH SOCIOLOGY

different answer in relation to different societies and different periods." (32)

In a paper on "The Scope of Sociology" (33) Ginsberg rejects the limitations offered by Simmel, Vierkandt, and others and maintains that the object of sociology is:

1. To determine the nature or character of the various forms of social groupings and the institutions by which they are regulated and maintained and to trace the line of their growth or development.

2. To determine, by means of the comparative method and as far as possible by the use of quantitative measurement, the inter-relations between institutions and the degree of correlated growth. In this connection the phenomena of diffusion and contact are of the greatest importance.

3. To formulate empirical generalizations or laws of such growth.

4. To interpret these laws in the light of the more ultimate laws of life and mind.

His concrete work has closely followed this formulation, and recognizing the need for more empirical research, he undertook one of the first thorough studies in England on social mobility, the results of which are contained in his paper "The Interchange between Social Classes." (34) His valuable research in the field of social biology is also deserving of mention and "The Claims of Eugenics" and "The Inheritance of Mental Characteristics" are authoritative reviews. Of especial importance are the essays "Causality in the Social Sciences" (35) and the "Concept of Evolution in Sociology." In the latter essay he takes up the position that "the problem of evolution in sociology resolves itself into the question whether, the history of human culture is a continuum within which charges occur in accordance with immanent causality." He concurs with the view "That in some sense elements of culture such as language, religion, science are continua, possessed of a certain unity and immanent nature."

It should be an interesting experience for an American sociologist to compare the heavy and bulky tomes on sociology in this country with Ginsberg's little book Sociology (1934) which concise-

---

32 *Ibid.*, p. 14.
33. "The Scope of Sociology," *Sociological Review*, June, 1927. Later reprinted in *Studies in Sociology*.
34. These and other essays are included in his *Studies in Sociology* (1932).
35. *Proceedings of the Aristotelian Society*, 35: 253-270, 1934-5.

ly and clearly covers the fundamental problems in the subject. He is perhaps still too much under the influence of Hobhouse and, if he has been diffident in publication— his magnum opus is still to come —, as a scholar, teacher and inspirer of his students he is second to none in England.

III

Sociology and the Social Sciences Today. The relationships between general sociology, at long last established as a subject of study, and the other social sciences have become much closer in recent years. The three Conferences on "The Social Sciences" (36) held in London, in 1935, 1936, 1937, in general endorsed this closer co-operation (although not all of the participants were sure as to how this could best be done), and bear eloquent testimony to the work of Hobhouse, Ginsberg, and the Institute of Sociology. To review all the papers and discussions that took place is out of the question, but some of the more important may be noted. In the discussion on History and the Social Sciences, Professor M. Oakeshott denied the possibility of deriving from history any generalizations of the kind which belong to social science, while Professor G. N. Clarke was alarmed by the facile way in which sociologists dealt with such large entities like civilization, race and national character. Dr. M. Postan, speaking of historians, shrewdly observed that "The garb of fictitious concreteness may sometimes be so thick that the underlying implications may remain invisible to the author himself, and many a respectable historian would be shocked to find that he wrote Sociology." (37) As to political science, Professor J. L. Stocks was sceptical of a positive science of sociology, and Professor H. W. Brogan deplored the lack of organizing ideas on the subject. This position was challenged by Professor H. J. Laski, who pointed to the fruitfulness of the Marxian analysis in politics. In economics, the desirability of closer co-operation with sociology was stressed by all the participants, although Professor J. R. Hicks was not too hopeful and thought

---

36. Conference on the Social Sciences: Their Relations in Theory and Teaching. First conference 1935; second, 1936; third, 1937. The reports were issued later by the Institute of Sociology, and though printed are loosely bound, and the pagination irregular. The present author attended these conferences.
37. First Conference, p. 7.

BRITISH SOCIOLOGY

that psychology has most to contribute to sociology at the present time. Professor P. Sargant-Florence urged upon sociologists the desirability to get to know the economist's framework of thought, which in turn should avail itself more and more of statistical methods and analyses. The field of social biology was explored by Dr. J. Needham and S. Zuckerman; anthropology by Dr. R. Firth, Dr. E. E. Evans-Pritchard and Mr. J. Layard; and psychology by Dr. E. Glover, Professor M. Ginsberg, and Professor G. H. Thomson.

In the discussion on sociology Professor A. M. Carr-Saunders looked somewhat askance at the striving for generalization and interpretation so prominent in its main exponents, and he pointed out, that because of this fact many scholars who work in political science, comparative religion, or comparative ethics would refuse to call themselves sociologists. Professor Ginsberg showed that the theoretical position of sociology is much stronger now. He cites Sidgwick's objections to sociology as a science on the grounds that Comte, Spencer and Schaeffle not only contradicted each other but arrived at completely different conclusions, and points out that an analysis of two modern comprehensive systems, those of Durkheim and Hobhouse, would reveal more similarities than differences. Professor K. Mannheim, whose presence in England augurs well for the development of social theory, asserted "that so long as in our reserch work and in our school and academic curricula, we do not introduce sociology as a basic science, so long we shall not be good specialists."

This is undoubtedly also the view of English sociology, and there is undoubtedly a greater trend toward cooperation between general sociology and the social sciences. However, this is not a new trend, but an intensification of something that has distinguished English social thought since the eighteenth century, and that has been called the sociological approach. What was implicit has become more explicit. And this trend is refleced not only in academic works but in art, the novel, and the drama. It is reflected in the *Sociological Review* which has been strenghthened under the editorship of Professor Ginsberg and Mr. A. Farquharson, in the periodicals *Politica, The Modern Quarterly*, and in the series entitled "Modern Sociologists" comprising books on Tylor, Comte, Veblen, Marx and Pareto. It is seen in the special Division of Social and International Relations of Science set up a few years ago by the British Association for the Advancement of Science.

TWENTIETH CENTURY SOCIOLOGY

There is this clear gain, of course, that sociology as a separate discipline has emerged and promises to grow, even though its birth has not yet been recognized by some English thinkers. And that a general sociology is needed now more than ever can hardly be denied in view of the increasing number of the separate social sciences and specialisms. To be useful instruments both for theorical understanding and practical manipulation the social sciences cannot remain isolated but must be brought together.

In the initial stages, there are dangers in such a procedure: dangers of discursiveness and diffusiveness, of which English sociology has not completely rid itself. It has rightly combined philosophy with science, but not always in the right porportions. The great promise of sociology inherent in the eighteenth century was not fulfilled for reasons which we have already considered. And this was in many ways unfortunate, since Spencer's influence deflected attention from history in which eighteenth century social thought was strong, to biology and biological explanations for complex social phenomena, so that for a time the survival of the fittest became synonymous with the survival of the richest. There were numerous ties with psychology, ethnography and anthropology, but too few with history. Preoccupied with problems of the social organism, the general will and the social mind, it ignored Spencer's dictum, which he too ignored, that "what Biography is to Anthropology, History is to Sociology." It used the comparative method, but not always critically, for the study of primitive societies, but historical civilizations and contemporary society it overlooked. It was left to Toynbee to point out that one of the most important tasks facing sociology is to study history.

The dominating role of the concepts of evolution, stages of evolution, progress, and development may possibly derive from the evenness of English historical development, from a social gradualness that not even the last war upset. On the other hand, the concept of social classes, class war, imperialism, planning and social engineering have only recently begun to receive serious attention. As social problems came up, they were fitted into the traditional framework, and that is why, as we have already seen, so much of what in other countries belongs to sociology is in England a part of anthropology, politics, economics or psychology. The growth of systematic sociology, and the urgency for its need, seems to reflect the increasing functional interconnectedness of the segments and institutions of social life, the trend toward administrative centrali-

BRITISH SOCIOLOGY

zation, and the monopoly state. The present war, with its profound economic and political changes, may be turning point in English sociology. But whether it will stimulate it or retard it depends on the social transformations the peace will bring about.

SELECTED BIBLIOGRAPHY

Barker, Ernest, *Political Thought in England from Herbert Spencer to the Present Day,* (London: Williams and Norgate, 1915).

Barnes, Harry Elmer, "The Fate of Sociology in England," *Proceedings of the American Sociological Society,* 12: 26-46, 1927.

Barnes, Harry Elmer, and Howard Becker, *Social Thought from Lore to Science,* vol. II, *Sociological Trends throughout the World,* (Boston, etc.: D. C. Heath and Co., 1938), Chap. XXI, "British Sociology.

Bartlett, F. C., Moris Ginsberg and Others, eds., *The Study of Society; Method and Problems,* (London: The Macmillan and Co., 1939).

Cattell, R. B., J. Cohen, and R. M. W. Travers, *Human Affairs,* (London: The Macmillan and Co., 1937).

Ginsberg, Morris, and J. A. Hobson, *L. T. Hobhouse,* (London: G. Allen and Unwin, 1931).

Ginsberg, Morris, "The Life and Work of Edward Westermarck," *Sociological Review,* 32: 1-28, January-April, 1940.

Ginsberg, Morris, *Sociology,* (London: Butterworth, 1934).

Harper, E. B., "Sociology in England," *Social Forces,* 11: 335-342, 1943.

Hearnshaw, F. J. C., ed., *The Social and Political Ideas of Some Representative Thinkers of the Victorian Age,* (London: Harrap, 1933).

Hobhouse, L. T., *Social Development,* (New York: Henry Holt and Co., 1924).

Marett, R. R., *Tylor,* (London: Chapman and Hall, 1936).

Palmer, V. M., "Impressions of Sociology in Great Britain," *American Journal of Sociology,* 32: 756-761, 1927.

Rockow, Lewis, *Contemporary Political Thought in England,* (London: Parsons, 1925).

Rumney, J., *Herbert Spencer's Sociology,* (London: Williams and Norgate, 1934).

Rumney, J., *The Science of Society,* (London: Duckworth, 1938).

Wallas, Graham, *The Great Society,* (New York: The Macmillan Co., 1920).

Jay Rumney, B. Sc. (Econ.), Ph. D. (Soc., London School of Economics), is Professor of Sociology at the University of Newark. Professor Rumney was graduated from the London School of Economics in 1926 and received his Ph. D. from the same institution in 1933. Formerly Rockefeller Travelling Fellow, 1930-1932; Institute of Social Research, London, and the University of London, 1933-1938; Institute for Advanced Study, Princeton, New Jersey, 1938-1940. Publications include: *Herbert Spencer's Sociology: A Study of the History of Social Thought,* 1934, and *The Science of Society: An Introduction to Sociology,* 1938. Writing at present on the sociology of war.

CHAPTER XX

GERMAN SOCIOLOGY

by

ALBERT SALOMON

I

Introduction: The Principles of Classification. We are used to classifying philosophy and the sciences according to their systematic problems or to the context of types of thinking. From this point of view it would be as ridiculous to speak of German physics as it would be to discuss the characters of American or French philosophies. However there is a principle of classification according to national differentiations. If we take this principle seriously, it indicates a scientific or philosophical frame of reference as established by a national society within which individual developments of universal problems take place. The national differentiations of scientific thinking are modern and historical phenomenon. They are as unintelligible to the medieval philosopher as to the moralist of the Enlightenment who are living for the universality of truth. The modern societies have stressed the national differences in thought and in reflection, since they have actively participated in the government of their own affairs. These trends toward considering

GERMAN SOCIOLOGY

the work of the mind as manifestation of national societies are modern indeed. They came into existence with Romanticism and the social movements of the nineteenth century. Sociology, in particular, appears from its beginnings, as the manifestation of a specific social and historical situation of French society. The historian of ideas is justified when he speaks of French sociology in order to articulate the specific significance of the Saint Simonian School and the work of Comte. These works do established a frame of reference within which the scientific developments that we call "French sociology" come into existence. There are scientists who may have joined a different frame of reference although they live in the French society. They simply do not belong to the national frame of reference. The German frame of reference is analogous and radically different from the French one. It can be described as the interacting and intertwined systems of Hegel and Marx. Within these two systems of dialectical spiritualism and materialism some German scholars have contributed to sociology and have created what may be called "German sociology."

It is the thesis of this chapter that, in Germany, there is no sociology, but sociologists. In America and in France sociology has an objective function in the context of the respective societies as an instrument of pragmatic enlightenment and of moral education. Sociology is a social institution. In Germany, the climate of opinion was political and opposed to anything that had to do with an independent society. Sociology became the concern of some scholars who, starting from different fields of research such as history, economics, philosophy, finally met in the development of sociology as theory and method. What has been the reason for their restlessness? Why did not they remain true to their special sciences? They were united by three common experiences which induced them to transcend the traditional scheme of sciences and to establish a theory and method of sociology. The first experience was the shock that they felt in face of the gigantic systems of determinism which Hegel and Marx had presented. These sociologists revolted against doctrines which assumed to know the meaning of the social process. They revolted in the spirit of the positive sciences which were imbued with a deep distrust in metaphysics and with humility regarding the infinite variety of experiences and events. They were willing to recognize the unity and the comprehensive character of the social process. However they wanted to discover the scientific tools which made it possible to escape the iron necessity of radical determinism. The second experience was the vision of the rapidly expanding rational institutions in the industrial world and the growing pressure of conditions imposed upon the individual. The third experience was the awareness of the problematic character of the thinking human person, of its individuality, of its solitude in a world of collective action. These three experiences made it possible that some scholars in different fields turned to a new science of society and of social conduct. This German sociology may be labelled the sociology of liberalism in despair as over against the optimistic liberalism of the Scottish School. It is important to know these origins in order to understand the prevailing interest in theory and the complete lack of all descriptive and practical studies. Under these circumstances it is obvious that this German sociology has mainly influenced philosophy, psychology and the history of ideas.

The Revolt against Hegel. We distinguish two trends in the rise of German sociology. The one comes into existence in the revolt against Hegel, the other one in the reexamination of the work of Karl Marx.

Hegel was attacked for three reasons. First the scholars who were brought up in the spirit of positive and empirical sciences revolted against the metaphysical arrogance. Second, some individuals were convinced that the modern scholars had lost the religious or spiritual horizon that made possible the belief into our knowledge of an objective meaning. Third, some scientists attacked the dehumanizing effect of the Hegelian system in which the human person was a puppet of the absolute mind. In this revolt some thinkers reflected on the very being of man in the Here and Now of the historical situation. In a true humanistic spirit these men made an effort to reestablish the world of meaning and significance by a complete description of man in his lifeworld, i.e. in history.

Jacob Burckhardt. Jacob Burckhardt had a chair for history in his native Basel. He is wrongly labeled a historian. His works which deal with certain periods of history are not concerned with historical causation. The profound American reviewer of his *Civilization of the Renaissance in Italy* (1) was well aware that the purpose of the author is not a historical presentation, but a description and interpretation of the variety of human behavior patterns in a historical situation. The reviewer did not know that Burckhardt

---

1. New York Herald, October 18, 1880, (Henry or Brook Adams).

had dealt with a similar period of transition in his first book on the epoch of Constantine the Great. He understood just the same that the author purposely selected a period of transition and disintegration. Such periods are fascinating for the modern observer who is aware of the problematic character of the modern person in a world that had lost unity and significance in its social context. Burckhardt selected such periods and situations in which nothing was taken for granted but the actuality of the human being in action. He describes the variety of human attitudes, of social behavior patterns of political, moral, and religious conduct as a phenomenology of human self-realization. This description is based on the humanistic assumption that in times of radical transition men are guided by their spontaneous and independent characters rather than by established social values. It has the philosophical implication that we know of human beings only as living in historical action or in the total immanence of the Here and Now. In this enterprise Burckhardt has discovered a new science: historical anthropology. It is an empirical division of a sociological theory. His works are destined to present the scientific justification of Pascal's thesis of the grandeur and misery of man. However Burckhardt's thesis is scientific, not theological. It is the response to Hegel's intellectualistic hybris that knows everything about the meaning of the world. What we are capable of knowing according to Burckhardt is the bravery and suffering, the heroism and martyrdom, the acting and being acted upon of the individual human being. We do not know an objective meaning beyond the elevation or degradation of the human subject. However we are able to establish a comprehensive phenomenology of the variety of human experiences and of human acts and attitudes which point out the range of human self-realization. It is a scientific and empirical investigation into the historical character of man or into human nature in history. Burckhardt has given a systematic and theoretical conclusion of the historical anthropology in his *Reflections on History*. (2) He has described the human historicity as the very constitution of man. He has elaborated a structural context of power, religion, and creative intelligence which are interdependent with each other and appear in a variety of changing concatenations. He analyzes the antinomies of human history as

---

2. *Force and Freedom, Reflections on History,* ed., by J. Hastings Nichols, (New York: Pantheon Books, 1943).

the perennial trends toward order, continuity, duration and the lasting tendencies toward independence, growth, and progress.

Burckhardt's work still remains relevant for philosophy as long as philosophical anthropology is a concern of the philosopher. It is still a powerful suggestion for the sociologists who are interested in elaborating historical sociology. It is true that his method cannot be imitated, but he has suggested a scheme of historical phenomenology that can be used for sociological analyses. His historical imagination and vision is unsurpassed. His philosophical intent remains valid. (3)

Wilhem Dilthey (1833-1912). It is indicative of the climate in which the revolt against Hegel took place that Burckhardt and Dilthey had rebelled against the religious traditions of Protestantism as well. Both were sons of patrician Protestant families in which the ministry was considered to be a social and moral responsibility of the oldest sons. Both had given up the theological career because they were aware that Christianity was merely a historical phenomenon in a world which had lost its spiritual and transcendental frame of reference. Both shifted to history and a philosophy of history. Under the modern conditions we can only establish a scientific philosophy when we take for granted the total immanence of man, his complete historicity. Dilthey has succeeded in integrating the sociological approach into the descriptive phenomenology of the Gestalts of historical life as far as sociology searches for the recurrent and typical patterns of conduct in the social process. Dilthey escaped the dilemma of idealism and of sociologism. He has overcome the dualism of the subject-object relationship and that of individualism vs. collectivism. He was aware of the stream of experience and of thought as a psychic ensemble. His revolt against the naturalistic psychologies of Taine and John Stuart Mill led him toward a philosophy of life in which the traditional philosophical and sociological alternatives were canceled. Philosophy of total life establishes the principle of total immanence. Dilthey postulates as the hypothesis of his approach that we cannot retreat beyond life. We are forced to understand life out of

---

3. Jacob Burckhardt, *Gesamtausgabe*, (Berlin and Leipzig: 1930-33, 14 vols.); American translation: *The Civilization of the Renaissance in Italy*. On Burckhardt: the best introduction is the preface by J. Hastings Nichols to the edition of *Force and Freedom*. See also Albert Salomon, "Crisis, History and the Image of Man," *Review of Politics*, 2: 415-437, October, 1940.

itself. His is the ambition to turn the wisdom of the great moralists and of the poets into scientific knowledge and thought. Life and world are his fundamental categories. They do not express any dualism. They are the opposite sides of the whole. Life appears as the unity of Self and world. It is more than subjectivity, it is life in relations, in perspectives, in action. Self and world are correlative to each other.

Philosophy has a specific function in this world of experience. It becomes the interpretation of the Self and of the variety of his experiences. This philosophy points toward action and the control of life. For we recognize ourselves only in action, when we meet the resistance of the external world. Human life is the dynamic action of men in history. Philosophy of life is the self-interpretation of man on the various layers and in the different spheres of historical existence. This is Humanism as philosophy. Dilthey refers the objects of the mind to the very acts of their creation. He does not speak of religion, but of piety, he deals not with poetry, but with the imagination, he analyses the types of human self-interpretation, not of philosophy. The variety of experiences and the diversity of these acts can merely be understood when the philosopher takes into account the sociological determinants of these human attitudes and of their changes. His books and essays which deal with poetry and criticism, the articles on the types of *Weltanschauung* and the works on romantic religion are model cases of a responsible and cautious use of the sociological method in the history of ideas.

Dilthey is the German William James. His work is Humanism and Radical Empiricism in his search for the scientific and objective standards of the social sciences which must be different from those of the natural sciences. His investigations on descriptive psychology and on the structure of the historical world have established the avenues which lead toward Gestalt psychology and the descriptive method of phenomenology. Dilthey has made an effort toward discovering the categories of historical life. He has analysed the structure of human experience, the context of significance, the temporality as destructive and constructive element, the potency of creative action and the establishment of freedom by the knowledge of the increasing set of determinations. He has devoted his efforts toward finding out the scientific conceptions that make it possible to connect the analysis of experience with the expressions of the experiences and their understanding. Like G. H. Mead he has wrestled with the problems of communications and the participation in a common nature which would enable the social scientist to b⸱ as objective as the naturalist. (4)

The work of Dilthey's remains as fascinating as that of William James. Both authors have an experience of the fathomless character of human life and of the never ending human efforts to throw bridges of reason and mind over the abyss of the irrational life. Both have a rare range of experiences and an unusual ability to express their visions. In particular. Dilthey's investigations into the changing attitudes in religion and in poetical imagination remain of lasting value for the sociologist who is interested in these fields. His attempts to present the history of philosophy as the various perpectives of human self-interpretation have very important sociological implications.

His methodological writings and his efforts toward establishing the foundations of a scientific theory of interpretation are still suggestive and useful. They are closer to the attempts of the phenomenological and Gestalt-school to find the scientific theory for the social sciences than are the essays by Max Weber. Dilthey's ideas and insights are not yet completely exhausted.

Hans Freyer. In this connection a scholar must be mentioned who has considerably promoted the progress of sociology as a science, in transforming the Hegelian system into a science of reality. Hans Freyer (5) has continued the work of Lorenz von Stein who had already discovered the revolutionary function of the new science of society as the theory of the social revolution. Freyer starts with the description of the structures which make the social process articulate. They are dynamic and living contexts because they consist of the mutual relationships of the concrete persons. The concepts of social structures are not formal categories. They have specific and articulate psychological connotations. They are historical and trans-historical likewise. They arise in a certain sequence. On the

---

4. Wilhelm Dilthey: *Gesammelte Werke*, (Berlin: 1914-1935, 12 vols.), in particular, vol. V, *Aufgaben einer beschreibenden Psychologie*, vol. VII, *Der Aufbau der geschichtlichen Welt*, vol. VIII, *Weltanschauungslehre*, and vol. IV, *Jugendgeschichte Hegels;* see also: *Die Jugend Schleiermachers,* (Berlin: 1922), *Das Erlebnis und die Dichtung,* (Berlin: 1910), *Von deutscher Dichtung und Musik,* (Berlin: 1933).

5. Hans Freyer: *Soziologie als Wirklichkeitswissenschaft* (1930), *Einleitung in die Soziologe,* (Leipzig: 1931), *Die politische Insel,* (Leipzig: 1936), *Theorie des objektiven Geistes,* 2nd ed. (1928).

other hand, they can coexist in time and be intertwined in the same social phenomenon when they have come into existence.

Freyer insists on the concept of historicity as a constitutive category of sociology. There is no universal character of society, nor is there a formal and empty concept of society as such. There are merely stages in the social process. All social forms are historical in the perspective of their origins. All structural patterns are dynamic and open to a variety of concatenations. They may be intertwined and interdependent in a hierarchical context of layers. As science of reality, sociology points to the conflicts and antagonisms of the contemporary societies. Sociology elaborates the potential solutions according to the strength and power appearing in the divergent trends of the social structures. In this sense Freyer calls sociology a science of the ethos that takes into consideration the actuality of values and of evaluation in the processes of social action.

Freyer's achievement was a remarkable one and of high standing. He has cautiously applied results of Dilthey's and of Max Weber's within the Hegelian traditions. His conviction that there is only a political solution to the social antagonisms induced him to be in favor of the Nazis. He remains a good sociologists just the same.

The Revolt against Marx. The second trend in the rise of German sociological thinking can be described as the reexamination and the critical analysis of the sociological work of Marx. As in the case of Hegel, the scholars attacked the absolute determinism of the system and questioned its scientific validity. They turned their attention to the specific and articulate problems which are relevant for the constitution of a society. They made a great effort to discover the fundamentals of societal relationships and of social structures in order to understand the dynamic problems of social change and of social evolution.

Ferdinand Toennies (1855-1936): *An Approach toward the Scientific Analysis of Social Structures.* We cannot discuss German sociology intelligently without considering the fundamental work by Ferdinand Toennies. He has established sociology as a science in its own right. It can be described as the scientific enterprise that analyses and describes the constitutive social structures as social and as historical phenomena. This pioneering effort was the positive critique which Toennies offered in order to preserve the scientific truth of Marx vision, and to eliminate the dogmatic and unscientific formulation. Toennies was a liberal socialist. He had devoted his main effort toward investigating the structure of capitalistic and non-capitalistic societies. In the analyses of the social fundamentals, he discovered that two basic structural types recur in the historical process. He calls these types community and society. They result from two fundamental modes of will-relationships. He distinguishes the essential and the arbitrary will. The arbitrary will expresses the subjective and egocentric intentions of an individual or a specific group. This attitude is the basis for the structure of society. Society is the structure of the pragmatic and rationalistic, urban and industrial civilization. In this civilization all societal relationships have continuity and duration by legal and rational agreements and contracts. Community is the opposite structural type. Here all societal relationships are united by the prevalence of non-conscious and and sentimental bonds. These types of social structure are historical and trans-historical. They are historical because they appear in a certain sequence of time. There is no society which is not preceded by a community. They are trans-historical because they can coexist and be intertwined in many institutions as family, party, church, State. The structures are psychological and trans-psychological. They are psychological as far as all social institutions are composed of living human beings. They are sociological (trans-psychological) as far as the continuity and duration of collective structures rests with inter-subjective bonds. Toennies' types of will structure present a premonition of a phenomenological description in Husserl's sense, a social phenomenology *avant la lettre*.

Essential will appears as the unifying bond in the structure of community. It establishes itself as the integration of all organic relationships as authority, piety, loyalty in primary groups, in particular. Arbitrary will creates all rational planned and well organized institutions, chiefly the technical, economic and political organization of the industrial and urban societies. These modern societis have found their adequate sociological interpretation in the secular Natural Law as developed in the work of Hobbes. Toennies devoted much time to presenting the thesis that Hobbes is the father of modern sociology. Toennies frequently stated that sociology as a science is going to be the substitute for the past Natural Law with the tools of the modern sciences. According to Toenniës, Hobbes created the perfect sociological theory of the structure of society, the Law of Nature of society. Toennies had the ambition to make sociology complete and perfect by adding the Natural Law of community. (*Gemeinschaftsnaturrecht*). His analyses of mores and folkways, of public opinion and of philosophical terminologies, serve the purpose of making more articulate the elements that constitute community. Toennies stresses the primacy of the We-relationships in the structure of community. He develops a casuistry of the we-relationships in space and time, as neighborhood in rural and urban districts, as the sequence of generations in time, as family-clan-nation relations. Toennies is aware that he can establish the sociological theory of community only on the basis of the wholistic approach. (6)

Toennies' work has been recognized and applied by many sociologists. Boas and Sorokin have acknowledged the importance of his work. (7) Today we appreciate the work as a pioneering effort. However, Toennies limited the soundness of his theory of the will structures by confusing these fundamental tendencies with instincts and habits. What he had in mind was a presentation of the typical dualisms of the structure of human experience. Toennies wanted to clarify the opposite types of that experience. He was of the opinion that human beings organize their experiences either under the spell of the whole or under the pressure of self-centered desires and ambitions. He is mistaken when he calls these modes of will "psychological." They point to a phenomenological method that reduces the contingent, historical, and individual moments in order to discover the pure phenomena of fundamental structures. Furthermore, he was wrong in limiting the types to two structures. A philosopher, Schmalenbach made a remarkable improvement when he criticized Toennies' scheme and discovered a third category. (8) Schmalenbach developed the thesis that the concept of community

---

6. Toennies: *Gemeinschaft und Gesellschaft*, (1887, 2nd ed. 1912), tr. by Charles P. Loomis as *Fundamental Concepts of Sociology*, (New York: American Book Co., 1940); *Kritik der oeffentlichen Meinung*, (Berlin: 1926), *Fortschritt und soziale Entwicklung*, (Karlsruhe: 1926), *Soziologische Studien und Kritiken*, (Jena: 1924-28, 3 vols.), *Die Sitte*, (Frankfurt: 1909), *Hobbes, Leben und Lehre*, 3rd ed., (Stuttgart: 1925), *Philosophische Terminologie*, (Leipzig: 1906). See also "In Memoriam Ferdinand Toennies" by Albert Salomon, *Social Research*, 3: 248-363, August, 1936.

7. See *Reine und angewandte Sociologie, eine Festgabe fuer Ferdinand Toennies*, (Leipzig: 1936).

8. Herman Schmalenbach, "Uber die Kategorie des Bundes" in Die Dioskuren, *Jahrbuch fur Geisteswissenschaften*, vol. I, 1922.

as defined by Toennies is unsatisfactory. He rightly blames Toennies for having confused the non-conscious but rational bonds of traditional allegiances, authorities, and established standards that are taken for granted with the emotional bonds of spiritual and religious loyalties. Schmalenbach proposes an additional category "Communion" that makes articulate the specific character of emotional decisions and voluntary subjection under a principle of salvation that makes men friends and brethren. It is different from the rationality of the traditional and established ways of life that are the characteristics of community.

This modification of Toennies is valid and a progress. It is still more valuable as an attempt to reconsider the whole problem of social structures. It is impossible to found a comprehensive typology on the basis of the dichotomy: rational-irrational. We need a new principle of inter-subjectivity and of reciprocal perspectives for describing the variety of possible structures.

Max Weber (1864-1920): *Historical-Interpretative Sociology.* Max Weber, the historian of law, the political scientist and economist, became a sociologist in a long and intense dialogue with the ghost of Karl Marx. His treatise on sociology bears the title *Wirtschaft und Gesellschaft.* It indicates that the main purpose of the author is to reexamine the Marxian sociological thesis. Weber analyzes the sociological problems of religion, of social control, of law, and of economic processes. He is always concerned with two aspects of the problem. First, he is eager to state scientifically that all these social phenomena have been relevant in some way to the economic processes. Second, he stresses the point that all social strata have a dynamics of their own and a specific autonomy that are superior to all economic influences.

This objection to Marx in the name of empirical science is the one aspect of his sociological approach. The second aspect of Weber's critique is the reinvestigation of the total historical determinism. His studies on economic ethics and the religions of the world are a gigantic and encyclopedic effort to refute this determinism as unverifiable by scientific research. Weber's main purpose is to clarify the individual and spontaneous character of the emerging capitalism rather than to assert a prevalence of spiritual as over against material powers. Weber's thesis is that modern capitalism is the product of individual historical circumstances, not the product of an inescapable historical necessity. Weber opposes to Marx's thesis the counter-thesis that there is potential freedom in social action. "The puritans wanted to be men of a calling, we have to be." This potential freedom becomes actual in times of transition when men question everything. In such situations, men are capable of deciding what course to take according to their own vision and evaluations. This is the element of freedom in history. This first response to Marx implies Weber's second thesis; in such situations of crisis and of potential freedom, the religious requirements for social action are relevant for all spheres of social life. Weber's painstaking research has carefully elaborated the magic, ritual, moral, and religious elements that prevented the rise of industrial capitalism in various civilizations, although political and economic conditions were rather favorable to establishing these forms of economic organization.

These empirical investigations on religion have established the thesis that the autonomous development of this sphere takes place according to the logic that is immanent in its material principle. They have, furthermore, suggested the thesis that the reality of the autonomous sphere is more powerful than its social conditions. Finally, they have developed the categories that are the pillars of Weber's sociological system: the concepts of social routine and of charisma. All forces that make for duration, stability and continuity of the social institutions are those of social routine. They present the elements of preservation, tradition, and legality. They are the manifestations of a perennial attitude of conservatism. The first dynamic element in history is "charisma." It can be defined as the belief of a group that a certain individual has the qualifications of a savior in the religious, social, or political spheres. According to Weber's definition it is irrelevant for the sociologist whether this belief is correct or not. The charisma is the one revolutionary force in history. It is destructive and also constructive. It destroys institutions that have lost their meanings and reestablishes new ones which are in conformity with the social process.

The second dynamic and revolutionary force in history is rationalism. Weber uses the term in a specific sense to indicate the pragmatic and scientific intelligence that is directed toward establishing the rule of man in the world. Weber's thesis is that the dualism between rationalism and the charismatic irrationalism is the very dialectics of history. This is the thesis that Weber opposes to Marx. It implies a material philosophy of history. There is an irreversible progress of rationalization in all spheres of life.

Potential counter-forces appear in charismatic leaders and may alter the course of history. This spontaneous growth of freedom is restricted to the moments of crisis. Weber's philosophy of history is more radical and more realistic than that of Marx. Weber is more radical than Marx because the inescapable logic and necessity of the technological-rational development of the modern world is as valid and fateful for socialism as it is for the capitalistic world. He is more realistic than Marx because he does not see any hope for a world of freedom under the conditions of the technical rationalism that is the destiny of the modern world. For this reason we may call Weber the bourgeois Marx. This term indicates the overwhelming grandeur of his historical analysis and the defeatist scientifism of a scholar who does not recognize the changing social ethos that makes it possible to control the fateful rationalism and to use it for the common good.

The principles of Weber's philosophy of history are fundamental for his sociological analyses. In his discussion of social control, we find again the dualism of rationalism and irrationalism, of charismatism and institutionalism, as the basis of his typology. The institutional types of control which present the situations of routine appear as traditionalism and legality. Traditionalism is defined as a social order that is based on the established values and authorities of the past. Legality is the rational consensus that recognizes an impersonal legal order as valid and binding for the members of the group. The legitimate order as the typical form of modern government appears in its actuality as rational administration. Weber calls this form of administration "bureaucracy." Bureaucracy means the rule by experts and specialists. Their rule is the most efficient management of social affairs as over against the administration by patricians and politicians. The emphasis on bureaucracy is the empirical justification of the philosophy of the progress of technical rationalism. It appears, in particular, in periods of transition from a charismatic form of control to its established everyday routine — institutions. The rise of a charismatic movement cannot be deduced from a set of social determinants; it can only be explained in terms of the conditions under which it succeeded or failed. Its tranfer into the everyday routine, however, is to a large extent the economic problem of adjusting the followers and partisans to the social institutions, and to provide continuous incomes, positions, and rewards for them. The lasting interaction between charismatic and institutional behavior is the nucleus of history.

The sociology of law is centered around the same dualism of rationalism and irrationalism, which appears in this sphere as the formal and material qualities of the law. Weber stresses the point that the development of a legal profession has created logical rationality and systematic thinking as the constructive elements of legal thought. The developments in the legal sphere are conditioned by the different characters of political organization, by the dynamic relations between the religious and profane institutions, and by the specific character of the jurist-patricians, which is largely determined by the political structure. Legal rationality is a product of the West. Although economic conditions have supported that process in the West, they have never determined the evolution which is primarily the result of the political pragmatism and rationalism of the Occident. As in all other analyses Weber stresses the relative autonomy of the respective spheres and the primacy of political as over against economic conditions.

Weber's analysis of the town is a model case for the thesis of his historical sociology. It is an ideal introduction to urban sociology. Weber presents the sociological perspectives that make it possible to unite the economic, political, and administrative theories on the evolution of the town and of township. The town is the origin of civilization and of continuous social institutions. It is the organiaztion of social peace and of legality. Weber never ceases to emphasize the military and political conditions and motives in the development of urban institutions. Even the superiority of the economic classes in the Italian cities of the later Middle Ages becomes a political reality merely by the integrated power that revolted against the feudal-patrician rentiers.

Weber has established a new field of sociology in these analyses: historical sociology. He has investigated the strata of religion, of law, of political control and of urban organization in their interactions and interdependences. He has pointed out that we can understand the specific character and function of the various spheres when we refer them to their specific frame of reference. He has discovered that there are institutional centers and structural units in every society around which the other spheres tend to gravitate. All these structured spheres of social existence develop a dynamism of their individual form which constantly meets with the pressure of the environment.

We may summarize the result of Weber's historical sociology in the following way: First, there is no general denominator that explains the social process as a whole. Rather we observe as sociologists a changing hierarchy of determinants according to the individual constellation in the development of history. There have been periods in which magical and religious needs controled social action in politics and economic life. There have been other times when politics or economics prevailed; second, this moving kaleidoscope of conditions depends upon the external pressure of the environment and upon the inner pressure of the forces that are inherent in the dynamic context of conditions. This means third, that the inner logic of the individual spheres of the social process has an autonomy of its own and is independent of the social context. This sociological research in the field of universal history made it possible to construct a general theory of social action according to the motives of the agents that come into existence under certain social conditions. "Interests (material and ideal) and not ideas govern the immediate acts of man. But the world views created by ideas have often served as switchmen who have opened the tracks upon which the dynamics of interests push foreward social action." Weber's typology of social action on the basis of the historical sociology is closer to the formal sociology than to his concrete historical investigations. He classifies the types according to the diminishing degree of rationality or to the increasing degree of irrationality. This is as problematic a classification as the formalization of the category "interest" so that it actually covers all acts and attitudes of human conduct.

Weber was one of the last encyclopaedic minds and a genius of historical vision. His critique of Marx remains a progress in scientific sociology. The historical sociology has opened new avenues toward a historical anthropology. However he was not aware of all the implications of the idea of the frame of reference and of the insight into the whole and the unity of the historical process. The sociology of religion will probably be the weakest part of the great work. The main objections, however, refer to the methodology which is to be dealt with in another essay of this symposium. May I only draw the attention of the student of Weber to the fact that Weber actually applies a different method where he practices his historical

GERMAN SOCIOLOGY

sociology from that which he has so carefully proposed in his methodological writings. (9)

Weber's Diversified Influence. Max Weber's efforts to reconcile history with sociology had many repercussions. His work suggested many new and specific ways of emulating his pioneering work.

Alfred Weber, his brother and a professor of economics, was induced by the work of Max Weber to reexamine critically the categories of the Comtian philosophy of history or sociology. He calls his enterprise *Kultursoziologie.* His empirical investigations of some historical structures of the ancient world brought him to the conviction that as scientists we cannot know anything about the meaning of the historical process. However we are able to develop a theory of historical structures and of the laws that rule the different layers of historical existence. Historical existence is composed of three processes. The social process establishes the frame of reference in which the living human beings cooperate and work out the institutions which make possible the continuity of society. It follows the laws of growth and decline. The process of civilization is the sphere of progress in reason and technical capacity. It is under the law of continuous growth. The process of culture is the sphere of the intellectual and spiritual creations by which men establish the unity of their worlds as contexts of meaning. They are perennial and are not tied up with a specific law. For this reason there is a multivariety of historical structures in spite of the universal elements of their constitution. For these three processes are interdependent in quite different moments of their respective movements.

This analysis of the typical structures of historical processes is a very valuable addition to Max Weber's historical sociology. MacIver (10) has recognized its significance for the theory of social change. (11)

Weber's studies in the sociology of religion have provoked a work that is considered to be fundamental for the development of a

---

9. Max Weber: *Wirtschaft und Gesellschaft,* (Tuebingen: 1922), *Gesammelte Aufsaetze zur Religionssoziologie,* (Tuebingen: 1921, 3 vols.), *Gesammelte Aufsaetze zur Wissenschaftslehre,* (Tuebingen: 1921, 3 vols.), *Gessammelte Aufsaetze zur Sozial und Wirtschaftsgeschichte* (1924).

10. Robert M. MacIver, "The Historical Pattern of Social Change," *Journal of Social Philosophy,* 2: 35-54, October, 1936.

11. Alfred Weber: *Ideen zur Staats-und Kultursoziologie,* (Leipzig: 1927), *Kulturgeschichte als Kultursoziologie,* (Leiden: 1935).

sociology of religion. Ernst Troeltsch (1865-1923) wrote the *Social Teachings of the Christian Churches* under the influence of Weber. He has applied Weber's sociological categories to the sphere of Christian religion without giving up the special character of the religious phenomenon as such. Thus far he escapes Weber's sociologism that makes his effort problematic. Troeltsch starts from the hypothesis that we can define the Christian religion as a religious phenomenon per se. It is a very complex object. It includes eschatological, mystical, moral, sacramental, and philosophical elements. This synthetic constitution makes possible a historical development of religion as determined by the characters of the groups which carry on and spread the one or the other aspect of the gospel. Urban societies have promoted the moral and pragmatic teachings of the Christian religion, the rural and military societies have always a preference for the sacramental and magical elements, the intellectuals are favorable to the mystical traditions. It is the merit of Troeltsch to have analyzed the life of the Christian religion in its social development and on the diverse layers of the social process. However this merit is considerably limited by the inadequacy of his theological scholarship. His chapter on Luther, in particular, is very unsatisfactory. (12)

The influence of Max Weber was also felt very strongly among the scholars who were deeply influenced by Marx. Emil Lederer (1882-1939) has reexamined his Marxist position in the light of Weber's ruthless realism. His sociological analysis of the new middle classes is a valuable correction of Marx's theory of increasing proletarization. His description of the social-psychological constitution of the contemporary era presents the thesis that the social attitudes in any period are decisively affected by influences emanating from the social sphere. In many essays he has substituted the category "social" as the "ensemble of human reciprocity" for the Marxian use of the concept "economic." In particular, his essay on the problems of a sociology of culture is a very suggestive attempt to show the limits within which a sociology of the arts and of poetry is possible; he himself has applied his method to the sociological interpretation of modern art. His last work is a contribution to the sociological analysis of the totalitarian State. Here he reconsidered socialist theories regarding collectivism and the classless society.

---

12. Ernst Troeltsch, *The Social Teaching of the Christian Churches*, (New York: The Macmillan Co., 1931, 2vols.); Eugene Lyman, "Ernst Troeltsch's Philosophy of History," *Philosophical Review*, 41: 443-465, September, 1932.

GERMAN SOCIOLOGY

His analysis of the social function of articulate, responsible group organizations as opposed to amorphous masses is an important contribution to the phenomenology of the totalitarian State. (13)

In this connection I should mention two important contributions to the sociology of poetry and literature that bear witness to the productive merging of Marx and Max Weber. The articles by Georg von Lukacs have the great merit of having indicated the possibilities of interpreting the changes and transformations of literary forms in the light of the changing ethos and horizon of the modern societies. (11)

The same productive synthesis between Marx and Weber is visible in the notorious work of Karl Mannheim that will be dealt with in another section of this symposium.

Among the opponents of Marx the liberal Oppenheimer has a special position. He certainly is much nearer to Comte and to Proudhon than to Hegel and Marx. For this reason he can be mentioned only briefly in this context. In his encyclopaedic theory of sociology he has emphasized the point that force is an organizing element in creating legal and social institutions. He has elaborated the thesis by Gumplowicz that the State is the product of military conquest. Military conquest is one means of satisfying economic needs. In the pursuit of this thought Oppenheimer develops the theory of the two means: the economic and the political. He discovered the dualism of these means in all strata of social action. He strongly stressed the point that all monopolies are relative to the political, not to the economic means. Likewise competition is not a purely economic category and shares in the dualism of the social means. Peaceful competition prevails in the individual economic struggle. Hostile competition results from the political means and creates all kinds of monopolies. It is Oppenheimer's merit to have stated that the modern sociologists have exclusively dealt with competition and control while they have neglected the only category that will make it possible to preserve freedom in the world of technical-economic solidarity, namely the category of cooperation. A society that is based on the free cooperation of a variety of special groups will destroy all monopolies and establish order by scientific thinking.

---

13. Emil Lederer: *The New Middle Class*, WPA Project 165-97-6999-6027, (New York: 1937); "Aufgaben einer Kultursoziologie," *Erinnerungsgabe fuer Max Weber*, vol. 2 pp. 145-172; "Kunst und Zeit," *Die Neue Rundschau*, Berlin, 1922; *The State of the Masses*, (New York: W. W. Norton and Co., 1940).

TWENTIETH CENTURY SOCIOLOGY

The work of Openheimer (14) is the work of a man of genius who is surrounded by a profound solitude in the German environment that is simply not the life-world of his thinking. In France, his work would fit neatly into the process of sociological thought that runs from Comte to Proudhon.

A Theory of Social Invariables: *Georg Simmel* (1858-1918). Simmel was primarily a philosopher. However, sociological thinking was a fundamental element of his philosophical reflection. His early works (16) are still in the tradition of Spencer, which is philosophical and also sociological. His own thinking led him to a philosophy of life in which his sociological thought played a remarkable role as method and as theory. Simmel's sociological interest was the result of Spencer's and of Marx's influences. Like Toennies and the Webers, Simmel was fascinated by the work of Karl Marx. He was of the opinion that it was possible to preserve the scientific truth that was hidden in this political eschatology. Over and over again he remarked that his efforts were directed to finding a more profound and comprehensive basis of the dialectical materialism in the very structure of the life-world of human being. Three times (17) he attacked this problem. He established the thesis that the very character of human existence is dialectical. According to Simmel, the unending continuity of the process of life clashes necessarily with the acts of individuation, with the creative acts in which the social institutions are established. These acts transcend the flux of life. Their achievements have a reality of their own, a being beyond the continuity of the stream of life. This is the inescapable destiny of man, his tragedy and the crisis of civilization. Simmel calls this dualism of life and the objects of the mind "the objectivation of the human mind." Marx had called it the self-alienation. Simmel asserted that this dialectic is not a historical phenomenon of capitalism, but the general destiny of mature civilizations. In such situations the works of men lose the human coefficient and are esta-

---

14. Georg von Lukacs, *Die Theorie des Romans*, (Stuttgart: 1916); *Zur Soziologie des modernen Dramas*, (Tuebingen: 1914).

15. Franz Oppenheimer: *System der Soziologie*, (Berlin: 1923-1933, 4 vols.) on Oppenheimer, see Eduard Heimann, "Franz Oppenheimer's Economic Ideas," *Social Research*, 11: 27-39, February, 1944.

16. *Einleitung in die Moralwissenschaften* (1890-1893), *Ueber soziale Differenzierung*, (1890).

17. "Der Begriff und die Tragoedie der Kultur," in *Philosophische Kultur*, (Leipzig: 1919), *Der Konflikt der Modernen Kultur*, (Leipzig: 1918), "Die Krisis der Kultur" in *Der Krieg und die geistigen Entscheidungen*, (Leipzig: 1917).

blished in autonomous contexts of their own. These intermediate layers of civilization threaten the genuine and natural unity between man and his values. In particular, all mature civilizations face this problem. Men have created such a diversity of products and works that frequently means are considered to be ends. Simmel states that the confusion of the means-end relationship and the clash between the subject and the objects of the world are the very contents of the dialectics of human life. Man always is in danger of being slain by the objects of his own creation. This thesis of Simmel's is the humanization of Marx's objectivation of the consciousness and of the theory of self-alienation.

In similar terms he announces, in the preface to the *Philosophy of Money*, the methodological intention to reexamine historical materialism and to find basic societal relationships which make it possible to understand the dynamics of the economic processes in terms of human nature. Simmel states that in the flux of life all social phenomena are a whole and that all aspects of a situation must be taken into consideration. It was the merit of Marx to have pointed out the due place of economic processes among the conditions of civilization. However, economic processes as such can only be understood when the sociologist refers to the psychological and intellectual, moral and spiritual forces that influence the behavior patterns of the economic societies. Simmel has called the consideration of the reciprocity and interdependence of all conditions the sociological method. He applied the method in his *Philosophy of Money*. He takes for granted Kapp's theory of money as his economic hypothesis. On this basis, he elaborates most carefully the implications for social conduct which arise in the transition from a natural to a money economy. Simmel analyzes as a sociologist what philosophers have described as a revolutionary change in philosophical conceptions, namely, the elimination of the category of substance in favor of the new scientific thinking in terms of function. In the new credit system the value of money shifts from that of a substance to that of a function. Money becomes a symbol of and an abstraction for values. This new technical device had tremendous repercussions on all ways of life. In a very slow process, this development has promoted the trend toward intellectualism and the spirit of calculation and abstraction as over against the primacy of feelings and of imagination. Simmel analyzes carefully the new attitudes and the new style of life among the ruling classes. Implicitly, he has established the thesis that these new behavior patterns cannot be ascribed to the middle classes in the modern sense. Rather are they the property of the ruling élite in the revolutionary absolute and sovereign state. Simmel rightly characterizes this élite as the first competitive society in which merit and efficiency are higher virtues than birth and fortunes. This again is a manifestation of the new pragmatic rationalism and intellectualism. The new economic technique produces positive and negative results. It restricts and levels down original and individual characters. On the other hand, it opens up new avenues to freedom and independence. It emancipates and subjects human beings at the same time. It frees men from the bondage of personal services; it subjects men to the rigidly expanding world of rational and technical institutions.

Unfortunately, the work has never received the recognition which it deserves. It is the sociological pendant to Jacob Burckhardt's *Civilization of the Renaissance in Italy*. It presents under the sociological aspect the problematic character of the modern independence and of the modern individualism after the disintegration of the social system of the feudal societies. Furthermore, Simmel's work remains highly relevant for the critical reexamination of Max Weber's thesis on inner-worldly asceticism and on the Puritan spirit. Simmel has made suggestions which point to a quite different solution.

Simmel frequently stated that the sociological method that he applied in this book is universal for all fields in the history of ideas. For the modern man has discovered the impact and pressure of collective institutions on all spheres of human thought and action. He has made this experience a lasting element of his consciousness. (18)

However sociology is not only a method. Simmel has developed the thesis that sociology exists as a special social science. He has even suggested a three-partite division. He calls the three branches formal, general, and philosophical sociology. (19)

He starts from the assumption that neither the economic nor any other material layer of reality helps us to know anything about the fundamental societal relationships and the human constitution of society. On the contrary, we discover that the same attitudes and relationships occur in all spheres and on all layers of social action. In religion and politics, in school and business, in sports and in the army, Simmel finds lasting and recurrent relationships between

---

18. *Philosophie des Geldes*, 4th ed., (Leipzig: 1922).
19. *Grundfragen der Soziologie*, 2nd ed., (Leipzig: 1922), *passim*.

GERMAN SOCIOLOGY

human beings. All social institutions are composed of reciprocal relationships between individuals that are independent of the changing contents that determine the institutions. These lasting and recurrent attitudes and relationships are the forms of society that are open to the description and interpretation by the sociologist. Simmel calls this branch of sociology: formal sociology. This is a very unfortunate terminology. It hints at a clasification according to a mathematical principle that recognizes merely formal and abstract relations as in geometry. However, Simmel uses the term "form" as the principle of individuation and organization in the formless stream of life. Forms are the irreducible invariables that present the pluralistic universe of intersubjective relationships. Control and allegiance, loyalty and competiton, self-preservation and defense, intimacy and strangeness, social distance and affinity are lasting forms of mutual relationships between men as individuals or men as a collective organization. These forms make it possible to establish the structural organization and the articulation of the stream of life and experience. These very forms enable human beings to develop a diversity of we and you-relationships and to demonstrate the density and qualification of his societal relationships. Simmel has made the two categories of continuity and of form the central concepts of his philosophy of life and of his sociology that can be defined as the empirical division of the philosophy of life.

Simmel's social forms are primary phenomena whatever might be the impact of the contents. The social forms are the fundamental attitudes which are the indispensable instruments for realizing the lives of men as bearers of meaning and of ends in the inarticulate stream of life. Even the negative forms as combat and conflict serve a positive end, they reestablish over and over again structure and balance in the articulation of life. Simmel's formal sociology is a tremendous progress in sociological theory. It closes the gap between the traditional dualism of individualism vs. collectivism that has ruled sociology in the past. Simmel recognized the necessity of understanding societal relationships as structured wholes that are composed of human processes and are specific attitudes in mutuality. His presentation of the pluralism of intersubjective invariables as an open typology makes it possible to reconsider the fundamental problems of intimacy and strangeness, of anonymous and personal relationships, as elements of sociability and as elements of social structures. This reflection opens up the way for a philosophical anthropology. (20)

General sociology is a by-product of the formal sociology. It deals with the specific conditions and presuppositions of collective institutions. Simmel is of the opinion that the accumulation of power and of pressure in collective institutions makes it necessary to analyze their specific functioning and process as over against the acts of the individual person. In particular, Simmel has analyzed the differences of the human level in organizations of varying sizes. He ascribed all these analyses to the general sociology.

Simmel called the final division "philosophical sociology." It is philosophical because the sociologist faces the problems of the limits of his method and the trans-sociological meaning of the creative person. Simmel practiced this approach in his intellectual biographies of philosophers and artists. These books point out the paradox of social existence. Although these men are conditioned and determined as all life in time and space, there remains an area of perfection and finality in their works that cannot be interpreted by a sociological imputation. The more refined our instruments are for discovering the conditions, the more articulate appears the profound solitude of the sublime and thoughtful person in the context of his social world. This negatively sociological analysis raises the problem of the historical character of sociology, of its limitations and of its merits. It opens the philosophical discussion on the problems of determination and of freedom, of individual and general standards, and of creative action and collective research.

The three branches of Simmel's sociology show the different perspectives that make it possible to overcome the traditional antagonism between individualism and collectivism. They establish a sociological humanism that describes the whole in terms of the invariables of mutuality.

The work of Simmel is living and problematical. It is problem-

---

20. *Soziologie* (1908).

The purely formalistic trend of Simmel's thought found a continuation in the work of Leopold von Wiese (*System der Allgemeinen Soziologie*, vols. I, II, 1926-1933, American translation, adapted and amplified by Howard Becker: *Systematic Sociology*, New York, 1932). His entire effort is dedicated to a detailed classification of social bonds and groups on the basis of a nominalistic interpreted "Beziehungslehre" (Cf. on von Wiese's classification Logan Wilson's paper on "Sociography of Groups," section on "Group Theory in Germany," in this Symposium).

atical because it was produced in a very unfortunate situation of philosophy and psychology. For this reason it is necessary to interpret his work very carefully and cautiously in order not to miss the *leitmotif* of his thought, which was the "philosophy of life." It is problematical because it is unsystematic and the conceptualization is closer to a concrete description than to a strict and rigid abstraction. It is living and suggestive because of the variety of human and social phenomena that Simmel has described with a rare sense of delicacy and subtlety. It will remain a living and creative work as long as social scientists think it worthwhile to cooperate with the philosopher in an attempt to overcome the antinomies of life and to reconcile its antagonisms. Simmel's work is still unexhausted in the analysis of attitudes that brought into existence the modern world. He has seen problems that the Phenomenological School applies to the analysis of the social phenomena.

II

The Influence of Phenomenology. Marx and Hegel remain of lasting importance for German sociology. Since the thirties, Husserl's philosophy and the phenomenological method are becoming increasingly influential and opening up new scientific roads for sociological analyses. This strictly scientific philosophy is beyond the dualism of the idealistic subject-object relationships and above positivism and its methods. It succeeds in describing the pure phenomena in the context of significances. This makes it possible to explain and to understand individual and historical phenomena as deviations from the pure structures under the pressure of attitude and of social conditions. The first student of Husserl's who has influenced sociology was Max Scheler.

Max Scheler. Scheler used the phenomenological method in a very arbitrary way in order to develop a theory of emotional aprioris and of moral intuitions. It is not necessary to discuss the merits of this enterprise in this connection. We need only mention that Scheler reconsidered Toennies' theory on the fundamental structures. He rightly aserted that the classification of the social structures cannot be based on types of will, but on types of affection. The types vary acording to the density and quality of mutual affections. Sympathy and sympathetic understanding are indispensable for all structures of community; love and the complete identification with a cause, a person or an idea creates a specific structure of universalism that is close to Schmalenbach's communion. Emotional affections produce superficial contacts and make possible the horde which Scheler wrongly identifies with the crowd. Thus Scheler's insight into the integrating force of collective intuitions indicates the progress that can be made in this field of sociology.

There is still another direct contribution to sociological theory scattered throughout his work. His theory of the "ethos" of societies is a valuable contribution to the analyses of social change and of social order. The social ethos is the system of preferences and of standards that is taken for granted by societies in nonconscious emotional attitudes prior to any rationalization. This theory makes it possible to find a sociological clue for the discussion of national characters. Likewise important is the theory of the social ideal images (*Vorbilder*). They present types of social personality which are the focussing points for the orientation of social actions in terms of ideals. There are social images of all ways of life and modes of self-realization. There are images of the professions, of the occupations, and of such personal perfections as the hero, the genius, the saint. Scheler rightly distinguishes the imitation and the emulation in the relations between *Vorbild* and *Nachbild*. He suggests a very important sociological analysis when discriminating the types of *Vorbild* and *Gegenbild*. In a few fragmentary notes he hints at the pseudo-mythologies of modern revolutionary images that establish the world of modern demonry. His remarks on the leader-follower relationship as over against the image-emulation relation remains highly important.

In various connections Scheler has established a sociological theory on the resentment toward changes of ethos and ethics. He defines resentment as the ideological transformation of suppressed hatred into the destruction and negative evaluation of the values of the ruling group. He applies the concept to the revolutionary changes in social values that came into existence with the radical social movements of modern times. The revolutionary changes consist of prefering the abstract values of humanitarianism and of a universal love of mankind to the immediate and concrete responsibilities for the next, the neighbor, the country, and the perfection of an individual soul. He ascribes this transvaluation to the resentment of the rising middle classes and of the following radical movements.

This leads to his most important contribution to sociology. He has applied a sociological method to the description of emotive phenomena. The clarification of the phenomenological structure of experience is indispensable to the sociological observer who analyzes these phenomena in their functioning in the flux of the social process. The phenomenological method makes it possible to establish a precise isolation of the universal elements in the structure of human experience and of social action. The phenomenological reduction discloses the very structure, the invariable elements of the emotional facts. Scheler the sociologist is then in the situation to understand and to explain the individual historical realizations of these fundamental structures and their changes in the social process. His descriptions as to shame, repentance, the consciousness of death, suffering, love, the renascence of virtue follow the same pattern: Scheler first posits the attitude or affection within the structure of experience, second he describes its functional significance in relation to the elements of the structure, and finally he understands the various historical realizations in terms of sociological imputations. All these essays contribute to the sociological problems of societal relationships and of social structures. (21)

Scheler's contributions are suggestions and invitations rather than definite results. The theory of resentment can be of value when carefully and cautiously applied. In Scheler's presentation it remains without any value because of the unscientific attitude toward modern society. The thesis can be fruitful only when applied in the right perspective of social interaction and in measuring objectively the positive and negative sides that occur in all social phenomena. Scheler has made a lasting contribution in the field of emotional phenomena. Here he has laid the foundations for a future sociology of attitudes. Likewise, the theory of images will suggest many valuable investigations on empirical evaluative tendencies. This might be a contribution to a study in social teleology.

In this connection, some authors who have applied the new philosophical method of Husserl's must be at least mentioned. Vierkandt (22) has called his method "phenomenological" in order to indicate that the varieties of societal relationships are based on various states of inner connectedness. He makes the differences in density and

---

21. Max Scheler: *Der Formalismus in der Ethik und die materiale Wertethik*, *Vom Umsturz der Werte*, (Leipzig, 2 vols.), *Wesen und Formen der Sympathie*, 3rd ed., (Bonn: 1931), *Schriften aus dem Nachlass*, (Berlin: 1933), *Moralia* (*Schriften zur Soziologie und Weltanschauungslehre I*) (Leipzig: 1923).

22. Alfred Vierkandt, *Gesellschaftslehre* 2nd ed., (Berlin: 1928).

quality the very principle of classification of social structures. He has coined the terms "relations close to sympathetic understanding" and "relations of regulated and planning institutions." Vierkandt defines sociology as the science that deals with the phenomenological description of the modes of inner connectedness, its modes and its types, its degree and its laws. He has not clearly made articulate the difference between social structures, societal realtionships, and social processes.

In contrast to Scheler, Alfred Schuetz has taken seriously the phenomenological method in the original sense of Husserl. He has applied the new scientific attitude for correcting Max Weber's theory of social action. He poses the problem of the limits of Weber's category of subjective meaning. In contrast to Weber, Schuetz sees the key to the problem of subjective meaning and of its interpretation in the understanding of the stream of consciousnes or in the knowledge of the concrete time as elaborated by Husserl, Wililam James, Bergson, and G. H. Mead. On this basis he analyzes the natural attitudes of the life-world. He succeeds in discriminating behavior and action. Behavior is defined as active experiences and reflections upon them. The distinguishing character of action is determined by a project which precedes in time. It implies impulse and premeditation. In the project we grasp the primary meaning of action. Schuetz clarifies the concept of meaning with the distinction of the because-and the in-order-to-motives. Another contribution refers to the different layers of social actions according to the concreteness or the abstractness of the experiences of intimacy or strangeness. He distinguishes four layers: the associates, the contemporaries, the predecessors and the successors. The associates are those with whom I actually come into contact and have experiences in simultaneity. The contemporaries are those with whom I have only indirect contacts. It is the world of the anonymous One and of Public Opinion. In this sphere the ideal type has its specific function as the most appropriate conception. Schuetz's analysis of the limits of the ideal type and of its diverse cases is a progress in the understanding of Weber's interpretative sociology.

His paper on the stanger is a fruitful application of his methodological studies. It points out the different layers of knowledge in the variety of experienced life-worlds and its distance to the areas of changing environments. It is an important contribution to the problem of solitude. Like Theodor Litt, Schuetz has elaborated the

GERMAN SOCIOLOGY

idea of the reciprocity of perspectives which makes it possible to overcome the dualism of individual vs. collective consciousness. (23)

---

23. *Der sinnhafte Aufbau der sozialen Welt,* (Vienna: 1932); "Phenomenology and the Social Sciences," in *Philosophical Essays in Memoriam of Edmund Husserl,* (Cambridge: Harvard University Press, 1940); "William James' Concept of the Stream of Thought," *Philosophy and Phenomenological Research,* 1: 442-452, June, 1941. "Scheler's Theory of Intersubjectivity and the General Thesis of the Alter Ego," *Philosophy and Phenomenological Research,* 2: 323-347, March, 1942; "The Stranger," *American Journal of Sociology,* 49: 499-507, May, 1944.

SELECTED BIBLIOGRAPHY

Aron, Raymond, *Essai sur la theorie de l'histoire dans l'Allemagne contemporaine,* (Paris: Vrin, 1938).

Aron, Raymond, La sociologie allemande contemporaine, *Nouvelle encyclopédie philosophique,* (Paris: Alcan, 1935).

Barnes, Harry Elmer, and Howard Becker, *Social Thought from Lore to Science,* vol. II, *Sociological Trends throughout the World,* (Boston, etc.: D. C. Heath and Co., 1938), "Germany and Austria," pp. 879-933.

Becker, Howard, "Historical Sociology," in Harry Elmer Barnes and Howard Becker, eds., *Contemporary Social Theory,* (New York: D. Appleton-Century Co., 1940), Chap. 15. (Deals with Max and Alfred Weber).

Friess, H. L., "Wilhelm Dilthey," *Journal of Philosophy,* 26: 5-28, January, 1929.

Goldenweiser, Alexander, "The Relations of the Natural Sciences to the Social Theory, (New York: D. Appleton-Century Co., 1940), Chap. 5. (Deals with Dilthey).

Gurvitch, Georges, *Les tendances actuelles de la philosophie allemande,* (Paris: 1930).

Jankevitch, Wladimir, "Simmel," *Revue de metaphysique et de morale,* 1925, pp. 213-257, 373-386.

Mannheim, Karl, *Ideology and Utopia,* (New York: Harcourt, Brace and Co., 1936).

Parsons, Talcott, *The Structure of Social Action,* (New York: McGraw-Hill Book Co., 1937), especially Chap. XII (on German Sociology), Chaps. XIII-XVII (on Max Weber), and pp. 686-694 (on Toennies).

Salomon, Albert, "In Memoriam Ferdinand Toennies," *Social Research,* 3: 348-363, August, 1936.

Salomon, Albert, "Max Weber," *Die Gesellschaft,* 1926, pp. 131-153.

Salomon, Albert, "Max Weber's Methodology," *Social Research,* 1: 147-168, May, 1934.

Salomon, Albert, "Max Weber's Political Ideas," *Social Research,* 2: 368-384, August, 1935.

TWENTIETH CENTURY SOCIOLOGY

Salomon, Albert, "Max Weber's Sociology," *Social Research*, 2: 60-73, February, 1935.

Stonier, Alfred, and Karl Bode, "A New Approach to the Methodology of Social Sciences," *Economica*, 4: 406-424, November, 1937. (Deals with Schuetz).

Wiese, Leopold von, and Howard Becker, *Systematic Sociology*, (New York: John Willey and Sons, 1932).

Williams, Richard Hays, "The Method of Understanding as Applied to the Problem of Suffering," *Journal of Abnormal and Social Psychology*, 35: 367-386, July, 1940. (Deals with Scheler and Schuetz).

Williams, Richard Hays, "Scheler's Contributions to the Sociology of Affective Action," *Philosophy and Phenomenological Research*, 2: 348-358, March, 1942.

Albert Salomon, Ph. D. (Heidelberg), has been Professor of Sociology in the Graduate Faculty of Political and Social Science, New School for Social Research, since 1935. He served as editor of *Die Gesellschaft* and docent at the Deutsche Hochschule fuer Politik, 1928-1931; Professor of Sociology, Teachers College for Vocational Schools, Cologne, 1931-1933; lectured at the University of Cologne. Editor of *De Torqueville selections* (Zurich: 1936), and author of articles on the history of sociology and on attitudes.

CHAPTER XXI

SOCIOLOGY IN LATIN AMERICA

by

ROGER BASTIDE

I

General Tendencies. In a large measure Latin American sociology is in the Twentieth Century a continuation of that of the Nineteenth. The freedom from colonial status, the suppression of slavery with the resulting economic crisis — specially in Brazil and the Antilles —, and the difficulties experienced by the local economies in becoming integrated with the rhythm of capitalistic economy had led to a chaos of ideas and sentiments, partly emanating from the milieu itself with its mixture of races and its creolism, partly imported from Europe. And the ideas did not move to a synthesis. This accounts for the necessity of seeking in sociology the means for putting a little order in this confusion of thoughts and emotions: a certain number of clear ideas, some classifications, and some constructive theories. These were the circumstances that were to assure the success of positivism, which proposed a complete system that even included the idea of incorporating the colored proletariat into Occidental civilization in Brazil and Chile; of the Catholic school of Le Play, which offered an example nomenclature for encompassing the complexity of reality (1); finally, more to the south, of the socialism of Saint-Simon and Fourrier and the Spencerian evolutionism, which are the true points of departure of Argentine sociology. (2) But instead of looking for the desired synthesis in an imported sociology, would it not be more worthwhile to turn one's attention upon the concrete problems of the time and place, and with the aid of geography and history discover the roots of a truly South American synthesis?

From these tendencies stemmed two currents that have sometimes been called the current of the Atlantic and the current of the Pacific, because the countries bordering the Atlantic and consequently nearer Europe have been more interested in theoretical sociology, while those facing the Pacific could meditate on the ruins of a rich pre-Columbian civilization and devoted themselves primarily to historico-social speculations. (3) However, it would be a mistake to think of this as a matter of geographical opposition. Actually there also existed in Argentina at the end of the Nineteenth Century a concrete sociology with Sarmiento and Mejía as principal representatives, (4) while the national sociology of the Pacific was also fed by European influences — anthropogeographical or racial theories. (5)

All this early sociology suffered, however, from certain evils which the Twentieth Century has slowly eliminated. First, because of the education given in religious colleges and faculties of Law, minds wore a mark more literary or judicial than scientific. If one adds that the problems posed by the upheavals of the political structure, the economic backwardness, and the racial miscegenation were

---

* In this paper we omit ethnography, and social psychology, despite their points of contact with sociology.

1. Sylvio Romero in Brazil, followed by Jorge Goulart.

2. If the ideas of Fourier were not unknown in Brazil cf. G. Freyre, *Un engenheiro frances no Brasil*, (Rio de Janeiro: 1930), the influence of Saint-Simon was much stronger in Argentina with Echevarría. (*Cf.* Raúl A. Orgaz, *La influencia de Leroux y del saint-simonismo sobre Echevarría;* José Ingenieros, *Sociología argentina*, (Buenos Aires: 1910).

3. Oscar Alvarez Andrews, "Introducción a la sociología americana," *Revista mexicana de sociología*, 4: 7-22, 1942.

4. Domingo F. Sarmiento, *Facundo* (1845); *idem.*, *Conflictos y armonías de las razas en América* (1883); José M. Ramos Mejía, *Las multitudes argentinas* (1899).

5. In Venezuela especially the European influence is strong in the work of I. G. Fortoul, *El hombre y la historia.*

problems urgently demanding solutions that could not await the results of detailed inquires, one may better understand why the books of national sociology remained brilliant essays, as much poetry as they were sociology. The works were characterized by contradictory ideologies: an optimistic dogma that affirmed the superiority of the *mestizo* or of the indigenous culture over Occidental civilization; and a pessimistic belief in the superiority of Anglo-Saxon colonization over the Iberic, tracing the inferiority of the latter to miscegenation, the Indian heritage, the Latin race, the tropical climate, the persistence of the colonial mentality, the lack of political education of the colonists, or the handicap of slavery. (6) It was evident that sociology, as a positive field of inquiry, could develop only after breaking with these fancies. The difficulty was that they appeared to their authors less the dictates of their imagination than the results of their observation, and they pretended to buttress them with the theories of European savants.

These were not, however, the only obstacles encountered on the route to a positive sociology. The immense territorial extension with a population dispersed in little gangliated nodules separated by vast stretches of forests, pampas, or deserts, prevented the co-operation of different investigators, while the means of transportation, oriented more to trans-oceanic than to coastal navigation, favored the imported sociologies that could be assimilated with more or less success. Finally, the ancient division of patriarchal families into hostile clans was reflected even in the social sciences, favoring the establishment of rival schools more preoccupied with defending *a priori* postulates than with verifying theories in the context of new facts.

The Twentieth Century has not completely changed this state of affairs, but a radical transformation is in process. Urban growth is modifying the social structure, substituting secondary for primary contacts, outmoding the former sociology of familism or personalism, and tending to replace the dogmatism of the chapels with the syncretism of the schools. This syncretism is favored by the creation of chairs of sociology and, in the beginning, by the self-instruction of their first occupants. (7) Of course this offers some

---

6. Alvarez Andrews, *loc. cit.*

7. The first chair of sociology dates from 1896 (Buenos Aires). Since that date the number has expanded greatly, and particularly since the First World War.

new dangers in perspective: the desire of professors to show their familiarity with all that has been written, research in extension rather than in depth, the desire to be "at the page" and the consequent high valuation of fashionable ideas rather than their critical examination — these are the characteristiscs of auto-didactism. One must take into account the professional conscience that wants students not to be ignorant of the group of works of other thinkers. But it is not necessary to confuse research with teaching of sociology. Latin American sociology is still in many places at the stage of manuals and instructional treatises. The strengthening of university work is, however, now leading beyond this stage.

Chairs of sociology are now to be found in nearly all the American republics — in the Faculties of Law, in the Faculties of Pholosophy, in the Faculties of Social Sciences, or in Schools of Sociology—, and not only in the State but also in the Catholic universities. The need has been recognized of joining to these instructional posts some centers of research *in loco*. Thus, there have been created several Institutes, like the Institute of Sociology at Buenos Aires under the presidency of Ricardo Levene, the Centro of Pesquizas of the Faculty of Philosophy at Sao Paulo, the Bolivian Institute of Sociology at the University of S. F. Francisco Xavier in Sucre, and the Institute of Social Investigation in Mexico. Some specialized reviews have also been founded, such as the *Boletin* of the Institute of Buenos Aires, *Sociología* (Sao Paulo, Brazil), the *Revista interamericana de sociología* (Caracas, Venezuela), and the *Revista mexicana de sociología* under the able direction of Lucio Mendieta y Nuñez. All this has aided Latin American sociology to progress from didactism to personal research. In Brazil sociology is not only a field of advanced instruction but also part of the programs of secondary and normal school curricula. Thus students entering the University Faculties already have a little factual equipment, and the professors can devote themselves to more fundamental studies. Finally, it is necessary to add the contribution of the foreign professors, whether political refuges like Nicolai in Argentina, José Gaos and José Medina Echavarría in Mexico, or secured directly from abroad by the universities of South America, like Lambert, Arbousse-Bastide, Lévi-Strauss, Davies, Lowrie Pierson, and myself in Brazil, and R. Caillois in Argentina. These professional contacts assure the liaison between Latin American sociology on the one hand and the European and North American on the other.

SOCIOLOGY IN LATIN AMERICA

A great volume of research is thus set in train. But, as we were saying at the beginning, it is going along avenues already opened in the Nineteenth Century, correcting and perfecting more than changing directions. We may then speak of two sociologies, a theoretical sociology and some national sociologies, which are moreover interpenetrating more and more. The latter comes about through the fact that the same scholars often devote themselves to the two types of work, and through the fact that the theoretical sociology more and more takes into account local facts for illustrating or criticizing general theories, while the national sociologies tend to draw regional observations from universally valid laws.

II

Theoretical Sociology. Although cooperation among the several states of Central and South America is increasing, it is still necessary to start from the initial isolation. The resemblances among the sociologists, when they existed, derived more from the identity of external circumstances to which they were subject than from intercommunication.

In Argentina, the legacy of the Nineteeth Century to the Twentieth was organicism on the one hand, economic determinism on the other. The role of Jose Ingenieros was to attempt a synthesis between these two currents. For him society is a biological aggregate, but an economic organism rather than an animal organism. Economic processes are simply the continuation in the human domain of the biological laws of struggle for existence and adaptation to environment: "Human societies evolve within biological laws. They are conditioned in the first place by the environment in which they live, and from which they draw their subsistence. In this environment every social aggregate — race, nation, trice, etc. — is a group of individuals who struggle for existence with the purpose of preserving certain functions (customs) and certain organs (institutions) that represent a collectively acquired variation in the biological unity of the species." (8) A reaction against this naturalism could not fail to take place; it was the work of Antonio Dellepiane, who refused to consider society as a realm of nature but rather turned in the direc-

---

8. José Ingenieros, *Sociología argentina,* (Buenos Aires: 1910).

tion of psychology to the study of the laws of association between individual psyches. (9)

Here there were two opposed points of view. Was it possible to synthesize them, as previously Ingenieros had been able to synthesize the economic determinism and the organiscism of his predecessors? Carlos Octavio Bunge considers society as an organism, that is as a reality superior to the individuals that constitute it, but it is not an aggregation of cells. Rather, it is a psychic organism that has its own mind, deriving — and here his view approaches that of Giddings — from the instinctive sentiment that men have of beloging to the same biological species. On still another point Bunge effects a synthesis of the two different doctrines. He accepts from naturalism the laws of natural selection and struggle for existence, but he makes of them laws derived from a more primitive and more essential law, that of aspirability ("man is an animal who desires"), which is a spiritual law, an "idée force" as Fouillée would say.

The conflict which seemed to disappear has been renewed, however, primarily because French sociology, with Durkheim and Tarde, toward which the Argentine intellectual élite is oriented, presents the two currents of sociologism and psychologism. Thus one has a Maupas who continues Durkheim and a Martínez Paz who defines the social by some phenomena of interrelations. The conflict has also been renewed because following the First World War German ideas infiltrated into Argentina, with the biologism of Nicolai, the Spenglerism of Quesada, the cultural sociology of Baldrich, and the phenomenology of Renato Treves. (10)

In order to achieve unity of thought there remained no other possible solution but methodological syncretism. This is the solution arrived at by Raúl A. Orgaz and Alfredo Poviña. The former defines sociology as "the science that studies the processes of interaction and their products," that is, collective institutions. By this

---

9. Antonio Delepiane, *Estudios de filosofía jurídica y social*, (Buenos Aires: 1902).

10. See Carlos Octavio Bunge, *Principios de psicología individual y social* (1903); *El derecho* (1915); *Nuestra América* (1918); Maupas, *Concepto de sociedad* (1913); Enrique Martínez Paz, *Elementos de sociología* (1911); *Apuntes de sociología* (1914); Nicolai, *Fundamentos reales de la sociología* (1936); Baldrich, *Libertad y determinismo en la sociología de Max Weber;* Renato Treves, *Sociología y filosofía social;* Ernesto Quesada, *La sociología relativista spengleriana* (1921); *La evolución sociolóoica del derecho según la doctrina spengleriana* (1923).

procedure the two sociologies, relationist and psychological, institutional and objectivist, are reconciled. Far from being opposed to each other, they constitute two aspects of a single science. Poviña is more sensitive to the German influence, but he also seeks to reconcile sociology as a positive science, the inductive sociology of Durkheim, with sociology as a science of the spirit, the conceptual historicism of Max Weber. Poviña looks to Freyer for his inspiration: the object of the science of societies is both internal and external, formed by history and by the thinking and acting subject. (11)

Thus Argentine sociology appears in a dialectical aspect that gives it a certain living unity. On the other hand in Brazil the schools are farther apart, whether because in contrast to Argentina where the universities are relatively concentrated the Brazilian institutions are spacially separated, or because familism has lasted longer in Brazil, or finally because the elements of sociology having already been taught at the secondary levels it was possible for the university professors instead of treating general theories to work rather profoundly within the current of ideas that appeared more correct to them.

Fernando de Azevedo carries on the Durkhemian tradition at Sao Paulo. His *principios de sociología*, although naturally taking into account other valuable contributions to the study of society, attempts above all to give students that spirit of objectivity defined in *Les règles de la méthode sociologique*.

His *Sociología educacional*, which is clearly distinct from the sociology of education as defined by North Americans, takes as a point of departure Durkheim's *Sociologie et éducation;* but, he adds quite correctly, "it is curious to note that, once the way to that conception of the science of education (educational sociology) was opened by E. Durkheim, there still has not appeared in France a work in which there has been attempted a sociological study of the facts and institutions of education." It is precisely this still missing work that Fernando de Azevedo has accomplished with rare skill.

At Rio de Janeiro, in the contrary, it is the North American influence that is important, represented in the instructional treatises of Delgado de Carvalho, who sets forth the procedure of the experimental techniques in use in the United States; and in the work of

---

11. Raúl A. Orgaz, *Introducción a la sociología;* Alfredo Poviña, *La sociología como ciencia de realidad* (1939); *Historia y lógica de la sociología* (1941).

TWENTIETH CENTURY SOCIOLOGY

Carneiro Leao, who utilizes the idea of rural and urban sociology, social control, and ecology for application to Brazilian realities, and who opposes to the superstition of theories the necessity of making concrete studies within the framework of the region. (12)

Pontes de Miranda represents the German current of influence; not only the relationism of von Weise but also the Einsteinian physics. Human societies are in fact only a particular case of a very general phenomenon, which is that of aggregation. It follows that "physical laws are applicable to sociology because to admit the contrary would be to destroy universal principles and laws, to accept the possibility that in one domain of the universe they are not valid." However, if "social facts obey physical and biological principles," for example if social space is equally a space-time, if social space only appears where also appears social energy — as the field of gravitation only appears where energy appears — if the biological law of accommodation is the great law of cultural complexes it is no less true that these universal laws in passing into the domain of human societies become differentiated and clothed in new characteristics. An entire school follows Pontes de Miranda that may be called the school of Recife, although it has extended beyond the boundaries of that city to include even Rio de Janeiro. The group uses mathematical symbols. Two sub-groups may be distinguished: that of Djacir Menezes, for whom "changes in social space are given by economic coordinates," and "the economic rhythm is the one that has the role played by gravitation in physical space"; and that of Mario Lins, who is closer to Pareto and refuses to accord to the economic a privileged place among variables. (13)

Tristande Athayde represents Catholic sociology in Brazil characterized by the preponderance given finalism over mechanicism, and by the voluntaristic confusion of sociology with social philosophy, what we call sociology only constituting for him the lower stratum of a science that goes beyond facts to arrive at norms.

All these diverse schools are to be found in the other Latin

---

12. See Fernando de Azevedo, *Principios de sociologia* (1935); *Sociologia educacional* (1940); *A cultura brasileira* (1943); Delgado de Carvalho, *Sociologia* (1931); *Sociologia educacional* (1933); *Sociologia experimental* (1934); *Sociologia aplicada* (1935); *Sociologia e educacão* (1935); A Carneiro Leão, *Fundamentos de sociologia* (1940); *La sociedad rural* (1941).

13. Francisco Cavalcanti Pontes de Miranda, *Introducion a la sociologia geral* (1926); Djacir Menezes, *O principio de symetria e os fenomenos economicos;* Marion Lins, *Espacotempo e as relações sociais* (1940).

SOCIOLOGY IN LATIN AMERICA

American republics. Positivism, introduced in Chile by Lastarria, is continued there in the Twentieth Century by Letelier and his dual law of consensus and evolution, as well as by Lagarrigue whose *Nociones de sociología* constitute only a resume of the final volumes of Comte's *Cours de philosophie positive*. Positivism may also be detected in the work of Victoriano Ayala (San Salvador), although mixed with other influences. Spencerism is clear in the *Principios de sociología* of Cecilio Béez (Paraguay), who incorporated the laws of human evolution within the general framework of evolution. L. Vallenilla Lanz (Venezuela) likens human societies to organisms, similar in all points to animal organisms. Angel Modesto Paredes (Equador) studies the formation of biological species and the processes of heredity in order to apply the results to the human order in *Los resultados sociales de herencia*. From this double tendency, positivistic and organismic, stems the interest of South American sociologists in problems of evolution, so that even when this infra-structure of theories collapses books of *genetic sociology* are still written, as for example the collaborative work of Guillermo Valencia and Lucrecio Jaromillo (Colombia). The Catholic school is represented in Colombia by Alejandro Bermúdez, who accepts the idea of social laws—static, dynamic, and cinematic—but views their operation as safeguarding human liberty, and constructs his sociology by the study of the social reforms proposed by the Church. The psychological current is apparent in the work of Pane (Paraguay), for whom sociology has for its object the study of the "social psychim," (14) and in that of V. Gabriel Garcés (Equador), who defines sociology as the examination of inter-human relations, the actions and reactions of individuals among each other, and between these and the social group. (15)

However, since Latin American sociology is a sociology born from the instruction in the universities, the dominant tendency everywhere is syncretism. Bustamante (Bolivia), in giving society a physical base and "a psychological organization," reconciles anthropogeography with idealistic sociology. (16) Justo Prieto (Paraguay), in distinguishing in every collectivity a physical base, a network of psychic actions and reactions, and a systematic series of

---

14. J. A. Pane, *Apuntes de sociología*.
15. V. Gabriel Garcés, "Ensayo de interpretación histórico-sociológica de las nacionalidades en América," *Revista interamericana de sociología*, No. 7.
16. *Principios de sociología* (1909).

norms, brings together anthropogeography and the work of Ellwood and Stammler. (17) But the two most interesting works from the point of view with which we are now concerned are certainly the *Sociología general* of Mariano H. Carnejo (Peru) and the *Sociología genética y sistemática* of Antonio Caso (Mexico).

Carnejo is admirably familiar with all the sociological literature of his time, especially the European materials, and although he also knew the North American sociological developments, he preferred the ethnography of the latter region. Like Spencer and Wundt he proceeds by induction, drawing general societal laws from a mass of facts generally referring to so-called primitive peoples. He is thus able to unite the institutionalism of Tylor and Spencer with the ethnic psychology of Wundt and the psychic interpretations of the French sociologists. (18) Caso starts with geography; he thinks societies are originally subject to the external environment, but to the extent that man passes successively from the savage state to civilization this dependence ceases because of human inventions and their diffusion to the entire group through imitation. Thus culture is formed, existing independently of individuals. Caso analyzes the various elements composing culture, from the family to the State, basing his analysis on the well known distinction between community and society. Thus it my be seen that he integrates successively within his system sociography, the work of Tarde, institutionalism, and Toennies' theory of forms. (19)

If the particular ideas vary from one sociologist to another, there is nevertheless a ground common to all: the concern for scientific construction and for methodological preoccupation, and the sentiment, well expressed by F. Lles y Berdayes (Cuba), that social nature is subject to laws whih can be discovered. (20) There is also the common tendency, which is expressed even in the works of those who are partisans of organicism and psychologism, but which is of course more precise among others, to consider sociology as a distinct and relatively antonomous science with a special object. In addition to the names already cited, this tendency is especially notable in the

---

17. Justo Prieto, *Síntesis sociológica* (1934).
18. Mariano H. Carnejo, *Sociología general* (1908).
19. Antonia Caso, *El concepto de la historia universal y la filosofía de los valores* (1923); *Sociología genética y sistemática* (1925); *La existencia como economía, como desinterés y como caridad* (1932). See also Eugenio María Hostos, *Tratado de sociología* (1904).
20. F. Lles y Berdayes, *El individualismo, la sociedad y el Estado* (1933).

SOCIOLOGY IN LATIN AMERICA

views of López de Mesa (Colombia), Mendoza (Venezuela), Agramonte (Cuba), and McLéan y Estenós (Peru). (21) A final common characteristic of this theoretical sociology is the primary interest in general problems. Nevertheless, a false impression would be left if the more specialized works were neglected. The most numerous of the latter concern legal and political sociology, whether because sociology was born in the law faculties, or because of the problems posed by the difficulties in establishing democracy in recently colonial countries. Contributors to this field includes Arteba (Bolivia), Barragán (Mexico), Cr. Benítez (Venezuela), Eguiluz (Mexico), Lles y Berdayes (Cuba), Letelier (Chile), J. B. Genta (Argentina), and Pontes de Miranda (Brazil). Related special fields include: sociology of war (Baldrich and Orgaz in Argentina and Cornejo in Peru) and sociology of revolution (Orgaz and Poviña in Argentina and Grompone in Uruguay). Other specialties are also to be found: educational sociology (Ramón Elizondo and Poviña in Argentina; F. de Azevedo, Carneiro Leao, and D. de Carvalho in Brazil; Mario Rodrígues in Colombia); sexual sociology (McLéan in Peru); familial sociology (A. J. Tregui in Colombia); social morphology in the demographic sense of the term (Jorge Rosa in Cuba); economic sociology (Fr. Delancour in Haiti); sociology of religion (J. M. Rosa in Argentina); sociology of ideologies (E. Gil Borges and J. R. Mendoza in Venezuela). Finally, the very curious *Sociología de la autenticidad y simulación* by C. Betancour of Bolivia and Colombia may be noted.

American Sociologies. Three periods may be distinguished in the establishment of an American sociology: (1) the period of myths and, in reaction to them, of sociographies of a historical tendency; (2) then, after 1918, the introduction of the comparative method in order to proceed from particular cases to laws valid for all of Latin America; (3) finally, after 1930, the subdivision of national sociologies into a multitude of regional or particular problems, each treated with all the rigor necessary for a study to merit the designation "scientific." But it would be a mistake to think that each stage *ipso facto* insured the disappearence of the previous state

---

21. L. López de Mesa, *Sociología* (1931) and *Disertación sociológica* (1939); José Rafael Mendoza, *Manual de sociología* (1934); Roberto Agramonte, *Tratado de sociología* (1937); Roberto MacLéan y Estenós, *Exégesis sobre el contenido de la sociología* (1930), *Del salvajismo a la civilización* (1936), *Sexo* (1936), *Ficha sociológica de la urbe* (1938), *Sociología* (1938), *and Sociología peruana* (1942).

of development: on the contrary, the myths and sociographies persist even today.

The Twentieth Century was ushered in by two outstanding works: *La ciudad indiana* by Juan Agustín García in Argentina and *Os sertoes* by Euclydes de Cunha in Brazil. García wished to do for the colonial city of Buenos Aires what Fustel de Coulanges had done for the ancient city. But it is evident that the explanatory principle of the city of antiquity, religion, could not serve for a city of colonists who migrated from Spain and mixed with the natives. This is why García's method is closer to that of LePlay: he starts with the nature of the country (the pampas) to derive a labor economy (livestock raising), and, from the latter, the structure of the family, the social psychology of the Argentinian, and finally the reflection of this structure and psychology in the urban development of Buenos Aires in the course of the colonial period. Thus the economy, as an intermediary between the soil and the society, becomes the principal explanatory factor, and Argentine independence is less the product of a political ideology than of the antagonism of interests between the colonists and the homeland. Euclydes de Cunha, who knew well the campaign of Canudos against the mystical rebels, sought to give a sociological explanation of the Brazilian religious fanaticism. The campaign of the soldiers against the *sertanejos* of the *caatinga* (22) becomes in this way the fight of the seaboard against the *sertao*, and since the seaboard has been affected by European influences while the *sertao* is chiefly under native influences, the struggle between two different levels of culture. But for Euclydes it was not a simple matter of distinguishing the two Brazils, for it was also a question of understanding this *sertaneja* culture, both mystical and warlike. It is in the geographical conditions — the barren and desert-like soil and the dry climate — that he looks for his explanation of the psychology, the qualities of courage and endurance, of the "cow hand" and *mestizo*. Thus the analysis of a pathological phenomenon, religious fanaticism, ends up as an apology for men enmeshed in telluric forces.

Actually, it is the pathological cases that primarily interest the partisans of concrete sociology. And if the Brazilian pathology results in fanaticism, that of Agentina results in *caudillismo*

---

22. *Sertao*: the Brazilian interior to the extent that civilization has as yet made little penetration; *sertanejo*: inhabitant of the *sertão*; *caatinga*: type of desert vegetation characterized by small shrubs and cactus.

SOCIOLOGY IN LATIN AMERICA

(feudal war-lordism). The latter became the center of interest of Argentine sociologists at the beginning of the Twentieth Century. In *Nuestra América* (1918) Bunge seeks the explanation of this phenomenon in racial psychology: the Argentinian has derived laziness from the Indian, unhappiness from the Negro, and arrogance from the Spaniard; this explains his passivity that makes him abandon the destiny of his country to dictatorial leaders who are the successors to the colonial *caciques,* instead of concerning himself with the matter. Ayarragaray attempts to be more complete in his work, *La anarquía argentina y el caudillismo* (1904). He notes the influence of race, the absence of political education of the creole, and economic factors. His institutionalism brings us closer to true sociology: the upsurge of the forces of anarchy emerged from the sudden disappearance, at the time of national independence, of the colonial control that had inhibited them. But, as is readily apparent, the disappearence of certain control institutions is basically only a condition, not a cause, of the phenomena of disorder and *caudillismo* that followed; it is necessary to seek further for the cause in racial heritage, which in the last analysis brings us not very far from the formulation of Bunge. The work of A. Alvarez *Adonde vamos* (1904, on the other hand, brings us a little nearer to sociology, at least to the extent that the latter is defined as the study of collective representations. The author shows that under the influence of Catholicism there was established in Spain a certain "mental environment"; it is this heritage, theocratic and medieval, that was carried to America, where it has continued to operate as an obstacle to further civilization. We are here then at the other extreme from a racial explanation, since it is no longer the race that accounts for the collective psychology, but rather the changes in the ethnic group depend on changes in the mental environment; the mental heritage is actually not transmitted biologically but by the education of new generations by older ones. It follows that intervention, a mental revolution, is possible, and, according to Alvarez, this will be the work of the school.

In Argentina therefore we see a transition from geographical and racial to social explanations. This movement is duplicated in Brazil. We have noted the importance of the soil and climate in the work of Euclydes. The geographical factor still today inspires a number of Brazilian studies, such as those of Florentino de Menezes, and its importance is fortified by all the influence of the LePlay school. In this regard it is necessary to call attention to an especially typical case, that studied by Jorge de Goulart in his *Formation social du Rio Grande do Sul*. The country was settled by Azorians, that is, by a people characterized by a particularist family; now, in migrating to the region of the pampas, the family was transformed as a consequence of the influence of the environment into a quasi-patriarchal family. The racial factor dominates the work of Oliveira Vianna, who believes in the unequal capacity of the races and attributes an influence in Brazilian history to an opposition between the Portuguese blonde of German descent and the Portuguese brunette, more or less mixed with Arabian stocks. (23) The work of Gilberto Freyre, to which we shall return below, may be considered also as a reaction against these currents, by substituting ecology for anthropogéography, (24) and sociology for racial determinism.

If sociology in the South of the continent starts as a social pathology, the same is true of the North, but the ideologies are more contradictory in the latter region. Against the condemnation of miscegenation the region has developed an opposing tendency. Palza S. Humberto (Bolivia) justified the Hispanic man and the mestizo in close contact with nature who utilizes his cultural resources, José Vasconcelos (Mexico) arrives at a glorification of the "cosmic man," by a sort of American Bergsonism. Thus the evil comes primarily from the importation of Western civilization, particularly liberal democracy, in contradiction to tropical nature. (25)

All these brilliant essays have not been in vain. They have contributed a taste for national history treated sociologically or for sociography. The example of Alcides Arguedas (Bolivia) is very neat from this point of view; he starts with an essay, *Pueblo enfermo* (1909) and ends with a *Histoire de la Bolivie* (1922). If in these sociographies the importance of the geographical factor is often preponderant — as with Mendoza (Bolivia), Lauréano Vallenilla Lanz (Venezuela), and even in large part with Macléan y Estenós (Peru) (26) — in general we find here again the same tendency

---

23. See Oliveira Vianna, *Populações meridionâes do Brasil* (1920) and *Evolução do povo brasileiro* (1923).

24. Besides ecology, the influence of the French geographical school is to be noted in the work of Freyre.

25. José Vasconcelos, *La raza cósmica* (1925); R. Chavez González *Democracia y tropicalismo*.

26. Jaime Mendoza, *El factor geográfico en la nacionalidad boliviana* (1925); Laureano Vallenilla Lanz, *Cesarismo democrático* (1930), and *Disgregación e integración* (1930); R. MacLéan y Estenós, *Sociología peruana* (1942).

to syncretism that we have already noted in theoretical sociology. The studies in fact synthesize the factors of physical environment, race, economic and political influences, and pass in review the evolution of the family, the property regime, the church, and the State. These works seem for the last few years to be oriented more and more toward cultural sociology, and this is especially marked with Gonzáles (Paraguay), Moreno (Ecuador), and above all Fernando de Azevedo (Brazil) who tries to explain the whole of the ideal values of his country more by the social structure than by external factors. (27)

But was it not possible to go beyond the terrain of description and explanation of national pecularities, to see if there were not phenomena common to the diverse Latin American republics, to see if by the comparative method it was not possible to proceed from purely causal investigations to inductive laws of correlation or succession? This second stage was opened with the *Estudios de sociología venezolana* (1918) by P. M. Arcaya, who compares the Venezuelan situation with that of Argentina. But undoubtedly the greatest representative of this development is the Chilean, A. Venturino, with his three series of books (1920-1930) on Chilean sociology, American sociology, and general sociology The first series provides the base for the whole construction: the existence of a dual determinism — geographical determinism and historical materialism. The comparison of what has taken place in Chile with what has happened in other American republics arrives then at a specification of both differences and similarities: differences, since the physical environments that leave their marks on man differ — pampas, tropical forests, and rugged mountains imposing on individuals different modes of life and isolating them in clusters separated from each other; similarities, since all the American States grew out of the same regime of colonial economy and have undergone the same counter-influences of capitalist economy. Thus there emerges from the study of Latin America a very general law, the law of interdependence that is basically only an aspect of the great law of solidarity: cosmological interdependence, interdependence of culture levels (for example, between pre-Columbian and Iberian civilization), interdependence among the several American States,

---

27. J. Natalicio Gonzales, *Proceso y formación de la cultura paraguaya* (1938); J. E. Moreno, *El sentido histórico y la cultura* (1939), and *Para una sociología ecuatoriana* (1940); F. de Azevedo, *A cultura brasileira* (1943).

and intercontinental interdependence that results in every American retrogression having its counterpart in Europe and *vice versa*. Venturiano thus thinks that he has arrived at some results for general sociology, for, he says, until now sociologists have devoted themselves to discovering particular correlations and have not taken account of the integral correlation revealed by the study of colonial regimes.

It is not, however, in the direction of a global sociology that the most contemporary researches in concrete sociology seem to be oriented. Was sociology, in so far as it is a positive science, in fact sufficiently definitively established to permit such generalizations? Durkheim maintained that general sociology could only come in last place after particular sociologies had been achieved, and in North America vast syntheses were followed by fragmentary studies and field investigations that permitted, by their very limitations, a greater methodological certainty. Latin America is following this movement, with a little lag. The creation of the Instituto de Sociología at the University of Buenos Aires, with its program of work, corresponds in Argentina to this new state of modesty and technical precision in sociology. This development is parallelled in Mexico by the Instituto de Investigaciones Sociales of the University of Mexico. The founder of the latter institute, L. Mendieta y Nuñez, has himself given the example for this new type of sociology with his studies on *O problema agrario* (1937), *La habitación indígena* (1939), and *El alcoholismo entre las razas indígenas* (1939).

It is in this current that in my opinion it is necessary to place the work of the Brazilian, Gilberto Freyre, who utilizes the methods of both ecology and social history, studying an enviroment — the Brazilian Northwest region of sugar cane — and a period that extends from the colony to independence. His subject is the patriarchal family, its structure, its strength, and its disintegration with the appearance of a new type of life — the urban. But the family leads to a series of interrelations, between husband and wife, parents and children, the lord of the mill and the chaplain, masters and slaves, proprietor and agregado (a peon or serf). It is these different types of relations that are modified through time, particulary with the climbing on the social scale of the "bachelor" and free mulatto. And in order to study these transformations it is necessary to locate them in their habitat, because of another and still more essential relation: that between the

SOCIOLOGY IN LATIN AMERICA

type of life and the architecture of the house. It is this last relation that is represented in the titles of his books: *Casa grande e senzala* (1935), house of the master and living quarters of the slave in the colonial period and in the period of independence; *Sobrados e mucambos*, which are the ancient *casas grandes* and *senzales* transported from the country to the city and taking on a new and unaccustomed aspect because of the street that joins the houses. The books of Freyre, because of their value (they have become classics of Brazilian sociology), have inspired other works of unequal merit, like *O outro Nordeste* by Djacir Menezes on the *sertaneja* society, the *Marcha para Oeste* by Cassiano Ricardo on the Paulist *bandeirante* society — a book in which poetry presses upon science.

At the Centro de Pesquisas of the Faculty of Philosophy and at the Ecole Libre de Sociologie (Sao Paulo, Brazil), work is confined to still more limited studies; the most important of those published to date is *Roteiro do cafe* by Sergie Milliet on the correlations between economic and demographic phenomena through the displacements of coffee cultivation from old, exhausted land to new land. But the most interesting phenomenon that Brazil presents to sociology is certainly the double contact of races and ethnic groups: white, black, and red races, and European and Japanese immigrants. With respect to races, Freyre had already shown in the works previously cited how slavery separates colors and fuses cultures at the same time. Arthur Ramos, who started with ethnology, comes ever closer to sociology in studying the phenomena of acculturation, more particular under the form of religious syncretism — Negro-Catholic-cabocle-spirite fetishism. With respect to ethnic groups, the investigations inaugurated by Oliveira Vianna (*Raca e assimilacao*, 1931) on the intermixture of Brazilians and immigrants and their descendents have been continued with other methods, in view of the difficulties in using statistical data, by Emilio Willems in a recent book, *Assimilacao e populacoes margines do Brasil*, devoted to the descendants of Germans. But Brazil is not the only country in which not only biological miscegenation — the only type hitherto studied with respect to the opposing doctrines of the superiority or inferiority of the *mestizo* — but also cultural intermixture exists. It does perhaps present a unique case in that it unites the racial problem and that of European and Asiatic immigrants. In Mexico also there exists miscegenation of whites and Indians; in the Antilles, the mixture of whites and Negroes. Their study may lead to some discoveries of importance; already in Cuba Fernando Ortiz has formed a critique, accepted by Malinowski, of the term acculturation, substituting the term, trans-culturation. (28) It seems that this change of name corresponds to a more basic modification of significance.

III

Critical Appraisal and Conclusions. In these currents, those of theoretical sociology and concrete sociology, there has been thus constant progress through the progressive elimination or correction of doctrines superceded: geographic determinism, racial inequality, historical materialism, Spencerian organicism; through the rejection of dogmas from outside sociology favorable to the literary essay; through the greater and greater and greater attention, resulting from university instruction, to the explanation of the social by the social and not by something outside of it, and to the utilization in each case of the most appropriate and precise methods. But, if we examine the actual points at which these two currents have arrived we find ourselves in the presence of two opposing attitudes: synthesis and syncretism on the one hand, analysis and fragmentation of research on the other. It is these two attitudes that we must understand.

The syncretism reflects a very comprehensible state of mind: that of retaining from each theory the portion of truth that it contains, of presenting to students a vision of "the social" that leaves no part in the shade. If truth be defined as the convergence of thoughts, it is evident that it would be fortunate to find a synthesis that could command the unanimous support of scholars. But it appears at once that syncretism does not itself escape subjectivism, since there are as many types of synthesis as there are searchers who devote themselves to this type of work. Moreover the only possible synthesis would be one that rejected theories in order to investigate the duly established facts and particular laws and to coordinate them. Undoubtedly, even here, there would remain a difficulty, namely, that facts are never apprehended except through concepts — logical categories deriving from systems. But the difficulty is still greater when one attempts, as in Latin America, to coordinate instead of facts the systems themselves. For these systems contradict each other; they are not juxtaposed. When Angel M. Paredes, for

---

28. Fernando Ortiz, *Contrapunteo cubano del tabaco y el azucar* (1940).

SOCIOLOGY IN LATIN AMERICA

example, seeks to conciliate in *La conciencia social* the voluntarism of Durkheim and the psychologism of Tarde, and, even beyond that, organicism, making social life a combination but proclaiming that in order to understand it it is necessary to study the constituent elements — tracing the psychic bond to a biological instinct, sympathy — he unites what cannot be united. If social reality is a combination, then it is by nature different from individual psyches, and the only possible method in sociology is to study collective actions. This is the more the case in view of the fact that the fusion of consciences takes us away from natural organization.

In a more general way, Latin American sociology is seen as a genetic sociology, a philosophy of history, and at the same time giving a preponderant place to immobile factors such as geographical environment and race. This again is contradictory, for a genetic sociology ought to explain the social by the immediately preceding social; if appeal is made to external interpretative factors, then development is only apparent and dynamic laws only illusions.

A more defensible syncretism is that which makes of diverse systems, not elements of a totality, but dialectical periods — thus separate and progressive — in the development of sociological doctrine. But then syncretism cannot unite everything; it is only partial. Thus Orgaz reconciles Tarde and Durkheim by making of them two successive chapters in a single science, the former laying the bases for micro-sociology (interrelations), the latter, for macro-sociology (the institutions that result from the contacts among individuals). But there would still remain the reconciliation of sociology as a general science of culture (and no longer simply of formal connections) with sociology as a *corpus* of the social sciences. This is why there are almost as many syncretisms as there are sociologies chosen to be synthesized. And from this it is understandable why Brazilian sociologists have in general preferred to work with a single current of influences — Durkheimian, North American, or German — in order to extend it and draw from it new results. It might be objected that they thereby only avoid one danger to fall into a greater one, that of an *a priori* dogmatism. But there is actually none of this, for it its noticeable that they attach themselves less to dogmas than to the general spirit; they tend to convert the theories into methodologies for research and techniques for the exploration of reality. They do not content themselves with what has already been said; they seek rather to exhaust the inventive fecundity of a certain orientation of thought, of a certain way of apprehending the social. Now here a new syncretism becomes possible, which would consist in the successive clarification of a problem with the aid of various theories, no longer taken as systems but now as methods — just as the light of different projectors in the four corners of a sports arena are thrown upon the ring. Thus G. Freyre starts with cultural anthropology, studying material objects (houses, furniture, etc.), but with the object of discovering thereby the society, that is, what Durkheim has called collective representations; his work leads to a community, explored with the aid of ecology, but since ecology as an inventory of the environment runs the risk of hiding the institutional structure that operates more basically, he has recourse to the historical method. (29)

But with Freyre we have already passed from theoretical sociology to Americanist sociology. That interests us more. It is probably in thinking of the latter and of the results that it has already obtained that the Viennese, A. Menzel, wrote: "Sociological thought in Latin America, beginning with the independence movement, has been notably fecund; however, it remains partly unknown because, in a large measure, its contents are still to be explored and put in order." What has delayed this exploration and ordering is the fact that many sociologies of America fall into a pure and simple history, sociology being relegated to a very general introduction, or even in the text set side by side some regional descriptions and some morsels of sociological theory without any connection between the two. Venturino marks an advance, for instead of applying some imported theories to new data, going from the general to the particular, he starts with Chilean realities and, by comparisons, attempts to arrive at a universal law: he goes from the particular to the general. But his attempt, although interesting, came perhaps too soon, before the exhaustive study of the continent was achieved, and this is why the law with which he ended, that of interdependence, if it be correct, is more of a "generality" than a general law. It is understandable thus why the researchers orient themselves more and more toward limited studies, which gain in depth what they lose in extensity. It is not necessary to fear monographs; everything depends on the way they are done. As M. Mauss well said in his study on *Les variations saisonnières chez les Eskimos*, a single case will studied can reveal a law of extreme generality. Latin American

---

29. P. Arboresse-Bastide, Preface to G. Freyre's *Un engenheiro frances no Brasil* (1940).

sociology however will still have in this regard an obstacle to surmount, the facility with techniques of the North Americans. These have been so well pointed up, standardized, and industrialized that one is tempted to apply them without more ado; a certain phobia of intellectual effort runs the risk of substituting a sociology consisting of a quasi-mechanical application of imported methods for a sociology of imported doctrines. This has given rise to the danger cry by Echevarría in Mexico. (30) We think personally that each objective requires its appropiate technique, and that the method is not independent of the material to be encompassed, an empty form that can be molded indiscriminately to any sector whatever of social reality. Each time a sociologist reaches a new terrain, he should forge a new Methodological Discourse. How could the ancient Discourses — the European ones made for crystallized societies, American ones made for societies in formation — be valid for these paradoxical societies "both traditional and without roots, institutional and without consistencies," dynamic and fixed, as are the societies of Central and South America?

Shining through all these difficulties, however, the Latin American sociologies have arrived at some results that are not negligible, and which in conclusion it remains for us to review.

Durkheim distinguished, besides mechanical solidarity and organic solidarity, a pathological form of solidarity, with a forced division of labor, that he called colonial solidarity. Now, if the first two have been amply studied, the last remained to be explored. It is this methodical exploration in the first place that Latin American sociology gives us, and it provides us with an original explanation in showing that colonial solidarity is the juxtaposition in superimposed strata of mechanical solidarity on the part of the Indians or Negro slaves and of organic solidarity on the part of the white colonists who brought with them in their feudal regime a nascent capitalism. The disappearance of this forced solidarity at the moment of Independence clarifies another problem of importance, that of the relations between social structures and collective values, or, if one prefers, between the body and the soul of society. When, for example, the democratic ideology was introduced in South America, it was apparent that the struggle between parties had only the effect of continuing the contest between the patriarchal clans or families, without truly effective participation on the part of the colored

---

30. J. M. Echevarría, *Sociología contemporánea*.

plebeians. The study of religions also shows that spiritual values become diversified in accordance with social stratification, giving rise to as many Catholicisms as there were races in contact, and with the evolution of cults parallelling the transformation of races into hierarchized classes.

To a certain degree the Latin American present clarifies the European past. An entire series of phenomena which had taken place before — the formation of ethnic groups by a fusion of races, the formation of religions by the syncretism of beliefs, the passage from feudal economy to urban development — we encounter as phenomena of today analyzed by Portuguese-and-Spanish-American sociologists. "To a certain degree," we have said, for the more recent phenomena are also more rapid, and sociological duration, like the psychological, cannot be foreshadowed without thereby changing even its qualitative nature; the differences in rates involve a difference in the social reality. Moreover, the historic institutions that we find again in Latin America, like, for example, familial patriarchalism or the feudal regime, cannot be assimilated to the patriarchalism of the ancient world or the feudalism of the Middle Ages, because they are part of quite another world with a predominatly capitalistic mentality.

Latin American sociology is therefore of considerable interest, and its contribution valuable, for it shows the existence of general trends and at the same time of trends specialized with respect to time and place. It is accordingly potentially suited for reconciling the two neighboring sciences, sociology and social anthropology, that today hold in dispute the same domain.

In sum, Latin American sociology has arrived at that fortunate time in its existence when it has realized the special place reserved for it in the whole of sociology, as a revealer of new concepts, at the same time that it is in process of constructing its own instruments for research and analysis of reality.

SELECTED BIBLIOGRAPHY

Alvarez Andrews, Oscar, "Introducción a la sociología americana," *Revista mexicana de sociología*, 4: 7-22, 1942.

Barnes, Harry Elmer, and Howard Becker, *Social Thought from Lore to Science*, vol. II, *Sociological Trends throughout the World*, (Boston, etc.: D. C. Heath and Co., 1938), "Latin American," pp. 1119-1134.

SOCIOLOGY IN LATIN AMERICA

Bernard, L. L., "The Development and Present Tendencies of Sociology in Argentina," *Social Forces*, 6: 13-27, September, 1927.

Bernard, L. L., "Latin America," in "Introduction II—The Social Sciences as Disciplines," *Encyclopaedia of the Social Sciences*, 1: 301-320.

Bernard, L. L., "Topical Summaries of Current Literature: Sociology in Argentina," *American Journal of Sociology*, 33: 110-119, July, 1927.

Congrès de l'Institut International de Sociologie, "Rapport sur la sociologie contemporaine au Brésil," Sent to the Congress in 1937, *Revista do arquivo municipal de Sâo Paulo*, vol. XXXXVIII.

Ingenieros, José, *Sociología argentina*, (Buenos Aires: 1910).

Mendieta y Nuñez, Lucio, "Integración de las investigaciones en las Américas," *Revista mexicana de sociología*, 4: 125-137, 1942.

Mijares, Augusto, "La interpretación pesimista de la sociología hispano-americana," *Revista interamericana de sociología*, vol. I.

Moore, Wilbert E., "Rural-Urban Conflict in Argentine Sociological Theories," *Rural Sociology*, 6: 138-143, June, 1941.

Poviña, Alfredo, *Historia de la sociología en Latinoamérica*, (México, D. F.: Fondo de Cultura Económica, 1941). This is the only complete book dealing with Latin American sociology.

Roger Bastide, Agrégé de Philosophie, Paris, Professor of Sociology, University of São Paulo, Brazil. Author of *Les Problèmes de la Vie Mystique*, 1930 and *Eléments de Sociologie Religieuse*, 1935. Numerous papers in Brazilian periodicals

CHAPTER XXII

ITALIAN SOCIOLOGY

by

COSTANTINO PANUNZIO

Introduction. Sociology, as this writer understands it, no longer aims to make the grand synthesis Comte conceived of, but simply seeks to develop into an empirical, autonomous discipline, working in a specific field; to create its own body of theory and hypotheses, methodology and techniques; gather its own data; and arrive at its own generalizations.

As to subject matter, systematic sociology, as now conceived, seeks primarily to study human group life, particularly the social group. Groups are clusters of individuals held together by common characteristics and objectives, and having varying degrees of person-to-person, frequent, compulsive, repetitive, and routined relationship and interaction. Social groups are relatively small groups in which sociality is intensively at work.

A systematic sociology seeks to discover the dynamics, origins and development, the structures and functional processes, the maladjustments, the telesis and disorganization of groups; it aims to establish the correlations between group life, on the one hand, and various aspects of physical nature, biological nature, and culture; and it seeks to discover the regulations or "laws" which govern group life. In all its work, it keeps the group, and especially the social group, as the focal point of its investigation.

Since groups consist of individuals and since they form parts of institutions, societies and cultures, sociology studies these also; but only with respect to the group. A rigidly systematic sociology investigates only those aspects of the individual's biological and mental life, his private mode-of-living routine, personal habits, which may have, as they often do have, group bearing. Likewise, a systematic sociology studies what we ordinarily term the "social institutions," but only with the group as a frame of reference (*e. g.*, the group's position in or its influence on the governmental institution or war, the influence which the mechanization of economic life has or has not on group life, or group life on mechanization). In like manner, it investigates society or societies, in respect to the position, function, influence of group life, particularly social-group life, on a given neighborhood, parochial, communal, regional, national society, or a society as a whole. And, finally, systematic sociology studies culture, not in respect to culture traits, complexes, patterns or the rise and fall of civilizations, etc., but only in regard to the position or function of the group in a given culture (*e. g.*, the stamp which previous culture places or does not place on the groups, the extent to which the group is or is not the ultimate residuary and transmitter of culture, the degree to which culture modifices group life or group life culture).

In short, a systematic sociology is concerned only with group life and keeps the group, especially the social group, as the focus of all its investigation and theoretical work.

I

Early Italian Sociology. If this is what we mean by "Twentieth Century Sociology" then we may say in a word, there is as yet in Italy — as everywhere else for that matter — very little sociology. In his essay on "Status of Sociology in Italy," (1) Robert Michels names some hundred and fifty titles, but, on close scrutiny, very few of these turn out to be sociology as we now understand it.

Italian pro-sociologists, like those in other countries, were spellbound by Comte's positivist, evaluative, reformist, synthesizing program; and they devoted three or four decades almost wholly to

---

1. *Social Forces*, 9: 20-39, October, 1930.

attempts at assembling and synthesizing, or to making encyclopedic catalogues, of the findings of the social sciences. The early volumes of the *Rivista di sociologia*, which began publication in 1897, though containing articles by some now well-known names (Gumplowicz, Durkheim, Loria, Fauconnet, Kowalewski, Pareto and others), lump literally everything together, and pass it out as sociology. These volumes draw on ethnography, ethnology and anthropology, history and political economy, economics and social economics, on criminology, social ethics, social reform and social work; they discuss such topics as slavery in the Americas, war and peace in ancient Athens, immigration to the United States, social doctrines, the process of civilization, demography, class struggle, Greek proverbs, etc. The product certainly is not sociology; it might better be called hodgepodge-ology or catch-all-ogy.

In time, Italian sociologists turned to a delimitation of the field, to an inquiry into precisely what sociology should aim to do, what its basic hypotheses, its methods and techniques should be. Most of these early efforts, however, were unsuccessful. Icilio Vanni, for example, in his *Prime linee di un programma critico di sociologia* (First Outlines of a Critical Program of Sociology, Perugia, 1888) acknowledges that "sociology is discredited or suspect in the minds of many....," but he is so lost in Comte's synthesis scheme that he proceeds to do the very thing he criticizes. More or less the same thing is true of A. Asturato, *La Sociologia, i suoi metodi e le sue scoperte* (Sociology, its Methods and Discoveries, Genoa, 1897), which, though frequently cited in subsequent works, makes general pronouncements on cultural, societal, institutional, and some intergroup phenomena, but barely touches the group itself and the social group scarcely at all.

At the turn of the century, several works apeared. Of these mention may be made of Achille Loria, *Sociologia* (Verona, 1901) Fausto Squillace, *Dottrine sociologiche* (Roma, 1902), and Francesco Cosentini, *Sociologia genetica*, (Sassari, 1903). Allesandro Groppali poured forth six sizeable volumes bearing sociological titles in that many years; only two of these, however, namely, his *Saggi di sociologia* (Essays on Sociology, Milan, 1902) and *Elementi di sociologia* (Elements of Sociology, Genoa, 1905) even remotely approach scientific sociology. Next came Francesco Cosentini, *Sociologia* (Turino, 1912), and Amerigo Namias, *Principii di sociologia e politica* (Principles of Sociology and Politics, Rome, 1923). Of all these books, only those of Loria, Squillace

ITALIAN SOCIOLOGY

and Cosentini throw some fundamental light or make quasi-sociological contributions. Squillace comes close to scientific sociology in the work mentioned above and in his somewhat limited *Dizionario di sociologia* (Palermo, 1911).

Works Outlining the Objective of Sociology. There are two small books, however, which make theoretical sociological sense. One of these is Emilio Morselli, *Elementi di sociologia generale* (Elements of General Sociology, Milan, 1898). In it the author comes very close to a definition of scientific sociology. Much in the manner of Ginsberg's *Sociology*, it sets forth a cogent and meaty discussion of the origin of sociology, a classification of social phenomena, the idea of social development, the main "social laws," the methods and problems of sociology. The work is well worth perusing even now.

The second book is Filippo Carli, *Introduzione alla sociologia generale* (Introduction to General Sociology, Bologna, 1925). Significantly enough, Carli, as Robert Michels tells us, was General Secretary of the Chamber of Commerce at Brescia when Corrado Gini, then Professor of Political Economy at the University of Padua and later well-know as demographer, secured him to give a sort of extension course in general sociology at the University of Padua.

Carli's *Introduzione* which, the author states, "reproduces part of the course the author gave at the University of Padua during the academic year 1924-25," is well conceived, competently executed, and comes to grips with the basic problem of the objective of sociology. Its three parts discuss "the Field of Sociological Investigation," "The Ends and Means of the Investigation" and "Fundamental Systematizations." Its eight chapters consider the meaning of the social relation or *rapport*, the group, the limits and subdivisions of sociology, sociological laws, the sociological method, characteristics and classification of social forces, and the classification of social facts.

But while Carli sees very clearly that it is the task of sociology to study group life and especially social interaction, he merely draws together materials from history, psychology, economics and political sciences; he indulgesin the easy task of theorizing and making outlines about what should be done; but does not get down to the grilling job of doing even a little of it; and, apparently without realizing it, he koes on making of sociology a grand systhesizing science, almost wholly forgetting the group. As Shakespeare would have said, if to do were as easy as to know what were good to do, sociology shelves would be shorter and its tomes richer and more significant.

Such general sociology as was in process of development in Italy, like most other such work, suffered a setback with the rise of Fascism — a stark illustration of what societal crises will do to some academic minds. The serious student almost completely vanished and became prostrate before the Buffoon of Palazzo Venezia and prostituted to his demagogy. The demographers Gini and Savorgnan, for example, lost their scientific grip. Carli, who gave promise of accomplishing something significant, was lost to the discipline and devoted himself to a defense of the Regime and the economic function which he thought it was performing.

General Sociological Works. When we pass from the works aiming to state what sociology should do to the doing of it, we encounter in Italy, as elsewhere, very few works of importance. Vilfredo Pareto is the most important. Pareto, who was discovered and exploited *ad nauseam* in the United States about a decade or so ago, was trained in physics; he became a consulting engineer and superintendent of iron mines; and, after searching in vain for a university post in Italy, became Professor of Political Economy at Lausanne. As a scholar he was basically an economist, not a sociologist.

Although Pareto has been called the founder of mathematical sociology, his monumental work in three volumes, *Trattato di sociologia generale* (3 vols., Florence, 1916), ably recast into English as *The Mind and Society* (4 vols., New York, 1935), is not really sociology. As Spencer tried to twist society into a sort of biological structure, so Pareto attempted to fit all superorganic phenomena into Comte's social-physics mold and then squeeze from it the "social equilibrium" law. His enormous work, however, scarcely deals at all with social phenomena; it is concerned, rather, almost wholly with the equilibrium between nations, historical periods, classes, etc., which is conceived in mechanistic terms, and reduced to mathematical equations.

This, of course, is not to dismiss Pareto as of no value whatever to the sociologist. The distinction he drew between the logical and non-logical in human action; his emphasis upon the necessity of non- evaluative observation and investigation; his definition of the logico-experimental method; his stress on the plurality and interplay of causes; his theory of the residues and derivations — to mention his main ideas—are of importance to sociologists. How-

ITALIAN SOCIOLOGY

ever, some of these concepts were known from the days of Francis Bacon on, while others are but stated and not at all applied in the work itself. Pareto himself is often illogical, evaluative, subjective and confusing (if not confused); he employs imputations as if they were actual data; and his final product is a highly speculative examination of the supposed broader processes of society or of history, couched in highly complicated mathematical formulas; formulas which will be about as useful in the development of empirical sociology as integral calculus is to semantics. In the last analysis, Pareto's is societal philosophy, social ethics, and philosophy of history, rather than sociology.

Before leaving Pareto mention should be made of the *Compendio di sociologia generale* (Florence, 1920). In this work Giulio Farina, a disciple of Pareto, removes much of the chaff and reduces the eighteen hundred pages of Pareto's original to about six hundred small pages. Although even this is not overclear or systematic, someone could render a service to non-Italian students by adapting it for their use, much in the manner in which Howard Becker recast von Wiese in *Systematic Sociology*.

Luigi Bellini, *Saggi di una teoria generale della società* (Essays on a General Theory of Society, Milano, 1934) is more systematic than Pareto. It considerers the dynamics and morphology of society as a whole. It, too, barely touches the social, and is highly mechanistic.

The works of Guiseppe Pitrè (1841-1916) deserve more than a passing mention. Pitrè was born, raised and passed nearly his entire life in Palermo. After fighting under Garibaldi, he became a physician by profession, but devoted much of his life to the study of history, philosophy, and folklore. During the last six years of his life, he taught *demopsicologia* (folk psychology) at the University of Palermo.

Although Pitrè's twenty-five slender volumes, *Tradizioni popolari Siciliane* (Sicilian Popular Traditions, initiated in 1871 and completed in 1913) are in essence folklore, still they contain considerable material of a near-sociological character dealing with usages. The volumes are all the more valuable because, apart from the historical items, they contain records of minute observations, made by an identified-observer, native to the culture he is describing, covering a small area (Sicily) intensively, and confined largely to the author's own period. They constitute a veritable treasure house of Sicilian folkways and mores. Pietrès also published *Tradizioni popolari in*

Italia (Popular Traditions in Italy, 1894). While these volumes do not contitute a systematic study of group phenomena, the wealth of data they contain could be of use to the sociologist specializing on folkways and mores.

While mentioning usages, a passing reference should be made to Fausto Squillace, *La Moda* (1912) which treats the subject in a somewhat sociological manner.

Social Origins. When we turn to the special fields, we find Italian sociologists, like their comperes of other nationalities, often being lured by the primitive. Presumably they are tracing the origins and continuities which form the basis of the present social order, or are making comparative studies. But they seldom do or can do either scientifically. With virtually no direct data and only meager indirect materials (archeological, ethnographical, anthropological) at their disposal, they are obliged to rely mainly on "scientific imagination." Sometimes they observe W. I. Thomas's "contemporary ancestor," but usually they can witness only public acts and even those superficially, and being non-indigenous they cannot even remotely approach the social. Even at their best, their findings throw very little light on the group life of modern Western societies.

The Italian material on the primitive is voluminous; but one looks in vain for any real social origins or social continuities. Massimo Colucci, *Principi di diritto consuetudinario della Somalia meriodionale* (Principles of Ceremonial Right in Southern Somaliland, Firenze, 1924) is a case in point. The book is readable and well-done, and is as frequently referred to as Hobhouse, Wheeler and Ginsberg, *Material Culture and Social Institutions of the Simpler Peoples* is in English-language works. But the neat, novel-like picture it presents evokes suspicion. In any event, it casts as much light on Western social origins as an American scholar might by studying the peoples of Samoa. G. Sergi's *Origine umane* (Human Origins, Torino, 1913) is also well-known, but it is largely physical anthropology.

The Individual in Society. Occasionally Italian sociologists deal with the place of the individual in society. Francesco de Sarlo, *L'uomo nella vita sociale* (Man in Social Life, Bari, 1931) aims to do this. It draws a neat distinction between the individual-group and the individual-society relationship; but the work is vitiated by the broad conclusion that "The natural world is *found as is*, the human world is the product of the activity of man: the natural order is realized by means of forces (causes) and according to laws which, though necessary (sic), are blind and fatal, while man's order is realized by the action of *motives* and with the confluence of factors, in great part psychological in nature." The reader of these pages needs not have pointed out that after all the actions of men, their motives, their psychological activity are as much natural in the social realm as are "natural" phenomena in the physical universe.

Stratification Sociology. There are a number of works which deal with the various strata, classes or segments of society. Giorgio Arcoleo, *Forme vecchie, idee nuove* (Old Forms, New Ideas, Bari, 1909) contains a discussioin of the disoriented intellectual; Guido Cavaglieri-Eugenio Florian, *Vagabondi*, (Vagabonds, Turin, 1907) presents an able description of the wanderer and the vagabond; Mario Morasso, *Contro quelli che non sanno* (Against Those Who Don't Know, Palermo, 1901) shows that property-less and dispossessed classes are such because "don't know any better": Enrico Loncao, *Considerazioni sulla genesi della borghesia in Sicilia* (Considerations on the Genesis of the Bourgeoisie in Sicily, Palermo, 1900), considers the rise of the bourgeoisie in Sicily; Pasquale Rossi wrote three volumes analyzing the influence of the persecuted, martyrs and mystics on the masses: *I Persequitati* (The Persecuted, Cosenza, 1894), *Mistici e settari* (Mystics and Sectarians, Milan, 1900), and *Suggestionari e la folla* (The "Suggestionaries" and the Crowd, Torino, 1902); Roberto Michels, *Proletariato e borghesia* (Torino, 1907) considers the academic socialists. A. Guarnieri-Ventimiglia, *Conflitti Sociali* (Social Conflicts, Torino, 1905) advances the thesis that antagonism is as natural in society as in all realms of nature. Michels also considered the "lower" classes in his *Saggi economico-statistici sulle classi popolari* (Economico-statistical Considerations on Popular Classes, Palermo, 1911).

Closely related to these are Roberto Michels, *Sociologia del partito nella democrazia moderna* (Sociology of the Political Party in Modern Democracy, Torino, 1910) in which the author advances the proposition that in proportion as a political party grows in size and power it loses its hold on the people, while the latter resist it for fear of losing such gains as have been made under it. Gina Lombroso, *Vantaggi della degenezione* (Torino, 1904) considers "the advantages of degeneration," advancing the thesis that as occupational or other dangers increase resistance to the degenerative processes also increases; Federico Chessa discusses the "hereditary transmission" of professional ability in *Transmissione ereditaria delle professioni* (Torino, 1912); Napoleone Colajanni sees a relation between socialism and crime in his *Socialismo e criminalità* (Roma-Napoli, 1903); Gaetano Salvemini, *Tendenze vecchie e necessità nuove nel movimento operario italiano* (Old Tendencies and New Necessities in the Italian Labor Movement, Bologna 1922) considers the post-First-World-War labor movement in Italy; Ivanoe Bononi-Carlo Vezzzani, *Movimento proletario Mantovano* (Proletarian Movement in Mantua, Milano, 1901) presents one of the few local studies.

There are numerous similar works on the mendicant, the brigand, the composition of secret societies (e.g. the Camorra and the Mafia), on the *contadino* or farm worker, on the merchant, the leisure and the ruling classes. Nearly all of these works, however, as the titles cited above clearly suggest, are general, polemic, evaluative, and far from scientific. While highly interesting and significant as descriptions, they add little to the theory or to the systematic factual basis of a scientific sociology. (2)

Sociology of Sex and Marriage. Several works deal with the phenomena of sex, marriage, and the family. Pio Vazzi, *Lotta di sesso* (Sex Conflict, Milan, 1900) advances the theory that sex, rooted as it is in the organism, not only gives men and women different functions, but sets them into perpetual antagonism. Benini, *Principi di demografia* (Priciples of demography, Rome, 1901), though dealing principally with population in general, contains some items on sex selection. Corrado Gini's *Il sesso* (Sex, Bologna, 1908) is almost wholly a statistical analysis of sex at birth, sex distribution in the general population, sex and age etc. Moebius, *Inferiorità mentale della donna* (Mental Inferiority of Woman, Turin, 1904) considers the moot subject stated in the title far from scientifically; while Roberto Michels, *Limiti della morale sessuale* (Torino, 1912) considers, as the title suggests, the biological limits of sexual morality. Franco Savorgnan, *Scelta matrimoniale* (Matrimonial Selection, Ferrara, 1924) examines proximity, homogeneity, age, religion, and other elements as factors in marital selection; and A. Bosco's *Divorzi e le separazioni personali dei conjughi* (Rome 1908) examines divorce and personal separations of married people. The main sociological contribution these works make is to present considerable evidence which supports

---

2. For additional titles, see Robert Michels, *loc. cit.*, on which a few of the titles in this section are based.

ITALIAN SOCIOLOGY

the hypothesis that cultural proximity is a favorable factor in mating and marriage.

Sociology of Religion. There is a considerable body of Italian material which may be loosely termed the sociology of religion. These books, however, are not by sociologists, but are written almost wholly by Roman Catholic priests and prelates; they usually investigate religion not as a phenomenon of group life, performing certain social functions; they constitute, rather, attempts at a rationalization of Roman Catholic ideology, doctrine, dogma and usages; and they approach group phenomena almost wholy in terms of problems situations, maladjustment, and the necessity of religious reform.

Ugo Mioni, *Manuale di sociologia* (Manual of Sociology, Turin, 1932) is one of the widely-used of these. It sets forth the "grave sociological problems" that beset present-day society; analyzes these problems in terms of Catholic doctrine; then proposes solutions in keeping with those doctrines; and, finally, points a finger and adds a solemn "or else": or else society will enter on an era of intellectual and moral darkness and plunge itself into economic conditions worse than any ever experienced. "Let Russia teach us what horrors a wrong interpretation of the great problems will cause." Jacope Banchi, *Vita sociale* (Social Life, Vicenze, 1932) is another widely-used book. Though couched in quasi-scientific terms it does much the same thing as Mioni.

One may subscribe to the Christian or even to the Catholic position on the problems of society; one may even admit that there is a great deal sociologically sound in the Christian and Roman Catholic analysis and suggested solutions; and still he must reject books such as these as sociology. The reason for this is clear: a sound scientific sociology cannot build on preconceptions even though they appear to be sound. One of the great drawbacks of sociology is precisely that so much of it has been built on pathological-reform preconception. It cannot be too often stressed that we shall never understand society, or even its pathological aspects, unless first we know the total picture: the originating forces, the development, structure, the functional procedures, the ends which human beings pursue in society.

This is not to say that these books do not contain some illuminating pages. Mioni's passages on the individual and individual interdependence, his definition of the functions of authority, are illuminating and significant. Bianchi's book, likewise, contains a discussion of the individual in society, of the domination-subordination system, of the interaction between the component individuals and a family as a whole, which makes sociological sense. But when these authors and others discuss society mainly in terms of "social problems" and hurl condemnation at the "infected" humans, they fail to perform the fundamental task of sociology, as much as a botanist would if, instead of inquiring into the basic laws of plant life, he should devote himself mainly to an examination of plant disease, to a condemnation of deseased plants, and to suggesting cures based on preconceptions rather than on scientific knowledge.

Demography. Italian demographic works are very thorough and cover every conceivable aspect of population, from size, rates and "cycles" of population growth, to marital rates, the months, weeks, days and hours at which people marry, the male-female conception rates, and many other details. Benini made a good beginning in formal demography in his *Principi di demografia* (Rome, 1901), already mentioned. Napoleone Colajanni wrote an able "manual" in two volumes, *Manuale di demografia* (Napoli, 1909). Corrado Gini and Franco Savorgnan, however, and their co-workers have made or organized most of the recent scientific studies in this field. The work of Gini and co-authors *Demografia* is probably as exhaustive a compilation and analysis of scientific demographic data as may be found in one volume in any language. Gini's *Saggi di demografia* (Roma, 1934) contains many valuable items, some of them rare. There are also numerous works dealing with specific demography topics, as for example, Stefano Somogyi, *Aspetti demografici dei gruppi confessionali in Ungheria* (Demographic Aspects of Religious Groups in Hungary, Roma, 1936.) This, although somewhat technical, contains some sociological interpretation.

Savorgnan produced a nearly-model text, in the best European style, in his *Corso di demografia* (Course in Demography, Pisa, 1936). It is simple, direct, almost artistic; it presents the basic data and interpretations in a readable and pedagogical manner.

The Italians have done some specially significant work on the demography of war. Savorgnan's two small volumes on the demography of war: *La Guerra e la popolazione* (The War and Population, Bologna, 1918), and *Demografia di Guerra* (Demography

ITALIAN SOCIOLOGY

of War, Bologna, 1921), are particularly important. (3) *Fattori demografici del conflitto Europeo* (Demographic Factors of the European Conflict, Roma, 1919) deals more specifically with population as a factor in war; Achilla Loria, *Aspetti sociali ed economici della guerra mondiale* (Social and Economic Aspects of the World War, Milan, 1921) contains some sociological interpretations: and Corrado Gini, *Problemi sociologici della guerra* (Sociological Problems of the War, Bologna, 1921), does much the same thing.

While Italian works in demography contain a substantial body of excellent statistical data, they generally fail to grapple with the task of basic sociological analysis and interpretation. Savorgnan comes nearest to doing so.

Social Biology. There are two books by Livio Livi which, though dealing mainly with population, come very close to sociobiology. His *Lezioni di demografia* (Lessons in Demography, Padua, 1936) though examining principally economic life as a dynamic force, contains a discussion of several items (e.g. the relation between given characteristics of individuals and their associative tendencies and between economic status and modes of social behavior) which come quite close to sociology. He comes even closer in his *Fattori biologici dell'ordinamento sociale* (Biological Factors in the Social Order, Padua, 1937) which presents a cogent sociological analysis of the biological foundations of group life.

Bordering Fields. There are numerous works that border onto sociology and often contain material of value to the scientific sociologist: the books of Sighele, Bianchi, Rossi in "social" psychology; those of Loria, Colajanni and Ugo Spirito in "social" economics; those in political economy, jurisprudence and philosophy of history. Mention should also be made of governmental reports, which often contain valuable factual data. The *Annuario Statistico* and the *Compendio Statistico* are important. The latter often includes not only excellent statistical data, but quasi-sociological analyses. Also there are several reviews. *Rivista Internazionale di Scienze Sociali*, published in Milan by Jesuit Brothers, frequently has some able articles and reviews. *Scientia* also, published in

---

3. Parenthetically it may be mentioned that Savorgnan writing in 1918 computed that sometime between 1935 and 1940 France would feel the result of the First World War most keenly and that toward the middle of 1940 she would be weakest in manpower in her whole recent history.

TWENTIETH CENTURY SOCIOLOGY

Bologna, sometime has good sociological material, though rarely. *Metron*, published in Rome, is pre-eminent in demography. *Riforma Sociale* and *Critica Sociale* used to have excellent articles on reform programs and legislation, and the like. These last two stopped publication during the Fascist Era!

II

In a brief essay such as this, it is impossible to make a general appraisal. From what has already been said, however, it is clear that there is little that can be classed as systematic, empirical material, theoretical or factual, in the Italian writings that pass as sociology. This shortcoming, of course, is characteristic of much that passes for sociology not only in Italy but everywhere.

The status of Italian sociology is probably due mainly to Comtean influences. Comte's ambitious scheme to make sociology a kind of grand super-science that would systhesize the findings of all social science is probably at the root of the difficulty. Had Comte, by some miracle, conceived of his science as "groupology" and called it that, he might have saved us all a great deal of trouble. But such was not his concept. That Italian sociology has been influenced by the Comtean tradition is evident not only in the works examined above, but also from the fact that Italian sociologists or near-sociologists almost invariably still cling to that tradition. Gini, for example, writing as late as 1927, explicitly stated that it is the function of the "particular social sciences, such as demography, statistical economics, political economy, political science, social psychology" to observe the facts and ascertain the regularity of phenomena, while it "rests on sociology to gather together and systematize these in a concept of the whole." Pareto held to the same notion to his dying day, as may be seen from one of his two last books, *Fatti e teorie* (Florence, 1920).

In fact, it is probable that in Italy the Comtean idea has persisted even more than elsewhere, for a very good reason. In Italy the Comtean type of thinking had prevailed for centuries before Comte, through the works of Vico, Campanella, Machiavelli, Beccaria, and others, whose positivistic views were not unlike those of Saint-Simon and the direct founder of sociology. The idea of "society as-a-whole," of advancement or "progress," of "equilibrium," of "cyclical movements," etc., abound in Italian writings. Concepts such as these, taking in as they do large units of time and space, do not

ITALIAN SOCIOLOGY

conduce to the minute investigations necessary to building a body of scientific sociological theory and knowledge.

Italian sociology has given itself almost wholy to the grand synthesis for still another reason. Most Italian scholars dwell so greatly under the shadow of classical Rome that they seem almost incapable of dealing with phenomena in terms other than those of the Roman experience, much as American scholars are influenced by the American Revolution, or the French by the French Revolution. It follows that a great deal of Italian thinking and investigation deals with the rise and fall of nations and their causes, the equilibrium of nations, the circulation of classes, and the "cyclical" movement of all phenomena. Pareto, Mosca, Vaccaro, Gini, and many others have devoted almost their whole lives to these concepts. Their works, illuminating and well-worth studying though they are, cannot be regarded as scientific sociology, nor do they promote the detailed scientific study of group phenomena.

The development of scientific sociology in Italy has been retarded also by the fact that Italian scholarship is profoundly rooted in the philosophic, dogmatic, religious culture, so long dominant in Italy. For a thousand years or more, during the entire pre-Renaissance period, in Italy perhaps more than elsewhere it was "not proper" for man to study man, whether biologically, psychologically, or in any other aspect. In Italy that pattern of thought is far more lingering than elsewhere. It is for that reason, at least in part, that the scientific way of life, "good" or "bad" as it may be, has not influenced Italian life to the same extent as it has that of Germany, England, and the United States.

In any event, even the latest numbers of the *Rivista Italiana di Sociologia* available, those of 1939, clearly show that Italian sociology is still primarily dwelling on philosophies, on long term processes, and on society-as-a-whole speculations and deductions. Aside from the demographers, very few Italian scholars have undertaken those far more laborious, painstaking, essential tasks which we term scientific, namely, the setting up hypotheses and testing them by factual investigations.

And that is the only path of scientific virtue. If there is any hope of establishing a genuinely scientific sociology, that goal can be reached, not by speculative generalizations, but by inductively arriving at fundamental theories and hypotheses regarding group life; then by testing these theories and hypotheses by thousands

TWENTIETH CENTURY SOCIOLOGY

of detailed, painstaking, fact-finding studies; next by arriving at tentative generalizations; and so on, in a never-ending round of testing and retesting theories, hypotheses and the accummulated fund of knowledge derived from that process. It is a hard way, perhaps yielding no sounder fruits than that of the poet and seer. Still it is the only procedure that will produce the results which will ultimately give us the right to apply the term "science" to sociology.

SELECTED BIBLIOGRAPHY

Bellini, Luigi, *Saggi di una teoria generale della società,* (Milano: 1934).
Carli, Filippo, *Introduzione alla sociologia generale,* (Bologna: Zanichelli, 1925).
Colucci, Massimo, *Principi di diritto consuetuniario della Somalia meridionale,* (Florence: La Voce, 1924).
Gini, Corrado, Marcello Boldrini, Luigi de Berardinis, Gaetano Zingali, *Demografia,* (Torino: Unione Torinese 1930).
Gini, Corrado, *Il sesso dal punto di vista statistico,* (Milano: Sandron, 1908).
Livi, Livio, *Fattori biologici dell'ordinamento sociale,* (Padua: CEDAM, 1937).
Mioni, Ugo, *Manuale di sociologia,* (Torino: 1932).
Morselli, Emilio, *Elementi di sociologia generale,* (Milano: Hoepli, 1898).
Pareto, Vilfredo, *Trattato di sociologia generale,* (Florence: Barbera, 1916, 2nd ed., 1923, 3 vols.).
Pitrè, Giuseppe, *Opere complete di Giuseppe Pitrè,* (Roma: Libro Italiano, 1940).
Savorgnan, Franco, *Corso di demografia,* (Pisa: Nistri-lischi, 1936).
Savorgnan, Franco, *Scelta matrimoniale,* (Ferrarra: Taddei, 1924).
Ventimiglia, A. Guarnieri, *Conflitti sociali,* (Torino: Bocca, 1905).

Costantino Panunzio was born in Italy; came to the United States as a youth in the course of world-wide travel; remained in the United States; became a citizen in 1914; took his Doctorate at the Brookings School of Economics and Government in 1925; and he is now Associate Professor of Sociology at the University of California, Los Angeles.

His specialty is ethnic relations, especially as applied to the European immigrant in the United States. He has also written on aspects of demography, on the sociology of institutions, and on the sociology of Italy. For many years he has been active in the Free Italy and other liberal movements. He was designated by a committee of scientists of the New York World's Fair of 1940 as one of five hundred American minority-persons who, in the entire history of the United States, have made "outstanding contributions to American culture." His publications include *Deportation Cases* (1921), *The Soul of an Immigrant, Immigration Crossroads, How Mexicans Earn and Live, A Student's Dictionary of Sociological Terms, Major Social Institutions,* etc.

CHAPTER XXIII

SPANISH SOCIOLOGY

by

ALFREDO MENDIZABAL

The transition from the Nineteenth to the Twentieth Century in Spain coincides with a deep crisis in national thought. The anxiety sowed in the minds by the constructive pessimism of the generation of thinkers of '98 forces the Spaniards into an introversive sincere and unassuming position. At the time, Spanish culture was obliged to renew itself, or perhaps to be more exact, to be reborn, starting from the absolute zero that the exaggerated disillusionment of its intellectual leaders assigned to it at such a moment of depression. The result is that in the various fields of the sciences of doing, and in the sciences of knowing, many Spaniards, equipped with new techniques, are beginning to work with great eagerness.

If we try to analyze the Hispanic contribution to sociology, we find ourselves in the presence of abundant scattered material, without any coherent organization. Is there a Spanish sociology? It would be difficult to answer in the afirmative, if there is implied in the question a sociology worked out with pretensions towards completeness. Are there, at least, sociologists, specialists in this field? In the first stage up till 1918 we hardly find anything but "amateurs" of social subjects, men of action, rather than of thought, reformers of social conditions, almost always confused with the question of labor. Scientific sociology appears later, in the period that begins with the liquidation of the first world war. Only then do they leave the vague dissertation and adopt the methods in vogue in order to analyze systematically the multiform social reality, and acquire consciousness of the substantiveness of this science, formerly less appreciated or left to the vain currents of minds of the journalist type.

In the deontological root of the Spanish "psyche" we can discover the reasons for that scorn as regards sociology. The Spaniard is a man thirsting for the absolute, for the highest movings, for ultimate goals, for ideals, and even for utopias. At rare moments, he feels himself attracted by the real, or, in his line of behavior, by the feasible. "Imagine," says Ortega, "that you are condemned to devoting yourself to doing only that which is possible, that which by itself can be accomplished. What anguish! You would feel as though your life were emptied of itself. Exactly because your activity succeeded in its purpose, it would seem to you that you were doing nothing." In his effort to accomplish the impossible, man succeeds in many things: "what he never attains is what he plans." The impossible is "the only thing that has meaning." (1)

A science of reality like sociology, did not attract Spaniards, for the very reason that they seek especially in the social sciences the normative character that sociology lacks. The Spaniard always wants "norms" even though he is not distinguished because of his docility in conforming to the norms. He wants to know what to abide by, to know what "should be." What "is" is unimportant to him. He lives it, but it does not interest him as a subject for knowledge; and he even tries to see it only through the lens of his illusions. Through it, his behavior in the presence of reality is -- as in Don Quixote -- of a logic that would be perfect if things were such as he imagines them.

Sociology as a useful science and a science of limited pretentions (as regards it results, although limitless in the scope of its field of action) was until very recent times regarded unfavorably in the unutilitarian Spanish atmosphere. And the somewhat discredited title of sociologist was granted "with unbounded generosity and for lack of others, to anyone who in theoretic or practical form

---

1. José Ortega y Gasset, *El Libro de las misiones*, (Buenos Aires: Espasa-Calpe, 1940), pp. 144-146.

SPANISH SOCIOLOGY

had to deal intimately or distantly with any bit of the social reality." (2)

For a long time sociology, vague, or vagrant science, without a definite and established home, was cultivated bit by bit by professionals of other sciences, and particularly by jurists, philosophers and historians. Thus, works of a sociological nature or of sociological value of the latter were often mixed in researches in philosophy of history; and those of the former referred particularly to the domain of the philosophy of law, a branch of knowledge which, in Spain, had a double lineage, scholastic and Germanic. It is a fact that must be borne in mind that the chief developers of sociology are, in our time, jurists and legal philosophers and that therefore legal sociology is the branch most studied in that country. But only in these last years has sociology reached its own substantiveness as an empirical science, freeing itself from connected sciences of normative essence.

I

Four names stand out in the generation of '98, and can be linked and opposed to each other in twos: Joaquín Costa and later José Ortega y Gasset, Angel Ganivet and later Miguel de Unamuno. The two latter, although they are as significant as the two former, do not offer the same interest for this summary, because they do not work in sociology, and even would have been scandalized if anyone maintained that they did. And nevertheless, they themselves are typical men for a comprehension of the genuine social framework of Spain: they exhibit the individuality exalted in the Iberian temper, while Costa and Ortega, attracted by the movement of ideas in other peoples, rather than by the native, tried to Europeanize Spain.

In spite of the anti-sociologism of thinkers like Ganivet and Unamuno, there can be found in their works evaluations of society in general, and of Spanish society specifically, of interest to the student of social reality as it is, and as those authors would like it to be. "I do not believe," wrote Ganivet, "in metaphorical sociology that regards nations as organisms as well defined as individuals." For him, society is "only a resultant of the effort of its individuals";

---

2. José Medina Echavarría, *Sociología: teoría y técnica*, (México: Fondo de Cultura Económica, 1941), p. 151.

but "the individual is, in his turn, a photographic reduction of society"; and in this sense he considers the application of the psychology of the individual to social conditions, and of the pathology of the mind to political pathlogy, as advantageous. In the Spanish nation he finds the symptoms of a widespread disease: abulia, because in his day (he wrote this in 1896) it lacked acts of free decision, such as consciously intervening in the field of public affairs. "If in practical life, abulia manifests itself by inertia, in intellectual life it is characterized by inattention. For some time now our nation has been as though absent-minded in the midst of the world. Nothing interests it, nothing stirs it generally; but suddenly an idea appears, and unable to equilibrate itself with others, produces a rash impetus." In this feature, typical of the collective Spanish psychology, Ganivet sees the explanation of the aggressiveness which his compatriots show defending their ideals, fighting resolutely, not for their own, but rather against others who uphold opposing trends. Thus ideas become "pointed," sharp, in the social milieu in which they curdle; and are used as offensive weapons. (3) And doubtless, to a great extent, there lies in this the key of the agonistic and antagonistic attitude of the Spanish society of to-day and of some time back.

The most vehemently personal of the Spanish thinkers of the last half century, the mystic and prophetic Unamuno, believes that "human society in so far as it is a society, has senses which would be lacking to the individual if he did not exist within it": just as the individual, also the man who is, in his turn, "a sort of society" possesses senses lacking to the cells within him. But the "man" of Unamuno is not the abstract man (political animal, *homo sapiens, homo economicus, etc.*), is not the man who (pretending to belong to everywhere and to everytime) is of nowhere as well as of no epoch at all; he is "the man of flesh and bone" who "is born, suffers and dies — above all who dies —, who eats, drinks, plays, sleeps, thinks, loves"; and thus Unamuno corrects the well-known sentence of Terentius and says: *nullum hominem a me alienum puto*, since the adjective "humanus" seems as suspicious to him as the abstract noun "humanitas." He prefers the concrete noun "man" to both of them. (4) And through a character in fiction, Don

---
3. Angel Ganivet, *Idearium Español* (1897), pp. 140-141, 148-149 from the edition of Buenos Aires: Nueva Biblioteca Filosófica.
4. Miguel de Unamuno. *Del sentimiento trágico de la vida en los hombres y en los pueblos*, (Madrid: Renacimiento, 1913), Chapts. I-II.

SPANISH SOCIOLOGY

Quixote, much more real than his creator Cervantes, Unamuno extracts the permanent categories of the national soul. (5)

Costa, a deeply talented and unsociable man, devoted himself to historic and sociological subjects linked with legal matters. He especially emphasized agrarian questions in the Spanish economy, and he also wrote on customary law with a high competence. His studies on agrarian collectivism in the field of economic sociology and his analysis of the political phenomena of oligarchy and "caciquism" are of great value to understanding of social conditions in Spain. (6)

Ortega has brought to the study of society and of its structure the keen perception of his up-to-date philosophic talent, evaluating the functional character of the "mass" and of the individual in his possibilities of action and orientation on it. His theory, based on the diversity of both elements, nevertheless implies a "certain basic common ground between superior individuals and the crowd," since without such a community the work of the "individual absolutely heterogeneous from the mass would produce no effect whatsoever on the latter; it would glide over the social body without arousing the slightest reaction in it." This leads him to the study of the "idea of generations." The generation, "a dynamic compromise between mass and individual," is a human variety, in the strict sense that the naturalists give to this term. Its members come into the world, endowed with certain typical characteristics, which lend them a common physiognomy, distinguishing them from the preceding generation. So, the reactionary and the revolutionary of the Nineteenth Century are much more closely related to each other than anyone of them with anyone of us. Each generation represents a certain vital attitude, from which it experiences life in a determined fashion. If we take as a whole the evolution of a people each one of its generations appears to us as a moment of its vitality, as a pulsation of its historical potency. For each generation, living is a two-dimensional task: it consists in receiving the "lived" — ideas,

---

5. Unamuno, *Vida de Don Quijote y Sancho,* (Madrid: Fé, 1905).

6. Cf. Joaquín Costa, *Estudios ibéricos,* (Madrid: 1891); *El colectivismo agrario en España* (1898); *La fórmula de la agricultura española,* (Madrid: 1911-1912), 2 vols. *Reconstitución y europeización de España* (1900); *La vida del derecho* (1875), *Teoría del hecho jurídico individual y social* (1883), *Oligarquía y caciquismo como la forma actual de gobierno en España* (Madrid: 1902), *Derecho consuetudinario,* etc.

evaluations, institutions — from the proceding one; and, on the other hand, to allow its own spontaneity to flow. The spirit of each generation depends on the equation that those two ingredients form, on the attitude that the majority of its individuals adopts in reference to each one. There have been generations that felt sufficient homogeneity between what they received and their own. Then one lives in *cumulative periods*. Others have felt a profound heterogeneity between both elements: there are *periods of elimination and polemics*, generations of struggle. (7)

In *The Revolt of the Masses* (8) Ortega is devoted to the study of the fact that appears to him as the most important of our time: the accession of the masses to complete social power. Ortega's position is indeed aristocratic in essence. He is afraid to see mulitudes "precisely in the best places previously reserved to minorities: the multitude has suddenly become visible, installing itself in the preferential positions in society. Before it existed, it passed unnoticed, occupying the background of the social stage: now it has advanced to the footlights and is the principal character. There are no longer protagonists; there is only the chorus." (9)

Ortega tries to give a sociological notion of the mass: Society is always a dynamic unity of two component factors minorities and masses. The minorities are individuals or groups of individuals that are especially qualified. The mass is the assemblage of persons not specially qualified. By masses, then, is not to be understood, solely or mainly, the "working masses." The mass is the average man. In this way what was mere quantity — the multitude — is converted into a qualitative determination; it becomes the common social quality, man as undifferentiated from other men, but as repeating in himself a generic type. Strictly speaking, the mass, as a psychological fact, can be defined without waiting for individuals to appear in mass formation. In the presence of one individual we can decide whether he is "mass" or not. The mass is all that which sets no value on itself — good or ill — based on specific grounds, but which feels itself "just like everybody" and nevertheless

---

7. José Ortega y Gasset, *El tema de nuestro tiempo*, (Madrid: 1923), Chap. I.

8. Some of the ideas of this book has already been explained in *España invertebrada* (Invertebrate Spain) published in 1922. *La Rebelión de las masas* appeared in 1930. Its translation, *The Revolt of the Masses*, was issued in 1932 (New York: W. W. Norton and Co.).

9. *The Revolt of the Mases*, p. 13.

is not concerned about it. If the individuals who make up the mass believed themselves specially qualified, it would be a case merely of personal error, not a sociological subversion. The characteristic of the hour, according to Ortega, is that the commonplace mind, knowing itself to be commonplace, has the assurance to proclaim the rights of the commonplace and to impose them wherever it will. "As they say in the United States: to be different is to be indecent." (10) The mass-man is he whose life lacks any purpose, and simply goes drifting along. And the mass-men in revolt are placing in imminent danger the very principles to which our civilized standard of life owes its existence. If that human type continues to be master in Europe — Ortega concludes — thirty years will suffice to send our continent back to barbarism. The whole of life will to be contracted. For the rebellion of the masses is one and the same thing with what Rathenau called "the vertical invasion of the barbarians." (11)

Under the two different species of Syndicalism and of Fascism, Ortega considers a type of man "who does not want to give reasons or to be right, but simply shows himself resolved to impose his opinions. He wishes to have opinions, but is unwilling to accept the conditions and presuppositions that underlie all opinion. The average man finds himself with "ideas" in his head, but he lacks the faculty of ideation. He has no conception even of the rare atmosphere in which ideas live. Hence his ideas are in effect nothing more than appetites in words." The mass-man would feel himself lost if he accepted discussion. His intervention in the whole of public life is in the way of an inevitable process: direct action. At other times violence was the means resorted to by him who had previously exhausted all others in defence of the rights of justice which he thought he possessed. Force was, in fact, the *ultima ratio*, and civilization attempted to reduce force to being the *ultima ratio*. But "direct action" consists in inverting the order and proclaiming violence as *prima ratio*, or strictly as *unica ratio*. It is the norm which proposes the annulment of all norms, which supresses all intermediate process between our purpose and its execution. It is the Magna Charta of barbarism. For a man is uncivilized, barbarian, in the degree to which he does not take the others into account. Barbarism is the tendency to disassociation, and the barbarous

---

10 *Ibid*, pp. 13-15, 18.
11. *Ibid.*, pp. 53, 56-57.

epochs have been times of human scattering, of the pullulation of tiny groups, separate from and hostile to one another. The rebellion of the masses — Ortega adds — may, in fact, be the transition to some new, unexampled organization of humanity, but it *may* also be a catastrophe of human destiny.(12)

Dealing with the doctrine of revolutions, he affirms that "a revolution does not last more than fifteen years, the period which coincides with the flourishing of a generation, whose activity divides into two stages and takes two forms: during approximately one half, the new generation carries out the propaganda of its ideas, preferences, and tastes, which finally arrive at power and are dominant in the second half of its course. But the generation educated under its sway is already bringing forward other ideas, preferences, and tastes, which it begins to diffuse in the general atmosphere." (13) Here philosophy of history is starting out from sociological analysis. But the philosopher shows himself too categorically absolute in forecasting, before the monstruous growing of the modern State, the impossibility of any true revolution in the future, not assuredly because there are no motives for them, but because there are no means, since public power was brought to the level of social power: "Goodbye for ever to Revolutions! The only thing now possible is their opposite: the *coup d'état*." This problematical assertion is nevertheless founded by him in the paradoxical, tragical process of Statism, according to which Society that creates the State as an instrument has to begin to live for the State, and the people are converted into fuel to feed the mere machine which is the State. (14) Indeed, one could be led to think, starting from the same considerations, that liberation from the Statism will be the most revolutionary task offered to the present society by the actual conditions of common life, and the more the goal is momentarily utopian, the worthier it appears to the modern conscience.

II

The analysis of social deeds and of collective life has been advanced in Spain by designs of practical reform, rather than by an impetus of scientific knowledge. The founding of the "Instituto

12. *Ibid.*, pp. 80-83, 85.
13. *Ibid.*, p. 102.
14. *Ibid.*, pp. 131, 134.

de Reformas Sociales" (Institute for Social Reforms) as an advisory agency of the Government and as a center for study and for the preparation of legislative work in the social field, was — at the beginning of this century — a great step towards the methodic organization of sociologic research. It had the added merit, unusual in that country, of creating a milieu favorable to the collabaration on the different tendencies and schools of thought. The three most characteristic of them found adequate representation in the Institute: (a) the ethical-organicist trend stemming from Krausism (whose philosophy had a greater influence and more extensive development is Spain than in Germany itself); (b) socialism in both its aspects: socialism of intellectuals, and socialism of workers' organizations; and (c) social Catholicism, inspired by the doctrines of the Church and particularly by the Encyclicals of Leo XIII and later Pius XI.

Krausism, principally through the works of Roeder and Ahrens, was introduced in the second half of the nineteenth century, by a group of scholars among whom is outstanding first Prof. Julián Sanz del Río and then Prof. Francisco Giner, as the creator and guiding spirit of the "Institución Libre de Enseñanza" (Free Institute of Learning), a foyer for liberal education, founded on the fringe of the official University and of the then reigning orthodoxy in public teaching.

Giner is a philosopher of law, who proclaims the need for attention reflecting juridical experience through the observation of the legal phenomena of our lives and of the life about us. (15) Extending the idea of subject of rights beyond the limits of the individual, he maintains that since the end is that which causes a subject to be considered, and since there is nothing that can be denied finality, every being "in so far as the fulfillment of its ends depends in any respect on a free activity" will be a subject of pretensions; and thus he does not recognize rights of a plant with regard to the animal, but does recognize the rights of the plant and animal with regard to man, who through care and cultivation can bring about the fulfillment of their respective finalities. (16) In his studies

---

15. Francisco Giner de los Ríos, *Resumen de filosofía del derecho*, (Madrid: 1898), 12.

16. Cf. Fernando de los Ríos, *La filosofía del derecho en Don Francisco Giner y su relación con el pensamiento contemporáneo*, (Madrid: Biblioteca Corona, 1916), pp. 151-152; Adolfo Posada, "La idea de justicia en el reino animal" in *Literatura y problemas de sociología*, pp. 282-302.

on the social being, Giner develops his concept of the subject of sociology: society constituting a substantive unity and with its own personality. (17) For him, the notion of organism does not belong to biology, but to metaphysics. (18)

An eminent jurist, Prof. Gumersindo de Azcarate, presided over the "Instituto de Reformas Sociales" in its first period (1903-1917); and in addition to the orientation and direction of the work of such a center, we owe to his pen numerous sociological works (19), and an analysis of the vices and abuses in the working of the parliamentary system, as a means of restoring it to its ideal purity. (20) Azcarate forwarded in Spain the sociological studies based on a social realism of ideal substance. (21)

His constant collaborator in the Institute and also a professor in the University of Madrid, Adolfo Posada, joins to the study of public law that of sociology and published a treatise that expounds the principal trends of this science in the world. (22) According to him, the State should be the organ of the community itself, a living, active instrument, in natural communication with the social body, palpitating with it, its essential function being, precisely, to feel as its own the needs of the community, converted by thought into juridical problems, and with its means act to satisfy and alleviate them. (23) Posada analyzes Syndicalism as a social phenomenon characteristic of our time: Syndicalism is the organ of a collective function entailing the intensification of the teleological vision of human society. (24) He also examines the scientific trajectory of

---

17. Ginner, *Teoria de la persona social* (in *Obras completas*, Madrid: 1923-1924, vols. VIII-IX).

18. Cf. Adolfo Posada, *Teoria social y juridica del estado*, (Buenos Aires: J. Menéndez, 1922), p. 94.

19. Cf. G. de Azcárate, *Historia del derecho de propiedad, En concepto de la sociología* (Madrid: Academia de Ciencias morales y políticas), *Programa de sociología* (Ateneo de Madrid), *Estudios económicos y sociales*.

20. Azcárate, *El régimen parlamentario en la práctica*, (Madrid: Minuesa, 1931).

21. Cf. Azfirate, *Estudios filosóficos y políticos*, (Madrid: 1877).

22. Cf. Adolfo Posada, *Estudios sobre el régimen parlamentario en España*, (Madrid: 1891), *Teorías modernas sobre los orígenes de la familia, de la sociedad y del estado*, (Madrid: 1892), *El socialismo y la reforma social*, (Madrid: 1904), and especially, *Principios de sociología;* its first edition examined its process from Comte to Ward, the second (Madrid: Jorro, 1929, 2 vols.) continues the study to the time of publication.

23. Cf. Posada, *Teoría social y juridica del estado*, pp. 368-369.

24. *Ibid.*, p. 386.

SPANISH SOCIOLOGY

sociology and the elaboration of the concept of this branch of knowledge. For him, sociology, facing social reality, accomplishes an operation analogous to the determined function of the political science in face of political reality. (25)

A professor of penal law, Pedro Dorado Montero, has studied the phenomenology of public law with historical-sociological criteria; analyzing the function of law and of authority in simple groups, he considers the community as the creator of Law: the chief stimulus of conduct does not come from without, does not in the beginning reside in the order imposed by any being considered superior; it comes from within the very being who is acting. Between the performance and the norm there is no distinction at all; such a distinction appears later. In the made-up groups, the process of formation of the law has its origin in the differentiation of the conquering group, which imposes it, and the conquered group; and it perfects itself and develops throughout the "parasitic relation." For Dorado, the "whole social life, from its most humble manifestations to its highest, can be envisaged as an immense theatre of *parasitic relations*", and as such does he consider those of exchange of services, by virtue of which each individual lives in more or less intimate communion with the rest and from the product of the work of the others. But as the parasitic relation can not be so complete that the parasite makes the life of the victim impossible in all respects, since if this happened, the parasite would lose, the more intelligent the parasites, the better do they treat the exploited. This consciousness of the limit of exploitation, which should not be forced if one wishes to obtain better returns, is in Dorado's opinion one of the incentives of social progress consented to by employers on behalf of workers; thus, through *ego-altruism*, they have found the way of exploiting one's neighbor (utilizing his services) for the greatest advantage possible to him and all, in progressive forms of social cooperation. (26) Dorado, following Costa, attributes to "custom" an influence superior even to that of laws, in the creation and operation of law: custom produces an extra-legal social atmosphere, which acquires consistency and extension at the expense of the legal atmosphere; and laws are impotent when the social masses are not disposed to receive them,

---

25. Posada, *Principios de sociología*, vol. II Chapt. XVI.
26. Pedro Dorado, *Valor social de leyes y autoridades*, (Barcelona: Manuales Gallach, 1923), pp. 44-45, 64-67, 84-85.

whence comes the frequent divorce between legal life and real life, through which not a few official institutions are mere outward show, painted canvases, like theatre decorations. (27)

Among the psychological studies of Spanish society, those of Altamira on the national character, the causes of the decadence of Spain through the period of expansion and predominance in the world, the discontent of the Spaniards with themselves, and the social and cultural possibilities of a national rennaisance are outstanding, (28) and also those of Madariaga, who provides keen comparative analysis. (29)

In the field of ethnography, Arazadi and Hoyos have distinguished themselves. (30) One of the first sociological researches on social usages in Twentieth Century Spain which can be mentioned is the project suggested by the Section of Ethical and Political Sciences of the Ateneo of Madrid in 1901, which was carried out by means of a widely distributed questionnaire designed to obtain material for study on popular customs and proverbs related to birth (conception, gestation, birth, baptism, illegitimate sons), marriage (betrothal, agreements, banns, wedding, economic regime, adoption, adultery, separation, divorce, illegitimate unions, associations for married people), and death (preparations, death, burial, later practices, cult of the dead, cementeries). (31)

Criminal sociology is one of the most widely studied fields. Among Spanish penologists those who must be mentioned are Dorado Montero, (32) Salillas, with his most interesting works on the customs and language of delinquent, (33) Quintiliano Saldaña, Eugenio Cuello Calón, Constancio Bernardo de Quirós and Luis Jiménez de Asúa, in their books on criminology and in their peni-

---

27. *Ibid.*, pp. 131, 166-167.
28. Rafael Altamira, *Psicología del pueblo español*, 2nd ed., (Barcelona: Editorial Minerva, 1917).
29. Salvador de Madariaga, *Ingleses, Franceses y Españoles*, transl.: *Englishmen, Frenchmen, Spaniards*, (London: 1928). Cf. also: Ortega, *Invertebrate Spain* (ed. cit.), M. Sales y Ferré, *Psicología del pueblo español*, (Madrid: 1902).
30. Telesforo de Aranzadi and Luis de Hoyos Sáinz, *Etnografía: sus bases, sus métadas y aplicaciones a España*, (Madrid: Biblioteca Corona, 1917).
31. Cf. *Ibid.*, pp. 215-230.
32. Pedro Dorado Montero, *La psicología criminal en nuestro derecho legislativo*.
33. Rafael Salillas, *El delincuente español: el lenguaje; Hampa; Antropología picaresia; Poesía rufianesca*, etc.

tentiary studies, the complete list of which would make this account much too long.

Socialism, as well as social Catholicism, have in Spain made a considerable contribution to sociological studies, although the immediate preoccupations of both groups have been more of a practical nature, the reform of society. But in each group individually, and upon occasion both groups joined and collaborating in organizations such as the "Instituto de Reformas Sociales," "Instituto de Previsión," and the "Academia de Ciencias morales y políticas," some of the leaders devoted themselves to studies, according to sociological methods, of the concrete structure of the society to which their impulses towards reform were to be applied. In the first group are university professors such as Julián Besteiro and Fernando de los Ríos. Besteiro's position is perhaps most vigorously and thoughtfully presented in his study of Marxism and anti-Marxism, (34) in which can be followed the tendencies towards the infiltration of Marxist trends in the doctrines of its opponents, and the limited zone of emotional coincidence of one and the other; the point of contact between communism and fascism through their radical opposition; the possibilities offered by bourgeois society to effective socialist action. (35) Professor De los Ríos, whose philosophical and political attitude of humanist liberalism allows him to transcend the simple Marxist position, with a neo-socialism impregnated with ethical-esthetic and even religious values, is the author of a suggestive book which is a guide to his doctrine (36) and also of interesting monographs, especially on rural problems.(37)

---

34. Julián Besteiro, *Maxismo y Antimarxismo*, (Madrid, 1935); cf. especially pp. 108-115, 123-124.

35. On the proletarian movement, cf. Juan José Morato, *El partido socialista*, (Madrid: 1931): Gabriel Morón, *Política de ayer y política de mañana*, (México: 1942); from the anarchist point of view: Anselmo Lorenzo, *El Proletariado militante*, 2 vols. (Barcelona: 1901, 1923, 2 vols.).

36. Fernando de los Ríos, *El sentido humanista del socialismo*, (Madrid: Morata, 1926).

37. "Agrarian Problems in Spain" (in the *International Labor Review*, London, June 1925). Other important works aiming to give a sociological explanation of the peasant's position and the system of land ownership: Constancio Bernaldo de Quirós, "El Espartaquismo agrario andaluz" (in the *Revista general de legislación y jurisprudencia*, (Madrid, April 1919); Pascual Carrión *Los latifundios en España*, (Madrid: 1932); Julio Puyol y Alonso, *Proceso del sindicalismo revolucionario*, (Madrid: 1919); Julio Senador Gómez, *Castilla en escombros: las leyes, las tierras, el trigo y el hambre*, (Valladolid: 1925); Juan Díaz del Moral, *Historia de las agitaciones campesinas andaluzas*, (Madrid: 1929); Mateo Azpeitia, *La reforma agraria en España*, (Madrid: 1932).

TWENTIETH CENTURY SOCIOLOGY

Sociologist and man of action in the sphere of social Catholicism, Professor of Sociology at the University of Madrid, Severino Aznar, (38) directed the "Grupo de la Democracia Cristiana" and the "Semanas Sociales" (39) institution. Of a similar tendency, the works of Eduardo Sanz y Escartin (40) should be cited before those of Aznar; and along with the latter's those of Arboleya, P. Gafo, Llovera, (41) Sangro, and Viscount de Eza. (42)

José Medina Echavarría, passing from the field of juridical philosophy to that of sociology, is to-day one of the best prepared, among the professors of the last generation, to accomplish a systematic and scientific task that finally places Spanish sociology on the road of its maturity. His recent and already considerable work has fructified in exile on Mexican soil, there Medina has published the results of his studies and researches these past years. (43) A scientific sociology can not exist without a theory and without a technique of research, that is without a framework of categories, without a unifying plan, without a defined technique, subject to strict rules. This is his point of departure. (44) And as a function of such a prerequisite, Medina states the problem of sociology as a science of reality and as an orientation for life; he studies its methodology and its theoretic construction, as well as the techniques of social research.

Recognizing the limitations of the subject of this branch of

---

38. Severino Aznar, *Despoblación y colonización*, (Barcelona: Labor 1930); *Problemas sociales de actualidad*, (Barcelona: 1914); *La abolición del salariado*, (Madrid; 1921).
39. Cf. *Semana social de Madrid*, (Madrid: 1933).
40. Cf. especially Eduardo Sanz y Escartín, *El Individuo y la reforma social*, (Madrid: 1896).
41. José M. Llovera, *Tratado elemental de sociología cristiana*, 3rd ed., (Barcelona: 1916). This is more a theory of social morals than of sociology because of its constant preoccupation with deontology in aplication of principles.
42. Vizconde de Eza, *La concentración parcelaria en España*, Madrid: 1906; *El problema agrario en España*, (Madrid: 1915); *Agrarismo*, (Madrid; 1935). In this last work the agricultural structure of the country and the social structure of agricultural ownership are examined (Chapters I-II).
43. Especially: *Panorama de la Sociología contemporánea*, (México: Casa de Espana, 1940), a work of initiation and orientation for students, guiding then through the labyrinth of the most important schools and tendencies; *Sociología: teoría y técnica; Responsabilidad de la inteligencia*, (México: Fondo de Cultura Económica, 1943); *Prólogo al estudio de la guerra*, (México: Colegio de México, 1943).
44. Medina, *Sociología: teoría y técnica*, p. 8.

knowledge, he meets the objection of philosophers dissatisfied with the insufficient answers of sociology to the essential question: what is the social? Indeed, the answer capable of furnishing a necessary solution remains until now above or beyond what the sociologist can offer with his methods; but, he adds, the same reproach can be directed against other more developed sciences: can the biologist perchance define what "is" life, in a manner satisfactory to the philosophic conscience? There is nothing extraordinary, then, that the sociologist, leaping beyond what for him are *residual categories*, should feel himself attracted by the most terribly concrete themes of human living together. (45)

The dicotamous separation of natural sciences and cultural sciences, lacks sense in sociology, as Medina shows, since social reality appears to us both as nature and culture at the same time, and the phenomena that are objects of sociology and of the other social sciences "are forms of life, or as has also been said, forms of culture, if by this is meant what man adds to nature without setting nature aside, and insofar as it is an activity and not a precipitate." (46) In an analogous direction, another philosopher of law, Recaséns, presents law as a form of human life objectivized: "belonging to the domain of objectivized human life and constituting, within it, a normative form of collective or social character, directed towards the realization of some values." (47) And he considers the social processes that create, maintain, and renew the forms of the State, as processes of integration of its membres. To the reality of the State belong, says Recaséns, "all the relations, all the situations and all the social processes whose intentional meaning refers to the juridic"; that is, "every behavior tending to the creation of juridic norms, to their maintenance, their modification, or their abrogation." (48)

The problem lies, for Medina, in whether sociology — as a science — has to be satisfied itself with illuminating the conditions of action, or can take part in the decision itself. Reacting against the irrationalist tendencies of our time, and taking into account that the orientation which is asked of sociology is of a scientific nature,

---

45. *Ibid*, pp. 30-31.
46. *Ibid.*, pp. 58-60.
47. Luis Recaséns Siches, *Vida humana, sociedad y derecho*, (México: Casa de España, 1939), p. 61.
48. *Ibid.*, pp. 258-261.

that is, rational and empirical, deduced from the vigorous analysis of real facts, he believes that, although the ideal is that such an orientation should succeed even in dictating a decision to us, "in its present state sociology cannot completely fulfill this goal and we shall have to limit ourselves to demand of it, as well as of the other social sciences, as complete a rational analysis as possible, of the conditions of our action." (49) However, upon studying the function of sociology in the education, in the formation of man, the same author enlarges its field considerably, attempting to attribute to it nothing less than the role that corresponded to classical humanism, by giving a universal and many-dimensional sight of human social life, and a synthetic and organic sight of human destiny and of the incidents in its history, (50) which a philosopher of history would probably qualify as excessive. Perhaps this widening of the field, which may seem inadmissible, is based on an identification of functions with those of all the social sciences as a whole, which here the author does not differentiate sufficiently, upon pointing out the role which falls "to the social sciences, to sociology understood in a broad sense." Precisely on this amplification appears the imperialistic temptation from which it is so dificult for the sociologist to free himself, and from which at other moments the author defends himself perfectly.

Let us call attention, lastly, to the fertile labor of Medina in his essay on warlike typology (51) with his keen analysis of what civil war is (break up of a community, rent into abysmally separated parties) and what international war, which when total is equivalent to the pure type of absolute war, which civil war represents. The work of the investigator is prolonged on this subject in the research of the "Centro de Estudios sociales" conducted by him in the "Colegio de Mexico." His first collective seminar on the War constitutes a contribution of the greatest importance for the systematic treatment of the chief sociological problems raised by the war. (52) The presentation of the themes and of the plan of research proves in Medina the perspicacity and profoundness of the sociologist who is more than a sociologist.

---

49. Medina, *Sociología: teoría y técnica*, pp. 73-74.
50. Medina, *Responsabilidad de la inteligencia*, pp. 150-151.
51. *Op. cit.*, pp. 183 ff.
52. Cf.*Jornadas* (Colegio de México, Centro de Estudios Sociales, 1943-1944).

SPANISH SOCIOLOGY

SELECTED BIBLIOGRAPHY

General Treatises:

Medina Echevarría, José, *Panorama de la sociología contemporánea*, (México: Casa de España, 1940); *Sociología: teoría y técnica*, (México: Fondo de Cultura Económica, 1941).

Posada, Adolfo, *Principios de sociología*, (Madrid: Jorro, 1929, 2 vols.).

Political Sociology:

Costa, Joaquín, *Oligarquía y caciquismo como la forma actual de gobierno en España*, (Madrid: 1902).

Ortega y Gasset, José, *La rebelión de las masas*, (Madrid: 1930); Engl. transl.: *The Revolt of the Masses*, (New York: W. W. Norton and Co., 1932).

Juridical Sociology:

Dorado, Pedro, *Valor social de leyes y autoridades*, (Barcelona: Gallach, 1923).

Posada, Adolfo, *Teoría social y jurídica del estado*, (Buenos Aires: Menendez, 1922).

Recaséns Siches, Luis, *Vida humana, sociedad y derecho*, (México: Casa de España, 1939).

Psychology of the Spanish People:

Altamira, Rafael, *Psicología del pueblo español*, 2nd ed., (Barcelona: Minerva, 1917).

Madariaga, Salvador de, *Englishmen, Frenchmen, Spaniards*, (London: 1928).

Ortega y Gasset, José, *España invertebrada*, (Madrid: 1922); Engl. transl: *Invertebrate Spain*, (New York: W. W. Norton Co., 1937).

Rural Sociology:

Carrión, Pascual *Los latifundios en España*, (Madrid: 1932).

De Los Ríos, Fernando, "Agrarian Problems in Spain," *International Labour Review*, June, 1925.

Alfredo Mendizábal is Professor at the New School for Social Research, New York. Studied at the Universities of Saragossa and Madrid, Spain. LL. D. Madrid. Professor at the University of Oviedo, Spain, since 1926. Lecturer at the International University of Santander, at the F. de Vitoria Association (University of Salamanca), at the Social Weeks (Madrid). Member (co-founder) of the International Institute for Philosophy of Law and Juridical Sociology (Paris), of the National Academy of Jurisprudence and Legislation (Madrid). Lecturer in France, Switzerland, England, Ireland. Since 1942: Professor at the New School for Social Research, and at the Ecole Libre des Hautes Etudes, New York. Lectured at Queens College (N. Y.) and Rutgers University (N.J.), Universities of Havana (Cuba), Montreal and Quebec (Canada). Member of the Institut de Sociologie, New York.

Contributor: *Colosseum* (London), *Cruz y Raya* (Madrid), *Esprit* (Paris), *Internationale Zeitschrift fuer die Theorie des Rechts* (Brno), *L'Europe Nouvelle* (Paris), *La Vie Intellectuelle* (Paris), *Nouveaux Cahiers* (Paris), *Politique* (Paris), *Revista general de Legislación y Jurisprudencia* (Madrid), *Rivista Internazionale di Filosofia del Diritto* (Roma), *Univers* (Lille), *Universidad* (Saragossa), *The Commonweal* (N. Y.)

TWENTIETH CENTURY SOCIOLOGY

Author: *La doctrina de la Justicia en la Suma teológica* (Saragossa, 1925), *Los Tratados de Paz: su naturaleza, valor jurídico y eficacia* (Madrid, 1927), *Tratado de Derecho Natural* (with his father, Luis Mendizábal, 3 vols. 7th edition, Madrid, 1928-1931, *Aux Origines d'une Tragédie*: La Politique espagnole de 1923 à 1936 (Paris, 1937; English translation under the title *The Martyrdom of Spain*, New York, 1938), *Democracy and International Order* (in the book *For Democracy*, published by the People and Freedom Group, London, 1939).

CHAPTER XXIV

RUSSIAN SOCIOLOGY

by

MAX M. LASERSON

There is no other country in Europe in which the political history would be so closely connected with certain ideologies and premises as has been the case in Russia. And insofar as political mentality and philosophy of history are bound to be expressions of certain sociological trends it may be said that in Russia the sociological schools were mostly motivated by the political unfolding of their problems.

I

Several Fields Neighboring Sociology. The explanation for this phenomenon has to be found in the specific conditions of the country. Russian sociology in its first stages developed in a country where the interest in applied social sciences was very great, but where there was no freedom of thought and press and where the elaboration of social problems was always under the control and censorship of the regime. On the other hand, works of social science were the only place — in the absence of a free periodical press — where important problems could be adequately dealt with often enough.

TWENTIETH CENTURY SOCIOLOGY

There were some specific fields, neighboring to sociology, which helped to develop pure sociology in Russia.

The first such field is politics, namely the question of the essence of the peculiarity of the emergence, development and political affinities of Russia in the surrounding world. The deepest question in this field is the discussion between the Western (European) and Slavic coloration of Russia. In order not to go too far back we may say that this question was posed in the clearest way in the famous Instruction of Empress Catherine II, who in the first chapter of this book, built on Montesquieu, Beccaria and other "enlightened" authors, categorically asserted that "Russia is a European Power." Thus since 1770 when this book was printed in four languages (Russian, Latin, French and German) and down to the splendid book of Danilevsky *Russia and Europe* (1871) a whole literature has grown up around the discussion between the Slavophils and Westerners, and finds its latest expression in current Russian Soviet historical literature in which orthodox Marxism is giving up its old abstract universal construction in favor of a renewed Russian national historic school.

A second field of investigation relevant for the later Russian sociology was the field of *economics*. This field of Russian studies goes back farther than the first. It found its first clear expression in the book of Pososhkov *On Poverty and Wealth* (1754). In his field later on all battles pro and contra the economic uniqueness of Russia were fought. And among them the most important was that of the Russian community (obshtchina) with remnants of primitive communism. A rich sociological literature around this question grew up throughtout decades. This question was accompanied and sometimes conditioned by the questions of the destiny of capitalism in Russia and a future unfolding of socialist economy. The fight between Marxism and idealist Populism "Narodnishestvo," especially since the 1880's was most conspicuously expressed in the problem of whether Russia was due to undergo the same lines of capitalist economy as the Western states or would retain her own ways of economic growth different from Western patterns.

A third field of sociological investigation was connected with both of the preceding but, dealing with the very essence of Russian history, had to give an answer to the question of the role of the *personality*, as differentiated from the masses, in history. In Russia this question, dealt with in England by Thomas Carlyle, became especially important, both for the understanding of the past and the making of the future. Around this problem, too, the fight between Marxists and Populists became of great political importance. Marxists were inclined to diminish the role of the individual — they fought against the cult of heroes and heroism, while the Populist and other idealistic trends supported the idea of the importance of the person and his efforts to initiate and lead the decisive steps in the development of the country and her history.

The fourth field of investigation which became very helpful to sociology as such was *ethnology* and *ethnography* in the widest sense of these words. Embracing racial description, folklore, linguistics, folkways, specific economics, customs, and law, such investigations become decisive for very important conclusions of a general character.

Little wonder, therefore, that a splendid galaxy of ethnologists arose, many of whom were scholars and professors in jurisprudence, political science, history, and so on. In this relation investigators of the type of Maxime Kovalevsky (1851-1916), who investigated some ethnological peculiarities, especially legal ethnography in the Caucasus, are direct antidotes for such American scholars as L. H. Morgan, or such Englishmen as Sir Henry Sumner Maine. Russia being one vast territorially connected sub-continent was, and remains, to a certain extent, one of the last experimental fields of ethnological sociology. The description of the civilization of the whole variety of the hundred and fifty races, peoples, and tribes was in itself the basis for the necessary conclusion that there must exist certain causes of sociological nature which may explain this variety.

Of considerable importance for Russian sociology was the field of Russian *jurisprudence*. At no time was the purely dogmatic or analytical approach to legal science fully recognized. Even in civil and commercial law there existed some sociological trends; it suffices to mention such scholars as Pokrovsky, the author of *The Basic Problems of Civil Law* (1915) or Khvostov. To a larger extent sociological trends can be found in works devoted to topics of constitutional and criminal law and especially to the field of jurisprudence as such, which often was called "General Theory of Law" or Legal Encyclopaedia. Among the latter authors are B. Chicherin, V. Solovjov, Th. Kistiakovsky, P. Novgorodzeff, N. Korkunov (1833-1902), the founder of the positive school (see the English translation of his *General Theory of Law*).

Th. Kistiakovsky belongs basically to the idealistic Kantian School but later on he tried to bring it down in a revised way in his German sociological book: *The Individual and the Society* (1899). In his big work, *Social Sciences and Law* (Moscow, 1916), Kistiakovsky tries to delimit his methodology on the one hand from the usual dogmatic positivism, and from psychological positivism (of Petrazhytski) on the other. Legal philosophy has to be built on law as a cultural product and on philosophy of culture. Methodologically he advocates a pluralistic approach. For him there exist five notions of law: 1) the sociological, 2) the psychological, 3) the dogmatico-juridical or that of the State, 4) the philosophico-normative, and 5) the notion of law as an element of culture. In contrast to Petrazhytski, he denies emotion as a specific element of psychology and, what is more, he points out that the theory of Petrazhytski concerns in reality only the "psyche" of law but not law in the proper sense.

Otherwise Kistiakovsky has shown a very broad understanding of sociological and political problems. As far back as 1909 he gave a brilliant analysis of Russia's political mentality and activity and, it may be said, he predicted, if not expressly, the possibility of a social revolution in Russia.

Particularly important for the sociology of law was Leo Petrazhytski, the most prominent and original Russian legal and sociological thinker. Of Polish origin, after decades of creative work in Russia (Kiev and Petersburg) he returned to Poland (Warsaw) after the restoration of Polish independence. He created in Russia the so-called psychological theory of law and sociology.

This is not the proper place for detailed analysis of Petrazhytski's theory, but it suffices to say that his position was in an equal way foreign to Marxism, to Darwinist sociology, and to the dominant dogmatic or analytical jurisprudence of Europe. His theory was basically sociological in the sense that it found a new sphere of the existence of law as a specific ethical behavior including morals and law. If the most prominent German legal science remained normativistic and deemed every positive investigation of *what is* as belonging to sociology while jurisprudence has to deal with the *ought-to-be*, Petrazhytski induced sociological research into jurisprudence. Thereby his new research was based upon a revision of the old methodology and an entirely new psychological approach to ethical phenomena. New lines of distinction and differentiation, new fundamental qualities explained in their functional development, were adduced in order to create a theory of law included within a wider theory of sociality. A German translation of the *Methodology of the Theories of Law and Morals* (1902) appeared in 1933. An English translation of Petrazhytski's main work, *The Theory of Law and State* (1908, 1910, 2 vols.), under the editorship of Professor T. Babb, is nearing completion.

Under Petrazhytski's influence an entire school was created, the representatives of which investigated various fields of law and the social sciences under a more rigid or more flexible following of his theory. Among his followers we may mention A. Kruglevski, P. Lublinski, K. Sokolov. P. A. Sorokin, M. Laserson, and G. Gurvitch. Even under the Soviet regime, when the psychological theory of Petrazhytski was declared a bourgeois theory, some Soviet scholars, like M. Reussner, tried, nevertheless, to apply this theory in their works in a rather camouflaged way.

Max M. Laserson, (*General Theory of Law*; Riga: 1930; and *Russische Rechtsphilosophie*; Berlin: 1933), developed the theory of Petrazshytski in the direction of a deeper investigation of intuitive (non-positive) law. The intuitive law, in clear contrast to Petrazhytski, is divided by Laserson into two branches: (1) the individually adapted intuitive law and (2) the socially adapted intuitive law. This leads to an entirely new conception of natural law. Behind the Western doctrine of natural law, which is usually interpreted as the core of the problem, there is a permanent functional type of natural law that bridges individual ethical and legal consciousness with positive law and the established political order. Laserson has given a concrete description of the correlation between intuitive ethics and positive law, including the juridico-sociological phenomenon of revolution.

Georges Gurvitch, (*L'dée du droit social*, Paris: 1932; *Le temps présent et l'idée du droit social*, Paris: 1932; *L'expérience juridique et la philosophie pluraliste du droit*, Paris: 1935; *Sociology of Law*, New York: 1942), transformed Petrazhytski's psychological theory on the multiplicity of "normative facts" in jural life to a sociological conception. "Normative facts" according to him are social bonds, groups, and entire societies so far as they realize through their existence and activity positive jural values. The jural pluralism that Gurvitch developed on an "ideal-realistic" basis was further applied by him to the general problems of sociology, and especially to the problem of the "Sociology of the Human Spirit." In Gurvitch's theories on depth-levels of social reality, on immediate collective experience of values and ideas as embodied in social facts, on variable microcosms of social bonds in each group and on variable macrocosms of groups constituting each type of all-inclusive society, the influences of Petrazhytski, Durkheim, Bergson, James, and Phenomenology meet and synthesize. (Cf. *La morale théorique et la science des moeurs*, Paris: 1937; and *Essais de sociologie*, Paris: 1938. For further information on Gurvitch's sociology see the paper by C. Lévi-Strauss on "French Sociology" in this Symposium.)

A strong reaction against Petrazhytski is to be noted in the work of N. S. Timasheff, who has to be classified under Maxim Kovalevski's school of plural causation. As long ago as 1922 Timasheff made an attempt to orient the sociology of law toward social psychology rather than individual psychology as had Petrazhytski. (See his "Law and Social Psychology," in *Works of Russian Scholars Outside Russia*, vol. II.). In this study Pavlov's theory of conditioned reflexes was applied to the explanation of the fixation and automatism of legal behavior. The basic views of Timasheff are laid down in his *Introduction to the Sociology of Law*, (Cambridge: Harvard Committee for Research in the Social Sciences, 1939). In Chapter II of this book the author, developing his view on law as a social force and dealing with the ethical group conviction, rejects Petrazhytski's psychological theory as entirely based on individual psychology and therefore unable to reckon with the collective character of ethics. But he forgets that not only does Petrazhytski recognize the law as a product of mass adaptation but his emotional theory of law presupposes the existence and participation of intellectual images in the legal emotions. Thus there is given the channel through which collective ethics function and motivate behavior.

Translations of Foreign Sociological Works. Russian sociological science was paralled with a long series of translations, without which the development of Russian sociology is almost unthinkable. Translations of English, American, French, and Italian sociologists and German philosophers of history were published beginning with the 1860's down to the twenties of the present century.

Besides Herbert Spencer's and August Comte's works and all the basic writings of Utopian and Marxian Socialists with Karl Marx, Friedrich Engels, Ferdinand Lassale, and K. Kautsky in the lead, the following authors in the fields of pure sociology, philosophy of history, and the neighboring fields of political science, historical

RUSSIAN SOCIOLOGY

and sociological jurisprudence, etc. appeared in Russian translations:

P. Barth, *Die Philosophie der Geschichte als Soziologie.*
Beccaria, Cesare, *On Crimes and Punishments.*
Bentham, T., *Introduction to Morals and Legislation.*
Buckle, H. T., *The History of Civilization in England* (two different translations).
Carey, H. C., *Principles of Social Science* (appeared in Russian translation as early as 1869).
Carlyle, Th., *History of the French Revolution; On Heroes and the Heroic in History.*
de Condorcet, J. A., *The Progress of Human Reason,* and other works.
de Greef, K., *Social Progress and Regress.*
Gumplowicz, L., *The Outlines of Sociology; the General Theory of the State.*
Duguit, Leon, *Constitutional Law.*
Durkheim, E., *On the Division of Social Labor.*
Fouillée, *La science sociale contemporaine.*
Ihering, R., *The Spirit of Roman Law; The Struggle for Right.*
Kidd, B., *Social Evolution.*
Labriola, A., *Essays on the Materialistic Conception.*
Lacombe, P., *L'histoire considérée comme science,* (translated under the title: *Sociological Bases of History*).
Letourneau, Ch., *L'évolution de la propriété; La sociologie d'après l'ethnographie.*
A. Loria, *Sociology, Its Aim, Friends, and Sucesses.*
L. Levy-Bruhl, *Primitive Mentality.*
Maine, Sir Henry Summer, *Ancient Law; Village Communities; The Early History of Institutions.*
Mayr, *Die Gesentzniassigkeit in Gesellschaftsleben.*
Mill, John Stewart, *System of Logic; Liberty.*
Montesquieu, Ch., *The Spirit of the Laws.*
Masaryk, Th., *Philosophical and Sociological Outlines of Marxism.*
Morgan, L. H. *Ancient Society.*
Palante, G., *Outlines of Sociology.*
Ribot, T. A *Psychology of Sentiments.*
Richet, Ch., *Outlines of General Psychology.*
Rousseau, J. J., most of his works.
Romanes, *Mental Evolution of Man.*
Simmel, G., *Social Differentiation.*
Sorel, *Reflections on Violence.*
Stammler, R., *Wirtschaft und Recht nach der Materialistischen Geschichtauffassung.*
Sutherland, A., *The Origin and Growth of the Moral Instinct.*
Tarde, G., *Social Logics; Social Studies; Laws of Imitation* A. de Tocqueville, *Democracy in America; The Ancient Regime and the Revolution.*
Taylor, Edward B., *Researches into the Early History of Mankind; Primitive Culture; Anthropology, an Introduction to the Study of Man and Civilization*
Ward, L. F., *The Psychological Factors of Civilization* Wilson, Woodrow, *The State.*
Wundt, Wilhelm, *Ethics.*

TWENTIETH CENTURY SOCIOLOGY

The forgoing list does not exhaust the whole bibliography of translated literature in sociology and neighboring fields and is not so intended. Despite the variety of schools, approaches, and systems the following may be said as a general characterization. While in the fields of pure philosophy, legal philosophy, ethics, metaphysics, and philosophy of history Russian thought was to some degree influenced by German thinkers, in the field of the more modern sociological science the dominating influence and inspiration belongs to the Anglo-American and French scholarly literature.

At the same time the division on such lines was also a division of approaches. Various doctrines of positivism and of an objectivated progress prevailed in Anglo-Saxon and French literature of sociology; metaphysical aproaches, negation of positivism and exact research, higher evaluation of the uniqueness (Werteinmaligkeit) in contradistinction to general analysis was the basic trend of the German literature. We may say that while Anglo-American and French schools developed their theories towards positive sociology the bulk of German authors preferred to construct philosophy of history.

The Various Schools. It would be very naive to expect from the first stages of Russian sociology a purely objective non-evaluative approach. This was not the case in Western European countries either, where the claim to a sociology without evalutions of ideological suppositions was made a slogan. Decades of works on topics which were called sociological but did not belong to sociology in any sense have had to pass before works appeared which could be qualified as pertaining to sociology in the proper sense of this notion.

The School of Subjective Sociology. This school is the most original and chronologically emerged earlier than the Marxian School. One of the founders of this school was Peter Lavrov (1823-1900). He himself points out that his sociology is imbued with the spirit of anthropologism and considers as his precursors the ancient sceptics, A. Comte and L. Feuerbach, Spencer and Marx.

Basically his sociology is permeated with evaluative thinking; it is rather a philosophy of history which tends to show that there exists a progress both in anthropology and sociology. The starting point of every philosophical construction is the man (or personality) that develops together with the unfolding of the society.

Morality is not innate; not all men are able to elaborate moral stimuli in their psychology. An innate quality is only the striving after pleasure. The highly advanced man creates the delight of a moral life and places it at the very top in the hierarchy of pleasures. The majority does not go higher than utilitarianism. A critical attitude is a necessity in the process of the adaptation of the individual to the social development.

According to Lavrov sociology investigates the forms of appearance, the strengthening and weakening of the solidarity among conscious organic individuals, and therefore covers all animal societies, in which the individuals reach some extent of individual cognizance; on the other hand it covers all human societies and social ideals, with the help of which man strives to realize a just commonwealth. Progress according to Lavrov is the strengthening of conscious processes inside the individual and of social solidarity. The most popular and inspiring work of Lavrov was the *Historical Letters* (1870). In his last book, *The Principal Moments in the History of Thought*, he shows in what the real phases of historical progress actually consist. He finds the answer in the history of civilization which, according to him, shows "how the critical thought of the individual transforms the culture of societies, by striving to carry into their civilizations truth and justice."

K. N. Mikhailovsky (1842-1904). He is the second to Lavrov in the creation of the "Subjective" Russian sociology. He is to a certain extent more positivistic than Lavrov, but his ethical evaluation of social phenomena remains very strong. He considers it necessary to reconcile objective truth and justice. He bases it on a well known duplicity of the Russian word *pravda*. This word signifies two notions: truth (*istina*) and justice (*spravedlivost*). (1) Says Mikhailovsky: "I have never been able to believe it impossible to find a view wherein abstract truth and concrete justice could go together, each supplementing the other."

Despite the rather collectivist approach to political and economic problems in general he postulates as the final criterion of judgment the inlividual: "In all political questions as the focus of judgment must be made not the interests of the nation, not the government, not the commune, not the province, not the federation, but the individual."

In contradistinction to Spencer with whom he polemizes in his famous essay "What is Progress?" he claims that the objective method of Spencer and Comte makes any sociology impossible.

---

1. See my article, "Rights, Righthandedness, and Uprightness," *American Sociological Review* 4: 534-542, August, 1939.

Spencer's approach, says Mikhailovsky, is to such a high extent all-embracing that he does not even differentiate between epochs of development and epochs of decline. A purely objective approach seems to be impossible and undesirable.

"There is no absolute truth, but only the truth for man and beyond human nature there is no truth for man." This conclusion was made already by Comte. The big importance of Comte's line of thinking is diminished only by the basic shortcoming of his system, namely, by the elimination of the subjective method from the fields of sociology, ethics, and politics. The positivism did only half of the job: it established the legality of the human point of view on nature, but the human standpoint is the angle of the man who thinks and perceives, *i. e.*, of a complete individual who controls all organs and functions of the human organism. By such a common participation of all attributes of the individual, a truth is produced which is not an absolute one but the truth for the man. (2)

The evaluative character of Mikhailovsky's doctrine found its most conspicuous expression in the way by which he rejected Darwinism. It is in his eyes an anti-democratic and anti-social theory. "When converted into a sociological doctrine Darwinism only substitutes for the word "species," the "society"; for the term "differentiation of characteristics," "division of labor"; for the slogan "struggle for existence," "competition." This contradicts his formula of progress, which, according to Mikhailovsky is the gradual approach toward integrality of the indivisibles (individuals). Whatever retards this movement is immoral, or unjust, or harmful, or unwise, while in the progress visualized by Darwin the individual regresses.

The struggle for individuality against Czarism was also one of the most important premises of the political orientation of Mikhailovsky and the populist movement.

He was also much interested in the relations between the individual and the masses (see his *Heroes and the Crowd, Pathologic Magics*) ascribing, in contradistinction to Marxism, an important leading role to the personality.

It was mainly Mikhailovsky who stressed the accessibility of the subjective element in sociology. He went so far as to say: "I am convinced that an exclusively objective outlook in sociology is impossible and was never applied by anybody. (3)

---

2. N. K. Mikhailovsky, *Collected Works*, (1911) vol. I, p. 105-106. Appeared originally in 1869.

3. *Ibid.*, vol. III, p. 397.

RUSSIAN SOCIOLOGY

To that he adds: "The subjective way of research is, therefore, used by all where the human thoughts and feelings are analyzed. But it achieves the character of a scientific method only when it is applied consciously and systematically. That does not mean that the investigator must forget his sympathies and antipathies -- which is often suggested but never fulfilled by the objectivists. The sociologist has to state: This is desirable for me and that is not, beyond the truth as such. He does not deny that in the result some disagreements and important inconveniences are inevitable for sociology." Mikhailovsky and the other Russian subjective sociologists left the basic problem of how they understood the truth entirely unsolved and avoided any gnoseological inquiries.

Kareyev (1850-1931). In reality Kareyev is rather a philosopher of history than a pure sociologist, although during the last period of his life he wrote on sociology as such.

Being a progressively thinking idealist he negatively had to fight the old metaphysic conception of the Slavophiles and Romantics in his own field of history. Kareyev became in 1885 professor of history of the Petersburg University and is the author of *The History of Western Europe* in seven volumes.

Constructively Kareyev was a positivist like the other representatives of Russian Subjective Sociology. For him the central problem, remained that of the role of the individual in history. His main works were entitled *The Nature of the Historic Process and the Role of the Individual in History* (1890), *General Problems of the Philosophy of History* (1883), *Sociology* (1918).

Kropotkin. It scarcely needs to be stressed that for Prince Peter Kropotkin (1842-1921) social norms can by no means be attached to the non-evaluative or presuppositionless systems of sociology. In the introduction to his most interesting book, *Mutual Aid, A Factor of Evolution* (London: 1902), the author openly declares that his intention was the fight against amoralism which became particularly outspoken in the score of years preceding the 20th century. But the bulk of his argumentation and construction is built up not against purely meditative anti-moralism of the kind of Nietzsche but against Darwin, or rather against the conclusions made out of Darwin's law of mutual struggle for sociology and human ethics by Darwinists like Huxley.

And in this relation Kropotkin remains a unique case, because he himself was very far from any dogmatic moralization. Himself a scientist and naturalist, an observer of the animal life of Eastern

Siberia and Northern Manchuria, he was very well armed to make his conclusions and base them on his observations concerning mutual aid among animals. He points out the following against Darwin:

"Paucity of life, underpopulation — not overpopulation — being the distintive feature of that immense part of the globe which we name Northern Asia, I conceived since then serious doubts — which subsequent study has only confirmed — as to the reality of that fearful competition for food and life within each species, which was article of faith with most Darwinists." He came to the conclusion, which was at the same time his presupposition that besides the *Law of Mutual Struggle* there is in nature the *Law of Mutual Aid* which for the success of the struggle for life, and especially for the progressive evolution of the species, is far more important than the law of mutual contest.

From animal psychology Kropotkin steps to human ethics. He denies that love or sympathy are bases of human society; this is too evaluative for him. "It is the recognition," he says — "be it only at the stage of an instinct — of human solidarity. It is the unconscious recognition of the force that is borrowed by each man from the practice of mutual aid; of the close dependency of every one's happiness upon the happiness of all. Upon this broad and necessary foundation the still higher moral feelings are developed.

Almost twenty years later, as an anarchist and critic of the Communist movement and the Soviet State, he wrote (in 1921) his *Ethics*, published in Russia in 1922 and in an English translation in 1934 in New York. It is built in his first chapters on his Mutual Aid, particularly his analysis of the progress of morality and of the essence of the social instinct; in its greatest part, however, it is a historical analysis of the moral teachings from ancient Greece down to Herbert Spencer and T. M. Guyau.

De Roberty. A very important step nearer to modern sociology, although not deprived of an evaluative character, was made by De Roberty, a Russian who emigrated to France and returned to Russia only after the revolution of 1905. (4) He himself defines his theory as neo-positivism. He certainly rejects the Russian "subjectivism" and Marxism.

His sociological theory is based on the study of sciences of the superorganic world. What is the superorganic phenomenon and

---

4. *A New Program of the Basic Problems of Sociology*, Russian, (St. Petersburg: 1909) (Translated from the French with new additions).

which place does it take in nature? It' is the correlation between myself and the other (ego and alter), firstly a psychophysic and later on a psychological one. The first correlation, which is never surpassed by the animal societies, belongs to the province of biology; the other, on the contrary, is sociology in its specific sense, "There may once come the day," says De Roberty, "when super organic phenomena will be entirely reduced to their immediate source — to phenomena of the organic life. But this day is not near. Before sociality will disappear in life, the very concept of life will be replaced by the respective chemical notion; and prior to the time when the very word 'life' will become superfluous the chemical properties of matter will merge into the physical world of energy." Be that as it may, but if the superorganic phenomenon follows after the biological fact, it always precedes the psychological fact.

DeRoberty originally intended to improve Comte's method by applying to the study of social phenomena the descriptive method "as analytic as possible." But he did not succeed in this and he could not succeed because even modern sociology has to go a long way to achieve this aim. A sociological description without knowing exactly what has to be described is to the same extent fruitless and illiterate as the description of an illness by an unschooled nurse, or the description of a melody by one who does not know musical notes.

Instead De Roberty retreats from his original audacious intentions to the bridge leading from the superorganic phenomena to ethics. He finds that collective psyche is solidarity. Solidarity exercises a great influence upon the psychical development of the individual; it shapes the individual after itself and transforms him into a part of the group. Morality and sociality are identical. But sociality is in some way the progressive rationalization of life, of the great organic dominion, and in this manner of the entire universe.

Kovalevsky. One of the most prominent Russian sociologists was Maxim Kovalevsky (1851-1916). Although he, according to his basic academic work, was mostly creative in the fields of law and the history of political institutions, he at the same time wrote six volumes on the economic development of Europe and two great works on *Contemporary Sociologists* (1905) and *Sociology* (two volumes, 1910).

M. Kovalevsky was very far from the specific sociological discussions in Russia between Marxists and the Subjective Sociologists. In the beginning of his academic career he was compelled to leave

Moscow University and Russia, and the best years of his life, since 1887, he devoted to studies made mainly in England and France. Only in 1906 did he return to Russia, where he died in 1916.

In his economic works some critics tried to discover a similarity with the Marxian tendencies, while in reality Kovalevsky was an adversary not only of Marxism but of any other sociological monistic system with one exclusive or dominating factor. His view in this connection he himself formulated in the following way: Sociology can only achieve very much if the attempts to discover a factor or rather one main or prime factor are finally excluded from the sphere of its immediate tasks and if sociology, in full accordance with the complexity of social phenomena, limits itself to the indication of the existence of simultaneous and parallel effects and counter-effects produced by many causes. This plurality of factors was in itself a very important thesis. The explanation to that Kovalevsky saw in the relatively undeveloped status of social sciences which does not allow any broad causational generalizations. Instead he advocated the necessity of specific researches of particular phenomena and their monographic description.

The abolition of the traditional problem of factors does not mean the refusal of an establishment of functional links. But methodologically every attempt to describe the more and less important factors becomes senseless. Thus, Kovalevsky reaches almost the same conclusions concerning social causation as those maintained in modern sociology.

The idea of plural causation originally developed by Maxim Kovalevsky was in a clear opposition to the other schools of Russian sociology and particularly to the Subjective Sociology of the Populists and to the Marxists. It was the first serious attempt to get rid of an overloaded indeological burden of Russian sociology. His works on genetic sociology in special concrete fields like the history of the decline of the village community and its land ownership in the canton Waadt (1876), his numerous studies on the customs of Caucasians and particularly his *Common Law of the Ossetins* considered in comparative legal research (1893), on *Modern Custom and Ancient Law in Russia* (lectures delivered at Oxford, 1891) and so on, not to mention his splendid works on the history of democratic institutions — were the best proof of the scientific importance of a sociological research based upon the negation of monism.

If there was a certain school of Maxim Kovalevsky one of his most prominent followers and younger friends was Sir Paul Vinogradoff, a world famous Anglo-Russian historian and jurist (1854-1925), who stood in friendly relations with Kovalevsky throughout forty years. Both denied the analytical method as the only method of legal science; for both of them entire juridical institutions which existed throughout centuries were objects deserving a thorough investigation, which has to use the juridical phenomena in the light of historical and social (if not sociological) research, the latter including an economic analysis of the institution. The standard works of Vinogradoff were: *Villainage in England* (1892), *Growth of the Manor* (1905) and *English Society in the Eleventh Century* (1908).

At the same time Vinogradoff was deeply interested in the unfolding of political ideas. He delivered at Oxford a course of lecture on "Slavophilism and Western Ideas in Russian Culture."

Being simultaneously a professor of the Moscow and Oxford Universities, he was eager to bring the ideas of Anglo-American legal and political science to Russia.

It was always his idea that the Russian law schools and legal education were in a too high degree influenced, if not dominated, by German jurisprudence and its methods. This idea became particularly topical during the first World War when Vinogradoff together with Kovalevsky headed a new rapprochment toward Anglo-American political and legal ideas under the auspices of the newly created Russo-English Society.

As far back as 1907 Vinogradoff published a Russian translation of A. Dicey's *Introduction to the Study of the Law of the Constitution* with a preface by himself (1907) and produced a vivid reaction in Russian political science. During the War Vinogradoff published a Russian book, *Essays on Theory of Law* (1915), which was almost entirely based on his continuous work on Anglo-American law. This book opened to the average Russian jurists new horizons. The most important chapter was dedicated to sources of law illustrated by the court practice of England and the United States, a chapter dedicated to common law and equity with a briliant comparative study of Roman equitas and Anglo-Saxon equity, and a concluding chapter on natural law.

In connection with his professorial work he published a magnificent series entitled: *Oxford Studies of Social and Legal History*, (Oxford: 1909-1928).

A. Zvonitzkaya tries in her book the *Social Bond*, (Kiev: 1914) to go further in the direction of a divorce with Russian traditional evaluative sociology. Her system, if it deserves this title, is rather a combination of the doctrines of Tarde, Giddings, and Baldwin. She ascribes supremacy in sociology to the social bond. In revealing the nature of the social bond she finds that the psychology of the social personality bears the stamp of social relations. The obligatory (imperative) character of public consciousness is ununderstandable without social relations. In contradistinction to Giddings and Baldwin she seeks the explanation for social crises and the rupture of the social bond not in the conflicts between the individual and the society but in the clashes between various imperative norms. To a certain degree the theory of Zvonitzkaya reminds one of the theory of the German formal sociology of Georg Simmel.

A specific sociological work of research was done by E. Spektorsky. Out of his study on philosophy of law and the philosophy of social sciences (Warsaw: 1907) he came to the conclusion that the seventeenth century was the most productive epoch in the progress of physical and mathematical sciences and this led to the appearance of a unique social theory among whose exponent's Hobbes, Spinoza, and Weigel were the most outstanding.

The two volumes of Spektorsky's *Problems of Social Physics in the Seventeenth Century* (1910 and 1917) gave an exhaustive characterization of one of the most interesting phases of the history of social, political, and ethical thought. We get an exact picture of social mechanics and social dynamics, to the idea of which sociological thought returned in the 19th and 20th century. But Spektorsky does not reach any clear conclusion about the application of social mechanics at the modern stage of sociology.

In general it may be said that the independent non-evaluative sociology developed in the first two decades of the 20th century mostly in the frames of the Russian behavioristic school. It was built up by Ivan Pavlov, his pupils, V. Bekhterev. *General Foundations of Reflexology*, (Russian, 1918) and *Collective Reflexology* (Russian, 1921), W. A. Wagner, *Biological Foundations of Comparative Psychology*; and others.

Should there be a possibility of developing an independent non-evaluative sociology in Soviet Russia the first trend which will be renewed will be the behavioristic school, especially the bio-psychological works which were more or less tolerated in the special bio-psychological literature. This last mentioned was never in direct opposition to official Marxism or dialectical materialism. The other more sociological branch of behaviorism will have to wait for a renewal after the liquidation of the Marxist monopoly in Russian sociology.

The most outstanding representative of the present day Russian sociology is Pitirim Sorokin (since 1924, in the United States). In his short essay on "Russian Sociology" printed in 1927 in the *Publications of the American Sociological Society* (Vol. XXXI, pp. 58-69) he mentions himself under the representatives of the Russian behavioristic school. But since that time he overcame entirely this position and his criticism gave a death blow to behaviorism in the United States. He must be described as the founder of *sociological integralism*. The first term "*sociological*" aims to stress the facts that Sorokin views socio-cultural phenomena as a category *sui generis*, different from, and irreducible to, inorganic, organic, and psychological phenomena. It aims to indicate, further, that sociology studies this domain *per se*, and only indirectly the relationships between the socio-cultural and the inorganic, organic, and psychological phenomena. It means also that the main task of sociology consists in a specific investigation of the organization and life of this socio-cultural world, as well as an investigation of the main relationships between the chief classes of socio-cultural phenomena. It means, finally, that since the socio-cultural world is a category *sui generis*, sociology has to have its own framework of referential principles independent of those of the other sciences and fitted to the nature of the phenomena studied. In this respect Sorokin goes systematically so far as to attempt to create the categories of social time, social space, social relationship, and many others. These are to be distinguished from the categories of time, space, causal relationship, and so on of the natural sciences, which are regarded by him as unfit for an adequate study of social phenomena. Rejecting the fallacious simplifications of Durkheim, DeRoberty and other representatives of the sociologistic school, Sorokin carries the principles of this school much farther than they were carried by its earlier leaders.

The second word "*Integralism*" points out another fundamental aspect of Sorokin's theories. If we take his sociological methodology, integralism appears first in the principle that socio-cultural phenomena have two inseparable aspects: an inner — the aspect of meaning and mentality; and an outer — the aspect of the transsubjective materialization and objectivation of the inner aspect. Both aspects are inseparable and both have to be studied in any investigation of social phenomena. In this respect Sorokin deviates from the "overt behaviorists" who would study socio-cultural phenomena only as the trans-subjective phenomena; and from the sociological "introspectivist" who philosophize about the "inner meaning" of socio-cultural values but neglect to study their "objective" aspects.

Quite consistently with this "integral" standpoint, Sorokin's method demands the unification of the purely logico-epistemological approach, especially the "phenomenological" (in the Husserlian sense), with the "empirical" study of the relevant facts. The first is absolutely necessary in order to grasp and to understand the "inner" aspect of socio-cultural phenomena; the second, in order to study their overt aspect as it is "objectivized" in the empirical world of the senses. According to him, without a deep logical thought that analyzes the logical and epistemological assumptions, principles, forms and other aspects of the sociological problem studied, no more empiricism or "factualism" — whether statistical, historical, experimental, or observational — can yield valid results. On the other hand, in regard to many social problems it is possible to formulate several equally logical theories. Logic without the relevant facts is according to Sorokin sterile; the "facts" without logic and analytico-synthetic thought are not relevant facts at all, they are meaningless and have no cognitive value. Therefore, in all the important works of Sorokin one finds an attempt to integrate into one unity the logical and the "fact finding" methods: any important problem is first analyzed logically and epistemologically; and then is followed by the factual verification of the validity of a proposed theory by means of the relevant historical, statistical, observational, and some times even experimental data. Accordingly, Sorokin criticizes the one-sidedness of the "fact-finders," as well as that of the mere "logicians" who are isolated from the empirical reality.

The "integralism" appears also in Sorokin's conception of sociology as neither a mere encyclopedic depository of all the other social sciences nor a special discipline that studies its own single sector of socio-cultural phenomena, as Simmel and others claim. The "integralism" of Sorokin's system consists in a conception of sociology as *generalizing* science dealing with the socio-cultural world *as a whole;* and at the same time, as a special *systematic science* in the sense that it deals with this social world as a whole only along very specific and definite lines. The specific lines along which sociology deals with the whole social world have to do with its aspect of repetition or recurrence in time and space: recurrent forms and types, recurrent processes, recurrent relationships between various classes of social phenomena. Since they are recurrent they are not unique; if they are not unique they belong to the whole class of respective phenomena. The forms, processes, and relationships recurrent in al socio-cultural phenomena are those forms, processes, and relationships *common* to all those phenomena. Hence, sociology is a general and, at the same time, a special discipline. Its main task is to study the ever repeated forms and types of social structures, social institutions, and their logical and causal relationships; beginning with the universal — that which is common to all socio-cultural phenomena no matter where and when they are given — it ends with the repeated forms, types and relationships common only to a given definite class of social phenomena.

Consistently with his standpoint Sorokin rejects the concepts of "evolution," "progress," which he himself defended in his early works (5), and any generally linear conception of the direction of the socio-cultural and historical processes.

These remarks give an idea of the nature of the sociologistic integralism of Sorokin's system. These principles together with many others have been carried through all the more important monographic works of Sorokin, beginning with his Russian — *Sistema Soziologii* — and ending with *Social and Cultural Dynamics*, *The Crisis of Our Age*, and *Socio-Cultural Causality, Space, Time*.

II

Russian Marxism. Marxism as such is certainly not a specific school of Russian sociological thought, but in Russia the role and function of this school became a peculiar one. If in Western Europe and particularly in Germany Marxism was only a method to help in research of special social sciences, Russian Marxism became rather a key to interference in the historical process. In

---

5. For the sake of exactness, however, we must underline that even in these works (*The Review of the Theories and Problems of Progress* in the Symposium, New Ideas in Sociology (vol. III, 1914), Sorokin differentiates evaluative and non-evaluative theories of progress. The first category of theories is inevitably subjective while the non-evaluative theories of progress discover permanent tendencies of certain lines of evolution. Sorokin recognizes the positive role of the second category.

this relation Russian Marxism was the hostile twin-brother of the Russian Subjective Sociology. It is therefore little wonder that the first and best Marxian sociological work, namely that of George Plekhanov, *Toward the Development of a Monistic Conception of History*, was mainly construed as an anti-Populist and anti-Idealistic book, although dedicated to the founders of Russian Subjective Sociology. The theory of Plekhanov, based on Marx and Engels, put gravity center on the role of the individual in history besides the general dialectical conception of history. The question of progress and the role of the personality remained the key-point of Russian Marxism. To formulate it in a more concrete way out of the famous preface to Marx's *Contribution to the Critique of Political Economy* Western Marxism was more interested in the cognitive side, (in German terminology, *erkenntniss-theoretische Soziologie*), viz., in the dependence of the spiritual phenomena on the material conditions of life, taking as a starting point the aphorism of Marx that "the anatomy of civil society is to be found in political economy." Russian Marxism took as its basic postulate another thesis of the same preface, namely that saying: "It is not the consciousness of men that determines their existence but, on the contrary, it is their social existence that determines their consciousness."

Russian Marxism tried to use this formula to create a new existence. This tendency found its full expression in an entirely renewed volitional Marxism called later on Leninism. While Western Marxism remained a method to *explain* the historical development, Rusian Marxism stressed the trend to *re-make* the social and political existence. Lack of space does not allow us to go into details to prove it. This is so much the more complicated in that it did not find a clear expression in sociological terms or books but rather in the political Marxist press.

Plekhanov did not go far away from Engels. Immediately after the old Marxist assertion that the relations of production are the basis and all other ideological phenomena like law, morals, politics, religion, and art only superstructures, Plekhanov comes back to the second variation formulated by Engels, namely, the reciprocal influences of the superstructures upon the economics. Engels in his letter to Starkenberg (1894) formulated this somewhat changed description of historical materialism in the following way:

> The political, legal, philosophical, literary, and artistic development rest on the economic. But they all react upon one another and upon the economic

base. It is not the case that the economic situation is the *sole active cause* and everything else is merely a passive effect. Rather is there a reciprocity within a field of economic necessity which *in the last instance* always asserts itself.

Similarly, historical materialism does not deny the role played by social tradition in modifying the rate of change in the non-material aspects of culture.

In reality this new formula is a new conception. Because if there is a reciprocal action between the basis and super-structure under which the basis may be for a long time influenced by the superstructure or even dominated by it, the entire monistic system of Marxism ceases to be monistic and becomes multi-factorial.

This more deep-rooted and complicated variation was taken over by Plekhanov. In a very vivid way he describes this conception of Engels in the following words: (6)

"The factors are subject to reciprocal action; each influences the rest and is in its turn influenced by the rest. The result is such an intricate web of reciprocal influences of direct actions and reflected reactions, that whoever sets out to elucidate the course of social development begins to feel . . . an unconquerable necessity to find at least some sort of clue out of the labyrinth.

This is tantamount to a shift which brings Marxism nearer to all kinds of idealism. Because there are many factors or where the superstructure is able to influence and *ergo to* re-make the basis, no predominance of productive forces over various superstructures in a longer period of time is necessary. That means that law or politics are able to change the economic basis.

Plekhanov did not give a decisive answer to this basic question. The only conclusion he reached out of this discussion was that the first formula meant economic materialism, while true Marxism is the second variation, namely historical or dialectical materialism.

The objective truth is that this somewhat vague differentiation was incorporated by the later Soviet Marxism of the Stalinist coinage and on the basis of this same differentiation old pre-October Marxists like Prof. Pokrovski and Bukharin were stigmatized as economic materialists.

As to Plekhanov's view on the role of the individual in history his views were emphatically taken over by the later Russian (Soviet) Marxism. The limited role of the heroes or personalities was declared already by Plekhanov in his sharp polemics with the idealistic subjectivists as a vice of economical materialism which has

---

6. See George Plekhanov, *Essays in Historical Materialism*, (New York: International Publishers, 1940), p. 16.

nothing in common with real Marxism, *i. e.*, dialectical materialism. Hence the overstressed idea by Engels of freedom as the consciousness of necessity. The latter, according to Plekhanov, does not diminish the activity and the freedom of the individual but even strengthens the aspect of freedom. Plekhanov goes so far as to call Carlyle's definition of heroes or great men as beginners, a very apt description. "A great man," adds Plekhanov, "is precisely a beginner because he sees *further* than others, and desires thing *more strongly* than others." (7) Needles to say, these views were received enthusiastically by official Soviet Marxism.

Let us see what was added to this analysis by the most gifted Soviet Marxist sociologist N. Bukharkin (1888-1938). The new tendency brought in by Bukharin expresses itself in the sub-title of his book, namely, *"Historical Materialism, A System of Sociology."* (8)

There was always in Marxism a certain tendency to consider it only as a method of research and explanation. The founders of this doctrine appeared publicly with their most important works after Comte and at the same time as Spencer and other English, American, and French sociologists, and still they avoided calling historical or economic materialism a theory of sociology.

In the Soviet Union, in which from the very establishment of the proletarian dictatorship all non-Marxist doctrines or theories were stigmatized as "bourgeois" and therefore hostile to the Soviet regime, no system of sociology could be tolerated except pro-Soviet Marxism. This later was even counterposed to Western European moderate Marxism which was declared as belonging to the ideology of the petty bourgeoisie.

Being the only tolerated economic and social theory in the Soviet Union the "revolutionary" Soviet Marxism might have freely pretended to be the sociology, meaning the only recognized science of social phenomena. Most characteristically Bukharin writes in the introduction to his book:

> Some persons imagine that the theory of historical materialism should under no circumstances be considered a Marxian sociology, and that it should not be expounded systematically; they believe it is only a living *method* of historical knowledge, that its truths may only be applied in the case of concrete and historical events. In addition, there is the argument that the conception of sociology itself is rather vague . . . All such arguments

---

7. *Ibid.*, p. 59-60.
8. New York, 1925, Authorized translation from the third Russian edition.

are in error. In the first place the confusion prevailing in the bourgeois camp should not induce us to create still more confusion in our ranks. For the theory of historical materialism has a definite place, it is not political economy, nor is it history; it is the general theory of society and the laws of its evolution, i.e., sociology. In the second place, the fact that the theory of historical materialism is a method of history, by no means destroys its significance as a sociological theory. Very often a more abstract science may furnish a point of view (method) for the less abstract sciences.

The defense of historical materialism as the only correct and scientific sociology has in Bukharin's book an almost naive teleological character. Twice he comes back to this question. Firstly, in the introduction he gives the answer to the question "Why is Proletarian Science superior to Bourgeois Science?" and in the chapter on Determinism and Indeterminism.

The reason for the necessary rejection of the bourgeois sociology lies, according to the author, in the fact that the bourgeoisie is blinded by its desire to preserve capitalism and therefore bourgeois scholars did not foresee the (first) World War, the consequences of the world slaughter, the outbreak of revolution. "Not one!" insists Bukharin and explains why this happened. "They were all busily occupied in supporting their bourgeois governments and predicting victory for the capitalists of their own country." But this is a naive assertion. With much more right can one ask the representatives of Marxism (the moderate and radical left) whether they predicted the outbreak of the First World War, if anti-capitalist propaganda mentioning the military character of capitalism should not be misnamed as sociological prediction. And if "scientific prediction" and its exactitude is naively equalized by Bukharin for astronomy on the one hand and sociology on the other, let us ask whether in the twenties or thirties any Marxists (whether moderate or Leninist) have foreseen the rise of Hitlerism in Germany which led to a completely unpredicted turn in the totality of the "destiny" of the world. I am afraid "Not one" should be the truest answer. Both German moderate Marxists and Soviet revolutionary Marxists did not foresee even after the first parliamentary Nazi successes the near catastrophe, and both ridiculed the prospects of an internal victory of Hitler over (respectively) German socialism and communism. Was not one of the blinders — not less blinding than the blinders of some bourgeois sociologist — the dogma established by Marx as far back as in his *Communist Manifesto* and the 18th *Brumaire* that the petty bourgeoisie has to "vacillate" and to be disintegrated between the proletarian and the bourgeoisie? In reality in 1932-1934 the German working class and many other oppositionary groups were on the contrary re-integrated by the — call it petty bourgeois, if desirable — avalanche of German chauvinism permeated by the spirit of world conquest and domination. Even after the advent of Hitler, Soviet sociologists stubbornly "predicted" that Hitler is only a caliph of an hour; and furthermore, the onslaught of Nazi Germany of June 1941 was by no means predicted by those leading spirits who in the first crucial days of late June called this onslaught an act of perfid treachery.

Needless to say, if predictability is made the basic test of sociology no kind of Marxism including the Leninist or Stalinist stood this test. The same holds true for all other evaluative sociological theories.

Bukharin continues the old Marxist pattern of basis and superstructure. "Economy conditions politics" is also for him, as for generations of former Marxists, a kind of a key to sociological fiindings. "Laws are likewise conditioned by the level attained by the productive forces... It is on the basis of the economic conditions that law, customs and morals are evolved in any Society; they change and disappear with the economic system."

But he still is unable to solve the following question. If there is as Bukharin asserts, a relative equilibrium between the social technology and the social economy, why is it that the more "progressive" technology of the United States has as its superstructures the capitalist social economy while the much lower or backward technology of the Soviets, which throughout a quarter of a century has striven "to match" the American level of production, has as its superstructure "progressive" socialism?

In the old and basic issue of the factors Bukharin did not go very far away from Engels or Plekhanov. Neevrtheless his theses are more carefully formulated. He, too, asserts that the productive forces are the basis of social causation and at the same time, like Engels in his above-mentioned letter to Starkenberg, he speaks about the importance of the superstructures (politics, law, and science) for the basis. Bukharin in contradistinction to the old economic materialism rejects the theory of factors and *ergo* the prevailing economic factor. Speaking about the mutual interrelations among all the kinds of superstructures and their basis and vice versa he is unable — like his predecessors — to find out what the "productive forces" mean sociologically and in what consists their preponderance over all other causational or determining forces.

RUSSIAN SOCIOLOGY

Bukharin is aware of the importance of this issue. He himself says: "But if we recognize this mutual influence, what becomes of the bases of Marxian theory? For most bourgeois scholars admit a mutual interaction. May we still say that the productive forces and the production conditions are the basis of our analysis?"

He hopes to dispose of these doubts by a purely assertive statement in which the gravity center is transferred not to the static (structural) predominance of the basis but to the dynamic. He says: "At any given moment the inner structure of society is determined by the mutual relation between this society and external nature, i.e., by the condition of the material producttive forces of society; *the change in form, however, is determined by the movement of the productive forces.*" (My italics-M. L.)

But how will we ever be able to differenciate between the static, structural set of mutual relations where the productive forces are not necessarily decisive or predominant and the *change* or the movement where the productive forces become decisive? This irrefutable question remains unanswered in the works of one of the most serious and competent modern Marxists.

Leninism. The doctrine of Leninism was not exactly formulated by Lenin himself. Moreover, he never used this notion. Lenin's approach was in his own eyes that of an adherer of Marxism, who is obliged to resuscitate the real teachings of Marx after they have been distorted by Western moderate Marxists. But at the same time Lenin's interpretation of Marx was tantamount to involving voluntarism into Marxism, and meant the willingness to carry out those desiderata that for decades were proclaimed in Marxist programs without being achieved.

Objective prerequisites for the social revolution in Russia were set down not on an exact appreciation of economic possibilities. Moreover, they were to a certain degree removed and substituted by considerations of the "art of uprising." In this connection one of the most important documents is the letter written by Lenin on September 26-27, 1917 to the Central Committee of the Party in which some members were against the upheaval which became later known as the October revolution. The letter is directed not only against the moderate reformist Mensheviks and Socialist Revolutionaries, the supporters of the Democratic Kerenski regime, but also against the Bolshevik opposition. Lenin takes upon himself the reproach of being a "Blanquist," because the desire to be victorious in superseding capitalism in Russia as a basic "object-lesson" and precedent for a universal social revolution was the leading idea of this upheaval, no matter whether the previous economic analysis — even that of Lenin himself given in his work of 1899 — justified such a socialist upheaval in the most backward of all leading capitalist powers, with an industrial working class constituting about three and a half percent of the general population of the huge country.

The letter to the Central Committee asks only a "revolutionary upsurge of the people," and claims to find that all *psychological factors* are favorable for it. "The uprising," says Lenin in this letter, "must be based on the crucial point in the history of the maturing revolution, when the activity of the vanguard of the people is at its heights, when the vacillations in the ranks of the enemies, and in the ranks of the weak, half-hearted, undecided friends of the revolution are at their highest point." "Victory is assured to us," continues Lenin, "for the people are now very close to desperation, and we are showing the whole people a sure way out."

In addition to that it was only the conviction that "an international proletarian revolution is clearly rising" (*State and Revolution*) which inspired Lenin to initiate the revolution and to send his ultimatum containing his resignation from the Central Committee if his proposals were not accepted.

The leading idea which permeates Lenin's *State and Revolution* was the psychic and ethical negation of opportunism in the ranks of the moderate socialists of the Second International (1889 1914) among which the most guilty group are in the eyes of Lenin the German Social-Democratic Marxists who "vulgarized" Marx and "distorted" his doctrine (David, Kautsky, Scheidemann, Bernstein, Legien, Hilferding, etc.), because of their unwillingness and inability to lead a social revolution.

In the official Soviet literature, (9) these trends of Leninism, viz., the voluntarist approach which ignored the objective backward conditions of Russia in order to create the first experiment of a socialist State, have not been mirrored. In Lenin's conception which was a universalist one, Russia's dictatorship of the proletariat necessarily had specific features foreign to the advanced industrial countries, but nevertheless in Russia the conditions for a social revolution in the declining stage of the First World War were much more favorable than in Western Europe where the proletariat

---

9. Cf. the pamphlet of J. Stalin, *On the Foundations of Leninism.*

lost its revolutionary aspirations. In this connection orthodox Marxism is very far from Leninism, and cannot even be expressed in the terms of the original Marx's doctrine.

Stalin in his *Foundations of Leninism* gives the following definition of Leninism:

> Leninism is Marxism in the epoch of imperialism and of the proletarian revolution, or to be more exact, Leninism is the theory and tactics of the proletarian revolution in general, and the theory and tactics of the proletarian dictatorship in particular.

But most important is the fact that although this definition of Leninism ascribes to this "doctrine" no specific features, Stalin in this same work recognizes that there is a basic difference between Marxism and Leninism. This is done very cautiously and the recognition itself is only a partial one. Says Stalin:

> Others declare that Leninism is the revival of the revolutionary elements found in the Marxism of the forties of the nineteenth century, in contradistinction to the Marxism of subsequent years, when it grew moderate ... In discarding this stupid subdivision of the teachings of Marx into two parts, revolutionary and moderate, we must still recognize that this definition, in spite of its utter inadequacy and unsatisfactory character, *does contain a particle of truth*. That particle consists in the fact that *Lenin has indeed revived the revolutionary content of Marxism,* which had been submerged by the opportunists of the Second International. (Italics mine M. L.).

Stalin recognizes that Lenin added to Marxism some new elements simply because of the appearance after the emergence of imperialism of a new form of capitalism which did not exist in the times of Marx and Engels. He follows the admission of Lenin that out of the relatively backward character of Russia a socialism established in such a subcontinent must have necessarily mirrored these specific features, including the peasant problem and the nationalities issue.

Stalinism. As to Stalinism it is even less fixed that Leninism. But Stalin's conception of Socialism in a single country, in contradistinction to the outlook of Trotskyism, is in itself an approach which tends to deviate from all old principles and ideas of the orthodox Marxism. Stalin's conception was fostered and strengthened by the present Second World War, during which new ideological shifts slurred the old Marxian design. Basic changes in this direction are the rehabilitation of law as a regulator of human behavior, the rehabilitation of national history (Russian in particular and the national history of the partner nations of the federal Soviet Union); the revision of the approach to the family, education, and religion alters very much old ideological standards.

TWENTIETH CENTURY SOCIOLOGY

Stalin himself, as little as Lenin, in relation to Leninism, admits the existence of a specific teaching which would be possible to call Stalinism. Stalin, too, pretends to be merely an interpreter of Marxism. And there is no doubt that Stalinism as expressed in the most important writings of Stalin is like Leninism equally voluntarist. It is even more inclined to disregard logical or economic objections from the viewpoint of orthodox Marxism. Most significant in this connection is the answer given by Stalin in *Foundations of Leninism* to the argument that Russia at the time of the Bolshevist seizure of power had a negligible minority of three and a half precent of urban workers. This argument reads in part as follows:

> This is why statistical calculations based on the proportion of the proletariat to the population of a given country lose, in the solution of the question of the proletarian revolution, the exceptional importance so eagerly attached to them by the statisticians of the Socialist International, who have not understood imperialism and who fear revolution like the plague.

Sociologically speaking this argumentation hides behind Marxian phraseology a belief in the psychological factor, viz., in the willingness (audacity) or unwillingness (fear) to initiate a social revolution in a given country, independently of whether the productive forces or other social indications and factors are or are not present in a given country. Soviet Marxism has shown once more that behind traditional or stable labels new conceptions grow and create entirely new *idées-forces*.

The attempt to overcome old orthodox Marxism in the name of a new Leninist-Stalinist conception was made in two important publications of the Academy of Sciences of the U.S.S.R., the first one, *Against the Historical Conception of M. Pokrovsky* published in 1939, the second, *Twenty-five Years of Historical Studies in the U.S.S.R.*, published in 1942.

It is in these two volumes that Stalinism and the personal views of Stalin are confronted with the school of the late Professor M. Pokrovsky, one of the most serious Russian Marxian historians, who wrote mainly on Russian history. In these publications the school of Pokrovsky is "unmasked" as pure economic materialism, as unable rightly to appreciate the role of the individuality or leading personalities in history and even as a "nihilist approach towards the historic personalities, their actions and ideas" which was harmful for the development of historical science. And the last but not least charge against the school of Pokrovsky is its *sociologization* of history, meaning its inability to grasp the peculiarities and specific features of Russian history. The second volume goes so far to assert that the transformation of history of a given country into pure and abstract sociology with its respective schemes, instead of a concrete pragmatic link of events, was directly harmful to the education of the youth in the spirit of Soviet patriotism. (See the paper of A. M. Pankratova.) Stalinist slogans like "Historical materialism ought not only to explain the world but to remake it" and methodological recommendations about the periodization of Russian history might have been of some practical value but were unable to re-shape the basic sociological outlook of the obligatory state doctrine called Marxism-Leninism-Stalinism.

From the viewpoint of cognitive sociology Leninism and Stalinism did not add any new conceptions to the old ones as expressed by Marx-Engels and the Russian Marxists down to Bukharin.

Soviet Ethnography. The field of ethnography was always benevolently treated in Russia. This is certainly connected with the motley variety of the ethnographical character of this Euro-Asiatic subcontinent. Russian ethnography developed in the last three decades of the 19th century and particularly since 1903, when a special committee was established for the investigation of Middle and Eastern Asia from the historical, linguistic, and ethnographic point of view. At present there exists a special Institute of Anthropology and Ethnography of the Academy of Sciences of the U.S.S.R. This Institute publishes one of the best periodicals in this field, the quarterly review "Soviet Ethnography."

There is no doubt that the federal character of the Soviet Union and the positive attitude toward all kinds of national and ethnic self-determination of the constituent peoples together with a protective legislation in favor of the numerous national minorities, created an extraordinarily favorable environment for the unfolding and fostering of ethnography. As one of the impartial judges we could quote the Belgian scholar, M. Marinus, who in his study *Ethnography, Folklore and Archeology in Soviet Russia* (1934) stresses the objective character of this branch of Soviet Science and comes to the following conclusion: "I do not think that there is any other country in the world which could demonstrate greater achievements than the U.S.S.R."

Besides the above mentioned Maxim Kovalevsky, the leading ethnographers of pre-Soviet Russia were D. Anutchin, N. Kharusin, A. Maksimov, N. Marr, L. Sternberg, V. Yokhelson, V. Bogoras, V. Radlov and others. Some of them not only continued their work under the Soviets but produced their best work in the Soviet period and created new schools of young ethnographers. Among the latter are representatives of Caucasus and Central Asiatic Soviet Republics (G. Bagirov, A. Genko, P. Akritas, Meliksed Bekov, L. Muskeli, S. Lisitzian and many others).

Ethnography was the field of social science which remained the most remote from present political and social issues. Therefore, the highest degree of tolerance was shown by the educational authorities to non-Marxist scholars. It suffices to mention that L. Sternberg, V. Bogoras and Yokhelson — idealists or non-Marxists — not only continued their work under the Soviets but were appointed as directors of the most important ethnographic museums, institutes and so on. In 1936 the Academy of Sciences decided to publish all the ethnographical writings of M. Kovalevsky despite his prominently "bourgeois" and moderate democratic orientation.

Some attempts at Marxianization were made at the beginning of the nineteen-thirties (the archeologo-ethnographical conference in 1932), where resolutions were accepted against some bourgeois and idealistic trends and — on the other hand — against a nihilistic approach to the heritage of the bourgeois historical science. But much more important was the creation of new research and educational institutions such, for instance, as the Institute of the North with 400 students belonging to thirty various nationalities of the extreme North, or the Institute for the investigation of the peoples of the U.S.S.R. Among the youngest Soviet ethnographers the names of E. Kagarov, Krichevsky and M. Kosven, D. Selenin should be mentioned.

One of the prominent features of Soviet ethnographic research is the tendency, inherited from the pre-Soviet predecessors, viz, to remain in contact with the American ethnographical science. The American school of historical ethnology remains an important topic for the Review *Soviet Ethnography*: special articles are devoted to the present ethnography of the U.S.A.

Already before the onslaught of Germany the Soviet ethnography devoted a great deal of her research to the critique and refutation of German racial theories, but since Russia entered the Second World War considerable attention is given to the fight against the Nazi racial ideology. An important place is given to the research concerning the "ethnogenesis" of the Slavic peoples in contradistinction to the cheap Nazi propaganda literature, which was always particularly eager to demonstrate the inferiority of the

RUSSIAN SOCIOLOGY

Slavic peoples. A series of anthropological and ethnographical researches which go back to the fifth century B.C. were done and partly published. The Soviet scholars used the former works of Western Slavic scholars like Shafarik and Niederle but absolutely new results were gathered and different conclusions drawn. Among these scholars we may mention N. S. Derzhavin, with a record going back to pre-Soviet times and now a member of the Academy of Sciences, Tretyakov, A. Udalcov, B. Rybakov and others (see *Historical Journal*, a review of the Historical Institute of the all-Soviet Academy of Sciences, 1943).

Soviet Social Psychology. And finally a field which should not be entirely ignored by us because it is related to sociology is the new trend of psychology, and particularly social psychology. It is of great importance that here various investigators came by a round-about way to the recognition of moral motives in mass behavior, including the norms of the "ought-to-be." The genesis of new specific forms of human motivation is studied and emotional education of soldiers is a problem of this new psychology. (S. Rubinstein, "The Soviet Psychology under the conditions of the Fatherland's War' in the Review *Pod znamenem marxisma*, 1943, No. 9-10.)

SELECTED BIBLIOGRAPHY

Barnes, Harry Elmer, and Howard Becker, *Social Thought from Lore to Science,* vol. II, *Sociological Trends throughout the World,* (Boston, etc.: D. C. Heath and Co., 1938), Chap. XXVI, "Russian Sociology," and Notes, pp. 33-36.

Bukharin, N., *Historical Materialism, A System of Sociology,* (New York: International Publishers, 1925).

De Roberty, E., *Nouveau programme de sociologie,* (Paris: 1904).

De Roberty, E., *Sociologie de l'action,* (Paris 1908).

Hecker, J. F., *Russian Sociology,* (New York: Columbia University Press, 1915). (The author describes Russian sociology of the nineteenth century, while that of the twentieth century is dealt with very briefly. A revised and expanded edition, (New York: John Wiley and Sons, 1934) includes more recent materials concerning developments in the Soviet Union).

Kovalevsky, M., *Morale sociale,* (Paris: 1899).

Kovalevsky, M., *Russian Political Institutions,* (Chicago: 1902).

Kropotkin, P., *Mutual Aid, A Factor of Evolution,* (London: 1902).

Lenin, V., *State and Revolution,* in many English editions.

Lenin, V., *Collected Works,* vol. VI.

Plekhanov, G., *Essays in Historical Materialism*, (New York: International Publishers, 1940).
Stalin, J., *Foundations of Leninism*, (Publishing Society of Foreign Workers in the U. S. S. R., 1935).

After concluding his studies at the Imperial University of St. Petersburg and after getting the degree of magister of Public Law, Max M. Laserson was appointed in 1916 Assistant Professor at the same university in constitutional law and general theory of law. Became in 1924 Professor of International Law at the Riga (Latvia) Graduate School of Economics. In 1932 he was invited to Heidelberg University as a visiting professor. Lecturer at Columbia University, Dept. of Philosophy (1943-44 and 1944-45); at present connected with the Carnegie Endowment for International Peace.

CHAPTER XXV

EASTERN EUROPEAN SOCIOLOGY

A. POLISH SOCIOLOGY

by

EILEEN MARKLEY ZNANIECKI

I

At the Beginning of the Twentieth Century. As has frequently been pointed out, the course of Poland's history is reflected in Polish trends of thought. Disillusionment following the unsuccessful insurrection of 1863 led to the repudiation of romanticism and the development of positivistic and materialistic philosophies similar to those of Western Europe. But a reaction toward idealism soon set in. (1) In sociology this was expressed in the psychologistic theories of Sigismund Balicki, Edward Abramowski, and Leon Petrazycki. Balicki's unfinished work *Social Psychology* (2) followed the trend initiated by Le Bon and represented in America

1. Erasmus Pilz, ed., *Poland* (London: 1916), p. 301.
2. (Warsaw: 1919). Articles and books published in Poland are in the Polish language unless otherwise indicated, but titles are here given in English translation. The reader is warned that citations may not always be exact, as the author has been handicapped by lack of access to a Polish library. Dr. J. C. Gidynski, former secretary of the Polish Sociological Institute, has kindly furnished some information.

by McDougall, treating society as an integral psychological entity to which the same categories and principles can be applied as to the individual mind. Abramowski's psychosociology is still studied and admired by Polish sociologists, (3) chiefly for its rigorously scientific method and precise observations. Some of it has appeared in French and earned the approbation of Barnes and Becker for its freedom from bias and keen, critical analysis of human conduct. (4)

Petrazycki's theory of emotion as the fundamental element of both individual and collective life, a dynamic unit combining inseparably feeling and will, was developed in Russian (5) when he was lecturing at the University of St. Petersburg and translated into Polish under the title *Introduction to the Study of Law and Morality: The Foundations of Emotional Psychology*. And in 1930, when he was lecturing at the University of Warsaw, a collection of his works was published. His theory results in the most complete psychological atomization of social systems to be found in the history of social thought. Jarra, one of his disciples, developed in greater detail his principles as applied to the field of jurisprudence. His book *The General Principles of Law* became widely known to lawyers as part of the required reading for all law students. But in spite of Petrazycki's great reputation, his system — like Balicki's and Abramowski's — represents merely an individual effort, outside of the main curent of Polish sociology.

Before the World War, there was little opportunity for monographic research in sociology. No funds were available for the collection of concrete materials and moreover the occupying powers looked with suspicion on any one who studied empirical social phenomena. Only Austria permitted Polish universities to exist — at Cracow and Lwow.

Centers of higher education after the war. With the attainment of independence, one of the first tasks of the Polish State was to organize higher education on a suitable level. The older universities at Cracow and Lwow were at once taken over by the State and three new ones were established — at Warsaw, Poznan, and Wilno, In Warsaw, Ludwik Krzywicki occupied a chair of social history in

---

3. See Stanislaw Richlinski's article, "Sociological Phenomenalism of Edward Abramowski," *Polish Sociological Review*, 381-418, 1938.
4. Harry Elmer Barnes and Howard Becker, *Social Thought from Lore to Science*, (Boston: D. C. Heath and Co., 1938), pp. 1073-4.
5. (St. Petersburg: 1908).

EASTERN EUROPEAN SOCIOLOGY

the Faculty of Law from the opening of the University. In 1920, another chair was created in the same Faculty for Petrazycki, but after his death in 1931 this remained vacant. Later, two new chairs were established in the Humanistic Faculty for Stefan Czarnowski, the well-known Durkheimist, and the ethnologist Jan Bestron. From 1935, Joseph Chalasinski lectured as docent of sociology.

When Florian Znaniecki was invited to the new University of Poznan as professor of philosophy, his chair was at his request changed into a chair of sociology. For a time he lectured also in the Law School until Thaddeus Szczurkiewicz took over that course, which remained compulsory for students of economics. Later, Franciszek Mirek and Wladyslaw Okinski joined the staff as docents. The latter lectured on the sociology of education.

On the eastern limits of Poland, the University of Wilno and the University of Lwow went their own ways. Wilno University never developed any sociology, although Bronislaw Wroblewski, who held the chair in criminal law, applied the sociological approach to criminology. At Lwow, Franciszek Bujak both before and after the World War carried on extensive researches concerning the settlement and later conditions of the Polish population. He organized an Institute of Social and Economic History which, under his able editorship, produced a long series of studies of rural and small-town communities, thirty-three by 1939.

The oldest Polish University of Cracow, dating from 1364, did not recognize sociology as an academic discipline until in 1935 Bystrom asked to have his chair of ethnology changed into a chair of sociology and history of culture. When he transferred to Warsaw, this chair was occupied by Dobrowolski, a historian of culture. Close contact with sociologists was maintained by Zygmunt Myslakowski, professor of education.

Besides the State universities, there existed a Catholic University of Lublin, a Free University in Warsaw, as well as various schools for social work (mostly under religious guidance), commercial academies, agricultural colleges, schools of political science, and schools of journalism. In most of these sociology was taught, with emphasis, however, more on practice than on theory.

Let us briefly characterize the viewpoints of the sociologists who were most influential in training the youth.

Ludwik Krzywicki, hailed as the Nestor of Polish sociology, represented the historical, evolutionary trend, with emphasis on the economic aspect of social phenomena. In his most important book *Social Structure of Savagery and Barbarism*, (6) he developed the thesis that the different forms of social organization found in history are economically conditioned, depending on the possibilities of gaining a livelihood at the given technical level of each society. One of his most recent works was published in English, *Primitive Society and Its Vital Statistics*. (7) In this, the author investigated comparatively the population of primitive communities on the basis of their available statistics, showing that the size of these communities depended on their means of subsistence. In 1939, a collective volume devoted to his life and work was published to commemorate the twentieth year of his activity as Director of the Institute of Social Economy and the sixtieth year of his public service. (8) The 58-page bibliography of his writtings in French, German, English, Russian, and Polish gives a better idea of the magnitude and variety of his interests than any short discussion could do. Various phases of his work are reviewed by specialists in those fields. Among others, we find "Ludwig Krzywicki as Theorist of Historical Materialism," by Oscar Lange; "Psychological Problems in the Works of Ludwik Krzywicki," by Bohdan Zawadzki; "Ludwik Krzywicki as Historian of Social Evolution and Culture," by Alexander Hertz; "Sociological Importance of Ludwik Krywicki's Research on Primitive Societies," by Florian Znaniecki. Znaniecki finds that Krzywicki has succeeded in combining the historical study of social (mass) processes with a sociological analysis of typical and repeatable systems, and in this respect is in advance of most sociologists of the present time. (9)

Stefan Czarnowski, former lecturer at the Ecole Pratique des Hautes Etudes of Paris, applied to social phenomena the method of the Durkheim school, to which he belonged. His monumental work, *Le culte des héros*, (10) although well known to religionists, has never received from sociologists the attention it deserves. For Czarnowski, the social significance of the hero is that he has become a symbol of the common group values and a bond of social unity. In a smaller study, "Le morcellement de l'étendue et sa limita-

---

6. (Warsaw: 1914).
7. (London: Macmillan and Co., 1934).
8. Ludwik Krzywicki (Warsaw: Institute of Social Economy, 1938).
9. *Ibid.*, pp. 247-8.
10. (Paris: Alcan).

tion dans la religion et dans la magie," (11) Czarnowski developed his idea that space, like time, is not absolute, but relative, socially conditioned. This completes the sociology of knowledge of the Durkheim school, which tends to prove that all the Kantian forms, categories, and principles have a social origin and foundation. After his death in 1937, some scattered fragments of his works were published in a large volume, *Sociology and Culture*. (12) His discussions of methodological problems, of the sociology of knowledge, the sociology of literature, the sociology of culture, and the sociology of religion, as well as his characterizations of Greek, French, and Polish ideologies, justify the general regret that he did not put more of the results of his thinking into permanent form.

Florian Znaniecki. Although Znaniecki is well known in both Poland and America, it is doubtful if the full range of his thinking will ever be fully appreciated, for about half of his work is published in English and the other half — quite distinct — in Polish. He was led to sociology from a relativistic and cultural philosophy, which was partially expressed in *Philosophy of Values*, (13) *Humanism and Knowledge*, (14) *The Meaning of Evolution*, (15) *Cultural Reality*, (16) and a number of articles. His sociological viewpoint, applied in *The Polish Peasant* (17) (in collaboration with William I. Thomas) and later in his independent works, is that sociology is only one of the special sciences of culture, not a branch of biology or psychology nor an all-embracing substitute for a philosophical synthesis of existing knowledge. This viewpoint was developed in a volume entitled *Introduction to Sociology* (1922) (18) and later summarized in an article in the *American Journal of Sociology*. (19) (in English).

According to Znaniecki, the task of sociology is a comparative study of social systems and their changes. Every social system is structurally closed, but functionally connected with other systems.

---

11. Revue de l'histoire et des religions, Paris, 1927.
12. (Warsaw: 1938).
13: (Warsaw: 1910).
14. (Warsaw: 1912).
15. (Warsaw: 1913).
16. (Chicago: University of Chicago Press, 1919).
17. 2nd ed., (New York: 1927).
18. (Warsaw).
19. "The Object-Matter of Sociology," *American Journal of Sociology*, 32: 529-584, January, 1927.

TWENTIETH CENTURY SOCIOLOGY

There are four categories of social systems, differing in degree of complexity — social actions, social relations, social roles, and social groups. In 1925 Znaniecki published an outline suggesting how changes in social actions might be casually explained and in 1936 a systematic analysis and classification of social actions — both in English. He has published a number of monographic studies of social relations, social roles, and social groups, but as yet no systematic theories of those systems.

Jan Bystron, originally professor of ethnology at the University of Poznan, tranferred to the University of Cracow, where he combined ethnology with sociology and the history of culture. Later he moved to Warsaw, where a similar chair was created for him. He never developed a consistent theory of sociology, but applied the sociological approach to various problems in ethnology and history. Among his semi-popular monographs are: *The Social Significance of Books*, (20) *The Sociology of Literature*, (21) *Polish Surnames*, (22) a historical study of the origin of Polish surnames and the connection between different endings and the social classs they are supposed to indicate — probably the first attempt of its kind. Other contributions of his will be mentioned later.

Thaddeus Szczurkiewicz, docent of the University of Poznan, a pupil of both Znaniecki and Bystron, never approached them in facility of writing, but developed a keen, critical mind that promised great things in the future. For many years he and Czeslaw Znamierowski, professor of the theory of law, edited a sociological section of the periodical *Movement in Law, Economics, and Sociology*. In a volume *Race, Environment and Family*, (23) Szczurkiewicz analyzed critically the main anthropological, geographical and demographical trends in social thought.

Joseph Chalasinski was the Napoleon of Polish sociology. Of small stature like the original, he has shown indefatigable energy in his scientific work as well as great powers of organization. After attaining his doctor's degree and a docentship at the University of Poznan, he studied for two years in America and England with a Rockefeller scholarship. Strongly influenced by Znaniecki and by American sociology in general, he has produced a remarkable series of works in the sociology of education and rural sociology. These

---

20. (Warsaw: 1935).
21. (Warsaw: 1938).
22. 2nd ed. (Warsaw: 1936).
23. (Warsaw: 1938).

will be discussed later. We may merely state here that the close collaboration developed between the various school and institutes of Poznan and Warsaw was largely due to his untiring efforts.

II

Centers and Fields of Sociological Research. A distinctive characteristic of the development of Polish sociology was the rapid growth of institutes organized for sociological research. The most important of these were: The Polish Sociological Institute, under Znaniecki; the Institute of Social Economy, under Krzywicki; the Institute of Rural Sociology, under W. Grabski; the State Institute of Rural Culture, under Chalasinski; and the Nationality Institute. In surveying the work done in the various special fields of sociological research, we shall find that much of it was done in connection with these institutes.

The Nation vs. The State. "Nationality studies in Poland have a long tradition. The fact that the old Polish State during the last 200 years of its existence (1569-1795) was a multi-national State ... could not fail to emphasize the difference between the "State" and the "nation," which have for so long been somewhat obscure for the Western mentality, though very clear not only to intellectuals, but to the average citizen of Poland," says K. Symonolewicz in an article, "The Studies in Nationality and Nationalism in Poland between the two Wars (1918-1939)." He continues: "The conflict between the Polish nation and the partitioning powers and the nations they represented, was the first 'nationality problem' which the Poles learned in practice and the first they later began to study." (24) Symonolowcz lists 510 references in his bibliography, a veritable roll-call of practically all the names that are well known in the Polish social sciences.

The Poles consider the League of Nations to be a misnomer and a failure precisely because it did not represent the nations. If the new international organization established after this war is to be a success, its founders would do well to take into consideration the Polish studies of nationality.

Of course, national antagonisms also evoked great interest and formed the background for Gumplowicz's studies. In an illuminating article in the *Sociological Review* (25), Znaniecki traces them back

---

24. *Bulletin of the Polish Institute of Arts and Sciences in America*, 2: 59-60.
25. Vol. I, 1929.

to the primitive antagonism against everybody and everything that is foreign. In another article in English, written for the Baltic Institute and published separately, he emphasized the weakness of a purely defensive as contrasted with an ·expansive tendency in national struggles (26). Bystron, in *National Megalomania* (27), showed how nationality groups develop the illusion of their own superiority. Chalasinski discovered from his investigation of German-Polish relations in Upper Silesia that the borderlands on the frontiers of hostile nations offer a fertile field for sociological research, because the emotions are here intensified by the daily friction between individuals. (28) Dobrowolski studied the growth of national consciousness in two counties of this region. (29)

Other sociologists chose as their field of research the eastern provinces, the very territory that is now being claimed by Russia. In 1930 Orsini-Rosenberg drew up a plan for field studies in the province of Polessie. (30) They were carried out by J. Obrebski, a pupil of Malinowski's, who found this an ideal field for observation and eventual experimentation. In this backward province he studied not the clash of hostile nationalities, but a disintegrating traditional folk-culture, where literate nationality groups — like the Lithuanian and the Ukranian — had already emerged and more primitive nationality groups — like the White Ruthenians — were just beginning to emerge. In a series of articles in *Nationality Problems* (1936) and the *Sociological Review* (1936), he discussed "The Problem of Ethnic Differentiation and Its Sociological Treatment." He tried to explain the existing crisis, especially the revolt against tradition. Rejecting the old encyclopedic trend which treated a nation-state as an objective reality and tried to embrace all phases of its life, he insisted that the so-called sociological trend in nationality studies offered a much better tool for research. According to this, a nation is a subjective reality, a social group which arises, develops, and declines.

Sociological Ethnology. Many of these studies of nationality

---

26. *The Sociology of the Struggle for Pomerania,* (Torun: Baltic Institute, 1934).
27. 2nd ed., (Warsaw: 1935).
28. *Sociological Review,* III.
29. "The Growth of National Consciousness in the Polish Population of Spiz and Orawa," *Contemporary Review,* 1923.
30. *Nationality Problems,* (1930).

were actually on the borderline between ethnology and sociology. Ethnology in Poland has an old and respectable tradition, but as elsewhere it was mainly a study of cultural survivals and dialects, regional and local customs, art, technology, religion and magical beliefs and practices. The sociological approach revitalized this old museological attitude, and ethnologists began to use survivals as integral but changing components of present and active community life. Bystron applied this approach in his greatest work, *History of the Customs and Culture of Ethnic Groups in Poland* (2 vols., 1932-3). Malinowski's works in Polish add little to his general contributions to anthropology, ethnology, and sociology, which are too well known to need discusion here. Krzywicki's have already been mentioned.

Rural Sociology. Interest in nationality problems and Polish ethnology early led social scientists to study the rural population. Bujak was doing this from a historical and economic standpoint, even before the First World War. After the war, the crying poverty of the rural population presented the most pressing problem for practical reforms. Backed by government subsidies, the most rapid, successful, and original work was therefore done in the field of rural sociology. Grabski and Chalasinski with their staffs explicitly took *The Polish Peasant* as their starting-point and followed the lead of the Polish Sociological Institute in basing their conclusions on first-hand materials, particularly on autobiographies. Grabski undertook to write a synthetic system of rural sociology, but only the first two parts were published. (31)

The investigations of the State Institute of Rural Culture were synthetized by Chalasinski in a monumental work in rural sociology, *The Young Generation of Peasants* (4 vols., 2076 pages). (32) As Znaniecki said in his introduction: "This work pictures the present life of the young generation of Polish peasants with an accuracy that is not surpassed by any descriptions we possess of large human collectivities. In particular, the study of the schools in rural communities is a masterpiece." The first volume is devoted to the social foundations of the youth movements in rural Poland; the second, to the life, work, and tendencies of rural youth; the third, to the role of youthful rural circles in the eyes of the rural populations itself; and the fourth, to the rural school. There is no doubt that this work

---

31. *Annals of Rural Sociology,* I and II, (1936 and 1937).
32. (Warsaw: 1939).

would have formed the basis for extensive governmental reforms, if the war had not intervened.

Urban Sociology was less developed. A study of Warsaw as the Polish capital was made by Rychlinski for the Institute of Social Economy. One of the interesting conclusions reached in Znaniecki's synthesis of the investigation of Poznan (*The City in the Consciousness of its Inhabitants*) (33) was that the majority of citizens are indifferent to the city's institutions and functions and have no appreciation of all the services it furnishes them. Other problems connected with urban populations were studied by the Institute for Social Problems.

Closely connected with urban problems were the various studies of workmen and of the unemployed. Some of them were based on the large number of autobiographies of workmen collected by the Polish Sociological Institute. If space permitted, we would consider in greater detail the famous autobiography written by Jacob Wojciechowski. It might be termed the "infamous" autobiography, for after considerable doubt and reflection the Institute finally published all the facts concerning his sexual life which the author most frankly and openly described. It was greeted by a storm of protest from the conservative part of the public but enthusiastically by the literary set. Discussion over the matter raged from one end of the country to the other and never completely died down. It no doubt contributed to the extraordinary popularity of the autobiography.

All this interest in autobiographies stirred even Cracow to do some collecting. Zygmunt Myslakowski and Felix Gross published a volume in 1938 entitled *The Workmen Write: Memoirs of the Industrial Proletariat.* This was the result of an investigation conducted with the aid of the workmen attending the sociological seminar of the School of Social Science in Cracow. The object was to discover the cultural tendencies of the industrial proletariat and its share in educational and self-educational activities. Using the same material, Felix Gross wrote a volume, *The Proletariat and Culture.* (34)

Very valuable were the studies of unemployment made by the various institutes. The volume of autobiographies of the unemployed published by the Institute for Social Economy contained striking revelations concerning the individual and family disor-

---

33. (Poznan: 1931).
34. (Warsaw: 1938).

ganization that resulted from unemployment. (35) The Polish Sociological Institute by means of a contest collected about 600 autobiographies of the unemployed in the province of Poznan. This formed part of the material for a cooperative study of the social role of the unemployed which was carried on for three years by the students and assistants of the University of Poznan. It was supplemented by continuous observation and contact with about 1,000 families of the unemployed.

In connection with nationality problems and with rural and urban investigations, naturally the problem of emigration cropped up and some studies were made of immigrants in Siberia, North and South America. Many of these were printed in a periodical entitled *The Emigrant*. Perhaps the most interesting from a sociological point of view is Chalasinski's study of a Polish-American community that had been investigated 15 years earlier by Thomas and Znaniecki. The results were published in the *Sociological Review*. (36) His field study of the effect of emigration and re-immigration on rural life was partly financed by funds from America.

The attention of other sociologists was directed towards the new Polish emigration to France, and since France also was interested in the problem some cooperation between French and Polish sociologists developed. For instance, S. Wloszczewski wrote a study in French about Polish immigrants, when he was an assistant to Celestin Bouglé. W. L. Langrod discussed "The Role of Polish Immigration in French-Polish Relations," in the *Contemporary Review* (1932). Of. the two volumes of *Emigrant Memoirs* published by the Institute of Social Economy (1939), the first volume gave the memoirs of 37 emigrants to France and the second volume the memoirs of 27 emigrants to South America. (37)

The Sociology of Education. Interest in education rivaled and perhaps surpassed interest in rural conditions, and many studies of it were made by both educators and sociologists. In the notes to his chapter on "Educational Guidance" in *Social Actions*, (38) Znaniecki makes a clear distinction between their respective fields: "The task of sociology is neither to educate nor to tell educators how they should educate in order to attain certain purposes nor yet to deter-

---

35. (Warsaw: 1931).
36. Vol. II, 1933.
37. Five from Argentina, twenty from Brazil, one from Paraguay and one from Uruguay.
38. (New York: Farrar and Rinehart, 1936), pp. 673-4.

mine what ought to be the purposes of education. Its only concern is to make an objective, theoretic study of facts, and the facts it studies must be social facts. To be sure, every one nowadays agrees that education is a 'social process.' But what makes it social is that certain people — educators — act upon other people — educands; therefore, sociological investigation must concentrate on the activities of educators ... the norms to which they are subjected, and the purposes which communities and groups seek to attain in having people educated. ... The sociologist ... studies the actual influence which educational activities exercise upon the social participation of persons who have been subjected to them, and the effects of this participation upon communities and groups."

Znaniecki published two volumes on the sociology of education. The first deals with the social forces that condition education; the second with education as a social process. (39) A third volume was intended to deal with the social consequences of education as manifested by the participation of educated people in social life. But only an outline of the latter was published, (40) based partly on a two-years' investigation of well-educated Americans conducted at the invitation of Teachers College and Columbia University and partly on the continuation of this research in Europe. The life-histories of well-educated men were compared with those of working-men and of political and military "playboys." His hypotheses about the latter were applied by Alexander Hertz to Nazi politicians in one of his analytic sociological studies of contemporary European politics, which were published in *Knowledge and Life*. (41) The lives of Polish men-of-Letters were analyzed in a volume under that title by the Institute of Social Economy and ten autobiographies of physicians were published in one volume by the State Insurance Institute. (42)

Rychlinski in one of his articles in the *Sociological Review* on the English social structure discussed "The Educational Ladder in England." (43) Education as a means of social advance was studied by Bronikowski, *The Ways of Advance of the Peasant*, (44) and

---

39. (Warsaw: 1927-9).
40. *The People of Today and the Civilization of Tomorrow*, (Warsaw: 1934).
41. (Warsaw: 1937).
42. (Warsaw: 1939).
43. Vol. V, 1937.
44. (Warsaw: 1935).

EASTERN EUROPEAN SOCIOLOGY

by Chalasinski, *The Workman's Ways of Advance*. (45) Chalasinski's doctor's thesis was a socio-historical treatise on *Education in a Stranger's Home as a Social Institution*. (46). In 1935 he published *The Social Background of Adult Education* and in 1936 *The School in American Society*. The latter work traces the development of the American school system and points out how social, political, and economic conditions and ideologies have influenced it at various periods. His thesis that the school is a product of social groups, reflecting their struggles for existence and expansion, provoked the ire of a philosopher of education, who criticised it very sharply in an article in the *Sociological Review*, "Sociologism as a Menace to the Science of Education," (Vol. IV, 1938). Chalasinski's answer to this "Speech from the Throne by Professor Sergius Hessen" is a masterpiece of devastating satire.

Myslakowski, Professor of Education at the University of Cracow, published a book on *The Rural Family as a Source of Education*, (47) based on materials which were published in a separate volume. Mrs. Helena Radlinska, a specialist in educational problems at the Free University of Warsaw, was the editor of a collective work on *The Social Causes of Success and Non-success in School*. (48) She also studied "Propaganda; Its Types and Methods," *Sociological Review*, 1938.

Applied Sociology. Much of the published and unpublished work of the various schools and institutes mentioned above (with the exception of the Polish Sociological Institute) was practically rather than scientifically motivated. The enormous task of rebuilding the Polish State, solving the tremendous problems left after the period of partition, and repairing the destruction caused by the First World War naturally stimulated interest in practical reforms. We cannot survey the work done in this field, but may mention that the first attempt since Lester Ward to build a systematic applied sociology, taking into consideration all possible applications of theoretic sociology to the solution of practical problems, was begun by Dr. Valerian Adamski in his *Outline of Applied Sociology*. (49) Only the first out of three or four projected volumes has so far appeared.

45. (Poznan: 1931).
46. (Poznan: 1929).
47. (Warsaw: 1931).
48. (Warsaw: 1937).
49. (Poznan: 1929).

TWENTIETH CENTURY SOCIOLOGY

Sociological Method. The new attempts at systematization of sociological knowledge and especially the rapid growth of monographic studies obviously called for considerable methodological reflection. Many articles and the prefaces to most publications of materials discussed specific problems in sociological methods and techniques. Znaniecki, in particular, has been keenly interested in such problems, perhaps because of his training in logic and epistemology. *The Method of Sociology* (in English) presents his conception of analytic induction as the basic method by which modern sciences reach exact conclusions from empirial data, in contrast to Aristotelian deduction, which is the logical foundation of the statistical method and leads to merely approximate conclusions. Znaniecki has been criticised in America for failing to include concrete materials in his recent works. His answer is that a scientist does not need to describe all the individual instances on which he bases his conclusions; physical and biological scientists usually give only descriptions of the common empirical pattern that they have discovered by comparing individual instances. Only when an individual instance is exceptional should it be presented in concrete detail.

In conclusion, we may say that all the major fields of modern sociology were found in Poland in a more or less flourishing state. None may be said to be characteristic of Polish sociology, unless perhaps the unusual development of sociological studies of "nations" as groups united by a common culture, in distinction from "States," as political, organized, territorial groups. It may also be mentioned that Polish sociology made a greater use of autobiographical material than any other. Of course, all kinds of material — direct observation, questionnaires, documents, etc. — were also widely used; but the collection of autobiographies agglomerated in the archives of Polish research institutes is quantitatively and qualitatively unique.

The Future of Polish Sociology is exceedingly doubtful. Most of the older generation of sociologists mentioned in these pages have died or been executed by the Nazis. The fate of the younger generation who remained in Poland is entirely unknown. A few sociologists — among them, Felix Gross, Alexander Hertz, Gustav Ichheiser — are in America and doing interesting work here. They will in any case form a nucleus for the future development of Polish sociology. But what direction it will take cannot now be foreseen.

EASTERN EUROPEAN SOCIOLOGY

SELECTED BIBLIOGRAPHY

The works here indicated represent English summaries of sociological developments in Poland. The important sociological works are indicated in the text and not here repeated, while secondary materials in the Polish language are omitted as being inaccessible to most readers of English.

Barnes, Harry Elmer, and Howard Becker, *Social Thought from Lore to Science,* (Boston: D. C. Heath and Co., 1938), pp. 1069-1078.

"Sociological Institute of Poznan," *American Journal of Sociology,* 28: 335-336, 1923.

Symonolewicz, Konstanty, "The Studies in Nationality and Nationalism in Poland between the Two Wars (1918-1939)," *Bulletin of the Polish Institute of Arts and Sciences in America,* 2: 57-125, October, 1943.

Znaniecka, Eileen M., "Current Sociology in Poland," *American Sociological Review,* 2: 421-424, June, 1937.

Znaniecka, Eileen M., "News from Universities and Colleges," *American Sociological Revue,* 3: 573, 575, August, 1938.

Znaniecka, Eileen M., "Sociology in Poland," *American Sociological Review,* 1: 296-298, April, 1936.

Eileen Markley Znaniecki (in Polish, Znaniecka), J. D. (Chicago), on her marriage to Florian Znaniecki in 1916 gave up her law career to assist her husband in his work. She was preparing a history of Polish sociology in English when the war interrupted her work. A few fragments have been published in the *American Sociological Review.*

B. CZECHOSLOVAK SOCIOLOGY

by

JOSEPH S. ROUCEK

I

The peak of the development of Czechoslovakia's sociology was reached only during the two decades of Czechoslovakia's independence. But its genesis is intimately connected with the career and philosophy of **Dr. T. G. Masaryk,** the founder and first President of Czechoslovakia, whose career began in the nineteenth century as a philosopher. Hence, it is necessary to note the roots of Czechoslovakia's sociology in that period.

The Roots of Czechoslovakia's Sociology. Sociology in Czechoslovakia originated from, and until recently was influenced by philosophy. (1) Nineteenth century Czech philosophers had few traditions at home and turned to Germany for models. Hegel's idealistic philosophy influenced several. But his exaggerated intellectualism did not satisfy Czech thinkers who sought harmonious solution of actual national problems. They swung from Hegel to the empiricism of Herbart. Thus the first systematic Czechoslovak treatise on sociology was written under the influence of Herbart's philosophical, psychological, and pedagogical doctrine. (2) But it was only with Masaryk's teaching that the Czech scientific world began to take permanent interest in sociology and especially in the theories of Comte and Spencer.

Thomas Garrigue Masaryk as Sociologist. Dr. Thomas Garrigue Masaryk (1850-1937), former Professor in Charles University, Prague, is identified with a complete departure from Herbart's and

---

1. See: Joseph S. Roucek, *The Development of Sociology in Czechoslovakia* (an unpublished M. A. thesis, School of Education, New York University, 1937); otherwise no comprehensive and systematic treatment of the past and present status of sociology in Czechoslovakia is known to the author. For available scattered material, see: Josef Kral, *Ceskoslovenska Filosofie*, (Prague: Melantrich, 1937), Chapter IX, "Sociologie," pp. 183-220; I. A. Blaha, "La sociologie tchèque contemporaine," *Revue internationale de sociologie,* 29: 225-248, 1921; and "Die zeitgenossische tschechische Soziologie," *Jahrbuch fuer Sociologie,* 2: 441-461, 1926; "Contemporary Sociology in Czechoslovakia," *Social Forces,* 9: 167-179, December, 1930; E. Chalupny, "La Sociologie tchécoslovaque pendant les derniers dix années," *Revue internationale de sociologie,* 38: 411-419, 1930, Z. Ullrich, "Ceska sociologie" (Czech Sociology), Supplement, in P. Sorokin, *Sociologicke Nauky Pritommosti (Contemporary Sociological Theories,* trans., Prague: 1936), pp. 680-688; reprinted as *Vyvoj socialni psychologie; The Evolution of Social Psychology,* (Prague: 1936), pp. 60-68. The most valuable source remains the *Sociologicka revue,* a quarterly, edited by I. A. Blaha for the Masaryk Sociological Society, at Brno, between 1930 and 1939.

2. The first prominent Czech sociologist was Gustav Adolf Lindner (1828-1887), Professor of Pedagogy in the University of Prague. His work *Ideen zur Psychologie der Gesellschaft, als Grundlage der Social Wissenschaft (Social Psychology as a Foundation for Social Sciences,* 1871), appeared before Spencer's and Tarde's contributions, and before the rise of the organic and psychological schools of society in France, America and Germany. In fact, Lindner's *Manual of Empirical Psychology as an Inductive Science,* (trans., Boston: 1890) was quite popular as a college textbook in psychology in American colleges at the end of the nineteenth century.

Lindners' highly speculative theories, and represented the trend in his country which favored the more positivistic and realistic sociology of Western Europe.

Masaryk, as sociologist, is comparable to the great sociologists of his times, such as Ward, Giddings, Tarde, Durkheim, Toennies, Simmel, and Karejev; but it is more appropriate to consider him in relation to the development of Czech sociology. Nearly all internationally known great sociologists of his generation offered great sociological systems, but Masaryk never attempted to originate or synthesize a sociological system. However, he did analyze quite a number of the problems of abstract and applied sociology. Otherwise his sociological work is limited to numerous articles and several monographic studies. (3)

Masaryk began his scientific and research activities with sociology. His first literary productions were sociological articles and his first great work a sociological monograph on suicide. (4) His *Concrete Logic* (5) is characterized by himself (6) as being sociologically colored and contains quite a detailed chapter discussing the methodology and history of sociology. His ecological study, *Man and Nature* (7), was published in 1890. It studied the influence of natural phenomena on the individual and society. In

---

3. Cf. Joseph S. Roucek, "Masaryk as Sociologist," *Sociology and Social Research*, 22: 412-420, May-June, 1938. The only available complete bibliography of Masaryk's scholarly contributions can be found in: K. Capek, *Mlceni's T. G. Masarykem (The Silences with T. G. Masaryk,* Prague: 1935), pp. 27-31; his studies pertaining to sociology are cited in Roucek, *The Development of Sociology in Czechoslovakia.* Other scattered sources on Masaryk's life and contributions are: Roucek, "President Masaryk of Czechoslovakia," *Current History,* 21: 1109-1112, March, 1930; Roucek, "Thomas Garrigue Masaryk," *World Unity,* 6: 413-425, September, 1930; Roucek, "Thomas Garrigue Masaryk, as Politician and Statesman," *Social Science,* 6: 272-278, July, 1931; C. J. Street, *President Masaryk,* (London: Geoffrey Bles, 1930); E. Ludwig, *Defender of Democracy, Masaryk of Czechoslovakia,* (New York: Robert M. BcBride and Co., 1936); K. Capek, *President Masaryk Tells His Story,* (New York: G. P. Putnam's Sons, 1935); K. Capek, *Masaryk on Thought and Life,* (London: Macmillan and Co., 1938).

4. *Sebevrazda hromadnym zjevem spolecenskym moderni osvěty (Suicide as a Social Phenomenon of Modern Civilization,* originally in German, Vienna; 1881; Czech edition, Prague: 1904; 3rd ed., 1930).

5. *Zaklady konkretni logiky (Concrete Logic,* Prague: 1885; in German, Vienna; 1887).

6. *Zaklady konkretni logiky,* pp. v-vi.

7. "Clovek a priroda," *Cechovy kvety,* 12, 1890.

1898 his *Social Question* (8) appeared. It is a sociological and philosophical analysis of Marxism as a collectivist and economic theory of history and society. In 1900-1901 appeared the methodological part of his *Handbook of Sociology.* (9) This was really the second edition of the chapter on sociology from his *Concrete Logic*, brought up-to-date, and included a brief history of sociology. Shortly before World War I, Masaryk published his famed *Russia and Europe*. (10) During the war he contributed two lectures: *The Problems of Small Nations in Europe's Crisis*, (11) delivered at the London University, October 19, 1915, and *The Slavs Among the Nations* at Sorbonne, February 22, 1916. (12) As the President of Czechoslovakia, Masaryk wrote his *The Making of a State*. (13) Therein he formulated his latest concepts of philosophy, of history and of several sociological problems, particularly those of nationalism and internationalism.

We have not cited a number of smaller articles and pamphlets, some of which deal with the sociological aspects — as the *Philosophy of Nationality, The Difficulties of Democracy* (14) — or are related to it. In fact, all the more important Masaryk's studies are sociological in emphasis. To him sociology is the core of his scientific activity. But it is frequently difficult to distinguish between Masaryk's philosophical and sociological view points.

To understand Masaryk's conception of sociology, we must first turn to his concepts of philosophy. Masaryk endeavored, at first, to construct his philosophy as an ally of science. He believed that a philosophy which satisfied all human needs would bring order and harmony to the intellectually, morally disintegrated individual and to society. He was concerned especially with society. He believed that such a philosophy required that our knowledge be classified and

---

8. *Otazka socialni*, (Prague: 1892, 2nd ed., 1935; in German, Vienna: 1899; in Russian, Moscow: 1900).
9. "Rukovet sociologie," *Nase Doba*, 8, 1901.
10. (2 Volumes, originally in German, Jena: 1913; in Czech, Prague: 1919-1921, 2nd ed., 1930-1931; English translation as *The Spirit of Russia*, New York: 1919, 2 vols.).
11. (London: 1916; Chicago: 1917; in German, Prague: 1922; in Czech, 1926).
12. (London: 1916; published as *Les slaves dans le monde*, Prague: 1919, 3rd ed., 1924).
13. (New York: Frederick A. Stokes Co., 1927).
14. *Narodnostni filosofie doby novejsi*, (Jicin: 1905, 2nd ed., Prague: 1919); *Nesnaze demokracie*, (Prague: 1913).

tested, scientifically and critically. He classified the sciences and human activities, and developed a unified and natural system of human knowledge. He showed the relationships between the sciences in content and in method, and how the dogma of a science corresponded to its historical development. As far as sociology is concerned, Masaryk distinguishes abstract from concrete and practical sociology. They must not be mixed from the standpoint of method. He classifies ecology, the study of population problems, the science of the family, ethnology, economics, political sciences, education (as a moral organization) and history as concrete sociological sciences. In the practical sociological sciences he includes politics, in the broadest sense of the word. As social politics, and politics in the narrower sense of the word, he classifies state politics, law-making administrative sciences, and economic and military politics. Every branch of concrete and practical sociological science can be either general or specialized.

Abstract sociology, according to Masaryk, is the fundamental science for the whole social and historical sphere. It deals with the foundations of the social organization and evolution. It is divided into social statics and dynamics. Social statics is the explanation of the social characteristic of man and those social forces which keep society together during its constant evolution. Social dynamics deals with the concept of progress, it includes a general evolutionary theory and it names the moving forces in the evolution of human spirit religion, morality, science, art, politics, etc.

Masaryk recognizes in social events the role of the individual as initiator, and his part in the formation of social life. On the other hand, also, the influence of the social organization is a definite, ideal whole, which is the collective, objective possession of the group.

Masaryk takes the middle road between extreme individualism and extreme collectivism. He himself described his point of view as that of "critical realism." Society, to him, is a dynamic organization of subsidiary organizations. It is not composed of individuals, but of associations. Between the organizations exists a mutual interdependance, a reciprocal relationship, a social consensus, of which Comte, Mill, Ward, Karejev, and others speak. This concensus cannot be identified with the concept of equilibrium. In the last analysis, however, the individual must be the unit of society. By way of analysis, we achieve, finally, an individual point of departure and individual consciousness (for a separate social consciousness does not exist). The social explanation, generally, implies a psychological explanation. Since the fundamental social factors are individuals, psychology is the direct foundation of sociology. Social phenomena are, at the same time, psychological phenomena. Sociology studies in them only that which makes them social, historic. Our consciousness justifies us in assuming that the cognition of the individual is of equal value with the cognition of the group, and must precede it. Thus the real history of the human spirit is reflected in the history of sociology, for Masaryk, as it was for Comte.

For Masaryk the sociological methods are observation, especially of the common and daily phenomena, statistical observations, comparative method, historical method, and the classification by series, as emphasized by Comte. He feels that Hume is not justified in claiming that mathematics only is certain, and that our empirical knowledge is also logically justified. We achieve knowledge of final causes not only through long experience, that is, through psychology, but often on the basis of a single case which allows us to see cause and effect. This conclusion is the result of logical thought, genuine judgment. Of course, scientific method must be used in psychology; not a mathematical method, as Herbart wished, but an empirical one. In fact, Masaryk claims that our ethical perceptions, our religious emotions, are facts, and these facts of inner experience cannot be excluded from sociological observations. We must not exclude search for ultimate causes.

In this connection we must outline Masaryk's conception of religion. Positivism conceives of religion in purely intellectual terms. Religion is also a ritual and moral code, but not a completed thing. It is necessary, however, to distinguish beeween the religion of the church and religion in Masaryk's sense. The first does not satisfy. It is vanquished by life. The other realms of culture achievement — philosophy, art, science, business, medicine — have escaped from the domination of the church. The same process will occur with regard to religion itself. Science and philosophy are in conflict with the religion of the chuch but not with religion itself. Religion must, like all else, be considered from a genetic viewpoint. The religion of the church is one stage of religious development; religion must be carried on to a higher stage, led to completion, to the stage of a scientific religion. There are not varieties of truth, but one truth, only, that of science, critically tested and accepted. The religion of the modern world must rest on scientific truth, on conviction, not on faith. (15) Blaha characterizes Masaryk thus: "Masaryk thus attempts to correct Comte and his followers with the evolutionary point of view of Spencer, adapting it to the sphere of religion."

The Evaluation of Masaryk. Masaryk cannot be appreciated without understanding his activities at home and abroad. His prewar sociological writings reflect Czech political and national conditions. Subjected to the Austro-Hungarian Monarchy, the Czech leaders were interested mainly in utilizing their social energies, and their research and investigation, for the promotion of national interests. Everything in the field of culture and sociology was measured from a utilitarian standpoint. Masaryk's writings are characterized in this respect, by practical aims, more than by emphasis on theory. Whatever theoretical bases of sociology were laid by him, were almost immediately applied practically.

From this standpoint Masaryk belongs to the group who consider sociology as philosophy. Masaryk answers perfectly the description of a sociologist made by Dean E. Payne. "If there is anyone in the world who should philosophize, who needs to philosophize, who has to philosophize, it is the sociologist." (16) One needs only recall the famed program laid down by Masaryk for his nation: "What is needed is an inner renovation, without which there is no meaning in political liberty. What is needed is an active love for one's neighbor, without which there is no true patriotism. What is needed is to love, to seek, and to defend the truth. What is needed is to establish public life upon the basis of morality and truth." (17) Masaryk read this humanitarian ideal into Czech history. That same ideal led him to become a university professor, a political and moral philosopher, a member of parliament, a party leader. It convinced him that Austria was false, violent, and incapable of reform, and that she was an obstacle to the progress and national development of her non-German peoples. For that reason Masaryk began revolutionary activities in 1914. (18) These resulted in the formation of

---

15. Masaryk, *V boji za nabozenstvi* (*The Battle over Religion*, Prague: 1904); *Prehled nejnovejsi filosofie. Nabozenstvi* (*Introduction to the Most Recent Philosophy of Religion*, Prague: 1905); *Inteligence a nabozenstvi* (*Inteligentsia and Religion*, Prague 1907); *Veda a cirkew* (*Science and the Church*, Prage: 1908).

16. E. G. Payne, "Scientific Reaction to Philosophy," in E. G. Payne, ed., *Readings in Educational Sociology*, (New York: Prentice-Hall, 1933), vol. I, p. 20.

17. Cited in *President T. G. Masaryk*, p. 5.

18. See especially his *The Making of a State*, Chapter X, "Democracy and Humanity," pp. 368-441.

the Czechoslovak Republic in 1918. Among world-famous sociologists Masaryk belongs to that pre-war group of sociologists who followed Comte and Spencer and call sociology an independent science.

Finally, Masaryk is one of the few sociologists in the world who was able to apply his sociological and philosophical principles. It is not our task to analyze his contributions as the President of Czechoslovakia from 1918 to 1935. But Czechoslovakia carried out Plato's recommendations that philosophers be placed upon the throne.

Eduard Benes as a Sociologist. Dr. Eduard Benes has been the the most famous follower of Masaryk. His career started with an instructorship in the Czechoslovak Commercial Academy, Prague, Czechoslovakia. He joined Masaryk's revolutionary activities in 1915, and returned to Prague as Foreign Minister, a post which he held from 1918 to 1935. During this period he was also Professor of Sociology in Charles University, Prague. In 1935 he succeeded Masaryk as President of Czechoslovakia; he resigned after the Munich agreement on October 5, 1938, left Czechoslovakia on October 22, lectured at Chicago University subsequently and lived in England after July, 1939. After the outbreak of World War II, Dr. Benes took the lead in the movement for the restoration of Czechoslovak freedom. On July 21, 1940, London recognized the Provisional Government with Benes as President, a step soon followed by other Allied nations. (19)

Benes began his career by registering at the Charles University in 1904. His interest centered in the so-called practical philosophy, propounded by Masaryk, including his wide theoretical sociological basis for solving important public questions. Masaryk was

---

19. For Benes' career, see: E. B. Hitchcock, *Benes, The Man and Statesman* (London: Hamish Hamilton, 1940); Pierre Crabites, *Benes, Statesman of Central Europe* (New York: Coward-McCann, 1935). Benes sociological ideas are surveyed in Joseph S. Roucek, "Eduard Benes as a Sociologist," *Sociology and Social Research*, 23: 18-24; September-October, 1938, Roucek "Eduard Benes," *World Unity*, 14: 136-146; June, 1934, Roucek, "Eduard Benes," *Social Science*, 10:200-201, April, 1935; Roucek, "Fiftieth Birthday of Dr. Eduard Benes, *"World Affairs Interpreter*, 5: 154-158, July, 1934. For the various articles by Benes and by sociologists on Benes' sociological contributions, see: Roucek, *The Development of Sociology in Czechoslovakia*. Benes has not systematized his sociology; his ideas can be, however, found in English in his *My War Memoirs*, (Boston: Houghton Mifflin Co., 1928), and *Democracy Today and Tomorrow*, (New York: The Macmillan Co., 1939).

EASTERN EUROPEAN SOCIOLOGY

Benes' inspiration. In 1905 Benes registered at the Sorbonne at Masaryk's suggestion. In 1908 he published his doctorial thesis, *Le problème autrichien et la question tchèque* (Paris: 1908), a study which already showed his sociological inclinations; its theses supported the decentralization and federalization of the Austro-Hungarian Empire. In 1908 Benes received his doctorate from the University of Dijon and became Professor of Political Economy in Prague. In a little volume, *The Nationalistic Question* (1909) he describes his sociological understanding of the problem. In 1910-1911 he published three volumes on modern socialism. (20) In 1912 Benes's first important sociological study, *The Party System*, (21) appeared; it was his "habilitation" thesis which won him the appointment as "Privat Docent" in Sociology in Charles University in 1913 and a year later in the Czech Technical High School.

This book in political sociology cannot be considered of great sociological importance. It has all the weakness of a doctorial thesis and depends extensively on foreign literature. It examines, from the static point of view, a much discussed problem concerning which as yet so little of a purely theoretical and general character had been done in sociology. It surveys the theories of the origin and classification of political parties, criticizes them and then proceeds to describe sociologically the aims and functions of political parties, their organization, and their relation to other social elements.

After the opening of World War I Benes published a sociological study, *War and Culture* (*Valka a Kultura*, Prague: 1915). During the same year he joined Masaryk abroad and worked for Czechoslovakia's freedom. Since then he has had little time to devote himself to theoretical studies, although he has published several smaller contributions particularly in the field of political sociology.

In summary, Benes' best contributions concern political sociology. Politics, for him, is a social activity purposing to adjust the social environment so that people may best satisfy their needs and aims. The adjustment may change by shifts in the relationships between individuals in his group. When the value of human per-

---

20. Benes, *Strucny nastin vyvoje moderniho socialismu* (*A Short Outline of the Evolution of Modern Socialism*), vol. I, *Podminky vzniku a vyvoje moderniho socialismu* (*The Conditions or the Origin and Evolution of Modern Socialism*, Brandys Laben: 1910; vol. II, Prague: 1911 vol. IV, 1911); vol. III has never appeared.
21. Benes, *Strannictvi. Sociologicka Studie,* (Prague: 1912).

sonality is high, the adjustment favors the widest masses, and vice versa. The aristocratic system has always organized the environment for the benefit of the few. Democracy aims at such adjustments to increase general welfare and satisfy general needs. (22)

Politics, according to Benes, is a lofty social occupation, from the moral as well as the material standpoint. It is an art and a science. As a science it studies with the help of law, history, geography, economics, etc., the real state of man and society; it seeks that which is regular, planned and permanent in sociology. It is obvious that for the politician, the social sciences, psychology, and biology, are important. Therefore, the scientist-politician must vivisect society; must study society as a map. Important to him are: (1) natural, material, and physical realities (the earth, climate, the nation, its characteristics, etc.); (2) motives, ambitions, plans, and needs of the individual and of his collectivties, with their emotions, passions, and instincts; (3) social incidents, uncontrollable social forces, and movements.

A practical politician must be a good sociologist and must know well the natural and social environment of a certain society. The politician as a good sociologist must know how to analyze conditions, to observe these systematically and scientifically and reach, eventually, the correct understanding.

Such a politician must be a good psychologist. He must know people. He must analyze behavior and public and party opinion correctly. He must be tactful, also, which is another expression for the knowledge of practical psychology.

But it is not sufficient to be a good sociologist and a psychologist. He must have the synthetic spirit of an artist, good sense, have keen intuition, and keen emotions. Those in politics who can control their emotions by reason, and their reason by emotions, and can establish an equilibrium, are great politicians.

From this discussion it is obvious that Benes takes into account both social and political processes, the individual and society. He does not emphasize, one-sidedly, the social factor, as Durkheim,

---

22. The best exposition of Benes' sociological theories is his article: "Sociolog-Teoretik a Politik-Praktik" ('The Sociologist-Theoretician and the Politician-Practician), *Sociologicka Revue*, 8: 7-20, 1936. Other of Benes' recent contributions are cited in: "Literature on Czechoslovakia and the Czechoslovak Cause," *News Flashes from Czechoslovakia under Nazi Domination* (Czechoslovak National Council of America, Chicago, Release No 201, September 6, 1943).

but utilizes psychology also. He understands the social factor in its widest sense, not allowing himself to be deceived by socialistic, juristic or any other school. When analyzing the individual, he does not forget that rationalism is determined by irrational factors, such as instinctive impulses, emotions, intuitions; thus he agrees with such thinkers as Thorndike, McDougall, and Pareto. But as a critical realist, Benes does not overemphasize either intellectualism or emotionalism, but harmonizes both. If the politician is too much of a scientist and rationalizes too much, he does not know how to create intuitively for the future, or to have great conceptions. He becomes a dry, limited politician. On the contrary, if the politician lets himself be carried away by his intuitions and emotions, he follows phantasies, impossible combinations, politics of passions and hate. Politics must analyze the social reality scientifically. Such politics are important in a democracy. This demands leaders. Democratic institutions are not enough; the people must be convinced of the ideals of democracy. It is difficult to govern with corrupted and poor institutions, difficult to lead poor people. Hence the problem of democracy is primarily the problem of education for democracy, the moral problem. Concurrently, this democratic problem is interrelated to the problem of nationalism. "Humanitarianism is basic to modern democracy, e.g., to a nation's claim to a political, economic and cultural liberty." (23)

In conclusion, Benes' own words express his sociological approach to politics most clearly: (24)

"Without giving up his high ideals, the modern statesman must propound a practical policy. He must observe all elements of the public life of the state and nation, evaluate all factors of political, economic, social and moral life, must strictly evaluate the strength of the different material and moral component parts, recognize and know the value of political parties and individuals . . . From all this he forms his political synthesis and makes daily decisions destined for the immediate and distant future. He never gives up his program and ideals, makes no compromise in principles, but understands, on the contrary, no policy of personal ambitions and egoism . . . never goes back, stays only one moment when forced by circumstances to consolidate gains and gather force for the further journey. This is the concept of idealistic realism."

Our evaluation of Benes parallels that of Masaryk. Both base their sociology on philosophy and each was a fortunate sociologist able to impress his principles on his political and cultural pattern

---

23. Benes, *My War Memoirs*, p. 494.
24. Cited in Roucek, "Eduard Benes," *World Unity*, 14: 142, June, 1934.

— his native country. Benes wrote less on theoretical sociological topics but his literary productivity in the post-war period, especially, has by no means been negligible. In fact, his interest in sociology gave a tremendous impetus to the interest in sociology in Czechoslovakia. The first organization of the Czechoslovak sociologists was named the Masaryk Sociological Society. Benes was one of the founders of the outstanding Czechoslovak sociological quarterly, *Sociologicka Revue*, to which he contributed articles from time to time.

Other Czechoslovak Sociologists. The most prolific follower of Masaryk was Dr. I. A. Blaha, Professor of Sociology in the Masryk University of Brno, founder and leader of the so-called "Sociological School of Brno" and editor of *Sociologicka Revue*. Blaha favored philosophical and applied sociology, while the so-called "Prague School," propounded empirical and "non-evaluating" sociology. Blaha's numerous books and articles covered the sociology of city life, the sociology of education, the sociology of peasant and laborer. In fact, Hodza, former Prime Minister of Czechoslovakia and one of the founders of the Czechoslovak Agrarian Institute (one of the many Czechoslovak institutions interested in sociological problems of the country), himself a sociologist, stated publicly that "It was really Blaha who discovered the peasant for us." It is true that Blaha's work was not so carefully done as W. I. Thomas' and F. Znaniecki's *The Polish Peasant in Europe and America*, but it was produced independently, with less financial support, and is quite original. In the years preceding Munich, Blaha was particularly interested in the sociology of intellectuals, and the growing crisis of society in its various branches.

Dr. Josef Kral, Professor of Sociology in the Charles University, the leader of the "Prague School," also may be classed as a follower of Masaryk's "critical realism." He devoted himself to the studies of Herbart and Masaryk's sociology and the editorship of *Socialni problemy (Social Problems)*, another well-edited Czechoslovak sociological quarterly. (25)

Dr. E. Chalupny, Docent in Sociology in the Masaryk University in Brno, in the Institute of Technology in Prague, and Pro-

---

25. For other sociological periodicals of Czechoslovakia, cf.: Roucek, "Sociological Periodicals of Czechoslovakia," *American Sociological Review*, 1: 168-170, February, 1936; Roucek, "Czechoslovak Journals," 2:270-271, April, 1937.

fessor of Sociology in the Free School of Political Sciences in Prague, was the first Czechoslovak sociologist to attempt to build up a sociological system. He aimed to summarize all the knowledge of society in his eighth (of the promised 15) volumes. His texts are, however, not so much original contributions as a synthesis and systematization of available sociological knowledge, with references to various sociologists the world over. Chalupny conceives sociology as the science of civilization. The elements of human life belong either to nature, culture or to the sphere of spirit. Sociology is not interested, according to him, in the spiritual and natural elements, but in the cultural elements. The foundation is the fusion of subjectivity and objectivity. Hence Chalupny places sociology between biology and psychology; after psychology comes logic, which ends the cycle beginning again from mathematics, as in the system of Comte. (26)

II

Contributions to Educational Sociology. To more than a usual degree Czechoslovakia's sociologists paid attention to the field of "Educational Sociology" or "The Sociology of Education." (27) Lindner can be considered a founder of Educational Sociology. Masaryk's sociological analyses were frequently interested in education; the same applies to Benes. The *Sociologicka Revue* published a regular section entitled "Sociologie Vychovy" (The Sociology of Education), which contained short articles and regular reviews of the literature in that field. Jan Uher, who studied in the United States and was later to be executed by the Nazis as Professor in Brno, published numerous valuable studies on American education and various sociological aspects of Czechoslovakia's education. Other sociologists published their findings about the educational

---

26. If anything, the post-war Czechoslovak sociology was characterized by numerous contributions made by sociologists working mostly in other fields. It is only fair to notice such sociologists as: Joseph Hanc, Antonin Obrdlik, Antonin Ullrich, F. Modracek, J. L. Fischer, Bruno Zwicker, Antonin Ralis, O. Machotka, Jan Mertl (an able young sociologist who was reported to have turned a "Quisling"), Antonin Bohac, Jaroslav Auerhann, Zdenek Peska, etc.

27. Cf. Roucek, "Some Contributions of Sociology to Education," in Harry E. Barnes and Howard Becker, eds., *Contemporary Social Theory*, (New York: D. Appleton-Century Co., 1940), Chap. 22, pp. 793-833; Roucek, "Trends in Educational Sociology Abroad," *The Educational Forum*, 3: 488-494, May, 1939.

problems of America, Poland, Yugoslavia and Russia. In general, Educational Sociology was most interesting to the Czechoslovak sociologists and educators, although it was not there noetically so well-defined as in the United States.

Conclusions. It can be safely stated that of all the Central-Eastern-Balkan countries, Czechoslovakia's contributions to sociology in the post-war period were most numerous, outstanding and valuable. Not only the government of that country but the sociologists themselves made every effort to develop specific fields of sociology at home, and to keep themselves informed of the sociological trends abroad. (28) Numerous leading foreign sociological works were translated into Czech (Robert Michels, Durkheim, Comte, LeBon, Kidd, Giddings, Sorokin).

Until very recently, Czechoslovak sociology was closely connected with philosophy. The influence of the strong personality of Masaryk gave the Czechoslovak sociology certain definite characteristics, which set it apart from sociology in other countries. In many other nations, Comte and Spencer were closely associated in their developments of sociology. In Czechoslovakia this influence was not so marked. But here the general approach is colored by the national and social and cultural needs of the country. But no sociological "ism" dominated the Czechoslovak sociology as in the surrounding dictatorial countries. The Czechoslovak sociology meant much more in public life in Czechoslovakia than in most other nations where it has remained mostly an academic subject. Compared to America, the influence of the Czechoslovak sociologists on their public life was far advanced.

The geographical situation of Czechoslovakia conditioned, partly at least, the international character of Czechoslovakia's sociology. There was hardly an outstanding American or foreign sociologist unknown in Czechoslovakia. Thus, the Czechoslovak sociologists escaped being as provincial as the American and Anglo-Saxon sociologists.

The development of Czechoslovakia's sociology was favored by an unusually large number of excellent sociological periodicals or

---

28. *Sociologicka revue* had its board of "foreign" editors: C. Bouglé of Paris, G. L. Duprat of Geneva, V. Ganeff of Sofia, M. Kosic of Belgrade, M. Mirkovic of Subotica, G. Richard of Bordeaux, and a circle of "American" editors (C. C. Eubank, C. W. Hasek, P. A. Sorokin) headed by Roucek. The Masaryk Sociological Society elected several oustanding American (and other) sociologists as "Corresponding Members."

periodicals granting space to sociology, all of them supported by private or governmental funds. But in contrast to developments in the surrounding dictatorial countries, the Czechoslovak sociology remained one of the few countries in the world where sociological research was made public without hindrance or interference of government or press groups. In fact, Czechoslovakia, like America, while free, supported a number of exiled scholars from neighboring countries. (29)

All in all, Czechoslovak sociology was young, if compared to the developments in other nations. In fact, one of its chief leaders, Benes, is still living. Considering its short span of existence, its striving for scientific basis, its international character, it is possible to conclude that the Czechoslovak sociology made remarkable progress and that much can be expected of it after World War II.

---

29. Thus Professor P. A. Sorokin, now an outstanding American sociologist, Harvard University, was Massaryk's guest after World War I, as well as Professor Georges Gurvitch, now well known French sociologist, at the University of Strasbourg, France, and Director of the French Sociological Institute, Ecole Libre, New York.

SELECTED BIBLIOGRAPHY

Barnes, Harry Elmer, and Howard Becker, *Social Thought from Lore to Science*, vol. II, *Sociological Trends throughout the World*, (Boston: D. C. Heath and Co., 1938), Chap. XXVII, "Sociology in Eastern Europe, the Balkans, and Turkey," pp. 1060-1101, and particularly "Czechoslovakia," pp. 1060-1067, and bibliographical references, pp. xxxvi-xxxviii.

Blaha, Innocence Arnost, "Contemporary Sociology in Czechoslovakia," *Social Forces*, 9: 167-179, December, 1930.

Obrdlik, Antonin, "Sociological Activities in Czechoslovakia," *American Sociological Review*, 1: 653-656, August, 1936.

Roucek, Joseph S., "Czechoslovak Journals," *American Sociological Review*, 2: 270-271, April, 1937.

Roucek, Joseph S., *The Development of Sociology in Czechoslovakia* (unpublished M. A. thesis, New York University, School of Education, 1937).

Roucek, Joseph S., "Eduard Benes as a Sociologist," *Sociology and Social Research*, 23: 18-24, September-October, 1938.

Roucek, Joseph S., "Masaryk as Sociologist," *Sociology and Social Research*, 22: 412-420, May-June, 1938.

Roucek, Joseph S., "Sociological Periodicals of Czechoslovakia," *American Sociological Review*, 1: 168-170, February, 1936.

Roucek, Joseph S., "The Trends in Educational Sociology Abroad," *The Educational Forum*, 3: 488-494, May, 1939.

TWENTIETH CENTURY SOCIOLOGY

C. RUMANIAN SOCIOLOGY

by

A. MANOIL

I

Some Introductory Considerations. Among the so-called social sciences, sociology still has a special position; there are still discussions about its field and methodology, and especially, its position as a science. These various discussions appear as a result of the fact that sociology, by its very nature, oscillates between becoming a pure science or a normative and applied science. These oscillations, or tendencies, are reflected throughout the development of sociology as a science.

The way in which Rumanian sociology follows this general pattern will constitute the Rumanian sociology in the twentieth century.

Beginnings of Sociology in Rumania. The beginnings of sociology in Rumania are interwoven with various philosophical conceptions. Sociology is considered either in the light of a particular philosophical system or as an aspect of the philosophy of history. To this stage in the development of Rumanian Sociology belong Vasile (Basile) Conta and A. D. Xenopol. (1)

For Conta, in accordance with his determinisic philosophy, "...fatalism dominates the social phenomena" and the proof is given by statistical study of social facts. "Statistics," as Conta writes, "gives the most convincing proofs of the existence of fatalism in the domain of social facts" (2); also, social phenomena are perfectly comparable with the biological ones, and sociology as a science cannot progress without the help of biology. (3)

---

1. The name of Ion Eliade-Radulescu, *Echilibru intre antiteze* (Equilibrium between antithesis), (1859), may also be mentioned. (After G. Vladescu-Racoasa, "La Sociologie en Roumaine," *Revue internationale de sociologie,* 37: 2, 1922)

2. V. Conta, *Theorie du Fatalism,* (Paris: Mayolez; Bruxelles: Germer-Baillere, 1877), p. 12.

3. Id., *Teoria ondulatiunii universale,* (Iasi Saraga: 1876), p. 260.

EASTERN EUROPEAN SOCIOLOGY

As an attempt at a system on applied sociology, Conta left a rude outline on "The art of behaving and governing in society." (4) It constitutes the first trace of an embryonic Rumanian sociological system.

For Xenopol, (5) "sociology is a science based on laws as stable and immutable as those which guide the movement of celestial bodies, though **not so precise as the latter**." (6) But that is applicable exclusively to static sociology, which considers only coexistent social facts. Dynamic sociology, which has as its object the study of development, and consequently, considers the successive facts (7), cannot engender any more ideal conceptions, except in an absolutely abstract region outside the reality of facts, so that " . . . history or dynamic sociology will have to be satisfied only with having a glimpse of the direction these facts will follow in the future." (8) The method to be applied can be neither the inductive nor the deductive, but the inferential, the only characteristic method of history as a science.

Another historian who has contributed to the development of Rumanian sociology is N. Iorga. For him, history must deal with particular facts and sociology with their general aspect. (9)

Some Data on Rumanian Theoretical Sociology. A Rumanian

---

4. "L'art de se conduire et de conduire dans la société," published and commented on by D. Gusti after an inedited manuscript; in D. Gusti, *Sociologia Militans,* (Bucharest: 1935), pp. 539-544.

5. A. D. Xenopol, well known author of a History of the Rumanians, wrote *Les principes fondamentaux de l'histoire,* (Paris: Leroux, 1899), which constitutes a most remarkable contribution to the philosophy of history and is, at the same time, one of the clearest critics of the position of sociology as a science. This book was republished in 1908 under the title of *La théorie de l'histoire.* See also the critical review of this book by G. L. Duprat, *Revue internationale de sociologie,* 16: 384-390, 1908.

6. *Op cit.,* p. 209.

7. The distinction between coexistent and successive facts is used by Xenopol, in proposing a new classification of sciences: Theorical sciences (coexistent phenomena) concerning (a) matter: Physics, chemistry . . ., (b) the spirit: psychology, logic . . . static sociology; Historical sciences (succesive phenomena) concerning: (a) matter: geology, paleontology . . ., (b) the spirit: history or dynamic sociology.

8. *Op. cit.,* p. 17.

9. See N. Iorga, *Essai de synthèse de l'histoire de l'humanité,* (Paris: 1926), and, as directly connected with Xenopol's Theory of history, *Doua conceptii istorice* (Two historical conceptions), Academia Romana, Discursuri de receptiune, (Bucharest: G. Gobl, 1911).

author on the same theoretical level as the authors mentioned above, although with more sociological preoccupations, is G. Scraba. (10) For him, sociology has as its ideal the harmony between society and the individual; sociology must be considered as a philosophy and a science, and its object the social future. (11)

In another category of Rumanian sociologists enters Spiru C. Haret. (12) He makes the first attempt to construct a scientific sociology on a mathematical basis. The work of Haret, particularly appreciated by Gaston Richard, (13) is an attempt to apply rational mechanics to the study of social phenomena. (14)

This work of Haret remains without followers, although we may mention Al. Alexandrescu (15) who tries to develop some of Haret's conceptions but without his mathematical apparatus.

A Rumanian sociologist known better as a philosopher is D. Draghicescu. (16) For him, "The logical situation of an objective sociology is untenable." Sociology cannot be but subjective, and somehow a complement to psychology. "Sociology, conceived as subjective sociology," writes Draghicescu, "shall be an effort of complementing the introspective psychology by having it provided with a really causal explanation,..." (17)

Another sociologist who considers sociology as a philosophical discipline is N. Petrescu. (18) For him, sociology is a science of the general; it considers reality in its totality as against other sciences

---

10. *Dialectique historique*, (Bucharest: 1922). (After Gaston Richard, see below).

11. See: Gaston Richard, "La méthode sociologique en Roumanie: l'oeuvre du Prof. D. Gusti," *Archiva pentru stiinta si reforma sociala*, 13/14: 404, 1936.

12. *Méchanique sociale*, (Paris: Gauthier-Villavs; Bucharest: C. Gobl, 1910).

13. *Loc cit.*, p. 402.

14. See also G. Titeica, *Din vieata si activitatea lui Spiru Haret* (About the life and activity of Spiru Haret), Academia Romana, Discursuri de receptiune, (Bucharest: 1914).

15. *Originile Civilizatiei* (The origins of civilization), (Bucharest: 1930).

16. Two of his most important sociological works are: *Du role de l'individu dans le déterminisme social*, (Paris: Alcan, 1904); and *La réalité de l'esprit; Essais de sociologie subjective*, (Paris: Alcan, 1928); also, *Le problème du déterminisme social*, (Paris: Alcan, 1903).

17. *La réalité de l'esprit*, p. xiii.

18. See *The Principles of Comparative Sociology*, (London: Watts and Co., 1924); *The Interpretation of National Differentiations*, (London: Watts and Co., 1929); "Sociologia ca disciplina filosofica" (Sociology as a philosophical discipline), *Revista de Filosofie*, 18 (3-4), 1933; *Fenomenele Sociale in Statele Unite*, (Bucharest: Cultura Nationala, 1921).

which consider it in its parts. (19) As for comparative sociology, which is the science of social differentiations, the basic element has to be the identical ground of man's social manifestations. "Every discipline of the so-called sciences of the spirit," writes Petrescu, "takes into account the identical ground of man's manifestations in society. Without the existence of such an identity, it would be impossible to obtain unity in these sciences..." (20)

Another Rumanian sociologist with a philosophical point of view is Traian Braileanu. (21) For him, society is an autonomous system, and the social phenomena a positive negation of the individual. Sociology must prove "the real and complete disappearance of the individual from the moment of the birth of society." (22)

A Rumanian sociologist who sustains a strictly scientific point of view in sociology is P. Andrei. (23) "Any attempt to transform sociology into a practical instrument...," writes Andrei, "means changing its nature. The application of the results of sociological research cannot be confused with sociology proper." (24) As for the object and methdology: "Any cultural or social phenomenon is subject of study for sociology, and any special science can take a sociological point of view... but, sociology proper considers the social phenomenon in its totality and utilizes the special knowledge provided by the social sciences." (25)

Other authors who may be mentioned are M. Ralea, who wrote a very interesting study on the idea of revolution in the socialistic doctrines, (26) and an Introduction of Sociology. C. Dobrogeanu-

---

19. *Sociology as a Philosophical Discipline*, p. 12.
20. *The Principles of Comparative Sociology*.
21. *Sociologia Generala*, (Cernauti Tip. Mitrapolitul Silvestru, 1926); *Introducere in sociologie* (Introduction to Sociology), (Cernauti: Ostasul Roman, 1928).
22. See Vladescu-Racoasa, loc. cit., p. 15.
23. P. Andrei, *Sociologie Generăla*, (Craiova: Scrisul Romanesc, 1936); Id., *Das Problem der Methode in der Soziologie*, (Leipzig: O. Harrassowitz, 1927).
24. *Op. cit.*, p. 69.
25. *Ibid.*, p. 72.
26. *L'idée de révolution dans les doctrines socialistes*, (Paris: Riviere, 1923). For other contributions of Rumanian sociologists see G. Vladescu-Racoasa, loc cit., pp. 1-21.

TWENTIETH CENTURY SOCIOLOGY

Gherea, (27) a socialist rather than a sociologist; E. Sperantia, (28) and L. Blaga. (29)

II

Present Status of Rumanian Sociology. The authors we have mentioned above, by their different points of view, have contributed to the development of sociology in Rumania, and some of their works will certainly have an influence on its ulterior development. Their contribution, however, remains for the moment on a theoretical level.

The first Rumanian sociologist who succeeded in creating a school of sociological thought and for the first time introduced sociology as a science in the Rumanian culture is Dimitrie Gusti. He and his school represent the last and the most comprehensive stage of sociology in Rumania.

D. Gusti and Present Trends of Rumanian Sociology. Gusti and his school, (30) by the value attached to the sociological mo-

---

27. *Conceptia materialista a Istoriei,* (Bucharest: Socec, 1892); *Neo-Iobagia,* Bucharest: 1910). (See also G. Vladescu-Racoasa, *loc. cit.,* p. 10).

28. *Problemele sociologiei contemporane* (The problems of contemporary Sociology), (Bucharest: Societatea Romana de Filosofie, 1933).

29. L. Blaga, *Elogiul satului romanesc* (Eulogy of the Rumanian Village), Academia Romana, Discursuri de receptiune, LXXI, 1937; as regards this author, see also: H. H. Stahl, "Satul romanesc. O discutie de filosofia si sociologia culturii," *Sociologie Romanesca,* II, III, 1937.

30. For data concerning this sociological school and its various contributions see: Vladescu-Racoasa, "La sociologie en Rumanie," *Revue international de sociologie,* 37: 1-22, 1929; *Id., L'Institut Social Roumain, 15 ans d'activité,* (Bucharest: 1933); *Id.,* "Profesorul D. Gusti (viata, opera si personalitatea lui"), *Arhiva pentru stiinta si reforma sociala,* 14: 1070-1092, 1936; Mircea M. Vulcanescu, "Dimitrie Gusti, Profesorul," *Arhiva,* 14: 1198-1287; *Id.,* "Teoria si sociologia vietii economice; Prolegomene la studiul morfologiei economice a unui sat,"*Ibid.,* 1932, pp. 206-222; Traian Herseni, *Teoria monografiei sociologice; Cu un studiu introductiv: Sociologia monografica stiinta a realitatii sociale de D. Gusti* (The theory of sociological monography. With an introductory study: Monographic sociology, science of social reality, by D. Gusti), Ed. Institutul Social Roman Biblioteca de Sociologie, Etica si Politica, Seria A, No. 1, (Bucharest: 1934); *Id., Realitatea Sociala; Incercare de ontologie regionala, ibid.,* Seria A, No. 4, (Bucharest: 1935); H. H. Stahl, *Tehnica monografiei sociologice* (The technic of sociological monography), *ibid.,* Seria A, No. 2, (Bucharest: 1934); *Id., Monografia unui sat* (Monography of a village), (Bucharest: Fundatia Culturala Regala, "Principele Carol," 1937); Gaston Richard, "La méthode sociologique en Roumanie: l'oeuvre du Prof. D. Gusti," *Arhiva pentru stiinta*

noraphy, give a new orientation to the Rumanian sociology. According to Gusti, (31) sociology is the science of social reality. Upon this social reality are constructed the objective culture and social institutions of an epoch so that scientific knowledge of this reality shall constitute the very substance of sociology. Accordingly, sociology would be a system of knowledge about the present social reality. "This social reality (human reality)," as Gusti writes, "is not suspended in the air," but forms a complex system of parallel manifestations of various social units influenced by the social will. The social will and the motivation of the creative social activity define the essence of the sociology. The result is what Gusti calls the phenomenological existence: units, relations, and social processes.

The social reality originates from conditions and potentialities (genesis) and goes toward actuality (objective values); social activity, social processes, take place within the environment which may be analyzed into two categories of frames or cadres of phenomenological existence. These two categories are the natural (subdivided into cosmological and biological) and the social (subdivided into psychical and historical). Any social fact can be studied

---

si reforma sociala, 13-14: 339-407, 1936; Philip E. Mosely, "The Sociological School of Dimitrie Gusti," *Sociological Review*, 28: 149-165, 1936; Joseph S. Roucek, "Sociology in Rumania," *American Sociological Review*, 3: 54-62, 1938. For details on various researches on Rumanian sociology see *Arhiva pentru stiinta si Reforma Sociala*, which began to be published under Gusti's direction in 1919, and especially the two volumes published in 1936; I. *Mélanges D. Gusti, XXV ans d'enseignement Universitaire;* II. *Omagiu profesorulus Gusti;* also *Sociologie Romanesca*, mostly dedicated to monographical research which began to be published at Bucharest in 1936, and is edited by D Gusti. For the last research, just before the war, intended as papers for the XIVth International Congress on Sociology, scheduled to take place at Bucharest in 1939, see "XIVe Congrès International de Sociologie, Liste de titres de resumés des rapports et communications," *Revue internationale de sociologie*, 47, 1939.

31. See D. Gusti, *Sociologia Militans; Introducere la Sociologia Politica*, Institutul Social Roman Biblioteca de Sociologie, Etica si Politica, Seria A, No. 3; *La monographie et l'action monographique en Roumanie*, Institut de droit comparé, Etudes de Sociologie et d'Ethnologie juridiques publiées par René Maunier, (Paris: Domat-Montchrestien, 1935); Traian Herseni, D. Gusti; Un systeme de sociologie ethique et politique, *Arhiva pentru stiinta si Reforma Sociala*, 13-14: 225-241, 1936.

according to this scheme. (32) As for the social manifestations, they also may be analyzed into two categories: the regulative category (subdivided into political and juridical), and the constitutive category (subdivided into economical and spiritual). The frames and manifestations of social reality resolve in the law of sociological parallelism. This law concerns parallel interrelations between social will and manifestations, between frames and manifestations, and among social manifestations themselves. The result of this process will resolve into tendencies and social evolution. On one side we shall have the politics considered as a system of means for the realization of social and ethical values and norms; on the other side, the ethics conceived as a system of aims or ethical ideas. From this global system of sociology, politics, and ethics, we may consider the future social reality.

All monographical research in Rumania so far has been made in accordance with schemes and principles established by Gusti in his sociological seminary of the University of Bucharest. The results obtained, besides giving a more accurate knowledge of the Rumanian social reality, define as the basis of Rumanian national sociology the Rumanian village. (33) By that, Gusti slides somehow toward transforming sociology into a science of the State, into a science of the nation. (34) But, if we disregard this aspect, which, although of great social importance is beyond the boundaries of sociology as a science, the results of monographical research in Rumania are the more remarkable. It is due to this work of Gusti and his school that some of the characteristics of the Rumanian village are scientifically known. Under this aspect, the affirmation of Roucek is absolutely correct "that social science there (in Rumania) has grown in its research and influence on certain aspects of national life, to a point

---

32. As an example of the way this scheme works see H. H. Stahl, *Monografia unui sat;* Roman Cressin, "Monografia comunei Sant," *Sociologie Romaneasca* I, No. 6, 7, 9, 1936; see also various articles in *Sociologie Romaneasca,* and *Arhiva pentru stiinta si Reforma Sociala,* 1932, containing various studies concerning the villages: Cornova, Dragus, Fundul Moldovei, Runcu, etc.

33. See H. H. Stahl, "Piedici mai vechi in alcatuirea unei sociologii romanesti (Old hindrances to the constitution of a Rumanian Sociology)," *Sociologie Romaneasca,* 2: 5-11, 1937.

34. See D. Gusti, "Stiinta Natiunii," *Sociologie Romaneasca,* 2: 49-59, 1937; A. Golopentia, "Rostul actual al Sociologiei (The present reason of Sociology)," *ibid.,* 26 12-19; see also the critique made by P. Andrei in *Sociologie Generala,* pp. 69, 70.

EASTERN EUROPEAN SOCIOLOGY

nowhere else attained in the countries of southeastern Europe." (35)

As is shown by this summary exposition, Rumanian sociology seems to have followed divergent directions. There are various currents of thought which, up to a certain degree, are absolutely independent of each other. The first time we meet a group of scientists following a system and having unity of purpose is when we consider the school created and directed by Gusti. Since that is the only Rumanian sociological group so far, Rumanian sociology is to be considered through the principles of this school. On a theoretical plan, this school is characterized by a global sociological approach in the sense that all the aspects of social reality are to be considered almost simultaneously; on a practical level, this system asks for a collaboration of various sciences but under the direct and immediate supervision of the sociologist. On a theoretical level as well as on the practical one, this Rumanian sociology is markedly monographical. Since these monographic researches represent only a first step toward a systematic accumulation of Rumanian sociological data, we may reasonably expect a perfection of the sociological system proposed by Gusti. The accumulated data and the perspectives on theoretization they provide will certainly enrich sociological learning and constitute a valuable contribution to sociology as a science.

---

35. Joseph S. Roucek, "Sociology in Rumania," p. 54.

SELECTED BIBLIOGRAPHY

Andrei, Petre, *Sociologie Generala*, (Craiova: Scrisol Romanesc, 1936).

Braileanu, Traian, *Sociologie Generale*, (Cernauti: Tip. Mitropolitul Silvestru, 1926).

Draghicesco, D., *Du rôle de l'individu dans le déterminisme social*, (Paris: Alcan, 1904).

Gusti, Dimitrie, *Le monographie et l'action monographique en Roumanie*, Inst. du droit comparé, (Paris: Domat-Montchrestien, 1935).

Gusti, Dimitrie, *Sociologia Militans; Introducere in Sociologia Politica*, (Bucharest: Inst. Social Roman, 1935).

Haret, Spiru C., *Mécanique sociale*, (Paris: Gauthier-Villars; Bucharest: C. Gobl, 1910).

Herseni, Traian, *Teoria monografiei sociologice* (With an introductory study, "Sociologia monografica, stiinta a realitatii sociale" by D. Gusti), (Bucharest: Inst. Social Roman, 1934).

Moseley, Philip E., "The Sociological School of Dimitrie Gusti," *Sociological Review*, 28: 149-165, 1936.

Petrescu, N., *The Principles of Comparative Sociology,* (London: Watts and Co., 1924).

Petrescu, N., *The Interpretation of National Differentiations,* (London: Watts and Co., 1929).

Ralea, M., *L'dée de révolution dans les doctrines socialistes,* (Paris: Riviere, 1923).

Richard, Gaston, "La méthode sociologique en Roumanie: l'oeuvre du Prof. D. Gusti," *Arhiva pentru stiinta si reforma sociala,* 13-14: 339-407, 1936.

Roucek, Josph S., "Sociology in Rumania," *American Sociological Review,* 3: 54-62, 1938.

Sperantia, Eugen, *Problemele sociologiei contemporane,* (Bucharest: Soc. Romana de Filosofie, 1933).

Stahl, H. H., *Tehnica Monografiei Sociologice,* (Bucharest: Inst. Social Roman, 1934).

Adolf Manoil, B.S. (Roman, Rumania) 1926, Licentiate's Degree (Bucharest) 1929, Ph.D. (Bucharest) 1932, Diploma of "Corso di Orientamento Professionale," R. Istituto Industriale (Torino) 1934, Diploma of "Institut National d'Etudes du Travail et d'Orientation Professionelle" (Paris) 1940. Formerly Assistant in Psychology, University of Bucharest, 1930-1933; Prof. of Psychology, "Ecole d'Auxiliaires Sociales" (Bucharest) 1930-1933; Lecturer, Catholic University of Milan (Italy) 1937; Assistant to J. M. Lahy (Ecole Pratique des Hautes Etudes), Industr. Psychology (Paris) 1933-1939. At present, Associate Editor, Head of the Rumanian Section, Morale Services Division, Language Unit, Army Service Forces, War Dept., New York.

D. SOCIOLOGY IN YUGOSLAVIA

by

JOSEPH S. ROUCEK

I

In Yugoslavia the development of sociology has been strongly influenced by national problems and history. For centuries the Turks exploited the people. Peoples migrating between Europe and Asia crossed its territory. Between the two World Wars the country was agitated by the question how to weld these various Southern

Slavs, imbued with the idea of decentralization and autonomy, into a strong, unified Yugoslav nation. In addition, none of Yugoslavia masters was able to lessen the danger of the country's international position. All these facts are clearly reflected in the social theories developed in the country.

Obstacles in the Development of Empirical Investigation. The Serbs began their first fight for liberation in 1804-1813 and the foundation of a new Serbian State were laid between 1815 and 1830. The nineteenth century saw the national consciousness of the Croats and Slovenes strengthened; in consequence, a fierce political struggle resulted when the Hungarians did everything in their power to absorb them. It was, therefore, quite natural that the spirit of nationalism was reflected in intelectual pursuits. On the whole, up to 1918, the Yugoslav had supported their nationalism by intellectual romanticism. Thereafter their main problem was to decide what form their State should take — centralized or federalist. Hence political struggles, international and internal, have consumed the nation. (1) In social struggles little tolerance and appreciation for the opponent's viewpoint is allowed; consequently the political, social and cultural background of the national mentality has been and still is unfavorable to a scientific approach in the social sciences in Yugoslavia.

Even the social structure of the State presented handicaps. The villages and small cities formed the backbone of the nation. Localism operated here in a very effective way. Everybody knows everybody else, including the outsiders who carry on business with them. Very few sense any problems in the social life of the peasant people, and, generally speaking, they themselves take their *status quo* for granted. The conditions are so simple they seem to need no examination. To make a social investigation is "insulting" to the locality.

The inclusion of powerful minorities in the new State only added to

---

1. See: J. S. Roucek, "Social Character of Yugoslav Politics," *Social Science,* 9: 294-304, July, 1934; "Social Character of Balkan Politics," *World Affairs Interpreter,* 5: 68-86, Spring 1934; *The Politics of the Balkans,* (New York: McGraw-Hill Book Co., 1939), Chap. II, "The Political Pattern," pp. 10-25, and Chap. IV, "Yugoslavia," pp. 55-83.

such difficulties. The social investigator discovered, for instance, "Jewish" or "German" blood in an individual whose very existence depended upon making his livelihood in a community antagonistic towards minorities. Furthermore, social investigations were often considered subterfuges of political opponents to provide themselves with political weapons. At other times, the social investigator asking political opinions found himself in jail for political doubtfulness. At any rate, local patriotism was a weapon not only against social research but against any kind of empirical investigations. Were not professors removed by the post-war governments of Yugoslavia as "politically undesirable"?

The Roots of Yugoslavia's Sociology. In addition to the nationalistic conditions which are fully reflected in the growth of Yugoslavia's sociology, we must also note foreign influences. Around the nineties the evolutionary and deterministic doctrines of general cultural history were spread in Serbia. There appeared the translations of Buckle, Draper, Kolb, R. Ihering's *Zweck in Recht*, Laveleye's *La Propriété*, and Bagehot's *Physics and Politics*. On them were based the contributions of the only Yugoslav philosopher of history, Boza Knezevic, who spent his life in one of the dullest small Serbian towns teaching in secondary school. (2)

From the beginning of the twentieth century, four social movements were creating interest in modern sociology: (1) Socialism gained because of the growing industrialization of the country and proletarization of the weakest social classes. (2) Nationalism needed to settle theoretically the problems of the national union between Serbs and Croats. (3) Feminism was imported from the outside and helped to dissolve the patriarchal family. (4) Christian Socialism among the Slovenes and partly among the Croats was organized on the same basis and with the same aims as in other Catholic countries. After the World War was added (5) Agrarianism. The main question since 1918, however, has been the form of the national state. Nevertheless, much work has been done in the social sciences, especially in

---

2. *The Principles of History* (1898); *The Order in History* (1898); *Proportions in History* (1901).

the fields of ethnography, anthropo-geography and history. Economic and political sciences have been less stressed. (3)

"*National Sciences*" *of Bogisic and Cvijic.* The growth of nationalism among the Yugoslavs, especially among the Serbs and Croats, awoke early and bore fruit in the remarkable researches in the field of "national sciences" by the school headed by Bogisic and Cvijic.

Baltazar D. Bogisic (1834-1908) was Professor in the University of Odessa and then Minister of Justice of Montenegro (1893-1899). His main contribution was the *Collection of the Contemporary legal Customs in Southern Slovenia* (Zagreb: 1874). The results of his research were interpreted to the Western European countries by F. Demelic in *Le droit coutumier des Slaves meridionaux d'après les recherches de M. V. Bogisic* (Paris: 1876). His contributions induced Polish, Russian, Czech and Roumanian national societies to follow his example. In collaboration with C. Jirecek, (4) Bogisic edited the *Liber statuorum civitas Ragusii* (Zagreb: 1904), the famous

---

3. Several sections of the subsequent discussion have been adopted from M. M. Kosic, "Stav sociologickeho studia u Jihoslovanu" (The Status of Sociological Studies of the Yugoslavs), *Sociologicka Revue*, 2: 190-194, and 3: 334-339. Other information has been secured from the *Narodna Enciclopedija Srpsko-Hravatsko-Slovenacka* (*The Serb-Croat-Slovene National Encyclopaedia*), 4 vols., ed. by St. Stanojevic, (Zagreb: Bibliografski zavod, 1928-29, 4 vols., and *Masarykuv Slovnik Naucny*, (Prague: 1925-1933); both of these publications contain the most complete biographical and bibliographical data on the Yugoslav social scientists. See also Dinko Tomasic, "Sociology in Yugoslavia," *American Journal of Sociology*, 47: 52-69, July, 1941; Nicholas Mirkowich, "Beginnings of Rural Sociology in Yugoslavia," *Rural Sociology*, 5: 351-354, September, 1940; Harry Elmer Barnes and Howard Becker, *Social Thought from Lore to Science*, (Boston: D. C. Heath, 1938), vol. II, pp. 1081-1086.

4. Jirecek, although a Czech, deserves to be mentioned in connection with Yugoslav's sociology. He served as Secretary General of the Ministry of Education of Bulgaria, and as Minister of Education 1881-1882; thereafter he was appointed Professor of General History, Prague, 1884, and Profsesor of Slavonic Philology in the University of Vienna, 1892-1910. His researches created scholarly interest in the Balkan countries and related geography to history. The most important work in regard to Serbia is *Staat und Gesellschaft im mittelalterlichen Serbien*, (Vienna: Holder, 1912, 2 vols.). For additional information on Yugoslav social scientists, see P. R. Radosavljevich, *Who Are the Slavs?* (Boston: R. G. Badger, 1919, 2 vols.), *passim*, which is a veritable mine of scattered, but most useful information.

law book of his native city, Ragusa (Dubrovnik), composed originally in 1272. (5)

With the exception of Albania, Yugoslavia is the outstanding Balkan country which furnishes the most original and fruitful field for sociologists and psychologists interested in ethnology. But Yugoslavia's sociologists have paid little attention to tribal formations, settlements, ecology, mechanisms of social interaction, conflict, accommodation, stratification, assimilation, selection of leaders, division of work, and gradual dissolution. The greatest specialist in this field was Jovan Cvijic (1865-1927), Professor of Gography at the University of Belgrade, whose greatest work was *La peninsule balkanique: géographie humaine* (Paris: 1918). He also published numerous valuable articles in other languages, as well as in English. (6) He organized an extensive anthropogeographic examination of the Balkan Peninsula and his school (The Geographic Institute of Belgrade University), gathered and published substantial factual material about settlement formations, migration movements, economic forms, psychic and cultural differences among the Balkan nations, especially in Serbia. Thus the sociology of the Balkans was given a good geographic and ethnographic basis.

Cvijic's researches were connected with the political aspirations of Serbia before World War I. He considered the Macedonians, a branch of the Balkan Slavs, ethnically able to join either the Serbs or the Bulgars (opponents in the nationalistic ambitions of the Serbs). (7) Cvijic was furiously attacked by the Serbian press and nationalists. Thus was repeated the experience of Masaryk, a great Czech sociologist, when he dared to question the scientific value of Czech nationalistic writings. At any rate, Cvijic's ideas "greatly influenced Serbia's cultural and political life, and her historians, sociologists, and politicians undertook studies and political activities in accordance with them." (8) In particular, they cultivated

---

5. See S. C. Lobingier, "Bogisic, Balthazar Anton," *Encyclopedia of the Social Sciences,* 2: 618.

6. J. Cvijic, "The Geographical Distribution of the Balkan Peoples," *Geographical Review,* 5: 346-360, 1918; "The Zones of Civilization of the Balkan Peninsula," *ibid.,* pp. 470-482. Cvijic is mentioned in H .E. Barnes, ed., the *History and Prospects of the Social Sciences,* (New York: Alfred A. Knopf, 1925), pp. 83, 314. See also Tomasic, *op. cit.* pp. 54-57.

7. Roucek, *The Politics of the Balkans,* Chap. VIII, "Macedonians," pp. 138-161, is a survey of the troublesome Macedonian problem.

8. Tomasic, *op. cit.,* p. 55.

his basic theory that Serbia was to be the "Piedmont of Yugoslavia" and all other "inferior" types in Yugoslavia were going to be transformed into useful subjected groups under the leadership of Serbia.

Among the follwers of Cvijic was the late Professor Stanojevic, a leading Serb historian, who especially stressed racial factors, and emphasized the "state-making qualities of the Serb race." (9) Another sociologist and historian, D. J. Polovic, Professor of Sociology in the University of Belgrade, inspired by similar ideas, was interested in the formation of Serbia's upper classes, especially its merchant class, and in the problem of *hajduks* (highway brigands) who, according to him, had a leading role in the formation of nineteenth-century Serbia but, as ordinary highway robbers and mountain brigands, could found no State. So he tried to make a distinction between "good *hajduks*" and "bad *hajduks*. (10) "Good *hajduks*," of course, had high morals and statesmanlike qualities and played their proper role in the organization of the modern Serb State. Dragoljub Jovanovic, former Professor of Economics at the University of Belgrade and a Serb politician, propounded the theory that Serbia, like the United States, could assimilate every newcomer and Serbians "represent the best human material which could be found on the Balkan Peninsula and some or the best in Europe." (11) But his outstanding contribution is *Agrarian Politics*, (Belgrade: 1930), which is defined as "only one sphere of science or belonging to the competence of one Ministry only; it is a social policy, a certain orientation of spirit, an ideological and political aim" (p. 10). Obviously Jovanovic does not unterstand agricultural policies as an exclusive economic science, such as developed in Central Europe under German influence. Man, not goods, is Jovanovic's goal. His ideal is family property without hired help. He conceives the problem of agriculture as the question how to strengthen the family as a social unit to oppose all adverse economic tendencies and economic crises. Jovanovic's international reputation, however, is based on *Les effects économiques et sociaux de la guerre en Serbie*, (Paris: 1930), a Carnegie Foundation publication, which gives a magnificent description of the cultural situation of Serbia before the World War and the effects of that conflict in the country. He makes

---

9. St. Stanojevic, *Postanak srpskog naroda*, (Belgrade: 1934).
10. Dusan Popovic, *O hajducima*, (Belgrade: 1930).
11. Dragoljub Jovanovic, *Socijalna struktura Srbije*, (Belgrade: 1932).

the unbelievable statement that every family in Serbia during that period was in flight (p. 27). Interesting is his viewpoint that "it is difficult to say whether, from the spiritual and moral standpoint, Serbia gained or lost in the War" (p. 229). In support of his premise he states that some 10,000 refugees studied abroad, especially in France; numerous political and artistic works appeared in foreign countries; the peasant woman become the head of the family; and the peasant-soldier really fought for his family and soil and only later learned the concept of the fatherland and the State (p.287).

The Influence of Marxism. Cvijic's school of thought, though dominant, was not, however, the only sociological school in Serbia. Much earlier than Cvijic another sociologist, Svetozar Markovic, appeared in Serbia. As a student in Petrograd and Zurich, Markovic came under the influence of anarchist and socialist ideas and of the writings of Chernishevski, Bakunin, and especially Marx. He very early engaged in political and promotional activities and came to be the leading sociologist and revolutionist of nineteenth-century Serbia. He compared the Serbian *zadruga* to the Russian *mir* and held that the conversion of the whole land into one *zadruga* would bring about a communistic society, without the intermediate stages of capitalistic economy and violent class war. Although he died at the age of twenty-nine, he exerted more influence on the social and political currents in Serbia than any other individual before or after him. (12) His friends and associates later became leaders of the National Radical Party, which for half a century was the dominant political cluster of Serbia. But in post-war Yugoslavia the party eventually came to believe the exact opposite of Markovic's teachings favoring extreme conservatism and national chauvinism.

Although Marxism had no social reason for its existence in Serbia, it dominated the thinking of the growing intelligentsia of Serbia for a decade after Markovic. Around 1880 Auguste Comte was translated into Serbian and Spencer's teachings were propagated. Social Darwinism was introduced by the late Vladimir Jovanovic in his

---

12. D. Jovanovic, "Markovic, Svetozar," *Encyclopedia of the Social Sciences,* 10: 144-145; S. Jovanovic, *Svetozar Markovic,* 2nd ed., (Belgrade: 1920); J. Skerlic, *Svetozar Markovic,* 2nd ed., (Belgrade: 1922); H. Wendel, *Aus dem suedslavischen Risorgimento,* (Gothe: 1921), pp. 135-165 and *Aus der Welt der Suedslawen,* (Berlin: 1926), pp.. 205-210; M. Mirkovic, "Social Teachings of Svetozar Markovic," *Sociologicka Revue,* 10: 87-95, 1930; Radosavljevich, *op. cit.,* pp. 193, 199; Markovic's publications are gathered in *Collected Works,* (Belgrade: 1889-1899, 8 vols.).

EASTERN EUROPEAN SOCIOLOGY

Social and National Struggle for Existence (1885); but Marxism persisted. The Marxists published most translations. Marxist periodicals lived longest of the social periodicals, and imitated foreign examples; but they produced nothing original. The only "original Marxian sociology" is probably Filip Fillipovic's *The Evolution of Society* (1924), but really nothing more than a compilation of Bukharin's and Bogdan's works on historical materialism.

The Spell of Zadruga. Around the middle of the nineteenth century, great interest was taken in the *zadruga*, a very interesting social organization. (13) The attention given it was exceeded only by that given the Russian social organization *mir*. A long series of studies began with Croat Utjesenovic's *Die Hauscommunion der Suedslaven,* (Vienna: 1859) and Serb Milicevic's *La Zadrouga, étude sur la vie en commun,* (Paris: 1860). Both domestic and foreign scholars (F. Demelic, Doppsch, Ivich, L. A. Janitch, Laveleye, R. Millet, J. Peiskert, M. Zoriricic, Sir Henry Maine, Kadlec, Strohal, and others) wrote about the *zadruga*. It was also a very convenient theme for Yugoslav aspirants for doctorates in foreign universities. (14) However, no definite sociological study has been made of the *zadruga* treating its socio-psychological and socio-morphological relations and its place and function in the tribal and national unit. In fact, most ethnographic investigations concerned folklore. Only Tihomir Gjorgjevic, Professor of Ethnography in the Belgrade University, who, during the World War came into contact with the modern English ethnology, showed an understanding of the important sociological problems of his field. He was especially interested in the forms of sexual and family life. Here belongs his collected work, *Our National Life,* (Belgrade: 1930, 2 vols.).

---

13. See P. A. Sorokin, C. C. Zimmerman, C. J. Galpin, *A Systematic Source Book in Rural Sociology,* (Minneapolis, Minn.: University of Minnesota Press, 1932), vol. II, pp. 57-67; A. Smith, "Zadrugas, The Strength of Serbia," *Contemporary Review,* 107: 515-520, April, 1915; Radosavljevich, *op cit.*, vol. II, pp. 110, 114, 121, 142-151, 155, 163, 210, 295, 376; H. J. E. Peake, "Village Community," *Encyclopedia of the Social Sciences,* 15: 253-259; Demelic, *op. cit.,* pp. 23-63; S. Troyanovitch, "Manners and Customs," in *Servia and Servians,* edited by A. Stead, (London: 1909), Chap. XII.

14. For instance, M. D. Novakovitch, *La Zadrouga,* (Paris: 1905) a thesis for D. J.; M. Glouchtchevitch, *Le self-government local en Serbie,* (Paris: Larose and Tenin, 1911), a thesis for D. J.; etc.

TWENTIETH CENTURY SOCIOLOGY

II

Modern Sociology in Yugoslavia. It was only in 1910 that more modern sociological ideas found recognition in Yugoslavia. Gustave Le Bon's *Psychologie des foules* had appeared in translation as well as Gumplowicz's *Geschichte der Staatstheorien* (1909). Most modern tendencies in sociology, however were introduced in 1912 by Mirko M. Kosic, the outstanding sociologist of his country. As Professor in the Universities of Belgrade and Subotica, he translated or gave support to the translation of Sombart, Oppenheimer, Toennies, Vierkandt, Michels, and Lederer. His writings deal principally with the problems of national society and techniques of national struggle, sociological principles of the declining birth-rate and sociology of the Yugoslav countryside. Of the first group is the *Die Suedslavenfrage*, (Zurich: 1918). The second group is represented by his *Der Gebuertengruckgang in Ungarn*, (Munich: 1914) and *Die Soziologischen Grundlagen der Gebuertenbeschraenkung*. (Munich: 1917). Rural sociology has interested him since the World War, especially as it was influenced by the agrarian reform. His *Introduction to the Sociographic Study of the Village*, (Novisad: 1920), a small pamphlet, has been used quite extensively, as well as his *Agrarian Policies* (1925). Of value also have been his *Sociology of the Magyar Revolution 1918-19* (1920), *The Idea of Progress in Contemporary Sociology* (1924), and the *Leadership* (1930).

Lately Kosic studied the "Social Situation and the Trends of Ideas among the Yugoslav Youth." (15) He showed therein how the game of politics disgusted Yugoslavia's youth which tended to favor either communistic or romantic agrarian ideologies. In his *Introducsion to Sociology*, (Navisad: 1934), he states definitely that sociology is not a kind of "reformology" or method of solving crises, and is not social philosophy, philosophy of history, or an encyclopaedia of social sciences. Instead, it determines and describes generalities pertaining to all concrete social phenomena, of social groups, of social relations and social processes. The work also surveys American sociology and contains an excellent bibliography. The book is excellent, in fact, equal to any work written in English by American scholars. (16)

---

15. *Sociologicka Revue*, 5: 76-80, 1934.

16. Of the same high quality is his *Problems of Sociology* (Belgrade: 1934), which also contains a chapter on the development of Yugoslav sociology.

EASTERN EUROPEAN SOCIOLOGY

Sociology in Croatia. The geographical position of Croatia has influenced to a considerable degree the mental attitudes of the Croatian spokesmen. In constant contact with Latin culture as the settlers on the shores of the Eastern Adriatic, the Croats have also been in contact with the Roman church and western European civilization. But while the peasantry retained many patterns of its original social organization, ways of living, beliefs, attitudes, and language, the thin upper layers of the Croatian intelligentsia and townsfolk were more influenced by these relations with the Western world. The cultural dualism of rural and urban life determined the two basic trends in Croatian sociology and politics: the "autochthonous culture" movement on the one hand, and the tendency toward "Europeanization" on the other. The same dualism stimulated sociological research and brought sociology into close contact with politics, so that the leading Croatian sociologists were also the leading Croatian politicians. The two outstanding representatives here were Anton Radic (1868-1919) and Milan Sufflay (1879-1932). (17) Radic studied the autochthonous culture of his own people, the folk culture of Croatian peasants. The material collected was published in numerous volumes by the Academy of Sciences and Arts at Zagreb. Upon his ideas, a peasant political movement was started under the leadership of Radic's brother, Stjepan Radic. Its basic philosophy was that peasants, who are the original producers of material and spiritual goods, should have political power in their hands in order to bring about a new all-human, equitable and pacifistic world. (18)

Suffay, Croation historian, sociologist, and politician, born in Croatia of a family of Hungarian origin, stressed the racial, cultural, and mental difference between Serbs and Croatians and concluded that no durable union was possible. Croation nationalism was necessary for the preservation of all that was good in western European civilization. He was assassinated for his ideas which,

---

17. See Tomasic, *op. cit.,* pp. 61-66, for a detailed analysis of their ideas.

18. Radic was influenced by J. Michelet's (1798-1898), *Le Peuple* (1848) and A. Fouillée's (1838-1912), *Psychologie du peuple français* (1898). Radic's predecessors in Croatia had been Juraj Krizanic (1618-83) and Baltazar Bogisic (1814-1908). Krizanic, originator of the pan-Slav idea, conceived a separate Slavic world and Slavic civilization as contrasted to the Greco-Roman world and western European civilization. Bogisic, on the other hand, was first to discover the richness of South Slav folk culture.

TWENTIETH CENTURY SOCIOLOGY

however, became the backbone of the ideology of one part of the Croatian separatist movement.

Sociology in Slovenia. Unlike Croatians and Serbs, Slovenes never in their history organized an independent State of their own. When in the second part of the nineteenth century the beginnings of Slovene bourgeoisie were formed, its sons attended German universities in Austria and Germany where they became impressed by the strength of pan-Germanism and influenced by the ideas of cultural, political, and economic liberalism. As a reaction to this liberal trend the Catholic clergy inaugurated a strong counterliberalistic movement which dominated Slovene cultural, political, and economic life until the end of World War I. The spiritual leaders of this counter-liberalism were professors at the Slovene schools of theology: A. Mahnic, J. Krek, and A. Usenicnik, (who were influenced by such German, French, and English Catholic writers as V. E. von Ketteler, de Mun, Manning, etc., whose ideas formed the backbone of "Christian socialism" or the "Christian social movement"). While Krek started a cooperative movement among Slovene peasants, Usenicnik published his *Principles of Sociology*, (Zagreb: 1920), wherein he asserted that sociology should be based on philosophy, and especially the scholastic philosophy of the Middle Ages as elaborated by Thomas Acquinas.

After 1918, the liberal bourgeoisie of Slovenia got strong support from the liberal bourgeoisie of the rest of Yugoslavia, and the increased industrialization of Slovenia resulted in the growth of the proletariat and a rapid spread of the ideas of Marxian socialism. The control of the Catholic clergy over Slovenia was challenged, and this induced the reorientation of Slovene Catholic sociology. Andriga Gosar, Professor of Economics in the University of Ljubljana criticized in his *Principles of the Sociological and Economic Reform of Society*, (Belgrade: 1933) the former Cathlic sociologists for not succeeding in attracting to their sociology the larger layers of the proletariat.

The Use of Sociological Approach by Yugoslav Social Scientists. After World War I, interest in sociology grew in Yugoslavia. The works of LeBon, Ferri, Sighele, Eisler and Giddings have been translated in Croat. Kjellen's and Ostrogorski's works in political sociology can now be read in Serbian. The number of Yugoslav sociologists also was growing. Kosic's efforts are now reflected in the contributions of numerous others among whom are a number who deserve mention. Dragic Lapcevic, a leading Serbian socialist publicist, devotes his *Our Musselmans* (1923) to the sociology of the Yugoslav Mohammedans; the same problem interests C. Mitrinovic, whose book of the same title (1926) ably treats the accommodation and assimilation processes among this Yugoslav minority. Gjorgje Tasic of Belgrade University published abroad his investigation of the relations of Duguit to the new French positivist sociology. Mijo Mirkovic of the Law Faculty of the University of Subotica has investigated the social background of Serbia's political parties, (19) and related the life of Masaryk (20). Vladimir Dvornikovic, Professor of Philosophy in the University of Belgrade, (21) has published not only in the field of philosophy but also in that of sociology; his *Psychology of the Yugoslav Mentality*, (Zagreb: 1925) was translated into Czech (1926); the same applies to his *Masaryk as Philosopher and Sociologist*, (Prague: 1926). Possibly his best work is *Our Cultural Orientation in Europe of Today*, (Zagreb: 1931). A young Zagreb sociologist, Mirko Kus-Nikolajev, a member of the Zagreb museum, is also well-known for his sociological studies. Among them are *Problems of Biological Sociology*, (Zagreb: 1924), *The Theory of Socialization*, (Zagreb: 1926), researches into peasant life, and his latest, *Sociology of the Environment* (Belgrade: 1929). Julka Chlapec Djordjevic specializes in the sexual problems in sociology and Ilija P. Peric in social legislation. Masaryk's sociological views interest Albert Bazala (*Masaryk als Denker*, Zagreb: 1934).

Rural Sociology. It is not hard to understand that, in a country where the predominant majority of the population were peasant farmers, there was a special interest and need for the development of rural sociology. The work in this field was, however, confined to Belgrade and Zagreb, both having different projects and practically no contacts, due to the internal political antagonism. (22) During the years 1936-1938 field work was done in Northern Serbia, but, for the lack of proper experience, there were no special results. "Lack of experience in field work and methods of inquiry was very

---

19. M. Mirkovic, *op. cit.*
20. Mijo Mirkovic, *Tomas Masaryk*, (Belgrade: 1930). His *The Solution of the Slovak Question*, (Novisad: 1928), deals with the problem of Slovakia in Czechoslovakia.
21. Dvornikovic's biography and bibliography can be found in *Who's Who in Central and East-Europe 1933-34*, (Zurich: Central European Times, 1935), p. 231.
22. Nicholas Mirkowich, "Beginnings of Rural Sociology in Yugoslavia," *Rural Sociology*, 5: 351-354, September, 1940.

characteristic of the Belgrade group, most of their leading members having a purely theoretical background." The Zagreb group, headed by Dinko Tomasic, Professor of Sociology in the University of Zagreb (who had been trained in the University of Chicago) spent a great deal of time working on the development and character of the *zadruga* institution in Croatia. (23)

Yugoslav Sociology Abroad. During the post-Munich years, Tomasic and Mirkowich continued their sociological researches in the United States and both have published numerous and valuable studies in this country. While Tomasic specialized in the sociological problems of Croatia and in political sociology, (24) Mirkowich, on, the other hand, has devoted himself to the reconstruction aspects of Yugoslavia's main social problems. (25) Nor should we fail to notice the contributions of Paul R. Radosavljevich, a specialist in "experimental education" or New York University, whose numerous books and articles published in Amerisa and abroad have a good sociological basis and are characterized by the knowledge of sociological works in all modern European languagues. (26) His *Who Are the Slavs?* still remains the best available study in English of the social life of the Slavs. His "Introduction" to W. A. Lay's *Experimental Pedagogy*, (New York: 1936) is the best evaluation of the social basis of that field available today. Nor should we forget the sociological implications of the popular works of Louis Adamic, which more than any other publications have made the American reader aware of the ethnic and peasant customs of Yu-

---

23. Cf. H. J. E. Peake, "Village Community," *Encyclopedia of Social Sciences,* 15: 253-259.

24. Tomasic, *op cit.*; "Peasants and Propaganda in Croatia," *Public Opinion Quarterly,* 1: 68-73, 1937; "Constitutional Changes in Yugoslavia," *Political Science Quarterly,* 55: 582-593, 1940; "The Struggle for Power in Yugoslavia," *Journal of Central European Affairs,* 1: 148-156, 1941; "Personality Development in the Zadruga Society," *Psychiatry,* 5: 229-261, 1942; "Croatia in European Politics," *Journal of Central European Affairs,* 2: 64-86, April, 1942; "Reconstruction in Central Europe," *American Political Science Review,* October, 1943; 37: 888-903.

25. Mirkowick, *Yugoslav Postwar Reconstruction Papers* (published by the Office of Reconstruction and Economic Affairs, Government of Yugoslavia, New York, 1942-1943).

26. See Radosavljevich's biography and bibliography in *Who's Who in America.*

goslavia and the impress made by the minorities groups in the United States on America's culture. (27)

Conclusion. While between the two World Wars there were but a few departments of sociology in Western Europe, (28) in Yugoslavia there were six universities and colleges having sociology in their teaching program. All these departments were established only after 1918 and the chairs were held mostly by rather young people, most of them educated on the lines of thought of French positivism and the Durkheimian school. Since the new departments were hardly older than a few years, their work was still experimental, consisting of search for methods and objects. Obviously, Yugoslav sociology lacked special institutions and organizations for a development. Professor Kosic periodically tried to found a sociological magazine (1921 and 1930) and a sociological library. The Sociological Society of Zagreb conceived of sociology as being all social sciences in their broadest sense. As a special subject, sociology was taught only in the University of Zagreb. Introduced in 1906 in connection with criminology, it spread the teachings of Spencer, Gumplowicz and Giddings. After the War, Professor Kosic lectured on general sociology, statistics and economics in the University of Ljubljana. But many non-sociologists cultivated sociology (like Baltazar Bogisic) without teaching it. Others published their results abroad (especially Kosic of Belgrade and M. Mirkovic of Subotica).

On the whole, Yugoslavia's contributions to sociology have been more valid and durable than they are generally known. We must especially appreciate them when we consider the enormous difficulties facing the Yugoslav sociologists from the standpoint of political and religious conditions, not to mention the general philosophical hang-over from the last century. But, despite these great handicaps, Yugoslavia can boast of having advanced furthest in sociology of all the Balkan states, with the exception of Rumania (and Czechoslovakia — a Central European States).

---

27. Louis Adamic, *The Native's Return,* (New York: Harper and Bros., 1934); *What's Your Name,* (New York: Harper and Bros., 1942); *My Native Land,* (New York: Harper and Bros., 1943); etc.

28. Cf. Earle S. Eubank, "European and American Sociology: Some Comparisons," *Social Forces,* 15: 148-150, December, 1936; P. A. Sorokin, C. C. Zimmerman, and C. J. Halpin, *A Systematic Source Book in Rural Sociology.*

TWENTIETH CENTURY SOCIOLOGY

SELECTED BIBLIOGRAPHY

Barnes, Harry Elmer, and Howard Becker, *Social Thought from Lore to Science,* vol. II, *Sociological Trends throughout the World,* (Boston, etc.: D. C. Heath and Co., 1938), "Yugoslavia," pp. 1081-1088.

Mirkowich, Nicholas, "Beginnings of Rural Sociology in Yugoslavia," *Rural Sociology,* 5: 351-354, September, 1940.

Roucek, Joseph S., "The Development of Sociology in Yugoslavia," *American Sociological Review,* 1:981-988, December, 1936.

Tomasic, Dinko, "Sociology in Yugoslavia," *American Journal of Sociology,* 47: 52-69, July, 1941.

Joseph S. Roucek, Ph. D., Chairman of the Department of Political Science and Sociology; Hofstra College, Hempstead, Long Island, was born in Czechoslovakia, and was naturalized in the United States in 1927. He is on the editorial board of *New Europe, Social Science,* and *World Affairs Interpreter,* and author, co-author, or editor of numerous works, including *Our Racial and National Minorities* (1937, 1939, 1945), *Contemporary World Politics* (1939, 1940), *Politics of the Balkans* (1939), *Contemporary Europe* (1941), *Sociological Foundations of Education* (1942), and *Twentieth Century Political Thought* (1945). He has taught in a number of educational institutions in this country (New York University, Pennsylvania State College, San Francisco State College, College of the Pacific, Reed College, the University of Wyoming) and in summer schools of Czechoslovakia and Rumania.